Human Intelligence

This book is a comprehensive survey of our scientific knowledge about human intelligence, written by a researcher who has spent more than thirty years studying the field. It takes a nonideological view of a topic in which, too often, writings are dominated by a single theory or social viewpoint. The book discusses the conceptual status of intelligence as a collection of cognitive skills that include, but also go beyond, those skills evaluated by conventional tests; intelligence tests and their analysis; contemporary theories of intelligence; biological and social causes of intelligence; the importance of intelligence in social, industrial, and educational spheres; the role of intelligence in determining success in life, both inside and outside educational settings; and the nature and causes of variations in intelligence across age, gender, and racial and ethnic groups.

Earl Hunt is Professor Emeritus at the University of Washington, where he has been a faculty member since 1966. He has also taught at Yale; the University of California, Los Angeles; and the University of Sydney, Australia. His other books include *Concept Learning* (1962), *Experiments in Induction* (1966), *Artificial Intelligence* (1975), *Will We Be Smart Enough?* (1995), *Thoughts on Thought* (2002), and *The Mathematics of Behavior* (2007). He has received the International Society for Intelligence Research's Lifetime Achievement Award for his contributions to the study of intelligence and has been named the 2011 recipient of the Association for Psychological Science's Cattell Award for lifetime contributions to applied psychological research.

Human Intelligence

EARL HUNT

University of Washington

CAMBRIDGE UNIVERSITY PRESS
Cambridge, New York, Melbourne, Madrid, Cape Town, Singapore,
São Paulo, Delhi, Dubai, Tokyo, Mexico City

Cambridge University Press
32 Avenue of the Americas, New York, NY 10013-2473, USA

www.cambridge.org
Information on this title: www.cambridge.org/9780521707817

© Earl Hunt 2011

First published 2011

Printed in the United States of America

A catalog record for this publication is available from the British Library.

Library of Congress Cataloging in Publication data

Hunt, Earl B.
Human intelligence / Earl Hunt.
    p.   cm.
Includes bibliographical references and index.
ISBN 978-0-521-88162-3 (hardback) – ISBN 978-0-521-70781-7 (pbk.)
1. Intellect.   I. Title.
BF431.H814   2010
153.9–dc22   2010038696

ISBN 978-0-521-88162-3 Hardback
ISBN 978-0-521-70781-7 Paperback

Contents

List of Figures

List of Tables

Introductory Remarks

After spending some thirty years studying human intelligence, I decided to write a book. Why? It must be that I have something new to say.

Well, I do and I do not. Virtually everything that could be said about human intelligence has been said. It is or isn't important, it is or isn't evaluated by the tests, it is or isn't genetically based, and on and on. This book does not say anything that has not already been said. It could not. What it does do is attempt to bring up to date the information on the various conflicting views. My contribution is to moderate these views, because I do not think that any of the extreme statements that have been made can be supported.

There is a saying that has been traced back to the days of classic Greece;

The fox knows many little things; the hedge-hog knows one big thing.

It is not entirely clear what that means, but some philosophers have interpreted it as saying that some people summarize issues with detailed, nuanced views, while others make bold, simple statements. I am a fox. I think the field of human intelligence has had far too many hedgehogs. There are major individual differences in cognitive power; these differences have important implications for human behavior; they do not have a single cause, nor do they ever act outside of the context of the current problem. We need to understand intelligence in its full complexity.

Intellectual foxes have a problem. They are more likely to be right than intellectual hedgehogs (there is actually data on this!), but they are less likely to be believed (there is data on this, too). Nevertheless, being a fox, there is nothing I can do but try to locate the burrows of as many intellectual hedgehogs as I can, and try to dig them out. It is my nature, and that is what I have tried to do. Complete intellectual objectivity is impossible to achieve. I have tried to present as fair a picture as I can of a much-studied, much-debated topic. The result is a book that may sometimes be difficult to read, but I hope that it is a comprehensive presentation.

Any effort of this sort is impossible unless you receive support. My first and greatest debt is to my wife, Mary Lou Hunt, who has put up with years of papers scattered all over the house, a somewhat grumpy husband, and mutterings as I uncovered the tracks of one or another of those intellectual hedgehogs.

My second debt is to Cambridge University Press, which put up with my being late, late, late, but let me persevere. I also owe a special debt to Jeanie Lee, for her substantial assistance in ensuring that permissions for reproduction were obtained. Too many books on intelligence wave words at the reader about what the data said. Thanks in no small part to Ms. Lee's assistance, this book will often let the reader see what actually was found.

I owe favors to colleagues around the world who were willing to read pre-publication versions. Special thanks go to Tom Bouchard Jr., who engaged me in lively e-mail discussions over virtually every chapter; to two of my sons, Alan and Steven, who discussed and commented on different topics (very different – Alan's a biophysicist and Steve an industrial-organizational psychologist); to Wendy Johnson of the University of Edinburgh for her comments on genetics; and to Diane Halpern, for comments on the introductory chapters. Naturally, I am responsible for everything in the final product!

And I suppose I owe an apology to all those authors whose works I should have read but did not. All I can say is that life is short and there are an awful lot of you.

Bellevue, Washington
April 2010

Human Intelligence

CHAPTER 1

The Issue of Intelligence

So it is that gods do not give all men the gifts of grace... neither good looks nor intelligence nor eloquence.

Homer, The Odyssey

There's many a man has more hair than wit.

Shakespeare, Comedy of Errors, act 2, scene 3

1.1. The Idea of Intelligence

Homer and Shakespeare lived in very different times, more than two thousand years apart, but they both captured the same idea; we are not all equally intelligent. I suspect that anyone who has failed to notice this is somewhat out of touch with the species. However, we cannot simply sort people into the "intelligent" and the "not-so-intelligent." Homer observed that few people have great gifts. Shakespeare, more pithily, observed that all too many of us do not do terribly well at problem solving. Most of us, though, fall in between Homer's desire for eloquence and Shakespeare's worry about lack of wit.

In this book I will talk about the nature of intelligence, its causes, who has it, and how it is used. I will do so without the eloquence of Homer and Shakespeare. I will take a scientific view. Modern psychology has a great deal to say about intelligence, and somehow a great deal that has been said has been seriously misunderstood. The popular media sometimes report that the psychologists who study intelligence say almost the opposite of what the psychologists actually said.[1]

There is a reason for this. The study of intelligence is not an isolated academic topic; our intelligence has social consequences. We want our leaders to be intelligent, and exhibit concern if we think they are not. There were politically motivated attacks on the intelligence of Presidents Lincoln, Truman, Harding, and Ford. Serious concerns about mental competence

---

[1] See Tannenbaum (1996) for a discussion of this issue and references to earlier discussions of the topic. Gottfredson (2005) provides a spirited discussion of how failing to consider the implications of psychological research on intelligence can be costly to society.

were raised about Wilson and Eisenhower, following strokes, and Reagan, due to early symptoms of Alzheimer's disease. Lincoln and Truman, who received the most vicious attacks, are now considered two of our finest presidents. Eisenhower recovered to function well; Wilson did not. The effect of Reagan's illness upon his second term is still a matter of debate.

Concerns about intelligence are not confined to concerns about our leaders. Our school systems use cognitive tests to stream high school students into different programs. Colleges use cognitive tests to screen applicants for higher education programs. These tests are never called "intelligence tests," but they correlate highly with them.

Testing is not confined to the educational system. Volunteers for the United States military services must obtain passing scores on a test of general mental competence, the Armed Forces Qualifying Test (AFQT). Similar tests are used in many other countries. Toward the bottom end of the scale there are a variety of special assistance programs for people who simply do not have the cognitive competence to cope with the complexities of the modern world. Low intelligence test scores can be offered as evidence of diminished mental capacity during the penalty phase of a criminal trial.

While there is broad agreement that some people are smarter than others, things become more complex when we try to be precise. I think that every knowledgeable person would agree that Albert Einstein and Thomas Jefferson were both highly intelligent. Who was the more intelligent? That is hard to say; they were brilliant in different ways at different times. It would be easy to find other examples of the same point. There are clearly varieties of cognitive skill, especially at the top. As a result some modern observers have concluded that there is no single dimension of intelligence.

This idea is not new. In the sixteenth century the Spanish physician/philosopher Juan Huarte de San Juan[2] drew a remarkably cogent picture of individual differences in human thought. Huarte believed that when people attack problems some will use their imaginations to envisage how a solution might work out, while others will rely on their memories of solutions that have worked in the past. Huarte also defined "understanding" (*entendimiento*) as a separate capacity, implying that one can be bright without having a good understanding of a situation. Huarte's distinction between problem solving by imagination or by memory is mirrored in contemporary theories that distinguish between the ability to do abstract reasoning and the ability to apply previously learned solution methods.[3] Robert Sternberg, a prolific modern writer on intelligence, has emphasized the distinction between analytic intelligence and the ability to understand complex social situations.[4]

Huarte anticipated another modern idea, the need to have a biological explanation for intelligence. Huarte offered a theory based on the sixteenth-century notion that the body is governed by four "humors" – blood, bile, black bile, and phlegm. This theory of biology has long since been discarded. The idea that there should be a biological explanation for individual variations in cognition has been retained. One of the most active areas of modern intelligence research deals with the relation between intelligent behavior and the brain.

Let us leap from the sixteenth century to the nineteenth, and to one of the most colorful characters in the history of science, the Victorian physician, mathematician, and explorer Sir Francis Galton. Galton explored in Africa, made major contributions to the development of statistics, and conducted research in psychology, most noticeably on intelligence. He wholeheartedly endorsed the theory of evolution proposed by his cousin Charles Darwin. Galton believed that human intelligence was largely inherited. He also maintained that intelligence was one manifestation of a person's overall constitutional fitness. Therefore,

---

2   Huarte de San Juan, 1575/1991.

3   Horn & Noll, 1994.
4   Sternberg, 2003.

it should be possible to learn something about a person's intelligence by examining his or her physique, including brain size, and by determining the efficiency of the person's nervous system by doing such things as recording the speed with which he or she reacted to a signal to strike a bag. These ideas are alive, in much expanded form, today.

The next step was taken at the start of the twentieth century, when the Frenchman Alfred Binet developed the first intelligence tests to be used in schools. Testing has dominated the study of intelligence since then, so we need to look more closely at the idea.

1.2. Testing

If you want to go beyond saying "people are different" you have to offer some way of measuring those differences. There is an imperative to develop such measures if a society wants to assign different roles to different people, based on their personal characteristics. Not all societies do this, all the time. There was no intelligence test for the ruler in the hereditary kingships of medieval Europe. The Hindu caste system pre-assigned people to social roles, based upon their birth. It is notable, though, that both these societies experienced a good deal of conflict due to their restricting people's social roles.[5]

In village-based societies personal knowledge of individuals plays a major role in assigning people to jobs. When American pioneers began to move into the northern plains states Sitting Bull, the paramount chief of the Lakota (Sioux) Indians, selected Crazy Horse to be war leader from among people whom he knew personally.[6] That

technique does not work in today's large societies, where there are many positions to be filled in both government and industries. Leaders cannot possibly know all their subordinates, let alone the subordinates' subordinates. Our society requires formal machinery for selecting candidates either into employment, directly, or into educational systems that serve as channels to future employment.

Many societies solve this problem by an elaborate form of recommendations. A boy or (historically less often) a girl who is thought to be talented is sent off for training and/or apprenticeships. While the details have been lost, this appears to be the way the ancient Egyptians selected children to be trained as scribes. It was also the way in which second, third, and fourth sons were recruited for the priesthood (or the army) in medieval Europe. The person was not needed at home, and somebody had connections enough to start them on a career. The use of connections is certainly not unknown in modern times. But we do rely on another method of personnel selection: testing.

There have been many objections to testing. In evaluating them it is well to keep one thing in mind. Society needs a mechanism for personnel selection. Not everyone can have whatever they want. Students have to be selected, jobs have to be filled, and when behavioral problems arise, mental competence must be assessed. If you do not like testing, what is your alternative?

1.2.1. *Testing Before Psychology*

Modern psychologists did not invent testing. In the days when the Chinese emperor claimed to rule "the Earth, the Moon, and three quarters of the Sun" an elaborate series of local, regional, and nationwide tests was used to select officers for the imperial bureaucracy. Candidates had to write traditional poetry and to explain the importance of fearing the will of heaven and knowing the words of the sages. Evidently it was assumed that a person who could do these things could collect the imperial taxes or be an ambassador to the Mongols.

---

5 During the Hundred Years' War between England and France (roughly 1350–1450) the French court was disrupted when Charles the Foolish inherited the throne. He probably suffered from a bipolar psychosis. In India the Sikhs were formed largely as a protest against the rigid social structure enforced by the Hindu caste system.

6 He did well. Crazy Horse defeated General Custer at the Battle of the Little Big Horn. This was the most stunning Native American victory in the history of the western expansion.

Some centuries later the British Empire emulated the Chinese Empire. Until after World War II career positions in both the Indian empire and the British upper bureaucracy were filled largely from the ranks of people who had read history, classics, and occasionally economics at the elite universities, especially Oxford and Cambridge. The British assumed that someone who could do well on oral and written examinations of the writings of Horace and the wars of Caesar would have the ability to administer India or to ferret out secrets while on Her Majesty's Service.[7]

Such techniques of personnel selection may sound quaint to us, but, on the whole, they worked. The Chinese bureaucracy held the empire together in a way that no succession of able emperors could ever have done alone. Properly educated British gentlemen administered India reasonably well for two hundred years. The classics program at Cambridge University produced at least four remarkably effective twentieth-century spies. Unfortunately, they spied against Britain for the Soviet Union, but that is a motivational rather than a cognitive aberration.[8] They were good at what they did.

Why did these exercises in testing apparently irrelevant knowledge do a reasonably good job of selecting people able to run very large, complex empires? Or for that matter, able to fool a modern counterintelligence agency?

What the British and the Chinese had stumbled on, and what we today attempt to evaluate, was a collection of mental traits that, collectively, we call *intelligence*. These traits define individual differences in skills that have broad application in many settings. One of the most important aspects of intelligence is an ability to learn. You demonstrate this by showing that after exposure to knowledge you have learned something. The skills needed to learn the wisdom of Confucius or the philosophical ideas of Socrates are not exactly the skills you need to run an empire, *but there is an overlap*. For that matter, the skills needed to do well on a college entrance test are not exactly the skills you need to acquire a bachelor's degree, *but there is an overlap*. That is why both the classic and the modern testing systems work. It is also why they work imperfectly.

1.2.2. *Alfred Binet Invents Modern Intelligence Testing*

At the start of the twentieth century the French Ministry of Education had a problem. The idea of universal public education had been accepted, but the schools did not seem to work for some students. How did this problem arise?

France, like all modern democracies, was (and is) committed to providing public education for all its citizens, so that all children have an opportunity to compete for desirable positions in society. This goal is not easy to achieve.

Modern schooling is an historically unusual form of education. Before 1800 most humans were educated "on the job" – observing and then helping adults, and serving as apprentices. Universal education, the requirement that every child learn by practicing seemingly esoteric exercises in a setting divorced from everyday life, is a late nineteenth-/early twentieth-century idea. By 1900 it was apparent to educators that some children have a great deal of trouble learning in this manner. The French educational administration needed to have a way of identifying such children, so that they could either be dropped from the system or channeled into an educational program more suited to their capabilities.

The fact that France was a democracy imposed an added constraint. French educators needed an objective method, in preference to the subjective impressions of "persons in authority," the teachers and principals. In an authoritarian regime there is no

---

7 Gardner, Kornhaber, & Wake, 1996, pp. 12–16.
8 Anthony Blunt, George Burgess, David MacLean, and Kim Philby. Burgess, MacLean, and Philby fled to the Soviet Union when they were about to be exposed. Blunt stayed in England, undiscovered, and became a distinguished art historian. His espionage role, which seems to have lasted through the 1940s and 50s, was not publicly revealed until 1979.

need for such a method; if the authorities don't like you, you're out.

So from the very first, testing was embedded in the society that required it.[9]

In order to meet this challenge the Education Ministry hired Alfred Binet, who had worked for a while with Galton. Binet began by making two important assumptions. The first was that mental competence increases over the childhood years. The typical six-year-old can solve problems a four-year-old cannot; a four-year-old can solve problems a two-year-old cannot, and so on, at least from birth to the late teenage years. Therefore, it makes sense to talk about *mental age* (MA) – the level of mental competence at which a child is operating.

Binet took a pragmatic approach to the measurement of mental age. He asked experienced teachers what sorts of problems children could solve at different ages. Once he had a set of problems typical of the ones children could solve at age six, seven, eight, and so on, he could determine a person's mental age by finding the most difficult problems that a child could solve. Mental age could then be compared to chronological age (CA), to determine whether a child has been performing below, at, or above the cognitive level that would be expected.

Binet then made his second, more arguable, assumption. He assumed that a child's relative standing in mental development, compared to his age group, will remain fairly constant as the child grows up. If Sammy and Tommy are both six, but Sammy has a mental age of eight and Tommy one of five, Binet assumed that four years later, when they are both ten, Sammy would have a mental age higher than ten, and Tommy a mental age lower than ten. Therefore, it follows that if you test children on entrance to school (age six or seven), and you find that some are markedly behind (i.e., have mental ages in the three-to-four range), those children are likely to be behind their classmates at all ages, and therefore are candidates for removal from the normal school program. That is what the French education system wanted to know.[10]

The Education Ministry accepted Binet's argument. The modern era of intelligence testing had been born.

1.2.3. *The Intelligence Quotient (IQ)*

Binet did not use the term *Intelligence Quotient* (IQ) because the concept of mental age was sufficient for classifying children who were entering school. As mental testing expanded to the evaluation of adolescents and adults, however, there was a need for a measure of intelligence that did not depend upon mental age. Accordingly the intelligence quotient (IQ) was developed. There have been changes in the definition and use of the term since its introduction. The details are provided in panel 1.1. Here we proceed directly to the modern use of the term.

The term IQ is used in two ways, which I will call the *narrow* and *broad* uses of the term.

The narrow definition of IQ is a score on an intelligence test, developed according to a scoring protocol where "average" intelligence, that is, the median level of performance on an intelligence test, receives a score of 100, and other scores are assigned so that the scores are distributed normally about 100, with a standard deviation of 15. Some of the implications are that:

1. Approximately two-thirds of all scores lie between 85 and 115.
2. Five percent (1/20) of all scores are above 125, and one percent (1/100) are above 135. Similarly, five percent are below 75 and one percent below 65.

9   The contrast between the French and the Chinese and British imperial systems is informative. The Chinese and British systems were designed to select a sufficient number of qualified candidates for government functions. So long as the supply of young officers and bureaucrats was adequate, there was little concern that the system might have shut out potential candidates. The French testing program was designed to staff society, without favoring some citizens over others. Any government has to solve its staffing problems. Only democracies have to justify the staffing system to the citizens.

10   Binet & Simon, 1905.

Panel 1.1. The Intelligence Quotient (IQ)

Mental age is inadequate as a means of comparing the intelligence of two children of different chronological ages (CA). Suppose a six-year-old and a ten-year-old both have a mental age (MA) of eight. Cognitively, they are likely to be very different individuals, for one is developing rapidly and the other is developing slowly. The need for a measure of mental development that is independent of chronological age led to the concept of the *Intelligence Quotient*, IQ, which was originally defined as the ratio of mental age to chronological age, multiplied by 100.[*]

$$I Q = 100 \cdot \frac{MA}{CA}. \qquad (1.1)$$

To illustrate, a ten-year-old who can solve problems at the level of difficulty expected of a twelve-year-old would have MA = 12, CA = 10, IQ = 120. An IQ of 100 indicates that the child's cognitive development is proceeding on schedule, an IQ above 100 indicates acceleration, and an IQ below 100 indicates slowed development. In the case of our hypothetical six-year-old and ten-year-old, both of whom have a mental age of eight, the first child would have an IQ of 133 and the second an IQ of 80. In modern educational terms the first child might be considered for an accelerated program, while if the second's IQ score were accompanied by difficulties with schoolwork he or she would be a candidate for a special education program.

This method of calculating IQ will not work with adults, because intelligence does not increase linearly with age past childhood. A man of sixty whose mental powers are equal to those expected of a forty-year-old would not be considered a case of retarded development! Therefore, the IQ ratio just described has been replaced by a measure based on the notion that IQ should reflect a person's relative standing within his or her own age group.

Intelligence tests are *standardized* by giving them to a relatively large sample of people chosen to be representative of the population for whom the test is intended. In the case of a test intended for broad use, such as establishing the mental competency of adults, this is essentially the entire population of the country, so attempts are made to obtain a large representative sample of the United States, the United Kingdom (for the British version), Spain (for the Spanish version), and so forth.[†] The sample should be sufficiently large that a distribution of scores can be obtained for different age groups.

The *raw* test score is based on the number of items correctly answered and/or the difficulty level of the item. (The scoring algorithm varies somewhat with the test, as discussed in Chapter 2). The IQ score is derived from the raw score in the following way.

Let Y be a raw score for a person in a particular age group, and let M be the mean and S the standard deviation for all scores in the reference group.[‡] The corresponding *standard score* is

$$z = \frac{Y - M}{S}. \qquad (1.2)$$

The IQ score is derived from this by the conversion

$$I Q = 15 \cdot z + 100. \qquad (1.3)$$

If the raw scores were normally distributed, then the resulting IQ scores will be normally distributed with a mean of 100 and a standard deviation of 15. The graphic depiction of this distribution is the famous "Bell Curve." The Bell Curve for IQ distributions is shown in Figure 1.1.

Why not record scores in the standard score format? Statisticians, psychometricians, and research workers would probably prefer to do this. The advantages have to be weighed against two countervailing trends: tradition and public relations. IQ scores were introduced almost a century ago; people are used to them. Standard scoring is a bit esoteric for the nonstatistician. For a statistician, having a scale with a mean of zero and a standard deviation of 1 is a convenience, nothing more. If a (nonstatistical) parent were to be told that their child had scored a zero on an intelligence test, they might interpret this as a claim that their pride and joy had the intelligence of a rock! Half the people who took the test would receive negative scores, which could lead to all sorts of misunderstanding. Appearances can be important.

* The concept of IQ was developed by the German psychologist William Stern, not by Binet.

† This procedure contains the implicit assumption that the distributions of intelligence are the same across populations. Thus if you consider a score of 100 on the Spanish form of the test to indicate the same thing as a score of 100 on the American version of the test, you are implicitly assuming that Americans and Spaniards have equivalent intelligences, on a population basis. Such assumptions have been vigorously debated. The controversies are discussed in detail in Chapter 11.

‡ The standard deviation is a measure of the amount of variation in a population. More details are given in Chapter 2.

Thus IQ, in the narrow sense, is a score indicating a person's relative performance on an intelligence test, compared to the performance of people in an appropriately chosen comparison group. This does not completely clarify the matter, because there can be debate about what counts as an intelligence test. This matter is also discussed on page 8. I will attempt to be clear about how the term is being used in various contexts.

In the broad sense the term IQ is used as a synonym for intelligence, that is, as a shorthand term for individual differences in cognition. This can lead to confusion, so I shall attempt to use IQ only in the sense of a test score. The term *intelligence* will be used to refer to the broader concept of individual differences in mental ability. In my usage, a person who has high intelligence will probably have a high IQ score, but the distinction between the two is important.

In interpreting IQ scores it is often useful to think of percentiles, which indicate the percentage of people in the referent group whose scores are below a certain level. What that level is will be determined by the IQ score and by the properties of the Bell (normal) Curve itself. Table 1.1 gives some important reference scores. The properties of these scores follow from the assumption that IQ scores will follow the normal distribution, which is illustrated in Figure 1.1.

As a result, in terms of the modern scoring, if someone says that their child has an IQ of, say, 120, this does not mean that the child's mental age is 20% higher than his chronological age. It means that the child has a test score in the top 9% of test scores at the child's age.

Why can we assume that IQ scores are distributed normally? The answer is simple. IQ tests (and many other tests) are constructed by choosing appropriate numbers of easy, intermediate, and hard items, so that the total scores will be normally distributed in the population for which the test was intended. The Bell Curve is an artifact of the way the test is constructed! There is no definition of IQ independent of the tests themselves. This contrasts with a variable like height, which is defined independently of yard sticks or meter sticks. Height happens to be distributed approximately normally, within the populations of adult males and females. The distribution of height is a fact of nature. The fact that IQ test scores are normally distributed is an outcome of the test construction procedure. Nevertheless, it is a reasonable thing to do. Why?

IQ scores are used to describe people *relative to each other*. They are also used to

Table 1.1. The distributions of standard and IQ scores in terms of the percentage of people above or below selected scores. An IQ of 65 would, if accompanied by other indications of mental incompetence, be cause for considering a person mentally disabled. If IQ is distributed normally, about one percent of all people have IQ scores this low. Average IQ is, by definition, 100. Approximately half of all scores lie between 90 and 110. About 16% of the scores lie above 115, 2% above 130, and 1% above 135. *MENSA*, an organization whose members have high IQ scores, defines the 4 *sigma* group, people with IQs over 160. (*Sigma* is a term frequently used to refer to the standard deviation.) This level of score would be expected three times in every 100,000 observations.

Standard Score (z)	IQ Score	% Below	% Above
−2.33	65	0.982	99.018
−2.00	70	2.275	97.725
−1.00	85	15.866	84.134
−.67	90	25.249	74.751
0.00	100	50.000	50.000
.67	110	74.751	25.249
1.00	115	84.134	15.866
2.00	130	97.725	2.275
2.33	135	99.018	0.982
3.00	145	99.865	0.135
4.00	160	99.997	0.003

make predictions and to indicate associations, as in predicting a student's likely academic progress or investigating the association between intelligence and income. There are technical reasons for wanting to deal with normally distributed scores when we apply the statistical methods used for making predictions and analyzing associations.

There is another, less technical reason for requiring that IQ scores be normally distributed. Many other human qualities that can be measured on scales with physical interpretations, like height and weight, are distributed normally. It seemed to many of the early researchers that if we could measure intelligence in some physical manner, such as measuring the efficiency of the nervous system, these measures would probably turn out to be normally distributed. Therefore, it seemed appropriate to require that IQ scores be normally distributed.

In the late nineteenth and early twentieth century this reasoning seemed compelling, because the normal distribution itself was regarded (almost mystically) as a Law of Nature. Today we are a bit more skeptical, but there is still a good argument for assuming normality. If a person's intelligence is due to a large number of independent causes, each of which has a small effect, intelligence would be distributed normally across the population.

A certain amount of the confusion between the broad and narrow senses of IQ is due to the way in which cognitive tests are described. Some tests are explicitly marketed as intelligence tests. But because the term IQ, and sometimes even the term *intelligence*, have acquired a bad taste in certain circles, many tests of cognitive skills are not marketed as intelligence tests, even though these tests are highly correlated with tests that *are* marketed as intelligence tests! For instance, in a widely read and highly controversial report, Richard Herrnstein and Charles Murray used the Armed

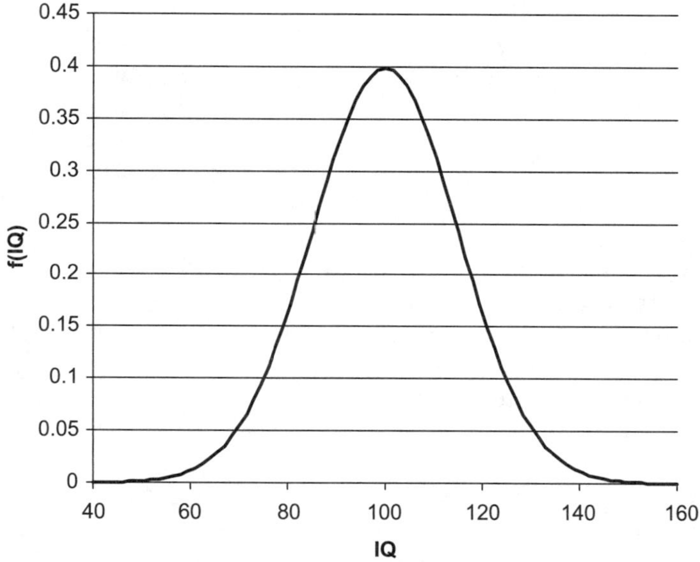

Figure 1.1. The "Bell Curve" for IQ. The area under this curve represents 100% of the population. The area under the curve and to the left of a given IQ value (on the abcissa) represents the fraction of people in a population who have IQs lower than the indicated IQ. Conversely, the area to the right indicates the fraction of people who have this IQ or a higher one. For example, 50% of the area under the curve lies to the left of IQ = 100, indicating that half the population has an IQ of less than 100. Nine percent of the area under the curve lies to the right of 120, indicating that only nine percent of all people have IQs of 120 or higher. The Bell Curve for IQ scores is a special example of the normal, or Gaussian, distribution. At the extremes, the curve never quite touches the abscissa ("x axis"), but this cannot be shown on the graph.

Services Qualifying Test (AFQT) as a measure of intelligence, and treated AFQT and IQ scores as being virtually synonymous.[11] The US Department of Defense never refers to the AFQT as an intelligence test. Similar confusions arise with the SAT. Many research projects have used SAT scores as a measure of intelligence, although the test's publisher, the Educational Testing Service, does not describe it as an intelligence test.

There is great controversy over whether or not IQ scores should be treated as real indicators of mental ability. Panel 1.2 presents a historical debate that took place in the 1920s, but in many ways foreshadowed contemporary arguments. I shall come down squarely in the middle of the controversy. I will argue that the scores certainly do mean

something, but they may not mean as much as some enthusiasts claim.

1.2.4. *What Binet Discovered: "Drop in from the Sky" Testing Works*

Let us take a closer look at what Binet assumed and what he found.

Binet's assumption that mental competence increases as children grow older is certainly correct. Mental competence may decrease in old age, but that is another story, and was of no concern to Binet. He was also correct that there are marked individual differences in the rate at which mental competence increases.

His second assumption, that relative standings remain constant as children age, is true on the whole, but there are exceptions. As a toddler, Albert Einstein was a relatively

11 Herrnstein & Murray, 1994.

Panel 1.2. Defining Intelligence: The Debate between Mr. Lippmànn and Professor Boring

In science clarity of definition is essential, for good definitions make clear what the important questions are. The study of intelligence has been plagued by a lack of precise definitions. The debate between Lippmann and Boring, early in the twentieth century, shows how the failure to define terms introduced confusions that continue to this day.

Following the use of tests in World War I, intelligence testing became a growth industry. So, inevitably, it attracted the attention of learned commentators – people who, if there had been TV in those days, would have appeared as talking heads on the Sunday morning pundit shows. One of the most respected of these commentators, Walter Lippmann, did not at all like the new technology. He was particularly incensed by a claim, based on analyses of the Army Alpha data, that the average American had a mental age of fourteen. In Lippmann's own words:

> *The intelligence test, then, is an instrument for classifying a group of people, rather than "a measure of intelligence." People are classified within a group according to their success in solving problems which may or may not be tests of intelligence. They are classified according to the performance of some Californians in the years 1910 to about 1916 with Mr. Terman's notion of the problems that reveal intelligence. They are not classified according to their ability in dealing with the problems of real life that call for intelligence.*
>
> *(Lippmann, 1922a)*

Lippmann argued that the test developers had produced a barrage of statistics that had the trappings of science, but were not scientific. The tests themselves were based on hunches by people such as Terman that this or that behavior indicated intelligence, rather than on any scientific theory of what constituted intelligence. Lippmann also doubted that a classification of people on the basis of test scores would map onto a classification according to their ability to "deal with problems of real life that call for intelligence."

Academia responded. The Harvard professor E. G. Boring* clarified the matter by asserting:

> *Intelligence is what the intelligence tests test.*
>
> *(Boring, 1923)*

So there!

The exchange between Lippmann and Boring foreshadowed a debate that is active today. Should a test be developed inductively, by the pragmatic procedure of identifying people who are believed to vary in intelligence, seeing what behaviors distinguish those who are intelligent from those who are not, and then incorporating these behaviors into a test? Or should a test be based on a theory of how individual differences in cognitive power come to arise?

The answer is not a simple one. To see why, consider the following analogy. I think that everyone would agree that people differ in their physical fitness. But what is physical fitness? You could take the approach of an athletic coach, and ask people to run, jump, throw weights, and so forth in order to determine physical fitness. Alternatively, you could take a medical approach. Physical fitness depends on muscular adequacy, reaction, and the ability of the heart and lungs to provide fuel to the muscles. So let us take measures of cardio-pulmonary capacity and construct tests of the strength of isolated muscle groups and the speed of neural impulses.

Binet, Terman, and their many successors took the coach's approach. Lippmann seems to have wanted a more theoretically justified approach, although he did not offer one. (After all, he was a journalist, not a scientist.) Lippmann did not deny that something called intelligence exists, for he spoke of dealing with problems that call for intelligence. His objection was to the tests offered to evaluate it.

Boring's response, identifying intelligence with a test score, strikes many (including me) as somewhat arrogant, for it confounds the concept of intelligence with a score on an imperfect indicator of intelligence. However, it does lead to a research agenda.

The first item on the agenda is to ask whether or not the tests identify people who would otherwise be considered intelligent. Lippmann said they would not, but that was his opinion, not an observation of fact.

To some extent the way in which the tests were developed ensured that they did identify "the intelligent." Binet and Terman began with groups who had known variations in cognitive competence (e.g., younger and older schoolchildren), and then developed tests whose scores reflected the variation. Lippmann pointed out that this procedure makes the definition of intelligence dependent upon an appropriate choice of examinees for the initial (*standardization*) testing. This was an important observation. Today there is a lively debate over the appropriateness of using intelligence tests that have been standardized in the post-industrial world to evaluate intelligence in the developing nations of Africa, Asia, and Latin America.

But Boring had a point, too. If test scores are accepted as good indicators of intelligence, the tests become a powerful tool for investigating individual differences in cognition. You can determine how test scores are related to variations in brain structure and/or process, genetic makeup, schooling, family support, and a variety of other causal factors. Test scores can also be used as predictors of success or failure in all walks of life. We can then consider different explanations for observed relationships. Science advances by accounting for relationships between observables, not by debating beliefs about what ought to be the case.

Boring's view has lead to the *psychometric* approach to intelligence. It has resulted in a viable research agenda. But it contains a weakness.

If intelligence is equated with an IQ score, the study of intelligence is reduced to an analysis of the causes and consequences of test scores. So if the original process of test construction missed something important about intelligence, the assertion that intelligence is what the tests test makes it hard to incorporate new perspectives. Lippmann was right to be concerned over the conceptual limitations of a fascination with test scores.

The argument between Lippmann and Boring foreshadowed future developments. There are many advocates of the psychometric approach today. It is not entirely devoid of theory. In fact, the analysis of pragmatically defined test scores has suggested theoretical positions about intelligence that can then be expanded to include new measures. Some of these efforts will be presented in later chapters.

There are also contemporary psychologists who accept Lippmann's concerns (although he is seldom cited!) and then go beyond criticizing to try to develop a theoretical basis for intelligence and intelligence testing. Such a theory will be useful if it leads to a coherent picture of how individual differences in cognitive power arise and influence human experience from birth to death.

In Section 1.4 I present my own views about what such a theory has to deal with, and explain the difficulties that it encounters.

* Boring, 1923.

late talker! Most of us can think of someone who was not terribly impressive in grade school or high school, but who had a great college career. Things go the other way, too. The smartest kid in grade school does not always become a Phi Beta Kappa in college, let alone becoming a prize-winning physicist or a fabulously wealthy entrepreneur.

Such examples are striking, but they are exceptions to a general rule. Past the age of about ten, indicators of relative cognitive competence are fairly stable. A Scottish study found a substantial correlation between intelligence test scores taken at age eleven and subsequent measures taken when the examinees were in their sixties and seventies.[12] In psychological jargon intelligence is a *trait*, a characteristic of the individual that is reasonably stable over time and that is revealed in many situations.

Binet's third assumption was the unnoticed 600-pound gorilla in the room. Let us accept that there are individual differences in the mental competencies required to be successful in modern society.[13] These competencies, collectively, are what we mean when we say "intelligence." Binet assumed, and then showed, that it is possible to make reliable measurements of a substantial number of the traits that constitute intelligence, within the space of three or four hours.

I suggest that the reader go back and weigh each clause of that sentence. Binet showed that *some* of the cognitive traits important to success can be evaluated within a single testing session, conducted outside of the context of everyday activities. I like a term originally coined by Robert Mislevy,[14] *Drop in from the Sky* testing, because it captures the examinee's view of the out-of-context nature of the assessment. Much of

the research in the century following Binet can be looked upon as an attempt to refine and expand the measurements that can fit into the "Drop in from the Sky" paradigm.

Throughout this book I shall argue that by accepting the conventional testing paradigm as a given, intelligence researchers have too often ignored traits that cannot be measured within the paradigm but that, by any reasonable definition, are part of intelligence. Nonetheless, a nontrivial subset of human cognition does fit into the "Drop in from the Sky" paradigm, and hence can be evaluated using conventional testing methods.

1.2.5. *Expansions of Binet's Work: The Stanford-Binet and Wechsler Tests*

Binet's tests excited a great deal of interest. Educationally, the need for classifying students was a problem for the burgeoning public educational systems of the early twentieth century. Intellectually, the tests provided a foothold for applying the new, but rapidly developing, science of psychology. Lewis Terman, a professor at Stanford University, translated and modified Binet's tests for use in the United States. Due to the interruptions caused by World War I, Terman did not complete his work until the 1920s. The resulting test, the Stanford-Binet Intelligence Test, is still used in regularly updated form today.

The Binet and Stanford-Binet tests were intended for use with schoolchildren, roughly age fifteen and younger. In the late 1930s David Wechsler, a clinical psychologist working at New York City's Bellevue Hospital, created a similar test for adults, the *Wechsler-Bellevue* test. It has subsequently been modified into the *Wechsler Adult Intelligence Scale* (WAIS). It and a companion test for children, the *Wechlser Intelligence Scale for Children* (WISC), are the most widely used individually administered intelligence tests today. The Wechsler tests are often referred to as the "gold standard" for intelligence tests.[15] As of 2010 the fourth

---

12 Deary et al., 2000.

13 Individual differences in mental competence probably occur in every human society, although the relative importance of specific competencies may vary from society to society. The ability to locate one's self in space is less important in a society that has street signs and global positioning systems than in a society of hunter-gatherers.

14 Mislevy, formerly at ETS and now a professor at the University of Maryland, is a highly respected specialist in the field of psychometrics, the mathematical analysis of test scores.

15 Matarazzo, 1972.

revisions of the tests, WAIS-IV and WISC-IV, were in use.

Both the Wechsler and the Stanford-Binet tests are individually administered. The examinee sits down with a trained examiner and attempts to solve a series of problems, divided pragmatically into problems that do or do not involve language, and that vary in the demands that they place on memory. Wechsler has described this as an opportunity for the examinee to display his or her cognitive skills during a standardized interview with an experienced observer.[16]

The resulting IQ scores have proven to be highly useful, both in the educational system and in other settings. For instance, the WAIS is widely used to evaluate a person who, for whatever reason, is of suspected mental disability. Examples of such use are the adjudication of legal competence and the analysis of status following brain injury. Other applications of these tests, and there are many, are extensions of these ideas. The focus is always on the individual. The cost of testing is evaluated relative to the potential benefits of the results in making judgments about an individual case. Are the decisions made about this person improved by knowing test scores, and if they are, is the value of a typical decision enough to justify the costs of the test?[17]

The Wechsler and Stanford-Binet tests are not the only individually administered intelligence tests. However, they have played a very important role in the development of testing. Some further tests will be discussed in Chapter 2, where the tests are described in more detail.

1.2.6. *The Development of Group Testing*

The next major step in intelligence testing was a spin-off of technology from a military application. When America entered World War I the army had to make rapid mental evaluations of large numbers of incoming soldiers. The War Department[18] sponsored development of a test that could be administered to large groups of recruits. Psychologists responded with the *Army Alpha* Test, a written test suitable for group administration, and the *Beta* test, which could be given to nonliterates.[19]

The program was considered a success. Today the militaries in virtually all developed nations routinely use cognitive tests to screen recruits. The tests that the U.S. military uses will be described in Chapter 2.

The military tests are examples of personnel classification tests. Cognitive tests for personnel classification are widely used in the civilian sector as well as in the military. The costs and benefits of testing within a personnel classification system are not the same as the costs and benefits of testing intended for individual counseling and/or placement. In a personnel classification system correct classifications have a value and incorrect classifications have a cost, as seen from the perspective of the institution setting the test, rather than as seen from the perspective of the examinee. A classification test is economical if, on the average, the cost of administering the test is less than the value of improved decision making. This view shifts the focus from decisions about an individual to the average value of a decision, calculated over the entire population. The shift greatly affects the economics of testing. A cheap test, which makes only a moderate improvement in the accuracy of the selection decisions, administered to thousands of or even millions of people, can be a valuable classification instrument.

---

16 Wechsler, 1975.
17 The law provides a dramatic example. The United States Constitution prohibits "cruel and unusual punishment" but does not define it. Several of the states and the current federal code include capital punishment for treason and for particularly vicious cases of murder. The Supreme Court has held that it would be cruel and unusual punishment to execute a mentally retarded person for committing a capital crime, on the grounds that the person, though guilty, could not understand the crime or its consequences. As of 2009 a defendant's attorney could offer an IQ test score as one piece of evidence of mental retardation and, hence, as a reason for not assessing the death penalty.

18 Now renamed the Department of the Army and absorbed into the larger Department of Defense.
19 In the United States today illiteracy is almost a signal that the individual is of suspect intelligence. That was not true in 1917–18, for universal public education was not the case. Many people of normal intelligence were illiterate, especially in rural areas.

Well over a hundred group-administered classification tests have been developed. They include the Scholastic Ability Test (now renamed by its acronym, the SAT) used in the college admissions process, and the General Aptitude Test Battery (GATB), which for years was used by the United States Department of Labor to provide a test score to guide in industrial hiring, and many more.

Describing all the tests in use today literally takes a volume, and the volume has to be updated annually. Some of the more prominent tests are described in detail in Chapter 2. The important point is that since the 1930s intelligence testing has been widely used to make important decisions about people's academic and vocational careers. Testing is also used as a guide in medical rehabilitation, such as evaluating the course of treatment following insults to the brain. The tests are also widely used in research on the description, causes, and consequences of being intelligent.

1.3. Do the Tests Work? Efficacy and Controversy

There has been a great deal of debate about how well intelligence tests work. The debate is not surprising, because the issue is inherently complicated. How accurate does a test have to be before we say that "it works"? There can be different standards for different purposes. How well do we understand why the tests work? People are uncomfortable using indicators that they do not understand. To the scientist interested in intelligence, though, this question ought to be a challenge. What are the consequences of basing important decisions about education, employment, and personal planning on test scores?

We will look at the question of test accuracy in considerable detail in Chapter 10. Here I will do three things: explain the criterion by which tests are judged as being accurate or not, provide just a few interesting statistics (saving the rest for Chapter 10), and then describe the controversies.

Tests would be perfectly accurate if, whenever a test score was used as a predictor, there was some critical score such that everyone who had a score equal to or higher than the critical score succeeded, and everyone with a lower score failed. No such intelligence test exists, and none ever will. Test scores are not perfect indicators of a person's cognitive power; other things besides intellectual talent determine success; and success itself is not an either/or thing. The question is not whether or not test scores can be used to make perfect predictions of success or failure; the question is whether or not using test scores reliably improves our ability to predict who will succeed or fail. Tests that do this are said to be *valid*. Validity is a matter of degree; the more using a test improves prediction, the higher the test's validity.

Here is an example that illustrates the issue.

In the 1930s the Scottish psychologist Godfrey Thomson conceived the impressive plan of testing virtually the entire nation of Scotland. And he managed to do it. In 1932 Thomson's *Moray House* intelligence test was given to almost every eleven-year-old in Scotland, more than 80,000 in all.

About seventy years later Ian Deary, a professor at the University of Edinburgh, and his colleague Lawrence Whalley traced 2,300 of the people whom Thomson had tested. Figure 1.2, taken from their report, shows the fraction of the original respondents to the 1932 test who were still alive at different times from the 1930s until the start of the twenty-first century. The data is shown separately for men and women from the upper quartile (top 25%) and lower quartile (bottom 25%) of the distribution of test scores. Intelligent people live longer!

An intelligence test score obtained in childhood was a valid statistical predictor of length of life. This ought to catch the reader's attention.

Now let's use this fact to uncover some of the complications dealing with test scores, and by implication, intelligence itself, as a predictor.

We first must determine whether or not we are dealing with an artifact due to

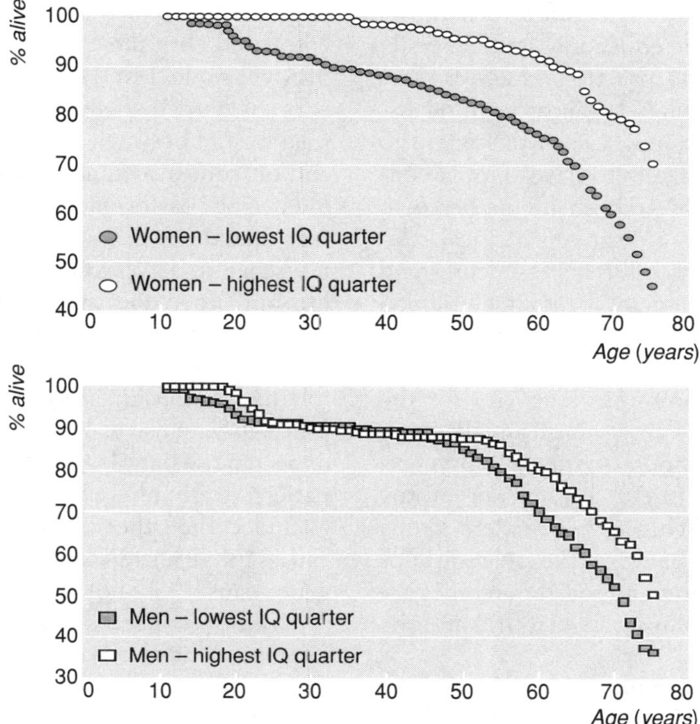

Figure 1.2. The fraction of individuals surviving to various ages for a cohort of approximately 2,200 Scottish children tested at age eleven, in 1932. From Whalley and Deary, 2001, Figure 1. By permission of the authors and the *British Medical Journal.*

some relationship that is forced between test scores and the outcome of interest. For instance, in the United States the SAT scores of people who enter college are higher than the test scores of people who do not enter college. That fact, alone, is uninteresting, because test scores are one of the determiners used to decide who gets to go to college. However, this sort of problem did not arise in the Scottish study, for it is unlikely that a score on a test taken at age eleven has any direct influence on mortality. The statistic indicates some meaningful relationship between mortality and whatever the test measures. But what?

I can imagine three different reasons why a test score might predict mortality. There might be a direct relationship. We know, today, that intelligence test scores are partly determined by the state of the brain. This statement will be documented in detail in Chapters 6 and 7. It could be that the test scores (imperfectly) revealed the state of the brain at age eleven, and this state carried forward over the years, producing an association between test scores and later mortality. This explanation would have appealed to both Galton and Juan Huarte de San Juan.

There could be an indirect relationship. Perhaps intelligence, as revealed by the tests, makes people less likely to do unhealthful things, like drinking alcohol to excess, or driving a motor vehicle after drinking to excess, or forgetting to take vaccinations against influenza, and so on. This explanation – that intelligence is related to finding smart solutions as you navigate your way through life – would have appealed to Binet.

Finally, it might be that the relationship is not due to intelligence at all; it is due to a third variable that both causes test scores (although it is not intelligence as we normally think of the term) and also influences mortality. Parental socioeconomic status (Parental SES) is a term used to refer to the general "place in society" occupied by a child's family. It includes such things as financial status, education, and generally beneficial lifestyle practices, such as having children inoculated against common diseases. It is also an indicator of the extent to which a child is likely to have "family connections" to help establish his or her own lifestyle. There is a positive statistical relationship between children's test scores and Parental SES. It might be that childhood test scores predict mortality because Parental SES assists in the development of a lifestyle that promotes longevity (or the opposite, for low test scores and Parental SES). The contemporary American psychologist Richard Nisbett, a professor at the University of Michigan, has made a strong argument that many of the relationships between test scores and social outcomes are actually relationships between SES and the outcomes.[20]

Which of these explanations do you think accounts for the Whalley and Deary data? Could two or more explanations both be true?

There are *probabilistic* relationships between test scores and a variety of interesting outcomes in life. In general, the higher a person's test score, the more likely that person is to have good things happen to them. These include educational achievement, on-the-job performance, income, marital status, health and longevity.[21] Most of the statistical relationships are high enough to be economically valuable evidence to guide decision making, both in personal life planning and in personnel classification. But because the relationships are probabilistic they have to be understood in statistical terms. This demands some expertise on the part of the person who tries to interpret the facts.

Test scores are not only correlated with outcomes in life, they are also correlated

with a variety of other measures that are correlated with the outcomes. The Parental SES example just given is illustrative. It is often hard to determine why there is a relationship between intelligence test scores and outcomes such as educational achievement, job performance, and health. The fact that there is a correlation between an IQ score and X, where X is almost any life outcome, does not prove, alone, that "intelligence causes X." There will almost always be several plausible interpretations for the relationship, and they are often not mutually exclusive. In the intelligence–life expectancy example three alternative explanations were offered, and none of them excluded the others. The questions "What causes intelligence?" and "What does intelligence cause?" are not easily answered.

Do not expect simple answers about intelligence in this book. I shall try to be as clear as I can, but some things are necessarily complex.

If you encounter simple answers somewhere else, my advice is to be very, very suspicious.

1.3.1. *The Controversies*

Because test scores are used to make major social decisions, it is hardly surprising that they have been controversial. One of the first of these debates occurred in the 1920s, when the social commentator Walter Lippmann published a series of articles criticizing intelligence testing in *The New Republic*, an influential magazine in liberal intellectual circles. Lippmann's articles provoked a furious response by Terman and, in somewhat more measured terms, a critique by the Harvard professor E. G. Boring. Boring's reply included the somewhat famous definition of intelligence as whatever the tests test.

The debate between Lippmann and Boring is described in Panel 1.2. Their argument touched on concerns about intelligence testing that are still raised today. Other concerns have also been raised. Most of these concerns deal with complicated facts about what intelligence is worth, and who has it – topics that are discussed in detail in

---

20 Nisbett, 2009.
21 There are a great many studies backing up these assertions. See Neisser et al. (1996) for the statement of the situation by a review panel of the American Psychological Association, Gottfredson (1997, 2007b) for reviews, and Herrnstein and Murray (1994) for a comprehensive analysis involving the AFQT. Chapter 10 discusses the topic in much more detail.

Chapters 10 and 11. Here I will foreshadow the discussion of the controversies briefly, by introducing the objections to the tests and outlining the nature of the responses.

Objection 1. The tests cannot possibly work. It is unreasonable to believe that performance on a "Drop in from the Sky" test, made up by people who do not know the examinee, could possibly reveal important mental traits.

A slightly more sophisticated way of saying this is that the objector believes that human thought is so subtle that its nature could not possibly be captured in a single interview. This makes the objection seem much less anti-intellectual, but it amounts to the same thing as my original, italicized version.

I do not know whether to call Objection 1 a Know-Nothing attitude (I don't want to learn) or a Know-All attitude (I already know the answer, so your tests are not necessary). In any case, this objection dominated the debate between Lippmann and Boring (Panel 1.2), and it still arises today. I do not believe that it is productive.

Objection 2. The tests don't work. There are people who have only modest test scores and do well, and people who have very high test scores and are not doing notably well.

Here the objector asks that all predictions made on the basis of test scores be accurate. This is an impossible goal. Intelligence is not the only thing that determines success or failure, in academics or in life in general.

I conjecture that the objection is rooted in two facts – a psychological one and a sociological one.

The psychological fact is that when people have to deal with probabilistic relationships they try to get an intuitive feeling for the relationship, rather than analyzing numbers. This leads to an overinterpretation of exceptional cases. Because the tests do work pretty well, on the average, failures stand out. People remember the case of the person with low test scores who did brilliantly, or the one with high test scores who did miserably. The fact that most people perform about as well as their test scores predict, with a small amount of variation, just does not stick in memory.

The sociological fact is that many of us live in a cognitively stratified society. Children of parents with high, middle, or low SES go to schools with children of the same background as their own. Academic testing mechanisms stratify college students on the basis of SAT or similar test scores. In the workplace our coworkers tend to be of roughly the same intelligence as we are. When we deal with people of greatly varied intelligence we tend to do so in a stereotyped way. A sales clerk, for instance, encounters customers of highly varied intelligence, but does not interact with them in a way that would reveal their intelligence. Stratification occurs at home, because there is a great deal of residential segregation by socioeconomic status; therefore, neighborhood life is "stratified by intelligence."

The result is that within a person's local society there will not be a great deal of variation in intelligence, so other factors, such as variations in personality, will play a role in determining social success. Therefore, when people try to evaluate intelligence by referring to their personal experiences they are likely to undervalue the role of intelligence in the general society.

The poor statistician has an uphill climb when trying to show that intelligence really is an important part of the big picture.

Objection 3. The tests work only in the academic arena.

This objection flies in the face of the evidence. The point will be addressed directly in Chapter 10, where evidence will be given showing that test scores predict success in both the academic and the industrial/economic sphere. Because the argument has to be made statistically, it has to counter the results of the intellectual stratification of the workplace, as described in the response to objection 2.

There is also another problem. Leaving aside spectacular cases, like billionaires heading companies that pioneer new technology, it is hard to establish who is succeeding in the workplace on an individual basis. This makes the statistical analyses more complex than they are in the case of analyzing academic success, and hence harder to explain to the nonstatistician.

Objection 4. The tests work only for certain demographic groups, notably middle-class whites. The tests do not predict well for other groups.

This issue will be addressed directly in Chapter 11. Foreshadowing, while some data is lacking, it is usually found that test scores have about the same power to predict achievement in all demographic groups.

Objection 5. The tests should not be used because they are prejudiced against minority group members, who tend to get low scores.

This objection raises one of the most incendiary topics in psychology: the possibility that there are individual differences in intelligence across racial and ethnic groups. The topic is discussed in detail in Chapter 11. Here I present a brief statement of the issue.

In the United States, and in other industrially developed nations, there are differences in the average intelligence test scores of different racial/ethnic groups. In the United States the order of scores, from highest to lowest, is Asian-derived groups, European-derived groups, Latin-American–derived groups, and then African-derived groups. The Asian-European gap is reliable, but rather small. The European-Latino and European-African gaps are substantial. The debate is not over the existence of differences, it is over their meaning and their implications for action. These are two separate issues.

If the tests predicted performance only in the white group, discrepancies in test scores across groups could simply be disregarded. However, that is not the case; the test scores do predict performance in all racial/ethnic groups. Although many strong opinions have been expressed, there is no consensus about the causes of group differences in IQ scores. Because this debate requires a good understanding of intelligence itself, I have postponed the discussion of racial and ethnic differences until the next-to-last chapter.

Should test scores be used in personnel screening if doing so would reduce the proportion of minority applicants who are accepted for employment or education? There is no justification for using a test that would have an adverse impact on one group or another if that test is *not* a valid predictor of performance. If the test is a valid indicator – as intelligence tests usually are, to some degree – then the policy maker is faced with a trade-off. Should the best people be selected, regardless of group membership, or should some effort be made to balance rates of acceptance across racial and ethnic groups? This is a policy issue, not a scientific one. Scientific research can provide information about the costs and benefits of a policy, but the decision is up to the policy maker.

1.4. A Framework for Thinking about Intelligence

1.4.1. *Manifest and Latent Variables: Definition and Diagramming Conventions*

Many of the arguments over intelligence have been less informative than they might be, because the arguers have not been clear about what their concept of intelligence is, or about what they think the relation is between test scores and intelligence, in the more general sense of individual differences in mental competence. Here I present my own views. They represent an expansion of a model of the causes and consequences of mental competence that I developed together with Jerry Carlson, a professor at the University of California, Riverside.[22] We did not present a new theory of what intelligence is, nor do I here. The goal is to provide

22 Hunt & Carlson, 2007a.

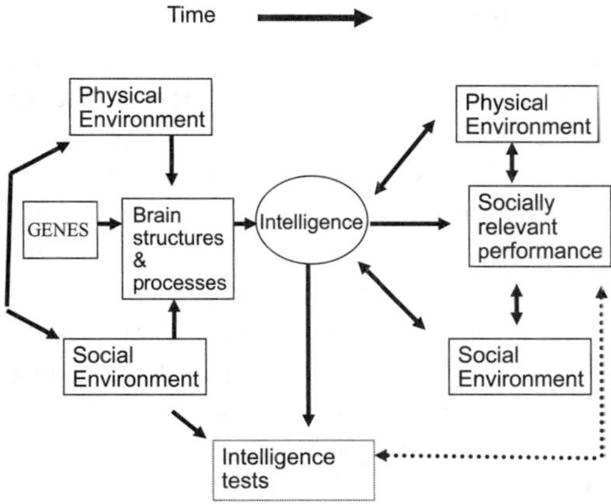

Figure 1.3. A model of the development and utilization of cognitive abilities ("Intelligence"). Intelligence is a latent variable, indicated by manifest variables that include but are not limited to intelligence test scores. Intelligence influences, and is influenced by, a number of environmental and biological variables.

a framework for discussing theories and facts about intelligence.

Figure 1.3 presents the model I will use throughout this book. Before discussing its content a word is in order about the notation used in the figure, for these notational conventions will be followed throughout this book.

Rectangles will be used to represent *manifest variables*, things that can be seen and, in principle, measured. Test scores, grades, and salaries are examples of manifest variables. Ellipses will represent *latent variables*, conceptual entities that are used in theories. Intelligence, cultural knowledge, and socioeconomic status (SES) are latent variables. They can be defined only by their (imperfect) manifest indicators. Latent variables are never defined or measured directly; their values are inferred from observation of the appropriate manifest variables. For example, SES is inferred from education, wealth, and residence. Intelligence is inferred from test scores and, in many cases, other indices of cognition.

We also have to distinguish among three separate relations between variables: causation, reciprocal causation, and correlation. Causation will be indicated by a single-headed arrow. For instance, in Figure 1.3

there is a single-headed arrow between genes and brain structure, because genetic makeup does determine brain structure. Reciprocal causation, in which one variable causes another and then the second feeds back into the first, will be indicated by a double-headed arrow. The double-headed arrow between intelligence and the social environment indicates that a person's intelligence partly determines his or her social environment, which in turn influences the further development of intelligence. Correlation, in which two variables tend to occur together, without any implication of causation, will be indicated by a double-headed arrow with a dashed line between the arrowheads. There is an example of this in Figure 1.3, and we will encounter examples of correlation without causation in other diagrams.

The debate between Lippmann and Boring can be cast in terms of manifest and latent variables. Lippmann thought of intelligence as a latent variable, but failed to grapple with the question of how it should be related to manifest variables. Boring either did not make the distinction, or wanted to assert that his manifest variable, the test score, was a perfect indicator of the latent variable. I do not think that either position can be maintained.

1.4.2. *The Causes of Intelligence*

Now let us turn to substance, working from "the beginning," at the left side of Figure 1.3, toward the expression of intelligence represented on the right-hand side.

It all starts with the genes. A person's genetic makeup determines his or her potential for the development of brain structures that support all activities, including cognition. There are individual differences in genetic makeup; otherwise we would all be clones. These differences do have implications for the development of intelligence, even though most people probably operate well below their genetic potential.

Although the genotype is established at conception, parts of the genotype may not be expressed until certain ages are reached.

For example, there are a number of medical conditions, such as Alzheimer's disease, that have some genetic basis, but are not displayed until well past childhood.

The extent to which the genetic potential is realized depends upon the extent to which the environment encourages the development of intelligence. In modern developed societies it appears that somewhere upwards of 50% of the variance in IQ scores can be statistically associated with genetic variation. However, no one, ever, inherited a test score in the same sense that they inherited the color of their eyes. People do differ in the extent to which they have inherited brain mechanisms that allow them to deal with their society in a way that produces the mental capabilities required to solve the problems proposed on a cognitive test. My apologies for a complicated sentence, but I cannot think of any other way to make this very important point. Genetic capacities unfold throughout life. In fact, the association of genetics with intelligence test scores is higher in old age than in adolescence.[23]

The extent to which the genetic potential is realized is determined by the physical and social environment. Here is a striking example.

If a pregnant woman abuses alcohol her child may be born with *fetal alcohol syndrome*, a serious form of mental retardation. The likelihood that this physical condition will occur depends on the social environment. Fetal alcoholism does not incur in societies that enforce abstinence. It can be a substantial problem in societies where alcohol is freely available as a recreational drug, especially if the social stresses that lead to alcohol abuse are present.

Social influences also act upon the developing mind. At this point, though, we have to shift from the concept of *brain* to the concept of *mind*. Ultimately everything is in the brain. Nevertheless, it is often useful to distinguish between mental capabilities that are determined by a person's capacity to process information in the abstract and capabilities that are determined by the possession of information, either about the world or about how to solve problems in the world. Information and problem-solving styles are heavily influenced by the society within which a person lives.

Arguably the most striking example is literacy. The ability to read appears to be associated with willingness to evaluate abstract arguments and to take multiple perspectives, a behavior that is tested in many intelligence tests.[24] These can be considered direct influences of literacy upon intelligence. Literacy also has an indirect influence, for it opens the door to formal education, and education is, by definition, a major avenue for passing on culturally acquired knowledge. Literacy facilitates the transmission of cultural knowledge, and cultural knowledge allows us to behave more intelligently.

Medicine offers an example. Modern health workers wash their hands when they move from patient to patient. Prior to the mid nineteenth century this was not seen as necessary. Does this make today's physicians more intelligent than the physicians of George Washington's day? In an important sense, they are. Knowledge is cognitive power.

There is a two-way interaction between brain and mind. One of the major limitations on knowledge acquisition is the ability to concentrate mental effort on a topic, in the face of distractions. The ability to concentrate depends on how well certain brain structures work, primarily but not exclusively in the forebrain. It also depends upon how efficiently information about the external world is coded inside the nervous system. The coding systems people use depend very much upon their experience with the topic at hand.

Intelligence is a personal trait produced by an interaction between genetic potential and environmental support. Where do IQ scores fit into this picture?

23 McGue et al., 1993.

24 Cole, 2005; Wolf, 2007.

1.4.3. *The Measurement of Intelligence*

The center portion of Figure 1.3 makes a point that is obvious when you think about it, but that is surprisingly often forgotten.

A person's intelligence test score is produced by two things: the social decision to construct an intelligence test in a particular way and the examinee's ability to deal with the test once it has been constructed. Different societies might construct different tests, depending upon the mental capabilities that each society values. This does not mean that tests are narrowly culture-bound, for some mental qualities are seen as vital in all societies. For instance, all societies demand that their members learn their native language. On the other hand, societies may differ in the emphasis that they place on other aspects of cognition.

Both these points were illustrated nicely by an anecdote told me by Manuel de Juan-Espinosa, a Spanish psychologist who has studied conceptions of intelligence held by the Fang, a society of mixed agricultural-ists and hunters in Equatorial Guinea. When you ask people in Western society to list the attributes of an intelligent person, you generally get statements about the ability to solve abstract problems and the ability to comprehend and use language. Spatial orientation, the ability to locate oneself in the physical environment, is either not mentioned or mentioned far down on the list. When the topic is brought to their attention people do agree that it is intelligent to be able to find your way around the neighborhood. In our society, though, this is usually not an important skill. Our intelligence tests include only a few evaluations of spatial orientation.

When the Fang list the qualities of an intelligent person they say, "Intelligent people do not get lost in the forest." This does not mean that the Fang devalue the sorts of verbal skills that Westerners mention. In fact, they stress verbal skills, in much the same way that Westerners do. If the Fang were to construct intelligence tests they would include tests of verbal skills, as ours do. The Fang might look into the matter of spatial orientation in more detail than we do.

IQ tests, and tests related to IQ tests, such as the SAT and AFQT, are artifacts of the cultures in which they arose. They test some aspects of intelligence but not others. However, the tests are not arbitrary.

IQ tests would not have survived, as arti-facts, unless test scores could be used as (imperfect) predictors of what our society sees as socially important behaviors, such as academic and social achievement. Because the test scores do meet this criterion, the tests must either evaluate mental skills that are used by the society or they must evaluate mental skills that are not used, in themselves, but whose possession is highly corre-lated with the possession of skills that can be used. That is, the tests might be like an Army physical examination where the candidate is required to do push-ups. Soldiers are not going to do push-ups in combat, but the ability to do push-ups is correlated with the ability to move heavy objects (e.g., carrying artillery shells to a gun position), which soldiers may have to do. The same argument may apply to the mental gymnas-tics required to perform well on intelligence tests.

While all human societies are not identical, there is a core set of cognitive skills that all societies rely upon. All societies demand that their members learn to speak the native language, be able to control attention, and, by the standards of all other animals in the world, remember events very well. Therefore, an intelligence test that is valid in one culture is unlikely to be entirely invalid in another, although its validity may be reduced.

Individual differences in cognitive skills might, in principle, either be due to posses-sion of a great many special-purpose brain mechanisms or be due to possession of very general information-processing capa-bilities that can be applied to all men-tal challenges. Intermediate solutions are possible; we might have a single general processing capacity, augmented by special processors. To the extent that the evolu-tion of our species has produced a general problem-solving brain, it does not matter precisely how that brain is evaluated, for a person's behavior in one cognitively challenging situation will predict how well he or she deals with other situations.

There is a surprising amount of evidence that evolution has taken the general problem-solving solution.

1.4.4. *The Uses of Intelligence*

We now come to the right-hand section of the diagram, dealing with the results of intelligence.

People use their cognitive abilities to define their environments. Consider good health practices. Sometimes very bright people become alcoholics and/or crash cars, both activities that can lead to brain damage. But, on the average, people with high intelligence test scores do not do such things, and so enjoy better health.[25] Once again, we see how intelligence and the environment interact.

Cognitive abilities are not the only abilities that we have. Differences in behavior are also produced by individual differences in a variety of emotional-motivational traits. These are lumped together loosely under the title "personality." It is not clear where to draw the line between intelligence and personality. For instance, *conscientiousness*, the tendency to fulfill obligations to others (including one's employers) is usually considered a personality trait. However, it is possible to see conscientiousness as an offshoot of intelligence. It makes sense to be conscientious in fulfilling obligations to people who control resources that you want.

This is hardly a new observation. Machiavelli's famous sixteenth-century discourse on political behavior, *The Prince*, contained cogent arguments for displaying certain personality traits, including honesty and conscientiousness, because such behavior is in one's enlightened self-interest. It is intelligent to be thought trustworthy and reliable.

We can make a distinction between cognition and personality by asking if we are talking about whether a person *can do* or *will do* a certain behavior. To the extent that the answer is "can do" the mental acts controlling the behavior are part of cognition, and hence individual differences in them are part of intelligence. To the extent that the answer is "will do" the mental control is part of motivation, and individual differences are part of personality.

Any particular action has to satisfy both "can do" and "will do" requirements. Although this is hardly a profound statement, it is surprising how often explanations of behavior focus on personality to the exclusion of intelligence or vice versa.

1.4.5. *The Results of Intelligence*

Intelligence shows itself in two ways: by test scores and by socially relevant behaviors. Test scores are easy to analyze; socially relevant behavior is hard to analyze. Nevertheless, socially relevant behaviors are far more important than test scores.

There are statistical associations (correlations) between intelligence test scores and measures of socially relevant behavior including academic achievement, income, health, and occupation of prestigious positions in society.[26] These associations are facts. Arguing about why they occur is a reasonable thing to do. As every student in elementary courses on experimental design is told, correlation does not imply causation. Rather, the fact that intelligence test scores and measures of socially relevant behaviors are correlated suggests a number of possible causes, all of which are worth investigation.

Performance on an intelligence test and performance in socially relevant situations might both depend upon the same cognitive processes. This is what most researchers on intelligence believe. However, the statistical associations, although not negligible, are not compellingly large. They generally range from a correlation coefficient of .2 to

---

25 For a typical study recent study, see Batty et al., 2006.

26 Gottfredson, 1997; Herrnstein & Murray, 1994. See the extensive discussion in Chapter 10.

.5, and in a few situations correlations as high as .8 have been reported. Just what these statistics mean is explained in more detail in Chapter 2. Temporarily, I ask readers to take on faith the statement that the correlations are high enough to indicate that test scores and behaviors tap some common traits, but low enough to indicate that the traits that affect the tests and the behaviors are not exactly the same.

It could be that the test scores themselves are causing the behaviors but that the cognitive capabilities required by the tests are not. This might happen in two ways. One is that knowledge of a high or low test score could cause other people to treat the examinee differently. It has been claimed that this is the case in education, because teachers may respond differently to students with high or low IQ scores.[27]

Test scores will influence behavior if the scores are used to decide who is offered a chance to behave in a certain way. The SAT, the ASVAB, and the Department of Defense's Officers Qualifying Test (OQT) are examples. Other things being equal, the people with the highest test scores will be allowed to enter a prestigious university, be commissioned as an officer in the armed services, and so forth. Subsequent behavior will be guided by the experience of having been in the university, been a commissioned officer, and so forth. On the one hand, it can be argued that this is appropriate. If a test correctly identifies people who have the cognitive capability to, say, benefit intellectually from an Ivy League education, then the test is an appropriate gatekeeper. On the other hand, it could be argued that the benefits one gets from being allowed to enter a certain social stratum depend very little on cognitive abilities. Colloquially, it's not what you learn

---

27 Should teachers know their students' IQ scores? There are rational arguments for and against the practice. If teachers know students' IQ scores they might offer special instruction to students they think are bright, or they might give up on teaching low-scoring students. Looked at another way, the information could be used diagnostically, helping teachers tailor instruction to the student.

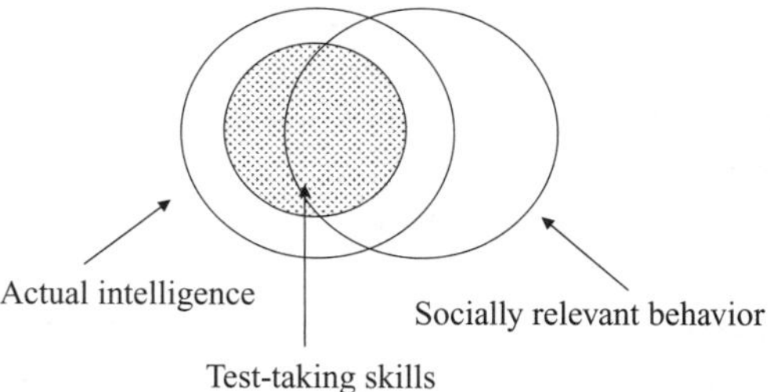

Figure 1.4. People possess cognitive skills (conceptual intelligence) to varying degrees. Some of these skills are evaluated by the tests. Of the skills evaluated by the tests some are specific to the test situation, and others are relevant to social behavior in general.

at Harvard (Yale, Stanford, Duke, Oxford, or Cambridge) that determines your subsequent success in life, it is who you meet in college. Either of these mechanisms could produce a correlation between test scores and later success, on a between-institution basis, because the test scores were used to determine who got in, but not on a within-institution basis, because the test scores did not tap the abilities required to benefit from the experience.

The two explanations are not mutually exclusive. My own bet is that both factors operate.

Figure 1.4 summarizes the argument. Socially relevant behaviors are partly determined by cognitive skills. Variations in these behaviors are, conceptually, intelligence. Some of the skills that define conceptual intelligence are reflected in test scores. Other socially important cognitive skills that are part of intelligence are not reflected in test scores, and test scores also reflect test-specific skills that are not related to socially relevant behavior.

Lippmann was right that IQ scores do not measure everything, Boring was right that they do measure something.

Intelligence tests do a good job of evaluating an examinee's ability to respond rapidly to problems of varying degrees of complexity. In the following chapters I discuss evidence showing that IQ and similar tests are statistically related to the cognitive abilities that underlie socially relevant behaviors, ranging literally from becoming a judge to becoming a criminal. However, important cognitive abilities required for socially relevant behavior are not tapped by the tests. What might these be?

Any testing method that relies on the conventional "Drop in from the Sky" paradigm cannot evaluate abilities that reveal themselves over a relatively long period of time, such as the ability to plan, to allocate time for extended courses of action, or to integrate information from multiple sources. It is difficult, if not impossible, to tap these skills in a test that seldom takes more than three hours and that consists of unrelated problems that, individually, take only a few minutes to solve. Overreliance on conventional testing has greatly limited modern research on intelligence.

1.4.6. *Cause and Effect in Intelligence Research*

The arrows going back and forth in Figure 1.3 highlight how hard it is to determine cause and effect when studying intelligence. If everything were simple we would place causal variables on the left, intelligence in the center, and the effects of having intelligence on the right. To some extent this can be done. Genetics and a child's physical and social environment do produce intelligence, and a person's intelligence does produce socially relevant behavior, and thus alters the person's environment. The problem is with the feedback. Intelligence influences a person's environment, and feedback from the environment alters intelligence.

Take the case of aging. As we grow older two different processes influence intelligence. There is a decline in brain function. At the same time, as people live they acquire "wisdom," better and better knowledge about how the culture runs. There are huge individual differences in both of these processes. Some people remain cognitively fit until great age; others descend into near-senility at little past fifty. Some people acquire wisdom as they pass through the world; others only have experiences. In both these situations intelligence appears to act

as both cause and effect. Other things being equal, more intelligent adults are more likely to maintain healthy lifestyles than less intelligent ones, and are more open to engaging with, and thus extracting wisdom from, the world about them.

The interaction between intelligence and the environment has posed a major problem for researchers. We know far less than we need to know about the development of cognitive power over the adult life span. It is reasonably easy to measure cognition and other psychological variables as long as people are in the educational system. Similarly, it is relatively easy to obtain access to retired people, through social and medical support institutions, ranging from gray-haired hikers pausing at an elder hostel to the patients in a medical care facility. It is much harder to obtain access to people in the working years, for the simple reason that they are busy at work and raising families.

This is a serious situation, for adult intelligence is not inert. It rises to meet environmental challenges.

1.5. Reaction Ranges and the Challenge Hypothesis

Imagine a hypothetical person, Harry P., at age fifty. We want to estimate Harry's intelligence without actually measuring it. Here is what we can do.

1. Our initial estimate is the average intelligence of a person at age fifty.
2. Collect facts about Harry's physiological status, including genetic background, medical history, present eating and drinking habits, and so on. Use these to compute a biological correction factor to the initial estimate.
3. Collect facts about Harry's social environment, including education, marital status, hobbies, profession, and so forth. Compute a social correction factor, and add it in. The twice-adjusted figure is our estimate.

The result will be an estimate of current intelligence. We would not know how that

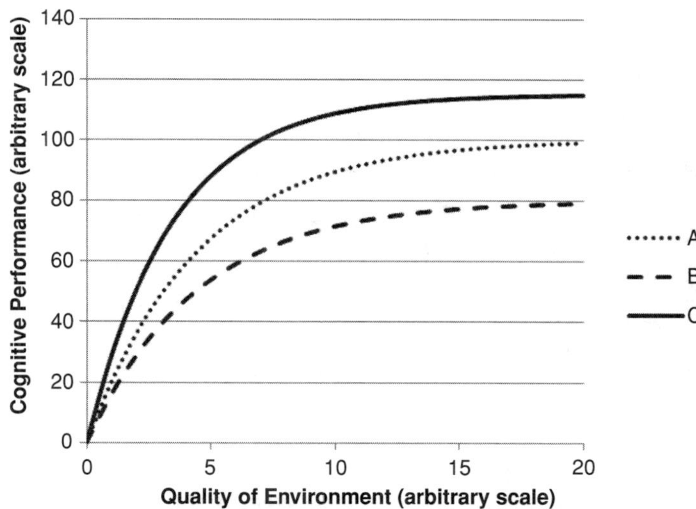

Figure 1.5. The concept of reaction range. The ordinate represents the quality of observable performance, and the abcissa represents the extent to which the environment supports development of cognitive skills. A person's level of cognitive performance is determined by the combination of reaction range and quality of the environment. Persons A, B, and C each have a unique potential for cognitive performance, indicated by the three lines. Their actual performance will be determined by the quality of the environment. If the environment goes from very poor (at the far left of the figure) to moderate (toward the middle), there will be considerable improvement of performance. Going from moderate to good environments (towards the right) does not result in a great deal of improvement.

intelligence had been acquired. Estimation alone does not explain the dynamics of intelligence.

A person's genetic makeup does not provide that person with a certain number of "intelligence units," any more than it provides a person with a certain number of points on an IQ test. Genetic status provides a *reaction range*, a range of levels of intelligence. Environmental factors determine where the person will operate within that range.

Figure 1.5 displays three hypothetical reaction ranges. Cognitive functioning is shown on the ordinate (y-axis), the level of favorableness of the environment on the abscissa (x-axis). Three different reaction ranges are shown. Where a person actually functions is determined by the point at which a vertical line drawn from the environment's rating crosses the reaction range

line. Observable cognitive performance is determined by the combination of genetic reaction range and environmental quality. The level of genetic inheritance cannot be inferred from IQ scores unless environmental quality is known, nor can environmental quality be inferred from IQ scores unless genetic inheritance is known.

Varieties of this theme will appear throughout our discussion of intelligence. For example, any difference in the cognitive performance of identical (*monozygotic* or *MZ*) twins can be attributed to the environment because MZ twins, having identical genotypes, will have identical genetically determined reaction ranges.

The concept of reaction range applies to the environment as well. This can be seen in Figure 1.6, which is simply a "cleaned up" version of Figure 1.5, in which three vertical lines have been drawn upward from

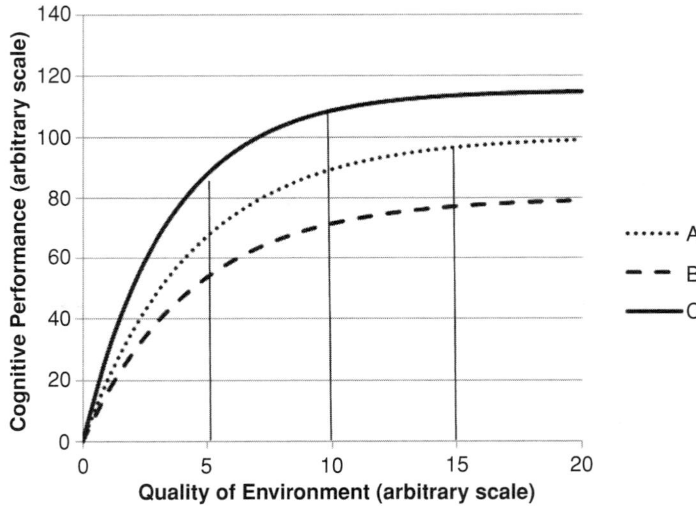

Figure 1.6. Environmental reaction ranges. Suppose the environmental quality is fixed (arbitrarily) at a quality of 10 for all individuals. Differences in cognitive performance will occur due to individual differences in genetic potential. However, if individual A is placed in an environment of quality 15 and C in an environment of quality 5, A will outperform C even though C has greater genetic potential.

the environmental quality axis, each line representing a different quality of environment. Each of the lines intersects the different genetically determined reaction ranges at different points, resulting in a variety of cognitive performances, even though the environment is identical for all individuals.

Figures 1.5 and 1.6 show the genetic reaction ranges as negatively accelerated curves that rise steeply at first, and then flatten out as they approach an asymptotic value. This was an arbitrary choice, for both the cognitive performance and environmental quality axes are shown on arbitrary scales. I chose to display negatively accelerated curves because of my conjecture that, in fact, attempts to improve cognition will result in negatively accelerated curves. Why do I make this conjecture?

There are a number of ways of producing physical environments that greatly constrain the development of intelligence. Prolonged famine is one; infection of the brain is another. Once these disaster states are avoided, the incremental effects of improving the physical environment are probably rather small. The same thing is true for the establishment of genetic potential. There are many "catastrophic" genetic conditions, where the presence of a single anomaly greatly restricts cognitive development, but if there is no anomaly genetic potential seems to depend upon the combined effects of a large number of genes, no one of which contributes a great deal. These matters are discussed in some detail in Chapters 8 and 9. There are lots of ways to restrict intelligence, but we know of relatively few ways to expand it. This implies negatively accelerated growth curves.

Having a reaction range does not mean that you use it. Cognitive skills are acquired by investing time and energy. Willingness to invest depends upon one's perception of the likely outcome of the investment. I propose the following conjecture.

The Challenge Hypothesis:

Intelligence is developed by engaging in cognitively challenging activities. Environments vary in the extent to which they support such challenges, and individuals vary in the extent to which they seek them out.

The development of intelligence depends upon the extent to which the individual wishes, is allowed to, or is required to meet environmental challenges.

Consider one of the linchpins of human cognition – language. Every human being is required to learn a spoken first language, and all normal people do so. Only in the last two hundred years have societies begun to demand literacy, which is a much harder skill to acquire. It is worth the effort. A literate person has acquired a cognitive skill that makes him or her more intelligent than an illiterate one with an identical, but unrealized, biological potential for intelligence.[28]

The example expands. Literate societies dominate the globe. They have developed formal education systems that force further intellectual development. Mechanisms of education such as the school, the newspaper, and the World Wide Web are different from, and far more challenging than, the educational systems of the nineteenth century. As a result, today's children are more intelligent than children in the past. As a reflection of this phenomenon, IQ scores rose throughout the twentieth century.

Literacy is an example of a compulsory challenge; individuals have to meet it or suffer severe consequences. In other cases there may be options. Learning about statistics and probability provides a good example. On a population basis, relatively few people study statistics. Students who graduate from, and understand, elementary statistics courses can solve problems that Pascal and Gauss could not solve. I do not think that the typical student in a modern statistics class has the biological potential for intelligence that Pascal and Gauss had. There is a sense in which they are more intelligent, for they are more powerful problem solvers.

Robert Sternberg has identified three ways a person has of responding to cognitive challenges.

1. *Adapting*: Changing your own cognitive behaviors to meet the challenge. Studying is a way of adapting, though certainly not the only one.
2. *Shaping*: Changing the environment to adapt it to your current capabilities. If you have difficulty doing arithmetic, buy a hand calculator.
3. *Selecting*: Finding a new environment that does not present the challenge you want to avoid. If you are a college student majoring in engineering, but math classes are difficult for you, consider switching majors.

Sternberg's three strategies have different cognitive demands of their own. Both adapting and shaping require a willingness to engage with the environment. This is in itself a reliable individual trait. Philip Ackerman, a professor at the Georgia Institute of Technology, has conducted research showing that willingness to engage in intellectual challenge is characteristic of the people who hold the occupations and avocations that we think of as requiring intelligence.[29] Selecting can be rational in some situations, but it has the danger of becoming a way to avoid intellectual challenge, and hence, to avoid the development of one's biological potential for intelligence.

1.6. Intelligence Is Part of a System

Defining intelligence solely in terms of test performance is an impoverished view. It focuses our attention on explaining variations in test scores, which are not important in themselves, at the expense of studying individual variations in socially relevant behavior, which are important. However, it would be foolish to disregard the considerable amount of information about intelligence that is incorporated in test scores.

One of the major reasons for studying intelligence is to understand how individual differences in cognitive competence, intelligence in the broad sense, are related to individual differences in the display of socially

28 See Wolf (2007) for a very well-argued, extensive expansion on this point.

29 Ackerman, 1996; Ackerman & Beier, 2005.

relevant behaviors. In practice, there are two problems. Variations in socially relevant performance are determined by noncognitive as well as cognitive factors. Success (or failure) is based on both "can do" and "will do." In addition, the display of socially relevant behaviors depends upon the opportunity to display them, which may be quite beyond a person's control, no matter what his or her personal characteristics are. Here are two historical examples.

In the early twentieth century Joseph P. Kennedy, an American financier, amassed a considerable fortune. Subsequently three of his sons – John, Robert, and Edward – became United States Senators. In 1960 John became President of the United States. One can argue, probably correctly, that Joseph Kennedy provided his sons the genetic capability to become very intelligent. But his fortune certainly helped their political careers, if only to relieve them of the need to earn a living outside of public service.

Now let us look at an example of restriction. The Declaration of Independence of the United States, written in 1776, contains the statement, "All men are created equal." At that time women were disenfranchised, and the slavery of Africans was condoned. Over two hundred years later Condoleeza Rice, an African American woman, who had served in many high-level positions, including Secretary of State, observed that when the Declaration was written, "They weren't talking about me." Dr. Rice's impressive achievements, which depended very largely on her intelligence, would have been impossible in 1776.

At the start of the twenty-first century the Darfur region of the Sudan was wracked by drought, famine, and vicious ethnic warfare. Children born in Darfur in the year 2003, no matter what their genetic potential, did not have good life prospects.

The point of these examples is that both the causes and effects of intelligence are embedded in a matrix of other variables. This makes good research on intelligence hard to do. The task is difficult, but it is not impossible. While an ideal study may be impossible to implement, a great deal can be learned from less-than-ideal studies. Progress can be made by investigating the issues that can be studied, and hopefully by holding down excessive interpretations and conclusions where we do not have the right evidence.

It is fairly easy to determine the correlation between test scores and other measures of interest, such as grade point average (GPA) and performance at work. Such studies provide important data. However, they bias our knowledge toward finding out the role of intelligence in certain institutions, such as the schools and the military, that, while certainly important, are not the whole of society. In addition, the study of bivariate correlations, in isolation, fails to stress an important fact. Intelligence is just one of the variables in the system defined by human society. What does this mean?

A *system* is a set of interdependent variables, in which each variable influences the others. In *closed systems* the interdependence is complete. The value of each variable is completely determined by the other variables in the system. In *open systems* some variables are influenced by conditions outside the system. The real-world systems we study are always open. Therefore, it is important to distinguish between *system variables*, which exert measured reciprocal influences on each other, and *external variables*, which influence the system variables but are not (to any great extent) influenced by the system variables.[30]

To illustrate, consider a hypothetical study of the roles of genetics, family influence, and intelligence during primary school, middle school, and high school. The following relations hold:

1. A child's intelligence on the first day of school has been determined by genetic inheritance and family environment prior to entering school.
2. Intelligence on entering middle school is determined by intelligence on entering

---

30 In economics the terms *endogenous* and *exogenous* variables are used.

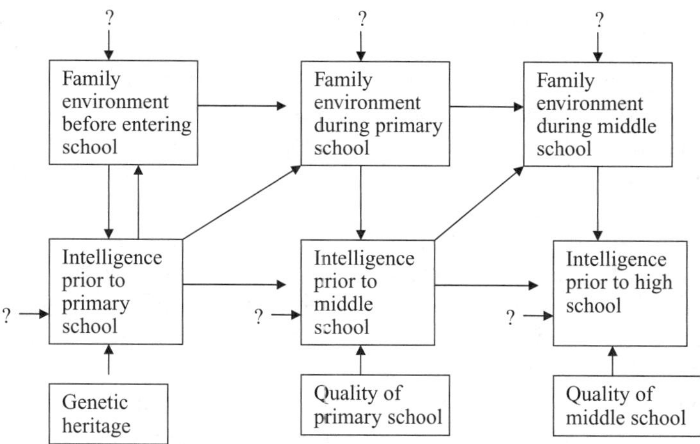

Figure 1.7. A systems' view of the relationship between intelligence, family environment, and the quality of schooling. Intelligence and family environment are system variables. Genetic heritage and quality of school are external variables. Unknown sources that influence the system variables are indicated by a question mark.

primary school, the quality of the primary school, and family environment during primary school, but not by the environment prior to entry into primary school.

3. A child's intelligence on entering high school is determined by intelligence on entering middle school, family environment during middle school, and the quality of the middle school.

4. At any time family environment is determined by prior family environment and by the child's intelligence. (People, including children, influence their environment.)

Figure 1.7 diagrams the system. Intelligence and family environment are system variables, because they influence each other. Genetic potential and quality of schooling are external variables, because they exert influences on other measures but are not influenced by them. If we can obtain measurements of all these variables, we can use modern statistical methods to evaluate the relative influences of each variable upon the others.

Then we come to the external, unmeasured variables. Figure 1.7 makes no provision for extrafamilial influences on the family environment, such as financial emergencies. Nor is there any provision for extrafamilial and extra-educational influences on intelligence, such as physical injury. Therefore, we have to allow for the "unknown unknowns," the influence of unmeasured external variables. These are indicated by the "?" symbols in the figure. While we cannot identify these variables, modern statistical techniques do allow us to estimate the size of their influence compared to the influence of the measured system variables on each other. Hopefully the influence of the "unknown unknowns" will be small; if it is large, analyses within the system will account for only a small part of what we need to know.

We can learn a great deal by comparing systems models to each other. The intelligence-education system displayed in Figure 1.7 treats genetic influences as a one-shot effect – genetics influences intelligence prior to entering school – but has no direct influence subsequently. In fact, though, some genetic effects unfold over time. For example, individual differences in the rate at which connections are developed in the forebrain during adolescence may result in differences in the ability to control impulsive behavior, which may influence how much a student learns in middle school, and so forth. These influences could be modeled by extending arrows from the genetic inheritance box to the boxes representing measurements of intelligence at each time period, not just at the point of school entrance. The extension is needed only if the added arrows produce a system that (reliably) explains more of the variation in intelligence than did the simpler system.

System analyses of this sort allow researchers to move far beyond arguments over the meaning of a correlation between IQ scores and just one other variable, in isolation from the system in which both occur.

Still, problems remain. Systems incorporating human intelligence are so complicated that no one study can ever include adequate measures of all relevant variables. The size of the influence of unknown variables can be evaluated, but what those variables are and how they exert their influence will remain unknown. Therefore, we cannot explain all the causes and ramifications of intelligence, all at once. We can identify and analyze reasonably closed subsystems, dealing with a particular aspect of intelligence. No one such study will tell us all about intelligence, but, taken together, they will tell us quite a lot.

1.7. Summary and Prospectus

Individual differences in cognitive capacities – *intelligence*, for short – are an important part of human variation. Intelligence is partially tapped by intelligence tests (IQ) and by other tests of cognitive achievement, but other important cognitive abilities lie outside of the tested realm. While intelligence does not completely determine success in life (or lack of the same), it certainly contributes to it. In order to get a complete picture we have to consider personality and motivational factors, and the extent to which the social and physical environments encourage some behaviors and discourage others.

Intelligence has both multiple causes and multiple consequences. In order to study intelligence it is necessary to isolate relatively closed systems of variables. This poses a challenge, because our ability to measure some variables, and hence to study systems involving them, is much greater than our ability to measure other variables. Test scores and measures of genetic variation are much easier to obtain than measures of success in society, or measures of variation in the physical and social environment. Therefore, we have to be vigilant against the error of studying what is easy to analyze, at the expense of missing amorphous but important effects. This tension will be reflected throughout the discussions in this book.

Some typical tests will be described in Chapter 2. Subsequent chapters deal with the description, causes, and consequences of intelligence. The book closes with a discussion of how intelligence is distributed across our society and, finally, some speculations about the development of research on intelligence in the future.

The Tests

I agree with you that there is a natural aristocracy among men. . . . the natural aristocracy I consider as the most precious gift of nature for the instruction, the trusts, and the government of society . . .

> Thomas Jefferson, letter to John Adams, 1813[1]

2.1. Introduction

Thomas Jefferson and John Adams, the men who wrote in the Declaration of Independence that "all men are created equal," believed in a natural aristocracy! They weren't hypocrites. Jefferson and Adams believed that all men had equal rights, not that they had equal talents. Adams's lifelong support of his alma mater, Harvard University, and Jefferson's investment in the University of Virginia showed how strongly both men supported the development of the natural aristocracy. However, neither Jefferson nor Adams said how the natural aristocrats were to be identified. Today we partially rely on tests to do this.

We all have an intuitive feeling about what a cognitive test is, for you are unlikely to grow up in post-industrial society without taking one. This chapter expands on intuitive notions by describing some of the typical tests, chosen to represent different types, and by commenting on the aspects of intelligence that they do, or do not, evaluate.

Most textbooks on testing stress the distinction between individual testing and testing people in groups. An equally important distinction is between tests composed of batteries of subtests and single-format tests.

Test batteries contain subtests that evaluate different aspects of cognition. For instance, many test batteries contain, as subtests, vocabulary tests and tests of simple arithmetic. Overall scores are constructed by combining subtest scores. The way the widely used Wechsler test batteries are scored is illustrative. The Wechsler batteries contain subtests involving verbal and nonverbal material. Subset scores are combined to obtain verbal IQ (VIQ) and performance IQ (PIQ) scores, and then verbal and

---

1 Quoted in Lemann, 1999.

performance scores are combined into a full-scale IQ (FSIQ) score.

The SAT, a college admission test that will be familiar to many readers, is a battery of subtests that evaluate different aspects of verbal and mathematical reasoning. We will look at this test in more detail in section 2.3.1 of this chapter.

Single-format tests are tests in which all questions are of the same type. Thus a single-format test looks very much like one of the subtests of a test battery, used alone. For instance, vocabulary tests are sometimes used alone, to get a rough indication of a person's general cognitive power. Obviously a single format test does not evaluate as many cognitive talents as a test battery does. However, if scores on a single format test are highly correlated with scores on the test battery as a whole (as vocabulary scores and VIQ scores are for the Wechsler tests), an estimate of a person's intelligence can be made, with some loss of accuracy and great reduction in cost, by using a single-format test that takes a few minutes instead of a test battery lasting several hours.

There is no board that certifies a test as an "intelligence test." Indeed, only a few of the many cognitive tests on the market are specifically labeled tests of intelligence. Why? The answer to this question requires a look at different tests, and a brief excursion into what might be called "political semantics." The case of the SAT provides a good example.

The SAT evaluates cognition. However, the Educational Testing Service (ETS), the company that constructs the SAT, never calls it an *intelligence* test. ETS says that the test evaluates the extent to which a person who has an American high school education is prepared to be a college undergraduate. This sounds very much like Binet's goal for the very first intelligence test, which was designed to assess children's readiness for the French public education system.[2] So why isn't the SAT an intelligence test? In fact, some researchers treat the SAT as virtually synonymous with a measure of

intelligence, no matter what ETS says.[3] The same thing is true of several other cognitive tests. Knowledgeable people call them intelligence tests, but their publishers do not.

What we have here is a problem of definitions, tempered by some political controversies. Historically, and contemporaneously, certain tests have been called intelligence tests. These include Terman's translation of Binet's tests, the Stanford-Binet test, and David Wechsler's Wechsler scales, to be described later. Both are battery-type tests intended to summarize the results of an evaluation of a wide range of cognitive skills, and to be appropriate for many different populations.[4]

These individually administered, battery-type tests did not fill two important niches. They were too expensive for mass personnel screening programs, such as military recruitment. Therefore, group-administered tests, such as the Army Alpha and the SAT, were developed. There was also a need for specialized tests, to be used when the examiner was interested in only a limited range of cognitive abilities or when the test was intended for use in a particular population.

Some comparisons involving the SAT illustrate all these issues. The SAT is a group test, while the Wechsler intelligence tests are individually administered. It costs much less to evaluate a person using the SAT than it does using the Wechsler. The Wechsler scales cover a greater range of cognitive skills than the SAT does. For instance, the Wechsler scales include subtests to evaluate visual-spatial reasoning. This is a reasonable thing to do, for visual-spatial reasoning is certainly part of human cognition. The SAT does not contain visual-spatial reasoning tests, on the grounds that this ability is not required throughout the college curriculum, while verbal and logical reasoning abilities are required everywhere.[5]

2   Binet & Simon, 1905.

3   E.g., Jackson & Rushton, 2006.
4   Matarazzo, 1972; Wechsler, 1975.
5   Perhaps it should. A case can be made for considering visual-spatial reasoning as an ability required in majors such as art, architecture, and engineering. See Humphreys & Lubinski, 1996, for a more extended discussion.

Now consider the SAT compared to the Armed Services Vocational Aptitude Battery (ASVAB). Both the SAT and the ASVAB contain subtests evaluating language skills. The questions on the SAT are harder than comparable questions on the ASVAB, on the grounds that a higher level of language skill is required to succeed as a college student than to succeed as a military enlisted person. Both tests evaluate linguistic skills, but in different ranges.

Here is a more extreme illustration of tests intended to evaluate different ranges of intelligence. The Mini Mental Status Examination is a test widely used in medical practice to determine if a person is seriously cognitively impaired. It contains questions like "What day is it?" and "Where are you?" At the other end of the scale, the Miller Analogies test, intended to screen entrants to graduate school, contains some very hard analogical reasoning questions.

Given this variety of uses, it makes sense to describe a test by the use for which it is intended, instead of using the omnibus term "intelligence test."

A second reason for avoiding the words "intelligence test" is dictated more by public relations than by a desire to provide an accurate description. The very word *intelligence* has a negative connotation to some people. Some social commentators associate the term with elitism and even racism. The reasons for this are discussed in Chapters 8 and 11. As a result some test producers deny that they are evaluating intelligence, resorting to terms like "ability" and "aptitude," both to avoid controversy and to increase marketability.

While the proliferation of test names is understandable, it has resulted in a good deal of inconsistency. In 2006 the authors of an article in the journal *Intelligence* extracted a score from the SAT that they referred to as an index of general intelligence.[6] Two issues later in the same journal, other authors referred to the SAT as a test of scholastic achievement, and tried to predict SAT scores using scores on a nonverbal, academic-content-free test called the Raven Advanced Progressive Matrices (RAPM). The RAPM did pretty well as a predictor (correlation of .39), but a vocabulary test did substantially better (correlation of .69).[7]

This example shows, in microcosm, what the situation is. On the one hand, virtually all tests of cognitive abilities correlate positively with each other. This shows that there is a tendency for cognitive skills to vary together, across people. If you have a high level of one cognitive skill, you probably do not have a low level on another. On the other hand, the associations between cognitive skills are far less than perfect, so there is a case for specialized tests in appropriate situations.

With these general remarks aside, let us look at some of the tests, as they could be described by data available in the 2007–09 period. New tests and revisions are published frequently, but they all are designed on the same basic principles.

2.2. A Description of Individually Administered Test Batteries

Individual testing is generally appropriate if there is concern about the mental capabilities of the examinee. For instance, in education a child might be examined for special placement in a remedial ("special") education program or, less frequently, for admission to a program for gifted children. Tests used for this purpose include the Stanford-Binet, a much-updated version of Terman's translation of Binet's tests, and the Wechsler Intelligence Scale for Children (WISC).

Adults are tested individually as part of a clinical assessment for a variety of behavioral problems. The judicial system sometimes uses intelligence testing to determine whether or not the examinee is sufficiently intelligent to be held criminally responsible for his or her (illegal) actions. Individual testing is also used in order to assess an adult's mental status following injury to the brain.

6 Jackson & Rushton, 2006.

7 Rohde & Thomson, 2007.

Intelligence tests are also widely used in research on individual differences in cognition. Researchers tend to prefer the less expensive group-administered tests, simply to save money. In some situations, however, individual testing is appropriate. As an alternative, it is often possible to administer some of the subtests of an individual test on a group basis, for a special purpose, such as the evaluation of vocabulary.

2.2.1. *The Wechsler Tests: The Adult Intelligence Scale (WAIS-IV) and the Wechsler Intelligence Scale for Children (WISC-IV)*

The Wechsler tests for adults and children (the WAIS and the WISC) are by far the best-known individual tests. They are regularly revised, as are other intelligence tests. Early versions of the WAIS tests provided three scores: a verbal IQ score (VIQ) calculated from scores on subtests involving language, a Performance IQ (PIQ) score based on scores from subtests that did not involve language, and a Full Scale IQ (FSIQ) based on a combination of the VIQ and PIQ scores. A memory scale could also be calculated. These scales, which are based on a pragmatic division of cognitive skills into verbal and nonverbal skills, are often reported in all but the most recent literature.

The current (WAIS-IV) test has a somewhat different structure, which reflects recent theoretical developments, and in particular the importance of individual differences in the speed of cognitive processing and in the ability to keep information in immediate memory while working on a problem. The subtests are grouped into tests involving verbal comprehension, perceptual (visual) reasoning, immediate ("working") memory, and speed of processing. An index is calculated for each of the groups. The Full Scale IQ score is calculated by combining the indexes. Within each of the groups there are core subtests, which are used to calculate the appropriate index, and supplemental tests that can be utilized if the examiner wishes to probe the examinee's abilities within a particular area.

Table 2.1 lists the core tests used within each group. It also includes brief descriptions of the cognitive skills required to complete each test.

Like the Stanford-Binet, the Wechsler tests represent a pragmatic approach to intelligence. They incorporate a widely accepted distinction between verbal and nonverbal reasoning. Otherwise the tests and subtests have evolved, and theories of intelligence have been induced from research on them, rather than psychologists having used a theory to generate the tests.

2.2.2. *Two Individual Tests Motivated by a Psychological Theory*

The pragmatic approach to theory exemplified by the early Wechsler tests contrasts with a more theory-based approach taken in the development of two other widely used tests: the Kaufmann intelligence tests (one for adults and one for children) and the Woodcock-Johnson test, which is used largely for adult self-assessment as an aid in career planning. These tests are based on a theoretical distinction between *crystallized* and *fluid* intelligence, first articulated by Raymond Cattell and developed further by his colleague John Horn.[8]

Cattell and Horn distinguished between solving problems by applying previously learned knowledge and/or problem-solving methods (*crystallized intelligence*, Gc) and solving problems by applying general reasoning methods to figure out a solution to an unfamiliar problem (*fluid intelligence*, Gf). This echoes Juan Huarte de San Juan's sixteenth-century distinction between problem solving based on memory or imagination,[9] and also resembles Spearman's distinction between inductive and deductive reasoning. Cattell and Horn

---

8   Cattell, 1971, 1987; Horn, 1985; Horn & Noll, 1994.
9   Cattell and Horn's ideas were developed independently of Huarte's work. Huarte's book on intelligence was first translated into English in 1594, but it appears to have had little influence on contemporary English-speaking psychologists. His ideas were reintroduced to us by Spanish psychologists in the 1980s.

Table 2.1. The subscales of the Wechsler Adult Intelligence Scale–IV (supplemental scales are indicated)

Name of Test	Content	Cognitive Skill Evaluated
Tests used to compute the verbal comprehension scale		
Vocabulary	Word definitions required	Vocabulary
Similarities	Given names of objects, explain how they are alike	Abstract reasoning. Detection of similarities
Information	Questions based on general cultural knowledge	Knowledge of culture
Comprehension (supplemental)	Oral questions requiring solutions to everyday problems	Verbal comprehension, knowledge of culture
Tests used to compute the working memory scale		
Digit Span	Repeat a series of digits either forward or backward	Short-term storage of information
Arithmetic	Simple arithmetic problems are to be solved "in the head."	Manipulation of information in immediate memory
Letter-number sequencing (supplemental)	Examinee hears a mixed sequence of letters and numbers, and repeats them back separately in their normal sequence	Manipulation of information in immediate memory
Tests used to compute the perceptual reasoning scale		
Block design	Assemble a set of colored cubes to form a specified design	Nonverbal reasoning. Visualizing object movements
Matrix reasoning	Recognize a pattern of changes in visual figures	Pattern recognition and application
Visual puzzles	Choose three of six pieces to make a specified design	Visualizing movement of objects. Visual immediate memory
Picture completion (supplemental)	An incomplete picture of a common object is shown. The task is say what is missing	Nonverbal reasoning. General knowledge
Figure weights (supplemental)	A balance scale is shown, with some objects in it. The task is to choose other objects to balance the scale. Object weights are to be inferred from examples of balanced scales	Nonverbal reasoning. The examinee is forced to deal with an unusual task
Tests used to compute the processing speed index		
Symbol search	Indicate whether or not designated target symbols appear in a group of symbols	Speed of visual processing. Short-term memory
Coding	The examinee is shown an arbitrary pairing of marks and numbers. The examinee is then shown a set of marks and must list the associated numbers	Paired associates learning. Speed of visual processing
Cancellation (supplemental)	The examiner describes values of attributes of objects, e.g., shape and color. The examinee must indicate which shapes in a set have the required combination of attribute values	Speed of visual processing. Also, the ability to disregard distracters, such as a shape that has one of the required attribute values (e.g., a red circle when the target shape is a red triangle)

Table 2.2. The subtests of the Kaufman Adult Intelligence Test

Name of Test	Description of Activity[a]
Crystallized (Gc) tests	
Definitions	A sentence is given with a missing word. Some letters of the missing word are given. The task is to find the missing word. Example: The jockey was riding a ___. _O_S_
Auditory comprehension	The examinee listens to a brief recording, and then answers questions that require either recall of information in the recording or drawing an inference from the message.
Double meanings	The examinee is given two sets of word clues. The task is to find a word that has two meanings, associated with each of them. Example: Clues: "Sport & Champion," "Music & Singing." Answer: Record.
Famous people (used for extended testing)	The examinee is shown a photograph of a famous person and a brief statement about that person. The task is to name the person.
Fluid (Gf) tests	
Rebus	The examinee is shown a "sentence" made up of pictures that stand for words. The task is to "read" the sentence. Example: Show cartoon pictures of an eye, a tomato soup can, and a fly. The sentence is "I can fly."
Mystery codes	The examinee is shown a set of pictures, each with a "code meaning," e.g., a large triangle representing "woman" and a black dot representing "new." The examinee is then shown a triangle with a black dot inside. The task is to determine what the meaning of the new symbol is ("girl").
Logical steps	The examinee hears or reads a set of premises, and then must deduce the answer to a question. Example: "At the Round Table, Gawain is to Arthur's left and Launcelot is between Gawain and Arthur. Who is to Launcelot's left?"
Memory for block designs (used for extended testing)	The examinee is shown a pattern composed of colored blocks. The examinee must then recreate the pattern from memory, using blocks and a form board.

[a] The examples are not of actual test items, in order to maintain the confidentiality of the test.

deserve credit for carrying this idea considerably further than their predecessors did.

Table 2.2 presents the subtests of the Kauffman Adult Intelligence Test (KAIT), grouped into subtests used to generate the Gc and Gf scores. As in the case of the WAIS, a "full-scale" score can also be generated. The Woodcock-Johnson test also generates separate scales for Gc and Gf, along with a full-scale IQ score.

2.2.3. *A Test Motivated by a Theory of How the Brain Works*

The Gc/Gf model and the distinction between verbal and nonverbal reasoning are models of how the mind works, for there is no direct connection to brain mechanisms. (In Chapter 7 we look at how such connections can be made.) The next test to be described, the Cognitive Assessment System (CAS), was motivated by a theory of how the brain works. The theory and related tests were developed by J. P. Das, a professor at the University of Alberta, and his colleagues.[10]

Shortly after World War II, Das, a native of India, had the opportunity to work in the then Soviet Union, with the noted neuropsychologist A. R. Luria. Luria had

10 Das, Naglieri, & Kirby, 1994.

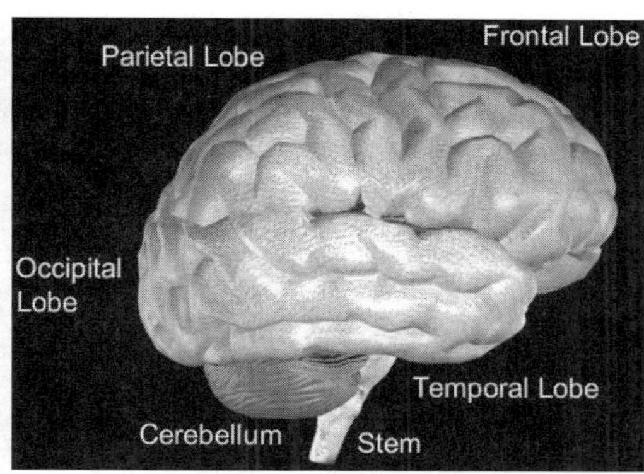

Figure 2.1. The four major lobes of the cerebral cortex. Copyright Matthew Holt, used by permission of the Washington University of St. Louis Internet Stroke Center.

examined a very large number of brain injury cases. He was struck by the fact that damage to different areas of the brain produced quite different behavioral deficits. Luria concluded that the four major areas of the cerebral cortex, the frontal, temporal, parietal, and occipital lobes (see Figure 2.1), are specialized for different types of information processing.[11]

It had already been determined that the occipital lobe is largely concerned with the mechanics of vision. Luria believed that the temporal lobe is concerned with processing information in series (e.g., comprehending a sentence as it is spoken), that the parietal lobe is concerned with parallel processing, as when one notices the symmetry of a figure, and that the frontal lobe is concerned with planning actions and with the control of attention.

Luria was mainly concerned with the results of substantial injuries to the brain. Das extended Luria's ideas to the analysis of normal behavior by healthy children. He reasoned that if different areas of the brain carry out planning, attention control, and serial and simultaneous functions, then individual differences in behavior within the normal range should reflect individual differences in the development of each of the four brain areas. Das coined the acronym PASS, for Planning, Attention,

Serial, and Simultaneous (PASS) model, and constructed a number of tests to evaluate each function. Das's colleague Jack Naglieri subsequently developed a comprehensive test battery, the cognitive assessment system (CAS), incorporating subtests for the four dimensions of the PASS theory.[12]

Table 2.3 shows the subtests used in the CAS. The score on each subtest is based on both the speed and accuracy with which a child answers questions. An effort was made to construct test items that were as nearly as possible void of cultural content. This, and the emphasis on the speed with which simple tasks are done, is consistent with Das's and Naglieri's desire to evaluate the effectiveness of brain processes rather than mental competencies tied to cultural knowledge.

Although Das was inspired by Luria's neuropsychological work, it is not clear that the CAS scores map onto discrete brain functions, for our understanding of the brain is greater than it was in Luria's day. The PASS model is stated in terms of cognitive behaviors: planning, attending, and processing information in either a parallel or serial manner. These are characteristics of the mind as an information-processing device, not characteristics of the brain as a physical device. The mapping to brain locations is not quite what Luria's theory predicts. For instance, tasks that involve planning draw heavily upon both frontal lobe and parietal lobe mechanisms.[13] Also, the Das-Naglieri assignment of tasks to the four PASS functions seems (to me) to be sometimes insightful and sometimes arbitrary. As an example of a good assignment of task to function, the planning connections task is a variant of a "trail making" task, which is widely used as an indication of damage to the frontal cortex. However, it is less clear that one should regard the matching numbers and planned codes tasks as examples of planning.

In the last analysis, though, the proof of the pudding is in the eating. There are two questions that we have to ask about any proposed battery of tests. First, do the test

11 Luria, 1962/1980.

12 Naglieri, 2005.
13 Jung & Haier, 2007.

Table 2.3. The subtests of the Cognitive Assessment System

Tests of planning	
Matching numbers	The examinee is shown rows of eight numbers. Two of the numbers are identical. The task is to underline the identical numbers. Several pages of rows are shown. The measure is the time needed to complete the task.
Planned codes	The examinee is shown a set of letters and a code form for each, e.g., A = OX, B = XX. The examinee then examines a number of rows of letters and replaces them with their code form.
Planned connections	The examinee is shown numbers arranged haphazardly on a page. The task is to draw a line ("trail") starting with the lowest number and proceeding in order to the highest. In a harder problem, numbers and letters are intermixed, e.g., 1-A-2-B
Tests of attention	
Expressive attention	This is a variety of the Stroop task, in which a person is shown words in different-colored ink and must call out the color of the ink. The words are color names, as in BLUE printed in red ink.
Receptive attention	The examinee is presented with pairs of letters, e.g., AB, Aa, AA. The task is to identify which ones have the same name.
Simultaneous processing tasks	
Matrix task	This is a progressive matrix task, similar to the matrix task on the WAIS-R. It evaluates nonverbal reasoning.
Verbal-spatial relations	The examinee is shown six simple pictures and asked a question. The examinee indicates which picture is the best answer to the question.
Figure memory	The examinee is shown a geometric pattern, and then must find it embedded in a larger pattern.
Successive processing tasks	
Word series	The examiner speaks an arbitrary string of words. The examinee repeats the words in order.
Sentence repetition	The examiner speaks a syntactically correct sentence, which is composed of color words and has no obvious semantic content, e.g., THE BROWN GREENS THE YELLOW. The examinee repeats the sentence.
Sentence questions	The examiner speaks a sentence as in sentence repetition, then asks a question about it, e.g., WHO GREENS THE YELLOW?

scores predict real-world cognitive behavior? Second, if the test is based on a theory, do the patterns of scores on the subtests behave in a manner predicted by the theory? In the case of the CAS, are subtests within the Planning, Attention, Serial, and Successive groups more highly correlated with other subtests within the same group than they are with subtests in other groups? We postpone the answers to these questions, for the CAS and the other battery tests, until our discussion of psychometric theory, in Chapter 4.

2.2.4. *A Commentary on Individually Administered Tests*

Individual testing offers two advantages over group testing; *contingent item presentation* and *supplementary reporting*.

Contingent item presentation simply means that the next question that the examiner asks can be chosen on the basis of the answers that the examinee has already given. This is efficient and sensible, because the examiner avoids trying to find out something about the examinee that the examiner already knows. If you are evaluating a person's ability to do arithmetic and you have already seen the person multiply 24 by 72 "in the head," there is not much point in asking if he or she can add 32 and 18! In an examination of a person's knowledge of US history, if someone has already told you that Franklin Pierce was president of the US after Millard Fillmore, there is not much point in probing to find out if they know who followed Franklin Roosevelt. In addition to its efficiency, contingent item presentation makes the examination more like an interview than an examination, for the question–response–next question sequence follows the rules of normal conversation. Wechsler himself referred to his scales as providing a structured interview for the display of cognitive skills.[14]

Contingent item presentation can also be obtained by computer-controlled testing, a procedure that is becoming increasingly common. Computer-controlled testing assumes that the examinee has basic computer skills and is motivated to cooperate. Both assumptions are probably correct for healthy adults and older children, in industrial and post-industrial societies. They are suspect for young children, people who are infirm (e.g., the extreme elderly), and outside the post-industrial world.

Examiners typically write reports describing how the examinee reacted during an individual testing session. These comments can be very helpful. For example, if intelligence is being examined to determine recovery from a brain injury, the examinee's behavior during testing may be as important as the test score. However, there are two qualifications. One is that the observations and interpretations made during testing are only as good as the observer, which raises the issue of variations in skill across examiners, as well as examinees. The other is that both the cost and the difficulty of scoring the examiner's subjective impressions make it difficult to incorporate such observations into research programs.

The costs of individual intelligence examinations are in the $200–350 range.[15] Sometimes such costs are clearly justified. Suppose the purpose of the examination is to decide whether or not a student should be placed in a special (remedial) education program. The cost of supporting a student in an American special education program is about $17,000, more than twice the cost of supporting a student in a regular program.[16] Keeping a student in a regular classroom when he or she needs special education can be a disaster, both for the student and for the teachers who must deal with a person who cannot keep pace with his or her classmates. In such a case individual testing is worth it, from the viewpoint both of the institution and of the person being examined.

2.3. Group-Administered Test Batteries

Individual examinations are not economically feasible in many personnel selection systems. Consider some numbers. In 2005, US high schools graduated approximately three million people. Slightly under half of them took the SAT, the most widely used college entrance examination.[17] The US military screens over 100,000 potential recruits a year. A commercial testing company that specializes in screening applicants for hourly-wage positions uses computerized testing to screen an average of 40,000 people each workday. In such situations individual examinations are not an option. Group tests are needed.

14 Wechsler, 1975.

15 A fee of $250 was quoted on the website of the State University of New York, Stony Brook, Center for Psychological Services, January 2010.
16 This figure is based on the National Education Association's website, www.nea.org/specialed/index .html, 14 February, 2007.
17 National Council of Educational Statistics and College Board figures for 2005.

Table 2.4. The Otis-Lennon Test of School Abilities; selected subtests

Scale or Subtest	Description
Verbal tests	
Comprehension	
Antonyms	Given a base word, select from a list of target words the word most nearly opposite in meaning.
Synonyms	Same as antonyms, except that the word to be selected should have the same meaning as the base word.
Sentence completion	Select word needed to complete an incomplete sentence.
Verbal reasoning tests	
Classification	Given a set of words, identify those that are in the same class.
Analogies	Given two words as a base, and a target word, identify the relationship between the two base words and use it to select a word that has the same relation to the target word. Example: White is to black as up is to (sideways, below, down, behind).
Arithmetic reasoning with verbal problems	Word problems requiring simple computations.
Nonverbal tests	
Figural reasoning	
Figural analogies	An analogy test similar to verbal analogies, except that the relations are between parts of geometric figures.
Matrix patterns	A matrix test using geometric figures (see the discussion of progressive matrix tests in section 1.2).
Quantitative reasoning	
Number series	Given a series of numbers, where each number bears some relation to the proceeding ones, identify the next number in the sequence.
Number matrix	Matrix problems similar to those used for figures, but constructed using relations between numbers (see text below).

Note: The Otis-Lennon Test formats vary with grade level, the examples here have been chosen to illustrate the nature of the test.

2.3.1. *The Otis-Lennon Test*

Most group-administered, battery-type intelligence tests carry over the pragmatic distinction between verbal and nonverbal skills that characterizes the Wechsler and Stanford-Binet tests. Tests of quantitative skills are often added. In spite of the similarity between these batteries and the individual tests, test developers seldom use the term *intelligence*. Instead the tests are described as tests of "reasoning" or "scholastic ability."

A good example is the *Otis-Lennon Test of School Ability*. This is a descendent of Arthur Otis's *Otis Group Intelligence Scale*, first published in 1918, with the latest revision in 2009. Otis, who had studied with Terman, realized that most of the items on tests like the Stanford-Binet could be written in a form suitable for group administration.[18] Accordingly he designed such tests for use in the schools.

18 Robb, Bernardoni & Johnson, 1972.

Table 2.5. The scales and subtests of the Cognitive Abilities Test-3. (When the test is administered in classrooms, three class sessions are required, as indicated in the table)

Session 1:	**Verbal Battery**
	Test 1: Verbal Classification
	Test 2: Sentence Completion
	Test 3: Verbal Analogies
Session 2:	**Quantitative Battery**
	Test 4: Quantitative Relations
	Test 5: Number Series
	Test 6: Equation Building
Session 3:	**Nonverbal Battery**
	Test 7: Figure Classification
	Test 8: Figure Analogies
	Test 9: Figure Analysis

The Otis-Lennon test is actually a testing program. Below the fourth grade children are given individual tests. Group-administered, age-appropriate group tests are provided for grades five through twelve. Table 2.4 shows some of the subtests used. The test battery is divided into verbal and nonverbal sections. Within the verbal section a further distinction is made between verbal comprehension and verbal reasoning. The nonverbal section is divided into tests intended to evaluate "figural reasoning" (relationships between visual patterns) and quantitative reasoning. The test as a whole takes about three hours, but it is typically taken in several sessions.

2.3.2. *The Cognitive Abilities Test*

A similar approach to testing is seen in the *Cognitive Abilities Test* (CAT-3, for the third revision), developed by David Lohman, Robert Thorndike, and Elizabeth Hagen, and marketed through Riverside Press. The publishers claim that this test is the most widely used intelligence test in the United Kingdom. It has figured prominently in important studies of the relation between intelligence and educational accomplishment.

Table 2.5 shows the sections and subtests of the CAT-3. There is a substantial commonality between the Otis-Lennon and CAT-3. This is hardly surprising, as the tests were developed for the same purpose, for the same audience, using a pragmatic approach of building content on the content of previous tests, rather than conforming to a theory of intelligence.

2.3.3. *The SAT*

We now look at one of the best-known, most-discussed tests used in education, the SAT, which is widely used as part of the college admission process in the United States.

The SAT is a distant descendent of a college admissions test developed in the 1920s by Carl Brigham, a psychologist who had worked on construction of the Army Alpha Test. Brigham observed that the Army Alpha was easy for candidates who had some college education. He concluded that a test similar to the Army Alpha could be developed as a college entrance test, but that it would have to be made more difficult.

Brigham produced a test that was used on a trial basis by several universities during the 1920s and 1930s. In 1933 Harvard's president, James Bryant Conant, became interested. The tests that Harvard used at the time emphasized the content of courses available in a relatively small group of expensive Eastern preparatory schools. Conant knew that this gave an advantage to children from families who could afford to send their children to these exclusive schools. Accordingly, Conant asked one of his faculty members, Henry Chauncey, to look into developing tests that would identify gifted students who had not attended private schools.

Chauncey himself was a graduate of a private school, although he was not exceptionally rich. Nevertheless, in athletic parlance, he took the ball and ran with it. He was impressed by Brigham's test, but could not adopt it due to the disruptions caused by the Depression and World War II. After the war ended a US presidential commission concluded that there was a need to open up college admissions procedures to a wider range of applicants. The commission's conclusion mirrored the concerns Conant

Table 2.6. The subtests of the SAT-I

Test Section	Item Type	Comment
Verbal comprehension		All questions are multiple choice.
Reading comprehension	Read short passage and answer multiple-choice questions	The questions deal with the meaning of words in context, information in the passage, and information implied by the passage but not explicitly stated.
Sentence completion	A sentence is presented with some words omitted.	The examinee selects words to complete the sentence.
Mathematics		All questions are multiple-choice or require a numerical answer.
Numerical operations	Calculation	Calculators are permitted.
Algebraic functions	Algebra problems	Covered to the level of a second-year high school course.
Geometry	Geometric problems	Questions cover Euclidean geometry up to three-dimensional solids
Statistics and probability	Questions in elementary statistics and probability theory	Questions include interpreting graphic displays of data.

had expressed, and Chauncey was prepared to respond.

Chauncey established the Educational Testing Service (ETS), a nonprofit corporation, in 1948. The ETS took over administration and development of the SAT, and continues to do so sixty years later. The SAT has become a watchword for students intending to enter college, and ETS has become a major developer of both yearly updates of the SAT and numerous other educational and professional tests.[19]

The present SAT is taken in two parts. The first part, which the ETS refers to as the SAT-I, deals with skills that entering college students are expected to have, but that are not tied to specific optional parts of the curriculum. The second part of the SAT contains subject-matter specific tests. We will generally be concerned only with the first part, which will be referred to simply as the SAT unless there is a reason to distinguish between parts I and II.

The SAT is divided into three sections. One, introduced in 2005, is a writing test in which examinees are given twenty-five minutes to write an essay on a specified topic. The inclusion of a writing examination is a good example of the demands placed on a screening test, as opposed to a test designed to evaluate general mental competence. Essay writing is a not a universally required skill in our society, but it is a skill that is used in college. The writing examination was included in response to complaints by college and university faculty members that some students who had received acceptable scores on the pre-2005 SAT turned out to have poor writing skills.

As yet there is insufficient data to show how well the writing test score relates either to the other tests or to the later performance of college students.

The other two parts of the SAT are the "critical reading" (formerly verbal comprehension) and mathematics sections. Table 2.6 describes the sorts of questions asked. Scores on the sections can range from 200 to 800. Mean scores on the individual

19 Lemann, 1999.

Table 2.7. The Subtests of the Armed Services Vocational Aptitude Battery (ASVAB)

Name of Subtest	Commentary
General science	Questions about science roughly at the level of courses taught in US middle schools.
Arithmetic reasoning	Numerical calculations.
Word knowledge	A vocabulary test.
Paragraph comprehension	Read a paragraph and answer questions about it.
Mathematics knowledge	Apply simple mathematical formulae.
Electronics information	This and the next test are designed to identify enlistees who would be good candidates for training in appropriate technical specialties.
Auto and shop information	See above.
Mechanical comprehension	Tests the understanding of common mechanical problems.
Object assembly	Evaluates skill in seeing how objects should be assembled from diagrams.

sections are in the 550 range (varying somewhat from year to year), with a standard deviation of approximately 100. The overall score is determined by adding the two section scores, so 1600 represents a perfect score on the SAT. The writing test is scored separately.

The questions on the SAT are generally harder than similar questions on tests intended for the general population, such as the WAIS and comparable group tests, because the SAT is intended for the top two-thirds of high school graduates, rather than for the population at large.

2.3.4. *The Armed Services Vocational Aptitude Battery*

The Armed Services Vocational Aptitude Battery (ASVAB), administered and developed by the personnel branch of the US Department of Defense, is designed to evaluate potential enlistees and to identify candidates for training in the military's many occupational specialties, ranging from cooks to computer technicians. Like the SAT, the ASVAB is updated regularly. Table 2.7 lists the subtests of the ASVAB as of 2008. The tests may be administered either in paper-and-pencil form or, as is now usual in recruiting, via an interactive computer system.

The Armed Services Qualification Test (AFQT) score is a weighted combination of the Arithmetic Reasoning, Mathematical Knowledge, Paragraph Comprehension, and Word Knowledge scores of the ASVAB. This makes the AFQT a combination of assessments of mathematical and written verbal skills, as is the SAT total score. There is a correlation of .82 between overall scores on the SAT and the AFQT.[20] The SAT, being intended for a more cognitively powerful audience, is considerably harder than the AFQT.

The special-topic subtests of the ASVAB – General Science, Electronics and Auto and Shop Knowledge, Mechanical Comprehension, and Object Assembly – are used as indicators to see if a given recruit qualifies for specialized training courses (e.g., electronics repair).

Each service establishes a minimum AFQT score that must be achieved for enlistment. The Navy and Air Force, both of which have a large number of technical billets to fill, generally set higher minimums than the Army and the Marines. Recruitment standards in all the services vary from time to time, due to the needs of the services for new recruits, compared to the talent levels in the applicant pools.

20 Frey and Detterman, 2004.

In addition to its use in military recruiting, the ASVAB has been used by the Department of Labor in research on the US workforce.

2.4. Single-Format Tests

While tests like the SAT, CAT-3, and ASVAB are economical from the viewpoint of the institutions that use them, they still require several hours of the examinee's time. Industrial personnel screening and psychological research programs have a need for tests that make fewer demands on the people who take them, even though the resulting examination may be less detailed.

2.4.1. *Baddeley's Three-Minute Reasoning Test as an Illustration of a Speeded Test*

One strategy for designing a quick test of cognitive skill is to shift from measuring a person's accuracy in answering reasonably complex questions, to measuring the speed with which that person can answer simple questions. The argument for doing so is that those people who can answer hard problems, given time, are also likely to be able to answer easy problems, quickly.

The British psychologist Alan Baddeley developed a test of verbal intelligence based on a prototypical linguistic act, determining whether a sentence correctly describes a visual situation. Questions on this test take the form

---

A B The A is before the B   True____ False____
B A The A is not after the B True____ False____

Individually, these questions are easy; no one who reads English should ever get one wrong. The sentences vary in linguistic complexity, although that complexity is well short of the complexity that might tax a proficient reader. While only two pictures are possible, **A B** or **B A**, there are eight possible questions, composed by varying whether the question asks about the position of **A** relative to **B**, or **B** relative to **A**, whether

the relation specified is *before* or *after*, and whether the descriptive statement is expressed positively, as in the first example just given, or negatively, as in the second example. When taking Baddeley's test it is not hard to answer the question, but it may take a little effort to figure out what the question is.

The score on Baddeley's test is the number of questions a person can answer in just three minutes. Simple as it is, this score has a correlation of .6 with scores on verbal intelligence tests that take over an hour to administer.[21]

What Baddeley showed is that the ability to do certain simple verbal manipulations, rapidly, is correlated with the ability to do such complex things as comprehending a paragraph. Therefore, the quick test can be used to identify good verbal comprehenders without asking them to do much comprehension. This is the sort of finding that might have infuriated Walter Lippmann, because the test of comprehension only minimally involves comprehension. The same finding would have delighted Prof. Boring, because the test worked.

2.4.2. *The Wonderlic Personnel Test*

Baddeley's test was developed for research purposes, not for the commercial market. The principle behind Baddeley's test, evaluating intelligence by seeing how quickly people answer simple questions, has been incorporated into a widely used industrial test, the Wonderlic Personnel Test (WPT).[22] The WPT can be thought of as a hypercompressed battery in which examinees are asked to answer simple verbal questions, do arithmetic, and solve simple logical problems. The different types of questions are mixed up, so examinees have to switch rapidly from solving one type of problem to solving another. The WPT consists of fifty questions similar to those shown in Table 2.8. The score is the number of questions that can be answered correctly within twelve

21 Baddeley, 1968.
22 Wonderlic, 1992.

Table 2.8. Sample questions illustrating the Wonderlic Personnel Test, revised edition (WPT-R, 2007 revision)

Question 1 Which of the following is the earliest date?

A) Jan. 16, 1898   B) Feb. 21, 1889   C) Feb. 2, 1898   D) Jan. 7, 1898   E) Jan. 30, 1889

Question 2 LOW is to **HIGH** as **EASY** is to ___?__

J) SUCCESSFUL   **K) PURE**   **l) TALL**   **M) INTERESTING**   **N) DIFFICULT**

Question 3 A featured product from an Internet retailer generated 27, 80, 99, 115 and 213 orders over a 5-hour period. Which graph below best represents this trend?

A   B   C   D   E

Question 4 What is the next number in the series 29 41 53 65 77 __?_

J) 75   K) 88   L) 89   M) 98   N) 99

Question 5 *One word below is underlined. What is the OPPOSITE of the word?*

She gave a complex answer to the question and we all agreed with her.

A) long   B) better   C) simple   D) wrong   E) kind

Note: The items were provided courtesy of Wonderlic, Inc. The underlined word in example question 5 appeared in blue print in the original. Underlining has been added here to indicate the content of the question.

minutes. Research conducted well after the Wonderlic Test was introduced, in the 1970s, has shown that the ability to "change set" by switching between tasks is an important part of intelligence.

WPT scores are highly correlated with the full-scale IQ score of the much longer WAIS. This makes the WPT an attractive test for personnel screening, especially in situations where there is a concern that the applicant meet a minimum standard of cognitive ability. In one high-profile application, the National Football League has used the WPT to screen players trying out for a career in professional football. Having a high WPT score will not get you a lucrative American football career. Having a low WPT score may make the scouts and coaches think twice, for there is a cognitive component to the life of a professional player.

2.4.3. *Raven's Progressive Matrices Tests: A Non-speeded, Single-Format Test*

We next examine tests that use the *Progressive Matrix* item format, which is a format designed to evaluate inductive reasoning. These tests are widely used in research, and have also been used in personnel selection, particularly in Europe.[23] Progressive matrix tests represent something of a contrast between an emphasis on speed and accuracy. The item format can be used to present problems that vary widely in difficulty, so part of the score depends on how hard a problem the examinee can solve. The tests are usually given with a time limit, so the score also depends upon how quickly the examinee can find a solution.

Progressive matrix tests were developed by John C. Raven in 1938. Raven had studied with Charles Spearman, who believed that the defining characteristic of intelligence was the ability to detect and manipulate complex patterns appearing in observations.[24] He referred to this ability as *eduction;* most modern researchers would probably say "inductive reasoning." Raven constructed three tests to evaluate inductive reasoning: the Colored Progressive Matrices (RCPM) test, for children, the Standard Progressive Matrices (RSPM) test, for general use, and the Advanced Progressive Matrices (RAPM) test for evaluating people of above average intelligence, such as college students. The progressive matrix format has since been adopted for subtests in a number of battery-type tests, including the WAIS-IV.

Figure 2.2 shows two progressive matrix questions. The examinee is shown a 3×3 matrix, in which each entry is a geometric figure. The entries differ in some systematic way along both the rows and the columns. The lower right-hand entry (position (3,3) in matrix notation) is blank. The task is to select one of the alternative answers at the bottom in order to complete the matrix. In order to do this the examinee has to solve one problem defined by variation across rows, then keep the solution "in the head" while working on another problem defined by variation across columns. As Figure 2.2 illustrates, problems can vary considerably in difficulty.

The Raven tests take about forty-five minutes to complete, making them a cheap alternative compared to the SAT or the WAIS. A more recent form administered by an interactive computer system takes even less time.

Raven's own matrix tests always use figural patterns, as in the example. Progressive matrix tests can also be constructed using numerical and verbal material. What number should be used to fill in this matrix?

1	2	3
2	4	6
4	8	

It has been claimed that progressive matrix tests are the best measures of general intelligence that we have.[25] The claim is based on statistical evidence indicating

23 J. Raven & J. Raven, 2008.
24 Spearman, 1923. Spearman's ideas are further discussed in Chapter 3.
25 Jensen, 1998.

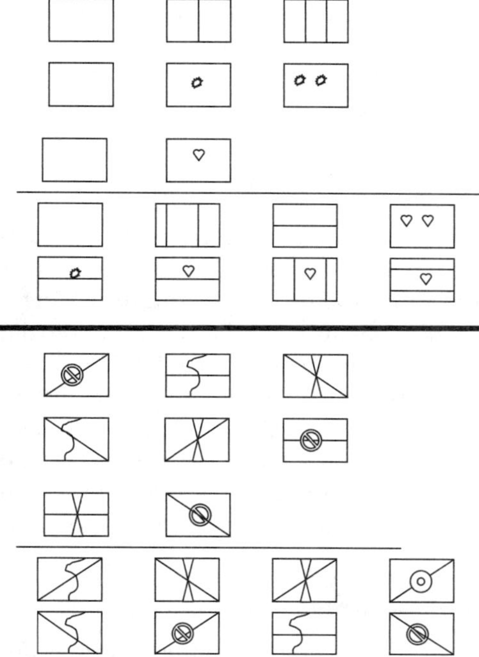

Figure 2.2. Two progressive matrix items. The task is to complete the 3 × 3 matrices by selecting the appropriate pattern from the eight patterns below the line. The items have been made up by the present author, to illustrate the technique.

that scores on these tests are associated with whatever common trait underlies performance on all subtests of a test battery, such as the subtests of the SAT or the WAIS. This argument will be described in Chapter 4.

A number of researchers have used progressive matrix tests in cross-cultural studies, and have sometimes made claims about the relative intelligence of different groups based upon the results. The argument for doing so is that the ability to find patterns in observations is a cognitive ability that is required in all societies. This is a very strong claim. It assumes both that the progressive matrix item format is appropriate and that the "Drop in from the Sky" testing paradigm is an appropriate means of evaluation outside of industrial and post-industrial societies. Such claims raise complex issues, for validity is not an "either/or" issue. A test may be valid to different degrees in different societies, and societies themselves do not fall into precisely defined categories,

such as "developed," "industrial," and "post-industrial" societies. This matter will be pursued further in Chapter 11.

We now turn to some general issues that are raised in the construction and use of the tests.

2.5. Themes in Testing

There is a great deal of commonality in the cognitive skills the various tests evaluate. Here are some of the recurrent themes.

2.5.1. *Language Use*

Virtually all battery-type tests evaluate language skills. There is a good case for doing so. Although a person cannot participate fully in human society without language skills, there are substantial individual differences in the degree to which people possess these skills. Everyone learns to produce and comprehend a passable version of his or her native language. Very few people reach the levels of comprehension and expression illustrated by Shakespeare and Cervantes.

In intelligence testing an important distinction is made between language familiarity and language comprehension. Language familiarity is usually assessed by a vocabulary test. Language comprehension is tested by asking examinees to explain the meaning of sentences or paragraphs. In theory one might argue for separate evaluations of comprehension of the written and spoken language. The case for doing so rests on a distinction articulated by the evolutionary psychologist David Geary, who maintains that we have genetically determined "primary" mental capacities, common to all societies, and socially acquired "secondary" capacities that are required in only some of them.[26] Use of the spoken language is clearly a primary capacity. Normal children learn to speak without explicit tuition, simply being reared by speakers of the local language. Literacy is a secondary skill. Reading and writing are acquired through instruction, and the

26 Geary, 2005.

success of this instruction varies greatly. It is possible, for instance, to be competent in the spoken language and still be nearly unable to read (dyslexic). Adults can suffer brain injuries that render them unable to read or write even though they can still speak. This is called *acquired dyslexia*. This contrasts with *developmental dyslexia*, which is manifested when an apparently healthy child has abnormal difficulty learning to read.

The dyslexias are an exception to the general rule that skills in spoken and written language are highly correlated, a finding that has been obtained in two different populations that have considerably different language skills: American college students and military enlisted personnel.[27] Finding that the same relationship occurs in different populations provides strong evidence for the generality of the relationship.

2.5.2. *Visual-Spatial Reasoning*

Almost all battery-type tests that are avowedly evaluations of intelligence measure some form of *visual-spatial reasoning*. The tasks used vary in the extent to which they involve perceptual or reasoning processes. At the perceptual end, some tests require the identification of a pattern hidden within another or identification of two patterns as the same, different, or perhaps one as a mirror reflection of the other. An example problem is shown in Figure 2.3. The reasoning end is represented by progressive matrix problems and similar tasks, in which a (possibly abstract) pattern must be extracted from visual displays.

There has been a good deal of controversy over whether visual-spatial reasoning tests should be included in test batteries used in educational and industrial personnel selection programs, such as the SAT and the ASVAB. At present (2010) neither battery assesses visual-spatial reasoning. Those who would include such tests argue that visual-spatial reasoning is an important

part of cognition in some courses of study, such as architecture and engineering, and in a variety of mechanical trades of use to the services.[28] Visual-spatial reasoning is assessed in some detail in personnel selection for some occupations, especially in aviation.

The argument against assessing visual-spatial reasoning is that there are many areas where the ability is not required. Visual-spatial reasoning is itself a complex domain. There are substantial male-female differences in performance on some tests of visual-spatial reasoning. Therefore, if a personnel selection program gave undue weight to visual-spatial reasoning, the selection system might be considered biased against women.

2.5.3. *Mathematical Reasoning*

Many, but not quite all, attempts to evaluate intelligence include some evaluation of mathematical reasoning. In the simplest case this amounts to nothing more than a test of how rapidly one can do simple arithmetic. See, for instance, the numerical problems on the Wonderlic Personnel Test (Table 2.8).

Are tests of mathematical reasoning tests of one's academic background, or are they tests of general intellectual competence? The answer is "probably a little bit of both." Citing Geary and the evolutionary psychologists once again,[29] humans are genetically programmed for some aspects of numerical reasoning, such as the idea of distinguishing specific numbers of objects rather than making a binary one-many distinction. These skills are rudimentary mathematics, compared to the calculus! Acquisition of substantial mathematical skill clearly depends upon having an appropriate cultural background. Therefore, in Geary's classification, mathematical skills beyond a rudimentary level are secondary skills. Nevertheless, there is a good reason to assess them. Skill in mathematics is central to functioning in developed societies.

---

27 Palmer et al. (1985) present data for college students; Sticht (1975) presents data for military enlisted personnel.

28 Hegarty, Just, & Morrison, 1988; Humphreys & Lubinski, 1996.

29 Geary, 2007a.

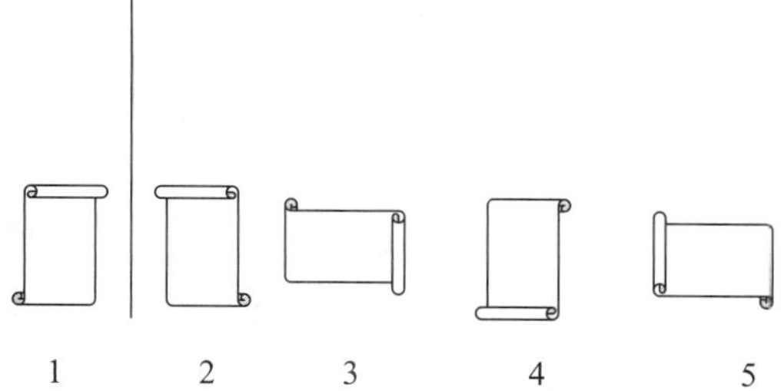

Figure 2.3. An example of a visual-spatial reasoning problem. Three of the four figures numbered 2 through 5 can be made identical to figure 1 by rotating them in the picture plane without lifting or turning the figure. Which of the figures *cannot* be made identical to figure 1 in this way?

2.5.4. *Deductive and Inductive Reasoning*

The ability to reason is widely accepted as a sign of intelligence. Two different types of reasoning are recognized, *deductive* and *inductive* reasoning. In deductive reasoning an examinee is told to assume that certain statements are true, and is asked to draw conclusions from them. Examples are

> *Categorical syllogism: All the girls in Ms. Jones's class went on the field trip yesterday. Ann and Sally are in Ms. Jones's class. Where were Ann and Sally yesterday?*
>
> *Deduction: John and Sam drink beer only when they are together. Yesterday John was in town and Sam was out of town. Did John drink beer yesterday?*

Inductive reasoning is the process of abstracting general rules from observation of specific cases. Progressive matrix tests were developed to evaluate this ability. Inductive reasoning is also evaluated using other formats. Here are some widely used ones:

> *Similarity: Which of the following cities does not belong in the group: San Francisco, Las Vegas, San Diego, St. Paul?*
>
> *Series completion: Complete the next number in the following series: 3:5:7 ____?*
>
> *Analogies: Choose the correct answer to complete the analogy: Black is to white as right is to: left, error, up, tight.*

There are logical and empirical arguments for evaluating abstract deductive reasoning.

Syllogisms and categorical reasoning are central to Western notions of mathematics, law, and rational argument. Mothers tell children, "If you don't eat your vegetables, you can't have dessert." Chocolate-loving children are supposed to draw an appropriate conclusion.

Empirically, scores on abstract reasoning tests can be used to predict performance on other applications of intelligence, such as paragraph comprehension, mathematics, and (to a lesser extent) the ability to solve visual-spatial reasoning problems. Because abstract reasoning predicts so many other types of thinking, it is reasonable to believe that abstract reasoning is either a central part of intelligence, itself, or that it is closely tied to something that is.

However, there is a case against stressing it too much. Although abstract reasoning is dear to Western academic and scientific circles, outside these circles some people think of abstract reasoning as a sort of word game, with little intellectual content. Let me give two examples.

In one of the Sherlock Holmes stories, "Silver Blaze," the great detective deduces that an intruder did not break into a stable to steal a horse because a watchdog did not bark in the night. This is an example of the classic syllogism:

> *Premise: A implies B. If there is an intruder the dog will bark.*
>
> *Observation: Not B. The dog did not bark.*
>
> *Conclusion: Therefore, Not A. Therefore, there was no intruder.*

When I used this example in an undergraduate class on critical thinking one of my students said that that was a nice made-up story, but that watchdogs do not always bark when strangers appear. Her more general point was that the real world is far more complicated than the abstract world of logical reasoning. She did not see the point in learning ways of thoughts that were useful only in the abstract world. She is not alone in her attitude.

Abstract reasoning is actually proscribed in some cultures. Consider the example of the two men who always drank beer together, given earlier as an example of a syllogism. The example is a paraphrase of an item that was used in an anthropological investigation of reasoning across cultures.[30] Rural Liberian tribesmen said that the question was not reasonable, on the grounds that they did not know the individuals involved, and one ought not to draw conclusions about things that one has not experienced personally.

Both these arguments can also be used against the inclusion of abstract inductive reasoning items in intelligence testing. In addition, there is another objection. The answer to an inductive reasoning problem is never uniquely determined. This is shown by the example in which an examinee was asked to find the dissimilar city in the set {San Francisco, San Diego, Las Vegas, St. Paul}. One could argue that the first three cities are in the Far West of the United States, while St. Paul is in the Midwest. Or that the first three cities have Spanish-derived names, while St. Paul does not. Or that Las Vegas is the only city not named for a Christian saint. There are many ways in which the four items can be compared; the question does not specify which one is to be used.

Similar arguments can be made against the use of series or analogy problems, including progressive matrix tests. In all cases the answer is determined by consensus, and the consensus opinion may be different in different cultures. Here is another example.

Which two of these animals belong together: fox, cat, dog?

When University of Michigan students were asked this question most of them said that the fox and the dog belong together because they are both canids. When Central American Amerindians were asked the same question their preferred answer was that the fox and the cat belong together because of

their similar behavior. The Michigan students preferred a taxonomic grouping; the Amerindians preferred an ecological one.[31] Who is to say which answer is correct?

This example is by no means an isolated one, restricted to a contrast between students in a post-industrial society and members of a (somewhat) traditional agrarian culture. Richard Nisbett, a professor at the University of Michigan who has made extensive studies of cultural influences on thought, has offered similar examples involving contrasts between the reasoning of American and Eastern (Asian) styles of thought. Nisbett has argued that the American-European emphasis on focusing on only the perceived relevant aspects of a situation, and applying formal logic to those aspects only, is a marked contrast to an Eastern emphasis on being sensitive to the total context of a problem.[32]

2.5.5. *Another Way to Look at Content: Aptitude versus Achievement*

A distinction is sometimes made between *aptitude* and *achievement* tests. The distinction can be illustrated by comparing three different college admissions tests: the SAT-I, the SAT-II, and the American College Test (ACT). The SAT-I is said to stress aptitude, because its content is not tied to specific course curricula. The SAT-II and the ACT contain subtests tied to courses, tests of history, literature, science, and mathematics.[33] What is the difference?

Achievement is simple enough. You have successfully studied English, mathematics, history, physics, or anything else if you know the relevant facts and principles. But what is meant by "aptitude?"

---

30 Cole et al., 1971.

31 Lopez et al., 1997.
32 Nisbett, 2009, pp. 162–170.
33 The ACT was originally developed by E. Lindquist, a psychologist who was involved in the early development of the SAT. Lindquist disagreed vehemently with Chauncey's decision to emphasize aptitude over ability. He believed that it was more appropriate to evaluate a person's readiness for further education by determining what the person had learned up to the point of testing.

According to Richard Snow, an educational psychologist from Stanford University, "aptitude" implies that a person has a talent for doing something – politics, music, athletics, and so forth.[34] "Achievement" implies that a person already has done something in a certain field. A person who has an aptitude for a field should do well if he or she trains in that field, but having "aptitude" does not imply that the training has taken place. You can have an aptitude for playing music without knowing how to play the clarinet. But if you have the aptitude, learning to play should be easy.

The SAT-I was once explicitly called a scholastic aptitude test because it was supposed to identify students who could be successful if they went to an American college or university, without stressing the knowledge acquired in particular courses. By contrast, the SAT-II and ACT test identified topics, such as mathematics. However, the SAT-I is not entirely knowledge-free. For instance, it assumes that examinees know the English language, but does not assume that they have had a course in English literature.

Progressive matrix tests are aptitude tests that make even fewer demands on knowledge. However, users of these tests assume that the examinee understands the basic testing situation, and there are various strategies for taking such tests that depend upon cultural knowledge.

The developer of an achievement test assumes that all examinees will have had certain experiences – for example, a course in American history. The test is intended to determine what the examinee learned from the experience. The argument for using achievement tests as screening devices is that one of the best predictors of how well a person will do at learning something in a new situation is how much the person has learned in comparable situations. By this logic, the best predictor of grades in first-year college physics is a test of how much the student learned in high school physics.

In educational settings it turns out that very much the same admission decisions are made regardless of whether an aptitude or an achievement test is used. While there are cases of people who score highly on the SAT-I and do poorly on the ACT, and vice versa, at the population level the SAT and the ACT predict success or failure for almost the same people.[35] On the whole, if you have an aptitude for academic studies, then you will have learned a lot from the classes you have already had; if you do not have the aptitude, you will not. This is not to deny the fact that late bloomers do exist; there are people who have the talent to succeed in academics but who, for a variety of reasons, have not learned very much in high school. Conversely, there are people who do not do well on abstract aptitude tests, but are quite good at learning academic material. These cases are exceptions to the rule. Academic achievement and academic aptitude test scores are highly correlated.

2.6. Test Creation and Use

We now move from a consideration of the content of cognitive tests to some more general issues about how the tests are developed.

2.6.1. *Item Selection and Evaluation*

The questions on intelligence tests have been the butt of quite a few jokes and sarcastic remarks. Here is what one popular science writer admitted that he believed prior to looking into the issue.

> *the questions on IQ tests are all written by graduate students from Connecticut and begin "Teddy leaves Sag Harbor on the brunchtime jitney . . . "*
> B. Maddox, *writing in* Discovery,
> *March 2008, p. 18*

---

34 Snow, 1996.

35 Koenig, Frey, and Detterman, 2008. These authors also show that the ACT has a substantial predictive correlation, .61, with the Raven Progressive Matrices test, which is in no sense an achievement test!

Maddox' s comment is not too far from Walter Lippmann's characterization of the first Stanford-Binet test, eighty years earlier (see Chapter 1). Neither criticism addresses the rigorous procedures used for item selection. And, in fairness to Maddox, later in his article he explains that his initial prejudices were wrong, and he delves into some of the issues surrounding intelligence testing in a reasonable way.

Candidate questions on all intelligence tests are initially developed either by identifying a group of people who are thought to be intelligent to varying degrees, and seeing what sorts of problems they can solve, or by generating questions from a theory of what intelligence is. The candidate questions are then given to a sample of people who are thought to be typical of the population for whom the test is intended. One way to do this is to insert a new question into an existing test. Answers to the new question are not counted as part of the score on the existing test, but statistics are gathered on them. If these statistics meet certain criteria, the new item is incorporated into the next revision of the test.

If a test question is a good one, scores on that question should be positively correlated with people's scores on the other items on the test. Consider an analogy between taking a test and a high jump competition, where competitors have to jump over a bar set at various heights. Suppose a competitor can jump over ("clear") a 1.75 m bar (5 ft., 9 in.), but cannot jump over a bar set to 1.83 m (6 ft.). We would expect this competitor to be able to jump over a 1.6 m bar, but not to be able to jump over a 1.9 m bar. More generally, if a jumper can clear a bar at height x, but cannot clear a bar at height y ($y > x$), we expect the jumper to clear all heights lower than x, and not be able to clear a bar at heights higher than y.

Suppose we wanted to construct a ten-item test of the ability to solve word problems. According to *psychometrics*, the term for the science of test construction, we should look for ten problems that (a) could be ordered in terms of difficulty, defined by the percentage of people who can solve each

problem, and (b) behave like the high jump bar – if a person can solve a problem at difficulty level x but cannot solve a problem at difficulty level y, where y is greater than x, then the person should solve all problems with difficulty level less than x and not solve any problems with difficulty level greater than y.

What I have just described is an ideal situation. In practice, there will always be some people who fail to solve a problem at one level of difficulty, but do occasionally solve problems at a higher level of difficulty. Therefore, a statistical technique called *Item Response Theory* has been developed to select questions that can be thought of as measuring the same thing.[36] Items that have this property are said to be *scalable*. The point to remember is that a great deal of care is taken to select test questions that appear to be evaluating the same skill, but at different levels of difficulty.

2.6.2. *Differential Impact*

Avoiding *differential impact* is part of item selection. Differential impact means that an item is selectively difficult for some sub-population of test takers, compared to the general population. The idea may be best illustrated by an example, once again using mathematics word problems.

> *Baseball problem, version 1. The Detroit baseball team was ahead of the Seattle team by one run. But at the very end of the game the Seattle team scored two runs.*
> *Did the Seattle team or the Detroit team win the game?*

This is a simple arithmetic problem. You can solve it without knowing very much about baseball. Now look at version 2.

> *Baseball problem, version 2. It was the bottom of the ninth and the Tigers were up by one. The first Mariner walked, and the next one up homered.*
> *Did the Seattle team or the Detroit team win the game?*

36 Embretson & Reise, 2000.

For anyone who knows baseball this is the same simple arithmetic problem as version 1. If you do not know baseball version 2 is harder than version 1, because version 2 has been written using baseball jargon. If you do not know that the names of the Detroit and Seattle teams are, respectively, the Tigers and the Mariners, all you can do is guess what the answer might be. Version 2 has differential impact on people who are or are not familiar with baseball.

This example was made up to make a point. However, it does resemble objections that have been made in realistic situations. For instance, on occasion tests have been attacked for differential impact on African Americans because they were written using the vocabulary and syntax of the majority population.

Differential impact does *not* mean that tests and items have to be equally difficult for all groups. To see why, consider again the high jump competition. Women, in general, cannot jump as high as men. (As of April 2010 the men's record was 2.45 m, and the women's 2.09 m.) If we were to set a high jump bar at a randomly chosen height between one and two meters, we would find that a higher percentage of men than women could jump over the bar. Nevertheless, high jump bars do not have differential impact, because they meet the criterion for equal scalability in both groups; the difficulty of jumping over a bar increases with height for both men and women. The same argument applies to cognitive tests. Tests and items do not have differential impact if they scale equivalently in each group. This means that the order of difficulty must be the same for all items, and in addition that the items must meet some further statistical criteria specified by item response theory.

This definition of differential impact is one based on psychometric theory. Law courts have accepted definitions of differential impact that are somewhat different, and that change from time to time and from jurisdiction to jurisdiction. The psychometric definition tells test developers what sort of items they should avoid. Satisfying the psychometric definition will generally, but not always, also satisfy the legal definition.

2.6.3. *The Distribution of Test Scores*

It is often said that intelligence is "normally distributed." The facts are a bit more complex. We need to distinguish between test scores, IQ and similar metrics, and the underlying concept of intelligence as a property of an individual. Again we draw on an analogy between intelligence testing and high jumping.

We can think of a high jump competition in the following way. The jumps are ordered by height, from the lowest to be considered to the highest. Competitors try to jump at each height, and are scored by the number of jumps they clear. A competitor's score would not depend on the order in which jumps were attempted. To see this, consider a person who has the ability to jump 1.5 m high, and a contest in which the jumps are, in order of height, 1 m, 1.5 m, and 2 m. That person will succeed on two jumps, regardless of the order in which they are presented. An Olympic-level athlete would almost certainly succeed on all three, and if I were to compete, I think I could manage to clear the lowest jump.

In a cognitive test each question is associated with a level of difficulty, just as the height of a bar is associated with difficulty in high jumping. The "raw score" on a test is the number of questions the person can answer correctly. (If the test contains multiple-choice questions there has to be a correction for guessing, but this is easily made.)

What would the distribution of scores be over the population of people who either compete, in high jumping, or take the test, in intelligence research? That depends upon two things; how high we set the bar (or how difficult we make the items) and how skilled the competitors (test takers) are.

If we were testing male high school–level competitors using the 1, 1.5, and 2 m bars, virtually everyone would clear the lowest bar, most would clear the middle bar, and a few would clear the highest bar (a little below the US national high school record). The distribution of scores would contain very few 0's, some 1's, mostly 2's, and a few 3's. We could change the distribution of scores by changing competitors. The score for male college jumpers would be mostly 3's, for female jumpers almost all 2's (for the highest bar is just under the world women's record). Or we could change the distribution of scores by changing the height of the bars. Suppose the bars were set at 1.4, 1.6, and 1.8 meters. The scores for male college jumpers would pile up in the 3's, and we would begin to see more 3's in the women's competition.

We could do exactly the same thing in cognitive testing, except that we would manipulate item difficulty instead of the height of the high jump bar. For a given population (high school students, military recruits, etc.) the distribution of *raw scores* (numbers of questions answered correctly) depends upon how many items the test contains at different levels of difficulty. For a given test, the distribution of scores depends upon the distribution of cognitive skills in the population.

Many cognitive tests are constructed so that they yield a normal distribution of test scores in their intended population. For instance, SAT scores are approximately normally distributed over the population of people who apply to American colleges and universities. This is a selected group of individuals of higher-than-normal intelligence. By contrast, scores on the WAIS are intended to reflect a person's intelligence relative to all people in the population. A student who receives a near-average score (somewhere around 1100 for the combined scales) on the SAT-1 would probably have an IQ score of over 100, simply because the mean intelligence level of the high school students who apply to college is higher than the mean intelligence level of all people in that age group.

As a result, raw scores on intelligence tests are (approximately) normally distributed because the questions on IQ tests have been selected to produce a normal distribution! Contrast this to height, which (within sexes) is approximately normally distributed. Since the measurement procedure for height is dictated by a theory of what length is, the fact that height is normally distributed is a discovery about nature. The fact that IQ and similar scores are distributed normally is a consequence of the way the tests are constructed.

There are marked advantages in requiring that test scores be normally distributed over an appropriate population. The statistical procedures for dealing with normally distributed scores are well known. If scores are normally distributed, the standard score metric (described in Panel 1.1) provides a convenient way of comparing individuals to each other in terms of different cognitive skills, measured on the same population. Suppose that we are told that a particular individual had a score of 555 on the verbal section of the SAT-1 and a score of 580 on the mathematics section. This does not tell us too much, for the scores on the two parts of the test are not comparable. By contrast, if we were told that the individual had a standard score of 0.1 on the verbal test and 0.0 on the mathematics test, we would know immediately that the person scored just slightly above the mean on the verbal test and received the mean score on the mathematics test.

When scores are normally distributed there is a well-known translation from standard scores to percentiles.[37] For instance, for a normally distributed set of test scores, a person with a standard score of 1 will have a score that is above the scores of approximately 85% of the population. Such interpretations are often useful. Since IQ scores are simply a translation of standard scores to a scoring algorithm with a mean of 100 and standard deviation of 15, compared to standard scores with a mean of 0 and a standard deviation of 1, the same sorts of statements about distributions can be made for scores using the IQ metric.

---

37 The same thing would be true for any known distribution of test scores, but the conversion may be more complicated. The normal (Gaussian) distribution is, by far, the most widely used.

2.6.4. *IRT Scoring: An Alternative to Using Raw Scores*

Raw scores are easy to compute and understand. Item Response Theory (IRT), mentioned earlier, provides an alternative method of scoring that has the advantage of depending much less on an arbitrary selection of item difficulties in order to force a normal distribution of scores, but has the disadvantage of being much harder to understand! I shall present the chief results of IRT, without attempting to present the mathematics.[38]

Return, for the last time, to the analogy between intelligence testing and a high jump competition. This time, though, suppose that the judges have lost their measuring devices, so they don't know how high the bars are! They can still conduct the meet, and assign sensible scores to the competitors. Here is how this would work.

We can safely assume that every competitor has a trait, jumping ability. Every bar, although of unknown height, has a quality we will call jumping difficulty. We can measure jumping difficulty directly, by seeing what percentage of people can clear a bar, even if we do not know how high that bar is. The insight of IRT is that jumping ability and jumping difficulty must have the same scale.

We now make an assumption – that in some *reference population* jumping ability is distributed normally, with a standard score mean of 0 and a standard deviation of 1. Arbitrarily, let us decide that the population of male high school students will be the reference population. We find the bar (of unknown height, it doesn't matter) such that half of all high school students can clear this bar. By our assumption of the normal distribution, half of all high school students have a jumping ability above the mean, and half below, that is, a standard score of 0. Therefore, the bar that just half the students

can clear must have a jumping difficulty score of 0. By the same token, if approximately 16% of the students clear a second, higher bar, then the second bar must have a jumping difficulty of 1. Why? Because, by the properties of the normal distribution, 16% of the population has a standard score above 1.

If we carry out the above *norming procedure* for, say, thirty bars of different heights, we will have a test of thirty items, each of which has a jumping ability defined by the percentage of people in the reference population who cleared each bar. Note that the raw scores (number of bars cleared) would not necessarily follow a normal distribution.

The analogy to cognitive testing is exact. We take a reference population, assume that the cognitive ability of interest (intelligence, verbal ability, etc.) is normally distributed in the reference population, and infer difficulty levels for questions by observing the percentages of people in the referent population who can answer each question.

The resulting test can then be used to measure ability levels in populations other than the reference population, using the scale derived from norming in the reference population. In the high jumping example, we could compare the scores of college-level women competitors to those of high school–level women competitors, using the scale established by the high school men! In an intelligence application, we could compare the intelligence level of, say, Harvard students to Yale students using a scale established at Stanford.

The only arbitrary assumption is that the underlying ability is normally distributed in the reference population. If the reference population represents a wide range of ability, this assumption can be defended. If intelligence is produced by the cumulative effects of many different causes – ranging from inheriting good genes to going to a good school – and if these causes are independent of each other and no one of them has a huge effect, then intelligence will be distributed normally. This follows from demonstrations of ways in which the normal distribution can be derived.

---

38 The basics of IRT were developed in the 1960s (Birnbaum, 1968). The method did not become feasible until the advent of modern high-speed computing. See Embretson & Reise (2000) and E. Hunt (2007) for further discussions.

2.6.5. *The Importance of Norming*

Choosing a reference population is an essential step in test construction, regardless of whether the raw score or IRT procedures are used to establish test scores. The appropriate reference population depends on the purpose of the test. The Wechsler tests are intended to be used on national populations. Therefore, an attempt is made to obtain a probability sample of an entire population (e.g., all Spaniards, Americans, or Germans for the appropriate version of the test) for norming purposes. Because these tests are intended to be applicable to all ages, the norming sample ought to contain a large number of people of different ages. This is an expensive proposition, so at times various compromises are used. For instance, some norming studies for the Raven tests were carried out in just one city, but the city was chosen because it had values on a variety of demographic variables that were thought to be "typical" of the country in question.[39]

The problem of norming is much easier when a test is intended for a clearly defined subset of a population. The SAT is intended primarily for students in the junior or senior year of an American high school and who intend to try to enter college, so norming is carried out in samples of college applicants. The ASVAB is normed by taking a population sample of all high school students, because of a legal requirement that the US military define its enlistment goals based in part on the distribution of cognitive skills in the high school population.

When we compare studies using different tests we have to keep in mind the effect of different tests having been normed in different populations. Four of the most widely used tests, the WAIS, the Raven tests, the SAT, and the ASVAB (or its subsidiary scale, the AFQT), are not strictly comparable. Studies have been done in which the same people take a pair of these tests. The investigators can then develop procedures for converting from one test score to another.[40]

39 J. Raven, 2000.
40 Frey & Detterman, 2004; Koenig, Frey, & Detterman, 2008.

Test developers try to make a test maximally sensitive to changes in the underlying trait (intelligence, verbal ability, or a similar cognitive trait) in the middle ranges of the reference population. This means that if a test is used to study a population that is very different from the reference population, the test may not do a good job of discriminating between people in the new population. To see this, imagine that for some perverse reason it was decided that the AFQT and the SAT should switch roles; colleges and universities use the AFQT, while the military uses the SAT. It would be hard to distinguish between the "better" and the "best" students applying to universities, because both groups would be getting very high scores on the AFQT, which is markedly easier than the SAT. This is called a *ceiling effect*. The military would find it hard to distinguish between applicants who were "marginal but acceptable" and ones who were "unacceptable" because both groups would be getting very low scores on the SAT. This is called a *floor effect*.

Of course, no one is going to switch the AFQT and the SAT. However, changes in reference populations do occur, and can have important practical consequences. Panel 2.1 describes one of them.

2.7. Some Issues Raised by the Use of Tests in Personnel Selection

How does cognitive testing fit into psychology, as a science, and into the cultural setting that produced the tests? These questions require a broader view than is provided by a narrow focus on test scores.

2.7.1. *Conflicts of Interest Are Inherent in Personnel Selection*

Personnel selection inevitably produces a tension between the selecting institution and the applicant. The argument is often framed as an argument over a test, but rationally it should be over the decision process using the test, not the test itself. The problem can be illustraten by the case of an idealized college admission process.

Panel 2.1. The Changing Definition of Mental Disability

Intelligence test scores rose steadily for most of the twentieth century.* This is true both for raw scores and for the underlying scores, derived by using the IRT methodology. The phenomenon is covered in detail in Chapter 9. For the moment, just accept the fact. The rise has had the unexpected consequence of raising questions about what we mean by mental retardation.

Prior to 1992 the American Association for Mental Retardation defined retardation as a child's having an IQ of 70 or less, measured by the Wechsler Intelligence Scale for Children (WISC). New norms are established for the WISC on a regular basis. The second version, the WISC-R, was normed on a sample representative of the US population in 1974; the third version, the WISC-III, was normed on a similar sample taken in 1991. But the 1974 and 1991 populations were not intellectually the same. It has been estimated that over that time period the mean on the full-scale IQ score for the WISC shifted upward by about five points. Therefore, the "zero point" (IQ = 100, standard score = 0) for the two tests was not at the same point on the underlying trait.

Tomoe Kanaya, a researcher at Cornell University, and her colleagues showed that this fact has serious implications for policies concerning the developmentally disabled.[†] Suppose that a child were to take the WISC-R in 1990. At that point the WISC-R, normed in 1974, would be the latest available test. Suppose further that the child obtained a score of 74. The child would not be classified as disabled.

Now suppose that the same child had been examined in 1992, instead of 1990, using the then-latest version of the test, the WISC-III. Presumably the child's mental capacities would be the same, but the reference point, the mean intelligence score, would have been moved up by five IQ points. Since IQ is determined by the deviation of a score from the population mean, the child would receive a score of 69 on the WISC-III, and hence be classified as developmentally disabled.

A similar example could be constructed at the other end of the scale. Suppose that in order to qualify for a "gifted student" program a child has to have an IQ of 130. Imagine a child who received an IQ score of 133 in 1990, using the WISC-R. The child qualifies as gifted. If the same child had been tested in 1992, using the WISC-III, the IQ score would be 128 and the child would not qualify as being gifted.

This forces us to think about what we mean by terms like "mental retardation" and "gifted." Do we want to define these groups by an absolute level of cognitive power? If so, qualifying scores should be adjusted so that the same people qualify as mentally disabled (or gifted), regardless of the population on which the test is normed. By this definition, if roughly 2.5% of the population of the US qualified as developmentally disabled in 1974 (IQ < 70 by 1974 standards), then only slightly less than 1% (IQ < 70 by 1974 standards, IQ < 65 by 1991 standards) would qualify in 1991 – not because the cognitive power of the mentally disabled had changed, but because the population as a whole had become more intelligent. The change in the incidence of diagnosed cases of retardation would have major public policy implications for, among other things, the amount of money needed for programs for the mentally disabled.

Another argument is possible. Suppose we define anyone who is in the contemporary bottom 2.5% of the intelligence distribution as being mentally disabled, regardless of where they would stand in the 1974 population. If we do

(continued)

Panel 2.1 *(continued)*

this, then the people who are classified as retarded using the 1991 test would, in a sense, be more intelligent than those classified using the 1974 test, which seems wrong. However, you could argue that if the population becomes more intelligent, everyday living will become more cognitively challenging. If this is true, then perhaps the definition of developmentally disabled ought to change, because people who were just able to keep up with society in 1974, those in the IQ 70–75 range on the 1974 test, cannot keep up with the more complicated society of the 1990s.

What do you think?

* Flynn, 1984, 2007.

† Tomoe, Scullin, & Ceci, 2003.

College and university applicants present evidence of their academic accomplishments and skills, often including their SAT scores. Figure 2.4 shows the six-year graduation rates of college students as a function of their entering SAT-I scores. There is a 7:1 difference between graduation rates in the highest, as compared to the lowest, SAT score interval. Admission officers should always prefer high scorers to low scorers.

The problem can be stated formally. Let x be an applicant's score on an entrance examination and let $p(x)$ be the probability that an applicant with score x will graduate.

The institution should set a minimum score, x_{mi}, (m for minimum, i for institution) and should reject all applicants with scores lower than this. The value of x_{mi} depends upon the benefits to the institution, B_i, if the student graduates, and the costs C_i, to the institution, if the student does not graduate. For an applicant with evidence x the expected benefits are $p(x)B_i$, and the expected costs $(1 - p(x))C_i$. The admission officer should accept the applicant if

$$p(x)B_i \geq (1 - p(x))C_i, \tag{2.1}$$

which is equivalent to

$$\frac{p(x)}{(1 - p(x))} \geq \frac{C_i}{B_i}. \tag{2.2}$$

The left-hand side of equation 2.2 is called the *odds on success*, and the right-hand side is the *cost:benefit ratio*. The odds on success are established by the evidence; the cost:benefit ratio is determined by the costs and benefits, as seen by the institution. The college should set x_{mi} to be the point at which expected costs equal expected benefits. The institution should accept the applicant only if the score is at or above the institution's critical value.

The applicant can reason in a similar way. There are individual benefits, B_a, for graduating from a college or university, and costs, C_a, for attending but not graduating. While the applicant and the institution should agree on the implications of the evidence, $p(x)$, and hence agree on the odds for success, they may disagree (legitimately) about the cost:benefit ratio. The applicant should establish a critical value, x_c, and should want to enter an institution only if his or her test score is above this value. Because the applicant's costs and benefits are not the same as the institution's, the applicant's critical value, x_c, may not be the same as the institution's minimum value, x_{mi}. The applicant and the institution should agree about acceptance when the applicant's scores are high enough to be above both critical values, and should agree about rejection when the scores are below both values. Disagreements arise if an applicant's scores are between the two critical values. If the applicant's cost:benefit ratio is lower than the institution's, there will be cases where the institution rejects an applicant who, from his or her perspective, ought to have been accepted. If the applicant's cost:benefit ratio is higher than the institution's, the applicant

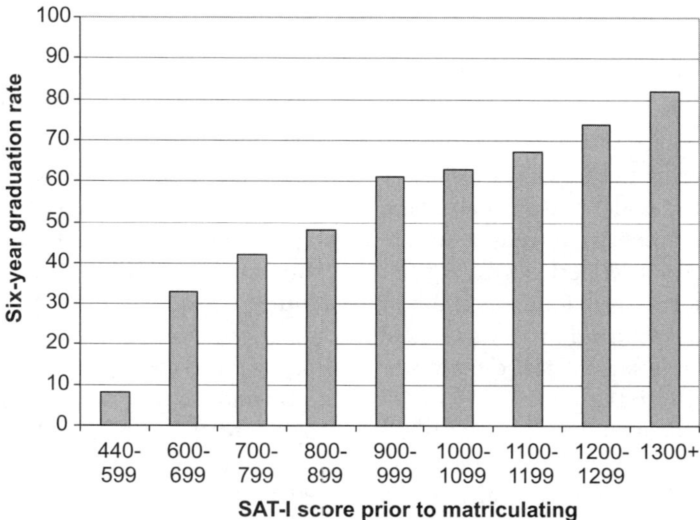

Figure 2.4. Six-year graduation rates as a function of entering SAT-1 scores. *Source:* The College Board, as reported in *The Washington Post*, Jan. 27, 2000, p. A11. The data does not reflect the use of a test of writing, which is now included in the SAT-1.

will reject an acceptance offer. In each case the disagreement is over the costs and benefits, not the implications of the evidence. In actual arguments over the use of tests in personnel decisions these different arguments are sometimes confounded.

2.7.2. *Missing Evidence: What the Tests Do Not Evaluate*

Arguments about the interpretation of cognitive tests take three forms. One, which is an argument largely carried out among researchers, is over the appropriate analysis of a particular study. While such arguments can be important, they are not the ones that catch the public's eye. Public concerns center on two things: systematic omission of certain abilities that might be tested but often are not, and omission of abilities that may be important to cognition but that do not fit into the conventional "Drop in from the Sky" testing format.

ABILITIES THAT COULD BE TESTED BUT OFTEN ARE NOT

Cognitive tests are designed to cover those skills that are required for all the situations where the tests are used, at the expense of evaluating cognitive skills that are required in only some of the applications. The SAT, for instance, evaluates cognitive skills that are common requirements across the undergraduate curriculum, but does not evaluate skills in, say, music or drawing, which are required in only some majors. There is also no opportunity for examinees to demonstrate a cognitive skill unless the examiner has decided that it is appropriate. The extent to which this is a problem depends upon the breadth of the applications for which the test is intended. The problem is reduced when a test is intended for personnel classification in a well-defined setting, such as the schools or the armed services. In such cases test developers can, and do, consult with the institution to determine what skills must be tested.

This policy, which is sensible in itself, creates a problem when a test is either used for research purposes, to study intelligence in general, or applied in a personnel selection setting outside of the one for which it was originally intended. In the former case, insisting that the current format of a test (or tests) is the definition of intelligence essentially puts a blinder on research efforts, because it amounts to agreeing with Boring that "intelligence is what the test tests," thus ruling out conceptual advances. Critics of intelligence research have claimed that this sort of thinking has hurt the field.

When a test is used outside the setting in which it was developed there is a substantial chance that the test will fail to evaluate some aspect of cognition that is, indeed, central in the new application. Robert Sternberg has referred to this sort of restriction as a failure to evaluate *practical intelligence*, knowledge and problem-solving skills that the examinee will actually need "on the job."[41]

Sternberg's concern over practical intelligence is closely related to his, and others', concerns that cognitive tests typically do not evaluate *social intelligence*, that is, knowing what to do in various social situations. Evaluating social intelligence sounds like a reasonable goal, but there are problems. A test can be designed to determine what an examinee thinks is right to do in a particular social situation, but that might not be what the examinee would do. If we are only interested in knowledge of the "correct" answer, then a test in social intelligence is very close to becoming a test of verbal comprehension. Finally, different segments of the same society may disagree about what the correct answer is. To take an extreme example, suppose a question on a social intelligence test asked what a deeply religious father should do if his daughter proposed marrying outside her family's faith. People in different cultures will have different views about what the right answer is.

There have been continuing concerns over the limited scope of tests of visual-spatial reasoning. Intelligence tests seldom evaluate examinees' ability to reason about moving objects, as might be required in a task as simple as crossing a street in the face of traffic, or maintaining one's orientation in the environment. There are substantial individual differences in the possession of both of these skills.[42] While they are hard to evaluate using the conventional paper-and-pencil format, appropriate tests can be incorporated into computer-controlled cognitive testing.[43]

ABILITIES THAT DO NOT FIT INTO THE CONVENTIONAL TESTING FORMAT
In normal life, thinking is distinguished by two important characteristics: problem solving is attempted because the solution has a value in itself, and finding the solution may require considerable time for planning and reflection. For example, US taxpayers are highly motivated to file their returns correctly and on time. Preparing a return takes anywhere from an hour to several working days. The task will be considerably simplified if the taxpayer has taken the trouble, in advance, to organize records of income and expenses. Doing so requires foresight, thoughtfulness, and personal discipline.

A test taker solves problems solely to be evaluated, outside of the context of normal events. Minutes, not days, are allowed for problem solving. There is no way to evaluate the examinee's skill in executing behaviors that, by their nature, take time. What might some of these behaviors be?

Learning: Learning, by definition, is change in behavior over time. Test developers may minimize opportunities for learning of content during a test because they want the difficulty of a question to be determined by the characteristics of that question, rather than by what an examinee has learned in answering other questions. This is called the *item independence* property. It is a cornerstone of the mathematical basis for modern theories of testing and scalability. But item independence defeats any attempt to evaluate learning.

Dynamic testing is a modification of conventional testing in which learning is evaluated.[44] The idea behind dynamic testing is that the examiner should first determine the level of difficulty of the hardest problem that a person can solve. This is said to establish a *zone of proximal development*. The examiner then provides hints and suggestions that the examinee can use

41 Sternberg, 2003.
42 Hunt, 2002.
43 Allahyar & Hunt, 2003; Hegarty & Waller, 2005.
44 Lidz & Elliot, 2000.

to solve more difficult problems. The procedure is continued until a point is reached beyond which the examinee cannot go, even with the examiner's support. The level of achievement reached after coaching is assumed to be the examinee's true ability.

Dynamic assessment is closely related to a form of educational testing called *formative assessment*.[45] Formative assessment has been shown to aid in learning complex concepts (e.g., introductory physics) in some circumstances.[46]

The value of either dynamic or formative assessment as an evaluation instrument is unclear. To establish the validity of this sort of testing as an assessment it would be necessary to show that scores obtained after coaching are better predictors of future performance than scores obtained prior to coaching. As far as I know, this has not yet been done.

The ability to reflect: Conventional testing does not allow any time for reflection over hard problems. When the Enlightenment philosopher Jean-Jacque Rousseau defined intelligence he placed the ability to stick with a problem, over time, on a par with the ability to think quickly. Reflection and persistence were the characteristics of Abraham Lincoln's style of thought.[47] Should a testing paradigm penalize people like Rousseau and Lincoln?

Creativity: Creativity is close to "ability to learn" on people's lists of desirable mental traits. The commonsense definition of creativity is that it is a talent for producing novel and admirable mental products. Biographical studies of people whom we all agree were creative (e.g., Picasso, Mahatma Gandhi, Einstein) invariably mention the time that they spent thinking about the issues before them.[48] This cannot be evaluated in the conventional testing paradigm.

There have been attempts to develop "creativity" tests that do fit into the normal testing paradigm, by asking examinees to respond to unusual requests within a brief time. Two example questions are "List as many uses as possible for a brick" and "Within x minutes, write an essay with the title "The Octopus's Sneakers."" Such tasks evaluate an ability to produce novelty on demand. But is this creativity?

SOME REFLECTIONS ON THE CRITICISMS
How serious are these limitations of the "Drop in from the Sky" paradigm? The answer depends upon what one wants to use the test for – identifying people who have a trait, or understanding the nature of the trait.

Identifying people who have a trait does not necessarily require that the trait be evaluated directly. Identification is possible if there is a statistical association between the trait(s) evaluated in the testing situation and the trait of interest. It has repeatedly been shown that the scores people achieve on conventional tests of cognitive ability predict their ability to learn rapidly in both academic and nonacademic settings. The relation between SAT scores and graduation rates (Figure 2.4) is one example of such an illustration.

The same argument applies to creativity. People whom society considers to be creative seldom have low intelligence test scores.[49] People with very high test scores are more likely to produce creative products than people with average scores or even above-average scores. David Lubinski, Camilla Benbow, and their colleagues at Vanderbilt University tracked the performance of people who, at age thirteen, took the SAT and achieved scores that put them in the top 1/10,000 (the 99.99th percentile) of test takers, for that age group. By their thirties members of this group had garnered an inordinate number of patents, well-received literary works, and appointments to positions where creativity was expected.[50]

Cognitive tests seldom evaluate reflectivity and creativity directly, because of the inherent limits of the conventional testing

45 Black and Wiliam, 1998.
46 Hunt & Minstrell, 1996; Minstrell, 2001.
47 Goodwin, 2005.
48 Gardner, 1993b.

49 Simonton, 1984.
50 Lubinski et al., 2006.

paradigm. However, people who are good reflective or creative thinkers may be identified by their scores on cognitive tests. The extent to which this is true is an issue to be decided by appropriate research, not by an attack upon or defense of the characteristics of the test.

2.7.3. *Public Policy Issues*

Tests used for personnel selection have public policy implications, for the public has a legitimate concern about how educational and industrial hiring decisions are made. Showing that a test is a statistically accurate predictor of academic or employment outcomes only partly answers these concerns, as the following example shows.

In 2001 the President of the University of California, Richard Atkinson, proposed dropping the use of SAT-I from California's admission program.[51] He was strongly critical of the use of abstract reasoning tests, and especially the use of analogies.

Atkinson pointed out that applicants could improve their scores by taking a special coaching course, which provides practice in solving artificial, out-of-context questions, such as analogical reasoning items. This concerned him for two reasons. One was that he thought that the prospective student's time would be better spent studying academic topics. The other was that the coaching courses are fairly expensive, so using such tests as part of the admissions process gives an advantage to students from wealthier families, who could afford to have their children coached.[52]

Generalizing Atkinson's concerns, when a test is used for personnel selection applicants will be motivated to acquire the skills the test evaluates. Decision makers who adopt a test have to consider whether they want to encourage such behavior. It may be that only some applicants (here, wealthy ones!) will have the opportunity to acquire the skills. Do the decision makers want to construct a system that gives some applicants an advantage over others?

There is another objection that Atkinson could have raised, but did not. Tests that are used to make personnel decisions have to both be fair (i.e., accurate) and appear to be fair. The public has little sympathy for applicants to universities who are turned down because they cannot demonstrate preparedness in English or mathematics. Applicants get more sympathy if the denial is based on their inability to answer analogy questions such as *Car is to Bus as Horse is to: Train, Airplane, Donkey, Stage Coach*. Students do not have to answer such questions once they are in college, so why should they have to solve them in order to get in?

Concerns such as these cannot be answered by appealing to statistics showing that test scores predict success. The tests must be perceived as fair in addition to having statistical validity.

2.8. Summary

There is no agency that certifies a cognitive examination as an intelligence test. Instead what we have is a collection of tests of cognitive abilities that, to varying degrees, assess different aspects of intelligence. This chapter has presented some representative ones.

Although different tests have been developed under different theoretical rationales, there is a surprising commonality of content across all tests. Methods for evaluating verbal intelligence, quantitative skills, and figural reasoning appear over and over again.

Some tests are given individually; others are given to groups of examinees. Beginning

---

51 Speech to the University of California Senate. Downloaded from www.senate.ucsb.edu/meetings/townhall/sat/abstracts/AtkinsonSpeech.pdf, 10 November 2008.

52 Atkinson constructively proposed using the SAT-II, which is a slightly better predictor of academic performance at the University of California than the SAT-I. SAT-II scores are less highly correlated with family socioeconomic status (SES) than are SAT-I scores (Geiser & Studley, 2002). We have come full circle. Atkinson's concern that the SAT-I favored the wealthy replaced Conant's concern, seventy years earlier, that a test like the SAT-I was needed to avoid favoring the wealthy!

around 1995 there was a movement toward presenting questions on computer screens. While this has advantages in terms of test administration, simply putting items on a computer does not change the nature of the psychological traits being evaluated; a vocabulary test is a vocabulary test.

Reliance on out-of-context, "Drop in from the Sky" testing severely limits what can be evaluated. Within this paradigm it is not possible to evaluate certain intellectual traits, such as a capacity for learning, reflection, or creativity, that certainly ought to be considered part of one's intelligence. This is a matter of serious concern.

When all is said and done, though, the tests are imperfect but not negligible predictors of success in academic and industrial situations. Validity coefficients range from .30 to .85.

Perfection is not a reasonable goal. An individual's success is not solely determined by his or her personal characteristics; situational constraints are often important. Nor can a test possibly evaluate all the personal traits that might be important in every situation. The fact that there are limits on predictive ability does not imply that tests should be disregarded. Test scores do reflect intelligence.

CHAPTER 3

On Theory

Then I would feel sorry for the good Lord. The theory is correct anyway.

> Albert Einstein (in reaction to a question from a graduate student about how he would have felt if the theory of general relativity had not received experimental support)[1]

3.1. Overview

This chapter and the next discuss theories of intelligence. This chapter describes the role that theory plays in our efforts to understand intelligence. The discussion is necessary because there has sometimes been a lack of clarity about what theories of intelligence are and how they are to be used. Hopefully the discussion here will provide some principles to apply in analyzing specific theories, as is done in Chapter 4.

The current chapter begins with a brief discussion of theory in general. It then moves to a discussion of some special problems facing theories of intelligence. Finally, I contrast two different goals for theories in psychology, and consider why these goals may produce different theories.

3.2. Scientific and Nonscientific Theories

Outsiders sometimes see science as a process of collecting facts. Theories are seen as secondary. Sometimes they are even derided. For example, proponents of *intelligent design*, the belief that life on Earth is the result of the actions of some all-powerful being, have insisted that schoolchildren be taught that the theory of evolution is "only a theory." This is not meant as a compliment to Charles Darwin. Less obviously, but perhaps more damagingly because the practice is so widespread, science courses below the college/university level too often emphasize memorization of facts and formulae, while deemphasizing the theoretical explanations that are offered to explain why these facts are facts, and why the formulae work.

1 Cited in Shapiro, 2006.

Theories are the glue that holds scientific observations together, for they summarize the chains of cause and effect that scientists use to understand how the world works. The theory of evolution, for instance, is a marvelously lucid explanation of why life on Earth is so diverse. Models of physical phenomena can be, and are, used to design complicated aircraft that fly (and land safely) on the very first attempt. Theory lets us look back to explain why something happened the way it did, and to look forward to predict what will happen under various assumptions about conditions in the future.

Theories are not unique to science. Many statements in philosophy, popular discourse, and religion are theoretical statements. The biblical explanation for plagues in Egypt amounts to a theory; the ancient Egyptians acted in a way that displeased Jehovah, who reacted with plagues of frogs, locusts, and disease. Subsequently Jehovah wished that a certain favored people, the Israelites, be permitted to leave Egypt. The waters of the Red Sea rolled back to let the Israelites pass, and then rushed forward again, engulfing the Pharaoh's army, in order that the Israelites might be safe. These are statements of cause and effect, and statements of cause and effect constitute a theory.

Scientific theories differ from nonscientific theories in three ways. The first is that they must refer to variables that are measurable in principle. The variables in a theory do not need to be measurable at the time that the theory is presented. The history of modern physics contains several instances in which theoreticians postulated the existence of subatomic particles before the technology to measure them had been developed. However, no variable can be admitted to a scientific theory if, in principle, that variable can never be measured. The theory of intelligent design is not a scientific theory because it postulates the existence of a being whose motives and powers influence our world, but whose nature cannot be known.

The second distinction between scientific and nonscientific theories is that scientific theories must be interpretable by objective means. Inspired gurus are not permitted, and personal faith is never to be confused with evidence. This does not mean that anyone, without training, should be able to understand a scientific theory. The necessary material may be hard to master, but the rules of mastery have to be open and nonmystical. Consider the following two cases.

Albert Einstein's theory of relativity was arguably the most important development in scientific theory in the twentieth century. When Einstein presented the theory of relativity he had to present a chain of assumptions and deductions that other, appropriately trained, scientists could (and did) follow. The theory was accepted by physicists on the basis of their analysis of Einstein's ideas, not because they attributed any mystic properties to Einstein himself. Contrast this to the decision of Saul of Tarsus – to accept Jesus as the Messiah and begin a new career as St. Paul, the Apostle to the Gentiles. St. Paul never claimed to have analyzed Jesus's philosophy; he claimed to have received a revelation from God.

The third distinction between scientific and nonscientific theories is that scientific theories must account for data. A scientific theory is vacuous unless it implies that certain observable events will happen – or, in more formal terms, that certain patterns will occur in data. There is no requirement that the observations be easy to make, or even that they be possible at the time that the theory is presented. Several of the predictions of Einstein's theory of relativity have only recently been evaluated, using technologies that were not available in his lifetime. The requirement for prediction does mean that the theory must be stated with sufficient precision that, given the opportunity to observe, we can tell whether the prediction was confirmed or denied. Newton's theory of motion predicted that large and small objects will fall at the same speed in a vacuum, regardless of their mass. And they do. The prophecies of the Delphic Oracle, Nostradamus, and other seers are notorious for their ambiguity.

3.3. Choosing between Competing Theories

Theories imply observations, not the other way around. When a theory correctly predicts an observation, this is evidence in support of the theory, but evidence can never prove that a theory is correct. However, if an observation is made that contradicts a prediction, then the theory has been disconfirmed. Accordingly, in the abstract, we do not ever determine the correct theory; all we do is to eliminate wrong ones, and continue to believe, with reservations, in those theories that have not yet been disconfirmed.

At this point statistics rears its ugly head. If theories always made exact predictions, and if we could be absolutely certain that our observations were accurate, then science would proceed in the way just described. In practice, that is not what happens. Predictions are often made in general terms, and measurements are never exact. Therefore, empirical results seldom completely rule out a theory. Instead, what we find is that the facts are more compatible with one theory than with another. This will modify our belief in the "winning" and "losing" theories, but not necessarily cause us to accept the winner and reject the loser. Indeed, it often happens that as more and more evidence accumulates our belief in all theories under consideration falls, and we have to develop new theories.

One of the most hotly debated topics in intelligence, the *Nature-Nurture* debate, provides a good example. In its pure form, the "Nature" side of this debate asserts that intelligence is inherited genetically. The "Nurture" side states that intelligence is obtained through experience, with the corollary that early childhood experiences are particularly important. Let us look at the logic of the argument, saving the details for Chapters 8 and 9.

Galton, who was firmly on the Nature side of the debate, observed that the eminent men and women of his own generation were highly likely to have had eminent parents or grandparents. Eventually he identified families who produced people of eminence, generation after generation.[2] Galton concluded that intelligence is largely inherited.

The hypothesis that intelligence is inherited implies that there will be a statistical association between the eminence of families from one generation to the next. The "null hypothesis" is that familial eminence varies randomly from one generation to the next. Galton found that the generation-to-generation associations of eminence were too strong to be accounted for by random variation. Accordingly, Galton had a strengthened belief in the hypothesis that intelligence (and hence eminence) is inherited.

Galton was correct that the data should strengthen his belief in the Nature (hereditarian) hypothesis *relative to the null hypothesis of no familial association*. The position relative to the Nurture (environmental) hypothesis is different. Most people inherit both their genetic composition and their social environment from their parents. Therefore, both the Nature and Nurture hypotheses predict associations of familial eminence from generation to generation. The association that Galton found was evidence for the Nature or the Nurture hypothesis against the null hypothesis that families don't matter in achieving eminence, but it was not evidence that could be used to decide against either Nature or Nurture.

As a side point, this example shows that, in general, simply testing a hypothesis against the null hypothesis is not likely to be very informative.

Proponents of the Nurture hypothesis can point to studies that show that children raised in unfavorable environments perform poorly in school and on intelligence tests, at least during the early school years. On its face, this evidence seems to support the importance of the environment. However, proponents of the Nature hypothesis can point out, correctly, that such children are not a random sample of children in their generation. Indeed, there is reason to believe that many of them are the children

2   Galton, 1869.

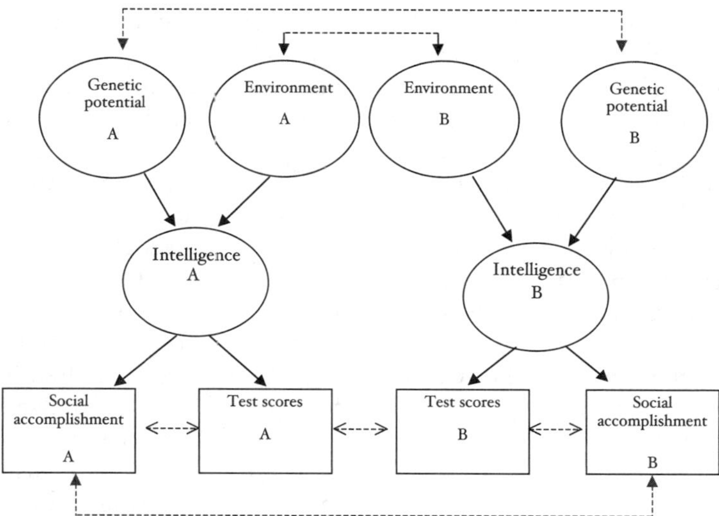

Figure 3.1. Genetic and environmental influences determine the extent to which the intelligences of any two individuals, A and B, resemble each other. This, in turn, will determine the resemblance between test scores and other cognitive behaviors of the two people. We can only observe correlations between manifest variables – test scores and other cognitive behaviors. In addition, genetic theory can be used to specify the degree of resemblance between the genetic potentials of A and B. The other resemblances between latent variables must be inferred.

of parents who were not terribly intelligent. The data does not discriminate between the hypotheses.

By the middle of the twentieth century the debate had become more refined. Scientists were willing to acknowledge that both heredity and environment do have a role, and that the issue is not to look for a single cause for intelligence, but rather to determine the relative influences of environment and heredity. At that point a much more sophisticated model of heredity began to be used. It is diagrammed in Figure 3.1. Its basic elements are (a) that there are both genetic and environmental components to intelligence and (b) that for any two individuals, the extent to which they share the genetic component of intelligence will be determined by their genetic relation, and the extent to which they share environmental components will be determined by their environmental relation.

While it is not immediately obvious, diagrams such as Figure 3.1 (and their associated mathematics) can be used to generate expected correlations between test scores. The values of the correlations depend upon the strength of the connecting links. Sometimes these strengths can be predicted from genetic theory. In a study of identical twins, for instance, the genetic link would have a strength of 1, indicating identical genetic constitutions. The link for fraternal twins would have a strength of .5, because fraternal (dizygotic, DZ) twins share half their genetic inheritance.

More generally, the contrast between theories, such as Nature versus Nurture, has been replaced in modern studies by a contrast between *models*, which can be thought of as assumptions about the strengths of particular links. The extreme Nature (heredity) model can be thought of as a specific case of Figure 3.1 in which the links from Environment to Intelligence are absent (strength = 0). We could also investigate intermediate models – for example, a model in which the Environment-Intelligence link is required to have half the strength of the Genetics-Intelligence link. In all cases we would come back to a basic test: which of the many possible models best reproduces the scores between observed variables, that is, the link between the four rectangular boxes (observable variables) in Figure 3.1?

We return to this example in Chapter 8. For the moment, the important thing to realize is that the field has advanced from evaluating broad assertions about the importance of heredity or environment, to a far more sophisticated competition between models whose parameters indicate the relative contributions of genetic and environmental causes of intelligence.

3.4. System Thinking Complicates the Issue

In Chapter 1, I argued that intelligence is not a directly observable trait; it is a latent trait that is inferred from observation of various manifest behaviors influenced by the trait. These include scores on IQ tests, school grades, and records of performance on the job. No one of these is entirely determined by intelligence, but each is influenced by it. This means that the definition of intelligence is, in a sense, something we make up, rather than being a directly observable trait. I also pointed out, in Chapter 1, that intelligence is embedded within a complex of other latent variables, including such things as genetic inheritance, socioeconomic status (SES), and educational opportunity. These variables have links between them – for instance, the link between the socioeconomic status of one's neighborhood and the quality of the schools.

When variables are linked into complicated systems there are both direct and indirect effects. (These are sometimes called *proximal* and *distal* influences.) Untangling them can be a problem. Here is an example dealing with verbal intelligence. Once again, I simply assert the facts, leaving the details for a subsequent chapter.[3]

Reading is one of the most important skills children acquire in the early school years. Subsequently, reading skills are used to facilitate learning. The sooner and more completely the learning to read–reading to learn shift is made, the more the child can get out of the educational system. Learning to read is associated with a child's family background. On the average, children from families in the middle and upper SES strata arrive at school better prepared to learn to read than children from a low SES background. This advantage is continued throughout the school years. Why?

There is a genetic explanation. To the extent that SES is linked to genetic potential, the children from middle-high SES families may be better learners simply because they are biologically smarter. There is also an environmental explanation. The parents in middle-high SES families, on the average, spend much more time reading to their pre-school children than do parents in low SES families. Indeed, some of this reading behavior comes very close to teaching reading, as in reading books that tell children that "A is for apple" and so forth.

We are dealing with a set of skills, embedded in a system. Furthermore, it is a system with feedback loops, for there is little doubt that as children learn to read their parents respond, and the manner of the response may vary with SES. The situation is depicted in Figure 3.2, which is only one of several possible models. It is forbiddingly complex.

Ultimately, every behavior has to take its action via the child's genetic potential. Parental genetic effects are of two sorts. Directly, parental genetics determine a child's genetics, and the child's genetic potential, interacting with the social environment, determines reading skills. Indirectly, parental genetics will partly produce parental child-rearing behaviors. These behaviors, influenced by the child's genetic potential, will produce the child's behaviors, which may include reading or pre-reading skills. The child's behavior, in turn, influences future parental behaviors, and the cycle continues. And this is only part of

---

3   See Bouchard, 2009, for further analysis of this point.

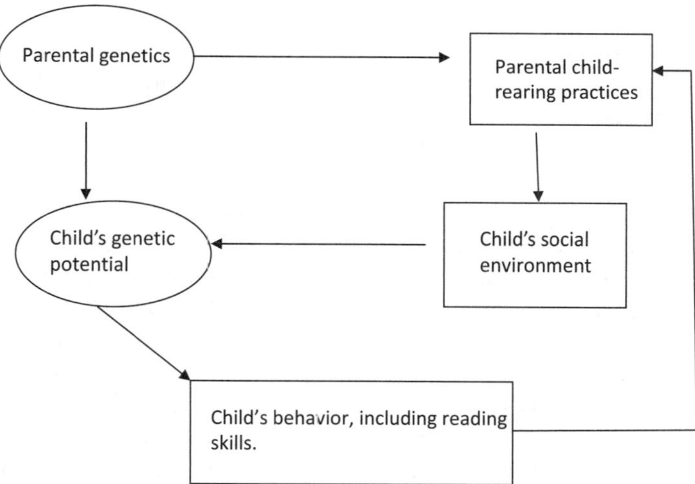

Figure 3.2. Influences on reading skills. Parental genetics will exert a direct effect on a child's genetic potential, and also may influence the parent's child-rearing practices (e.g., by increased sensitivity to a child's mood). Parental child-rearing practices establish a social environment that, acting through a child's genetic potential, produces a variety of behaviors, including reading skills. These behaviors, in turn, alter the parents' behaviors toward the child.

the system! I have not shown the effects of the parental social environment, which also influence parental behaviors, and many other influences besides. All the variables are enmeshed with each other.

This is the point at which many people begin calling for "controlled experiments." To continue the example of reading skills, it has been shown that extensive preschool programs, ones that are far more intense (and expensive) than the typical "Head Start" program, will improve children's cognitive skills during the early school years. There is even some evidence that the improvements last, in much weakened form, into adulthood. The studies in question involved comparisons between the performances of children who had participated in an intensive program compared to a matched group who had not, the classic experimental group versus control group study. The details will be given in Chapter 9. Such studies show that direct manipulation of a proximal variable, the child's social environment, can have an influence on the development of intelligence. However, this sort of study does not show that genetic

inheritance can be ignored. The reason that it does not is that random assignment of individuals to experimental and control groups, without measurement of, say, parental intelligence, effectively destroys any possible correlation between genetic potential and the child's performance, as an artifact of the experimental design.

Suppose that we improve upon the intervention design, by measuring parental intelligence and, by appropriate statistical manipulations, estimating how much the observed improvement in the child's performance can be attributed to the parent's intelligence, how much can be attributed to the intervention, and how much is due to some interaction between the two. Such designs have been approached, especially in the study of adopted children (Chapter 8). The resulting information is useful. However, it does not tell us what the controlling variables are in the world as it is, for we would be studying a "world as it might be," in which there are massively financed preschool programs.

The proper design for a study of intelligence depends upon what question we are trying to answer. It turns out that the proper theoretical model may also depend upon the question at hand. Intelligence, as a concept, can be introduced into different systems. Some questions deal with *control* issues in social systems – either how intelligence might be controlled within social systems, or how changing intelligence might alter those systems. Studies of the role of intelligence in education, personnel selection, and industrial operations focus on control issues. Other studies deal with *reduction* issues in biological systems – how intelligence can be derived from some more basic phenomena. Studies of the relation between intelligence and the brain, genetic influences on intelligence, and studies of the relation between physiological states and intelligence are reductionist. We want to conceptualize intelligence in a way that fits into the system being studied.

3.5. Intelligence as a Construct in Social Systems

We need theories and models so that we can think about how things work. We use them all the time to understand (not always correctly) how things like electrical circuits and mechanical pulley-and-lever systems function.[4] On a grander scale, economists argue (not always correctly) about the right model for the world economy, while epidemiologists use models (hopefully correctly) to forecast the seriousness of an outbreak of influenza.

Why should models be so ubiquitous? David Geary[5] has argued that humans have evolved a capacity to construct models of the world in order to satisfy an inherited drive to exert control over their environment. In order to accomplish this goal the various components of the model have to fit together in a way that we can think about. This means that we may have to conceptu-

alize the same thing in somewhat different ways, depending upon the world in which the thing is embedded. That is certainly true of intelligence.

Here is a case study.

During the 1970s two Stanford University educational psychologists, Lee Cronbach and Richard Snow, studied *aptitude x treatment* interactions in education.[6] They concluded that classroom environments that encourage active exploration and experimentation benefit students with high cognitive abilities, while students with lower cognitive abilities may do better in teacher-structured learning environments. Their findings have been replicated in situations as different as college students learning statistics[7] and elementary school children learning to read.[8]

Conceptually, Cronbach and Snow developed a model of the relationship between psychometrically defined general intelligence and educational practices. The variables they studied, psychometric scores and teaching methods, were measures and actions available to teachers. Statements about, say, the behavioral implications of the level of neural activation of children's forebrains during functional magnetic resonance imaging (fMRI) would be of little use in the classroom.

If we were to embed the cognitive behaviors that we call "intelligence" into another system, we might want quite a different conceptualization. Imagine a (hypothetical) study in which the investigator is interested in the use of drugs to ameliorate cognitive deterioration during aging. In that situation relating intelligence to the level of neural activation in a patient's forebrain might be a reasonable thing to do.

If a scientific model is to be used to inform decision makers – that is, to control a system – then the theory must be stated in terms of variables that the decision maker can measure and control.

---

4   Gentner & Gentner, 1983; Hegarty, Just, & Morrison, 1988.
5   Geary, 2005, 2007a.
6   Cronbach and Snow, 1977; Snow, 1982.
7   Shute et al., 1996.
8   Freebody & Tirre, 1985.

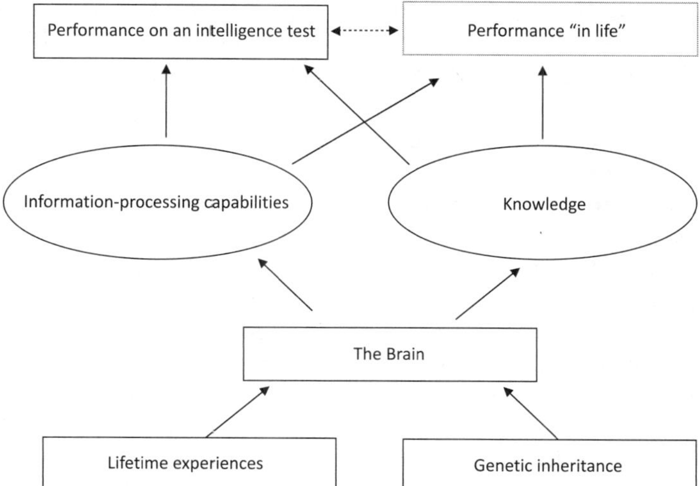

Figure 3.3. The levels at which theories of intelligence may be stated. Rectangles indicate physically measurable variables; ellipsoids indicate hypothetical variables.

3.6. Reductionism

Using scientific models to control variables is something of an engineer's view of the scientific enterprise. It is valid, it is important, and it is not the only use of theory in science.

The other use is pure understanding. Again the system concept is useful. A system is understood when it is completely closed, so that its behavior can be understood entirely from the actions of its elements. This produces an ordering of scientific topics: the properties of atoms are derived from the properties of subatomic particles and forces; the properties of chemical compounds are derived from their atomic structure; the properties of biological systems are derived from the chemical and physical properties of their components, and so on. The sequence is called *reductionism*.

Reductionist analyses have important implications for the study of intelligence. David Wechsler, the developer of the Wechsler tests, pointed out that intelligence is revealed by behavior.[9] Behaviors that we see as exercises of intelligence (or lack thereof) must be under the control of the brain. What is the alternative, the influence

of good and bad angels? Therefore, theories of intelligence that relate individual differences in cognitive power to individual differences in brain action are important as steps in reductionism. It is not clear that such theories would be manageable, let alone useful, in understanding how individual differences in intelligence influence academic learning or on-the-job performance. Models of these phenomena might well take as their primitive terms concepts such as general intelligence, verbal comprehension skill, and spatial orientation ability without any concern about how these abilities are produced by the brain – just as Newtonian mechanics accepts gravitational force as a primitive fact without further explanation.

Figure 3.3 diagrams the reductionist view of research on intelligence. All performance depends on the brain. At any moment the brain is the product of both a person's genetic inheritance and his or her environment. "Environment" has to be interpreted in the broadest manner. It does not just refer to obvious physical factors, such as nutrition or injury. It also refers to social factors, including education. Why? Because learning produces physical changes in the brain. This includes the storage of information, but there is more to it than that. The same

9 Wechsler, 1975.

external task may be processed by the brain in different ways before and after learning.

While the brain is ultimately the only thing that actually does something, it is often useful to deal with the results of brain action at the functional level rather than at the level of brain action itself. To illustrate, consider how a person recognizes his or her country's flag. In principle, it would be possible to describe flag recognition in terms of neural action in the occipital, temporal, and frontal lobes, but in practice it is simpler to say that visual pattern–detection and memory-recognition processes are involved. Individual differences in performance on the complex task, flag recognition, can then be related to individual differences in vision and memory. Failure to recognize the flag could be due to a distortion of either visual-recognition or memory-retrieval processes. Both processes are theoretical entities; there is a sense in which they do not exist. That is why information-processing functions are shown in ellipses in Figure 3.3, while physically observable brain and behavioral processes are shown in rectangles. Nevertheless, there is a place for descriptions of theoretical processes.

The top of the figure specifies two types of physically observable behaviors – performance on psychological tests and performance in life activities. In the physical sense both of these are produced by the brain. Conceptually, though, we can think of both behavior in testing situations and behavior everywhere else as being produced by information-processing capabilities combined with previously acquired knowledge.

The double-headed arrow between behaviors on tests and behaviors elsewhere indicates that the two different types of behavior are correlated, but that there is no causal link between them. Psychological test scores do not, in themselves, cause anything. (The social interpretation of a test score may be causal, but that is another issue.) What test scores can do is to indicate possession of knowledge and information-processing capacities that control behavior in life outside of the testing session.

The next three sections illustrate these principles by giving brief descriptions of studies that deal with issues at each of the three levels of explanation.

3.7. A Study at the Psychometric Level

Psychometric theories deal with the dimensions of individual ability that are believed to underlie performance on intelligence and personality tests. The goal is to simplify the tremendous amount of data contained in batteries of tests of cognition or personality, such as the various battery tests described in Chapter 2, by showing that the data from test batteries can be understood in terms of individual variations along a small number of dimensions of mental ability, called *factors*. Some details of the technique will be explained in Chapter 4. Here we concentrate on the results, using, as an example, a model that will be featured prominently throughout this book.

Two University of Minnesota researchers, Wendy Johnson and Thomas Bouchard, had available data from a study in which 436 adult participants had taken 42 different tests.[10] There were over 16,000 numbers in the data set, obviously more than a person could think about coherently. However, Johnson and Bouchard found that a large part of the individual variation on the forty-two tests could be captured by individual variation on just four factors: general intelligence, verbal skill, perceptual skill, and the ability to manipulate images "in the mind's eye," that is, to imagine how something seen from one perspective might look from a different perspective. They referred to their model as a general intelligence-verbal-perceptual-rotation (*g*-VPR) model.

Johnson and Bouchard's work is typical of hundreds, if not thousands, of psychometric investigations showing that variation on many tests can be summarized by variation along a small number of basic dimensions. Psychometric studies also provide measurements that are useful in understanding and

10   Johnson & Bouchard, 2005a.

controlling social systems, most notably in personnel selection. The SAT, AFQT, and WPC tests described in Chapter 2 are derived from psychometric studies, as are almost all college entrance and industrial screening tests.

Psychometric models are less useful when the task is to explain individual differences on specific cognitive tasks. To illustrate why, we take a look at an act of verbal comprehension.

Here is an excerpt from a newspaper editorial:

> *The citizens of Washington and the nation are spending millions and millions of dollars on efforts to protect salmon and save them and the ecosystem they support from the threat of extinction.*
>
> *These goals are being hurt by California sea lions that have outsmarted the system and now wait patiently for the fish to be corralled into the ladders at Columbia River dams.*
>
> Bellingham *(Washington)* Herald,
> *April 11, 2007*

From the psychometric perspective, in order to understand the editorial you have to have a certain level of verbal ability – in order to understand the passage at all – and a certain level of general reasoning ability to realize that the problem is that sea lions are eating too many fish to sustain the fisheries. This fact is not stated directly. It has to be inferred from an analysis of the text plus some general knowledge about sea lions, predators, and prey.

Psychometric research could be used to calculate the probability that a person with verbal ability level x and general reasoning ability level y would have probability z of understanding the passage. Something like this sort of analysis is used to design instruction manuals, where the prose has to match the reading and reasoning skills of the people who will read the manual. Psychometric analyses do not tell you what readers have to do in order to comprehend a manual. For that sort of analysis we must move to the information-processing level.

3.8. A Study at the Information-Processing Level

An examination of what has to be done to understand the editorial reveals that, without effort, we do quite a bit of information processing. Retrieving word meanings is only part of the task. It is complicated enough, for both semantic and syntactical information must be retrieved, and ambiguities must be resolved. Does the word *Washington* in the editorial refer to the city, the state, or the president? Then even heavier information-processing demands appear during the analysis of sentences and of the text as a whole.

The comprehension process has to operate on words as they appear. However, the meaning of a word, in context, often cannot be determined until following words are received. The initial *the* in the editorial has no meaning until it is attached to *citizens. The citizens of Washington and the nation* specifies which citizens and resolves the ambiguity of *Washington*. Next comes *are*. It appears that a descriptor is going to follow, that the collective just described (*The citizens . . .*) is going to be equated with something, as in *The citizens of Washington and the nation are taxpayers*. This interpretation is dashed when *spending* occurs, for now *are* must be interpreted as an auxiliary verb. *Are spending* is not a complete statement; the comprehender must find out what is being spent. The words *millions and millions* cannot be interpreted until *dollars* is encountered.

As this analysis shows, a language comprehender must have a cache for holding information to be integrated with information not yet received. In the current jargon of psychology, the cache is called *working memory*. It is an example of an *information-processing* concept, in the sense that it refers to an abstract ability to manipulate pieces of information in the mind, without specifying what these pieces of information mean in the world outside the mind.

The result of the construction is a *text model* summarizing what the text says explicitly. The text model alone is not enough! In order to reach full understanding the comprehender must construct a *situation model* of what the text means in the context in which it is presented.[11] This means going beyond the text to understanding things that are only referred to obliquely. The editorial is about sea lions eating salmon, but that is not stated explicitly!

Clearly working memory is central to the comprehension process. It follows that individual differences in the capacity of working memory ought to be related to individual differences in verbal comprehension. And they are. Marcel Just and Patricia Carpenter, professors at Carnegie-Mellon University, together with their colleagues, have conducted a substantial series of experiments investigating the link.[12]

In order to measure working memory Just and Carpenter used a procedure called the *memory span task*.[13] In a memory span task an examinee is asked to read a fairly complicated sentence aloud, and then remember the last word. Another, unrelated sentence is then presented. After k sentences the examinee is asked to recall the words. Just and Carpenter offer the following example, with $k = 2$:

Read:
When at last his eyes opened, there was no gleam of triumph, no shade of anger. The taxi turned up Michigan Avenue where they had a clear view of the lake.

Recall:
The examinee should then recall the last two words: *anger, lake.*

A person's memory span measure is defined as the highest number of sentences he/she can read and still recall all the ending words. The argument is that working memory is taxed by having to hold the ending words of previous sentences while the current sentence is processed. Thus the memory span is a measure of the capacity of working memory. College students' memory spans vary from 2 to 5.5, averaged over participants.[14]

The Carnegie group found that memory spans are associated with the ability to comprehend text.[15] One of the comprehension examples they used was the ability to detect ambiguities, as in

The experienced soldiers warned about the dangers. . . .

which could mean either that the soldiers warned some to-be-specified people or that the soldiers themselves had been warned by some unspecified person, as in

The experienced soldiers warned about the dangers conducted the midnight raid.

This contrasts with a phrase like

The experienced soldiers spoke about the dangers. . . .

where the soldiers are unambiguously doing the speaking.

Just and Carpenter argued that only people with high memory span could afford to keep two interpretations (alternative text models) in mind, and that this allowed them to achieve a better understanding of complicated texts than could be achieved by people with low memory span, and hence low working-memory capacities. They then conducted a series of experiments showing that their conclusion was correct. For example, high-span people read sentences faster than low-span people. However, high-span people read sentences containing ambiguous verbs, like *warned* in the illustration, more slowly than they read sentences with unambiguous verbs. Low-span people read both types of sentence at about the same rate. Evidently only the high-span individuals noticed the ambiguity and carried both meanings forward until the ambiguity was resolved.

This work is clearly reductionist. A psychometric construct, individual differences in verbal comprehension, was related to an

---

11 Kintsch, 1998.
12 Just & Carpenter, 1992; Just, Carpenter, & Keller, 1996.
13 Daneman & Carpenter, 1980, 1983; Daneman & Merikle, 1996.
14 Just and Carpenter, 1992.
15 See, especially, MacDonald, Carpenter, & Just, 1992.

information-processing concept, working-memory capacity.

3.9. Studies at the Brain Level

Explanations of behavior that use information-processing concepts such as working-memory capacity or retrieval of word meaning are less abstract than explanations based on terms like verbal ability or general reasoning ability, but they are still abstract. There has always been considerable interest in explaining individual differences in behavior in terms of individual differences in brain structures and processes. Historically, this was done by drawing inferences about normal behavior by analogy to extreme differences in behavior associated with damage to the brain, as in J. P. Das's development of tests for normal children based on Luria's observations of the results of brain injury. Today's advanced medical technology has made it possible to extend the approach, because we can take a limited look at the brain *in vivo*, as people are thinking. Chapter 7 reviews the current state of knowledge in this rapidly evolving field. Here a few quick remarks are in order, to show how models based on discoveries in the brain sciences fit into theories of intelligence.

The new technologies fall into three broad classes. A variety of imaging techniques have been developed that permit direct looks at structures in the living brain, at a much finer level of detail than provided by the X-ray imaging technique developed early in the twentieth century. (The X-ray method itself has become far more accurate.) Other technologies, and especially a technique called *functional magnetic resonance imaging* (fMRI), provide information on metabolism, and hence energy use, in different regions of the brain. These techniques have good spatial resolution, but, because metabolic processes themselves are slow, and hence reflect the brain's use of energy over a period of seconds, temporal resolution is poor. Techniques for recording the electrical traces of neural activity, such as the electroencephalogram (EEG), were developed in the mid twentieth century, but today's capability for recording electrical events is greatly enhanced over what it was as recently as the 1990s. Electrical recording techniques can detect events at the millisecond level but have relatively poor spatial resolution.

To give an idea of the current state of affairs, here are some results related to language processing.

Just and Carpenter's Carnegie-Mellon group[16] participants read sentences of varying syntactic complexity, such as

> *The reporter attacked the senator and admitted the error.*
>
> *The reporter that attacked the senator admitted the error.*
>
> *The reporter that the senator attacked admitted the error.*

while fMRI images were being taken of their brains. Metabolic activity increased in two areas previously known to be involved in language comprehension – a region in the left frontal cortex known as Broca's area, and a nearby region in the left temporal region known as Wernicke's area. As sentences increased in syntactic complexity the number of areas of the brain showing activation increased. Further studies of this sort, using linguistic and nonlinguistic stimuli, have shown that as the difficulty of a task increases, metabolism increases in the areas of the brain required to solve the task. However, studies of individual differences have shown that high performers (e.g., people with high verbal intelligence test scores) show *lower* metabolic rates than low performers when attacking the same task.[17] Evidently the harder the problem, the harder the brain has to work, but the more intelligent the person, the less the brain has to work. Intelligent people have efficient brains.

16 Just, Carpenter, Keller, Eddy, et al., 1996.
17 See Neubauer, 2000, and Vernon, Wicket, Bazana, & Stelmack, 2000, for reviews.

3.10. A Critique of the Levels Approach

Do we need three levels of theories?

There is a compelling argument for the psychometric level. The tests are needed, solely because of a requirement for the efficient measurement of intelligence in personnel selection and utilization, ranging from university entrance examinations to industrial employment programs. Since the tests are needed, some orderly way of thinking about the results is also required. Psychometric theories provide a way of doing this.

There is an equally compelling, but quite different, argument for brain-level theories of intelligence. They are an important step in understanding, for they link complex behavioral observations, such as verbal comprehension, to events inside the brain. Understanding these links is an essential part of the reductionist program of identifying the causal links between individual differences in brain processes and structures and individual differences in cognition.

Do we need a theory of intelligence at the information-processing level, intervening between models of individual differences in the brain and individual differences in test performance and in daily life? I believe that we do.

A complete information-processing theory of intelligence would provide (a) an understanding of the information-processing mechanisms that underlie thought, (b) measurements of individual differences in the power of these mechanisms, and (c) measurements of individual differences in the knowledge bases that are manipulated by the information-processing mechanisms. I see this sort of theory as a substantial advance on a theory that explains the way intelligence is expressed outside the laboratory in terms of correlations between measures of real-world cognition and either test scores or statistical summaries of them. I do not believe that a model of intelligence based on the brain can fulfill this role, because in practice we are often interested in individual differences in a capacity for processing information,

not individual differences in activation levels in this or that brain region. For instance, in assigning air traffic controllers it is important to know how many different aircraft a given controller can handle at one time – and there are individual differences in this ability. The requirement is stated in terms of information-processing behaviors. Psychological models to address this sort of issue must be stated in terms of information-processing capabilities.

This argument is not universally accepted. Ian Deary, a professor at the University of Edinburgh, has made a cogent argument against information-processing models of intelligence.[18]

Deary points out two weaknesses of current information-processing approaches. The first is that there is no guarantee that the tasks used to measure information-processing functions, such as the span task, measure what they say they do, because there is no agreed-upon theory of cognition at the information-processing level, and therefore no unassailable measure of the postulated functions. The second weakness is that many of the alleged elementary information-processing tasks require some of the same behaviors as the psychometric tasks. He does not see an advantage in restating a psychometric theory in information-processing terms.

Deary proposes that research on intelligence ought to try to link psychometric test scores directly to physiological measures.[19] Deary says that his view of the current state of theories of intelligence conforms to "the Scottish stereotype of dourness; stern and unrelenting."[20] I am somewhat more optimistic about the need to have information-processing levels of explanation, and a bit more dour, stern, and unrelenting concerning the utility of studying a system consisting solely of brain-based and psychometric variables.

The brain does not provide a place for a complicated trait like *intelligence*; it provides

18   Deary, 2000, Chapters 5–8.
19   Deary, 2000, Chaper 9.
20   Deary, 2000, p. 329.

a kit of tools, the information-processing functions, that, when guided by knowledge, can be assembled into intelligent behavior. The way in which the brain is organized, at the functional level, defines the kit of tools and tells us how they must be connected. Concepts like working memory, attention, and speed of information processing are useful ways of talking about the functional underpinnings of intellectual behavior, just as concepts like acceleration, deceleration, gasoline consumption, and turning ratio are useful ways of talking about the functional underpinnings of automobile capabilities.

The problem with going directly from brain-based variables to psychometric variables is that the steps are simply too complex to comprehend. While we now know a great deal about the involvement of different regions of the brain in different types of cognitive activity, we know much less about how networks of neurons create memories and conduct inferential reasoning, although we have interesting mathematical models of how neural networks might accomplish these functions.[21] Advances in the *cognitive neurosciences* will tell us what the neural bases of working memory, long-term memory storage, attention, and similar functions are. We will still need to understand how these functions are assembled to produce intelligent behavior. And we need to allow for the possibility that different people will assemble them in different ways.

I have somewhat more sympathy for Deary's "dour and unrelenting" view of current progress. He questions whether or not the tasks that have so far been used to assess information-processing concepts actually do this, and do this at a level that is more elementary than the behaviors required on a psychometric test itself. This issue can be resolved only on a case-by-case basis. It is true that there are disagreements about what the basic information-processing functions of the mind are, and about how each

function should be measured. However, the more research we do, the more psychologists seem to be converging on an agreed-upon information-processing model, including agreement on how its properties should be measured and how these measurements should be coordinated with information about how the brain functions. Thus there is no qualitative difference between my view and Deary's. It is just that we vary in optimism. Deary puts his eye squarely on the empty portion of the glass, albeit admitting that there is some liquid in it. My eye is more focused on the liquid, but I certainly admit that the glass is not full.

3.11. Summary

Theories are needed for two reasons – in order to develop models for predicting and controlling important systems and in order to reduce complex phenomena to more basic levels. Scientific theories are further distinguished by a commitment to empiricism, objectivity, and empirical verification.

Theories of intelligence can be stated at the psychometric, information-processing, and biological levels. All are needed, but for different purposes. Psychometric theories provide concise summaries of the dimensions of variation in cognitive competence. They also play an important role in personnel selection systems. Information-processing theories provide a functional description of why the variables at the psychometric level correlate in the way they do. This includes coordination with measures of brain processes. Biological theories relate intelligent behavior to individual differences in brain structure, brain processes, genetic inheritance, or any combination of these three.

Psychometric-level models and biological level models relate observables to observables. Information-processing models are, in a sense, fictions. They are extremely useful fictions. Indeed, they may be necessary. In addition to being the appropriate level at which to predict some aspects of socially relevant behavior, information-processing

---

21 This research is done under the general topic of connectionist modeling. See E. Hunt (2002, 2007) for discussions.

theories provide a vital link between the psychometric and biological levels.

Cogent criticisms can be directed at all current models at all levels. Criticizing current progress is not the same as denying the need for models. We never know when we have the "correct" model, for as we push our observations further we are almost certain either to change our current ideas or to decide that they are accurate within a particular set of observations, but need to be accommodated to allow consideration of other observations. This has been the nature of progress in every other science; there is no reason to expect it to be any different in the scientific study of intelligence.

CHAPTER 4

Psychometric Theories

The definition of an ability arises from systematic observations of individual differences in performance on a defined set of tasks. These observations constitute the empirical basis of ability measurement. They require no assumptions or exact knowledge about neurophysiological functions that might be responsible for performance levels, although specialists outside the strict field of psychometrics may find it possible and useful to seek such knowledge.

John B. Carroll, 1993, p. 23

Psychometric models of intelligence assume that variations in cognitive performance across different situations can be summarized by individual differences in a fairly small number of basic cognitive dimensions, such as general reasoning, verbal facility, and visual-spatial reasoning. In general, the effort to find these dimensions has been quite successful. In the last analysis, though, psychometric models are summaries of test scores, and are relevant to cognition in general to the extent that test performance itself is relevant to individual differences in thinking, as revealed in daily life. In Chapter 1, I argued that test performance is relevant, as an imperfect sample of the cognitive skills we use on a daily basis. This chapter concentrates on theories of cognition within that imperfect sample. The following chapter discusses expansion of these theories.

4.1. What Are Psychometric Models?

Whenever we summarize scores on different pieces of performance we are implicitly assuming that there is some common thread underlying each piece. This is a very common assumption. The SAT math and verbal scores are summaries of the scores on subtests, and these summaries are themselves amalgamated to produce an overall score. Similar summaries are used by the US Armed Services (summarizing subtests on the ASVAB to produce the AFQT), and on what are avowedly intelligence tests, like the WAIS (four index scores) and the Woodcock-Johnson (WJ) tests (fluid and crystallized intelligence, and a number of other scales.) Psychometric theories are basically expansions on this idea. Initially tests are chosen to represent the variety of cognitive performances that the investigator is interested in. Statistical analyses, which are reviewed briefly in the next section, are used to discover the latent traits underlying performance on ostensibly different tests. In the case of research programs the analysis often stops there. In the case of continuing programs of test development, such as the SAT and WAIS programs, the analyses of present tests are used to create improved revisions of the original test.

The next section is a brief description of *factor analysis*, a key statistical tool in test development. Following sections discuss the theories that have been developed using the tool.

4.2. Factor Analysis

This section is intended to develop an intuitive feeling for the method. It certainly is not a substitute for a text on modern factor analyts.

A psychometric model takes as the data to be explained the covariances (or correlations, in the case of standard scoring) among K observable measures. The explanation offered consists of a statement of M underlying hypothetical variables, called *latent traits*. The number of latent traits, M, should be substantially smaller than the number of tests, K. Further restrictions may also be implied.

Now let us unpack these mathematical ideas with a simple example.

4.2.1. *The Introductory Example*

Suppose that high school students were given the following tests:

Vocabulary: A test of their ability to define words.

Sentence comprehension: A test of their ability to define the meaning of sentences.

Numerical computation: A test of their ability to do computations involving the basic operations of addition, subtraction, multiplication, and division.

Algebra: A test of their ability to solve algebraic problems.

Word problems: A test of their ability to solve mathematical problems presented in words. (According to one cartoonist, the library in Hell contains nothing but books of word problems.)

Our intuitions, which in this case would be supported by a great deal of research, are that in a typical class there would be a strong tendency for the students who did well on one test to do well on the others. Conversely, students who did poorly on one test would tend to do poorly on the others. This condition, in which all tests in a battery are positively correlated, is called *positive manifold*.

Positive manifold is a matter of degree, for correlations between tests are seldom perfect. The best student on the mathematics tests might not be the best student on the language-related tests, but he or she would probably be toward the top. The same thing would be true of the worst student on the mathematics tests – probably toward the bottom on the verbal tests but not necessarily right at the bottom. To summarize, performance on one test would be a useful predictor of performance on the other tests, but the prediction would not be perfect.

The hypothetical example reflects the reality of intelligence testing. Virtually all tests of cognitive performance exhibit positive manifold to some degree, and they often do so quite strongly.

In the hypothetical case, it seems reasonable to suppose that there are two underlying abilities involved, verbal and mathematical ability. If the two abilities are themselves correlated, it might be appropriate to talk about a general cognitive ability. But how are we to find out, in an objective manner, whether we can reduce the five-dimensional space defined by the observable test scores to just two or three dimensions based on underlying traits? *Factor analysis* answers this question.

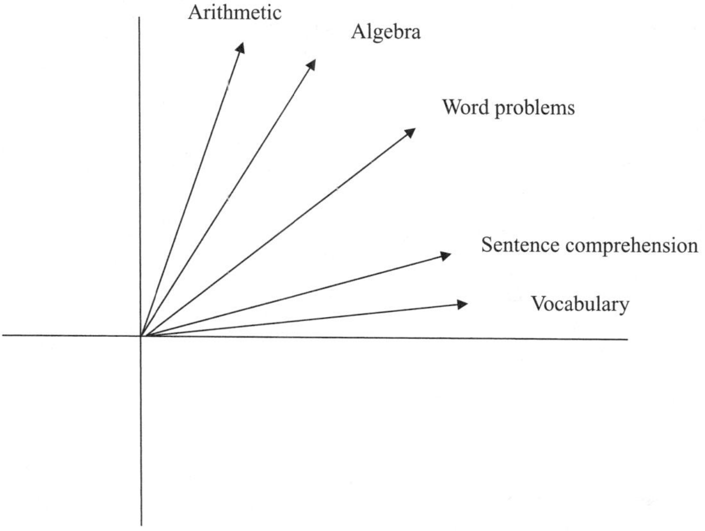

Figure 4.1. A hypothetical example in which five tests are given to a group of high school students. Each test can be thought of as an arrow that points outward from the origin (which represents zeroes on all tests). The more highly correlated the tests, the more their vectors will point in the same direction. In this example the mathematical and verbal tests form separate groups, and the word problems test, which contains both mathematical and verbal components, lies in-between the groups.

Factor analysis comes in two major varieties – *exploratory factor analysis* and *confirmatory factor analysis* – and several sub-varieties. First we consider the exploratory technique.

4.2.2. *Exploratory Factor Analysis*

Here is a geometric way of thinking about the five tests just introduced. Imagine that each test is an arrow, pointing somewhere in a space defining mental abilities, and that each person's score is a point somewhere along that arrow. If there is no correlation between any pair of tests, each of these arrows will be placed at right angles to (*be orthogonal to*) all of the others, so that the arrows would point along the axes of a five-dimensional space, and no further simplification would be possible. If the tests are positively correlated, the arrows will tend to point in the same general direction. The higher the correlation between any two tests, the more closely the arrows will point in the same direction. In the extreme, if the

correlation between two tests is one, the corresponding arrows will point in exactly the same direction.

The situation is shown in Figure 4.1, which is, of necessity, a two-dimensional projection of the directions of the arrows representing the tests. Exploratory factor analysis finds a line that, in a precisely defined mathematical sense (which need not concern us, other than knowing that the definition exists), best summarizes the common direction in which the tests are pointing. This is shown by the dashed arrow in Figure 4.2. It is called the *first* or *general factor* for the five-test battery. This provides a considerable simplification of the data. Instead of representing a person's score by five numbers, for five tests, we can represent the score by just one number, his or her *factor score* on the general factor. Obviously some loss of accuracy will result, just as a summary score on a test loses information about what problems a student did or did not answer correctly. But how much accuracy has been lost?

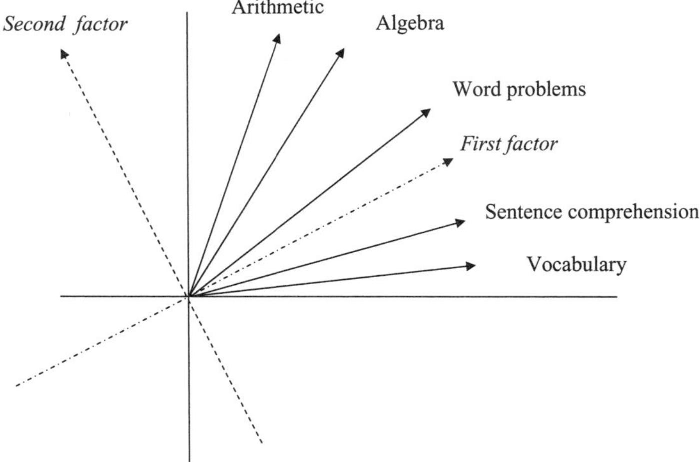

Figure 4.2. The first and second factors extracted from the hypothetical tests shown in Figure 4.1.

In order to answer this question we work backward, by determining the correlations between the first factor scores and each of the original scores. These are called the *loadings* of the original test on the first factor. Unless the loading is 1 on every test (which would imply that all the correlations between tests were also 1) there will be some loss of accuracy; the first factor score does not predict the original test scores perfectly. How great a problem is this?

Consider a particular student, Ignatz. Ignatz's score on the general factor will be influenced by his score on all five of the original tests. Suppose that Ignatz did exceptionally well on the vocabulary test, but poorly on the other tests. His score on the general factor will therefore be lower than would be expected from the vocabulary test score alone. Factor analysis represents Ignatz's vocabulary test score by two scores, the score predicted from Ignatz's position on the general factor and a residual, reflecting the difference between the actual score and the predicted score.

Residual score on vocabulary

    = Actual score – score predicted from

    first factor

Actual score = Score predicted from

    first factor + residual score

Repeating this procedure, the residual scores can be correlated, the machinery of exploratory factor analysis applied to the residual correlations, and *voila*, we have a second factor representing any common trend in the "directions" defined by the residual scores. However, these directions will be lines in a *four*-dimensional space, because one dimension has been "lost" to the first factor. The result of this process is shown by the second dashed line in Figure 4.2.

This process can be continued, analyzing residuals, then residuals of residuals, until the size of the residuals becomes so small that we may treat them as "noise." (When the number of factors extracted is equal to the number of tests, the residuals will be identically zero.) In most applications the residuals become small enough to ignore after only a few iterations. At that point we stop extracting factors. More generally, we say that we extract M factors from K tests, where M is always less than K, and in most cases substantially less. In our hypothetical example we stop at two factors, as shown in Figure 4.2.

The next step is to develop a psychological interpretation of the factors. At this point art supplements science.

In the example the first factor lies between the cluster of verbal tests and the cluster of mathematical tests. Let us call this

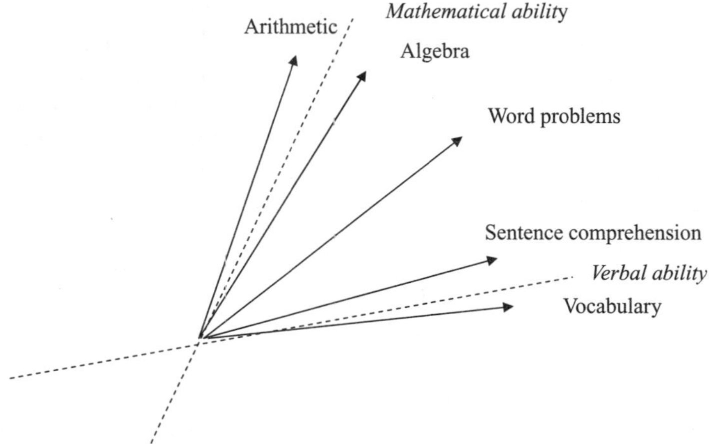

Figure 4.3. A correlated (oblique) factor solution for the hypothetical example, defining correlated verbal and mathematical abilities.

factor "general competence." The direction of the general factor is very close to the direction of the arrow representing the word problem test. This is reasonable, because solving word problems requires a combination of verbal and mathematical skills. The word problem test would be called a *marker* for the general competence factor, because the test and the factor point in nearly the same direction.

Because the second factor summarizes residual scores, the first and second factors must be uncorrelated. Geometrically, the arrows for the two factors will be at right angles to (*orthogonal to*) each other. The two verbal tests and the two mathematical tests point in different directions along the second factor. Mathematically, we would say that one set of tests has a positive loading and the other has a negative loading on the second factor.

One interpretation of the second factor in our hypothetical example is that it reflects negative correlations between the *residuals* of scores on the language and mathematical tests, suggesting that people can be classified as "relatively verbally skilled" or "relatively mathematically skilled," *after having taken account of their general competence.* The qualifying phrase is important. Findings like those in this example would not be evidence that people are either "good at math" or "good at language tasks," but not both. It is only after the effects of general ability have been removed that a tilt toward linguistic or mathematical problem solving appears.

This example is not completely made up. It is a simplification of an analysis conducted by Werner Wittmann, at the University of Mannheim in Germany. Wittmann analyzed scores achieved by fifteen-year-old students on the Program for International Student Assessment (PISA) mathematics and science examinations.[1] His two-factor solution resembles the one offered here.

The division of the two factors into a general factor and an orthogonal residual has been dictated by the requirement that the two factors be orthogonal to each other. While this simplifies the mathematical presentation, there is no compelling argument that a mathematically simple explanation will always lead to the clearest psychological explanation. An alternative way of proceeding is to use factor analysis to identify the number of dimensions required, two in this case, and then to rotate the dimensions so that each of the factors lies amid a cluster of similar tests. (These notions can be given a mathematical definition.) Figure 4.3 shows how this method of factor definition would be applied to the hypothetical

1   Wittmann, 2005.

example. This model identifies two psychologically interpretable factors: mathematical ability, with high loadings for the two overtly mathematical tests, and verbal ability, with high loadings on the two verbal tests. Instead of regarding the word problems test as a marker for a general competence factor, it is seen as a test requiring an amalgam of mathematical and verbal ability. This avoids the problem of dealing with a factor that seems to demand a negative correlation between abilities. The simplification has come at a cost. The mathematical model has been made more complex by adding an additional parameter, showing the correlation between factors.

In fact, one could argue that the fact that the mathematical and verbal ability factors are correlated is itself evidence for a general factor.

This example illustrates both the power and the weakness of exploratory factor analysis. The technique provides an objective and accurate technique for determining *how many* factors are required to account for individual variation in the scores, across tests. Assigning meaning to the factors requires a mix of further mathematical assumptions and intuitions about the psychology underlying the variation. Given this mixture of mathematics and psychology, it is not surprising that a good deal of the literature on intelligence from the 1930s through the 1960s reflected debates about how factor analyses should be interpreted. The field was considerably advanced by the development of *confirmatory factor analysis* in the 1970s.

4.2.3. *Confirmatory Factor Analysis*

Confirmatory factor analysis provides a way of deciding how well a theoretical model matches the observations in a psychometric study.[2] The investigator decides, in advance, the relationships that he or she believes hold between factors and tests, and for that

matter, between the factors. Computationally demanding algorithms are used to compare the observed relations between measures to the investigator's assumptions. This moves factor analysis from a method for inducing relations from data to a method for testing hypotheses about data – a preferable approach in data analysis. The following example illustrates the method. The example is due to Karl Jöreskog, a Swedish psychometrician who was one of the major developers of confirmatory factor analysis, and his colleague Dag Sörbom.[3]

Psychological tests can be given in either speeded or unspeeded conditions. In a speeded test examinees have to answer all questions within a fixed time period; in an unspeeded test examinees take as much time as they like. Jöreskog used confirmatory factor analysis to investigate the question of whether speed pressures influence some people more than others. The examinees in this study were given four vocabulary tests. Two of the tests, x_1 and x_2, were fifteen-item tests, administered with ample time to complete all fifteen items. The other two measures, y_1 and y_2, were seventy-five-item tests, administered under strict, tight time limits. The question of interest is whether the same trait, word knowledge, was measured in each condition, or, as is sometimes asserted, there are some people who just do not do well on speeded tests, even if they know the information? Table 4.1 shows the variance-covariance matrix for the four tests, which is what was analyzed. The bottom part of the table shows the correlation coefficients implied by the variance-covariance terms.

Jöreskog and Sörbom assumed that different, possibly correlated latent traits (*factors*) underlie performance on the two types of vocabulary tests. Their assumption is shown in Figure 4.4, using the graphic conventions introduced in Chapter 1. Causative relationships are indicated by single-headed arrows. For example, the first factor, f_1, is assumed to be a cause of performance on the

---

2 Confirmatory factor analysis is a subset of a more general statistical technique, *structural equation modeling*. As this method is fairly complicated I will touch on it only when necessary.

3 Jöreskog & Sörbom, 1979. The example is discussed on p. 52 ff. The original data is due to Lord (1956).

Table 4.1. The variance/covariance and correlation matrices in the confirmatory factor analysis example. Tests x_1 and x_2 are unspeeded vocabulary tests; tests y_1 and y_2 are vocabulary tests completed under a stringent time limit

Variance/Covariance Matrix	x_1	x_2	y_1	y_2
x_1	86.3979			
x_2	57.7751	86.2632		
y_1	56.8651	59.3177	97.285	
y_2	58.8986	59.6683	73.8201	97.8192

Correlation Matrix	x_1	x_2	y_1	y_2
x_1	1.00			
x_2	0.67	1.00		
y_1	0.62	0.65	1.00	
y_2	0.64	0.65	0.76	1.00

Source: Data from amalgamating information in Tables 2 and 3 of Jöreskog & Sörbom, 1979.

two unspeeded tests. Accordingly there are single-headed arrows from latent variable f_1 to observable variables x_1 and x_2.

The boxes, ellipses, and arrows establish the structure of a factor analytic model. The e's and the Greek letters indicate the three types of parameters to be estimated. The β variables indicate the relationship between the latent and the observed variables. These represent causation; the latent variable is seen as being one of the causes of the observed variable, and the value of β indicates the extent of the causal relation. The e variables represent residuals.

Residuals are not "error" terms in the sense that an error is a mistake. They represent the effects of all unmeasured factors that might influence the observable scores, but are not part of the model. In this example each residual term is uniquely

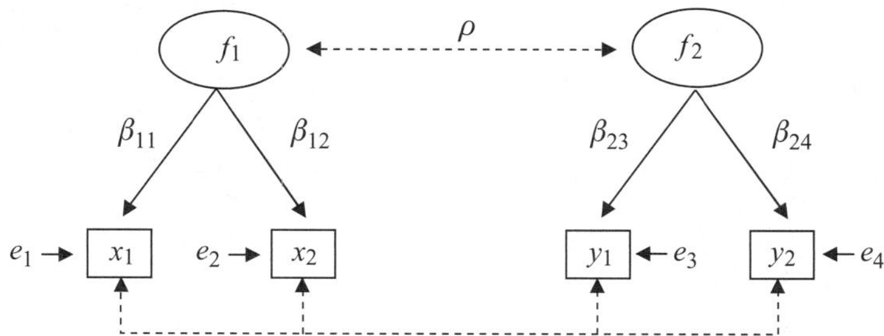

Figure 4.4. The two-factor model used by Jöreskog and Sörbom to summarize correlations between unspeeded (x_1, x_2) and speeded (y_1, y_2) vocabulary tests. The model assumes two latent traits, one representing the ability to do speeded tests and another representing the ability to do unspeeded tests. A correlation between the two latent traits is permitted, with the correlation, ρ, to be estimated from the data. The observed correlations are indicated by the lower dashed lines between the x and y variables. This model could be contrasted to a single-factor model by requiring that ρ be identically one. Note the residual terms showing external influences on each of the four tests. (Figure modeled after Jöreskog & Sörbom, 1979, Figure 3, p. 54.)

associated with a measurable variable. It is possible to construct models that postulate an unmeasured residual variable that influences several latent variables. If the system of variables were to be completely closed, so that the hypothesized factors were the only factors influencing the observable measures, the residuals would always be zero. In the social and behavioral sciences this virtually never happens. By examining residuals we can get an idea of the extent to which a model captures the variation between the observables. The smaller the residuals, the more the model captures the variations that are to be explained.

The ρ symbols indicate the magnitude of a correlation between variables, without any implication of causation. Therefore, the ρ symbols are always associated with double-headed arrows.

The absence of a link between two variables indicates that the model being tested assumes that the two variables are not linked, that is, that the appropriate β or ρ is identically zero.

This model makes strong predictions about the observed correlations among the four tests. Consider the two unspeeded tests, the x variables. If the model is accurate, the covariance between them, $Cov\ (x_1, x_2)$, should depend only on (a) their respective variances and (b) the two parameters β_{11}, β_{21}. A similar argument holds for the y variables. But consider the case of the covariance between an unspeeded and a speeded test, for example, x_1 and y_2. The covariance should depend on the test variances and three parameters, β_{11}, ρ, and β_{32}. Generalizing, any assignment of values to the parameters will imply predicted covariances (and therefore correlations) between all pairs of observed tests. These form the *predicted covariance matrix*, Σ. It can be compared to the *observed covariance matrix*, S. What confirmatory factor analysis does is to find the set of values for parameters that brings Σ as close as possible to S. This is exactly the same logic as is used, for instance, to estimate the mean and variance of a population from a sample. Only the details are more complicated.

4.2.4. *Statistical Evaluation and Model Comparison*

Let **M** be a collection of parameters, some of which have been estimated and some of which have been set by theory. We will refer to this as a *model*. Figure 4.4 is an example of a model. Any model **M** implies a predicted covariance matrix, $\Sigma(\mathbf{M})$, that can be compared to the observed covariance matrix, S. Statistical inference techniques can be applied to determine the extent to which the two agree. This is called the *fit* of the model to the data. Evaluations of fit can include determining whether or not the differences are greater than would be expected "by chance." This is logically identical to testing a null hypothesis, as described in introductory statistics courses. (The computations are quite a bit more complicated!)

It is often possible to go beyond evaluating fit. We can compare two different models, **M1** and **M2**, to each other. The simplest, and often the most useful, case is one in which the parameters to be estimated in **M2** are a subset of those to be estimated in **M1**. This can be illustrated using the model in Figure 4.4, which will serve as **M1**.

M1 assumes that two ability factors are involved, the ability to take speeded vocabulary tests and the ability to take unspeeded ones. However, the model allows for the (reasonable) possibility that the two may be correlated, that is, that people who do well on unspeeded tests tend to do well on speeded tests, but that the two talents are not exactly the same. The extent of the correlation is indicated by the ρ parameter, whose value is to be estimated from the data. A fairly obvious alternative is to assume that all vocabulary tests tap the same underlying trait, strength of vocabulary, and that it does not matter if the tests are speeded or not. If that is the case, Figure 4.4 should be modified to show just one latent trait, f, instead of f_1 and f_2. Call this model **M2**.

Here is an important insight. Saying that there is one trait is equivalent to saying that there are two traits but that they are perfectly correlated, $\rho = 1$. Therefore, **M2** has the same parameters as M_1, but, and it is a very important "but," in M_2 ρ is fixed at 1 instead of being estimated from the data. This has two important consequences. The first is that M_2 cannot have a better fit than M_1, because the computational techniques have ensured that in M_1 ρ has the best possible value it can have in order to get a good fit to the data. The second consequence is that we can compare the fits of the two models, to determine whether the difference between fits shows that M_1 is more accurate than M_2 than would be expected by chance. Going back to the example, we can determine whether the data requires that we assume separate vocabulary skills for speeded and unspeeded tests, or whether it is possible to make the simpler assumption that all the tests evaluate a single trait, vocabulary knowledge.

This illustrates a very important advance in theory construction. Confirmatory factor analysis permits testing of the relative accuracy of different models as summaries of the same data.

In this and subsequent chapters the reader will be presented with several models of the sort just described. The models will typically involve many more observable and latent variables, and the structure of the models will be more complex than in the simple example, but the principle of analysis will be the same. Confirmatory factor analysis allows us to establish a competition between models, and this is how science proceeds.[4]

4.2.5. *Limits on the Generality of Factor Analysis*

The development of modern factor analyses has greatly enhanced the precision of psychometric research. This point has not always been appreciated by critics, who sometimes appear to be attacking the field for deficiencies in techniques that were abandoned years ago.[5] Nonetheless, there are some limitations on generalizing the results of factor analytic research.

Factor analytic studies are often used to reveal the nature of underlying, unobservable traits, especially general intelligence. Tests with loadings close to 1 are important pieces of evidence, because a loading of 1 indicates that variation in observable test performance is perfectly linked to variation in the trait. For instance, the argument that the ability to detect patterns is an important part of general intelligence is supported by the fact that progressive matrix tests often have high loadings on the *g* factor, and that pattern detection is an important step in solving progressive matrix problems. In this case, we say that progressive matrix tests are *markers* for general intelligence.[6]

Unfortunately, it is easy to misinterpret this statement. A high loading between a trait and a test does not mean that the quality indicated by the trait is required for performance on the test in the way that, say, strength is required to push a piano across your living room. It means that variation in test performance, across people, is related to the way the trait varies, across people. Loadings are statements about individual differences as observed in a particular group. A person's standings on both trait and test are defined relative to the performance of other individuals in the group, not by the individual's absolute performance. The mathematics whiz in high school may not be that outstanding at MIT. This has an important implication for factor analysis.

The test loadings derived from factor analysis result from an interaction between the properties of the test itself, the other tests in the battery, and distribution of traits in the population being tested.

---

4 See Bouchard (2009). I have skipped over a number of technical details. It is possible, although rare in practice, to find situations in which alternative solutions have such close fits that confirmatory factor analysis cannot distinguish between them.

5 This is especially true of widely cited attacks by the evolutionary biologist Stephen J. Gould (1981, pp. 252–255). Surprisingly, the error was repeated in a revised edition of this work (Gould, 1996) even though the error had been commented upon by reviewers of the original work.

6 Jensen, 1998.

Some thought experiments illustrate what this means.

Here is a list of nine possible tests:

1. A vocabulary test.
2. A test of paragraph comprehension based on newspaper editorials.
3. A test requiring judgments of the syntax of English sentences.
4. A test requiring people to evaluate the logical argument contained in a political speech.
5. A test in which people are asked to judge whether or not meaningless patterns presented at different orientations are identical or whether one is the mirror image of another. This means that the examinee has to rotate figures "in the mind's eye." For this reason such tests are called *rotation* tests.
6. A test in which people view a room (e.g., an office) and then imagine that they are at one location, facing in a particular direction, and point to a target object. For example, "imagine that you are at the desk, facing the file cabinet. Point to the flower pot."
7. A test in which the task is to find a picture hidden in another; for example, finding a triangle in a Star of David figure.
8. A map-reading test.
9. A word problem test in which people read passages about an explorer going through a jungle and then answer questions about the spatial layout of objects. To illustrate: "As Henry proceeded southward, he realized that the python was keeping up with him on the right and the tiger on the left." Question: Was the python west of the tiger?

The first four tests evaluate language skill; the next four evaluate visual-spatial reasoning; and the last test evaluates both language skills and visual-spatial reasoning. Suppose that these tests have been constructed so that the scores are normally distributed in the high school population. Because visual-spatial and language skills are correlated in the high school population, it would be possible to extract a general factor and residual spatial and verbal factors.

Imagine two further studies. In the first we give the test battery to a representative sample of lawyers. In the second it is given to a representative sample of architects. What would happen to the factor loadings? I suggest the reader stop and think a moment.

Lawyers are highly selected for language-related skills. Therefore, the four tests of language skills, although appropriate for a high school sample, would be quite easy for the lawyers. As a result there would be little variation in scores on the verbal tests. Lawyers are not selected for their visual-spatial skills, so we might find considerable variation on the spatial tests. An analysis for a single general factor would result in a factor with high loadings on spatial tests, because that is where the variance would be. Test 9, which draws on both verbal and spatial skills, would have a high loading on the spatial residual factor and a low loading on the verbal factor.

The spatial skills tests would be easy for the architects, while tests of verbal skills should show more variation. Accordingly, it is likely that the general factor, as defined for architects, would have high loadings on verbal tests. Test 9 would now have a high verbal loading and a low spatial loading.

These changes in loading have nothing to do with the absolute abilities of the individuals involved. They are driven by the amount of variation in the population, not the level of skill. The examples are not contrived; they represent a situation that occurs often in the literature. It is common practice to conduct psychological studies using college students as participants. College students are selected largely on verbal skills and on general intelligence. As a result, the variation among college students on these traits is less than the variation in the population. Therefore, a study of the importance of intelligence in college students is likely to underestimate the importance of intelligence (or verbal skills) in the population at large.

The next thought experiment deals with another problem that limits the generality of factor analytic findings. The loading of a test on a trait can vary depending upon what other tests there are in the battery, even though the same population is studied.

Suppose that instead of using all nine of our tests we compose a smaller battery consisting of the first five tests – four tests of language skills and the rotation test. The test battery is given to a representative set of adults. We then extract a single general factor from the data. It would be defined by the traits required by the four verbal tests. The single spatial test (test 5) would have a low loading on the general factor and a large residual term. The vocabulary test (test 1) would have a high loading on the general factor, for it has repeatedly been found that people with high general verbal skills tend to have large vocabularies.

Now construct a new battery consisting of the vocabulary test and the four visual-spatial tasks, tests 5-8. The general factor will be determined largely by the visual-spatial tasks. The rotation test would have a high loading on this factor, while the vocabulary test would have a low loading and a high residual term.

These two thought experiments show what might happen, not what does. In practice, investigators use similar test batteries, which leads to replicability of results, but at the same time produces a restricted definition of intelligence, because the same mental skills are being evaluated from experiment to experiment, in only slightly different ways. Factor structures for a given battery are usually replicated across populations (college students, military recruits, population samples of adults), although there are occasional failures to replicate. The restrictions on generality developed here are warnings to keep in mind, not compelling arguments for throwing out all factor analytic studies.

4.3. The Theory of General Intelligence (g)

The *general intelligence* (g) theory is at once the best-known, most praised, and most vilified psychometric model of intelligence. The theory asserts that individual differences in cognitive performance are very largely due to individual differences along a single dimension of mental competence, general intelligence (g). Psychologists who advocate the g model acknowledge that there are other dimensions of mental performance, such as verbal or visual-spatial reasoning, but claim that these dimensions account for much less of the variation in cognitive performance than the g dimension does.

4.3.1. *Early Development of the Theory*

The g model was first stated by Charles Spearman, an Englishman who has some claim to be the first modern psychometrician.[7] After serving for some time as an army officer, Spearman entered academia, receiving a Ph.D. from Wilhelm Wundt's experimental psychology laboratory. He was attracted to Galton's concept of intelligence as generalized mental fitness, but did not share Galton's enthusiasm for what we would, today, call information-processing measures of cognition. Instead he thought that one should find a general factor through the analysis of complex measures of thinking, such as school grades. In order to investigate his ideas he developed both the basis for early factor analysis and the rank-order correlation coefficient, thus making substantial contributions to the budding science of statistics. David Wechsler, the developer of the WAIS, was a student of Spearman's, as was Raymond Cattell, whose work will be described later in this chapter. His work also heavily influenced the ideas of Philip E. Vernon, Hans Eysenck, Cyril Burt, and Arthur Jensen, all of whom have made major contributions to the field of intelligence.

Table 4.2 presents a table of correlations between a set of school grades that Spearman used as evidence for g. Following Spearman's practice, the classes are arranged in order of the average correlation between one grade and the other grades. To illustrate,

7   Spearman, 1904, 1923, 1927.

Table 4.2. The correlations between school grades used by Spearman as an illustration of the theory of general intelligence (g). The figures in parentheses are the predicted correlations when Carroll (1993) applied the theory using modern computing methods.

Class	Classics	French	English	Mathematics	Pitch	Music
Classics	1					
French	.83 (.84)	1				
English	.76 (.77)	.67 (.71)	1			
Mathematics	.70 (.72)	.67 (.66)	.64 (.60)	1		
Pitch	.66 (.64)	.65 (.60)	.54 (.54)	.45 (.50)	1	
Music	.63 (.62)	.57 (.57)	.51 (.52)	.51 (.48)	.40 (.43)	1

Classics, the first grade on the table, has the highest average correlation with the other grades.

Spearman argued that a student's grade in a class could be thought of as a measure of the sum of a student's generalized intelligence and the student's unique abilities and knowledge relevant to the class. Algebraically this is

$$x_{ij} = \beta_j g_i + s_{ij}, \qquad (4.1)$$

where x_{ij} is person i's grade on topic j, g_i is person i's general intelligence, and s_{ij} is person i's ability on a trait that reflects those aspects of test j that are not associated with general intelligence. β_j is a term that reflects the importance of the general factor in determining the grade in the jth class. In modern terms, β_j is the factor loading of test j on the general factor, and s_{ij} is the residual term for person i on test j.

There were no computers in Spearman's day, so he used clever but, by today's standards, archaic methods of estimating factor loadings. Almost one hundred years later a modern psychometrician, John Carroll, factor analyzed Spearman's data.[8] The resulting model is shown in Figure 4.5. The parenthesized terms in Table 4.2 are the correlations that would be expected if the g model were an accurate summary of the data. As can be seen, the observed and predicted correlations (the **S** and Σ matrices of section 4.2) are quite close. Spearman's theory is clearly supported by this data.

Although Spearman and his modern followers emphasized the importance of g, they recognized the existence of *group factors*, intellectual skills, such as facility with language or facility in dealing with visual-spatial patterns, that are less general than g but more general than an ability to take a specific test. Figure 4.6 shows a proposed analysis of our eight hypothetical tests in terms of Spearman's expanded model. All tests would be expected to load on the g factor, but the verbal tests would also be expected to load on a language skill factor, and the spatial tests would be expected to load on a visual-spatial factor.

In Figure 4.6 the g, language factor, and the visual-spatial skill factors are not allowed to correlate with each other or with g. (This is indicated by there not being any line connecting the three factors.) Spearman had to make this assumption because he did not have access to the computational power required to evaluate more complicated models. Modern computing allows us to consider a more sophisticated version, the *hierarchical model* shown in Figure 4.7. In this model Spearman's group factors are referred to as *(broad) second-order factors*, and g, a *third-order factor*, is inferred from the correlations between the second-order factors. We will see several other examples of hierarchical models subsequently.

4.3.2. *The Evidence for g*

Spearman's model has lasted longer than most psychological theories do. Arthur Jensen, a prominent modern advocate of

8 Carroll, 1993, p. 38.

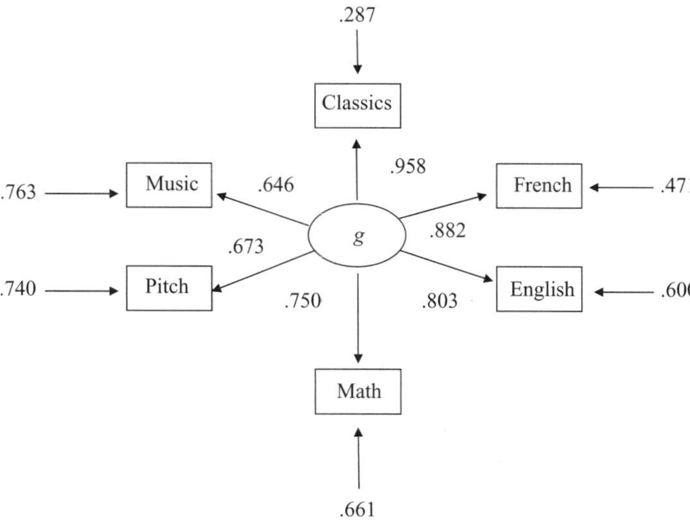

Figure 4.5. Loadings and residual terms when the *g* model was applied to Spearman's school grade data. Loadings calculated by Carroll (1993), residuals calculated by the author.

g theory, has claimed that after literally a century of exploration the *g* model provides a simple, accurate summary of a massive number of studies of intelligence.[9] Jensen built his case on three lines of evidence.

The first is the widespread observance of positive manifold. Virtually all tests of cognition are positively correlated. The second line of evidence is that measurements of general intelligence are among the best predictors of performance both in school and in the workplace. We will expand on this point in Chapter 10. The third line of evidence is that measures of *g* are related to a relatively small set of information-processing functions and, perhaps more importantly, to certain brain-based and genetic measures. This point is discussed in Chapter 6. Here we look only at the psychometric evidence.

Positive manifold is a widespread statistical phenomenon. The following examples show its ubiquity.

Gilles Gignac, an Australian psychometrician, analyzed four widely used American tests, the KAIT, the WAIS-R and WAIS-III, and a multidimensional aptitude battery (MAB) designed to cover a wide variety of cognitive skills.[10] While all analyses showed substantially the same results, the WAIS-III analysis is of particular interest because the standardization sample was constructed to represent the US adult population, using a sample of just under 2,500 people ranging in age from sixteen to eighty-nine.

Every subtest of the WAIS-III had substantial loadings on the general factor. The two highest loadings were on the Arithmetic (.79) and Vocabulary (.75) subtests.[11] This certainly fits the definition of a general factor, applying to a wide variety of cognitively demanding tasks. The lowest loadings were found on the Digit Symbol and Coding subtests (.53 and .56), which are essentially tests of short-term memory. A matrix test similar to the RPM described in Chapter 2 had a loading of .70, which is consistent with the argument that progressive matrix tests are good markers for general intelligence.[12]

In addition to being ubiquitous, the *g* factor was substantial. In Gignac's study the general factor accounted for from 30% to

---

9 Jensen, 1998.

10 Gignac, 2006. Gignac's model somewhat resembled Spearman's model (Figure 4.6), but the treatment of residual effects was much more sophisticated.

11 See Chapter 2 for a description of WAIS-III subtests.

12 Jensen, 1998, pp. 37–38.

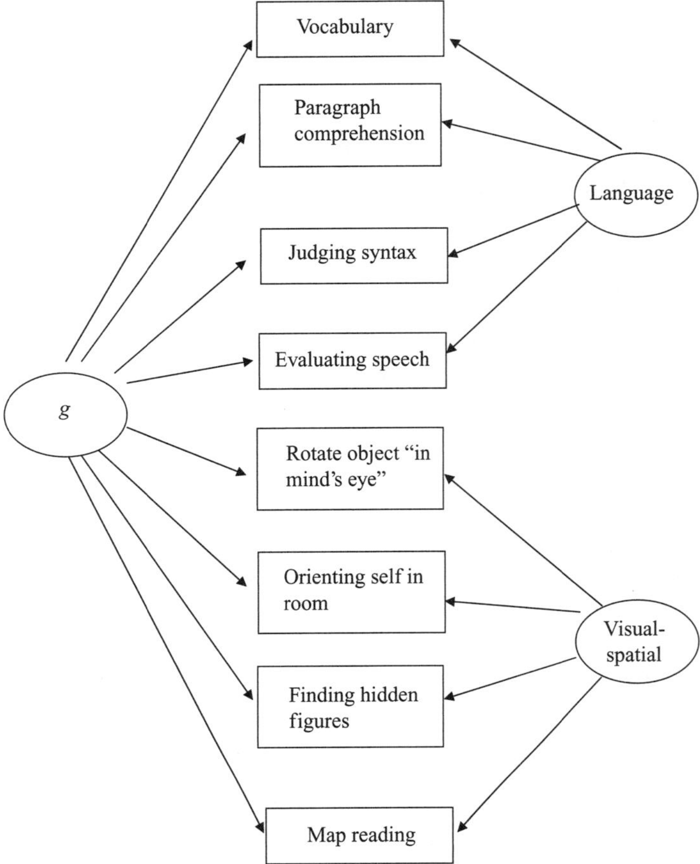

Figure 4.6. Spearman's *g* model expanded to allow for group factors. In this hypothetical example the battery consists of eight tests. All eight have loadings on the *g* factor. In addition, the four tests involving language have a loading on a language-skill group factor, while the four tests involving visual-spatial reasoning have a loading on a visual-spatial factor. The two group factors are uncorrelated.

60% of the variance in scores on individual tests.

The American results are mirrored by findings in other developed countries. Deary and his colleagues analyzed the results from a study in which the Cognitive Abilities Test was given to virtually all middle school children in England.[13] This test was designed to provide separate scales for verbal, quantitative, and nonverbal reasoning, but the scales are not necessarily statistically independent.[14] Indeed they were not. The general factor accounted for 70%

of the variance. In another British study Elliott[15] examined results from examination of schoolchildren of varying ages, using the British Ability Scales. Elliott's study was a challenging test of the *g* model, because the British Ability Scales were designed to provide clinical and educational psychologists with a more differentiated view of cognitive abilities than that provided by *g*-loaded tests, such as the WAIS. Nevertheless, the general factor accounted for 30% of the variance on these scales, even though they had been designed to deemphasize general intelligence.

13 Deary, Strand, Smith, & Fernandes, 2007.
14 See Chapter 2 for a description of this test.

15 Elliott, 1986.

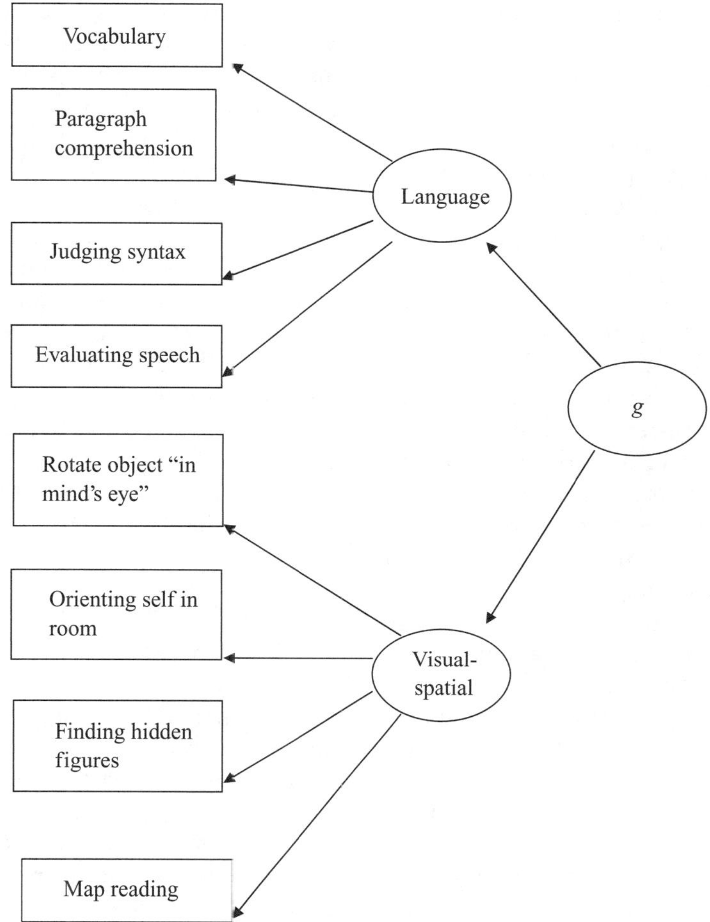

Figure 4.7. The example in Figure 4.6 reformulated as a hierarchical model. The two group factors are now partially caused by *g*, and thus would be correlated. This is the most widely accepted model of intelligence today.

Roberto Colom and his colleagues at the Universidad Autonoma in Madrid have analyzed the normative data from the Spanish version of the WAIS-III, doing separate analyses for groups with different levels of education.[16] The *g* factor accounted for 45% of the variance in the two least-educated groups, and 25% of the variance in the two better-educated groups. This turns out to be a typical finding. The general factor is often less powerful as cognitive skills increase.

Psychologists from the University of Tilburg in the Netherlands administered three different cognitive batteries to groups of immigrant and native Dutch students.[17] Depending on the battery, the *g* factor accounted for from 30% to 45% of the variance. The *g*-loadings of the various subtests were nearly identical in both the native Dutch and the immigrant groups. This suggests a similarity of cognitive structures over two different ethnic groups.

Similar results have been obtained in many studies. In 1993 John Carroll published an extensive survey of the results from many of the studies of batteries of tests that had been conducted up to that time.[18] He found evidence for a *g* factor in 146 different

16 Colom, Abad, Garcia, & Juan-Espinosa, 2002.

17 Helms-Lorenz, van de Vijver, & Poortinga, 2003.
18 Carroll, 1993.

data sets. There appears to be little doubt that analysis of virtually any battery of tests of cognition, in any population within an industrial society, will reveal a *g* factor.

As the thought experiments in section 4.2 showed, demonstrations of positive manifold in different populations and with different test batteries do not show that the different studies have found the same *g*. Carroll observed that in order to reach such a conclusion one would have to administer several test batteries to the same individuals, extract the *g* factor from each battery, and show that they were highly correlated.[19] Subsequently, Wendy Johnson and her colleagues at the University of Minnesota produced just such a finding. They administered three different test batteries to a group of just under 500 adults, of widely varying ages.[20] Their results strongly supported the contention that the *g* that is extracted by statistical analyses of widely used test batteries is the same trait, psychologically, regardless of the battery.

Because the Johnson et al. test provided such strong evidence for a general reasoning factor as both a statistical and a psychological phenomenon, we need to take a look at the study itself. The batteries they used were the WAIS and two batteries that had been designed to sample a comprehensive range of verbal, quantitative, and nonverbal reasoning abilities. Their sample consisted of adults from their twenties to their seventies who were participating in an extensive behavior-genetic study of adoptees. The participants were generally white, of middle or higher socioeconomic class, and from either a North American or a European country. Such a sample is certainly not statistically representative of the population of any country, let alone the world, but it is fairly representative of an important segment of the population within the industrial/post-industrial nations.

There is a massive amount of data showing a simple, clear-cut, and important fact. Within the culture of the industrial/post-industrial world, which is where these

studies were conducted, people can be reliably classified by the extent to which they display general intelligence (*g*), that is, a tendency to be cognitively competent in a wide variety of tasks. Anyone who asserts that individuals have to be described by several relatively independent cognitive traits is simply wrong. A person who is very good at verbal reasoning may not be the best at quantitative reasoning or reasoning about visual displays, but he or she is unlikely to be poor at these other tasks. The same argument applies, of course, to people who are very good at quantitative or visual reasoning. Their verbal reasoning may not be as good as their reasoning in their strongest domain, but it is unlikely to be bad.

4.3.3. *What Is the Nature of g?*

Positive manifold is a fact. There is no arguing with the existence of *g* as a statistical phenomenon. There is a great deal of argument over the reason that different evaluations of cognitive performance are virtually always positively correlated.

One possibility is that there is a mental trait, cognitive strength, analogous to physical strength, that people possess to different degrees and that, as is the case for physical strength, mental strength is useful in many settings. Let us call this the *unitary g* hypothesis. It implies that tests of cognitive competence will be positively correlated, as they are. But this is not conclusive evidence. Abstractly, if A (unitary *g*) implies B (positive manifold), and B is observed, then A might be the case, but B might have arisen for other reasons. What hypotheses other than the unitary *g* hypothesis imply positive manifold?

Positive manifold would arise if people possess distinct, rather specialized mental traits, such as verbal and visual-spatial reasoning, and these traits are correlated in the population, for either environmental or genetic reasons. Call this the *correlated traits* hypothesis. Correlated traits would be analogous to the statistical association between blond hair and blue eyes, neither of which causes the other.

19 Ibid., p. 596.
20 Johnson et al., 2004.

A third possibility is that there are separate cognitive traits but that over the life span there are positive interactions among these traits, so that high or low performance in one trait affects the development of others. The interaction could be due to biology, the environment, or some combination of the two. For example, children who appear to be highly verbal may be singled out for special instruction, which improves their cognitive capacity, opening yet further opportunities. The opposite may also happen; children who are perceived as being slow speakers or readers could be treated as if they were not too bright in general, leading to a self-fulfilling prophecy of failure.

The first position, that *g* exists as a trait, is the one held by most advocates of the general intelligence model.[21] But what is the trait behind the statistical abstraction? To quote from a statement by a US president, "it depends on what you mean by 'is',"[22] for the question can be answered at several levels. At the psychometric level general intelligence could be defined by examining the marker tests that have high loadings on the general factor, and attempting to identify the common cognitive challenges they present. At the information-processing level general intelligence could be defined by showing that the general factor is highly correlated with particular information-processing functions, such as working memory, the ability to control attention, and general speediness. At the biological level general intelligence could be associated with individual differences in brain structures and processes, and with variations in the genome. All three approaches have been tried. We will look at the psychometric evidence in this chapter, saving the information-processing and biological evidence for later chapters.

Spearman's belief that the ability to detect patterns is central to intelligence led his student John Raven to develop the Raven Progressive Matrices (RPM) tests described in Chapter 2. The effort was successful, for these tests do have high loadings on the general intelligence factor. Jensen states:

> *When the Progressive Matrices test is factor analyzed along with a variety of other tests it is typically among the two or three tests having the highest g loadings, usually around .80. Probably its most distinct feature is its very low loadings on any factor other than g.*
>
> *Jensen, 1998, p. 38*

This is what would be expected if Spearman were right, for a person who takes an RPM test does have to be able to notice visual patterns. However, the matter is not quite as clear as Jensen's statement suggests. Other tests, which appear to call forth very different sorts of problem solving than that required on the RPM tests, also have high loadings on *g*. In particular, vocabulary tests have nearly as high loadings on *g* as do RPM tests, a finding that has been found in samples as diverse as the WAIS-III normalization sample (representative of the US population),[23] Swedish schoolchildren,[24] and a large group of adults who volunteered for a research project.[25]

After reviewing findings from a great number of studies, Carroll[26] found that four different classes of tests were consistently found to have substantial loadings on *g*. These were tests of inductive reasoning, visualization (the ability to imagine movements of relatively complex forms), quantitative reasoning, and verbal ability. He concluded that

> *The eventual interpretation [of g] must resort to analysis of what processes are common to the tasks used in the measurement [of the abilities just listed] and to the analysis of what attributes of such tasks are associated with their difficulties.*
>
> *Carroll, 1993, p. 597*

---

21 See, e.g., Gottfredson, 1997; Jensen, 1998, 2006.
22 William (Bill) Clinton, commenting on the truth of his lawyer's statement that "there is absolutely no sex of any kind" in Clinton's relationship with a White House intern, Monica Lewinsky (Shapiro, 2006, p. 160).
23 Gignac, 2006.
24 Gustafsson, 1984.
25 Johnson et al., 2007. I calculated the loadings based on the data presented on p. 103 of their report.
26 Carroll, 1993, p. 597.

It is certainly unclear what single cognitive process underlies all four of the tests. Accordingly, let us look at the correlated traits hypothesis, the idea that there are some cognitive functions which, although not what we would normally think of as intelligence in themselves, are required for a large variety of cognitive tasks. Therefore, individual differences in these functions would produce g as a statistical phenomenon, even though no such thing as g exists as an underlying quality of the mind.

How would this work? Consider an analogy to carpentry. Carpenters use the same tools to make a great many things, ranging from tables and kitchen cabinets to fences. Suppose that there are individual differences in the quality of tools available to different carpenters. Instead of thinking of a modern carpenter, imagine a bit of time traveling, where we ask a modern carpenter, a medieval carpenter, a Bronze Age carpenter, and a Stone Age carpenter to make us some furniture, each using the tools appropriate to the historic era. We would not think of a saw, hammer, or adze as indicating carpentry skill, in itself. Nevertheless, across the ages, we could extract positive manifold in making furniture solely because of the quality of the tools.

Unlike carpentry tools (but like carpentry skills), psychological processes are dynamic. In an absolute sense, cognitive competence rises through adolescence, and declines in old age. Short-term memory processes and the speed of making simple decisions show a similar rise and fall with age. The same principle applies to knowledge. Knowledge acquired in mathematics can be utilized while studying physics. One way to find support for the correlated traits hypothesis is to show that practice in solving one task involving general intelligence will produce improvement on another, seemingly very different task.

There are not as many such studies as I would like to be able to cite. However, two studies do nicely illustrate the issue. In one, German children were taught to verbalize their strategies when attacking matrix problems, and then to solve the task by verbal reasoning. This improved scores on the (allegedly) nonverbal test.[27] A second, and even more dramatic, test involved training children to use the abacus.[28] As anyone who has learned to utilize the abacus can testify, this requires concentration of attention and recognition of visual patterns. Sudanese children were given an age-appropriate RPM test, and then divided into experimental groups that received substantial training in the use of the abacus, and control groups that did not. Prior to training, both groups had equivalent RPM scores. Following training, the experimental group outperformed the control group.

These two very different studies can be used to make the same point. There are certain cognitive skills that are useful in a variety of contexts. These include verbalization, which makes different aspects of the problem open to conscious inspection, and concentration of attention, which is a more primitive operation. No one of these skills, alone, is "general intelligence," but collectively they are. If the possession of one of these skills is statistically associated with the possession of others, positive manifold, and its correlate, g, will result even though no single cognitive skill can be pointed to as "intelligence."

Why should the skills that contribute to general intelligence be correlated? One possibility is that all these skills draw on a common biological capacity, such as efficiency of neural processing, and that there are substantial individual differences in that capacity. This argument makes positive manifold, and g, manifestations of a biological phenomenon.

Another possibility is that positive manifold emerges from interactions in which the development of one cognitive skill facilitates another. This is called *mutualism*. For instance, practicing verbalization during problem solving might facilitate the ability

27 Carlson & Weidl, 1992.
28 Irwing et al., 2008.

to control attention. If this is the case, the possession of key cognitive skills would become correlated, over time, even though they were initially uncorrelated.[29]

To summarize, the statistical evidence for *g*, positive manifold, could be produced by a pervasive general intelligence factor, or it could be produced by correlations between more specialized abilities. This leaves open the question of what these abilities are. Subsequently in this chapter we will look at a psychometric model that derives *g* from more specialized, correlated traits. First, though, we want to consider two reservations about the generality of findings on general intelligence.

4.3.4. *Reservations about g*

The extent to which a given study supports the *g* model depends on the extent to which the tests used show positive manifold. If the tests are highly correlated, the *g* model is supported; if they are not, it is not. It cannot be stressed too strongly that many, many well-designed studies provide results that are consistent with the *g* model. Nevertheless, two reservations are in order.

The first is that psychologists who have studied intelligence have been rather conservative in their decision about what sort of test is a test of cognition. The bulk of the evidence for *g* has been obtained by analyzing tests that fit into the "Drop in from the Sky" paradigm. If, as I urged in the first chapter, we expand our definition of intelligence to include problem solving in other situations, then other factors might be found, and *g* might or might not drop in power. What might happen is not what would happen. Whether studies of cognition in expanded situations would provide evidence for *g* should be decided by empirical research, not by the intuitions of people who support or oppose the model! There is a disturbing lack of data on this topic.

The second reservation is that studies of specialized populations often do not show strong evidence for *g*. In part this is simply a statistical phenomenon. Take the case of college students at a highly selective institution, such as Stanford, Harvard, or Cambridge. These students have been selected by a process that, to a considerable extent, evaluates their general reasoning ability. Therefore, within the selected group there will be a restricted range of *g*, and other factors will determine individual differences in test scores. The situation is analogous to the fact that height is not closely related to the ability to score points in professional basketball – because almost all the players are already very tall.

This poses a practical problem, because in general the populations that are easiest to study are the ones where such restrictions of the range of reasoning ability may occur. We do not have to go to highly selective colleges to see this effect; all college and university students have been subject to some selection on general reasoning ability. The same situation occurs when people try to obtain voluntary samples from the general population. A truly random sample is very hard to construct. It is much easier to recruit people from the middle and upper socioeconomic classes (SES) than to recruit people with low SES. This fact, and many other recruitment biases, operate to produce samples with restricted ranges on *g*, thus often underestimating the importance of the trait in the population.

However, that is not quite all there is to studies of populations with restricted ranges of *g*. There are some systematic changes in the ubiquity of *g* that are not solely due to statistical phenomena.

4.3.5. *Where g Is Not Found: There Are Very Few Universal Geniuses*

In the 1930s Leon Thurstone, a professor at the University of Chicago, challenged Spearman's *g* model.[30] Thurstone believed that intelligence is based on several distinct *primary abilities*, rather than on a single

---

29 Van Der Maas et al., 2006.

30 Thurstone, 1938: Thurstone & Thurstone, 1941.

general-reasoning factor. The primary abilities were:

Spatial reasoning: The ability to reason about figural representations. An example would be deciding whether two pictures did or did not represent the same object viewed from different perspectives.

Perceptual speed: The ability to detect simple figures in a display. For an illustration, try to find the browser icon on your computer desktop.

Number facility: The ability to do relatively simple numerical computations quickly.

Verbal relations: The ability to comprehend verbal statements.

Word fluency: The ability to produce simple words and statements rapidly.

Memory: The ability to recall information. Thurstone did not distinguish between short-term and long-term memory, as we certainly would do today.

Inductive reasoning: Spearman's ability to see patterns. A deductive reasoning factor was added in some of Thurstone's work.

Thurstone claimed that these abilities are essentially statistically independent; being good or poor on one of them does not predict whether a person is good, poor, or average on another. This conclusion is diametrically opposed to Spearman's claim that intelligence is largely produced by a single general-reasoning factor.

In the 1940s and 1950s there was debate over whether the discrepancy between Thurstone's and Spearman's results might have been due to different groups having used different factor analytic methods. The development of modern computerized techniques has essentially ended that discussion.

The discrepancy was probably due in part to restriction of range effects. In general, Spearman and other British psychologists analyzed data from the testing of schoolchildren. While Thurstone did similar studies, he also relied a great deal on studies of University of Chicago students. Chicago was, and is, a highly selective institution, so his college sample undoubtedly had a highly restricted range of scores on *g*. A third likely reason for the discrepancy has more psychological content. It could be that the structure of intelligence is more differentiated at high levels than at lower levels. In concrete terms, unusually high scores on a test of verbal reasoning might be only moderate predictors of unusually high scores on a test of mathematical reasoning, while unusually low scores on the verbal test could be very good predictors of unusually low scores on the mathematical test. To the extent that this is true, factor analysis would reveal relatively independent factors in a high-ability group, while revealing a strong *g* factor in a low-ability group.

Modern research has shown that this is the case. Douglas Detterman, a professor at Case-Western Reserve University, divided the WAIS-R and WISC standardization samples into five ability groups.[31] The strength of the *g* factor was highest in the low-ability group, and declined as group IQ score increased. Similar results have been obtained by other investigators, using other tests, in both national and international settings.[32]

This is an important result, because it is relevant to a social issue, the distribution of intelligence at high levels of cognitive functioning. High levels of talent appear to be fairly specialized, while marginal cognitive talent seems to have general effects. Why might this be the case?

In part it is probably due to experience. Modern society encourages specialization to a much greater extent than past societies did. Studies of expertise in a variety of fields, ranging from athletics to chess, have shown that acquiring a high level of expertise takes a great deal of time and effort.[33] At high levels of talent, therefore, social pressures lead to a differentiation of cognitive competences

---

31 Detterman, 1991; Detterman & Daniel, 1989.
32 Abad et al., 2003; Colom et al., 2002; Deary et al., 1996; Hunt, 1995a; Legree, Pifer, & Grafton, 1996. For some negative evidence see Sakolofske et al., 2008.
33 Ericsson, 1996; Ericsson et al., 2006.

due to specialized training. But this cannot be the whole picture, because the differentiation of abilities at high levels (or, conversely, generalization at low levels) occurs in children, as evidenced by studies on differentiation involving the WISC.

Whatever the reason for this, we will want to keep in mind the fact that high levels of talent are specialized when we come to a discussion of the implications of intelligence, in Chapter 10.

4.4. The Three-Stratum Model: Cattell, Horn, and Carroll's View of Intelligence

A widely cited alternative to the *g* model is the *Gc-Gf* or *three-stratum* model, originally developed by Raymond Cattell and John Horn, then modified by John Carroll.[34]

Cattell studied with Spearman in England, and then moved to the University of Illinois and finally to the University of Hawaii. He and his then-student at Illinois, John Horn (subsequently a professor at the Universities of Denver and Southern California), believed that Spearman's theory did not give sufficient weight to group factors. They were also skeptical of the idea that *g* is a trait. Instead they believed that positive manifold is due to individual tests drawing on several broad factors. To follow their argument, consider that bane of K–12 students, the mathematical word problem.

A train leaves station A and proceeds to station B, traveling at 60 miles an hour. At the same time that this train leaves A, another train leaves B, bound for A, traveling at 30 miles an hour. The distance from A to B is 270 miles. How long will it be before the trains meet?

A student who tries to solve this problem has to know the meaning of words and the syntax of English, *lexical retrieval ability* and *sentence comprehension*. Several facts have to be kept in mind as others are received, calling upon *short-term memory* ability. *Numer-*

ical facility is required. These narrowly defined abilities are examples of *first-stratum* or *primary* abilities. The first-stratum abilities are themselves grouped into broader, *second-stratum* abilities. According to Cattell and Horn the most important of these are *fluid intelligence* (Gf) and *crystallized intelligence* (Gc), which they defined as the ability to deal with new and unusual problems (Gf) and the ability to apply previously acquired knowledge to the current problem (Gc). In many contexts *visual-spatial ability* (Gv), the ability to deal mentally with visual images, is also important. The primary abilities of inductive and deductive reasoning are grouped under fluid intelligence; general cultural knowledge and lexical knowledge abilities are grouped under crystallized intelligence; and the abilities to compare spatial forms and to manipulate spatial forms "in the mind's eye" are grouped under visual-spatial ability.

As the theory has evolved additional second-stratum abilities have been defined. These include factors for retrieval from short- and long-term memory, the ability to deal with auditory as well as visual stimuli, quantitative ability, and two factors reflecting cognitive processing speed; cognition in general (*cognitive processing speed*, Gs) and another dealing with the speed with which very simple decisions are made (*decision reaction time*, Gt).

Cattell and Horn had long and active careers, during which they had colleagues who conducted research dealing with such things as the processing of auditory and tactile stimuli. In the typical extension of the theory a study would be conducted with a battery that included some tests already identified as a marker of abilities found by previous research, and some new tests that explored different primary skills. This process inevitably resulted in the definition of still more second-stratum factors. For instance, Stankov used this paradigm to extend the Gf-Gc model to tasks involving auditory stimuli, such as the ability to discriminate sounds.[35]

---

34 Carroll, 1993; Cattell, 1971, 1987; Horn, 1985; Horn & Noll, 1994.

35 Stankov & Horn, 1980; Horn & Stankov, 1982.

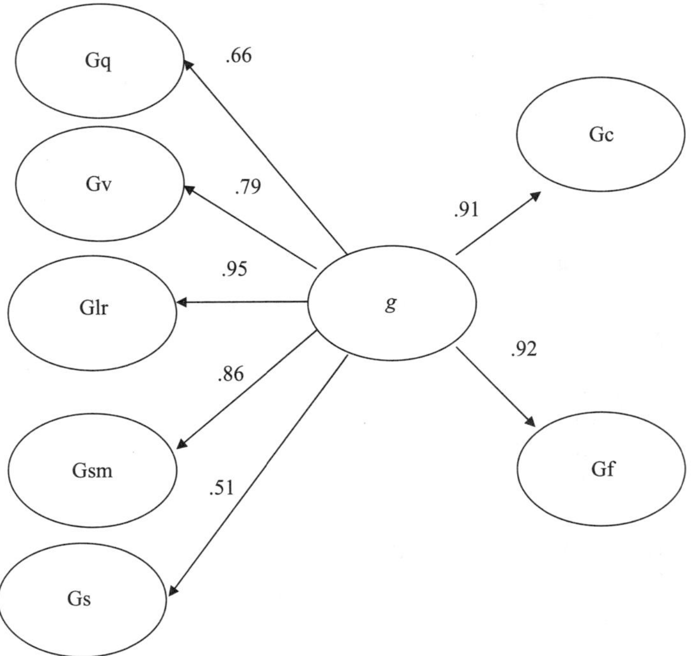

Figure 4.8. The structure of the second-stratum and third-stratum abilities in the WJ-III test. Codes: Gc – crystallized intelligence; Gf – fluid intelligence; Gq – quantitative ability; Gv – visual-spatial ability; Glr – long-term storage and retrieval in memory; Gsm – short-term memory; Gs – cognitive speediness; *g* – general intelligence. The loadings are those found in the WJ-III normalization sample, ages twenty to thirty-nine.

4.4.1. *Extensions and Applications of the Three-Stratum Model*

On the basis of his substantial review of the literature, Carroll[36] concluded that the Gc-Gf model provided a good fit to most of the over 450 data sets that he reanalyzed. However, in almost all cases abilities at the second stratum were themselves correlated. He took this as evidence for a single *third-stratum* factor, general intelligence. Conceptually this is the *g* factor advocated by Spearman[37] and, almost a century later, by Jensen.[38]

The resulting three-stratum theory has been used as a basis for several psychometric batteries, including the Woodcock-Johnson test battery[39] (WJ-III) and the revised Kaufmann Adult Intelligence Test (KAIT).[40] Table 4.3 lists some of the primary abilities evaluated by the WJ-III battery. In the interests of space, only enough of these abilities are listed to give the reader an idea of the theory.[41] In the WJ-III most of these abilities are represented by a single test, and therefore the structure at the first-stratum (primary-ability) level, per se, cannot be tested.

The heart of the theory lies in the broader, second-stratum abilities. These are shown in the left-hand column of Table 4.3. Reasoning abilities fall under Gf, while verbal comprehension and general knowledge abilities fall under Gc. The second-stratum abilities are themselves correlated. This gives the overall test the structure shown in Figure 4.8. All the second-stratum

36 Carroll, 1993.
37 Spearman, 1904, 1927.
38 Jensen, 1998.
39 McGrew, 2005.
40 Alfonso, Flanagan, & Radwan, 2005.
41 McGrew, 2005.

Table 4.3. A three-stratum grouping of primary abilities (middle and right-hand columns) into secondary abilities (left- and right-hand columns) in the three-stratum theory. The table is not complete, although the major secondary abilities are shown.

Second Stratum Ability	*Subsumed Primary Abilities*	*Brief Description*
Fluid intelligence (Gf)		The ability to solve novel problems.
	Deductive reasoning	The ability to reason from established principles or facts.
	Inductive reasoning	The ability to detect patterns in observations.
	Quantitative reasoning	The ability to reason using numerical and mathematical arguments.
Crystallized intelligence (Gc)		The ability to apply previously acquired knowledge to current problems.
	Linguistic development	The ability to follow an argument in one's native language.
	Lexical knowledge	The extent of one's native-language vocabulary.
	Information about culture	Knowledge of the facts about one's own culture.
General domain-specific knowledge (Gkn)		Breadth of knowledge of facts and principles in specific domains.
	Geographic knowledge	
	Mechanical knowledge	
	Other tests of knowledge within various domains	
Visual-spatial ability (Gv)		The ability to deal with structured visual stimuli.
	Visualization	Ability to recognize and match visual stimuli.
	Spatial relations	Ability to manipulate visual stimuli "in the mind's eye."
	Closure speed	The speed at which familiar visual stimuli can be recognized when obscured or hidden in other stimuli.
Short-term memory (Gsm)		The ability to apprehend and store information about the current situation.
	Memory span	The ability to repeat back, verbatim, information just presented.
	Working memory	The ability to execute cognitive processes on information held in short-term memory and to store the results.

(continued)

Table 4.3 *(continued)*

Second Stratum Ability	Subsumed Primary Abilities	Brief Description
Long-term storage and retrieval (Glr)		The ability to store information for long periods of time and to retrieve it.
	Associative memory	The ability to recall a complex piece of information given a previously learned association to it.
	Meaningful memory	The ability to store, retain, and recall meaningful pieces of information, especially biographical information.
	Free recall	The ability to recall, without cues, a long list of previously presented pieces of information, where each piece is unrelated to the others.
Cognitive processing speed (Gs)		The ability to execute easy, highly overlearned cognitive tasks.
	Pattern recognition	Quick recognition of familiar perceptual patterns.
	Numerical facility	The ability to execute simple arithmetic operations quickly.
Decision speed (Gt)		Speed of responding in simple decision situations.
	Choice reaction time	Choosing which of a small number of pre-defined signals has been presented.
	Semantic processing speed	Deciding whether a string of letters is or is not a word, e.g., CAT vs. TAC.
	Mental comparison speed	Time required to compare two familiar stimuli on some attribute, e.g., deciding whether the symbols 'A' and 'a' name the same letter.

Note: This table is based on a larger table presented by McGrew (2005), Table 8.3.

abilities have loadings on the single third-stratum factor, *g*.

The WJ-III was standardized on a sample of just under 9,000 examinees, of varying ages, who were chosen to approximate the distribution of a number of demographic variables (sex, age, ethnicity) in the United States. Table 4.4 presents the *g* loadings for several of the second-stratum tests, separately for different age groups.[42] The loadings are both high (in the .80 range and above) and remarkably stable over adulthood. The very high loadings of Gc and Gf on the *g* factor imply a correlation between Gc and Gf in the .80–.85 range.

The high loadings of second-stratum abilities on *g* have led some investigators to argue that the Gf-Gc distinction is a needless complication. For instance, Gustafsson has reported a study of over 1,000 Swedish sixth-graders in which the data was fit by a three-stratum model, with three broad-level abilities, Gf, Gc, and Gv. Gf had a loading of 1 (identity!) on the third-stratum *g* factor. The Gv and Gc loadings were .80 and .76, respectively.[43] Therefore, the

42 McGrew & Woodcock, 2001, Appendix F.

43 Gustaffson, 1984.

Table 4.4. The *g* loadings of the second-stratum factors on the WJ-III test, omitting Ga (auditory ability). Primary abilities are as shown in Table 4.3.

Broad Ability	Age 6–8	Age 9–13	Age 14–19	Age 20–39	Age 40+
Gc	.79	.86	.90	.91	.92
Gf	.96	.89	.92	.92	.94
Gq	.73	.74	.71	.66	.85
Gv	.85	.68	.77	.79	.85
Glr	.80	.75	.80	.95	.89
Gsm	.96	.91	.83	.86	.92
Gs	.61	.49	.49	.51	.75

Source: McGrew & Woodcock, 2001, Appendix F.

expected correlation between Gf and Gc would simply be the Gc loading, .80. This result contrasts with an earlier study, using rather different factor analytic techniques, in which correlations as low as .17 between Gf and Gc were reported.[44] I am somewhat at a loss to explain this difference. Taking the literature as a whole, it does appear that in the majority of cases fluid and crystallized intelligence are substantially correlated. But does this mean that they are both expressions of an overarching general intelligence, *g*?

4.4.2. *The Nature of g, Gc, and Gf in the Three-Stratum Model*

In the three-stratum model the second-stratum factors fall into three groups: the two cognitive factors, Gc and Gf; the short- and long-term memory factors; and factors relating to different sensory modalities, notably Gv (visual) and Ga (auditory). Almost any test involving cognition will involve Gc and Gf, to some degree. However, a battery might emphasize one or the other type of cognition. Whether or not memory or sensory modality factors are found depends upon the particular batteries used.

Two studies illustrate this point. Gustafsson's previously cited study of Swedish middle school children utilized a battery of thirteen tests. He recovered three second-order

factors – Gc, Gf, and Gv. Only two of his tests involved auditory presentations, and they were both memory span tests. Therefore, a factor involving these two tests, only, could be referred to as either a short-term memory or auditory skill factor. Gustafsson understandably chose to interpret variation in performance as due to short-term memory ability, as the only auditory component of the test involved hearing and remembering words or numbers. The composition of Gustafsson's battery contrasts with the extensive auditory tests (e.g., pitch discrimination) used in investigations that have successfully searched for Ga.[45] These differences certainly do not invalidate or weaken Gustafsson's study. They do drive home the point that how many human abilities are found depends upon how broad a range of behaviors is studied.

The second example involves a case that illustrates a common practice. Many investigators have extracted a general factor from tests that were designed for practical rather than research applications, such as the ASVAB and the SAT. Are the general factors derived from these tests reflections of the cognitive trait that is revealed by analyses of battery-type intelligence tests, such as the WAIS and WJ? According to the *g* model, they should be. Jensen, in particular, has argued that the identification of *g* is almost indifferent to the indicators used in a battery.[46]

44 Hakstian & Cattell, 1978.

45 Horn & Stankov, 1982; McGrew & Woodcock, 2001.
46 Jensen, 1998, p. 91; 2002.

From the viewpoint of the three-stratum model this is simply not accurate, as the following example shows.

The ASVAB was designed for a specific purpose, predicting performance as an enlisted person in the US military services. Some of the tests used in the ASVAB are combined into a general index, the AFQT. (See Chapter 2 for a more complete description.) A general factor that is highly correlated with the AFQT can be extracted from the ASVAB.[47] But is it *g*?

In their widely publicized *Bell Curve*,[48] Richard Herrnstein and Charles Murray correlated the AFQT with a variety of indicators of social behavior, ranging literally from education to divorce rate to salaries, and offered their results as evidence that general intelligence has a great deal of influence upon success in our society. We will discuss these results in some detail in Chapters 10 and 11. Herrnstein and Murray, and Jensen, assumed that *g*, as revealed by the AFQT, is equivalent to a general intelligence factor uncovered by other test batteries. Extending Gustafsson's argument, this could be called either *g* or Gf.

Richard Roberts and his colleagues at the Educational Testing Service tested this assumption. They combined scores on the ASVAB with scores on tests designed to measure Gf and Gc separately, and found that the general factor on the ASVAB is a measure of Gc rather than Gf.[49] This is not a small point. Virtually everyone acknowledges that Gc is responsive to education, while Gf is less responsive. Regarding the AFQT as a measure of Gc rather than a measure of *g* or Gf increases our optimism about the prospects of improving society through education.

Studies such as Roberts and colleagues' bring home the importance of a methodological point made in section 4.2. A factor is *not* an invariant property of a test. A factor is a statistic produced by the interaction between the abilities evaluated in a test battery and the distribution of those abilities in the sample being tested. The fact that g, Gf, and Gc keep reappearing shows that these traits are somewhat invariant across different situations. That is informative, for it suggests that they are indeed basic dimensions of variation in human cognition. Blithely accepting the ubiquity of *g* can produce misleading generalizations.

4.4.3. *What Is a Natural Kind; g, Gf, or Gc?*

A *natural kind* is a phenomenon that exists in nature and is to be discovered. This contrasts with an artifactual classification, which is constructed by human thought. The distinction between men and women is a natural kind; the distinction between legal and illegal residents of the US or the European Union is an artifactual one. Artifactual classifications can be quite useful in some settings. Nevertheless, they are the results of human action, not the action of a law of nature.

In studies of intelligence the broad sensory modality and memory factors are natural kinds, for they are defined as individual differences in human biological capacities. The distinctions among Gc, Gf, and *g* are debatable.

The Gf-Gc distinction is based upon an individual's social and cultural history. Consider how the following problem might be solved:

> *Two freight trains approach each other on a single track. Between them there is a brief side route capable of holding only one engine or box car. (See Figure 4.9.) How can the two trains pass each other?*

Most readers will see this as a novel problem, and solve it using a mixture of "reasoning about new problems" (Gf) and manipulation of visual images (Gv). In fact, it is a problem that occurs often in railroad switching yards, and has a standard solution.[50] The railroad-experienced reader will treat the problem as an exercise in Gc.

47 Ree & Earles, 1991.
48 Herrnstein and Murray, 1994.
49 Roberts et al., 2000.

50 Hayes, 2007.

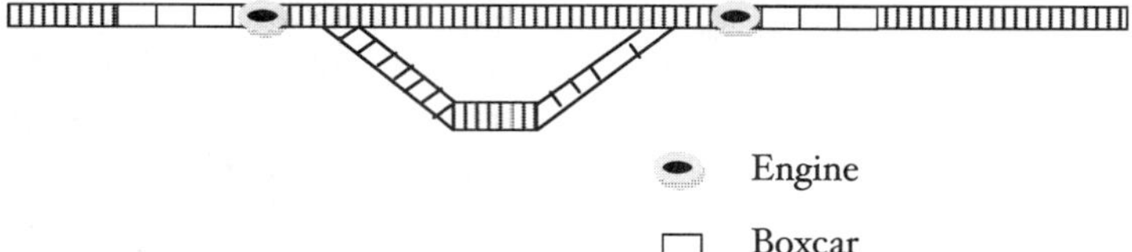

Figure 4.9. The railroad passing problem. Two trains approach each other. There is a side route that can hold only one engine or boxcar. Is it possible for the trains to pass each other and, if so, how?

Test developers get around such issues by restricting tests of Gc to tasks that draw upon "generally culturally accepted knowledge." This automatically restricts most Gc tests to the industrially developed countries, although the concept of "cultural knowledge" applies equally well to, say, a nomadic or hunter-gatherer culture. However, it would have to be tested using questions appropriate to the hunter-gatherer culture. A test of Gc in one culture could be a test of Gf in another. This is an important distinction, for the two types of intelligence make different demands on our information-processing capacities.

In order to solve a novel problem you must develop a way of representing it mentally. This can be a difficult task, involving the development of information structures to be held in short-term ("working") memory. In order to solve a problem by applying previously acquired knowledge you must have had appropriate experiences and coded them in long-term memory in such a way that they are accessible in the present context. Working and long-term memory draw on different brain processes and structures. This argument suggests that Gc and Gf are two different natural kinds of ability.

This argument is not vitiated by demonstrations that *g* exists as a statistical phenomenon. Cattell argued that we acquire Gc very largely by using Gf to discover appropriate problem-solving techniques, a process that he referred to as investing Gf in the acquisition of Gc. If two people enter into some experience that is unfamiliar to both of them, the one with the higher Gf will learn more from the experience, and end up with a higher Gc than the other person. Repeated throughout life, this would

produce a correlation between Gf and Gc, and hence statistical evidence for *g* even though there is no natural kind that corresponds to general intelligence.

The contrary argument, made most notably by Jensen, is that there are pervasive individual differences in brain processes that cause general competence, and that these differences are causes of differences on both Gc and Gf tasks.[51] There is no way to decide between the Cattell and Jensen positions from an analysis of the psychometric data alone. There is an important nonpsychometric argument in favor of Cattell's proposal.

Experimental psychologists show that two underlying human capacities are different by showing that they respond to a change of conditions in different ways. For instance, one of the strongest pieces of evidence for a distinction between conscious and unconscious memory systems is that conscious memory retrieval falters when a person is distracted, while unconscious retrieval does not.[52]

This sort of argument can be used to distinguish between Gc and Gf, using a universally occurring experimental condition, aging. Performance on tests that mark for Gf (e.g., matrix problems) declines with age over the adult life span. Performance on tests that mark for Gc (vocabulary tests and tests of cultural knowledge) does not. In fact, measures of Gc may increase until advanced old age.[53] This provides striking

---

51 Jensen, 2006.
52 Jacoby, Toth, & Yonelinas, 1993.
53 Horn, 1985, 1986. Horn argued that the decline of Gf began as early as the late 1920s. Horn relied mainly on data from cross-sectional studies. This may have led him to overestimate the decline, because it has since been shown that there are cohort effects on Gf

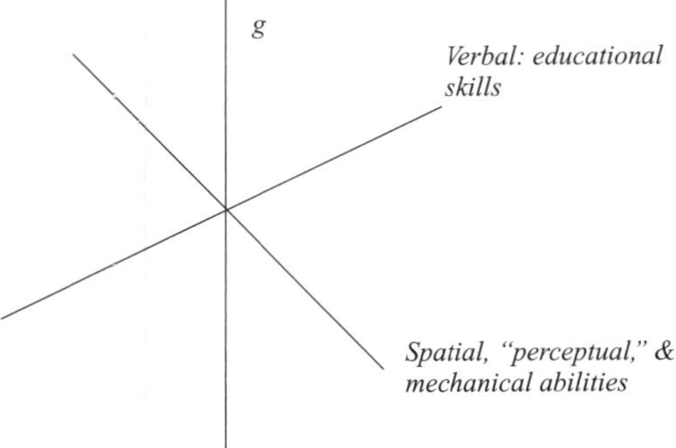

Figure 4.10. Vernon's structure of intelligence model. The model contains a *g* factor and two orthogonal group factors – the verbal-educational factor and the perceptual-mechanical skill factor.

evidence that Gf and Gc are indeed two separate processes. We look at this evidence in more detail in Chapter 11.

The body of evidence favors the three-stratum theory over a simple general intelligence model. However, a revision of *g* theory, the *g*-VPR model, deals with the evidence even better.

4.5. Johnson and Bouchard's *g*-VPR Model

By 2000 the three-stratum model had been widely accepted. Then, in 2005, two University of Minnesota scientists, Wendy Johnson and Thomas Bouchard, Jr., published new analyses that both questioned the three-stratum model and offered an alternative.[54]

Johnson and Bouchard began with a model of intelligence that had been proposed by the Canadian psychometrician Philip E. Vernon in the 1960s,[55] but then almost forgotten. Vernon himself barely mentioned his model in a 1979 book on heredity, environment, and intelligence![56]

Vernon's *structure of intelligence* model is shown in Figure 4.10. It contained three factors: a general factor (*g*) and two factors orthogonal to *g*. One he identified as a *verbal:educational* factor, reflecting the emphasis upon verbal skills in the educational system, and the other as a *perceptual:motor* factor representing skill in identifying and manipulating objects. Vernon also suggested the presence of a third special factor, mathematical skills, but felt that this was related to the perceptual:motor factor.

Johnson and Bouchard proposed a four-stratum model, with the structure shown in Figure 4.11. The first, bottom, level consists of the primary traits evaluated by individual tests, such as a test of the ability to do simple computations or to solve anagrams. The second stratum consists of broader but still fairly narrow abilities. For instance, at this level there is a distinction between word fluency, which is essentially a measure of speed of producing verbal associations, and verbal comprehension (their term, "verbal"), which is characterized by vocabulary and the understanding of proverbs. A similar distinction was made between memory for meaningful material and memory for arbitrary, experimenter-presented associations, such as arbitrary lists of number-noun pairs. In all the data sets analyzed they found substantial correlations between second-level factors, which indicated a need for a third stratum, in which the number of factors would be reduced, and where a second-level factor could have loadings on more than one third-order factor.

The third stratum, which is the heart of the model, contains three factors – Vernon's verbal and perceptual skills factors and a third "perceptual" ability, the ability to envision motion of a static figure, most clearly seen in tasks that require rotation of a visual figure "in the mind's eye." As was the case for Vernon's model, the Johnson and Bouchard model does not contain a memory factor. This is consistent with research in cognitive psychology, which has shown that there are many different types of memory.

Johnson and Bouchard's third-level factors were highly correlated, indicating a

marker tasks. These are discussed in more detail in Chapters 10 and 11. For the point being made here it does not matter whether the cause of the change in Gf and Gc scores is due to aging per se or due to cohort effects. The important finding is that the two abilities change differently over time.

54 Johnson & Bouchard, 2005a.
55 Vernon, 1964, 1965.
56 Vernon, 1979.

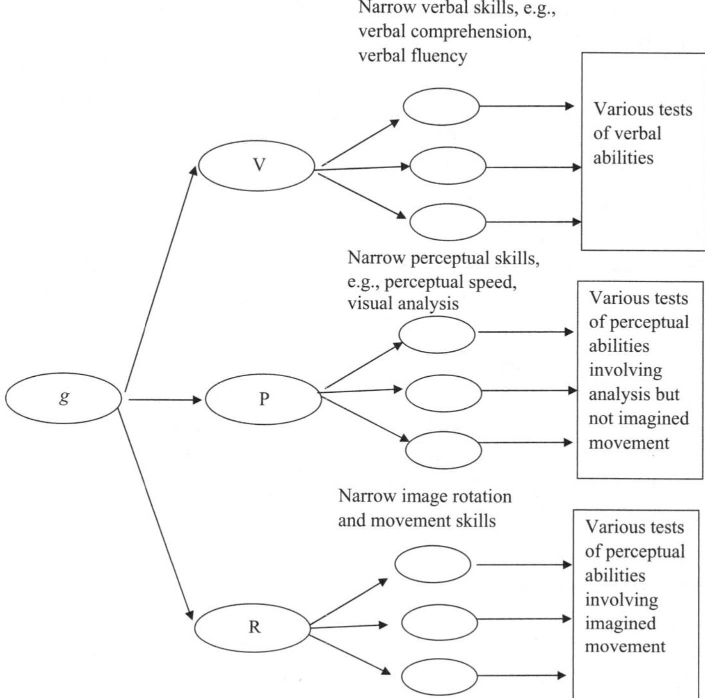

Figure 4.11. The structure of Johnson and Bouchard's VPR model. In the interests of clarity, the figure shows a hierarchy. However, the model is better described as having a lattice structure, for individual tests may have loadings on more than one second-stratum factor, and second-stratum factors may have loadings on more than one third-stratum factor.

need for a fourth stratum. They found that they needed only one factor at this level, which they identified as general intelligence, g.

Developing an acronym from the names of the third-level factors, Johnson and Bouchard refer to their model as the *g-VPR* model.

4.5.1. *Psychometric Evidence for the g-VPR Model*

Johnson, Bouchard, and their colleagues have presented two arguments for preferring the *g*-VPR model to either the *g* model (which it amplifies, rather than replaces) or the three-stratum Gf-Gc model. The first argument is based on psychometric evidence, the second on biological plausibility. We look first at the psychometric evidence.

Johnson and her colleagues made a comparative analysis of three different data sets, in which they compared the *g*-VPR model to the Gc-Gf model and Vernon's model of orthogonal verbal and spatial abilities.[57] The first data set came from 400 adults who participated in the Minnesota Study of Twins Raised Apart. This is an extensive study of twins and their relatives, which will be described in detail in Chapter 8, panel 8.7. For the present purposes, we can think of the study as a large data base in which the same adults completed three different battery-type tests. The investigators then reanalyzed one of the data sets Thurstone had used to justify his primary mental abilities model. Thurstone's data set contained scores from a study done in Chicago in the 1930s. Some

---

57 Johnson & Bouchard, 2005a,b; Johnson, te Nijenhuis, & Bouchard, 2007.

of the participants had taken sixty different tests. The third data set was based on 46 different tests given to just over 500 seamen in the Dutch Navy in the 1960s.

In all three data sets, the *g*-VPR model fit better than any of the other models. A comparison to the three-stratum model is particularly informative. Johnson and her colleagues subsumed Gc into a verbal factor (V), identified the Gf factor with *g*, and split the Gv factor into their two perceptual factors, roughly the analysis of static visual images (P) and the ability to conduct mental manipulations of visual objects (R). Because none of the batteries that they considered contained tests involving auditory presentations, they had no opportunity to uncover an auditory (Ga) factor.

The V, P, and R factors were not orthogonal, but, as would be expected, the correlation between the P and R factors was higher than the correlation between the V factor and the other two. While none of these samples can be claimed to be representative of a particular population, as opposed to the standardization samples for the WAIS, ASVAB, and WJ tests, one has to be impressed by the uniformity of the results, obtained over a wide variety of tests and using markedly different samples.

Johnson and Bouchard did not find a need to identify broad memory factors, although they did identify some specific memory factors in the second stratum. This does not mean that memory is unimportant to cognition; obviously it is. What it means is either that memory factors are subsumed by one of the broad reasoning factors or that memory abilities are highly specific to the type of material being memorized. As we shall see in Chapter 6, there is evidence for subsumption of the ability to deal with short-term memories into *g*, and to view long-term memory abilities as being highly specific.

Johnson and Bouchard regard their psychometric evidence as a disconfirmation of the three-stratum model. This is a strong statement. Whether you accept it or not depends upon your approach to statistical hypothesis testing.

If one takes the classic approach to hypothesis testing, none of the models, including the *g*-VPR model, accounted for the data. In every comparison there was a "statistically significant" deviation of the data from that predicted by the Gc-Gf, three-stratum, original Vernon, or VPR model. Johnson and Bouchard took the relativistic approach of comparing the models to each other, using a sophisticated elaboration of Bayes' law.[58] This analysis identifies the best model within a set of models to be compared, rather than testing to see if there are significant deviations from a particular model. The *g*-VPR model was the clear winner in this competition, although it did not account for all the data in an absolute sense.

4.5.2. *Logical Arguments for the g-VPR Model*

Johnson and Bouchard were also critical of the Gf-Gc distinction on logical grounds. I will present an expansion on their argument.

Gc is supposed to represent the use of previously acquired knowledge to solve the current problem. But how are you to construct a test for this ability? It makes little sense to test a person's level of a skill unless the examinee has had a chance to acquire the skill. Therefore, tests of Gc have to be tests based upon information that is widely available in the examinee's culture. Indeed, most Gc markers are of this nature. The vocabulary tests used as markers of Gc are roughly at the level of vocabulary used in television dramas.

Suppose that tests have been constructed such that we can be certain that every examinee has been exposed to the information needed to do well on the test. Individual differences in test scores will then be produced by differences in examinees' ability to extract this information from their common experiences. A great deal of cultural knowledge is based upon induction from

---

58   See Hunt, 2007, for a discussion of Bayes' law. The test used was the Bayesian Information Criterion (BIC) developed by Raftery (1995).

experience, rather than explicit instruction. This is especially true of our ability to understand the meaning of words in different contexts. "How are you feeling?" spoken by a waitress at a restaurant is a different question, and requires a different response, than "How are you feeling?" spoken by a physician in an emergency room. In order to understand such distinctions a person has to recognize patterns of usage. Pattern recognition is, by definition, Gf, and Spearman's *g*.

This muddles the Gc-Gf distinction. A test of Gc is either not fair, because it evaluates information to which the individual has not been exposed, or it is actually a disguised test of Gf.

Johnson and Bouchard also point out another problem with the Gc-Gf distinction, one that had actually been raised by Horn some time earlier.[59] If Gf is an initial ability that is invested to produce Gc, then Gf measures should be more responsive to individual biological variables than Gc measures. In at least one case this is simply not what happens. The heritability coefficients for Gc and Gf are approximately the same, in violation of the argument that Gc reflects cultural experiences, while Gf does not. By contrast, heritability analyses (to be discussed in Chapter 8 in more detail) show a coherent pattern of genetic association for the variables in the *g*-VPR model.[60]

The *g*-VPR model aligns with well-known neuroscientific findings. The ubiquity of *g* suggests that there are individual differences in some pervasive brain processes. Three candidate processes have been suggested: individual differences in the ability to control attention, individual differences in the speed and accuracy of neural conduction, and individual differences in the plasticity of neural connections, all of which would affect the ability to acquire and retrieve information. Language processing and perceptual processing are carried out by separate brain systems. At least one biological distinction mirrors the distinction between mental rotation and the analysis of static figures. There are large male-female differences, in favor of males, in the ability to conduct rotation-like tasks.[61] The male-female differences in other perceptual tasks are much smaller, and in some cases are in favor of women.

All in all, Johnson and Bouchard make a persuasive case for their model.

4.6. Summary and Evaluation of Psychometric Theories

Which psychometric theory is correct?

Any psychometric theory of intelligence has to account for the degree to which positive manifold exists. People who do well (or poorly) on a test of one type of cognitive skill generally do well (or poorly) on tests of other cognitive skills. This tendency is stronger at the bottom than at the top; poor performance on test A is a better predictor of poor performance on test B than good performance on A is of good performance on B. There is very little, if any, evidence for a negative correlation between cognitive skills. People who are highly competent with language may not be as good at visual or mathematical tasks as they are at verbal tasks, but they are unlikely to be bad at those tasks. The opposite reasoning holds. Mathematicians and physical scientists are generally not novelists, although there have been a few exceptions, but they are very unlikely to be functionally illiterate.

These facts indicate that a theory of intelligence has to include something like *g*. But *g*, alone, is not enough. The debate is over the appropriate structure of the broad, but not completely general, abilities that lie below *g* in the structure of intelligence.

The *g*, three-stratum, and *g*-VPR models can all account for the psychometric data in a general way. If we look at relative accuracy, the extensive data gathered by Johnson and her colleagues strongly indicate that the *g*-VPR model is a statistical winner. However, statistical criteria are not the

59 Horn, 1998.
60 Johnson et al., 2007.

61 Halpern, 2000.

only criteria by which a theory should be judged. Two other issues are relevant: the utility of a theory as a decision aid and the extent to which a theory at one level, here a theory of psychometric data, fits into theories and facts at a more basic level, here information-processing and biological models of thought.

In many personnel classification and training situations the Gc-Gf model has a great deal to recommend it. It makes sense to distinguish between candidates who do not know but can learn (low Gc, high Gf) and those who already have the requisite knowledge (high Gc). It is also worth noting that in industrial and military personnel screening the issue is usually whether a person has a particular cognitive capability, not how he or she came to have it.

Both the Gc-Gf and g-VPR distinctions can be fit into information-processing models. The Gc-Gf model matches the distinction between problem solving based on the manipulation of working memory and problem solving based on retrieval of previously acquired information. The g-VPR model matches the distinction between brain structures involved in working memory and the control of attention (i.e., the g and Gf components of the models can be identified with the same brain structures). The VPR components of the g-VPR model are closely tied to pathways of sensory information processing. As Carroll noted, the Gc component of the three-stratum model is very closely associated with verbal reasoning.[62]

While g implies positive manifold, so do the other models. Positive manifold could be produced by the development of separate modules of cognition that had positive influences on each other's development. Cattell and Horn's idea that Gf is invested in learning to produce Gc, creating positive manifold as an epiphenomenon, is an example of this sort of argument.

My conclusion is that a pure g model is too simplistic, although useful in some situations. Whether one should favor the g-VPR or three-stratum model depends a good bit on what the theory is supposed to do – provide a starting place for a theory that connects psychology to biology, or provide a model for using human intelligence in academia and the workplace.

Saying that the way you describe the situation depends upon the problem you want to solve is more in the spirit of engineering than of pure science. Both are legitimate worldviews.

And there is another worldview. All of these models are attempts to find structure in the data from conventional cognitive testing. In the next chapter we look at theories that attempt to expand theories of cognition beyond the data obtained from the "Drop in from the Sky" paradigm.

62 Carroll, 1993.

CHAPTER 5

Taking Intelligence Beyond Psychometrics

Newton said that if he had seen further it was because he had stood on the shoulders of those who had preceded him. In Psychology we stand on their faces.

> The late R. C. Bolles, Professor and historian of Psychology, the University of Washington, personal communication

Walter Lippmann had more to say about intelligence than was quoted in Chapter 1.

> *[The intelligence test] does not weigh or measure intelligence by any objective standard. It simply arranges a group of people in a series from best to worst by balancing their capacity to do certain arbitrarily selected puzzles, against the capacity of all the others.*
>
> *Lippmann, 1922b*

This criticism strikes at the heart of psychometric theory. Lippmann believed that "real" intellectual talent has little to do with a talent for test taking. His criticisms have been echoed, with surprisingly little change, in today's world.

The gist of the modern criticisms of intelligence testing is that the tests capture a very narrow slice of human cognition. The following quotes are from books written for the general public:

> *Almost everything you know about intelligence – the kind of intelligence psychologists have most often written about – deals with only a tiny and not very important part of a much broader and more complex intellectual spectrum.*
>
> *Sternberg, 1996, p. 11*

> *The score on an intelligence test does predict one's ability to handle school subjects, though it foretells little of success in later life.*
>
> *Gardner, 1983, p. 3*

The evidence does not warrant such skepticism. In fact, perhaps because of a perceived need to keep things simple in popular books, these quotes are oversimplifications of the authors' opinions. Both Gardner and Sternberg are considerably more circumspect when they write papers addressed to a professional audience.

Nonetheless, the public clearly wants to hear the attacks on testing. Why?

Possibly one of the strongest reasons is a gut feeling that tests with at best a tenuous resemblance to real life problem solving should not predict how well people can solve important everyday problems. This was the basis of Lippmann's objection to the first Stanford-Binet test battery. Imagine what Lippmann would have to say about a Progressive Matrices test!

Distrust is magnified by a certain amount of defensiveness. Burt Green, a respected psychometrician at Johns Hopkins University, once told me that people think that a fair question is one that they can answer. There is something to this. Sternberg opens one of his popular books with a diatribe about how he, personally, did poorly on an intelligence test.[1] His anecdote will resonate with anyone who feels that their test score does not reflect their true mental capability.

Anecdotes about how tests failed to predict outcomes are very common. There are many stories of people who did well despite their IQ, and a few stories of people (whom the story teller usually did not know or did not like) who did poorly even though they had high IQs. I have never met anyone who complained that their IQ score overestimated their ability.

Those defending testing reply *The plural of "anecdote" is not "data."* No one has ever claimed that IQ scores are either a perfect predictor or the only predictor of social outcomes. Depending upon the situation and the statistical assumptions one wants to make, the correlations between the trait underlying cognitive test scores and either academic or industrial performance are on the order of .5 or even higher. (See Chapter 10 for elaboration.) Cognitive tests, in some form, are given to literally millions of people annually, so there is plenty of room for anecdotes about how a test did not predict for a particular individual, even though the test is a valid predictor for the population as a whole. The argument is valid, but it will resonate more strongly with members of the American Statistical Association than with members of the general public, for statistical reasoning is very much an acquired skill.[2]

Another reason that people may distrust the tests is due to valid but limited personal experiences. Interviews with "successful people," including managers, regularly produce assertions that personality variables, such as self-discipline and openness to experience, are more important than intelligence. This contradicts the evidence, for in fact the correlations between indices of success in the industrial world and personality variables are about half the correlations between success and intelligence test scores.[3] Why the discrepancy?

People's personal social circles are highly selective. College graduates generally associate with other college graduates; industrial workers talk with other industrial workers. Intelligence plays a role in determining the people we know. Therefore the extent of variation in intelligence among one's acquaintances is likely to be smaller than the variation in intelligence in the general population. Providing that we avoid outright psychopathology, there is no comparable restriction on variations in personality traits. Intelligence may have less influence over behavior than personality variables do, within each person's own social circle, but more influence over behavior than personality variables do, when considered across the entire society.

Finally, two philosophic biases may lead some people, especially social liberals (the dominant social philosophy among academic writers), to downplay the concept of intelligence, as defined by psychometric tests.

Test scores are correlated with familial socioeconomic status (SES); the higher your family's SES, the higher your test score is likely to be, and vice versa. Therefore, there is concern that using test scores in personnel selection, and especially as a

---

1　Sternberg, 1996, p. 13.

2　Amsel, Langer, & Loutzenhiser, 1991; Gigrenzer et al., 2007.

3　Hunt, 1995b.

criterion for admission to higher education, will reinforce the existing social order. The concern is somewhat ironic, because one of the purposes of adopting cognitive tests as screening devices was to reduce the hold that the upper social class had on access to higher education![4] Nevertheless, the concern is valid. If test scores alone were to be used in admitting people to educational institutions, there would be a tendency to select applicants from families with moderate to high SES. The extent to which one sees this as a problem depends upon one's philosophy about the purpose of higher education, a topic that is far beyond the scope of a discussion of intelligence.

The second philosophic bias is closely related to the first. There are differences between demographic groups on virtually all cognitive test scores, including the SAT, ACT, and ASVAB. In the United States Whites and Asian-Americans generally have higher scores than African Americans and Latinos. The gap in test scores mirrors the gap in various measures of socioeconomic status, such as income and health statistics.[5] If you accept the test scores as valid indicators of intelligence, in the broad sense, then you may appear to have accepted differences in intelligence as a partial explanation for the gap in the socioeconomic statistics. This important and very complex issue is discussed in detail in Chapter 11.

Wanting something to be so, even for the best of reasons, does not make it so. What sort of evidence would make us want to either replace or expand the model of intelligence developed from psychometric studies? In order to answer that question we have to consider how intelligence, in the conceptual sense, rather than intelligence in the sense of test scores, influences behavior. This requires an amplification of the argument presented earlier, in Chapter 1.

The problem is illustrated diagrammatically in Figure 5.1. What we are ultimately interested in is how intelligence produces socially relevant behaviors. To investigate this we have to measure both intelligence and the behaviors. In the case of academics, we might want to know how intelligence, in the conceptual sense, determines what a person learns in school. This is a relation between concepts. All we can measure is the relation between test scores and grades, while admitting that the test scores do not perfectly measure intelligence and that grades do not perfectly measure what students have learned. A similar argument can be made for using test scores to evaluate workplace performance.

Intelligence is not the only thing influencing grades, and for that matter it is not the only thing influencing test scores. Grades will be influenced by a variety of nonintellectual factors, such as self-discipline and interest. Conventional psychometric test scores can also be influenced by nonintellectual factors. Sternberg amplified upon his own example by claiming that his IQ test score was dramatically influenced, not for the better, by a definable personality characteristic called *test anxiety*, which means what the name implies, a tendency to become panicked and underperform when tested.[6]

To further complicate things, social behavior is not solely the product of the individual doing the behaving. Behaviors can be elicited or constrained by properties of the situation. Gardner has provided a compelling example, in a series of biographical essays on creativity, as illustrated by such disparate figures as Einstein, Picasso, T. S. Eliot, and Mahatma Gandhi.[7] Each of the creative geniuses Gardner wrote about benefited from the support of people who, often at considerable sacrifice to themselves, played supporting roles so that the geniuses could concentrate on the work that, ultimately, made them famous.

The following sections examine several attempts to expand traditional psychometric models of intelligence. I will start with the simplest approach, expanding the conventional range of cognitive tests, and then

---

4 Lemann, 1999. See the discussion of the development of the SAT in Chapter 2.
5 Herrnstein & Murray, 1994.

6 Sternberg, 1996, Chapter 1; Sarason, 1980.
7 Gardner, 1993b.

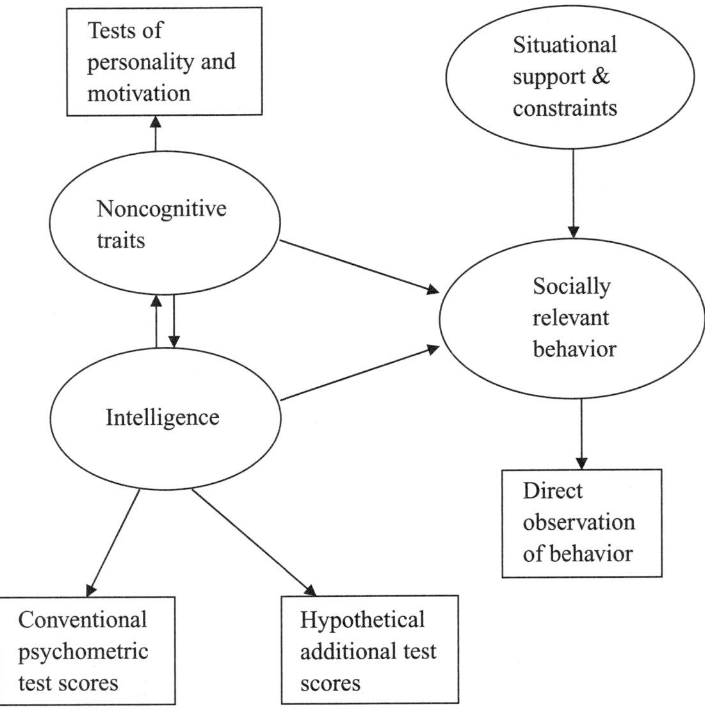

Figure 5.1. The relation between underlying traits, social constraints, test scores, and socially relevant behaviors. Test scores can predict but do not cause socially relevant behaviors. Both the behaviors and test scores are constrained by noncognitive variables.

move to a discussion of personality and motivational issues.

5.1. Gardner's Theory of Multiple Intelligences

Howard Gardner's *Multiple Intelligences* (MI) model, presented in his 1983 book *Frames of Mind*,[8] became instantly popular as an alternative to psychometric theories of intelligence. *Frames of Mind* was selected by five book clubs and translated into seven languages. The theory has since received a few modifications, but the basic message has not changed.[9] While Gardner has stressed the application of his ideas in grade school education, he has not hesitated to discuss possible applications in other domains.

As the name implies, MI theory is based on the assumption that there are many types of intelligence, ranging from linguistic skills to musical intelligence and bodily/kinesthetic intelligence. Gardner regards the purpose of schooling to be the development of each child's type of intelligence, without forcing all children to focus on developing a narrow set of linguistic and reasoning skills that, he feels, are needed much more in conventional schools than they are in the world outside school. While Gardner has made this contention in many forums, to my knowledge he has never offered evidence showing that the validity of IQ and similar educational tests is confined to academics.

Why did Gardner's view become so popular? One reason is that he presents an optimistic view of education. MI theory offers hope that the child who is not doing well in conventional subjects may have superior talents in art, music, social interactions,

8   Gardner, 1983.
9   Gardner, 1993a, 1999; Chen and Gardner, 2005.

or even bodily movement. It follows, then, that it is the teacher's job to identify and develop those talents. This approach to education is morale-building for students, parents, and teachers. The students and parents are assured that there are ways to success for every child. The teacher is encouraged, for the theory stresses the teacher's role as a diagnostician and facilitator. This is a far more professional view of teachers than the view that the role of the teacher is to transmit the assigned lesson to the class, en masse.

By contrast, proponents of the general intelligence (*g*) model are often interpreted by educators as saying "some children are smart and some aren't and there is not much that you, the teacher, can do about it." Therefore, the teacher's role is to transmit information, which either will or will not be picked up by the students, depending upon their pre-set intelligence.

In fact, *g* theorists have never said this. What they have said is a somewhat subtler message: "Some children are smart and some are not. There is a great deal that you can do to raise (or lower) the average level of competence in a class, but there is little you can do to lower the fact of variation. The bright children will learn more than the not-so-bright children, and this is a fact that a teacher has to live with."

The MI model is far more egalitarian than the *g* model. According to it, if the cultural situation (i.e., the classroom) is appropriately shaped, every child can have his or her potentials drawn forth. Gardner tells teachers that they can make a difference for all children, providing that they structure the classroom so as to encourage the appropriate talent.

It would not be logically contrary to anything Gardner has written to assert that even if there are many intelligences, there are some children who simply do not have much of any potential. However, that message is downplayed, and to some extent negated, by Gardner's assertion that the different intelligences he has identified are not highly correlated. This is an assertion about data, and can be evaluated – as we shall do.

Now let us take a closer look at the theory.

5.1.1. *The Multiple Intelligences*

MI theory is based on two premises. The first is that there is no general trait of overall mental competence. In Gardner's view positive manifold is a statistical artifact that arises because conventional schools emphasize only a limited range of skills – language, abstract reasoning, and rapid responding – and because virtually all the tests are presented using language. In Gardner's view, psychometric studies look at intelligence through a "verbal lens."

The second premise is that there are, in fact, a variety of different intelligences, ranging from linguistic intelligence to bodily/kinesthetic intelligence. But what are they? The way Gardner identified the dimensions of intelligence could not have been further from the way the psychometricians investigate the topic. He says of his preparation for his first book, in 1983:[10]

> *I had always been intrigued by the challenge and promise of examining human cognition through a number of discrete disciplinary lenses. I enjoyed investigating psychology, neurology, biology, sociology, and anthropology as well as the arts and humanities. And so I began reading systematically in these areas in order to gain as much information as possible about the nature of various kinds of human faculties and the relationships among them.*
>
> *Gardner, 1999, p. 33*

This method of analysis, broad reasoning followed by reflection, is quite different from the emphasis on data collection and analysis that characterizes psychometric research. Gardner himself has observed that he has little concern for measurement.[11] This makes his method of inquiry more akin to inquiry in the humanities than to scientific inquiry. That does not make the method

10 Gardner, 1983.
11 Gardner, 2006a,b.

wrong; humanistic inquiry is a legitimate method of investigation. It has lead Gardner to an updated definition of intelligence:

A biopsychological potential that can be activated in a cultural setting to solve problems or create products that are of value to society.

Gardner, 1999, pp. 33–34

This definition has been amplified by the identification of four criteria for an intelligence:[12]

Biological: The trait in question should be the product of a biological system, and therefore it should be isolatable by brain damage and should exhibit a development over evolutionary history.

Psychological: The trait should be improvable by specific training. Indicators of the trait should be correlated with other indicators of the same trait, but should have only a low correlation with indicators of other traits.

Developmental: The trait should have a distinct developmental history, with a definable set of expert-level endstate performances. There should also be special populations who display unusual development of the trait, such as *idiot savants* (who have a single exceptional talent, but are otherwise somewhat or even profoundly below the norm) and prodigies.

Logical: Each intelligence should have a definable core set of operations that can be expressed in a symbol system. The obvious case here is language, which is a symbol system whose structure and use are determined by the rules of syntax, semantics, and pragmatics appropriate to the language and culture involved. Music and choreography would also qualify by these criteria.

Gardner uses these criteria somewhat loosely, for most but not all of his intelligences satisfy all the criteria. Here are the intelligences that he has identified:

Linguistic intelligence: This refers to skill with verbal and written language. Writers and poets are prototypes of individuals possessing this skill.

Logico-mathematical intelligence: Skill in mathematical, numerical, and abstract logical reasoning. Mathematicians and computer programmers are offered as prototypes.

Spatial intelligence: A skill possessed by graphic designers and architects. It is the ability to perceive and manipulate spatial and visual images.

Bodily/kinesthetic intelligence: The skills displayed by dancers and athletes. They deal with the ability to control bodily movements.

Naturalistic intelligence: This skill is critical for archeologists and botanists, two rather different fields. It involves skill in dealing with elements in the natural environment.

Interpersonal intelligence: The skills politicians have to have! The skills required to deal with people, as opposed to ideas or things.

Intrapersonal intelligence: Skill in understanding and regulating one's own emotions, strengths, and desires.

These are certainly desirable traits, but is it useful to call all of them "intelligence"?[13] Gardner himself has admitted that his use of the term "intelligence" was a calculated attempt to capitalize on what he saw as a tendency in Western culture to value mental competencies, rather than an attempt to further the study of what others had defined as "intelligence."[14] Does grouping these various traits together lead to a *natural kind*, a set of behaviors that have similar causes and lead to similar effects?

---

12 Chen & Gardner, 2005.

13 Hunt, 2004.
14 Gardner, 1999, p. 33.

5.1.2. The Evidence for the Theory of Multiple Intelligences

MI theory resonates with popular ideas about intelligence. The idea that there are multiple talents and that people can be high on one (e.g., artistic skill) while low on others (e.g., analytic skills) accords with popular conceptions of the distribution of talent. Surveys have consistently shown that the popular concept of intelligence, in both developed and undeveloped countries, is broader than the range of talents evaluated in tests. Social skills, in particular, are given more weight in the popular mind than in the classic testing paradigm. When people are asked to rate themselves and others on Gardner's multiple intelligences, they see the task as reasonable. But when people are asked to give ratings of overall intelligence this is also seen as a reasonable task, and verbal, mathematical, and spatial skills are the biggest contributors to the overall ratings.[15] Whether or not you get popular acceptance of the MI model or of something closer to the g-VPR model depends a good deal on how you phrase the question.

In any case, popular opinion is hardly scientific evidence. We need a source of facts, not opinion. Evidence for the utility of a theory of intelligence comes from three sources: the theory's utility in explaining displays of human abilities both in the school and in the workplace, and from psychometric studies intended to evaluate the theory.

The MI model has been an easy sell to educators. They have developed a number of educational programs based on the multiple intelligences, usually for the early childhood and primary school years. The prototypical program first assesses children, and then provides educational interventions designed to develop their strengths. The intervention is followed by a final assessment. Consistent with Gardner's view, assessment is typically done by engaging children in a (hopefully) interesting task, rather than by formal testing. These programs have been reviewed favorably by Gardner himself,[16] and with somewhat more reservation by some of the authors in an edited volume examining evidence for the theory.[17]

These studies show that children in kindergarten and the early elementary school years become more engaged when they participate in activities that suit their individual talents, than when they must conform to activities chosen for a class as a whole. Not surprisingly, these talents are then further developed, for you learn to do what you practice doing.

But how relevant is this to the development of intelligence? Or, for that matter, to the design of school programs? To answer these questions we would have to compare the later performance of children who had gone through one of the MI programs to the later performance of comparable children who had gone through a standard early education program. To my knowledge no such test has been reported. I also worry that if such an experiment did not provide support for the popular Multiple Intelligence model the report would suffer from the bias against reporting negative results.

I doubt that negative results would have much influence, for Gardner and his supporters can offer two plausible explanations for them. Gardner claims that higher levels of instruction (e.g., middle school, high school, and college) are organized toward the development of traditional verbal and analytic skills. Therefore, the results obtained by training other intelligences during the primary school years would not be valued as children progressed up the educational pipeline.[18] A second reason for

15 Furnham, 2001.

16 Gardner, 1993a; Cheng & Gardner, 2005.
17 Schaler, 2006.
18 A good case can be made for the argument that schools are oriented toward developing analytic and verbal skills, at the expense of developing skills in artistic and social endeavors. But is this a bad thing? Are schools supposed to develop children's varied talents, or are they supposed to train a workforce for a post-industrial society? Educators tend to take the first view. Many observers from outside the educational field take the second view. The National

disregarding negative results is that a program designed to develop multiple intelligences may not have been properly organized. Gardner has said that he approves of some implementations, and not of others. This offers him an out; if a Multiple Intelligences program does not show success, it must be because the program was improperly implemented. And of course this could be true. But no definition of proper implementation has been given other than that the results should be in accord with the theory.

As far as I know, there has never been a rigorous attempt to evaluate the Multiple Intelligence approach as a guide to selection or evaluation of personnel in workplace settings. Indeed, the evidence is strongly in favor of the use of general measures of intelligence – that is, g-loaded measures – as predictors of workplace performance. This is not to say that special skills are irrelevant in certain extreme situations. Poets and airplane mechanics do different things! However, the advocates of MI have been primarily concerned with education.

Three Canadian psychologists, Beth Visser, Michael Ashton, and Philip A. Vernon, took a psychometric approach to the evaluation of MI theory.[19] They constructed two different behavioral tests for each of the eight intelligences. For example, linguistic ability was tested by a vocabulary test and by a test requiring people to identify a word that had the opposite meaning from a target word. Social intelligence was assessed by a task in which participants saw several cartoon drawings depicting part of a story and then had to choose a final cartoon indicating a logical completion of the story, and by a task in which participants had to determine what a word or phrase meant, in context. In addition to tests that evaluated the intelligences specified by MI, participants took the Wonderlic Personnel Test

(WPT) test, which is a g-loaded test that stresses rapid responding to simple problems. (See the description of this test in Chapter 2.)

The 17 tests were given to 200 adult volunteers drawn from a university community. Participants were recruited from students in thirty different departments, thus maximizing the chance that the sample would include people with diverse sets of talents.

The Visser and colleagues study stacked the deck in favor of the MI model. The participants were adults with different training and interests, and were of above-average general intelligence. As noted in Chapter 4, greater differentiation of ability is typically found in above-average samples than in below-average samples. Nevertheless, the results did not support the model. The tests of what everyone would agree are cognitive abilities – the linguistic, mathematics, and spatial tests – had strong loadings on a general factor and substantial correlations with the WPT. So did the tests of natural intelligence, which evaluated a person's knowledge about the biological world. This result, and other results in the literature,[20] are contrary to Gardner's frequent denial of the strength of the general factor in intelligence. The tests of noncognitive factors, such as the tests of bodily/kinesthetic intelligence, had low loadings on the general factor. This is consistent with the argument that combining all these variables under the name "intelligence" forms a class of behaviors that is no longer a natural kind.

A second result was also damaging to the MI theory. According to MI theory the correlations between different tests evaluating the same intelligence should be high. For instance, after accounting for the effects of general intelligence there should be a high correlation between the two linguistic tests, the two mathematical tests, and so on. In general, there was not. The two linguistic tests had a residual correlation, after

---

Academy of Science (NAS) report *Rising Above the Gathering Storm: An Agenda for American Science and Technology* (2007) can be read in places as expressing concern that our system is training too many poets, authors, and business managers, and not enough engineers and scientists.

19 Visser, Ashton, & Vernon, 2006.

20 Brody, 2006. See also Carroll's (1993) discussion of lack of evidence for Gardner's view of general intelligence.

removing the effects of *g*, of .29. None of the other seven correlations between tests of the same intelligence exceeded .18, and the average correlation was .10.

In sum, this study provided no evidence whatsoever that MI theory actually describes the distribution of cognitive skills in college students.

Gardner[21] dismissed these results, on two grounds. He disputed the appropriateness of some of the tests, and he rejected the idea that it is even appropriate to evaluate the theory using the standard psychometric testing paradigm. He concluded that Visser and her colleagues got the results that they did because they recreated the standard scholastic testing situation, with a strong emphasis on logical reasoning.

Gardner's rejoinder to Visser and her colleagues was typical of his reaction to attempts to assess his ideas. In his own words,

> *As I have often explained except for Project Spectrum I have not devoted energies to the devising of tasks that purport to assess MI. I have no objection to others doing so though the efforts so far have been modest. In my own experience, I have been impressed by efforts to create environments in which the use of multiple intelligences is highlighted.*
>
> Gardner, 2006b, p. 504

5.1.3. *An Evaluation of MI*

Despite the popularity of the MI idea in some educational circles, there is virtually no objective evidence for the theory. The attitude toward measurement that Gardner expressed in his reaction to Visser and her colleagues does not lead to good science. Scientific ideas are tested by their ability to account for data, and such tests cannot be carried out unless there is a commitment to means of measurement. Gardner cannot simply dismiss results such as those of Visser and her colleagues unless he offers an alternative means of measurement.

The fact that children can be enthusiastic about a program that plays to their own task-assessed strengths is interesting, although fairly obvious. However, there appears to be little evidence, positive or negative, that early childhood training using Multiple Intelligences theory translates into good performance later on in the educational process. One can blame the educational process for this, arguing that the later educational stages stress formal, analytic reasoning to the detriment of other intelligences. Whether such an attack is valid or not depends upon what one thinks formal education is for. (See footnote 18 for an expansion on this idea.)

There is no evidence that expanding the notion of intelligence beyond obvious cognitive characteristics, to include such things as musical and bodily/kinesthetic "intelligence," creates a natural kind. These noncognitive characteristics are all admirable talents. They can and should be studied separately. Forcing them under the umbrella of intelligence will lead to an unmanageable topic of study. It has been said that science proceeds when it defines tasks that carve nature at its joints. If this is true, Multiple Intelligence theory is not a map for scientific progress.

Having said this, I close with a strong endorsement of one of Gardner's positions, as being useful for science, and a more qualified endorsement of another, as a way of thinking about education.

Gardner makes a good point when he advocates expanding the evaluation of intelligence beyond the conventional psychometric testing paradigm. The field could definitely profit from more analyses of individual differences in performance of everyday tasks, in fields ranging from the evaluation of surgeons, mechanics, and lawyers, to the observation of schoolchildren. Indeed, in industrial-organizational psychology there is considerable concern that personnel assessment is limited by our ability to record details of on-the-job performance.[22] Gardner deserves credit for highlighting the problem, although (possibly due to his

---

21 Gardner, 2006b.

22 S. Hunt, 2007.

disdain for assessment) he has not provided a solution.

The qualified endorsement is that any humane person ought to agree with Gardner that schools should, insofar as possible, encourage students to develop their personal abilities and interests. I would like to see students given much more opportunity to develop talents in music, the performing arts, and even, for all students rather than just for selected stars, athletics. However, I also want students to be prepared for the advanced, post-industrial society that they are going to live in. In order to meet this goal schools have to stress the development of linguistic and mathematical skills. The extent to which other topics can be taught depends on how much time and money society is willing to invest in education. Defining the curriculum is a matter for educational policy, not for science.

5.2. Robert J. Sternberg's Theory of Successful Intelligence

The next theorist whose work will be discussed, Robert J. Sternberg, has, like Gardner, attempted to expand our views of intelligence beyond psychometrics. Unlike Gardner, though, Sternberg's research is grounded in previous research, and he has assiduously conducted experiments to support and expand his ideas.

Sternberg has been a strong advocate for the adoption of his theories in education and in industry. To that end he has written widely and made many presentations to nonspecialists, including both the general audience and policy makers. By contrast, most developers of psychometric theories have written mainly for other scientists. When evaluating Sternberg's work one has to consider both what he is saying, either about his own work or that of others, and the audience to whom he is saying it, either specialists or nonspecialists.

I will first consider Sternberg's views on the work of others. This provides a motivation for the development of his own theoretical position.

5.2.1. *Sternberg's Criticism of Previous Work on Intelligence*

Sternberg has shown a great deal of awareness of previous work on intelligence. This is evidenced by his excellent review of the field as it stood in 1990.[23] In it he presented a carefully balanced analysis of different theoretical approaches to intelligence, as they existed at that time. He was dissatisfied with the field because of what he saw as its myopic view of the range of human intelligence. He also felt that an appropriate goal for intelligence research was to provide useful information to guide educators and industrial leaders in the development of people's capacities, rather than simply cataloging individual differences. To satisfy this goal he has written numerous books and articles directed to the general public and to educators. Some of these contain harsh criticisms of the field. I have already quoted from one of these books. Here is what he has to say on the next page of the same work.

Almost everything you know about intelligence – the kind of intelligence psychologists have most often written about – deals with a tiny and not very important part of a much broader and more complex intellectual spectrum.

Harsh words indeed! In his writings in the technical literature Sternberg takes a more measured tone. For instance, he has been very much involved in developing educational programs that combine testing with educational programs that use the tests to tailor instruction to student strengths and weaknesses.[24] Here is what he has to say about the results of a large project involving an attempt to improve the prediction of success in college (after citing several meta-analytic studies of prediction of college performance, which produced validity estimates for predicting freshman GPA ranging from .4 to .6):

All together these results suggest good predictive validity for the SAT for freshman

---

23 Sternberg, 1990.
24 Sternberg, Grigorenko, & Zhang, 2008.

college performance. But as is always the case for any test or type of test, there is room for improvement. . . . Thus the theory [of successful intelligence] does not suggest <u>replacing</u>, but rather <u>augmenting</u> the SAT in the college admissions process.
Sternberg, 2006, p. 322; emphasis in
the original text

This is a correct analysis of the current situation, and a reasonable proposal for expanding the study of intelligence. What is the nature of the expansion Sternberg proposes?

5.2.2. *The Theory of Successful Intelligence*

Because Sternberg has written so much, and because his thinking has (appropriately) evolved over his career, it is sometimes difficult to assess just what his current position is. My comments will be based largely on the arguments presented in his book *Practical Intelligence in Everyday Life*,[25] published in 2000, and subsequent related publications. *Practical Intelligence* is a narrative account of research conducted over the previous twenty years, and thus provides a good jumping-off place for an analysis of his ideas.

Sternberg distinguishes three classes of intelligence: analytic (sometimes called academic), creative, and practical intelligence. He believes that conventional psychometric and personnel screening tests, such as the SAT and AFQT, are essentially measures of analytic intelligence. The analytic intelligence tests that he and his colleagues have developed intentionally resemble conventional cognitive aptitude tests. They do not seem to have the predictive power of tests like the SAT and AFQT, but that could be because they are much briefer and because, after all, the conventional tests now in use have been refined over the course of decades. Sternberg claimed that any major expansion of our ideas of intelligence will require the development of tests of creative and practical intelligence.

CREATIVITY

There is a long history of trying to develop tests of creativity apart from tests of intelligence. This has proven to be a difficult task, for a simple reason. What is the criterion? It is easy to collect anecdotes about undeniably creative individuals, especially those with very high levels of accomplishment. Albert Einstein is a frequently cited example. However, it is difficult to go further because highly creative people are rare.

Dean Simonton, a professor at University of California, Davis, who has made an extensive study of high levels of creativity, has pointed out that, unlike most human traits, creativity is not normally distributed. The majority of truly creative contributions are made by a very small fraction of the workers in any given field. (If a contribution is commonplace it will probably not be considered creative.) Simonton also points out that creative contributions are usually specialized. This could be because the psychological traits required to be creative are specific to a particular field. There is no compelling argument that being a creative chemist and being a creative artist draw on the same traits. It could also be that only a tiny, tiny percentage of people are creative in more than one field because there simply is not enough time. There is very little, if any, evidence for the existence of effortlessly creative people, who can contribute to one field after another without working very hard in any of them. And finally, both creative accomplishments and their recognition depend very much upon the social setting.[26]

These considerations make it difficult to draw generalizations from the study of people who we all agree are creative. Therefore, scientists who want to study creativity often wind up studying people who are believed to be creative in everyday life. This is not easy, either. Extrapolating from Simonton's analysis, the difficulty may be that there are not that many such people. Or it might be that they are there, but are not motivated to reveal themselves, because we do not want to have to be creative on a daily basis. The

---

25 Sternberg et al., 2000.

26 Simonton, 1984.

world works much better if, most of the time, the problems that people encounter are ones that they know how to solve. A day on which none of the problem-solving methods you have learned works is a bad, frustrating day.

This presents a problem for a test constructor. Psychologists construct intelligence tests by identifying people who display different levels of cognitive competence, as indicated by grades, supervisor ratings, and objective tests of on-the-job performance, and then designing tests that discriminate between performers and nonperformers. If creative behaviors themselves are rare or hard to identify, test constructors do not know where to begin.

It is possible to measure a sort of creativity referred to as *divergent thinking*. Examinees are shown a situation or object, and asked to list as many ways the test stimulus can be used or interpreted as they can – for example, asking people to list the different ways you can use a brick. The response is then assessed by judges. Such tests are face-valid as measures of the ability to produce many and/or unusual responses. But does this have anything to do with the creation of creative products? More particularly, does a creativity test requiring divergent thinking measure a useful trait that is not measured by intelligence tests?

There is evidence that it does. E. Paul Torrance, a professor of psychology at the University of Georgia, developed a widely used series of creativity tests along the lines just described. During the 1960s they were given to elementary school children in two selected schools. The students were also given the Stanford-Binet intelligence test. Torrance's participants were quite bright; the mean IQ was 120. Creativity was assessed by records of performance in adulthood, in some cases as much as forty years later. A modern analysis of Torrance's data[27] has shown that in this high-IQ sample creativity measures taken in childhood made a substantial contribution to predicting lifetime creativity, independently of predictions based on childhood IQ scores.

Sternberg is on firm ground in calling for an expansion of intelligence testing to consider creativity. Would the effort be worth the expense? That is hard to say. Statistically, the gains in prediction would probably be small. However, identifying creative people could be extremely important for economic and social reasons.

PRACTICAL INTELLIGENCE

Practical intelligence refers to the ability to deal with ongoing, realistic, and at times ill-defined problems. Sternberg has placed great stress on the importance of measuring this trait. He claims that tests of academic/analytical intelligence are incomplete because they rely on abstract problems in which all necessary information is presented. The practical intelligence problems that Sternberg and his colleagues have developed either ask for specific, task-relevant knowledge or describe situations claimed to be realistic, and ask examinees what they would do.

Table 5.1 shows some examples of questions that have been asked on tests of practical intelligence. Many of these questions resemble current industrial personnel selection practices. Asking for an analysis of a hypothetical situation is a low-fidelity simulation of performance on the job. In industrial-organizational psychology, tests that do this are called *situational judgment tests*, and have been used for years. It is of interest that within industrial-organizational psychology they are considered to reveal personality traits, such as preferences for certain types of action, as well as containing a cognitive component.[28]

Sternberg and his collaborators have stressed the importance of *tacit knowledge* as a component of practical intelligence. By this they mean knowledge that is not explicitly taught but that is required in many situations. Tacit knowledge is often procedural knowledge, knowing what to do, rather

---

27 Plucker, 1999.

28 S. Hunt, 2007, pp. 69–70.

Table 5.1. Examples of tasks used by Sternberg and his colleagues to assess practical intelligence

Setting	Item Type	Item	Reference
Evaluating knowledge of folk medicine in rural Kenya.	Knowledge of the uses of traditional remedies.	The examinees (Kenyan children) are given a description of a person's symptoms, the Kenyan name of the illness, and asked which of five native herbal medicines are appropriate for the case.	Sternberg et al., 2001.
Prediction of success of graduate students in an American business school.	Skills in solving a practical problem.	The examinee is given the role of the human resources manager of a manufacturing plant facing a personnel shortage. Employees are working excessive amounts of overtime and morale is low. The examinee is to suggest a course of action. Materials provided: current employment figures and job-satisfaction survey results.	Hedlund et al., 2005.
Prediction of graduate student success in an American business school.	Situational judgment test.	The examinee is presented with a personnel problem similar to the one just described, but with considerably more detail given. The examinee is then asked to rate several possible solutions, including hiring temporary workers, hiring full-time employees but warning them that they may be let go if product demand drops, mixing the two solutions, or letting each division within the plant decide upon its own solution.	Hedlund et al., 2005.

than declarative knowledge, knowing how to describe the situation. This is a notion worth examining.

The environment offers different degrees of support for acquiring knowledge, ranging from presenting examples offered without comment to presenting ideas in formal instruction, either in or out of school. People will vary in the extent to which they can articulate how or why they take certain actions. For instance, most people learn sports like bicycling and skiing by being coached. However, relatively few skilled skiers and bicyclers become good coaches, in part because they cannot verbalize what the novice is supposed to do. The concepts of tacit knowledge and explicitly instructed knowledge represent end points on a continuum, rather than mutually exclusive classes. In the narrowest sense, tacit knowledge should be knowledge that people acquire by observation and experience, without any form of instruction. As an amusing example, think of the way that pre-adolescents learn to curse. The learning phase usually includes some hilarious misuses of improper language.

At times Sternberg and his colleagues write as if tacit knowledge were identical to practical knowledge. This blurs an important distinction. Much practical knowledge is acquired through formal instruction. For example, airline captains have a great deal of job-relevant knowledge about how to fly aircraft. Much of it is acquired in flight school. As late as the 1960s Polynesian navigators in the Marianas Islands went to formal schools to learn how to sail outrigger canoes across vast reaches of the Pacific.[29] Simply showing that knowledge is practical does not ensure that it has been acquired tacitly.

This restriction does not deny the importance of tacit knowledge. Most apprenticeship learning is tacit. The master and the student have a problem to solve, and the master solves it, with the assistance of the student, who, hopefully, will later be able to act on his or her own. During problem solving the master may or may not explicitly instruct the student, but what instruction there is is almost always in the context of practical problem solving.

The research issue is whether different cognitive skills are required for learning by observation, apprenticeship learning, and formal classroom learning. It could also be that general intelligence is a substantial requirement for all forms of learning. The question is one to be settled by investigation, not by arguments that one or the other conclusion must be true.

5.2.3. *The Evidence for the Theory of Successful Intelligence*

Validation of Sternberg's theory requires that tests be defined for each of the three abilities, that the abilities be substantially uncorrelated (for otherwise they might simply be reflections of the pervasiveness of general intelligence), and that the

uncorrelated portions of the tests of academic, creative, and practical intelligence predict important behaviors both within and outside of an academic environment. In the book *Practical Intelligence in Everyday Life*, and in several publications since then, Sternberg has claimed that these criteria have been met.[30] This claim has been disputed.[31] It would not be possible to go through point and counterpoint of every study. I have selected a few examples to highlight the issues involved.

Three studies are relevant to the prediction of academic knowledge in three different educational settings.

In one study Sternberg and his colleagues administered tests of analytic, creative, and practical intelligence to over three hundred students attending a pre-college preparatory course at Yale University. At the time the students were also taking an introductory psychology course. This made it possible to construct a three-by-three experimental design, in which students were categorized as having strengths in analytic, creative, or practical intelligence, and then were assigned to study sections where the instruction stressed analytic, creative, or practical problem solving. Sternberg claimed that students performed best when the method of instruction matched their strengths in the appropriate type of intelligence.[32]

Nathaniel Brody, the author of several textbooks and a number of scholarly commentaries on intelligence, made several criticisms of this study.[33] He noted that the sample had been pre-selected to be high on general intelligence, for they were, after all, students intending to enter an extremely selective university. The factorial experiment supporting the crucial aptitude x treatment interaction dealt with only 199 of the 324 students in the study. When the entire

---

29 Hutchins, 1983.

30 Sternberg et al., 2000. See also his reply to criticisms (Sternberg, 2003b) and a claim for the utility of his measures in the selection of college students (Sternberg, 2006, 2007) and in general education (Sternberg, Grigorenko, & Zhang, 2008).

31 Gottfredson, 2003a; Hunt, 2008.

32 Sternberg et al., 1996, 1999; Sternberg, Grigorenko, & Zhang, 2008.

33 Brody, 2003.

sample was considered there was no evidence of an aptitude by treatment interaction. Finally, Brody reanalyzed Sternberg's data and concluded that the predictive ability of the three allegedly independent tests of different types of intelligence was due solely to a common trait that underlay them all. Brody felt that this represented general intelligence.

Sternberg replied to Brody by saying that he regarded the Yale study as a preliminary one, that he and his colleagues had developed better tests of creative and practical intelligence, and that positive results would shortly be forthcoming.[34] Sternberg subsequently published the results of a very large-scale study, the RAINBOW study, involving a number of universities and colleges, in which an attempt was made to predict first-year grade point averages (GPA) from a combination of SAT scores and scores on tests of analytic, creative, and practical intelligence.[35] The RAINBOW study covered a diverse set of institutions, ranging from California community colleges to Ivy League universities. One of the tests of creativity did improve predictivity beyond the predictivity achieved using the SAT alone, but the tests of practical ability did not add anything beyond predictions using the SAT alone.

In a nontechnical note addressed to college administrators, Sternberg claimed that predictivity was increased by 15%, in terms of variance accounted for. This is a substantial gain indeed.[36] Since the SAT predicts 10–15% of the variance in performance of accepted students, if we accept Sternberg's statement at face value, a test program that incorporated Sternberg's creativity tests along with the SAT or ACT could predict somewhere between 15% and 25% of the variance in first-year GPA.

Given this claim, a close look at the data supporting it is in order.

The added predictivity was due to a single test of creative ability, in which exami-

nees saw a collection of pictures, then made up and told the examiner a story about the pictures. Thus the test was rather like viewing comic book pictures without the captions, and then telling the story. Surprisingly, there was no gain in predictivity if the examinees had to write the story. Asserting that "Creative Intelligence" added to predictivity is something of an overgeneralization, since one test worked and the other did not. More generally, it is difficult to interpret the RAINBOW results because of a statistical problem.

An attempt was made to establish a relationship using multiple tests of both practical and creative intelligence, and one of them worked. This is a reasonable model for exploratory research, but it opens the gates to capitalization on chance results. In such cases the only thing to do is to attempt to replicate the findings.

Because a result could have been obtained by chance does not mean that it was. The result is consistent with previous research on creativity, especially Torrance's work, cited earlier. According to Sternberg the RAINBOW project is to be expanded.[37] If the results do replicate, a good case will have been made for including tests of the ability to produce fictional material as an evaluator of college readiness.[38] This is an important theoretical finding. Whether or not this means that Sternberg has provided a theoretical case for Creative Intelligence, apart from the sorts of testing of linguistic competence that occur in conventional testing, is a somewhat different question.

In order to make a case for creativity as a predictor Sternberg and his colleagues will have to show that several creativity measures predict success in college, beyond the prediction that can be obtained using

---

34 Sternberg, 2003b.
35 Sternberg, 2006.
36 Sternberg, 2007.

37 ibid.
38 The most recent versions of the SAT include a test of writing ability. If Sternberg and colleagues' results depend upon verbal fluency, they should not add to predictivity beyond that obtained by the expanded SAT. If the key point is creativity, however, then their tests should be unique predictors, because the SAT writing requirement is, in terms of content, rather prosaic. Grading is for English usage rather than for literary merit.

standard tests, such as the SAT and ACT. Ideally there should be some nonverbal creativity measures, to avoid confounding creativity and verbal performance.

The RAINBOW study failed to support Sternberg's theorizing in one important way. None of the measures of practical intelligence in an academic setting added to the amount of prediction that could be obtained with the SAT alone. This finding is consistent with Gottfredson's claim[39] that tests of practical intelligence are actually evaluating general intelligence (g) rather than evaluating a separate dimension of ability, as is claimed in Sternberg's Theory of Successful Intelligence.

Recognizing this and similar concerns, Sternberg and his colleagues have acknowledged that the Theory of Successful Intelligence provides one among several possible ways of motivating the empirical studies and organizing their results with respect to academic accomplishment.[40]

The RAINBOW study attempted to do many things, using a complicated design. It is useful to look at a more focused study, in which Sternberg and his colleagues attempted to predict the performance of students in their first year of a Master of Business Administration (MBA) program at the University of Michigan.[41]

Students in the Michigan program took two tests of practical intelligence – a test of their ability to analyze and recommend actions on realistic business problems, and a situational judgment test similar to the one described in Table 5.1. An attempt was made to predict their first-year course grades, either using the two tests and the students' scores on the Graduate Management Admissions Test (GMAT), which they had taken prior to entry, or using only the GMAT. The tests improved prediction over the predictions based on the GMAT alone. This finding is clearly what would be predicted by the Theory of Successful Intelligence.

Sternberg and his colleagues have completed a number of studies outside of academic settings. These include both studies of industrial performance and studies of intelligence in developing countries. A study of military leadership is of particular interest, both for its own importance and because it is illustrative of potential industrial applications.[42]

The first part of the study consisted of an extensive review of military leadership skills, including examinations of leadership duties at three different military levels: platoon leaders, company commanders, and battalion commanders. The distinction is important because the type of leadership required differs across these levels.

Platoon leaders lead by direct, face-to-face contact with from twenty-five to forty soldiers. Platoon leaders are almost invariably lieutenants, recently commissioned officers. They are assisted by three to five sergeants, noncommissioned officers who have had less formal command training than the lieutenants, but may have had considerably more experience in the military.

Company commanders are usually captains or senior first lieutenants. In the American services they will have had roughly five to ten years' experience in the military. Depending on the type of company, they will command from one to two hundred soldiers, organized into three or four platoons. The company commander has a small staff, including an executive officer (usually a lieutenant) and a few senior sergeants. His job mixes administrative duties with a good deal of face-to-face leadership of platoon leaders and sergeants.

Battalion commanders are majors or, more likely, lieutenant colonels. They will have had at least ten years' experience as officers. Depending upon the type of battalion, they will be in command of anywhere from three hundred to six hundred soldiers, organized into companies or analogous units. Battalion commanders are essentially administrative leaders. They are assisted by staffs containing experienced

39 Gottfredson, 2003a,b.
40 Sternberg, 2006, p. 322.
41 Hedlund et al., 2006.

42 Hedlund et al., 2003.

officers and senior sergeants, who develop plans and relay orders to company commanders and, rarely, individual platoon leaders.

Sternberg and his colleagues developed three measures of what they describe as tacit knowledge of military leadership for each level of command. These covered a number of practical aspects of leadership, ranging from motivating subordinates to communicating with senior officers. In addition they utilized a standard measure of verbal reasoning (similarities and analogies), and a measure of tacit knowledge developed for use with civilian managers. The officers were rated for their leadership ability by their superiors, peers (except for battalion commanders), and subordinates (except for platoon leaders).

The question of interest is whether the measures of military tacit knowledge predicted leadership ratings, over and above the prediction possible from use of the verbal reasoning measure. A secondary question is whether the measures designed for the military are more accurate predictors of leadership ratings than the measure derived for use in civilian settings. According to the theory, the military measures should be more accurate because they evaluate knowledge required by the local situation.

The results presented a mixed bag. The military knowledge tests were the best predictors of leadership ratings, but no test did particularly well. The six possible correlations between the military knowledge questionnaires and rated leadership ranged from .46 to −.11. What is even more puzzling is the pattern of correlations. The .46 represented a positive relation between the military knowledge test and the effectiveness ratings of battalion commanders by their superior officers. The −.11 represents a relationship between the same test and the ratings the same battalion commanders received from their subordinates! Similar but not quite so puzzling anomalies were found in the ratings of platoon leaders and company commanders. A further statistical analysis showed that knowledge of military leadership did have some predictive validity

beyond the other measures. However, the effects were far from spectacular. Only three of the seven possible comparisons were statistically reliable, and only one, prediction of superiors' ratings of battalion commanders, was large enough to be of practical importance.

As in the case of the studies of academic performance, this is the sort of study that is suggestive, but replication is required before strong conclusions can be made.

The studies in non-Western cultures include studies of a pastoral/farming community in rural Kenya, health practices in a Russian city, and hunters in an Alaskan Inuit community.[43]

The Alaskan study[44] provides typical results. The participants were Yu'pik Inuit adolescents residing in several small towns. The people in this area are best described as semitraditional; they live in settled towns, go to Alaskan state schools, and participate in the normal American economy. They also do a considerable amount of hunting and, to some degree, follow traditional social customs. Scores on a test of knowledge of hunting lore and Inuit terms were largely independent of scores on conventional tests of intelligence. The scores on the tests of Inuit knowledge correlated with estimates of hunting skills. Similar results were found in a study in Kenya, where the targeted information was knowledge of traditional medicine.

Both these studies illustrate a simple principle. People will learn to solve the cognitive challenges their societies present. There will be individual differences in the amount of learning, and such differences will predict performance in that society.

5.2.4. *Evaluation and Critique of the Theory*

Sternberg's approach can be evaluated on three grounds; his criticisms of other theories, the logic of his own theory, and the evidence he offers for it.

43 Sternberg, 2004.
44 Grigorenko et al., 2004.

CRITIQUE OF THE ATTACK

Sternberg's attacks on other theoretical approaches are excessive, especially when he writes for nontechnical audiences. "Everything people have been told about intelligence" is not false, and intelligence tests do not solely evaluate "narrow abilities of use only in school settings." He makes a case against conventional tests by offering anecdotes about failures in prediction, including some of his personal experiences. This is an effective rhetorical device, but it is not a valid argument, unless he is arguing against a claim that the tests are perfect predictors of performance. No one has ever made such a claim. The claim that is made, and supported by massive evidence, is that the tests, although far from perfect predictors of performance, are the best predictors that we have, both in academic and industrial settings.[45]

Nonetheless, Sternberg has a serious point. Since Binet's time psychometricians have seen their task as one of measuring intelligence, and then simply reporting the result. There has been a great deal of research on increasing test validity and making test administration more efficient. What has been missing is concern for what happens after test scores have been obtained. There is an implicit (and often not-so-implicit) assumption that personnel decision makers will establish a cut score, and then either accept or reject candidates. Reality is more complex. Educators have to do something with the students they have; industrial supervisors have to design jobs and training programs suitable for the available workforce; and military commanders have to lead the troops who have enlisted. What Sternberg has done is to move away from a pure selection model for the use of test scores to a model where test scores are meshed with training and educational decisions.

This is not a novel idea, for industrial-organizational psychologists have been doing this for some time, especially in military settings. For instance, in addition to the AFQT, the ASVAB battery provides scales indicating skills or knowledge in special fields (e.g., electronics). These scales are then used, along with other criteria, to assign soldiers to training programs for various military specialties. In educational and most civilian industrial applications, though, it is much more common for test scores to be used to determine whether an applicant is to be selected or not, without using test scores to tailor experiences for the individual after he or she has been selected. As was illustrated by the Yale study, Sternberg has called educators' attention to the possibility that training after selection could be guided by test scores indicating the student's strengths and weaknesses. This is an ambitious, needed step forward that has been totally ignored by most psychometrically oriented researchers in the field.

CRITIQUE OF THE THEORY

To what extent have Sternberg and his colleagues offered new theoretical insights about intelligence? In order to answer this question it is important to make a distinction between pragmatic advances in predicting important behaviors and theoretical advances in the study of intelligence. Both are valuable, but they are not the same. It is possible to make an important pragmatic advance in personnel selection, by calling attention to the importance of some aspect of intelligence already covered by other theories, but not being used for selection, without making any advance in the study of intelligence.

In my opinion, Sternberg's work on creative intelligence represents a pragmatic advance. Sternberg was not the first to distinguish between creativity and intelligence, nor was he the first to develop creativity tests. He has made an important contribution by calling attention to something that was in the literature, but had "dropped off the radar" of current test designers.

Sternberg's notion of practical intelligence is, at the theoretical level, close to Cattell and Horn's view of crystallized intelligence (Gc). Both tests of practical

45 For reviews, see Gottfredson (1997), Hunt (1995), and Schmidt & Hunter (1998). The topic is explored in Chapter 10.

intelligence and tests of Gc stress the use of previously acquired knowledge to solve a current problem. Where Sternberg and his colleagues differ from conventional test developers is in how they have instantiated the concept to create tests.

In conventional psychometric batteries tests for Gc are designed to evaluate people's ability to use the knowledge and ideas that are needed in industrial/post-industrial societies, and that are often explicitly taught in our schools. They are therefore culturally limited, albeit to a very large, important culture. They are further limited by concentrating on the evaluation of a sort of common denominator of what people in modern cultures are supposed to know. This is reasonable if the test is to be used for some broad swath of the population in an industrial/post-industrial society, such as applicants to college. Sternberg and his colleagues have demonstrated the feasibility of developing tests of Gc, their "practical intelligence," for non-Western, nonindustrial societies and for specialized segments of the sprawling post-industrial society. Cattell said that this would have to be done over half a century ago.[46] Sternberg did it. He was not the first to do so. Industrial-organizational psychologists have been developing specialized tests for years. Situational judgment testing is a good example. Sternberg and his colleagues have done an effective job of showing the need for such specialized testing in other areas.

When Sternberg and his colleagues question the utility of a test of, say, knowledge of English vocabulary to predict performance in rural Kenya, they are not attacking the concept of Gc. They are attacking the overgeneralization of the conventional realization of that concept, beyond the context in which the test was developed.

All in all, Sternberg's emphasis on practical intelligence, if heeded, will represent an important, albeit not unique, pragmatic advance in testing.

The concept of tacit intelligence is a unique theoretical contribution. A great deal of mental competence is based on information and skills that we acquire without explicit instruction. This is particularly true of the acquisition of language and social customs. Billions of people – literally – speak their native language and get along in their society without explicit knowledge of either the rules of syntax or the rules of etiquette.

Although Sternberg and his colleagues do not stress this, there are both input and output issues in the use of tacit intelligence. On the input side, are some people more able than others to pick up the unspoken rules? Is this a general talent, or is it specific to particular social situations? On the output side, recent research in decision making has shown that in some situations people are well advised to accept their gut reaction, rather than making decisions based on conscious reflection. In other situations conscious reflection is important.[47] Are some people better than others at deciding when to act with or without reflection? These are interesting research questions. Although the general field of unconscious cognition has blossomed since the beginning of the century, there has been little study of individual differences in either implicit learning or unconscious decision making.

There is no need to comment on Sternberg's analytic intelligence component, for, as he says, this is equivalent to standard views of general reasoning.

Sternberg has also extended his interest to ask how intelligence is used. He distinguishes three intellectual styles. By analogy to government, he identifies an *executive* style, which is an interest in putting ideas into place; a *legislative* style, which is an interest in creating ideas in the first place; and a *judicial* style, which is an interest in analyzing the implications of ideas and efforts to put them into place.[48] The extension stresses an interaction between the "can do" concept of intelligence and "how to" personality and interest issues. This work is in its beginning. The approach is an interesting one, for the borderline between

---

46 Cattell, 1957, 1971.

47 Klein, 2009.
48 Sternberg, Grigorenko, & Zhang, 2008.

intelligence and personality research is underdeveloped.

EVALUATION OF THE EVIDENCE
FOR THE THEORY

In *Practical Intelligence* (and in several articles since that book was published) Sternberg and his colleagues claim that there is ample evidence for the three different types of intelligence, and that practical intelligence, in particular, is an extremely important aspect of mental competence. I have already expressed some reservations. Other reviewers have expressed their reservations with more vehemence.

Linda Gottfredson, a professor of education at the University of Delaware who has frequently and ably defended classic psychometric theory, published a detailed analysis of the evidence that Sternberg and his colleagues provided in *Practical Intelligence*.[49] She concluded,

> [The authors of *Practical Intelligence*] *exaggerate the strength of the empirical support they summarize. They do so by presenting the most favorable results, overstating even those, interpreting inconsistent data in ways that produce consistent support, and giving citations to back up strong statements but which do not actually provide independent support (many are just earlier summaries of the same thing) or that even contradict the claim in question.*
>
> *The authors simultaneously discourage the close analysis that would reveal the inadequacies of their data and presentation. They do so partly by appealing to many people's strong desire to believe them, specifically by tapping the popular preference for an egalitarian plurality of intelligences (everyone can be smart in some way) and a distaste for being assessed, labeled, and sorted by inscrutable mental tests. These sentiments are evoked again by casting aspersions on research and researchers that have helped reinstate the concept of g, or general intelligence.*
>
> Gottfredson, 2003a, p. 392;
> emphasis in the original

Sternberg replied to Gottfredson but, as she pointed out, did not address the specific criticisms she made of his work.[50] Sternberg's reply did make a point that Gottfredson failed to address. He argued that focusing on individual studies can cause one to fail to appreciate the broad range of support for the theory. There is validity to this argument.

My own evaluation is this.

Sternberg's critiques of previous work are too broad, especially in articles and books written for nonspecialists. Nevertheless, they have a grain of truth in them, particularly in his criticisms of the work of researchers who have, either implicitly or explicitly, accepted the idea that intelligence is what the intelligence tests test. The theoretical ideas are not as new as some of his writing would lead one to believe, but they do advance the field. I point especially to his expansion of the concept of Gc by the development of practical intelligence tests, which could just as easily be described as tests of the development of Gc in specialized contexts. His ideas about possible individual differences in the acquisition of implicit (tacit) and explicit knowledge are very interesting, and deserve further exploration. He is also to be applauded for attending to the important issue of meshing assessment, training, and educational methods.

In order to support his theory he and his colleagues have carried out a staggering number of experiments. Taken individually, many of these studies are fairly weak. Taken together, they indicate that the augmentation of conventional tests would improve prediction. While the improvements would not be large, they would be of practical significance for very large personnel selection programs, such as admission to college or selection of military officers.

5.3. Ackerman's PPIK Theory

Philip Ackerman, currently a professor at the Georgia Institute of Technology, has

---

49 Gottfredson, 2003a.

50 Sternberg, 2003; Gottfredson, 2003b.

developed a theory of adult intelligence that combines cognitive processes, personality, interests, and knowledge, hence the *PPIK* model. In contrast to Gardner and Sternberg, Ackerman has been careful to point out that his ideas are extensions of ideas proposed by earlier researchers. These include R. B. Cattell's Gf:Gc distinction and J. L. Holland's discussion of adult vocational interests. Ackerman's extensions are a substantial and innovative contribution to our understanding of intelligence.

Ackerman was motivated by a paradoxical finding in the literature. Many studies have shown that psychometrically defined general intelligence (*g*) and, even more telling, fluid intelligence (Gf) decline over the adult years, beginning at about twenty-five.[51] Yet the world seems to be run by adults over the age of thirty-five. Ackerman offers the following example. When the president of Russia, Boris Yeltsin, had a heart attack, one of the attending surgeons, Michael De Bakey, was in his eighties. Age was not the point; Dr. De Bakey had performed several thousand cardiac operations.

This is not an isolated example. As we entered the twenty-first century more than half the physicians in the United States were over forty-five.[52] Most presidents of the United States took office when they were in their fifties. This group includes Washington (fifty-seven), Lincoln (fifty-two), and Franklin Roosevelt (fifty-one), arguably the three greatest presidents. As of 2007, 90 of the 100 United States senators were over 50, and 25 were over 70. Perhaps the intelligence tests are missing something.

Following Cattell, Ackerman[53] argues that as people age they increasingly rely on past knowledge to solve problems, rather than solving problems by using general problem-solving techniques. This is certainly true for extreme cases. Studies of expert performance in fields ranging from chess to athletics have repeatedly shown that very high levels of performance are reached after a great deal of deliberate practice, resulting in well-organized knowledge in the domain of expertise.[54] The same principles apply, to a lesser degree, to all adults. Older people do worse than younger ones on conventional intelligence tests, especially those that stress fluid intelligence, but they do better than younger ones when asked to generate solutions to realistic problems, ranging from an adolescent's desire to leave home to problems in credit management and personal health.[55]

Ackerman was also impressed by the extent to which adult knowledge is specialized. Physicians, business entrepreneurs, salespeople, mechanics, and farmers have to meet the challenges of their particular social niche. The situation is somewhat analogous, although not so extreme, to the conditions that led to Sternberg's emphasis on culture-specific knowledge. Ackerman distinguishes between general cultural knowledge (Gc) and knowledge of the more specialized culture in which the individual lives (Gk). Moreover, specialization is not limited to professional and technical knowledge. People in our post-industrial society will share experiences and interests with others in groups that are broadly defined, coherent within themselves, but different from each other. Experienced university professors, military officers, businessmen, and physicians will all share some cultural knowledge (Gc) of modern society, but they will differ in the particular knowledge that they have acquired within their domains of interest (Gk). These differences have to be considered when evaluating their intelligence.

5.3.1. *PPIK Theory*

Ackerman proposes that evaluations of adult effectiveness consider four traits. The first two of these are what we might normally consider aspects of intelligence. *Intelligence as process* refers to the ability to deal with

---

51 This topic is discussed further in Chapter 11.
52 Commission on Graduate Education in Medicine, sixteenth annual report, 2005.
53 Ackerman, 1996; Ackerman & Heggested, 1997.
54 Ericsson, 1996.
55 Baltes & Smith, 1990; Baltes & Staudinger, 2000.

novel, arbitrary, abstract problems. This aspect of intelligence corresponds closely to the Cattell–Horn view of fluid intelligence (Gf), and to the mental dimension of general reasoning (*g*) advocated by Jensen, Gottfredson, and others. *Intelligence as knowledge* is divided into two components: general cultural knowledge (the Cattell–Horn Gc, as conventionally measured) and knowledge relevant to the individual's interests and general role in society (Gk), including but not limited to the person's economic role.

Ackerman stresses the development of intelligence from the later childhood years through adolescence and on to maturity. His view is that over these periods intelligence is developed by a series of investments of current cognitive competence into knowledge-building experiences that both increase and temper the nature of future cognitive competencies. A person's personality and interests determine what experiences he or she will have, and therefore will guide the developmental process.

During childhood and adolescence competence is largely guided by the process aspect, as the child acquires general cultural knowledge through interaction with a relatively uniform environment, at least in the range typical of middle-class society in the developed countries. The situation is gloomier for children in extremely poor home or school environments, which simply do not offer much opportunity to acquire the early stages of Gc (e.g., skill in reading). In the later school years knowledge begins to build on knowledge, so that Gc acquired during, for instance, the first six years of school combines with maturing processing capacities (Gf) to guide acquisition of cultural knowledge in the next six years. This accounts for two observed phenomena, the increasing stability of test scores as children progress through school and the high validity of IQ scores obtained in early middle school as predictors of accomplishment by the end of high school.

Opportunities for specialized experiences arise in the later high school years, and continue through young adulthood, in the choice of jobs and/or college majors. By the early to mid twenties there will be a shift from acquisition of general knowledge of the culture to acquisition of knowledge relevant to specific sectors of society. Throughout both the school and early adult years intelligence plays a crucial role, for this is what makes the difference between having experiences and acquiring knowledge. Table 5.2 makes this point, by showing the correlations between tests of intelligence and tests of domain-specific knowledge. Ackerman and Beier have also demonstrated this point experimentally. Adults were first tested for their knowledge of the management of personal finances, clearly an important topic to us all. They were then given instruction, and tested again. Both pre-test and post-test performance and improvements in performance were predicted by tests of Gf and Gc. Perhaps the smart do not just get smarter over time; they may also get richer.

While environmental constraints undoubtedly play a part (a variable that Ackerman does not discuss), in a noncaste society personal interests and personality will play a substantial role in the person's choice of social niche, and therefore in the subsequent development of knowledge. This means that people who differ in how much they know about various domains will differ in other ways as well.

At the same time, due to biological effects associated with aging, there will be a decline of the processes supporting intelligence, that is, a decline in Gf. However, this does not mean that older people are less intelligent. Intelligence begins to differentiate. There is a decline in the processes supporting reasoning (e.g., concentration of attention, short-term memory, time to retrieve information) but an increase in the efficiency with which those processes are used, providing that the person is operating within a domain where his or her previously acquired knowledge is relevant.

Ackerman[56] has identified five domains of knowledge that are at once broader than the knowledge associated with professional

56 Ackerman & Heggested, 1997.

Table 5.2. *Selected data on the relation between knowledge and intelligence test scores and age. All participants were college graduates twenty-one to sixty-five years old. Twenty-five percent had advanced degrees. Due to restriction of the range of the test scores the estimates of correlations with intelligence are probably underestimates of the correlations in the general population.*

Content of Test	Correlation with Gf	Correlation with Gc	Correlation with Age
Chemistry	.516	.385	−.240
Physics	.568	.515	−.316
Electronics	.347	.451	.200
Law	.186	.379	.189
Geography	.320	.525	.150
Art	.168	.468	.224
World Literature	.156	.600	.248

Source: From Ackerman, 2000, Table 4. By permission of Oxford University Press and the author.

skills, yet narrower than the general cultural knowledge evaluated by a typical test for crystallized intelligence. The domains are knowledge about physical science, mathematics, the arts, literature, and social science.

Knowledge in each domain is not isolated; it is part of a *trait complex* that includes the intelligence required to work in a domain along with the personality and interests that lead someone to decide to work in the domain in the first place. To give these ideas some content, imagine a longitudinal study in which we followed students who, as they leave high school, vary in Gc and Gf, as conventionally measured, and also vary along the dimensions of interest in abstract investigations or social issues, and in conscientiousness. Subsequently, when they are in their thirties and forties, we test this group for their knowledge of scientific and social topics. According to the PPIK model we would find the following relationships:

1. Interest in abstract investigations, measured upon graduation from high school, would be related to adult knowledge of science. Interest in social issues, once again measured as a high school student, would be positively related to knowledge of social situations.
2. Knowledge of social situations and knowledge of science would be posi-

tively related to general intelligence (*g*), measured as an amalgam of scores on tests of Gf and Gc. (We expect the two to be substantially but not perfectly correlated.) However, the relative weightings given to Gf and Gc might differ depending upon whether we were trying to predict knowledge of science (which is often relatively abstract) or knowledge of concrete social situations.
3. With Gf and Gc and interests held constant, statistically, there should be a positive relationship between conscientiousness and knowledge.

As far as I know, this hypothetical study has yet to be done. However, Ackerman and his colleagues have reported cross-sectional studies that closely resemble it.[57] These studies revealed four trait complexes, produced by the correlations between domain knowledge, intelligence test scores, interests, and personality traits. They are

1. *The science and math complex*: This complex is defined by relatively high fluid intelligence (*g* or Gf) and by interest in realistic problems and in investigation of abstract issues. People with high knowledge of science and mathematics

[57] Ackerman, 2000; Ackerman & Beier, 2006; Ackerman & Rolfhus, 1999.

issues tend to have high scores on this complex.

2. *The conventional complex*: This complex is defined by interest in conventional topics, conservatism, and conscientiousness. Abilities are widely distributed across this complex.

3. *The social complex*: This complex is associated with an interest in social relations and extraversion. Abilities are widely distributed across this complex. Some studies indicate that the social complex should be split into two complexes, one identifying people interested in social power and leadership, and the other identifying people who value close social relations.

4. *The intellectual/cultural complex*: This complex is associated with knowledge of the arts and humanities. It is also characterized by the personality traits of openness to experience and a tendency to become absorbed in intellectual activities. The trait is also associated with relatively high scores on tests of Gc.

These descriptions are my gloss of results from Ackerman's studies. Slightly different complexes, with slightly different descriptions, have been found in each study. This is not surprising, for the studies generally involve from one to two hundred participants, recruited opportunistically (e.g., by newspaper advertisements) rather than by random sampling from a definable population.

5.3.3. *Evaluation of the PPIK Theory*

I believe that the PPIK approach has a great deal of potential. Ackerman and his colleagues have demonstrated the need to consider domain knowledge as an attribute of adult intelligence and the importance of considering how personality and interests guide the investment of current intelligence to produce future knowledge.

I suspect that there is more to Ackerman's concepts than the current studies have sug-gested. As of 2010, Ackerman's studies have concentrated predominantly on the study of college students and adults who have had at least some college. It seems likely that if studies of trait complexes were to be extended beyond the largely middle-class, college-educated urban population, more trait complexes would be uncovered. Their influence may be very powerful indeed.

5.4. Personality Variables Related to the Development and Use of Intelligence

The study of personality has developed almost independently of the study of intelligence. This is a bit surprising, given the amount of research on each topic. There is a difference in the sense that intelligence is a "can do" concept; it refers to the potential for dealing with and extracting useful information from the environment. Personality traits are generally "will do" concepts; they refer to a person's disposition to take certain actions and not others. Explanations of "can do" and "will do" complement each other. Psychology would benefit by an integrated approach to the two topics.

5.4.1. *Intellectual Engagement*

Ackerman's ideas on the topic provide a good place to begin our discussion. Ackerman has introduced the idea of *intellectual engagement*. He argues that people differ in the extent to which they engage conceptually with their experiences, especially when such engagement is not required for any immediate purpose. Imagine two stock brokers, both of whom carefully check the financial news, but only one of whom reads the rest of the newspaper. The second broker has more intellectual engagement than the first.

We can go beyond thought experiments. Goff and Ackerman developed a scale of intellectual engagement, based upon self-reports to questions about such things as manner of reading a newspaper. Scores on this scale can contribute to the prediction of academic performance, over a three-year period, after the prediction due to differences in intelligence is accounted for.[58]

This research is just in its beginning. The concept of intellectual engagement has a great deal of promise as an explanation of why some people learn broadly, while others become progressively narrower in their thoughts as they age.

5.4.2. *Self-Discipline*

Intellectual engagement refers to the way people like to behave. A related approach is to look at attitudinal variables that determine how much effort a person will put into doing something he or she should do. This brings us to the topic of self-discipline, which I interpret as the willingness to do something you perceive as worthwhile in the long run, even though it means forgoing immediate pleasures.

There is a substantial body of research showing that the personality trait of *conscientiousness*, that is, showing up for work and keeping on task, is the best, and in many cases the only, predictor of workplace performance after the prediction associated with general intelligence has been accounted for. The message is clear: success in the workplace is associated with both intelligence and willingness to work.[59]

The contribution of conscientiousness, alone, as a predictor is much smaller than the contribution of intelligence. This may be because in many workforce situations behavior is sufficiently constrained that conscientiousness is literally forced to fall into a narrow range. The time clock in manufacturing is a prototypical example of such a situational constraint.

The role of self-discipline seems to be especially important in the school years. Modern society educates its young using a form of instruction, formal schooling, that

depends upon the student's accepting the idea of delayed gratification, for students are asked to trade present fun for rather nebulous future gains. How well students meet this challenge will determine, in part, where they stand on the Gc scale when they graduate. Two small, but important, studies in social psychology have shown how important the relationship between self-discipline and success is.

The first study was conducted by a research group at Columbia University.[60] In the initial phase of their study pre-school children were offered a choice between two rewards that varied in value. The catch was that the children could either have the lesser reward immediately, or they could have the more valued one if they waited for a few minutes. (That is an eternity to a four-year-old.) Some fifteen years later the researchers obtained the SAT scores that the children had received upon their applying to college. There was a correlation of about .4 between the time the children had been able to wait for the desired reward, as toddlers, and their SAT scores as adolescents.

Duckworth and Seligman[61] made the same point in a study of self-discipline in middle-schoolers. The children were measured on academic achievement, intelligence, and a variety of self-discipline measures at the beginning of the academic year. One measure struck me as particularly ingenious. Students were offered a choice between \$1.00 during the testing session or a promise that the experimenter would give them \$2.00 the following week. This task was accompanied by several other questions in which students rated their choices in hypothetical situations where they could either take an immediate reward or wait for a delayed reward. The measures of self-discipline turned out to be better predictors for both grades and final test scores than measures of intelligence. The relative value is somewhat suspect, as the study participants were students in a selective "magnet"

58 Goff & Ackerman, 1992; Chomorro-Premuzic, Furnham, & Ackerman, 2006.
59 Hunt, 1995b; Schmidt & Hunter, 1998.
60 Shoda, Mischel, & Peake, 1990.
61 Duckworth & Seligman, 2005.

school, so there was probably a limited range of intelligence. However, the basic principle remains the same: self-discipline counts.

These two studies were laboratory demonstrations, using selected and probably rather talented participants. They need to be replicated. However, our confidence in their conclusion is strengthened because they complement many studies that have found positive relations between study habits, self-discipline, and academic performance.[62]

The moral to draw from this line of research is that you will not get smart if you do not try to get smart. But people will usually not try something unless they think that they have a reasonable chance of success. This brings us to another attitudinal variable, *mind-set*.

Carol Dweck and her associates have conducted a large number of studies on the relation between belief in one's own efficacy and what people actually accomplish.[63] Dweck's argument, which goes well beyond the study of intelligence, is that to a considerable degree success depends upon having a positive attitude toward chances of success and the self-discipline to get up and act, even when success is not guaranteed. As Henry Ford said, "It does not matter whether you say you can or you can't. Either way you're right."[64]

Ford was a bit optimistic. In our society a person with a tested IQ in the 70s or 80s is not a good candidate for graduate school in mathematics, no matter how hard he or she tries. Along with Dweck and Ackerman, I do believe that, for any fixed amount of intelligence, considerable variation in accomplishment can be associated with individual differences in self-discipline, intellectual engagement, and in an attitude of being willing to challenge oneself. It is not necessary to set up a competition to see whether intelligence or personality measures do the best job of predicting perfor-

mance. They are both important. Which one is more important will depend upon the particulars of the situation.

5.4.3. *Emotional Intelligence*

The study of intelligence has focused on individual differences in people's ability to think, when they are thinking coolly and rationally. We do not always act that way. What about individual differences in our ability to deal with emotionally charged issues? This question brings us to the topic of *emotional intelligence*.

The idea of emotional intelligence has generated a great deal of popular discussion, although it is not always clear just what is being discussed. Professional discussion has revolved around three points: the extent to which emotional intelligence ought to be regarded as an intelligence rather than a personality trait; the extent to which emotional intelligence is different from other, better-researched personality and intelligence traits; and the extent to which measures of emotional intelligence are useful predictors of achievement in cognitive tasks, over and above conventional measures of intelligence.

There is a good case for the existence of emotional intelligence.[65] Intelligence is defined as the ability to process information. Verbal intelligence refers to the ability to process verbal information, visual-spatial intelligence to the ability to process spatial and visual information, and so forth. There is a class of information that, loosely, can be referred to as emotional information. This includes internal cues about one's own emotions and observations of the behavior of others, which provide clues about their emotions. Dealing with emotional information is as much a cognitive activity as dealing with verbal material.

Before investigating emotional intelligence, we have to decide how it is to be measured. By far the most common measure is a behavioral inventory, in which people are

---

62 Credé & Kuncel, 2008.

63 Dweck, 2006.

64 Sign posted at the Henry Ford Museum, Dearborn, Michigan.

65 Mayer, Salovey, & Caruso, 2004; Salovey & Mayer, 1990; Salovey & Grewal, 2005.

either asked to describe themselves or asked how they would act in a hypothetical situation. A second, more expensive method of assessment is to determine the accuracy with which people can identify emotional displays or perform some emotion-laden task. For example, an examinee might be asked to identify the emotion displayed by a person in a photograph or video display, or to list physiological signs known to be associated with different emotions.

Self-descriptions do not fare too well as measurements, for they are contaminated by respondents' tendency to exaggerate their good qualities. This, in itself, is a confounding individual trait, for there are marked individual differences in the extent to which people bias their self-descriptions toward what they perceive as socially desirable ones. In the broad sense this is not surprising. Shakespeare said as much some years ago.[66] Even if we disregard a tendency to self-glorification, there is no reason to believe that people are able to accurately report their strength in assessing and controlling emotions, relative to other people. Doing so would require considerable insight both into one's own emotional intelligence and into the emotional intelligence of one's acquaintances. Self-reports of talents are not as objective as test scores.[67]

Behavioral measures of emotional intelligence are technically better measures than self-reports and have a firmer logical basis. Such measures of emotional intelligence are only modestly correlated with conventional measures of cognitive intelligence. This is evidence that we are indeed dealing with two separate abilities.

Further evidence comes from the neurosciences. Following certain types of brain injury patients display greatly reduced ranges of emotion. In other clinical situations the affected person will fail to discriminate emotions in others. Individuals who have received injuries in those areas of the brain that control emotion may display problems in interpersonal adjustment, but have no deficit in abstract cognitive performance.[68]

There is no contention that the brain mechanisms for dealing with "hot" and "cold" cognition are entirely separate. All that needs to be shown is that they are somewhat different. We now know that the perception and activation of emotion are both associated with the limbic system, especially the amygdala, and the ventromedial prefrontal cortex.[69] This contrasts with findings on the neural correlates of intelligence, which indicate heavy involvement of the lateral prefrontal cortex and the anterior parietal cortex in cognitive activities.[70]

The combination of the neuroscientific and correlational evidence makes a convincing case that there is such a thing as emotional intelligence, and that it is not the same as cognitive intelligence, although there is a small correlation between the two. A practical question remains. Does emotional intelligence predict academic and workplace performance as well, better, or in addition to measures of general (cognitive) intelligence?

Here there seems to be a great deal of "sound and fury" but, at this time (2010), rather little reliable evidence.

In his popular book on the topic Goleman[71] asserted that emotional intelligence is a much more important determinant of behavior than cognitive intelligence. He made his case largely by anecdote and informal reports. There are a number of studies showing that emotional intelligence, if measured alone, correlates with desirable outcomes in life. The key question, though, is whether measures of emotional intelligence can predict important behaviors, *beyond those that can be predicted by conventional intelligence and personality measures*. Few such studies have been reported,

66 Edwards (1959) discusses the issue of social desirability. As for Shakespeare, in *King Henry V* the king predicts that veterans of the battle of Agincourt would recount "with advantage" their heroic deeds.

67 Brody, 2004.

68 Bar-On et al., 2003.

69 Damasio, 1994, 1998.

70 Jung & Haier, 2007.

71 Goleman, 1995.

and those that have appeared have received sharp criticism.[72]

Despite the present record, though, I would not dismiss the potential contribution that emotional intelligence may make to the study of intelligence. I suggest that these contributions will be greatest when we examine "will do" rather than "can do" performance, over a fairly long period of time, and when the performance being evaluated requires interpersonal interaction, in face-to-face situations. A salesperson taking orders in a telephone call center for a ready-made clothing store does not have to have high emotional intelligence; a salesperson in an expensive clothing boutique does.

5.5. Closing Comments on Models to Expand Beyond Psychometric Intelligence

It is unlikely that dissatisfaction with conventional tests and testing will go away. While the critics have made some good points about the shortcomings of modern testing, they have not come up with good alternatives. If we are going to develop a scientific understanding of any topic, including human intelligence, there has to be some way of measuring what we are studying. Any claim that intelligence, as currently measured, is not important simply flies in the face of the facts. However, progress depends upon going beyond the known.

Consider another of Gardner's complaints about modern psychometric theory:

> Frankly I find it difficult to find a publicly-discussable reason why researchers should devote their energies to yet one more study of the role of 'g' in arenas ranging from job performance to longevity or yet one more effort to document racial or ethnic differences in intelligence.
>
> Gardner, 2006, p. 300

This is a pugnaciously worded claim that psychometric research is spinning its wheels. While I would not be as strong as Gardner

in making such a complaint, a great deal of current work is highly repetitive. The field could use a paradigm shift. I do not see how this can come about without the development of new methods of measurement. Where are we in this endeavor?

Instead of standing on the faces of those who went before, as psychologists are wont to do, let us stand on their shoulders. Any new theory of intelligence will have to deal with the facts established by present psychometric findings. General intelligence, g as measured by conventional testing, exists, and is a trait associated with accomplishment (or lack of it) in virtually all aspects of our society, not just in scholastic endeavors.

There are two acceptable models for the psychometric data: the three-stratum model and the g-VPR model, both described in the previous chapter. New models should build on the insights contained in these two approaches. Which one a new theorist should choose to emphasize depends to a great extent on what that theorist wants to accomplish.

If the goal of the new theory is to explain how intelligence functions in society, as Ackerman and his colleagues wish to do, the three-stratum theory is a good starting point. If the goal is to probe more deeply into the processes of intelligence, especially to the point of establishing the biological basis for individual differences in cognitive power, the g-VPR model may be the best starting point. I elaborate on this idea in the next chapter. In either case there has to be a starting point.

Attempting to develop theory without considering history is simply not a good idea. Of the three "new intelligences" reviewed here I believe that Gardner has disregarded the historical record, to the considerable detriment of his ideas. Sternberg has built on previous work. Two of his ideas, the need to study tacit knowledge and the need to incorporate research on creativity into research on intelligence, are clearly a step forward. Ackerman and his colleagues have built on previous research findings. Their work points a way toward a better understanding of intelligence in everyday life.

---

72 Brody, 2004; Matthews, Zeidner, & Roberts, 2005.

While these new theorists have not produced any revolutionary new paradigms, they have outlined an agenda for the future. It turns out that it can be summarized by an e-mail message that I received just as I finished writing this chapter. The message, which was intended as a joke, contrasted examinations in engineering and psychology.

The question for psychology was:

Based on your knowledge of their works, evaluate the emotional stability, degree of adjustment, and repressed frustrations of the following: Alexander of Aphrodisias, Ramses II, Gregory of Nicia, Hammurabi. Support your evaluation with quotations from each man's work, making appropriate references. It is not necessary to translate.

The question for engineering was:

The disassembled parts of a high-powered rifle have been placed on your desk. You will also find an instruction manual, printed in Swahili. In ten minutes a hungry Bengal tiger will enter the room. Take whatever action you feel appropriate. Be prepared to justify your decision.

Leaving aside the humor, these questions illustrate some important principles for the design of new assessment methods.

The question about psychology is humorous because answering it requires retrieving and rearranging knowledge. The task itself, writing a report, is a natural one. Doing so requires the exercise of important cognitive skills that, by their nature, take time to execute. Such skills cannot be evaluated within the testing paradigm. Nevertheless, they are very important aspects of cognitive competence.

What about the engineering question? Given proper training, assembling a rifle is not difficult. Soldiers and marines in modern armies all learn to do this. During learning the trick is to be able to visualize how the various parts should be moved to fit together. This is an exercise in visual rotation, the R dimension in the g-VPR model and the second-order Gv trait in the three-stratum model.

What we have here is a test of domain knowledge, Gk in Ackerman's expositions, and of visual-spatial skills.

The problem is the tiger, not the rifle. The task must be done in a hurry (*upesi* in Swahili). Interfering thoughts of tigers must be suppressed. The examinee has to manage his or her emotions in a way that facilitates the cognitive task rather than paralyzing it.

A similar problem occurs during knowledge acquisition. Military boot camp, where you learn to assemble a rifle, is (intentionally) an emotional experience. Learning is possible only if motivation can be maintained and emotions can be suppressed. In boot camp the emotions to be suppressed may be fear and confusion. In school and the workplace different emotions are involved (boredom? self-consciousness?), but the point is the same. Understanding the development of intelligence as knowledge requires an understanding of how intelligence interacts with motivation, personality, and situational constraints to produce understanding.

The present attempts to expand intelligence only scratch the surface of these issues. Too much effort has been spent trying to claim revolutionary new advances or, even more destructively, setting up oppositions between cognitive abilities, personality characteristics, and environmental variables. Past cognitive abilities, personality characteristics, and interests interact to increase intelligence. Progress depends on our developing an agenda for research that will describe the interaction.

CHAPTER 6

The Mechanics of Intelligence

I believe I have an unfair edge over most of my colleagues right now – my mind works better than my mouth does.

> U.S. Senator Tim Johnson, from a speech in Sioux Falls, South Dakota, announcing his intention to return to the Senate following a brain hemorrhage that left his speech impaired, August 28, 2007

Psychometric theories use what Sternberg has called a geometric analogy for intelligence; people are seen as varying along dimensions of intelligence in much the same way that they vary along the dimensions of height and weight.[1] Different theories identify different dimensions, but the geometric analogy is maintained. This is a useful way of summarizing variations in intelligence across populations, but it has a serious shortcoming. The geometric analogy does not explain the processes that make up thinking.

To see what this means, imagine two individuals, Ignatz and Horatio. We first determine their psychometric intelligence, in terms of the g-VPR model, and then ask them to attack the following two problems. The first problem makes use of the English rules that permit *center embedding*, putting one relative clause inside another. Ignatz and Horatio are presented with sentences of the form

> *The rat ate the cheese*
> *The rat the cat chased ate the cheese*
> *The rat the cat the dog scared chased ate*
> * the cheese*
> *The rat the cat the dog the man owned*
> * scared chased ate the cheese.*
> *And so on*

and we determine at what point each person finds the sentence incomprehensible.

The second problem is one of those (in)famous mathematics word problems:

> *The distance between Seattle and San Francisco is approximately 750 miles by air. If an aircraft leaves San Francisco at 9 a.m. and travels toward Seattle at 500 miles per hour at an altitude of 37,000 feet, while at the same time an aircraft leaves Seattle and travels to San Francisco at*

---

1 Sternberg, 1990.

550 miles per hour at an altitude of 34,000 feet, when will they pass by each other, and how far is this point from Seattle?

To complete the example, assume that we had conducted an experiment, not involving Ignatz and Horatio, in which problems like these were included in a large psychometric study using the tests covered by the *g*-VPR model. If we knew Ignatz's and Horatio's scores on the *g*-VPR dimensions, we could determine the probability that each of them would correctly solve the two problems. We could not go beyond this because the psychometric approach does not provide models of the problem-solving process. Psychometrics does not tell us what the elementary steps are in the problem-solving process, or how individual differences in the ability to execute these steps translate into individual differences in problem-solving ability, including the ability to take intelligence tests. To go further we have to look at another branch of psychology: cognition.

6.1. The Cognitive Psychology Approach

Suppose that we were to ask a modern cognitive psychologist to explain Ignatz's and Horatio's problem-solving behavior. The cognitive psychologist would want to look at the requirements of the problem-solving task. The psychologist would first observe that Ignatz and Horatio would have to be able to retrieve word meanings. This, in itself, is not a trivial task. Then there is more. In order to untangle center-embedded sentences a person has to have some way of storing information about a noun phrase until it can be connected to its verb. To understand

The rat the cat chased ate the cheese

Ignatz and Horatio would have to have some way of temporarily storing the phrase *the rat*, processing *the cat chased*, attaching the result of the processing to *the rat* (i.e., the particular rat that the cat chased), and connecting the modified idea to the verb

phrase *ate the cheese*. The cognitive psychologist would want to know what temporary storage capacities Ignatz and Horatio had for holding unresolved noun phrases, and whether they could organize that storage so that the noun phrases would be available when their verbs were encountered.

Turning to the mathematics word problem, the cognitive psychologist would first observe that Ignatz and Horatio have to retrieve word meanings, and have sufficient temporary storage space in memory so that they can analyze the meanings of the sentences. However, the passage does not contain deeply center-embedded sentences, so sentence comprehension itself would not present a challenge to their capacity for temporary memory storage. There would be another challenge.

Using information extracted from the sentences, Ignatz and Horatio would have to develop an *internal representation* of the problem. This could either be in the form of equations or in the form of a "picture in the head." The cognitive psychologist would probably remark that both representations require internal storage of information, but differ in the kinds of information stored. A representation in terms of equations is a symbolic representation that at least approximates syntactical analysis. A maplike representation requires a visual-spatial memory store. The cognitive psychologist would also note that the problem requires answering two questions, the time the two aircraft meet and the distance from Seattle. The problem solver has to set up a goal-subgoal structure to decide which problem to attack first, work on that problem, and then switch to the second problem. The cognitive psychologist would like to have an estimate of how many goals and subgoals Ignatz and Horatio can keep track of, and how long it takes them to switch from working on one goal to working on another.

Stepping back from the particulars of the two problems, cognitive psychologists offer explanations of behavior in terms of *elementary cognitive tasks* (ECTs), such as retrieving the meaning of a letter or word, holding a piece of information in temporary storage, and switching attention from one cognitive task to another. Information-processing theories of intelligence attempt to relate individual differences in intelligence, *in the broad sense of the ability to function in the world*, to individual differences in the execution of elementary cognitive tasks.

The cognitive psychologist stresses that such explanations are bound to be incomplete, because problem-solving ability will be determined both by the information the person has (knowledge) and how well he or she can manipulate information, in the abstract. An information-processing model addresses only the second question. Incomplete as it is, it is an important question because information-processing capacities stand somewhere between psychometric models of intelligence and brain-based explanations of intelligence.

To see this, return to the example of the center-embedded sentence. Knowing where Ignatz stands in the geographic space defined by the *g*-VPR model tells us the probability that he will be able to understand a sentence with, say, three levels of embedding. Speculating a bit, based on the discussion of the brain to be presented in the next chapter, we might observe that when Ignatz tries to understand a center-embedded sentence the frontal, anterior parietal, and left temporal parts of his brain show heightened activity. Horatio might be located at a different point in the *g*-VPR space and have a different probability of understanding the sentence, and while trying to understand the sentence Horatio might show different levels of activation than Ignatz does. It is useful, even necessary, to have an explanation that stands somewhere between the psychometric and brain-based explanations, by explaining in functional terms how Ignatz and Horatio are limited by their information processing abilities.

6.1.1. *An Historical Note*

The idea that individual differences in cognitive power are partially due to underlying differences in the ability to perform elementary cognitive tasks is not new. In the mid nineteenth century Galton measured the speed with which people could perform simple tasks, such as making a simple movement in response to an auditory or visual signal, and attempted to find a correlation between reaction time and occupational status. The results were not impressive, so he apparently dropped this line of investigation. In 1901 Clark Wissler, a graduate student working under the supervision of James McK. Cattell, attempted to find a relation between tasks similar to those Galton had used and the grades of Columbia University students. This work was also considered to be unsuccessful, and for many years the "revealed wisdom" was that there is no correlation between intelligence and performance on measures of information processing.[2]

In retrospect the conclusion was premature. Galton and Wissler both expected to find very strong relationships between performance on elementary cognitive tasks (ECTs) and complex thought. Today we know that the relations are there, but that they are moderate. Both Galton's and Wissler's techniques for measuring reaction times were not close to modern standards. Probably the biggest mistake they made was that they did not take into consideration variation in the execution of an ECT within the individual. They would, for instance, determine a person's reaction time by averaging three or four attempts to execute the task, whereas today upward of a dozen measurements would be taken. (Even today cognitive psychologists sometimes criticize researchers interested in intelligence for basing their measurements on too few trials.) Wissler's study had low statistical power, which means that it was capable of detecting only large relationships. All in all, by today's standards the research was so poorly done as to be virtually useless.[3]

The deficiencies in the research were not appreciated at the time, so the perceived failure of the Galton–Wissler approach resulted in a virtual cessation of interest

2   Jensen, 2006, pp. 5–7.
3   Deary, 1994.

in individual differences in elementary cognitive tasks. Psychometric studies of intelligence flourished, and, especially after the mid-1950s, the study of information-processing models, under the title *cognitive psychology*, became the dominant method for studying human thought, without regard for individual differences. These fields were pursued as separate endeavors, however, involving different investigators and publication in different journals. There were a few calls for a rapprochement, notably in a paper by the educational psychologist Lee Cronbach in 1957.[4] However, very little was actually done until 1973, when my colleagues Nancy Frost and Clifford Lunneborg and I published a series of studies on the information-processing correlates of verbal and mathematical reasoning.[5] This work was followed by a blizzard of studies, certainly not limited to my laboratory.

6.1.2. *Modern Information-Processing Models*

In order to understand the attempts to connect information-processing models of thought to intelligence we must understand modern theories of cognition as information processing. These theories owe a great deal to concepts developed for designing digital computing systems. However, the modern view in no way implies that the digital computer can be used as a model of the mind. Rather, the contention is that any computation, including thought, has to rely on certain elementary actions, and that studying performance on the individual actions is a useful way to proceed when studying cognition.

Any computing device much more complicated than a light switch has to be able to do three things: sense the environment (perception), classify the environment into states relevant to the device (categorization), and relate these classifications to previously stored information (memory retrieval). The result of these computations is an *internal representation* of the current situation as interpreted in the light of memory of past situations. The internal representation may then be used to select a response (decision making). If the computing device operates continuously, in a dynamic, changing environment, it has to be able to maintain a record of the situations it has encountered (as interpreted), the responses that have been made, and the results of the responses. Therefore, we have to be concerned with the storage and retrieval of information in long-term memory, in a way that ensures its accessibility when needed.

Although one can conceive of a robot mind that executed each of the four tasks, perception through decision making, in serial order, in the human brain they are interleaved, with a great deal of feedback between them. A model of how this exchange of information takes place is called a *cognitive architecture*. Psychologists who study human information processing have converged on some version of the *Blackboard* model of cognitive architecture.[6] A version of this model is shown in Figure 6.1. The components of the model are as follows:

1. Information from the environment is sensed, and then classified into progressively higher-order categories, through arousal of related information in long-term memory. Long-term memory is not thought of as a static storage process, as is the case in computer systems. Items in long-term memory exist in various states of activation, depending upon how frequently and how recently they and related pieces of information have been attended to. Therefore, the interpretation of a percept will be influenced by the context in which it occurs.

2. The information from the environment, together with relevant information retrieved from long-term memory, is placed in *working memory*, a term

---

4 Cronbach, 1957.
5 Hunt, Frost, & Lunneborg, 1973.

6 Anderson, 1996; Hunt & Lansman, 1986; Meyer & Kieras, 1997; Newell, 1990. These references summarize the ideas that the various authors had put forward over a number of years. I certainly do not claim priority.

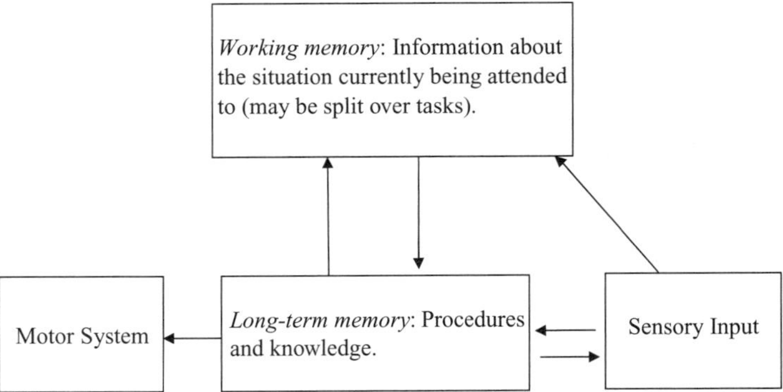

Figure 6.1. The blackboard model of cognition. Information about the current situation is held in a temporary working memory store. Sensory input enters working memory if attention is being directed to the appropriate input channel. Information on the blackboard and from the sensory input channel activates problem-solving procedures that have been stored in long-term memory. These place further information in working memory. Sensory information may also enter long-term memory directly, thus lowering the threshold required to activate some problem-solving procedures or, in some cases, initiating an action without placing information on the blackboard.

introduced by the British psychologist Alan Baddeley,[7] and widely accepted today. There further processing results in an *internal representation* of the current situation, as interpreted. The internal representation may include interpretations in contexts, and the identification of goals and subgoals in problem-solving. In totality, the processes acting on the internal representation are referred to as *executive processes*, whose role is to update the internal representation and establish priorities for action. One of the most important subsets of the executive processes are the *attentional processes* that highlight some pieces of information and suppress others.

3. Organizing information in this way enables a person to appear to be dealing with two or more tasks simultaneously – for example, talking while driving an automobile. The impression of simultaneity is something of an illusion, as both tasks will compete for space in working memory and for attention. When two tasks are done together, therefore, close examination almost always shows that one or both of the tasks are performed less well than they would be if performed alone.

4. Working memory acts as a "blackboard" that broadcasts information into long-term memory. Alternatively, you can think of long-term memory processes as actively watching working memory to see if their cue has been called, rather like actors at a stage production.

5. The storage section of working memory is thought of as being divided into modality-specific sections for linguistic, auditory-nonlinguistic, and spatial/visual information. There is no implication that working memory is located at a single place in the brain. It is a system resulting from the integration of processing at several different locations.

6. Information in working memory, as interpreted, is consolidated in long-term memory. This takes time. Therefore, the, probability that a piece of information in working memory will be stored

7 Baddeley, 1986.

in long-term memory is partially determined by the time it remains in working memory. Items briefly attended to are not likely to be remembered.

7. From time to time the information in working memory will initiate a process that calls for a motor response – speaking or making a physical movement. While many information-processing psychologists have been quite concerned with response production,[8] psychologists interested in intelligence have done rather little work on this aspect of cognition.

Cognitive psychologists are concerned with the typical characteristics of each of the processes in the cognitive architecture. Psychologists interested in intelligence want to know how individual differences in these characteristics are related to individual differences in intelligence, as measured by psychometric models. Using the g-VPR model as a guide, we will first look at two aspects of the architecture that appear to be related to individual differences in general reasoning, and then examine specialized processes related to verbal and visual-spatial reasoning.

6.2. The Speed of Mental Processing

The blackboard model depicts thinking as the shuttling of attention from one piece of information to another. To illustrate this, consider the common task of determining whether a view of a scene matches a description. The task could be as simple as answering the question *Are my car keys on the dining room table?* The listener must form an internal representation of the linguistic statement, form an internal representation of a visual scene, and compare the two. Different people use different strategies for comparing sentences to pictures,[9] but no matter which strategy they use, they have to shift back and forth from processing one piece of information to another.

All this has to happen quickly enough that the thinker can keep up with the environment. If a speaker is speaking at a normal conversational tempo, listeners are expected to keep up. See the example and elaboration in panel 6.1.

There is also an internal demand for speed in mental processing. Competing lines of thought vie for the limited storage space in working memory, and the competition is fierce. Have you ever been introduced to someone, immediately embarked on a conversation, and then realized that you did not know the person's name, even though the two of you had just been introduced? If information in working memory is usurped by another task, the original contents of working memory may be lost before it can be moved to long-term memory.

These considerations show why speed of processing should be important in thought. But is there a single speed of processing, or different speeds for different ECTs?

The reason for believing in processing speed as a pervasive trait is that all mental actions depend on neural processing. If people differ in the effectiveness of processing speed at the neural level, then there should be pervasive individual differences in processing speed no matter what the task.[10] Accordingly, speed of processing should be positively correlated with measures of g, the general reasoning factor. In order to test this hypothesis we have to find a way of measuring mental processing speed.

6.2.1. *Donders's Paradigm as a Way of Measuring the Speed of Mental Processing*

Elementary cognitive processes cannot be measured in isolation. Even the simplest tasks will require multiple mental steps, and may mix cognitive and noncognitive processes. In the nineteenth century Galton asked people to strike a bag upon a signal. He took the time interval between

---

8 For instance, Meyer & Kieras, 1997.
9 MacLeod, Hunt, & Mathews, 1978.

10 Jensen (2006) has developed this argument at considerable length.

Panel 6.1. Intelligence and the Speed of Language Comprehension

The speed with which people can comprehend simple speech is often taken as an indicator of intelligence. I will illustrate with an anecdote and an actual demonstration.

The anecdote is based on an incident in my laboratory. Most of my laboratory research effort at that time was devoted to studying individual differences in cognition in young adults, usually college students. However, one graduate student was interested in mentally disabled children. In order to communicate with the participants in her studies she learned to…talk…very…slowly. When she reported her results to her fellow graduate students she…drove… them…up…the…wall.

Recall Baddeley's three-minute test of reasoning, described in Chapter 2.* People were shown a picture and a statement, and asked if the picture described the statement. Two examples, one easy and one hard, are

Is the A after the B?   *AB*
Is the B not before the A?   *BA*

The score on this test was the number of items that could be answered in three minutes. It had a .59 correlation with scores on a formal intelligence test used to screen recruits in the British army. Tasks that require coordination of linguistic statements and visual information emerge as a way of evaluating *g*.

* Baddeley, 1968.

---

the signal and contact with the bag as a measure of speed of processing. A modern cognitive psychologist would point out that this reasoning is flawed. The interval between the signal and the strike contains many subprocesses: detecting that a signal has been received, interpreting it, selecting a response, and making the movement. The processes of detecting and interpreting the signal and constructing the response are cognitive acts, but hand movement is at best semicognitive, as the time taken to move the hand would depend on properties of the muscular-skeletal system as well as the nervous system. Someone with arthritis would strike a bag very slowly, but arthritis does not affect cognition. Some way has to be found to isolate each of the several cognitive actions that lie behind an overt response.

Franciscus Donders, a nineteenth-century Dutch physiologist, proposed a solution to this problem. Suppose that a task can be fractionated into a sequence of k steps that must be conducted in sequence. Suppose further that you can construct a second task that requires all the steps of the first task, and an additional $k+1^{st}$ step that has to be inserted somewhere in the series of steps required by the first task. The difference between the time required to execute the first task and the time required to execute the second task will be a measure of the time required to complete the inserted step. That is, if we let $R(x)$ be the time required to complete process x, then

$$R(inserted\ process) = R(task\ with\ insertion)$$
$$- R(original\ task). \quad (6.1)$$

This brief explanation does not really do justice to Donders's sophisticated ideas, but it is close enough for present purposes.

Donders's approach is based on three assumptions: that the processes involved must be executed in sequence, that for any pair of adjacent processes in the sequence the first process is not initiated until the second is completed, and that the speed with which a process is completed is independent of the speed with which any other process is completed. Collectively these conditions are referred to as the *independent serial processing* assumptions. The literature in cognitive psychology contains many discussions of how one can ensure that independent serial processing has occurred, for the issue is subtler than you might think.

Donders's logic applies only to situations in which the entire task is completed successfully. The effect of an error in any one of the processes is not defined. Therefore, a careful investigator should restrict his or her analyses to trials on which a correct response is made.

Unfortunately, researchers interested in intelligence have not always paid as much attention as they should either to the need to prove that the independent serial processing assumptions apply to their tasks, or to restricting their analyses to correct trials. In spite of these limitations, Donders's paradigm has proven to be useful. Panel 6.2 provides two examples of how Donders's method of subtraction has been used to measure the time required to access information in long-term memory. Panel 6.3 provides an example of how it can be used to measure the time needed to access information in working memory.

Experimental paradigms have also been designed to measure the speed with which a person can make an elementary decision, without reference to memory. Such studies are called *choice reaction time* (CRT) tasks. At the beginning of the experiment the participant is told that one of a small number of directly perceivable stimuli may occur. For instance, the participant might be told that either a red or a green light could be presented. The participant's task is to identify, as quickly as possible, which of the possible stimuli has actually been presented.

Choice reaction tasks differ in the number of possible stimuli that might be presented. Discriminating between red and green lights is an example of a *two-choice reaction time task*, denoted 2CRT. In a more complicated experiment, if the choice were to be among red, green, yellow, and blue lights, the task would be a 4CRT task. In practice experiments seldom go beyond the 8CRT task.

The 2CRT condition represents the time required to make a binary decision. On logical grounds, this should be central to cognition. However, the response time in the 2CRT condition will also include the time required to make the response. This contaminates cognitive and noncognitive processes. Suppose that an examinee had broken a finger prior to the experiment. Such a person would be slow pressing a button, and hence have a long reaction time. It would hardly be fair to infer that someone's brain was working slowly because of a broken finger.

To avoid such problem we can measure the manner in which choice reaction times increase with the number of choices. One such analysis is described in panel 6.4. As the panel explains, an analysis of how reaction time changes as the number of choices is increased can provide an estimate of cognitive processing speed, independent of motor processes.

6.2.2. *Identification Paradigms*

Donders's approach depends upon the assumptions of strict serial processing and independence of processes from each other. An alternative approach is to construct a task that is believed to be primarily responsive to a particular cognitive process, and use it as a measure of the time required for that process, ignoring the fact that other processes may also influence the measure.

One such paradigm is the *lexical identification* task, which is an attempt to measure the time required to retrieve information from long-term memory. An experimental participant decides that a letter string either does or does not constitute a common word, for example, MALEC or CAMEL. Reaction time (RT) is measured. A generalization of this task is the *semantic identification* task. In semantic identification an object name and a category name are presented, for example, CAMEL ANIMAL. The participant indicates whether or not the object named is a member of the category. In such tasks the reaction time reflects both retrieval of information from long-term memory and the motor processes involved

Panel 6.2. Using Donders's Logic to Measure Access to Long-term Memory

The following two examples show how Donders's paradigm can be used to measure the speed of access to long-term memory.

Example 1. Category identification

Task 1. The examinee sits in front of a computer monitor. A program presents single digits on a screen. The examinee is to depress the space bar as soon as a digit is presented.

Task 2. The procedure is identical, except that the space bar is to be depressed only if an odd digit is presented.

The first task can be conceptualized as

(1) Number presented. (2) Recognize number. (3) Press space bar. Let the time required to do this be RT(1).

The second task can be conceptualized as

(1) Number presented. (2) Recognize number. (3) Classify number and select response. (4) Press space bar if appropriate. Let the time required to do this be RT(2).

Applying Donders's logic, the time required to make a simple decision is

$$\text{Time to classify stimulus and select}$$
$$\text{response} = \text{RT}(2) - \text{RT}(1).$$

Example 2. Name identification and physical identification

This task was originally developed by Michael Posner and his colleagues at the University of Oregon.* Variants of it have been used widely in studies in cognitive psychology.

The examinee is shown two letters on a computer screen and is asked to indicate, as rapidly as possible, whether or not the two letters are identical. Possible letter pairs are

A A

A B

A a.

The answer for these three pairs depends upon what is meant by "identical." Does this mean that they are *physically identical*, or does it mean that they *name the same letter*? For the first pair the answer is "yes" in each case, for physically identical objects must have the same name. For the second pair the answer is "no." For the third pair, A a, the answer depends upon the instructions; the letters are physically different but refer to the same letter of the alphabet.

Now suppose that identification takes place in the following steps.

Physically identical (PI) steps

P1. Determine whether the two letters are physically identical.

P2. If they are, respond "yes"; otherwise respond "no."

Name identical (NI) steps

N1. Determine whether the two letters are physically identical.

N2. If they are, respond "yes"; otherwise go to step N3.

N3. Retrieve letter names.

N4. Determine whether the two letters have the same name.

N5. If they do, respond "yes"; otherwise respond "no."

In order to perform under name-identical instructions, the observer has to retrieve the names of letter forms, an act involving retrieval of information from long-term memory. This takes time. College students take about eighty milliseconds longer to execute the identification task under the NI than under the PI condition. Thus eighty milliseconds can be taken as a rough estimate of the time required to access highly overlearned information in long-term memory.

The eighty milliseconds is the average identification time taken by college students in general. If college students are split into two groups, one with high verbal comprehension test scores and one with low test scores, students in the high test score group take about sixty milliseconds to deal with the NI condition, compared to the CI condition, and students in the low test score group take about ninety milliseconds.[†]

---

[*] Posner et al., 1969.
[†] Hunt, Frost, & Lunneborg, 1973; Hunt, Lunneborg, & Lewis, 1975.

Panel 6.3. The Short-term Memory Scanning Task

The short-term memory scanning task was developed in the 1960s by Saul Sternberg, then a researcher at the (now disbanded) Bell Laboratories of the American Telephone and Telegraph Company.[*] Since then the paradigm has been widely used by many researchers. The procedure is as follows:

> *A memory set* of from one to six digits or letters is presented – for example, A Q X L.

> The memory set is removed and a probe item is presented – for example, T.

> The examinee indicates, by pressing a button, whether or not the probe was a member of the memory set. In this case the answer is NO.

> The procedure is then repeated, with a new memory set.

The scoring procedure illustrates the use of mathematical modeling. Let k be the number of items in the memory set, and let RT be the reaction time, that is, the time between the onset of the probe item and the point at which the examinee makes a response. We consider only correct trials. It is considered important to train participants until they make very few errors. Otherwise, individual differences in trading off speed and accuracy will influence the results. Unfortunately, this caution has not always been followed in research on intelligence. Empirically it has been found that after individuals have received enough training that they make errors on only about 5% of the trials, RT increases linearly with the number of items in the memory set:

$$RT = A + Bk,$$

where A and B are positive constants. The B parameter can be thought of as the increment in time required to scan the memory set when memory set size is increased by adding one item. This interpretation makes it a reasonable measure of the speed of access to information in short-term memory. The A parameter, by contrast, reflects all of the processes involved, including identifying the probe item and making the response.

Sternberg's analysis of memory scanning is a variant of Donders's method, because the estimate of the B parameter is sensitive to the successive differences in the times required for memory sets of one versus two, two versus three, and so forth.

---

[*] S. Sternberg, 1966.

Panel 6.4. Jensen's Choice Reaction Time Procedure

Arthur Jensen developed a choice reaction time procedure that is widely used in the study of individual differences.* The examinee is seated in front of a display that consists of (a) a bank of eight lights, with buttons immediately below them, and (b) a "home" button in the center of the display. Depending on the condition, the examinee is told that any one of two, four, six, or eight lights may be lit. When one of the lights comes on, the examinee lifts his or her finger from the home button and depresses the button under the light that has been lit.

This procedure yields two measures on each trial. The *decision time* is the interval between the time the light is illuminated and the time the examinee releases the home button. The *movement time* is the interval between the release of the home button and the depression of the button under the illuminated lamp. The idea behind measuring each interval is that the decision where to move is made before the examinee's hand is lifted. Therefore, decision time reflects the time required by the cognitive process of selecting a response. Movement time reflects a motor movement. Accordingly, decision time should be a better measurement of cognitive processing speed than movement time. The analysis assumes that the independent serial processing assumptions are true.

When people are asked to choose between k alternatives using an apparatus like Jensen's, *after an initial practice period*, their reaction time is a linear function of the logarithm of the number of choices,

$$RT(k) = A + B \, ln(k),$$

where A and B are positive real numbers. This is an interesting observation in itself, because it is the function that would describe the operation of a decision maker who was choosing between alternatives by making an optimally efficient sequence of binary choices between subsets of the alternatives. Therefore, B, the slope parameter, can be thought of as an estimate of the time it takes to decide which of two equally probable alternatives has occurred. The A parameter, by contrast, reflects general speed of processing, including movement time.

Both Sternberg's task and Jensen's task are based on Donders's reasoning. In each case the argument is that reaction times increase regularly with increases in the complexity of the decision process. The increase in time should be smaller for more intelligent people.

* Jensen, 2006. This reference summarizes over twenty-five years of research using the device.

---

in making a response. Because the reaction times obtained in identification tasks mix times for cognitive and motor processes, the times themselves are not easily interpretable. Somewhat surprisingly, though, the way these tasks are used avoids the interpretation process.

In cognitive psychology, without regard to individual differences, the typical experiment focuses on how experimental conditions change the reaction times in an identification task. For instance, one of the major uses of the lexical identification task is to study how observation of semantically related items changes the speed of identification of a target item. To take a frequently cited example, the word NURSE will be recognized faster if the immediately preceding word was DOCTOR than it will if it was BUTTER.

A similar logic applies to studies of individual differences. When we study the relation of elementary cognitive processes to intelligence, we are interested in the differences in reaction times between people who have been indexed by their scores on intelligence tests, or by some other measure of intelligence. The correlation coefficient is a measure of these differences; if people who have high intelligence scores are consistently faster in lexical identification tasks than people who have low scores, then this is evidence that at least one of the processes required for lexical or semantic identification is associated with intelligence. And this is the case. In the population of college students lexical identification RT has a correlation of $-.40$ with scores on tests of verbal intelligence.[11] The negative relation is expected because short reaction times are associated with high test scores. The magnitude of the correlation in a more heterogeneous population than college students would presumably be higher.

Nevertheless, it would be nice to obtain as direct a measure as possible of cognitive processing speed. To see this, consider some facts obtained from general experimental psychology. In the spirit of Donders, we can think of any cognitive process as consisting of the following steps:

Perceive the stimulus → Select a response

→ Make a response.

The middle step is what we normally think of as cognition; the first step reflects the sensory-perceptual apparatus, and the third step reflects motor processes.

In a modern information-processing study the participant reacts to information presented on a computer screen by pressing one of the keys on the keyboard. Studies in perception suggest that it takes from twenty to fifty milliseconds or less to detect a simple visual figure, depending on the illumination and the complexity of the surrounding visual field. It takes a healthy college student about 250 milliseconds to press a button indicating detection of a visual signal, in a situation in which the same button is to be pressed regardless of the identity of the stimulus. This condition minimizes the middle, cognitive step in the sequence. If a cognitive task is introduced, such as asking the student

to recognize whether or not CAMEL is a word, reaction time rises to 500–600 milliseconds. This means that of the roughly 550 milliseconds taken for the decision task somewhere between 250–300 milliseconds, about half the response time, will be taken up by perceptual and motor processes. The other half is taken up by cognitive processes. Therefore, the reaction time provides a measure of cognitive processing speed, albeit a contaminated one.

This analysis ignores an important issue. In general, the longer a person waits to make a response in a choice task, the more likely they are to make the correct choice. This is called the *speed-accuracy trade-off*. Different people adopt different criteria for accuracy; one person may be satisfied if his or her responses are correct on 95% of the trials, others may prefer 98%, a third may accept 92%. Studies of the speed-accuracy tradeoff have shown that above accuracy rates of 90% small differences in accuracy may be associated with substantial differences in reaction time. Therefore, if different participants adopt different criteria for acceptable accuracy another source of variation has been introduced, further confusing the interpretation of correlations between CRT and IQ scores.

6.2.3. *The Inspection Time Paradigm*

Most of the problems that arise in interpreting CRTs arise because a reaction time study lumps cognitive and motor processing together. These problems are avoided in the *inspection time* task. In the typical visual inspection time task two vertical lines are presented for a brief time, followed by a visual mask. The interval between the onset of the two lines and the onset of the mask is called the *inspection time*. Figure 6.2 illustrates the procedure. The participant then indicates whether the line on the right was longer than the one on the left or vice versa. The experimenter adjusts the inspection time until it is as short as it can be, while allowing the observer to maintain a fixed level of accuracy. This is usually set at 75% correct responding.

11 Palmer et al., 1985.

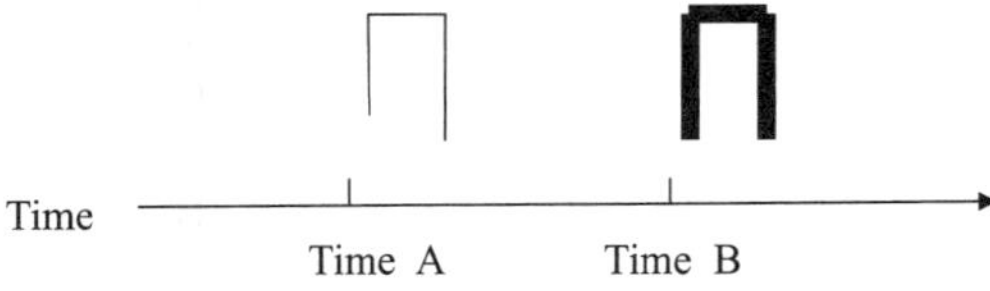

Figure 6.2. The inspection time paradigm. Two lines of unequal length are presented at time A, and displayed until time B. At time B the lines are replaced by a visual mask blanking out the stimulus. The observer then indicates which vertical line was longer. The time interval A-B is the inspection time. The experimenter adjusts the inspection time until the shortest time interval is found at which the observer can maintain a fixed level of accuracy, usually 75 to 80% correct.

Inspection times vary substantially, depending upon the apparatus, the transient illumination, and the age and intelligence of the participants. Some young adults can maintain accuracy at an inspection time of 30 milliseconds. Senior citizens may produce inspection times of 80 to 90 milliseconds. Within age groups and experimental conditions inspection times are negatively correlated with intelligence, that is, higher test scores are associated with lower reaction times. Correlations in the $-.3$ to $-.4$ range are typical. Various statistical corrections may raise this figure to $-.6$ to $-.7$

The inspection time paradigm avoids mixing cognitive process and motor responding. However, it does so at the expense of minimizing the cognitive processes involved, for the task is largely a perceptual one. Therefore, it is not surprising to find that when inspection time measures are included in an analysis of an intelligence test battery, the inspection time measures load on a "cognitive speediness" factor. This is a broad second-order factor in the three-stratum model. It has been suggested that if we broaden the study beyond analysis of results from young adults, inspection time might also indicate an ability to control attention.[12]

6.2.4. *The Relation between Processing Speed and Intelligence*

The correlations between intelligence test scores and various reaction and inspection time measures are typically in the $-.2$ to $-.4$ range, which is enough to show that there is a common core to the test scores and information-processing measures, but small enough to show that speed of mental processing and psychometric intelligence are not identical. If the correlations are corrected for various mediating effects, such as the restricted range of intelligence test scores found in university undergraduates, the correlations may climb to the $-.5$ to $-.7$ range, but the points about overlap and nonidentity remain.

This is reasonable. Early in the modern study of individual differences on information-processing tasks my colleagues Nancy Frost and Clifford Lunneborg and I pointed out that the study of individual differences in information processing is quite different from the study of psychometrically defined intelligence.[13] We saw the two as related, but not identical, enterprises. Therefore, we pointed out that the success of the endeavor would come from combining understandings of individual difference in intelligence, *conceptually defined*, from the two different perspectives of cognitive psychology and psychometric psychology.

The testing procedures required to evaluate elementary cognitive tasks are time-consuming and expensive. While there are a few laboratories where banks of computer-controlled test stations have been built, for the most part this research takes place using participant groups that range from a single individual to perhaps half a dozen people. Partly for this reason most of the research on individual differences in elementary cognitive tasks has been conducted using university undergraduates as participants.

The fact that so many studies are conducted on populations of young adults has led to contradictory results and some

12　Nettlebeck, 2001.

13　Hunt, Frost, & Lunneborg, 1973.

confusion in the literature. For instance, in a very well-done study of Spanish undergraduates, Roberto Colom and his colleagues found no reliable relationship between measures of information-processing speed and intelligence test scores. When they extended their study population to include high school students, a reliable relationship appeared. This study is notable because exactly the same procedures were used in each experiment.[14] An American experiment that contrasted information processing in university undergraduates and high-level mentally retarded patients found that both the evidence for a pervasive speed factor and the relation of that factor to intelligence test scores were much stronger in the mentally challenged group than in the university undergraduates.[15] In perhaps the largest study done to date, a Scottish representative survey of people from their late teenage years to their sixties found correlations between reaction times and performance on a complex arithmetic task in the −.3 to −.4 range.[16]

The potential size of the effects achieved by expanding the study of the information processing–intelligence relationship beyond the ubiquitous college population should not be underestimated. If we compare "fast" populations, such as college students, to "slower" populations, such as the elderly or mildly mentally retarded individuals, estimates of processing speed may vary by anywhere from 50% to a factor of five or more, depending upon the apparatus and parameter involved.[17]

There are also a number of other reasons for believing that current studies, done mostly on undergraduates, underestimate the strength of association between measures of speed of information processing and intelligence test scores. A few of them are discussed in panel 6.5.

What are we to make of the moderate but nontrivial relation between mental processing speed and psychometric measures of intelligence? Two extreme positions could be taken. One is that the various elementary cognitive tasks evaluate the speeds of different mental processes, each of which contributes to cognition. Under this view, for instance, the lexical identification task and the inspection time task are measuring different things. Therefore, each of the processes evaluated should make its own contribution to the prediction of performance on complex reasoning tasks, such as are present on intelligence tests. Another implication of this view is that any measure of processing speed that contains a substantial motor component should have markedly lower correlations with complex reasoning tasks than would measures associated largely with cognitive processes.

At the other extreme, it might be that all of the different information-processing measures reflect a fundamental speediness property of a person's nervous system. If this is the case, all the different information-processing measures would be regarded as measures of the same pervasive property and would have similar correlations with test scores.

The truth seems to lie somewhere in between. In general, overall measures of performance, such as the mean CRT in Jensen's paradigm, tend to have somewhat higher correlations with scores on intelligence tests and complex reasoning tasks than do derived measures of basic processing, such as the slope parameter, although the latter measures should, in theory, evaluate a specific cognitive process. In fact, the most important variable seems to be the total time required to complete the information-processing task. The longer the time required, the higher the correlation between performance on the task and on an intelligence test.[18] This is what would be expected on the assumption that all measures tap a single mental speed trait, for then

---

14 Colom et al., 2008. See particularly the contrast between the results of experiment 1 compared to experiments 2 and 3.
15 Detterman & Daniel, 1989.
16 Deary & Der, 2005.
17 Ibid.; Hunt, 1980, 1987; Salthouse, 1996.

18 Jensen, 2006.

Panel 6.5. Practical Limits that Obscure the Relation between Information-processing Speed and Intelligence Test Scores

The study of the role of mental-processing speed in intelligence is made difficult by some logistical restrictions.

When cognitive psychologists conduct reaction time experiments they almost always provide participants with a substantial number of practice trials. This is done to stabilize performance prior to measuring such parameters as semantic access or short-term memory scanning rates. The reason for doing so is that the cognitive psychologist wants to be sure that the procedure is measuring a stable process in each participant.

Psychologists studying individual differences need to have a large number of participants in order to obtain adequate statistical power for the analysis of correlations. This makes taking great care to obtain reliable measurements from each participant an expensive proposition. As a result, many studies of the relation between performance on elementary cognitive tasks and psychometric test scores are based on studies in which, by the standards of cognitive psychology, the participants simply did not have enough practice.

If the participants are trying to figure out how to use the testing apparatus at the time that measurements are being taken, an investigator could obtain a spuriously high correlation between the information-processing measure and an IQ score, because high-IQ individuals are quicker at finding out how to work the apparatus. Alternatively, the correlation might be spuriously decreased because individual performance on the information-processing measure will not have stabilized at the time of measure-ment. All we can say is that this feature of many experiments makes interpretation of the results confusing.

There is also a question of reliability. Psychometric tests of intelligence have internal consistency statistics (split-half reliabilities or Cronbach's α statistic) in the .80–.95 range. Reaction time (RT) measures typically have even higher analogous correlations, often in the .90–.95 range. Within a test session RT measures are highly reliable.

Things are quite different if we examine reliability across sessions. The correlation between equivalent measures of a conventional psychometric intelligence test, taken a few days apart, will typically fall in the .8–.9 range. Taken together with the internal consistency statistics, this shows that the trait being measured is quite stable over intervals of days or weeks. RT measures show much greater day-to-day variability. Test-rest correlations can drop to .6 at intervals of only one or two days.* Because the within-day reliability is much higher, the trait being measured must itself be variable from day to day. Such variability constrains the upper value of the correlation between an RT measure and a psycho-metrically measured trait. If we correct for this effect statistically, the estimated correlation between the traits measured by information-processing measures and intelligence test scores jumps from an observed .3–.4 to an estimated .6–.7.

It would be possible to conduct a study in which RT measures were taken over several days, and the trait common to them was correlated with psychometric test scores. Such a study would be fairly expensive and, as far as I know, has not been done.

*   Bittner et al., 1986.

the longer tasks would provide a better measure of individual differences in processing speed.

However, different tasks do have some specificity. For instance, lexical decision times correlate most highly with verbal intelligence measures, while inspection time measures correlate most highly with nonverbal tests. Nevertheless, the general trend is clear. General cognitive speediness is a reliable trait, and is certainly a part of what we mean by "intelligence."

Some critics of research on mental processing speed have attacked the idea that "it is good to be fast" on the grounds there are situations in which this is not true.[19] In fact, some societies distrust rapid responders, believing that the more intelligent individual is the one who stops to weigh alternatives before speaking.

This objection misses the point of the research. Studies of individual differences in processing speed are concerned with how rapidly a person can grasp a situation, given a fixed amount of information. Deciding to make an overt response is a separate action. Being a bit flippant, there is a difference between noticing the logical flaw in your father-in-law's political views and deciding to point out that flaw to him. These two separate acts of cognition both benefit from rapid thinking. Indeed, rapid thinking will probably help you suppress inappropriate or impolitic responses in many social settings. The assertion that there is an association between speed of information processing, measured by simple cognitive tasks, and the ability to reason in complex settings is not equivalent to saying that the intelligent individual necessarily has the fastest mouth in town.

6.3. Working Memory and General Intelligence

One of my colleagues once observed that since time is continuous the present just became the past. Therefore, perception is impossible; all psychology reduces to memory and imagination.[20] Leaving aside imagination, a great deal of our thinking does depend on memory.

Psychologists distinguish between two types of memory: immediate memory, which spans at most a few seconds, and long-term memory, in principle spanning the individual's lifetime, although retrieval becomes difficult as time passes. The Blackboard Model uses this distinction strongly. The blackboard is itself an immediate memory device, and is thought of as being a severely limited resource, while long-term memory is conceived of as being essentially limitless. We now want to take a closer look at the structure of the blackboard.

Battery-type intelligence tests, such as the WAIS, often contain separate subtests for short-term memory and long-term memory. Short-term memory is commonly evaluated by a *digit span* test. In a digit span test the examiner presents a randomly chosen series of three to eight digits, for example, "3, 9, 7, 4." The examinee's task is to echo the digits immediately after they have been presented. In the somewhat more challenging *backward digit span* task, the examinee must echo the digits in reverse order, "4, 7, 9, 3" in the example.

The forward digit span task is generally regarded as a test of a person's short-term storage capacity. Digit span tests typically have a loading of about .5 on the general factor of an intelligence test battery.[21] Backward digit span introduces a processing as well as a memory component; instead of "reading out" memory the examinee has to reverse the order in which information has been received. The backward digit span is more highly correlated with total test scores than the forward span. This suggests that we ought not regard the blackboard–immediate memory system as just a storage system. Nor shall we.

19 See, e.g., Sternberg, 1996.

20 Poltrock, 1977.
21 See Gignac, 2006, and O'Grady, 1983, for results on the WAIS, spanning more than twenty years.

When Alan Baddeley introduced the idea of working memory,[22] he pointed out that when people solve problems they have to hold key pieces of information readily at hand, even though they are not at the immediate focus of consciousness. In addition, information has to be transformed, mental representations have to be built, and attention has to be focused on information relevant to the task at hand, while irrelevant information must be suppressed. Baddeley's view of working memory, which is incorporated into the Blackboard Model, is that it is a mental workspace containing (a) modality-specific, passive memories (*slave memories*, in Baddeley's terminology) for small amounts of auditory and spatial-visual information and (b) a somewhat underspecified "executive" that supervises the flow in and out of the storage systems. Variants of this model that include an additional slave memory for abstract semantic information have since been proposed.[23]

Baddeley's "central executive" was not well specified. At the least, there has to be provision for a process that focuses attention on some information in working memory, to make it available for processing, while at the same time preventing (total) loss of information that is not currently at the focus of attention, but that has been accessed in the recent past and may be needed in the immediate future.

This idea is encompassed by the term "situation awareness," a phrase that has become popular in engineering psychology. The term refers to the need to be aware of what is going on about you, even if some aspects of the situation are not of immediate concern. For instance, an automobile driver has to keep aware of the positions of nearby cars, including those behind the driver's vehicle and hence not in immediate view.

Similar requirements occur in many situations, some quite far removed from driving. When attorneys question witnesses during criminal trials they have to be aware of jurors' reactions as they are interrogating the witness. When people attack problems in logic they have to be aware of different interpretations of the premises. When chess players consider a move they must evaluate different counters that the opponent might make. From an information-processing view, controlled manipulation of information in working memory is an extremely important part of cognition. Therefore, we would expect individual differences in the effectiveness of the working memory system to be related to general intelligence. And they are.

6.3.1. *Measuring the Capacity of Working Memory*

The *span* task is a popular technique for evaluating working memory capacity. In a span task a person is asked to perform a series of simple actions (e.g., reading a sentence) while holding more and more information in memory as each sentence is read. The simple task will be called the primary task; the act of holding information in memory is the secondary task. The idea is that the processing requirements of the primary task interfere with holding the information needed for the secondary task. Therefore the amount of information that can be held in memory in the face of the periodic interruptions by the primary task provides a measure of the storage capacity of working memory.

Two typical span tasks are shown in panel 6.6. When the primary task is reading, the span measure has a .5 correlation with measures of verbal comprehension, including the paragraph comprehension tasks that are often found on tests of verbal intelligence.[24]

When different types of span tasks are included in a comprehensive battery of reasoning and information-processing tasks it turns out that (a) all the span tasks reflect a common underlying factor, referred to as working memory capacity (WMC), and (b) WMC has a correlation of .64 with a

22 Baddeley, 1986; Baddeley & Hitch, 1974.
23 Hunt, 2002.

24 Daneman & Merikle, 1996.

Panel 6.6. Memory Span Tasks

The first, and still the most widely used, memory span task is the *reading span task* developed by two Carnegie-Mellon University researchers, Meredyth Daneman and Patricia Carpenter.* The examinee hears or is shown from one to five unrelated sentences, one at a time, and then is asked to repeat the last word of each sentence. An example is

> *He walked down Michigan Avenue in the face of the bitter wind.*
>
> *The restaurant was known for its creative preparation of fish dishes.*
>
> *All the cabinet wished the foreign secretary success on her vital trip.*
>
> RECALL
> The examinee is then supposed to recall *wind, dishes, trip.*

Randolph Engle, a Georgia Institute of Technology professor, and his colleagues have generalized this finding.[†] They point out that, abstractly, the span task requires processing some information (the sentences) while holding other information (the words) in abeyance. Therefore, a (somewhat) nonverbal span task, *processing span*, can be created. In the following example the task is to read and verify the arithmetic equation, and then store the word that follows the answer.

> *The examinee is shown*
> *IS (8/4) − 1 = 1?*

The examinee responds "yes." The word *bear* is then presented. This is followed by the following sequences:

> *IS (6∗2) − 2 = 10? (Response: YES)*
> *Beans*
>
> *IS (10∗2) − 6 = 12? (Response: NO)*
> *Dad*
>
> *RECALL*
> *The examinee replies "bear, beans, dad."*

Span tasks similar in structure can be constructed for a variety of operations in other domains, such as counting, keeping track of movements, and imagined rotation of visual objects.

*   Daneman & Carpenter, 1980.
[†] Engle et al., 1999; Kane & Engle, 2002; Kane et al., 2001, 2004.

general reasoning factor extracted from conventional intelligence tests.[25]

Span tasks are a special case of *dual tasks*, tasks in which people are asked to attend to at least two streams of information at once. A person who listens to the radio while driving a car is performing a dual task. Many laboratory tasks are formalizations of this everyday paradigm. In a dual task attention has to be switched from one stream of information to another, and then back again, with minimum loss of information during the switch. Dual tasks call on both the storage and attentional control aspects of working memory.

In a widely referenced series of studies by Patrick Kyllonen and his colleagues at the US Air Force's Armstrong Laboratory, Air Force recruits performed a number of working memory tasks, including span tasks, and also took highly *g*-loaded tests of reasoning. The recruits' scores on the ASVAB were also available. A common factor extracted from the working memory tasks predicted virtually all the variance extracted from the reasoning tests and from the general factor on the ASVAB test.[26] Similar findings have been reported by other investigators. This work is important for two reasons. First, the populations studied included US Air Force enlistees, thus broadening the studies beyond the usual range of college students. (While Air Force enlistees generally do not have the test scores of college students,

25 Kane et al., 2001.

26 Kyllonen & Christal, 1990; Kyllonen & Stephens, 1990.

they are of somewhat above-average ability compared to the general population.) Second, the number of different working memory tasks used ensured that the result did not depend upon the unique information-processing requirements of particular tasks.

The latter finding poses something of an intellectual challenge. As the Spanish psychologist Roberto Colom put it,

> *Working memory comprises the functions of focusing attention, conscious rehearsal, and transformation and mental manipulation of information.*
> *Colom et al., 2004, p. 277*

Kyllonen's work and the studies that followed it show that working memory, a complex information-processing concept, is related to general intelligence. But what part of working memory is crucial? Ian Deary, a professor at the University of Edinburgh,[27] has pointed out that we do not advance understanding by showing that one mysterious concept is linked to another.

There are two ways to reply to Deary's objection. One is to show that one, two, or all of the information-processing functions that comprise working memory make separate contributions to the relationship with *g*. That is, we reduce the intelligence–working memory link to links between intelligence and the component parts of working memory. The other is to accept the linkage at the intelligence–working memory level, and challenge the need for further reduction.

In order to discriminate between these possibilities we need to have separate measures of Colom and colleagues' four aspects of working memory. We require:

(a) Memory span tests, to evaluate the ability to store information while processing another concurrent task.

(b) Tests that evaluate short-term storage without processing – for instance, recall of a short string of digits without any intervening or concurrent processing,

(c) Tests that evaluate the ability to control attention without any memory component. An example of such a test is shown in panel 6.7.

(d) Tests that evaluate processing speed, such as a choice reaction time task. This is considered necessary because speed of stimulus identification, decision making, and rehearsal of information are all involved in the working memory tasks.

(e) One or more tests shown to be markers of reasoning, fluid intelligence, or general intelligence.

Structural equation modeling can then be used to identify latent traits underlying each of the five types of tests, and to determine the relationships between the traits.

Several such studies have been done, with somewhat confusing results. *Within* each of the studies a coherent picture emerges, often identifying a key component determining the relation between working memory and intelligence. *Across* studies there is very little agreement over what the component is.

The array of studies has an international flavor. Studies of American university students produce results indicating that the key component is the ability to control attention.[28] Studies of Spanish high school and university students[29] indicate that the storage process is the key component. Studies with German university students produce results pointing toward "supervision," which is described as the ability to keep track of the current state of variables that change over time – for example, the location of the car in the driving example given earlier. (This process is sometimes referred to as *updating*.)[30]

It seems unlikely that working memory would work differently in Spain, Germany, and the United States. And just in case you think it might, a study that explicitly compared the architecture of information processing in two different countries showed

27 Deary, 2000.

28 Engle et al., 1999; Heitz, Unsworth, & Engle, 2005; Kane et al., 2001, 2004.
29 Colom et al., 2008.
30 Oberauer et al., 2003.

Panel 6.7. An Attention-switching Task

Several different tasks have been devised to measure the ability to switch attention from one concurrent task to another. They all follow this general outline.

1. The observer is presented with two simultaneously presented streams of stimuli, and is told to search for targets on one. Stimuli are presented rapidly.
2. Aperiodically the observer receives a signal indicating that he or she should either continue to search for targets on the stream being monitored or shift to the other stream.
3. The dependent variable is the number of targets missed immediately after the signal is sounded. This is taken as a measure of the time required to fix attention on the new target stream.

The following example illustrates the procedure. The observer is told that he or she will see a sequence of pairs of letters presented on a computer screen. The letters will be presented reasonably far apart, but both letters will be within the visual field. Only one of these sequences is to be monitored at any one time.

The task is to press a button whenever a vowel appears in the position (right or left) currently being monitored.

At the start, monitor the right-hand sequence.

Subsequently, if a high tone is sounded, switch from the currently monitored sequence to the other (e.g., from the right to the left). If a low tone is sounded, continue to monitor the sequence being monitored before the tone was sounded.

Here is an example. Each line represents a time period.

Left-hand Sequence	Right-hand Sequence	
R	L	
K	X	
O	R	
Z	E	(target)
T	K	
(High tone sounds)		
(target) I	J	
N	S	
(Low tone sounds)		
Q	Y	
(target) U	C	

Doing well on this task hardly qualifies as intelligence, in the conventional meaning of the word. However, the ability to switch back and forth from one stream of information to another can be vital in certain jobs. Air traffic controller is a good example. Empirically, the ability to perform well on attention-switching tasks is statistically associated with scores on measures of fluid intelligence.[*]

[*] Duncan et al., 1996.

that the overall relations between structures were the same in each. The countries compared were Greece and China![31]

In spite of the confusing results, I believe the findings have a rather simple explanation. There is little doubt that working memory is an important component of general intelligence, although the two are not identical, either in the sense of being perfectly correlated with each other statistically or in the sense of being conceptually identical.[32] It is not surprising to find

31 Demetriou et al., 2005. Chinese children and adolescents were better than Greeks at tasks involving visual-spatial reasoning, but there was no difference in variables specifying the relation between working memory and reasoning.

32 In addition to the studies cited here, my conclusion is based on an excellent review of the literature by Ackerman, Beier, & Boyle (2005).

that the constraining features of working memory may differ in different populations. For instance, studies in the ubiquitous university student population show relatively small relations between processing speed and intelligence test performance. If we extend the studies over the full adult range processing speed becomes an important variable. Finally, confusion may result because studies that try to isolate *the* most important aspect of the working memory–intelligence relationship may be trying to carry the analysis to a finer level of detail than is appropriate. I now elaborate on this point.

6.3.2. *Brunswickian Symmetry: Working Memory and Intelligence as System Effects*

In a talk given at the University of Washington, the German psychologist Werner Wittmann made the point that when we compare two sets of behaviors it is important to maintain the same level of complexity for each behavior. Wittman referred to the balance as *Brunswickian Symmetry*, by analogy to some of the ideas of Egon Brunswick concerning decision making. Wittmann's argument can profitably be applied to studies of the relation between working memory and general intelligence.

The terms *general intelligence* and *working memory* both refer to systems of psychological functions, rather than individual functions. Consider the case of what many consider to be the best single measure of general intelligence, the progressive matrix item. A moderately difficult item of this sort is shown in Figure 6.3. What does it take to solve this sort of problem?

You have to be able to pick apart the individual elements of the figures, recognizing that each figure has certain attributes, rather than reacting to the figure as a whole. You have to be able to recognize that each attribute of a component of the figure appears once in each row and that each attribute of another component appears once in each column. Because visual attention is limited, you must be able to hold

in memory information about recognizing an item in a row as you look down the rows and across the columns. Then you have to fill in the missing pattern. Finally, you have to hold the correct pattern in short-term memory as you search the alternative answers provided, until you find one that matches the pattern. There is no one necessary working memory function. All of them are required.

Working memory and intelligence are both concepts that refer to the ability to coordinate a system of elementary functions into a coherent whole. There are relations at the system level, but trying to establish relations between the elementary functions, below the level of overall system functioning, is not likely to be useful. The quest for a single information-processing function that explains intelligence is no more likely to succeed than the quest for the Holy Grail.[33]

6.4. Verbal Comprehension

Verbal comprehension is the process of understanding written or spoken communication. In adult readers, the two processes are highly correlated.[34] Comprehension is somewhat different from production, although providing that one does not demand elegance in writing or speaking, the abilities to understand and to generate linguistic messages are closely related. Tests of verbal comprehension are contained in almost all battery-type intelligence tests. For instance, people who take the SAT have to show that they can extract meaning from passages that are roughly the length of a newspaper editorial, and that deal with serious topics.

Over the general range of ability, understanding language and general intelligence are closely intertwined, although not perfectly correlated. In extreme cases the processes do become distinct; poets are not necessarily good at high level mathematical reasoning, nor are mathematicians necessarily literary virtuosos. However, it is

33 Hunt, 1987.
34 Palmer et al., 1985.

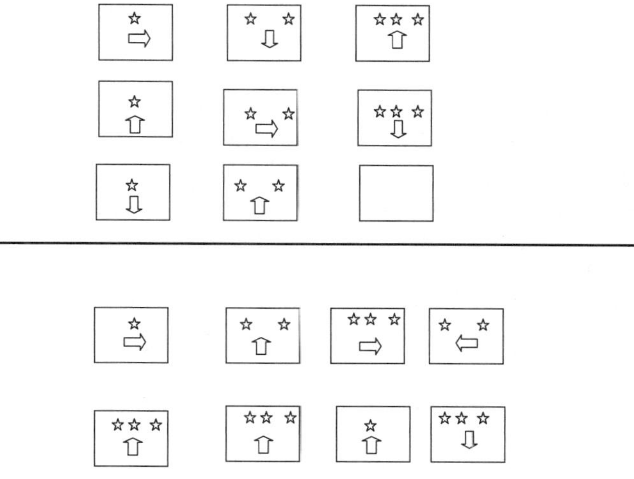

Figure 6.3. A progressive matrix item of intermediate difficulty. The task is to decide which of the figures below the line is needed to replace the blank item in the 3 × 3 matrix above the line. The problem was constructed as a demonstration, using Carpenter, Just, and Shell's (1990) rules for constructing progressive matrix items.

important to keep this distinction in perspective. People who have an elegant command of the language do not display incompetence in logical and mathematical reasoning, nor are logicians and mathematicians likely to be inarticulate.

At the other end of the intelligence scale, low general intelligence is almost always associated with a pervasive low level of verbal comprehension. On occasion, though, we find a disassociation between general reasoning and some aspects of verbal skill. Here is an interesting example.

Williams syndrome is a genetically determined type of mild to moderate mental retardation. Patients with Williams syndrome display language abilities that are considerably higher than their general reasoning abilities. At one time it was thought that this was evidence for a disassociation between linguistic skills and general cognition, but further research has shown that that is not quite accurate. Williams syndrome patients show surprising verbal skill, compared to other people suffering from the same level of general mental deficiency. However, their use of language lags behind that of age-matched children with normal mental capacities. One of the most interesting deficiencies is their tendency to react to

the literal meaning of statements, thus failing to grasp the meaning of metaphorical statements or irony.[35] A Williams syndrome patient might profoundly misinterpret statements like *He's full of baloney* or *I suppose he'll relax by going skydiving.*

To go further we have to consider what language comprehension is. Walter Kintsch, a University of Colorado professor, has developed a useful framework for understanding the comprehension process.[36] Kintsch distinguished three stages in comprehension. First there are the purely linguistic processes of retrieving word meaning (*lexical retrieval*, in technical terms) and applying syntactic rules in order to extract meaning from phrases and sentences. These tasks comprise *low-level* comprehension. Low-level comprehension is followed by *high-level* comprehension, in which sentence and phrase meanings are incorporated into a *text model*, essentially an understanding of what a text says. As the text model is built, some information is dropped out and other information is highlighted. The text model is then incorporated into a *situation model*, which represents the meaning of the

35 Mervis, 2003.
36 Kintsch, 1998.

text, in the light of other information that the comprehender has and sees relevant.

Kintsch presents text comprehension as a highly interactive process. Sentence comprehension, building the text model, and building the situation model do not take place in series; there are many feedback loops. Going into the theory in detail would be rather far afield from our concern with individual differences. Instead I offer examples in the spirit of Kintsch's analysis, without going into details.

The following statement was made by Senator John McCain, about Senator Hillary Clinton, at a time when McCain was a candidate for the 2008 Republican presidential nomination and Clinton was a candidate for the Democratic nomination.

> *In case you missed it, a few days ago, Senator Clinton tried to spend $1 million on the Woodstock Concert Museum. Now, my friends, I wasn't there. I'm sure it was a cultural and pharmaceutical event . . . I was tied up at the time.*[37]
>
> Senator John McCain, Oct. 29, 2007, at a Republican debate in Orlando, Florida

The following propositions make up my (informal) text base

> *Senator Clinton tried to spend a million dollars.*
>
> *The money was for the Woodstock Concert Museum.*
>
> *McCain was not at (the Woodstock concert).*
>
> *McCain believes the concert was a cultural and pharmaceutical event.*
>
> *McCain was occupied with other matters at the time.*

Certain statements in the text are unimportant – for example, the qualifier "in case you missed it." They drop out of the text base. Strictly speaking, the statement "I wasn't there" is ambiguous; it could refer

either to the concert or to the time when Senator Clinton tried to acquire money for the museum.

The situation model puts this in the context of unstated but widely known information about the Woodstock concert and about McCain himself. Of course, such a model depends upon the comprehender's knowledge. Here is what my situation model is. Information not specifically stated in the text base is shown in parentheses.

> *Clinton wants to appropriate one million dollars for a museum commemorating the Woodstock concert. (Government money, not her own.)*
>
> *The Woodstock concert was a cultural event. (It was the icon of the radical youth culture of the late 1960s and early 1970s.)*
>
> *There was a great deal of (illegal) drug use at the concert.*
>
> *At the time of the concert McCain was not present. (He was a prisoner of war in Vietnam, where he was badly treated, i.e., he was literally tied up.)*

An even wider situation model assumes that McCain was contrasting his undeniably patriotic record during the Vietnam War to Clinton's attempt to memorialize an event that many in his Republican audience considered an example of moral decay during the "hippy" era. Other readers might develop other models. In each case the situation model will depend heavily upon knowledge that the comprehender brings to bear. This depends upon both what the comprehender knows and what he or she sees as relevant to understanding the current statement.

Our interest is in the role of individual differences in information processing during both the low-level stage of understanding what the text literally says and the high-level stage of understanding what it means.

6.4.1. *Information Processing and Low-Level Linguistic Skills*

Every normal human being acquires a complex set of rules for speaking and listening,

---

37 McCain's statement was accurate. Clinton had joined with New York's other senator, Charles Schumer, in an attempt to secure funds for the museum.

up to the level of analysis of sentences and phrases, in a stunning display of tacit learning. But we are not all equally adept linguists. There are subtle differences among individuals in their ability to understand language.

Different people know different words. A score on a brief vocabulary test is a guide to a person's general intelligence.[38] For instance, the vocabulary test included in the WAIS has a loading of .80 on the general factor.[39] Having a small vocabulary does not necessarily reflect a deficiency in information-processing capability, for differences in vocabulary may simply reflect differences in a person's social environment. Word knowledge, in itself, is part of intelligence, for your vocabulary does, in part, determine how well you can function in society. Just knowing words, however, is not an information-processing component of intelligence.

People differ in the speed with which they can retrieve well-known words, which is an information-processing capability. People who have high scores on tests of verbal comprehension recognize common words more rapidly than people with low test scores.[40] They also recognize well-known semantic relationships, answering questions like "Is a deer an animal?" more rapidly than their low-scoring counterparts.[41] This appears to be partly a general processing-speed effect and partly a more restricted verbal skill.

There is one piece of the mechanics of word recognition that is not related to verbal comprehension test scores. In general, people are quicker to recognize a word when it is presented shortly after a related word. The word NURSE will be recognized more quickly if a person is first asked to recognize a related word, like DOCTOR, than if an unrelated word, like BUTTER, is presented first. This phenomenon is called *semantic priming*. While priming is obviously useful in verbal comprehension, there are only small individual differences in priming, and they are not related to individual differences in verbal comprehension.[42]

Moving from word recognition to sentence recognition, we find both effects of accuracy of lexical retrieval and effects of working memory. Marcel Just and Patricia Carpenter[43] measured people's working memory, using the reading span task described earlier. They then determined the time that their participants took to analyze complex sentences and how accurately they were able to analyze them. Here are two illustrations of their work.

Consider the two sentences

The evidence examined by the lawyer shocked the jury.

The defendant examined by the lawyer shocked the jury.

In the first sentence *examined* must introduce a relative clause modifying *evidence*, because *evidence*, being inanimate, cannot examine anything. In the second case *examined* might refer to an activity by the defendant or it might introduce a relative clause. The ambiguity cannot be resolved until the phrase *by the lawyer* is encountered. At an absolute level, people with high working memory capacity read both sentences faster than people with low working memory capacity. However, people with high capacity read the first sentence more rapidly than the second, that is, they took advantage of the ambiguity resolution afforded by the inanimate quality of *evidence*. People with lower memory spans read both sentences at about the same speed.

Now consider the following two sentences:

The experienced soldiers warned about the raid before the midnight attack.

The experienced soldiers warned about the raid conducted the midnight attack.

The phrase *The experienced soldiers warned about the raid* is ambiguous; it could

38 Carroll, 1993.
39 Gignac, 2006.
40 Palmer et al., 1985.
41 Goldberg, Schwartz, & Stewart, 1977.

42 Palmer et al., 1985.
43 Just & Carpenter, 1992; MacDonald, Just, & Carpenter, 1992.

refer to a warning either given by or given to the soldiers. The ambiguity is resolved when the word *before* or *conducted* is read. Readers with high working memory capacities slowed down when they encountered the ambiguity-resolving word. People with low working memory capacities did not. When asked questions about the interpretation of the second question, such as *Did anyone warn the soldiers?*, people with high spans were more likely to answer the question correctly.

Just and Carpenter interpreted these results as showing that the high-span (and, by inference, high-working-memory-capacity) readers carried forward both meanings of the ambiguous phrase until the ambiguity was resolved, while the low-span readers carried forward only the preferred alternative, that the soldiers did the warning.

Just and Carpenter also considered the effects of an extrinsic task on sentence comprehension. Recall that in the memory span task a person reads a sentence, stores the last word, then reads another sentence, and so forth. Memory span is determined by the number of words that can be recalled as more and more sentences are read. Just and Carpenter turned this procedure around. First they established people's memory spans, using a fixed set of sentences. In a separate procedure, they presented material to be retained in memory and then presented sentences of varying complexity, and determined whether or not the readers understood them. This gave them a measure of sentence-processing capability in the presence of a concurrent short-term memory load. Understanding decreased as sentence complexity increased, but people with high spans were less bothered by the concurrent memory load than were people with low spans.

Just and Carpenter concluded that working memory should be considered a capacity for processing, rather than a reflection of either accurate lexical retrieval or short-term storage capacity. I would put this somewhat more neutrally. Working memory is a system of storage, retrieval, processing, and attention control functions. The important thing is how well these functions work together to create a system for managing information. When dealing with verbal comprehension we regard working memory as a component of verbal ability; when we deal with reasoning more generally, we talk about the effect of working memory on *g*. In either case individual differences in the effectiveness of the working memory system are central to individual differences in cognition.

6.4.2. *Higher-Order Comprehension Processes*

It is difficult to distinguish higher-order verbal comprehension from intelligence, for some of the most complicated items on cognitive tests are verbal comprehension items. Doing well on the SAT requires comprehension of quite complex statements. It is somewhat more profitable to present an analysis of how texts are comprehended, continuing with an informal use of Kintsch's model. The analysis will indicate the points at which information-processing constraints become important.

The following rather convoluted passage appeared in the *Yale Alumni Magazine*.

> *Whatever fails to accord with the values of political liberalism fits uncomfortably within the range of possibilities that the prevailing conception of diversity permits students to acknowledge as serious contenders in the search for an answer to the first-person question of what living is for.*
>
> Kronman, 2007, p. 26.[44]

My first reaction when I read this was

Eh?

> *All-purpose word in Canadian English*

But, with an effort, this forty-five-word sentence makes sense. You just have to take it stage by stage.

> *Whatever fails to accord with political liberalism -> nonliberal ideas*

44 Kronman is a former Dean of the Yale Law School.

Parse phrase, refer to long-term memory for semantic references, and store in memory.

fits uncomfortably within the range -> is outside of, not permitted by

Parse phrase, refer to long-term memory for semantic references, store result in memory. Working memory now holds *nonliberal ideas not permitted by.*

of possibilities that the prevailing conception of diversity permits -> ideas permitted by the current concept of diversity

Parse phrase, refer to long-term memory, identify *possibilities* with *ideas.*

Working memory now holds *nonliberal ideas not permitted by the current concept of diversity.*

Next we encounter *students*. This changes the presumed grammatical structure of the sentence. It turns out that "concept of diversity" is the subject of the sentence, not the object of the preposition *by*. We have an example of updating, one of the functions of working memory. Appropriate rearrangement of the contents of working memory produces

The current concept of diversity does not permit students

and *non-liberal ideas* is free floating until the next word occurs.

to acknowledge

This anchors the term *nonliberal ideas*. Working memory now holds

The current concept of diversity does not permit students to acknowledge nonliberal ideas.

We next encounter a mouthful (memoryful?) of relative clauses.

as serious contenders in the search for an answer to the first-personal question of what living is for

These require similar parsing and analysis. I will not go through the steps. The result is fairly simple.

Current concepts of diversity do not let students consider nonliberal views.

We have gone from forty-five words in the statement to eleven in the text base. We

can move to the situational model by recalling that Kronman was writing in 2007, and that he was addressing Yale alumni. A completed part of the situation model is

There has been concern over academic biases against conservative thought.
Professor Kronman is trying to explain the current situation to the Yale alumni.
Kronman says that
   Views in favor of cultural diversity prevail on campus.
   These views do not permit students to consider competing ideas.

Perhaps Kronman could have written more simply. My purpose is not to edit his writing. It is to show that comprehension of language, a very important part of human intelligence by any definition, requires a complex interplay between the working memory and long-term memory systems. Long-term memory does not just act as a provider of information and syntactic rules. It also holds information needed to understand what the text means in the context in which it is stated. Neither McCain's nor Kronman's statement can be understood unless the comprehender knows, and sees as relevant, a great deal of cultural information about American political and social issues in the early twenty-first century.

The ability to bring such information to bear is an important part of intelligence. It has to be evaluated if one wants to make a serious claim that one's test measures verbal intelligence in any meaningful way. This poses something of a problem to the test maker. There may be situations in which the test maker does not want to evaluate possession of knowledge, because possession of knowledge depends upon a particular cultural background. At the same time the test maker does want to evaluate the ability to use knowledge to build a situation model. What to do?

The answer is to be clever. Here is an elegant example of evaluating an elementary school student's ability to build a situation model. It was a test item in an Australian examination intended to assess a student's ability to understand irony.[45]

> Text: *Lovely mosquito, sitting on my arm*
> *Stay right where you are, I mean you no harm.*
> *Still as a statue, stand right where you're at.*
> *I only mean to give you a pat.*
> Question: *Does the writer like the mosquito?*

The best of our computer programs for automatic language comprehension would have a hard time answering this question. I asked a reasonably intelligent fourth grader, who replied (with an evil grin)
He wants to kill it.

6.5. Information-processing Mechanisms Underlying Visual-spatial Reasoning

Visual-spatial reasoning is included in psychometric models as the Gv (visual intelligence) second-order factor in the three-stratum model, and by the perceptual and rotational dimensions in the *g*-VPR model.[46] The "visual" term is justified because the ability refers to the ability to detect, recognize, and analyze objects in the visual field, and in visual imagery, the ability to manipulate objects in the mind's eye. The two are closely related, although not perfectly correlated.[47] The "spatial" term refers to the ability to reason about real or imagined movement in space, including one's own position and movement relative to other objects (orientation). Orientation ability is not measured in the major battery-type intelligence tests, but it is evaluated in some personnel-selection situations, particularly in aviation.

Table 6.1. Correlations between different visual-spatial abilities

Narrow Factor	CF	CS	SR	VZ
CS	.65			
SR	.60	.32		
VZ	.58	.65	.77	
MS	.52	.43	.43	.46

Source: Data excerpted from Burton & Fogarty, 2003, with permission from Elsevier.

An analogous factor, auditory ability (Ga), has been identified in research on the three-stratum model.[48] Auditory ability was left out of the *g*-VPR model simply because none of the test batteries analyzed by Johnson and Bouchard contained any auditory tests. It is difficult to fit tests of audition into a paper-and-pencil testing paradigm, but the recent developments in delivery of computer-controlled music should make it easier to explore individual differences in auditory ability in the future.

A study by two Australian researchers, Lorell Burton and Gerald Fogarty, provides a good idea of the nature of visual-spatial ability.[49] Previous research on the three-stratum model had identified the following specialized factors for visual-spatial abilities.

> *Closure of forms (CF):* The ability to detect a hidden form in a larger display, particularly if the detection requires that the examinee "break a set" of looking at a larger or different figure. As an example, count the number of vertical lines in this sentence. To do so you have to detect features within familiar letters.
> *Speed of closure (CS):* The speed with which you can recognize easily detectable forms, such as a triangle or circle. This is closely related to the more general concept of processing speed.
> *Speed of rotation (SR):* The speed with which one can recognize a simple figure (e.g., a letter) rotated out of its usual orientation.
> *Visualization (Vz):* The ability to imagine what a visual figure will look like

45 I encountered this while attending a National Research Council workshop on assessment of student achievement. I reproduce it from memory, and may not have the verse absolutely correct.

46 Carroll, 1993; Johnson & Bouchard, 2005a.

47 Burton & Fogarty, 2003; Kosslyn, 1980; Poltrock & Brown, 1984.

48 Carroll, 1993; Horn & Stankov, 1982.

49 Burton & Fogarty, 2003.

Table 6.2. Loadings of visual-spatial and imagery first-order factors on a general visual-spatial reasoning factor

	CF	CS	SR	VZ	Image Quality	Image Speed	Image Self-report
Loading	.74	.69	.80	.87	.83	.59	.46

Source: Data excerpted from Burton & Fogarty, 2003, with permission from Elsevier.

if its orientation is changed. An example is the "paper folding" test, in which the examinee is shown a flat piece of paper with dotted lines on it. The examinee is to indicate what figure can be constructed from folding the paper along the dotted lines.

Memory for shapes (MS): The ability to hold a shape in short-term memory for a brief while.

In the terms of the *g*-VPR model these abilities would be second-stratum factors – more general than specific tasks but still highly specific abilities. They would be subsumed by the more general P and R dimensions at the third stratum of the model.

Tests of the abilities just listed, and a number of others, were given to slightly over 200 undergraduate students (approximately evenly split between men and women). Table 6.1 shows the resulting correlation matrix. The correlations are substantial and positive, an indication of a single factor, visual-spatial ability.

6.5.1. *Imagery*

Visual-spatial reasoning tasks force examinees to think about things that they can see. Studies of imagery require thinking about things that the examinees imagine. For instance, you could ask a person to imagine a letter E in its normal form, and then ask him or her to describe how it would look if it were to be rotated ninety degrees clockwise. An extensive body of research has shown that the sorts of operations that can be performed on images are at least loose analogs to the sorts of operations, like rotation, that can be applied to a percept.[50] If

operations on perceived and imagined figures use the same mental operations, individual differences in visual-spatial ability should be related to individual differences in imagery.

Burton and Fogarty included a number of objectively measured imaging tasks in their test battery. An example of such a task is given in panel 6.8. Performance on images reduced to two factors: *image quality*, the accuracy of information contained in a person's image, and *imaging speed*, how fast a person can construct an image. Table 6.2 shows the loadings of both perceptual and imagery factors on a single visual-spatial reasoning factor. Clearly imagery and visual-spatial reasoning are closely related. Note, though, that people's reports of their imagery have a lower relation to the visual-spatial factor than the behavioral measures of imagery do. This is interesting, because many studies of imagery have relied on self-report, which may not be terribly accurate.

6.5.2. *Spatial Orientation*

Spatial orientation is the ability to develop an internal representation of an exterior space, including one's own position in that space. There are very large individual differences in people's ability to do so. Some individuals seem to have a keen awareness of their spatial orientation, both with respect to objects in their immediate environment (e.g., what is immediately to your right rear?) and with respect to larger spatial layouts (e.g., can you draw the layout of the building you are in right now?). Others have a great deal of trouble answering these sorts of problems. This does not mean that these people go around lost! Instead they seem to rely on memories for routes between key locations. Panel 6.9 describes a case that

50 Kosslyn, 1980.

Panel 6.8. An Imagery Task

Here is an example of a *creative imagery* task. The instructions are

Imagine the letter A. (Pause) Now imagine a triangle to the right of the A. (Pause)

Imagine this triangle so that it is now facing upside down. (Pause) I want you to place the letter A inside the center of the triangle such that all end points or edges match up.

Participants were instructed to write down as many of the emergent forms as they were able to detect. They were told not to draw the image held in their mind until they had written down everything that they could see in their image.

A picture of what a participant might image is shown immediately below. The emergent forms detected might include one small triangle, two larger triangles, a diamond shape, the letter "w," and so on.

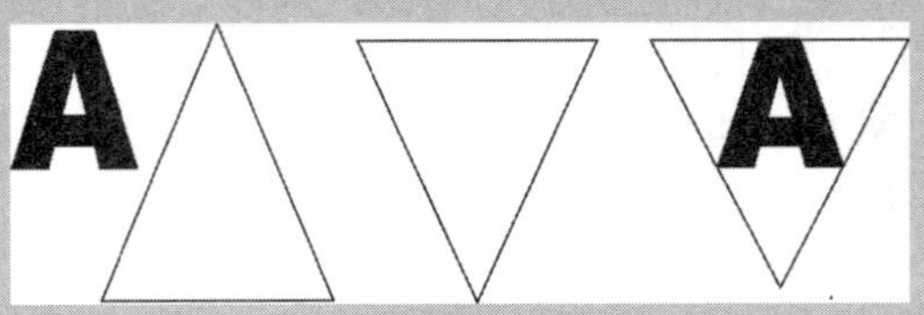

Panel 6.9. Lost in the Hospital

A study was conducted of the extent to which nurses understood the layout of a hospital in which they had worked for over a year. All the nurses regularly went about their daily activities without getting lost. The experimenter asked the nurses how they would go from one familiar location to another if their normal route was blocked. Some of the nurses could develop alternate routes; some could not.[*]

This is an example of a more general finding. When people explore a space, some of them will develop a mental representation functionally equivalent to a mental map of the environment. This is sometimes referred to as a "surveyor's representation." Others do not reach this level of understanding of their surroundings. Instead they develop memories for routes from one location to another.[†]

[*] Moeser, 1988.
[†] Hunt, 2002, Chapter 6, section 5.

illustrates, dramatically, how strong these individual differences can be.

A number of laboratory tasks have been designed to evaluate different aspects of orientation ability. This research has generally been conducted outside of the mainstream of research on intelligence, even though maintaining orientation is certainly part of the concept of intelligence.

The reason for this situation is understandable. In order to evaluate someone's orientation ability you have to determine how well they can explore an unfamiliar environment. This is an expensive, time-consuming process that does not fit into the classic testing paradigm. About the only way that orientation can be evaluated under normal testing conditions is to show the examinee one or two pictures of an object, taken from different perspectives, and ask what the object will look like from another perspective. This gets at one aspect of orientation, but only one.

Virtual environment technologies provide a way of getting around the logistical problems inherent in evaluating spatial orientation.[51] In this technology the examinee has to move through computer-generated artificial worlds. Large individual differences in orientation are found. These are related to, although not identical to, both conventional tests of visual-spatial ability, particularly spatial rotation and

51 Waller, Beall, & Loomis, 2004.

perspective-taking tasks, and skill at orientation in real-world environments.[52]

Spatial orientation serves as a shining example of a cognitive skill that is socially important, for which there are wide individual differences, and, as we shall see in the following chapters, that has both biological and cultural bases, but that has been almost ignored in research on intelligence due to overreliance on the standard testing paradigm.

6.5.3. *The Relation between Visual-spatial Reasoning and Information Processing*

How do information-processing models enhance our understanding of visual-spatial reasoning? The answer to this turns out, surprisingly, to be "very little," not because information-processing models are irrelevant, but because they are incorporated into several of the psychometric tests used to identify visual-spatial processing. This can be seen by contrasting two workhorse tasks used to define verbal intelligence – vocabulary tests and paragraph comprehension tests – to two workhorse tasks used to define visual-spatial reasoning – closure and rotation tasks.

The two verbal reasoning tasks are complex in themselves. Recognizing the meaning of a string of letters requires identification of the string as a word, retrieving its several meanings, and determining the correct meaning in context. The selection process is not trivial. In English, which appears to be a particularly ambiguous language, the typical word has 2.5 meanings.[53] Paragraph comprehension requires recognition of words, retrieval and selection of word meanings, plus analysis of sentences, and then the construction of text and situation models. Neither psychometric task goes to the level of detail in examining verbal processing that the information processing measures do.

Figure 6.4. A visual closure task. There are five topi (a species of antelope) in this picture. Can you find them? (Ngorongoro crater, Tanzania, August 2007. Photograph by the author.)

Closure tasks require the detection of lines, assignment of boundaries to objects, detection of surfaces, and development of representations of objects from representations of surfaces. There is something of an analogy to building a text model, or even a situation model. The example in Figure 6.4 illustrates this; perception is difficult until you (a) have a clue about what you might see and (b) are given an anchoring point. This level of detail is close to that used in experimental studies of figure detection.

In a rotation task a person is shown a relatively simple picture and asked what it would look like if it were to be presented at a different orientation. Figure 6.5 presents an example. There are strong individual differences in the ability to deal with tasks such

Figure 6.5. A rotation problem. If gear A is moved in the direction indicated by the arrow, which way will gear C move?

---

52 Hegarty & Waller, 2005; Waller, Knapp, & Hunt, 2001.
53 Hunt & Agnoli, 1991.

as this.[54] Rotation tasks actually appeared on psychometric tests of visual-spatial orientation before they were studied in experimental laboratories. The only difference between the psychometric and information-processing techniques is that the psychometric tests determine how many rotation problems a person can solve in a fixed period of time, while the laboratory procedures determine how long a person takes to solve individual rotation problems.

Visual-spatial reasoning factors generally have high loadings on the general reasoning factor, *g*. From an information-processing view this is not surprising. Visual-spatial reasoning tasks often require the development and manipulation of internal representations of visual-spatial information. Baddeley's model of working memory contained a "visual-spatial scratch pad." Subsequent research has shown that measures of Baddeley's scratch pad and operations on its content are apart from, although correlated with, measures of verbal working memory.[55]

As was the case in discussing the working memory–*g* relation, trying to pick visual-spatial working memory apart into separate tasks does not reveal any single, crucial process that explains visual-spatial reasoning. The visual-spatial working memory system is just that, a system. Reasoning about percepts, images, and space is an emergent property produced by the synthesis of storage, attention to, and processing of, percepts and images.

6.6. Summary Comments on Information Processing and Intelligence

Individual differences in information-processing capacity make a substantial contribution to individual differences in cognitive skills – in essence, to intelligence. However, the two are not identical. Rather, information-processing capacity constrains a person's intelligence.

Thought results from the development of internal representations of external problems. This means that there has to be a storage place (or places) for the representation of percepts and images. This includes the possibility that there are separate storage places for, say, linguistic and visual-spatial information. There have to be processes for fetching information and transforming it, in an orderly fashion. There has to be some way of prioritizing the processing of crucial information. That is what the control of attention is all about. Everything has to work together. And finally, it is better if everything is done quickly. The important question to ask about the information-processing contribution to intelligence is not whether this or that isolated process is efficient or deficient. It is whether the total system is functioning well enough, and quickly enough, to get the job done.

Information-processing capacities alone do not produce intelligent behavior. Intelligent behavior is evidenced by appropriate responses to external problems. Choosing the right response requires the construction and manipulation of an internal representation of a problem. Take an illustrative case, buying a new car.

In order to decide what car to buy you have to think about the different ways that you are going to use the vehicle, the capabilities of automobiles offered for sale, the price range, the cost of operation, and so on and so forth. Working memory is a shorthand for the mental workspace and tools you use to build and manipulate your representation of the situation. The more pieces of information you can consider at once, the better you can balance relevant information. The faster your processing speed, the less likely it is that information in the transient working memory stores will decay, and the more likely it is that you will be able to juxtapose relevant pieces of information. For instance, you must realize that economic considerations include both the purchase price and the costs of operation and insurance.

I could just as easily have taken an example from cooking, political decision making, computer programming, or any other

54 Hegarty, Just, & Morrison, 1988.
55 Ackerman, Beier, & Boyle, 2002; Logie, 1995.

field where people use their ability to think. Thinking about anything requires having relevant knowledge. In order to bring that knowledge to bear you have to use the machinery provided by your information-processing system.

Although no one of the components of the information-processing system dictates thought, each of the components constrains thought. Just how different constraints operate depends on both the situation and the person. We have seen examples of situational variation throughout this book. The Wonderlic Personnel Test (WPT, see Chapter 2) evaluates a person's ability to answer many simple questions, quickly. Processing speed and the ability to switch tasks (control of attention, executive functioning) constrain performance on the WPT. Now recall the convoluted sentence on liberalism written by the Dean of Yale's Law School. It took a big working memory to get through those forty-five words.

The nature of information-processing constraints varies in different populations. Comparing results from studies of intelligence in university populations and in the elderly, we find that the variations in processing speed are not major determinants of performance for sophomores, but they are for senior citizens. Sophomores are pretty good at thinking quickly. One of the most consistent findings in research on aging is that processing speed decreases substantially over the adult years, possibly beginning in the thirties.[56]

We can see a similar effect in studies of the role of attention, short-term memory storage, and information-processing measures in general. Studies that focus on intellectually capable young adults are examining a group in which individual differences in constraints due to information-processing capacities are small, relative to their role in other populations. Attentional control is weak in young children and the elderly; processing speed decreases markedly with age, even during an adult's working lifetime; and information-processing constraints appear to be much stronger in people of low intelligence than in those with normal or high intelligence, as assessed by test scores.[57] The relationships among these findings have not been ignored, but they certainly have not been studied adequately. In a review of studies of the relation between working memory and intelligence, Ackerman and his colleagues observed that less than three percent of the correlations reported involved participants over thirty years old![58]

Psychologists would do well to consider this fact:

All sophomores are human. Not all humans are sophomores.

Future research on the relation between intelligence and information processing ought to ask how information-processing capacities constrain intelligence in different populations, as well as how information processing constrains thought in people in general.

56 Salthouse, 1996.

57 Detterman & Daniel, 1989.
58 Ackerman, Beier & Boyle, 2005.

CHAPTER 7

Intelligence and the Brain

The human brain, a 3-pound mass of interwoven nerve cells that controls our activity, is one of the most magnificent – and mysterious – wonders of creation.

> President George H. W. Bush,
> July 17, 1990 (Presidential
> Proclamation 6158 designating the
> 1990s as the "Decade of the Brain")

He's a nice guy but he played too much football with his helmet off.

> President Lyndon Johnson,
> referring to Congressman (later
> President) Gerald Ford. Ford had
> been a collegiate football star.
> Attribution by Schnakenberg
> (2004).

The two presidents were right. President Bush (or his speechwriter) described the brain accurately – a very complex bit of circuitry. President Johnson's description of Ford may not have been accurate, but he was right that bouncing the brain is not a good thing. A modern playwright put the matter in a slightly different way.

> *Merkin's brain has a mind of its own.*
> *Act I of* Below the Belt, *a 1997 play*
> *by Richard Dresser*

Every expression of intelligence is due to actions of the brain. What actions a brain will take in a given situation depends upon both the brain's structure and its history. This chapter will focus on individual differences in brain structures and processes related to intelligence. The topic is exciting. Findings are coming in so fast that it is hard to make sense of all of them. My computer literature search for papers on BRAIN AND INTELLIGENCE retrieved 5,648 citations.[1] Neither I nor anyone else has read them all. There are some who believe that virtually all psychology, including the study of intelligence, will soon be reduced to studies of the brain. I do not think so. What I do think, and what will be stressed throughout this

1   Using PsycINFO, 30 May, 2009.

chapter, is that the relation between intelligence and the brain is very important, but has to be kept in perspective. Consider this analogy.

Orchestras vary greatly in their ability to play music. The same piece played by your local high school orchestra and by the New York Philharmonic may be recognizably the same piece, but the two orchestras do not sound the same. There is a positive correlation between size and musical quality. High school orchestras tend to be smaller than citywide amateur and professional orchestras, which are in turn smaller than the major philharmonics. However, there can be a good deal of variation in the quality of music performed by orchestras of the same size. Adding performers to your high school orchestra will not make it sound like a philharmonic.

There is also a correlation between intelligence and brain size, but the same cautions apply.

By analogy to studies of brain injury, imagine studying the essence of orchestral quality by removing one player at a time. To start, remove the conductor. The orchestra begins to play in a flat, hesitant fashion, and can play only those pieces for which it has a lot of practice. But it can play, and besides, there are inter-orchestra differences when the conductor is there. In addition, there is the puzzling problem that the conductor clearly influences the music being played, in spite of the fact that the conductor does not make any noise!

Now try removing all or part of the string section, the brass, the woodwinds, or the percussion instruments. Each removal would affect performance, but the effects would depend upon the work being played. Removing the strings would affect almost, but not quite, all pieces. Playing "76 Trombones" does not require a violin; percussion instruments are not needed to play chamber music. And there is still the problem that there is great variation in the performance of intact orchestras.

Now try an analogy to modern studies of how brain metabolism varies with mental activity. The orchestral equivalent would be measuring the sound level in different parts of the orchestra. You would quickly find that in all but the simplest pieces the sound comes from all over, and that the pattern of sound varies far more with the piece being played than with the quality of the orchestra. The same thing is true in cognition; all but the simplest problem-solving activities elicit neural activation across the brain, and the pattern of activation varies more with the activity than with the individual.

Instead of looking at activity all over the orchestra, suppose that we arrange a "laboratory study" that isolates the performance of individual players, so that we can rate their performance. This is what the information-processing psychologist does, by designing situations that isolate working memory or visual perception, instead of having them work together, as they do in everyday problem solving. You would find that you were getting somewhere, for there would be a substantial correlation between the quality of individual performers and the quality of the orchestra. Musicians in philharmonics are much better than musicians in high school orchestras. However, if you were to look at a narrower range – say, between the members of the New York, Cleveland, Chicago, and Seattle Philharmonics – you would find that the differences were very small.

Then there is the pesky problem of the conductor. You would find it very hard to evaluate a conductor without an orchestra. He or she would look more like a person suffering from a minor epileptic fit than a musician, and would not make any sound at all. How can you reconcile this with the fact that that orchestras play considerably better with a conductor than without?

In desperation you conduct a "metabolic" study, by looking at how much orchestras are paid. This is an indicator. Musicians in major orchestras earn considerably more than musicians in minor ones, and amateurs are not paid at all. But is this because being paid more produces better music, or is it perhaps the other way around?

Besides, the silent conductor is getting paid more than anyone.

The brain is more complex than an orchestra, and cognition is more complicated than musical performance. Cognition and music are emergent properties. They depend partly upon measurable qualities of the parts of the organisms that produce them, brain and orchestra, and partly upon the interaction between those parts. We can make progress in understanding cognition (and music) by making measurements on parts, but these measurements, alone, will not provide a full explanation. You should keep this in mind as we discuss the brain-mind relations that tell us a lot, but not the whole story, about intelligence.[2]

The following two sections provide an introductory discussion of the structure of the brain and of modern technologies for examining brain structures and processes. Readers familiar with both topics can jump immediately to section 7.3, which begins the discussion of major findings relating brain variables to intelligence. I urge readers not familiar with brain structure or the new technologies to refrain from jumping too quickly.

7.1. The Structure of the Brain

The human brain is a swelling that sits at the upper end of the spinal cord. Figure 7.1 presents a "cartoon" version of the brain, as viewed from the left. It is divided into four major anatomical structures, called *lobes* – the frontal, temporal, parietal, and occipital lobes. The occipital lobe, at the back of the brain, is primarily concerned with visual analysis. It also plays a role in visual reasoning. The cerebellum, sitting below and to the rear of the cerebral cortex, is largely concerned with automatic motor coordination, although it does have some function in cognition.

2   I am not arguing for a duality of mind and brain. If we knew the nature of every connection between the approximately five billion neurons in a person's brain, and if we knew the algorithms the brain uses to activate and alter these connections, we would know everything there is to know about that person's cognition. We are so far from having such knowledge that, for the foreseeable future, there is a place for nonbiological models of intelligence.

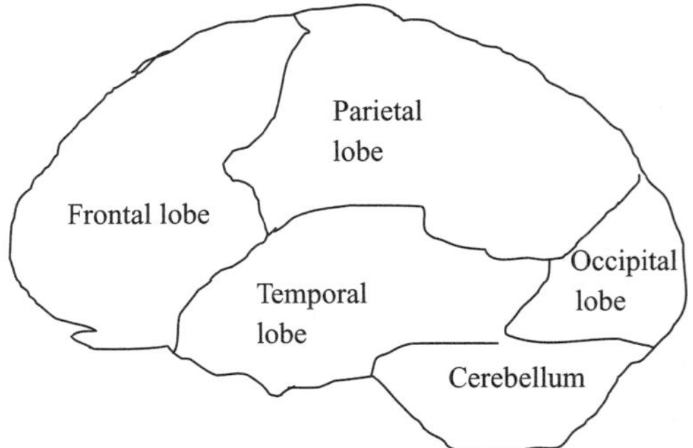

Figure 7.1. A sketch of the human brain, seen from the left. Sketch by the author.

If you view the brain from above you would see that a deep fissure divides it into left and right hemispheres, connected by neural bundles that bridge the fissure. The largest of these bundles is the *corpus callosum*, which provides the main communication link between the two hemispheres.

In general, somatosensory and motor information is represented contralaterally; the right side of the brain controls the left side of the body, and vice versa. There are some exceptions, notably in the analysis of information in the middle of the visual field, but these need not concern us. Certain functions that are not directly tied to a side of the body may also be differentially localized across the hemispheres. Language, which primarily depends on structures in the left hemisphere, is the best known of the lateralized functions.

There are individual differences in brain structures. Some left-handed people have their language centers located in the right hemisphere, and there are some differences between men and women in the localization of brain functions. These will be discussed in Chapter 11, section 3, which describes male-female differences in intelligence.

Figure 7.2 shows a diagram of several subcortical structures that are important in cognition. The *cingulate gyrus* functions as a communication system between various areas of the cerebral cortex. It also appears to be important in response selection. Below the cingulate gyrus is the *limbic system*, which contains the *hippocampus*, and the *amygdala*. The hippocampus

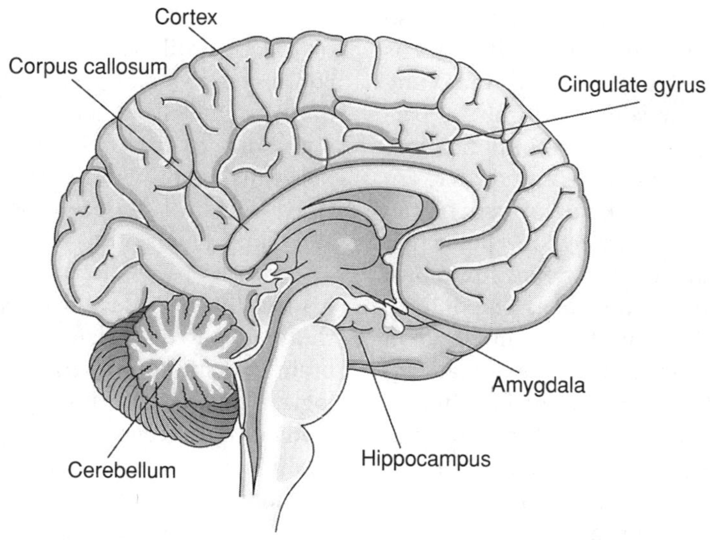

Figure 7.2. The cingulate gyrus and the limbic system. Drawing courtesy of the National Institutes of Health.

plays an important role both in memory and in spatial-visual reasoning. The amygdala, along with a midbrain structure called the *hypothalamus*, is involved with emotions.

Six terms are used to define locations in the brain. They are:

Frontal: The forward part of the brain or part of the brain being discussed.
Posterior: The opposite of frontal.
Ventral: Toward the bottom of the brain or the brain region being discussed.
Dorsal: Toward the top of the brain or brain region.
Medial: Toward the middle of the brain.
Lateral: Toward the side of the brain.

These terms may be combined. For instance, the *dorso-lateral prefrontal cortex* (DLPFC) is an area at the extreme front of the brain (prefrontal), on the upper (dorso) outside (lateral) surface. It is important in working memory.

All information held in the brain (memories) and all processing upon that information (thoughts, percepts, images) is determined by the physical form of networks of nerve cells, or *neurons*. The term "physical" is important; ultimately all thinking comes down to the manipulation of neurons. So is the term "network"; we store and process information by changing the configurations of networks of connected neurons, not by changing the states of individual neurons. Our memories of our grandmother, or of yellow Volkswagens, are coded as configurations of neural elements. Within limits, two different individuals may code the same information in somewhat different neural configurations.

Neurons can be classified, anatomically, as either *gray matter* or *white matter. White matter* refers to neurons whose axons are coated with a fatty substance called *myelin.* Gray matter consists of masses of neurons that are involved in computations within a local area of the brain. The white matter provides long-distance connections between brain regions. There is a loose analogy here to distributed computing, where networks of gray matter play the roles of local computing centers and the white matter provides the cabling that connects the local centers to each other.

Introductory textbooks often contain maps showing where different functions lie in the brain. The most famous examples involve speech. *Broca's area*, in the left posterior frontal region, is associated with speech expression, and *Wernicke's area*, in the left temporal lobe, is associated with retrieval and understanding of semantic and syntactic relationships. A great deal has also been written about how the left brain is specialized for analytic, sequential reasoning while the right brain conducts intuitive, parallel reasoning. This is an oversimplification.

The brain does contain centers that are specialized for certain kinds of processing, but it does not contain regions dedicated to broad cognitive or emotional functions. *The brain functions as a system*. The orchestral analogy is apt. In understanding human intelligence it is useful to consider what cognitive functions are carried out in different regions of the brain, but understanding as complex a behavioral phenomenon as intelligence requires understanding both where different specialized processes are and how they mesh to produce thinking.

7.2. Technologies for Examining the Living Brain

Until the discovery of X-rays at the turn of the twentieth century our knowledge of brain structure was based upon post mortem examinations. These provide a limited source of information about brain-mind relations, because post mortem examinations are biased toward studies of the elderly or those who have died an untimely death. In both cases the state of the brain following death may not accurately reflect its state when the person was alive and fully functioning. Nevertheless, a great deal of information about brain-mind relations was obtained in the nineteenth and first three quarters of the twentieth century by studying alterations in behavior following brain damage.

In one of the pioneering studies in this field, the nineteenth-century physician Paul Broca (1824–1880) determined that injuries in the left posterior frontal lobe are associated with deficiencies in speech expression but not in speech comprehension. This condition is referred to as *aphasia*. A century later, in 1957, the world saw a striking example of the malady. President Dwight Eisenhower developed a minor aphasia, probably due to a small aneurism in Broca's area. Eisenhower

recovered sufficiently to complete his term of office (until January 1961), although he continued to exhibit signs of mild speech impairment. Given the extremely demanding nature of the presidency, Eisenhower's performance provides a striking example of the dissociation between speech production and comprehension.[3]

Broca's observations began a long and fruitful line of research in *neuropsychology*, the study of the relationship between the brain and mental functions. Neuropsychological findings are highly relevant to the study of intelligence, but they are limited in an important way. Variations in intelligence within the normal range may not be produced by the same mechanisms that make it possible to perform a particular cognitive function in the first place. Consider the following analogy. Loss of a leg makes a dramatic difference in running speed. "Number of legs" is not a determining factor in running speed within the normal range of variation.

In order to go beyond neuropsychology scientists needed some method of examining the brains of healthy individuals. X-ray imaging, developed early in the twentieth century, was a beginning; but early X-ray images could not provide a clear picture of the soft tissue in the brain. In the 1970s much more powerful imaging techniques became available. They fall into two broad classes: techniques for measuring brain structures and techniques for measuring neural activity at different sites in the brain.[4] Panel 7.1 presents a brief, nontechnical description of the major technologies in use today. The development of new technologies continues, so my list will probably be outdated within a year of the publication of this book! The results from studies using these techniques are exciting, but we want to keep three recurring problems in mind.

---

3   Eisenhower recovered. Other leaders have not been so fortunate. In 1526 King Henry VIII of England received a blow on the head while jousting. His impulsive behavior following the injury, which disrupted both his personal life and English policy, suggests forebrain damage.

4   Haier, 2009.

Panel 7.1. Technologies for Looking at the Brain

This panel presents a brief view of the major technologies used, as of 2010, to relate brain structures and processes to intelligence. Each of these technologies was developed from basic discoveries in physics that made it possible to detect weak electrical and magnetic signals emanating from the brain. Making sense of the signals required the development of complicated computer algorithms and extremely rapid electronic computing machinery, whose development also required basic advances in physics. The imaging technologies represent a striking example of how basic research in one field can have important practical implications in other fields.

Technologies for Examining Brain Structures

Computerized Axial Tomography (CAT or CT Scanning)

CT scanning is derived from X-ray medical imaging. Marie Curie received the Nobel Prize for her discovery of X-rays in 1911. This started a string of Nobel awards building on Curie's discovery. The first CT scanning devices were announced in 1972, and the inventors were awarded Nobel Prizes in 1979.

In CT scanning, low-intensity X-rays are passed through the body from positions on a circular ring around the body. This contrasts with conventional X-ray imaging, in which a single picture is taken by passing X-rays through the body onto a photographic plate. After the X-rays have passed through the body they are collected by receivers that are far more sensitive than the chemical elements on a photographic plate. This permits the use of X-rays of low enough intensity that their passage is impeded by soft tissue, producing a soft-tissue image. The two-dimensional images, taken from many different angles, are combined by a computer program that determines the structure of various parts of the brain. The method is applicable to all parts of the body, not just to the brain.

Magnetic Resonance Imaging (MRI)

Magnetic resonance imaging (MRI) sprang from work in the 1960s and 1970s, based on discoveries about electromagnetism that date from the 1930s and 1940s, including Nobel Prize–winning research by Isidor Rabi. The first medical scanners were introduced in the early 1980s. The developers of modern MRI, Paul Laterbauer of the University of Illinois and Peter Mansfield of the University of Nottingham, were awarded the Nobel Prize in 2003.

In MRI, the person being scanned is placed in a tube that is surrounded by a large magnetic field. A radio pulse is then directed toward the part of the body being scanned. The pulse frequency is chosen to resonate with hydrogen atoms. This causes hydrogen atoms in the body to move out of alignment with the magnetic field. They then return to alignment and, as they do so, emit a detectable electromagnetic signal. This information is used to reconstruct locations in the brain or body.

Diffusion Tensor Imaging (DTI)

Diffusion tensor imaging (DTI) is a form of magnetic resonance imaging based on signals that are sensitive to the diffusion of water molecules along the myelin sheaths (white matter) that coat some of the neurons in the brain. Signals are transmitted along myelinated neurons considerably faster than they are along

(continued)

Panel 7.1 *(continued)*

unmyelinated neurons (gray matter). Columns of myelinated neurons are believed to be involved in transmitting signals from one region of the brain to another, while unmyelinated neurons are involved in local computations within a region. As a loose analogy, DTI provides a way of locating the cabling between the computing centers of the brain.

Technologies Used to Identify Brain Activity

Positron Emission Tomography (PET) Scanning

The basic ideas behind positoron emission tomography were developed in the 1950s. The first use in humans waited until the 1970s, due in part to the need for high-speed computing to support the sensing technology.

As radioisotopes decay they will emit positrons (anti-electrons). When a positron encounters an electron both are annihilated, emitting a gamma ray. In PET scanning a person is placed in a ring of sensitive sensors. A rapidly decaying radioisotope is then injected into the bloodstream. Rapidly decaying isotopes are required in order to avoid damage to tissue as the gamma rays pass through the body. The isotope will be taken up by tissue, roughly in proportion to the metabolic activity in neurons at that point. As the isotope decays it emits positrons, which are annihilated when they encounter electrons, producing gamma rays. The gamma rays will vary in strength according to tissue density and current metabolic activity at that point. Sensors detect the gamma rays as they exit the body. Computer programs are then used to calculate metabolic activity at various locations.

Functional Magnetic Resonance Imaging (fMRI)

Like MRI, fMRI is based on molecules generating an electromagnetic pulse in the presence of a magnetic field. The biological mechanism is different. When neurons are active they take up oxygen from the blood. This causes a change in the magnetism of the oxygen molecules, which can be detected by sensors. The signal is called the Blood Oxygen Level Dependent (BOLD) response. The BOLD response provides an indication of neural activity at a location.

Electroencephalograms (EEG) and Event Related Potentials (ERP)

Neural events generate electrical signals that can be detected by electrodes placed on the scalp. This was first demonstrated in 1929. It is the basis for the modern electroencephalogram (EEG). EEG recording is important in medicine because physiological states have characteristic EEG signatures. These include characteristic patterns for epilepsy and for different stages of sleep. The event-related potential (ERP) is an EEG signal in response to a specific external event, such as a flashing light. The ERP has proven to be a very useful tool in cognitive psychology, as different mental events have characteristic ERP signals. For example, when people hear semantically meaningless sentences, such as THE COOK ROASTED THE CEMENT, they display a characteristic ERP. Syntactically anomalous sentences, such as WOMAN THE LOVE CATS, have a different ERP signature.

Modern EEG signals are recorded from 50 to more than 100 sites on the scalp. Computer-based analysis is required to identify signature waveforms and to inter their location in the brain.

7.2.1. *The Spatial and Temporal Resolution Problem*

The MRI, PET, and CAT procedures described in panel 7.1 are accurate to within a few millimeters. Therefore, they can detect structures and processing activity in bundles of neurons, but not individual neurons. Timing presents a problem. Functional MRI (fMRI), the most widely used method, identifies neural activity by measuring oxygen uptake, referred to as the BOLD response. The BOLD response takes place over a few seconds. By contrast, cognitive operations such as word identification take place in well less than a second. Therefore, the BOLD response is useful in locating a place of brain action, but less useful in isolating the time course of the action.

There is activity all over the living brain, all of the time. In order to determine the place of action associated with a particular cognitive activity neuroscientists have to isolate the "signal," the brain activity associated with the cognitive action of interest, from the "noise," the background activity of the brain. In order to do this neuroscientsts use an analog of the Donders subtraction paradigm described in Chapter 6. The brain regions supporting different steps within a cognitive activity are located by comparing the BOLD response during an activity that employs the function of interest to the BOLD response during a control condition, which contains all the steps of the first activity except the one of interest. For example, in order to identify the neural structures associated with lexical identification the BOLD response obtained while a person reads words like CAMEL is compared to the BOLD response as he or she looks at a meaningless letter string, such as LEMAC. The BOLD response to LEMAC is subtracted, on a point-by-point basis, from the BOLD response to CAMEL. The areas of the brain that show more activity in response to CAMEL than to LEMAC are assumed to be involved in the retrieval of meaning. As in the case of the use of Donders's paradigm in reaction time studies, the comparison is valid only if the brain regions involved in executing the function of interest are uninfluenced by the execution of other functions that may be active at about the same time.

EEG/ERP recordings of electrical events are accurate to within a few milliseconds. The neural response to a stimulus will follow presentation of a light or noise by a few milliseconds, simply because there has to be time for the signal to get to the brain before it can be interpreted. It is difficult to determine the place in the brain that is the source of an EEG/ERP signal unless a large number of electrodes are placed on the scalp. Large electrode arrays did not become practical until the advent of high-speed computers, but this is no longer a serious concern.

7.2.2. *The Averaging Problem*

All of these technologies rely on the analysis of signals immersed in noise. Therefore, results are often reported in terms of the average signal observed, where the averaging is over trials and sometimes over individuals. A technology that may be sensitive enough to detect trends in averages may not be sensitive enough to detect individual differences around that trend. Accordingly, someone interested in individual differences in cognition – that is, intelligence – can rely on positive results obtained using the new technologies (subject, of course, to the usual cautions about the need for replication), but should be a bit cautious about results that report no difference. Are such results obtained because there really are no differences between individuals or because the technologies being used are not sensitive enough to detect them?

Average patterns of brain activity, computed over individuals, may not represent the pattern of activity in any one individual. For instance, male and female patterns of brain activity differ in a number of cognitive tasks. Therefore, it often does not make sense to report average brain activity, summed across men and women. This is a glaringly obvious distinction, for we know that there are many differences between men and women, and so are alert to errors based on averaging results across the sexes.

What is more worrisome is that there may be qualitatively different types of brain activitiy within each gender that are masked in averaged data.

7.2.3. *Logistical Problems*

All the new technologies except the EEG rely on large, expensive, immobile machinery. This is not a problem that is likely to be solved by technology, for the problems are due to the physical nature of the sensing apparatus. All the technologies use machines that must be shielded from extraneous electromagnetic fields. Magnetic resonance imaging requires a large, inherently heavy magnet.

Imaging experiments are time-consuming and involve some physical discomfort for participants. This can range from injections of radioactive materials (in PET scanning) to holding still in a noisy, uncomfortable chamber (in MRI). Therefore, there are pressures to use a small number of participants. For instance, one important study in the field reported correlations based on only eight participants. Thirty to fifty participants would be considered a large study. For statistical reasons alone, positive results can be trusted but negative results are indeterminate, due to the low statistical power of the experiment. In addition, using very few participants, often drawn from available rather than representative groups, raises the possibility that there are important individual differences in brain-behavior relations in the population at large that are not represented in the study group.

Because of the expense involved and the need to study relatively few participants, many studies are based on comparisons of extreme groups – often a contrast between "normals" (usually healthy, relatively young adults) and clinical populations. While such studies can be informative, they do exaggerate the size of findings. They can also miss important phenomena that appear only when the full range of intelligence is studied.

The new imaging and EEG technologies have provided types of data that the psychometricians of the twentieth century could only speculate about. Findings based on the new technologies have made, and will continue to make, great strides in our understanding of the biological basis of intelligence. Like any other technologies, these new ways of looking at the brain do have limits, and the limits should be kept in mind.

7.3. Brain Structures and Cognition

It would be nice if thinking were located in neat compartments in the brain. As the orchestra analogy suggests, this is a vain hope. Consider an important part of cognition, paragraph comprehension, that is evaluated in almost all battery-type intelligence tests.

From the viewpoint of a psychometrician, a test of paragraph comprehension produces a score that is an indicator of verbal intelligence. From the viewpoint of a cognitive psychologist or a neuroscientist, paragraph comprehension is staggeringly complex. It involves aspects of (at least) visual form identification (occipital and temporal lobes), control of eye movements (parietal lobes), retrieval of lexical information (left temporal lobe), retrieval of syntactic rules (left temporal lobe), execution of syntactical rules for sentence comprehension (left frontal lobe), and maintenance of attention on the topic (left frontal lobe, anterior cingulate cortex). It takes all of this, and more, to read *The Cat in the Hat* to a four-year-old child.

Nevertheless, we can make some generalizations about the functions of different brain areas:

Frontal cortex: The frontal lobe is involved in two major aspects of thought: the provision of working memory and the control of attention. Both working memory functions and the control of attention involve coordination between the frontal and parietal lobes, and the anterior cingulate gyrus (Figures 7.1 and 7.2). The frontal lobe is also important in inhibition of action, including inhibition of emotion-guided responses. Inhibiting such responses can be important, both in constructing plans and in

Panel 7.2. The Case of Phineas Gage

Phineas Gage was a nineteenth-century railway construction foreman. He was known as a good supervisor and a shrewd businessman. In 1848 an accidental explosion drove a steel rod through the forward part of Gage's skull. After he recovered he was irreverent, capricious, unable to concentrate, and often profane. Some reports remark on his tendency to make sexual comments, something that was far more proscribed in Victorian times than it is today. Gage lost his job as a foreman and became a stage coach driver. This job probably minimized social interactions, compared to his earlier job, but still required considerable skill. Ten years after the accident he developed epilepsy. He died in 1860. During his lifetime there was interest in his case. As late as the 1990s, Gage's skull was on display in Harvard's Library of Medicine.

Over a hundred years after Gage's death modern neuroscientists examined the skull and concluded that the iron bar had heavily damaged the frontal lobe.*

Here is a personal anecdote. For some years I supervised an undergraduate laboratory course in cognitive psychology. One day when I entered the laboratory I found that a graduate student leading one of the sections, a small woman, had been trapped in the corner of the room by a large man who was berating her for giving him low grades. His behavior was threatening and completely inappropriate. I intervened, and convinced him to leave. (Because he also exhibited very poor motor coordination I was sure that I was in no physical danger.) I noticed that he had scars on his forehead. Upon later inquiry I learned that he had suffered frontal lobe damage.

These two examples illustrate the impulsivity and inability to concentrate that is typical of people with damaged frontal lobes.

*   Damasio et al., 1994.

---

maintaining social order. People with damage to the frontal lobes are notoriously poor in both functions. Panel 7.2 presents a famous illustrative case and a relevant personal anecdote.

Temporal lobe: The temporal lobes are heavily involved in hearing. The left temporal lobe and the left posterior frontal lobe are important for the production and comprehension of speech. There is also some involvement of speech in the right temporal lobe. In about five percent of the population the speech areas are found on the right rather than the left. Such people are almost always left-hand dominant. (The converse is not true. Many left-handers have their speech center in the left hemisphere.) The posterior temporal lobe is also involved in the identification of visual stimuli, as explained in the following discussion of the occipital lobe.

Parietal lobe: The parietal lobes were once thought of as being responsible for analysis of tactile signals and for coordination of sensory-motor movements. These functions are carried out contralaterally; the left side of the brain receives sensations from and controls actions on the right side of the body, and vice versa. We now know that the parietal lobe is also involved in the allocation of attention to sensory input streams. In addition, the parietal lobe plays an important role in locating objects and in sensing motion. It acts in conjunction with the frontal lobe to support the working memory system.

Occipital lobe: The occipital lobe is specialized for visual analysis. This is where most "low-level" visual analysis takes place, including parsing the visual signal into connected surfaces and objects. During perception visual information from the occipital

Panel 7.3. The Case of H. M.

H. M. was a young Canadian architect's draughtsman who, in 1953, had his hippocampus, amygdala, and other parts of the limbic system removed in order to treat severe epileptic seizures. H. M. was the last person on whom this operation was ever performed. The surgery did control his epilepsy, but it destroyed his ability to form new declarative memories. As a result he had to live in custodial care until he died, in 2008, when he was in his eighties. At that time his identity, Henry Moulson, was revealed.

H. M. was studied extensively. One of the most interesting aspects of his behavior was the highly selective nature of his loss. After his operation his WAIS IQ score was in the above-average range. This is what would be expected, given his employment prior to surgery. Declarative memory – that is, the sort of memory that can be retrieved by an explicit cue to recall – was gone. For example, he could not recognize researchers who had worked with him for over ten years.

However, he could learn new motor skills, although he did not remember having learned them. He also showed some semantic memory for events that had occurred after his injury. Such memory was reduced compared to the memories of a noninjured person.

Although surgeons no longer perform bilateral hippocampal removals, a few cases of hippocampal loss due to injury or accident have been reported. They all resemble H. M.[*]

A good deal has been made of H. M.'s above-normal IQ scores, which have been used to argue that intelligence is unaffected by the loss of declarative memory. This conclusion defies logic. A capacity for declarative memory is an essential part of the concept of intelligence. Failure to evaluate it adequately on the WAIS is a deficiency of the test. You cannot say that a man who has to be provided custodial care due to a cognitive defect still has normal intelligence.

[*]   Milner, 2005; Milner, Corkin, & Teuber, 1968.

---

lobe moves along a pathway through the temporal lobes that is responsible for identifying visual objects, and along a pathway through the parietal lobes that determines object location and movement.

Two subcortical structures are important in cognition (Figure 7.2):

The limbic system: The limbic system consists of the hippocampus, the amygdala, and the fornix. The limbic system, and especially the amygdala, is heavily involved in emotional arousal, including fear. This is important for cognition, because affective reactions are important in capturing attention and in response selection. One of the important functions of the frontal and prefrontal regions is the inhibition of reactions based on affect, thus making cooler-headed reasoning possible.

The hippocampus is central to the construction of *declarative memory*, memories that can be recalled explicitly. People with hippocampal injuries may exhibit a profound anterograde amnesia, in which they are literally unable to form memories of experiences following their injury. Panel 7.3 presents the case of H. M., which may be the most-cited single case study in all of psychology. The hippocampus is also heavily involved in the learning of spatial layouts.

Cingulate gyrus: This large structure lies between the limbic system and the upper parts of the cerebral cortex (Figure 7.2). The cingulate cortex and the frontal system form a circuit that is important for the control of attention, in the sense of attending to certain aspects of the current problem and not others. This is sometimes referred to as "executive control."[5]

This description of the functions of different parts of the brain has not dealt with individual differences. We now turn to a discussion of how variations in brain structures and processes are associated with individual differences in cognition, that is, with intelligence.

7.4. The Brain and General Intelligence: *g* and Its Correlates

In a classic children's story Winnie-the-Pooh explains his mishaps by saying he is a "Bear of very little brain."[6] Is it true that the bigger our brains, the smarter we are? Panel 7.4 presents two cases in which men with large brains displayed considerable intelligence. But wait! The panel also contains a discussion of the problems of inferring scientific laws from single case studies. The answer to the question about brain size and intelligence depends on your perspective. Does a large brain imply greater intelligence? From an evolutionary point of view the answer is "Definitely!" Within our species, the answer is "Somewhat." It also depends on what type of thinking we are talking about and where in the brain we look.

7.4.1. *Evolutionary and Cross-species Evidence*

Cross-species and evolutionary records indicate a strong relationship between brain size and cognitive power. Compared to the brains of other mammals, the human brain is relatively large, and very large for our body size. Adult men have brains that are slightly above 1400 cc³ in volume and 1.30 kilograms in mass. Women have brains around eight to ten percent smaller. Brains also vary with age; they are obviously smaller in children, and shrink in advanced age. Brain size is positively related to body size, both within and across species. A comparison to another

large animal, the elephant, shows the human advantage in brain size after body size is considered.

The average weight of the elephant brain (which varies depending on whether the animal is male or female, and African or Asian) is 4.70 kg, more than three times the weight of the human brain. The elephant weighs from 7,500 kg (African male) to 3,700 kg (Asian female). Modern humans weigh around 75 kg (male) to 62 kg (female). Elephants are sixty to one hundred times heavier than humans, which makes the three-to-one ratio of brain weights look a little less important.

This example generalizes nicely. Across species there is a remarkably accurate relationship between brain size and body size,

$$E(B_i) = A_g S_i^{r_g},$$

where $E(B_i)$ is the predicted brain mass, in grams, of the ith species, and S_i is body mass in grams. This is called an *allometric equation*. The A_g and r_g terms are constants that depend upon the particular group of animals, *g*, being compared. If the exponential term, r_g, is less than one, brain size is a negatively accelerated function of body size, which means that the increase in brain size per unit weight of body size decreases as the animal gets larger. The human:elephant contrast illustrates this. The r_g term is about .75 across mammals, and .56 across birds.

Within a group of related species some animals will have larger brains than others, after accounting for their body sizes. The amount of variation that a particular species displays, compared to others in the same group, is indexed by the encephalization ratio, C_i, which is defined as the ratio of the observed brain size to the size that would be predicted on the basis of body size,

$$C_i = \frac{B_i}{E(B_i)}.$$

If C_i is greater than one, the species has a larger-than-expected brain size, calculated by considering brain size:body size ratios in comparable animals.

5 Posner et al., 2006.
6 Milne, 1926, Chapter 4.

Panel 7.4. Two Case Studies of Big Brains, and a Comment on Case Studies in General

Albert Einstein

The theoretical physicist Albert Einstein (1879–1955) is often held up as the prototypical example of high intelligence. Prior to his death Einstein gave permission for the scientific study of his brain. Einstein's brain was not remarkable, for a man of his age at time of death (seventy-six), except in one way. His parietal cortex was about 15% larger than the brains of other men who had died at about the same age.* Both the scientists who conducted the study and the popular press made a good deal of this, observing that the parietal cortex is involved in visual-spatial reasoning and mathematical reasoning[†] and that Einstein had said that his thoughts tended not to be verbal statements.

The First King of Scotland

Robert Bruce (Robert I of Scotland, 1279–1324) had a spectacular career. In 1309 he was supported by the Scottish church as King of Scotland, even though he had been excommunicated for murdering a political rival. In 1314 he defeated a much larger English force at the Battle of Bannockburn, establishing Scotland as an independent kingdom.

A modern Scot, Ian Deary, used magnetic resonance imaging (MRI) of a cast of Bruce's skull to estimate Bruce's cranial capacity.[‡] He then determined the relation between cranial capacity estimates and intelligence, using a modern survey of forty-eight adults, for whom he had both an intelligence estimate (a reading comprehension test) and measures of skull size. Bruce had an estimated intracranial volume of 1661.67 cc^3; the mean of the modern sample was 1492.50. Using the capacity:brain size relation in the modern sample as a guide, Deary and his colleagues estimated Bruce's IQ to be 128, approximately two standard deviations above average. Deary concluded that his estimate was consistent with Bruce's demonstrated skills as a political and military leader.

A Comment on Case Studies

Case studies make great reading. They are often useful in suggesting hypotheses about brain action, because they tell us what variables are worth examining further. What case studies do not provide is the sort of careful examination that rules out alternative hypotheses. Consider what the cases of Phineas Gage (panel 7.2), H. M. (panel 7.3), and Einstein and Robert Bruce contribute to scientific knowledge.

The case study of H. M. made substantial contributions to our understanding of the mechanisms of memory. But this case study was an unusual one. The initial report of H. M.'s cognitive deficits was followed by years of careful, well-controlled studies of his cognitive capacities. Similar cases were sought out and observed. The study of H. M. was valuable because extensive observations were possible, conceptual replications could be made, and various alternative hypotheses could be explored.

There was no systematic study of Phineas Gage. It has been possible to determine, to some extent, what his injuries were, but we have only anecdotal evidence about his behavior. The evidence is moderately strong that he got into more trouble after the accident than before, but Gage's behavior was never recorded in anything like the detailed records we have for H. M. However, we do have well-documented records of people whose injuries were similar to those of Gage. Gage's story makes a nice illustration of points about brain injury, but it is not scientific data.

The analysis of Einstein's brain is interesting, but hardly conclusive. Many measurements were made comparing Einstein's brain to the brains of lesser-known people. If many measurements are made, some of them are likely to meet conventional standards for statistical significance by chance alone. The fact that the difference was in the parietal lobe is suggestive, for neuroscientific studies have established that the parietal lobe is involved in visual imagery and arithmetic. Einstein did claim that his internal thought processes were visual rather than verbal. However, self-reports of imagery are not highly correlated with objective indicators of imagery.[§]

Deary and colleagues' estimate of King Robert's IQ is fun. Their conclusion is consistent with modern studies of brain size:intelligence relations, although Deary and colleagues' estimate of the IQ:cranial capacity size relationship was somewhat higher than is normally found. While their estimate of Bruce's IQ was 128, the margin of error was broad, with confidence intervals from 106 to somewhere above 130. Most national leaders probably have IQs in this range. IQ estimates for the first forty-two US presidents run from a high of 145–160 (Jefferson) to a low of 108–140 (Harding).[**]

And finally, whenever you deal with case studies, you have to be concerned about case studies that illustrate the opposite point, but that you are not told about. There are cases of eminent men who had rather small skulls.[††] But that does not make good press.

---

[*]   Witelson, Kigar, & Harvey, 1999.
[†]   Ganis et al., 2004; Piazza & Dehaene, 2004.
[‡]   Deary et al., 2007.
[§]   Poltrock & Brown, 1984.
[**] Simonton, 2006.
[††] See Gould, 1981, pp. 92 ff. for examples.

But what are "comparable animals"? The A and r_g parameters differ across classes of mammals. Therefore, it is more useful to compare the relative encephalization indices between two species, within a reference class. First the encephalization ratios are computed for all species within the class of interest. Then one species is arbitrarily assigned an encephalization value of one. Other species in the class are compared to that species, according to the equation

$$R_j = \frac{C_j}{C_i},$$

where j is the species of interest and i is the index species for the reference group.

Within the nonhuman primates, reports of innovation, tool use, and social reasoning increase with relative brain volume. The correlations are in the .5 range and above.[7]

This suggests taking a closer look at our own reference group, the great apes and, more specifically, the hominids.

Using modern humans (*Homo sapiens*) as the index species ($R_{human} = 1$) for the great apes, the chimpanzee has a relative encephalization index of .3. *Australopithicus*, the genus that preceded the genus *Homo*, and that last lived about 2.3 million years ago, had a relative encephalization index in the .4 to .45 range. Our immediate evolutionary ancestors, *Homo erectus*, first appearing about 1.8 million years ago, had an encephalization ratio of slightly less than .8. The fossil record indicates rapid increases in encephalization beginning about 500,000 years ago, with the first appearance of representatives of *Homo sapiens*. Our sometime contemporary, but now extinct "cousins" (i.e., descendants of a common ancestor, but not ancestral to us), the Neanderthals, had an encephalization ratio close to 1. (The exact value is hard to determine because

---

7   Reader & Laland, 2002.

we have only a few adequate fossils. Neanderthal brains were somewhat larger than modern human brains, but their bodies were also larger.) Encephalization appears to have peaked within *Homo sapiens* about 20,000 years ago, and may have decreased slightly since then.[8]

If you accept the idea that the progression from throwing sticks and making stone tools to throwing bombs and making plastic tools represents an increase in intelligence, then there is clear evidence that across species increases in brain size parallel an increase in intelligence. But does this relationship apply to individuals within the same species, us?

7.4.2. *Intelligence and Variations in Brain Size in Humans*

In the early nineteenth century there was widespread interest in *phrenology*, a pseudo-science whose followers claimed that they could diagnose intelligence and personality from the size and shape of the skull. They had little evidence to back up their assertions. The first objective evidence for a within-species brain size:intelligence relationship was obtained when Galton, and then his colleague Karl Pearson, found a correlation of .11 between Cambridge students' skull sizes and their grades.[9]

Galton faced a handicap. His study participants were alive. I am not being entirely facetious. In Galton's time the only way to measure cranial capacity, and by inference brain size, in a living person was to make a measure on the exterior of the skull. This method of measurement confounds thickness of the skull and cranial capacity.

To overcome this handicap several researchers, both in Galton's time and since, have estimated brain size by direct measurement of cranial capacity post mortem. This line of research was so popular in the late nineteenth and early twentieth centuries that it led to a lively – and, to the modern eye, quaint – technical dispute over the relative merits of measuring brain size by filling the cranial cavity with bird seed, shotgun pellets, or sand. An obvious shortcoming of such studies is that the investigators seldom had measurements of how intelligent the people whose crania they were examining had been when those people were alive. This did not stop the early researchers. They simply assumed that certain groups, usually Europeans as compared to non-Europeans, but sometimes men as compared to women, were smarter than others. The investigators then pointed to intergroup differences in cranial capacity as proof of their assumptions.

In 1981 the Harvard paleontologist Stephen J. Gould wrote an elegant, amusing, and scathing review of this line of research, as part of a more general, and equally scathing, analysis of virtually all aspects of research on intelligence.[10] He concluded that there was no reliable evidence relating brain size to intelligence. He also claimed that attempts to show group differences in brain size were motivated by racial prejudice. Gould had previously achieved considerable public credibility as a commentator on science, so his views were widely accepted in spite of negative reviews of his work in the technical literature.[11]

It is impossible to know whether Gould's imputations about investigators' motives were correct or not. Indeed, if the early investigators' facts were right it does not matter to science what their motives were. There have been several careful studies about the brain size–intelligence relationship. Gould had his facts wrong.

In 1992 J. Phillipe Rushton, a professor at the University of Western Ontario, analyzed records of the cranial capacity in American service men and women, taken as part of the physical examinations for military service. He found that the mean intracranial volume in officers was greater than that in enlisted men, even after considering body size. It is tempting to say that what one makes of this depends upon whether one

---

8 Geary, 2005, pp. 50–54.
9 Citation by Rushton, 1992.
10 Gould, 1981, 1996.
11 For an exceptionally comprehensive review, see Carroll, 1995.

served as an officer or as an enlisted person. More seriously, though, there is little doubt that the average IQ test score for officers is higher than the average for enlisted service men and women. In 1996 Rushton and his colleague C. D. Ankney published a review of similar studies that had been done to that date. They concluded that there is a correlation of .15 between estimates of cranial capacity based on skull measurements and measured intelligence.[12] Rushton also found differences between men and women, and between racial groups. These are discussed in Chapter 11.

In 1991 Lee Willerman, of the University of Texas (Austin), reported a reliable, positive correlation between intelligence and brain size measured using imaging techniques.[13] Willerman's study was followed by others. In 2004 a meta-analytic review concluded that the brain size–IQ correlation is about .33.[14] As the correlation between external estimates of the size of the crania and imaging estimates of the volume of the brain is about .5, we would expect the cranial estimate–IQ correlation to be approximately .16, in agreement with Rushton and Ankney's finding. More recent studies have suggested that the relationship is primarily driven by the density of gray matter, indicating the importance of local connections within each region of the brain. However, there does appear to be a smaller, but reliable, correlation with the density of white matter.[15]

As far as I have been able to determine, there is only one study in which investigators were able to correlate post mortem measures of brains with levels of intelligence.[16] Such a study is important, because direct measures of parts of the brain are more accurate than the estimates obtained through imaging. The results were confirming in some ways and confusing in others. There was a .6 correlation between overall brain volume and measures of verbal intelligence,

in right-handers. This is on the high side of the measures reported in the various meta-analyses. There was a much smaller relation between spatial-visual reasoning and brain volume in women, and essentially none in men. These findings indicate that in addition to size differences there may be qualitative differences in the way that the brain is organized in men and in women, and in right-handers as compared to left-handers. We explore this issue in the next section.

7.4.3. *Structural Differences in Various Regions of the Brain and Their Relation to General Intelligence*

While it would be naïve to think that intelligence is located in any one place in the brain, it is reasonable to believe that different parts of the brain participate to different degrees in producing intelligence. Brain density can be measured, on a region-by-region basis, using modern imaging techniques. When this is done there is a shift from measuring volume to measuring density of either gray or white matter, as discussed earlier. Definitive studies are difficult to accomplish, because the expense of imaging makes it difficult to obtain a large sample. This reduces statistical power, leading to a concern that small to moderate correlations may not be discovered. Nevertheless, some good studies have been done, and some things have been learned. Unfortunately, the results do not present a clear picture.

A wide-ranging review concluded that there were substantial correlations between measures of cortical density and intelligence, in a large number of cortical areas.[17]

Three studies have been conducted on large samples, chosen to be representative of the populations of the US (two studies) and Spain (one study).[18] These studies involved correlations using a general measure of intelligence, either *g* or a composite score, such as the full-scale intelligence

12 Rushton and Ankney, 1996.
13 Willerman et al., 1991.
14 McDaniel, 2005.
15 Luders et al., 2009.
16 Wittelson, Beresh, & Kigar, 2006.

17 Luders et al., 2009.
18 Colom et al., 2009; Haier et al., 2009; Karama et al., 2009.

quotient (FSIQ) of the WAIS. Whether or not the results were consistent depends on how closely you look. All the studies found that the density:IQ correlations were highest for areas within the frontal and parietal regions, and in the cingulate gyrus and the limbic system. However, they disagreed about precisely where the activity was within these broad brain areas. To illustrate, in one of the studies there were reliable correlations between density of gray matter and a *g* score in over forty different local regions of the brain. In another, using a different test battery that had a similar factor structure, there were reliable correlations in fifteen different areas. Reliability hardly captures the result; the probability levels for the findings are in the $p < .005$ region. However, there were only six areas of overlap, in which the same region was implicated in both studies.[19]

This is consistent with an earlier review, in which Richard Haier, at the University of California, Irvine, and his colleague Rex Jung, at the University of Arizona, determined the percentage of studies in which reliable relations had been found between the volume or density of a brain region and a measure of intelligence.[20] There was only one area of the brain, in the left inferior parietal lobe,[21] where 50% of the studies of brain imaging had shown a relation between size and intelligence. The densities of areas in the anterior frontal cortex, other parts of the parietal cortex, and regions in the cingulate cortex were correlated with general intelligence scores in 30% of the studies. Most of the areas showing effects were in the left hemisphere, reinforcing the idea that the sorts of information processing required for conventional intelligence tests and reasoning problems are carried out primarily by the left side of the brain.

Why would such inconsistent results be obtained? There are three possible explanations. The least interesting explanation, but one that cannot be ruled out, is a statistical one. In this research correlations are calculated between many densities of many different brain areas and some form of IQ score. In order to avoid reporting results that are high "by chance," investigators adopt stringent statistical criteria. This increases the chance that low to moderate correlations will be overlooked. The second possibility is that different people's brains are actually organized in somewhat different ways. The differences would not have to be major ones. There are changes in brain organization during childhood, and there is differential organization across men and women. There could be other small, but systematic changes due to other demographic variables. There is also a psychological possibility.

If a *g* measure is obtained using a battery-type test, such as the WAIS, an individual's score is determined by a weighted composite of scores on the subtest batteries. Therefore, two individuals can obtain the same *g* or IQ score in two different ways – for example, one person could have a high IQ score on the WAIS by obtaining a high verbal IQ and moderate performance IQ, while another person could obtain the same score with a moderate verbal score and a high performance IQ. More generally, when we ask someone to demonstrate "intelligence" they do not do so, because intelligence is an abstraction. They execute a medley of information-processing acts, using different parts of the brain for the different acts. If a *g* measure is obtained from a single marker, such as a progressive matrix test, the questions on the test will be fairly complex, and will yield to different strategies. The same principle applies as in the case of the battery-type test; two people may obtain the same score using different elementary processing actions. When this is the case they will not display the same pattern of brain activation, even though they obtain equivalent test scores.

7.4.4. *Efficiency Counts*

We have been discussing measures of structure. An alternative way to look at the relation between intelligence and the brain is

19 Haier et al., 2009, Table 4.
20 Jung & Haier, 2007. See especially their Figure 2.
21 Broadman area 40.

to examine measures of overall neural efficiency, thus exploring the idea that in addition to having bigger brains, intelligent people may have brains made of a better grade of neurons.

The rudiments of this idea can be traced back to Galton's studies of reaction time. It is also captured in modern studies of relations between intelligence and the speed of information processing during very simple tasks, as discussed in Chapter 6. However, the evidence connecting overt response speed to neural measures is at best indirect. Studies that have used the new imaging technologies to examine brain action during thinking are more informative, especially since it was not clear in advance what they should have found.

Suppose two people attack the same problem. One of the problem solvers has markedly higher intelligence test scores than the other one. Would you expect the person with the higher scores to show more or less metabolic and neural activity than the person with the lower scores?

A case can be made for either answer. A high metabolic rate might be a sign that highly intelligent people have more mental energy in a literal sense, for their metabolic systems might provide more energy to their brains. A low metabolic rate might be a sign that highly intelligent people have more efficient neural systems, and therefore need less energy per mental computation than less intelligent people do.

In 1988 Richard Haier's University of California, Irvine, group showed that the "more efficient" hypothesis is correct. They obtained PET scans from eight university students as the students solved Raven Advanced Progressive Matrices (RAPM) problems. The correlations between metabolic rates and RAPM scores were in the −.7 range, varying somewhat across areas of the brain.[22] As a result of the finding by Haier's group, the weight of the evidence shifted toward the hypothesis that intelligence is associated with brain efficiency, not energy generation.

Haier and colleagues' findings have been replicated, using fMRI and other techniques. A particularly interesting line of research has been followed by Austrian researchers using the very different EEG/ERP technology.[23] They found that the amplitudes of neural responses to verbal or spatial problems were negatively correlated with measures of verbal or visual-spatial reasoning, respectively. There was also an interesting male-female difference. The relations between EEG amplitude and test scores were strongest for males attacking spatial-visual problems and females attacking verbal problems, mirroring the differences between men and women in verbal and visual intelligence.

A study from Carnegie-Mellon University also bears on the issue of efficiency. University students were given the reading span test described in Chapter 6. On the basis of their scores they were divided into groups having high or low verbal working memory. All groups then attempted sentence comprehension tasks, with sentences that varied widely in their linguistic complexity (e.g., sentences with high or low frequency words, simple or complex syntax). Their brains were imaged using fMRI during the sentence comprehension task. Activation in areas associated with linguistic analysis decreased with working memory span, and increased with linguistic complexity.[24]

Two further studies are worth noting, because they illustrate the flexibility of the brain. In addition to finding that people with high verbal working memory spans showed less overall activation, the Carnegie-Mellon group also found that the high-span individuals showed a greater response to increasing linguistic complexity than did low-span individuals. There was evidence of greater coordination in activation of different areas of the brain in the high-span than in the low-span group.

The second study, by a different group, utilized the "three back" task. In this task a series of verbal or figural stimuli are

22 Haier et al., 1988, Table 2.

23 Neubauer, Fink, & Schrausser, 2001; Neubauer et al., 2005.

24 Prat, Keller, & Just, 2007.

presented. The participant is supposed to respond if the current figure is identical to one presented three items back in the series. As an example, using letters, suppose that the series was

A B C A R Q K K Q.

A "three back" response should be given to the second A and the second Q. These are called *targets*. The second K should not be responded to, because it is "one back" rather than "three back." Such items are called *lures*. Lures are frequently misidentified as targets. It evidently requires an effort to suppress responding, for fMRI scanning showed that when lures are presented there is an increase in metabolism in the frontal and parietal areas. This was interpreted as an indication that an inappropriate response was being suppressed. Scores on the Raven's Matrix test were positively correlated both with accuracy and with the size of the metabolic response.[25]

These results are typical of other findings. Several research groups have reported that when they contrast metabolic or electrical activity from people who, by other means (intelligence tests or, often, measures of working memory) have been shown to have different levels of cognitive skills, the more skilled tend to activate fewer brain sites.[26]

What happens when the brain is "on idle?" Haier's UCI group asked this question.[27] They measured brain activation while people were watching videos, but not otherwise engaged. In this admittedly exploratory study, high Raven Matrix scores were associated with greater integration between the object-recognition and linguistic-processing areas of the brain. There is an interesting resemblance between this result and Ackerman's contention (discussed in Chapter 5) that intelligent people show an above-average intellectual engagement with tasks that are not directly related to their work or study. Even when watching videos from commercial television, the intelligent brain does not completely disengage.

Both the structural and process technologies present the same basic message. Intelligence is associated with larger brains, and with more efficient brains. However, there is no single hot spot in the brain, associated with all aspects of cognition. The brain provides a tool kit for intelligent action. An intelligent person has somewhat higher quality tools, and organizes them more efficiently, than an unintelligent person.

7.5. The Brain and Specific Cognitive Functions

Accepting the idea that the brain is a tool kit, we now look at some of the specialized tools. We first look at the relation between working memory and brain functions, on the grounds that working memory is tightly enmeshed with general reasoning, and hence our most important single general processing capacity. We then look at the brain structures underlying other information-processing capacities that have been associated with various aspects of intelligence.

7.5.1. *The Brain and Working Memory: Evidence and the P-FIT Model*

Figure 7.3 summarizes the findings of over two hundred studies in which brain metabolism was measured as people did various activities related to attention and relatively short-term memory, including operations on information while it is being held in memory.[28] The reviewers summarized the study as showing that working memory tasks showed heavy involvement of the frontal and parietal cortices, and the anterior cingulate gyrus. Lateralization depends upon the

25 Gray, Chabris, & Braver, 2003.
26 Bornkessel, Fiebach, & Friederici, 2004; Caplan, Waters, & Alpert, 2003; Neubauer et al., 2005; Larson et al., 1995.
27 Haier, White, & Alkire, 2003.

28 Cabeza & Nyberg, 2004. See also Smith & Jonides, 1999.

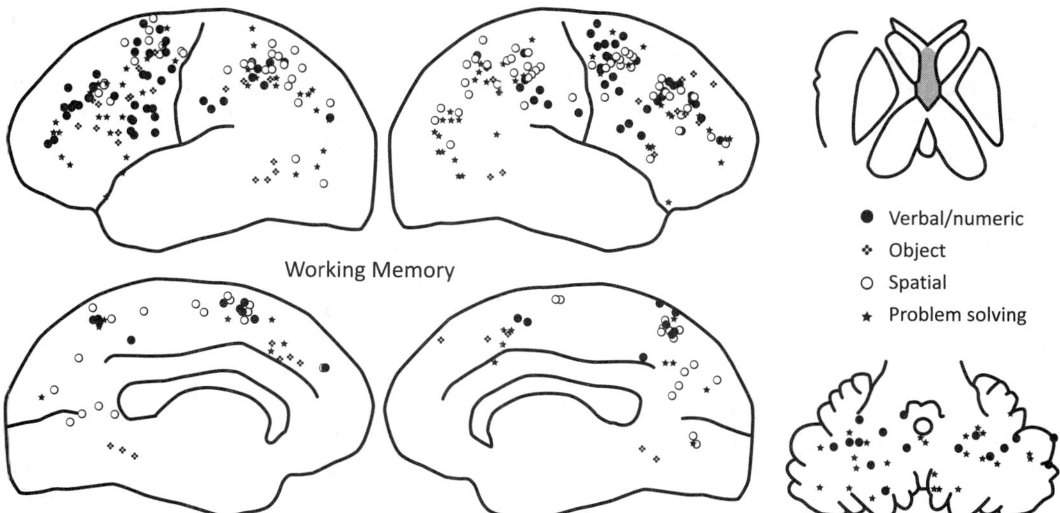

Figure 7.3. A sketch of areas of the brain that show activity during a variety of tasks involving working memory. The upper figures show a lateral view of the cortex; the lower figures show a medial view. From Cabeza & Nyberg, 2000, Figure 3. Reprinted with the permission of Massachusetts Institute of Technology Press Journals.

nature of the stimuli. In general, problems involving spatial and figural stimuli produce greater activation in the right than in the left hemisphere, while the reverse pattern is seen for problems involving language.

Figure 7.3 shows what parts of the brain are involved in working memory tasks in general. But to what extent are these areas related to individual differences in intelligence, and especially to either (depending on your theoretical predilections) *g* or Gf? One approach to this question is to take tasks that are known to have high *g* loadings in the intelligence literature, such as progressive matrix tests, and to determine what areas of the brain are active when people do these tasks. Another strategy is to determine what sort of brain injuries result in selective loss of the ability to deal with Gf-type problems, as opposed to Gc-type problems, where the solution depends largely on retrieving previously acquired information.

Both approaches lead to essentially the same answer.[29] Jung and Haier have

produced the *Parieto-Frontal Integration Theory* (P-FIT) theoretical model that does a good job of encapsulating our present knowledge.[30] They propose that our ability to do the sort of thinking captured by measures of Gf and working memory is supported by a system of brain regions involving the dorso-lateral frontal cortex, the parietal lobe, and the anterior cingulate gyrus. Each of these regions performs some of the functions needed for abstract reasoning and problem solving; no one of them is sufficient alone.

Jung and Haier's idea of the role of the frontal cortex is consistent with other observations, both of imaging results and of the sort of scattered thinking displayed by Phineas Gage, and by many other patients with frontal lobe damage. In general, the frontal lobes seem to be necessary to keep a person on-task.[31] In one study that nicely

29 Many studies could be cited. Some representative ones are Duncan, 1996, and Duncan, Burgess, & Emlie, 1995, for brain injury; Duncan et al., 2000,

and Haier, White, & Alkire, 2003, for differential activation of brain areas during imaging; and Colom, Jung, & Haier, 2006, for a discussion of the relation between neural density and *g* loadings.

30 Jung & Haier, 2007.

31 See Duncan et al., 1996, for a good discussion of this point. Shallice (2004), provides an independent review of frontal lobe functioning that is generally consistent with Jung and Haier's view.

illustrates the effect, it was shown that children who did not have a history of attention disorder prior to injury to the frontal and especially prefrontal-cortex displayed symptoms of attention deficit disorder after the injury.[32] One of the intriguing findings on this topic is that one area of the frontal lobe appears to be responsible for orchestrating thinking about things and abstract ideas, while another region orchestrates thinking about socially relevant topics.[33]

Jung and Haier argue that the parietal cortex is responsible for integrating information from various sensory modalities. This would be consistent with the parietal cortex's established role in controlling the deployment of attention externally, to particular regions of and objects in the sensory fields.[34] The role of the parietal cortex in providing temporary storage areas for information also appears to be well established. This seems to be an area where the lateralization is especially well marked; linguistic information, the phonetic loop in Baddeley's model, resides in the left (in most of us), while spatial and object information is held on the right.[35]

Jung and Haier propose that the anterior cingulate gyrus acts as a response selection device. It is responsible for directing decisions, albeit with substantial regulatory input from the frontal lobes. The anterior cingulate gyrus also seems to weigh the likely consequences of taking an action. Clancy Blair, a developmental psychologist at Pennsylvania State University, has pointed out that recent research, which it would take us too far afield to examine, has shown that emotional evaluation of outcomes plays an important part in response selection, even in situations where one would expect rational decision making to be the norm.[36] Combining Blair and Jung and Haier's views, an important part of the frontal cortex–cingulate gyrus interaction

may be modulation of the emotional and nonemotional aspects of decision making.

In summary, there is clear evidence that the working memory system, which we know is central to reasoning and general intelligence, is supported by a brain system involving regions of the frontal lobe, the parietal lobe, and the anterior cingulate cortex. I do not want to give the impression that these are the only areas involved, or that all the details of the involvement have been worked out. They have not, but the outline is clear.

Having disposed of g, we now look at brain correlates of the three secondary dimensions of the g-VPR model: verbal intelligence, perception, and spatial rotation. The discussions of perceptual and spatial-rotation dimensions will be collapsed into one, with an emphasis on the R dimension. This is because the imagination of movement in space is central to spatial reasoning, which seems to me more intellectual than detecting small differences in visual stimuli, and because the ability to visualize movement appears to be related to mathematical and numerical reasoning.

7.5.2. Structures Associated with Verbal Intelligence

Where is language in the brain? The answer to this question can be brief, not because so little is known but because so much is known that reference can be made to general textbooks and reviews. There is also what is known as the "issue of granularity." When we talk about a person having high verbal intelligence, we mean that the individual displays a high level of general competency with language. This includes a large vocabulary, and the ability to follow complex arguments. We do make a distinction between comprehension and expression, acknowledging that some people who comprehend well do not always express themselves well.

At this level of detail the neuroscientific basis of normal language comprehension has been known since late in the nineteenth century. There are major centers for language

32 Max et al., 2005.
33 Beer, Shimamura, & Knight, 2004.
34 Posner et al., 2006.
35 Cabeza & Nyberg, 2000. For a good illustrative study, see Smith & Jonides, 1999.
36 Blair, 2006.

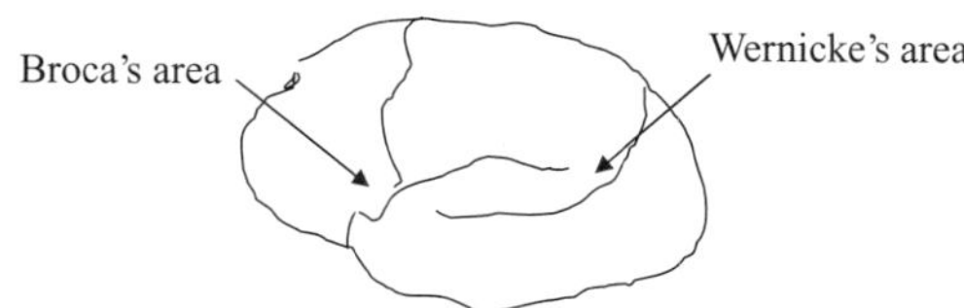

Figure 7.4. Broca's and Wernicke's regions on the left side of the brain. The display is for a right-handed individual. Sketch by the author.

comprehension in the left posterior frontal lobe (Broca's area) and in the left posterior temporal lobe (Wernicke's area). These are shown in Figure 7.4. These regions were identified on the basis of clinical studies. Patients with lesions in Broca's area understand language but are unable to express it. Patients with lesions in Wernicke's area can speak, but their sentences are often incoherent.

Imaging studies have confirmed the nineteenth- and twentieth-century neuropsychological findings. Figure 7.5 shows a summary of regions where imaging studies have identified brain activation associated with the perception and naming of words. While there is some involvement of the right hemisphere for listening, without a spoken response, the majority of the active centers are clearly in the left posterior frontal and temporal regions.

A similar picture is obtained in studies showing relations between verbal comprehension test scores and neural density.[37] One project (covering two studies, so self-replication was accomplished) obtained correlations greater than .7 between the density of gray matter in the posterior left temporal region and participants' scores on the vocabulary and information subtests of the WAIS, the two tests most associated with verbal comprehension.[38] Another has reported that adolescents with high scores on the vocabulary subtest of the WAIS show higher densities of gray matter in, somewhat surprisingly, the parietal lobe.[39] Two other reports

have indicated that reduced neural density in the temporal and frontal lobe regions associated with language identifies young children at risk for developing reading difficulties.[40]

If we move to a more complex task, sentence comprehension, we find a similar picture, with one addition. There begins to be more activation of the left frontal regions, those regions that are also involved in working memory tasks involving words or sentences.[41] This is hardly surprising. One of the more important findings, though, is that the more complex the sentence comprehension task the greater the activation level in all areas associated with language comprehension.[42] These findings are now so well established that research has moved forward to attempts to locate particular specialized functions – for example, processing a verb – rather than repeating studies looking for the general location of language. At this point students of individual differences are apt to lose interest, because of the need to maintain Brunswikian symmetry by trying to correlate concepts that are at the same level of granularity. Verbal intelligence is a broader concept than comprehending verbs.

7.5.3. *Structures Associated with Perceptual and Rotational Skills*

Verbal and Perceptual and Rotational skills (more properly, imagery and spatial-reasoning functions) are produced by different parts of the brain. To explain this we must consider how the brain conducts visual analysis.

Visual stimuli are initially analyzed in the optic tract and connected subcortical structures, prior to arriving in the occipital lobe, at the back of the brain. Analyses in the occipital lobes construct three-dimensional representations of an object from the two-dimensional pattern on the retina. The

---

37 Colom et al., 2009. Gc tasks tend to stress language ability (Carroll, 1993).
38 Colom et al., 2006, Tables 2 and 4.
39 Lee et al., 2007.

40 Deutsch et al., 2005; Hoeft et al., 2007.
41 Caplan, Waters & Albert, 2003; Colom et al., 2009; Cooke et al., 2006.
42 Prat, Keller, & Just, 2007.

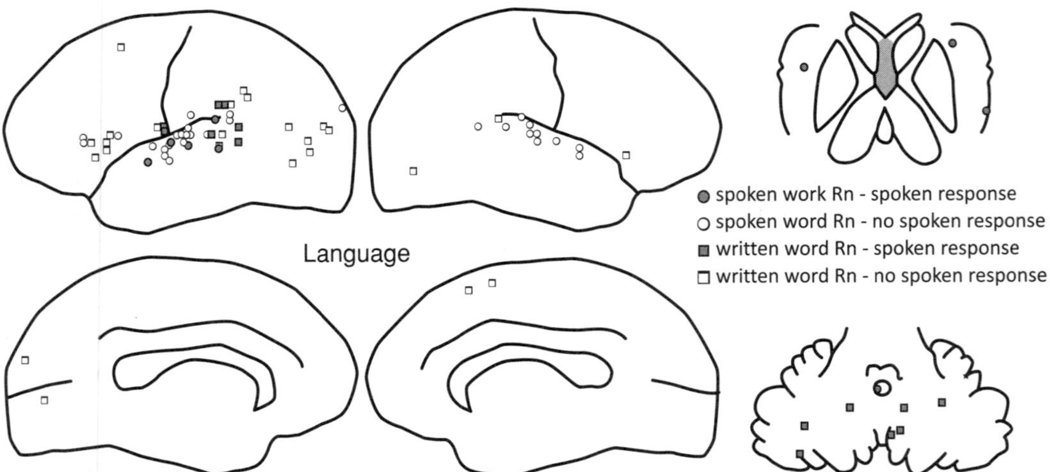

Figure 7.5. Areas that have shown activation during selected language comprehension tasks. Note the distinction between visual and auditory input, and between reception and reception accompanied by a verbal response. The upper figures show a lateral view of the cortex; the lower figures show a medial view. From Cabeza & Nyberg, 2000, Figure 6. Reprinted with the permission of Massachusetts Institute of Technology Press Journals.

(interpreted) visual image is then analyzed by two neural pathways. One goes from the occipital lobe along a dorsal route through the parietal lobe; the other moves ventrally into the temporal lobe. (See Figure 7.6). The ventral pathway is largely concerned with identifying what the stimulus is, including identification of its attributes (e.g., color). The dorsal pathway is concerned with where the stimulus is, and whether or not it is moving. Individual differences in visual-spatial reasoning, Gv in the three-stratum model and the PR dimensions in the g-VPR model, are related to gray matter cortical density along both pathways.[43]

Imagery and visual reasoning utilize brain structures that are close to, although not exactly identical to, the structures that support vision. Thus, as a rough approximation, we can think of the brain's visual analysis system as being driven either by the visual sensory system or by some "executive controller" in the brain itself.[44] In terms of the tool kit analogy, different parts of the brain can be used to attack a task, depending upon whether a verbal or a spatial-visual strategy is chosen. Panel 7.5 contains an example illustrating this point.

Male and female brains deal with visual-spatial tasks in somewhat different ways. This is interesting because there are marked male-female differences in visual-spatial reasoning, especially if the task involves visualizing motion. There is also a substantial amount of evidence indicating that the level of androgens influences visual-spatial reasoning. Prenatal influences seem to be

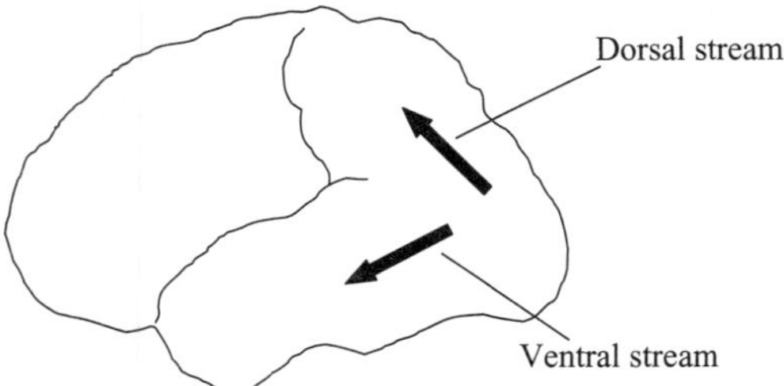

Figure 7.6. The dorsal and ventral visual streams. The ventral stream, through the temporal lobe, is primarily concerned with the identification of stimuli and their attributes. The dorsal stream carries information about location, movement, and configuration. Sketch by the author.

43 Colom et al., 2009, Figure 4. Note the Gv correlates indicated in this figure.

44 Ganis et al., 2004; Kosslyn, 1994.

Panel 7.5. The Sentence Verification Paradigm and its Neural Correlates

The *sentence verification paradigm* has been widely used to study verbal comprehension. The participant first reads a sentence describing a picture and then sees the picture. The task is to determine whether or not the sentence accurately describes the picture. Quite simple pictures are used. A favorite is the "plus above star" arrangement, where the picture is either

*

+

or

+

*

The simplest descriptions of these pictures are "star above plus" and "plus above star." More complicated sentences can be used, for example, "plus not below star." In either case the task can be regarded as a prototypical linguistic act, where the reader must coordinate verbal and perceptual information.

There are two strategies for sentence verification. In the visual strategy the participant reads the sentence and creates an image of the anticipated picture. When the picture is shown the participant decides if it matches the image. In the verbal strategy the participant first reads and memorizes the sentence. When the picture is shown the observer describes it, covertly, and decides whether or not the verbal description has the same meaning as the memorized sentence. College students can use either strategy.[*] Marcel Just's group at Carnegie-Mellon university took fMRI images of the same people when they were instructed to use either the verbal or visual strategies, thus relying on either verbal or visual working memory.[†] The centers of activation were in either the left posterior frontal region (verbal strategy) or the right parietal region (visual strategy), depending on the strategy used. Figure 7.7 illustrates the result.

This experiment shows that you cannot say that the brain controls this or that piece of cognitive behavior. It depends upon how the behavior is achieved.

[*] MacLeod, Hunt, & Mathews, 1978; Mathews, Hunt, & MacLeod, 1980.
[†] Reichle, Carpenter, & Just, 2000.

especially important. To show how general this is, the phenomenon can be produced in rats and mice. The situation seems to be quite complicated, but there is little doubt that individual differences in brain functioning do affect visual-spatial reasoning.

Orienting ability, the ability to develop a mental map of an area and to locate oneself in it, is worth special discussion. Orienting ability is certainly part of intelligence in the conceptual sense, but it is assessed only indirectly by conventional intelligence tests, due to the limitations of the conventional "Drop in from the Sky" testing format. This is one of the interesting cases where the argument that learning must influence the brain can be supported by evidence. London taxicab drivers show enlarged hippocampi, compared to appropriate control subjects.[45] In a more controlled setting, hippocampal volume is positively associated with how well people learn to navigate a computer-generated virtual environment.[46]

7.5.4. *Long-Term Memory*

Working memory is the workbench used to keep track of things related to the problem that is before us. Long-term memory refers to the ability to acquire some information, put it aside for awhile (which may be anywhere from a few minutes to a year), and then recall it when required. What brain structures are involved, and how do they

45 Maguire et al., 2003.
46 Moffat et al., 2007.

relate to individual differences in long-term memory? It turns out that the answers to these questions depend upon the sort of memory we are talking about. We have to distinguish between three different types of memory, and two different recall mechanisms.

Episodic memory refers to memory for specific events that have occurred in one's life – for instance, what you had for breakfast yesterday morning. *Semantic memory* refers to memories of how the world works; knowing that "hens lay eggs" is a piece of semantic memory. *Procedural memory* refers to knowledge of how to do things. Riding a bicycle is an often-used example. Logically, one might think that episodic memory would be central, and that semantic and procedural memories would derive from it. This is not the case. It is possible to acquire semantic and procedural information without storing an episodic record of how that information was recalled. The issue is not one of forgetting, which is normal. (Do you remember when you learned that hens lay eggs?) In some circumstances semantic and procedural information can be acquired even though no episodic record is ever laid down. To explain this we have to look at recall.

Recall can be *explicit* (declarative) or *implicit*. Recall is explicit if you are aware of the act of recall. If I ask you what you had for breakfast, you will be aware of recalling the answer. Whether you recall accurately is another matter.

Implicit recall is shown by a demonstration that behavior has been altered by an experience, even though that experience is not available for explicit recall. Implicit recall is dramatically illustrated by patients who have experienced electroconvulsive shocks to the brain, a form of therapy that actually has a history of benefits in some psychoses. The patient will typically not remember the experience but does show signs of nervousness if he or she reenters the room where the therapy took place. However, implicit recall is not solely associated with pathologies. It can be demonstrated in an undergraduate psychology laboratory, using quite innocuous procedures.[47]

Studies associating individual differences in memory with intelligence generally deal with explicit recall of episodic and semantic information. Many episodic memory studies deal with very short time intervals, often only a few seconds, as in the digit span test, which is part of many intelligence test batteries. Explicit recall of semantic memory is also tested, often under the title "test of general knowledge" or "vocabulary." It could be argued that semantic memory is a prototypical example of a crystallized intelligence (Gc) skill.

We have already seen, in the case of H. M. (panel 7.4) that someone who has lost his or her hippocampus will literally not recall a meeting that took place fifteen minutes earlier. H. M. had lost episodic memory. Similar dramatic losses of memory have been related to damage to the limbic system that is associated with alcoholism.[48] In these cases the frontal lobe may also show signs of damage. Dramatic losses of episodic and then semantic memory occur in Alzheimer's disease, a variety of senile dementia that can occur as early as fifty, affects 3–4% of people between sixty-five and seventy-four, and approximately half of all Americans over the age of eighty-five. Alzheimer's disease is associated with widespread reduction in brain volume, including both the frontal lobes and the hippocampal formation.

Are variations in brain structure also associated with individual differences in memory within the normal range? This is a difficult question to answer, because we have to distinguish among the various types of memories and how they are developed.

47 The technique used is to present people with very long lists of words, more than they can recall. Subsequently they are asked to perform some task that tests their readiness to use a word on the list, or some other word. There will be a tendency to use the word on the list, even though people cannot recall seeing it on the list. See Jacoby, Toth, & Yonelinas, 1993.
48 Sullivan & Marsh, 2003.

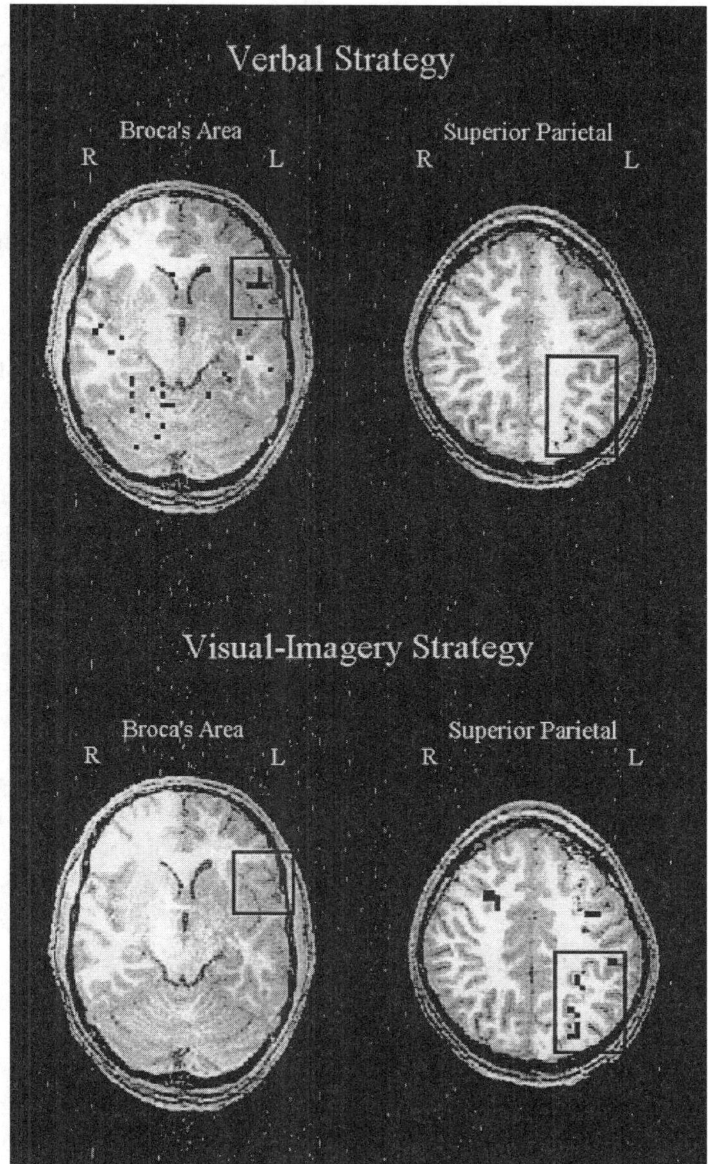

Figure 7.7. Regions of the brain activated within a single individual when that person was instructed to solve a sentence comprehension problem using either a verbal or a visual imagery strategy. The task is described in panel 7.5. From Reichle et al., 2000, Figure 3, with permission from Elsevier.

Consider how memories come to be. First, you have an experience. An internal representation of that experience will be created. This is a constructed representation of what is going on, an act of problem solving that takes place largely in the frontal-parietal-anterior cingulate circuit. The information in the coded representation is then transferred to long-term memory, along with its connections to information already in memory. This function is carried out by the hippocampus and other structures in the medial temporal cortex. The hippocampus is essential for the storage process, but, with the exception of maps of spaces, storage apparently takes place all over the cortex.[49]

Given this two-stage process, it is not surprising to find that individual differences in learning and memory have been associated with measures of volume in both the frontal lobes and the hippocampus and in related structures. The studies are small (in part because they are expensive), so there has been a tendency to focus on extreme groups, but the picture is consistent. Both the frontal-parietal-cingulate gyrus and the medial temporal cortex systems are required – one to decide what is to be remembered and one to carry out the storage process.[50] As is the case for virtually all findings in the rapidly developing field of neuroscience, all the details are not filled in.

One thing is quite clear. Memories do not reside in individual neurons; they reside in patterns of neurons. Accordingly, it has been suggested that intelligence depends upon the brain's ability to establish new connections between neurons, as well as any structural differences in the regions involved in memorization. What is the evidence for this?

7.6. Neural Plasticity

Human intelligence depends upon the ability to learn. When we learn something we change the brain, both in the sense that new memories are stored in the brain and in the sense that as we learn to do things (including learning how to solve problems), the brain is reorganized. The case has been made that differences in the ability to reorganize the brain in the face of experience, individual differences in *neural plasticity*, may be an important aspect of intelligence. Computer simulations have shown that things could work this way.[51] But do they?

The effects of increasing intelligence upon brain mechanism are mirrored by the effects of increasing practice; the more practice on a task, the lower the measured metabolic rate. In another set of PET studies by the UC Irvine group, Haier and his colleagues had students learn to play the computer game TETRIS, a highly demanding visual-spatial task. There was a marked decrement in metabolism as the task was learned. In addition, the greatest decrements were observed in people with the highest intelligence test scores. Similar findings have been observed with quite different tasks.[52]

Corroborating evidence comes from the study of infant intelligence. There have been many attempts to identify characteristics of infant behavior that could predict later intelligence. One of the most successful procedures is a technique known as *habituation*. In a habituation study an infant is shown a picture, and then shown the now-familiar picture along with a novel picture. Habituation is measured by the extent to which the infant looks at the novel picture. The idea is that this tests the ability to form a memory of the familiar picture, that is, to reorganize neural patterns to reflect experience. Habituation measures taken in the first year of life have a correlation of .36 (corrected for unreliability, .53) with IQ scores taken at age 21.[53]

Studies like these suggest that there is a relation between intelligence and the ability to organize neural patterns over a brief period of time. However, the neural reorganization is inferred rather than observed. An important study using the diffusion tensor imaging technique provided direct evidence, over a much longer period of time. During the early years of life the cerebral cortex first thickens, then thins. The process is not completed until late adolescence. It is believed to be associated with selective rearrangement of cortical neurons. The trajectory of development is much more sharply

49 Eichenbaum, 2004.
50 For typical work, see Habib, McIntosh, & Tulving, 2000; Rosen, 2003; Sullivan & Marsh, 2003; Tulving et al., 1999.
51 See Garlick, 2002, for an example of this sort of argument.

52 Haier et al., 1992. See also the conceptual replication, using a verbal memory task, by Habib, McIntosh, & Tulving, 2000.
53 Fagan, Holland, & Wheeler, 2007.

defined in individuals with high IQ scores (>120) than in individuals with lower scores.[54] This could be due to individual differences in the ability to reorganize the brain to incorporate new information, or it could be due to programmed (i.e., genetic) differences in the developmental progression of the neural system.

Many studies have shown that high intelligence test scores are correlated with faster learning, in contexts ranging from laboratory tasks through academic studies and on to workplace apprenticeships. Any learning has to be associated with some sort of reorganization in the brain. Individual differences in neural plasticity could produce such reorganization, but so could individual differences in other brain mechanisms. For instance, it could be that superior learning is mediated by a superior ability to focus attention, something that the intelligent clearly have. Why intelligence is associated with rapid learning remains in question. There may not be any one answer.

7.7. What Do We Learn from Studies of the Brain and Intelligence?

The brief answer to this question is "Lots, and there is more to come." A longer answer is more thoughtful, and a bit more reserved.

Intelligence is associated with multiple brain systems. General reasoning is supported largely by circuits between the dorsolateral frontal cortex, the parietal cortex, and the anterior cingulate cortex; verbal reasoning by structures in the frontal and temporal lobes, largely but not exclusively in the left hemisphere; spatial-visual reasoning (including rotation) by the occipital and parietal lobes; orientation by the hippocampus; and episodic memory by the general reasoning system, to decide what to remember, and by the hippocampus and related structures that carry out the process of writing information into storage locations all over the cortex.

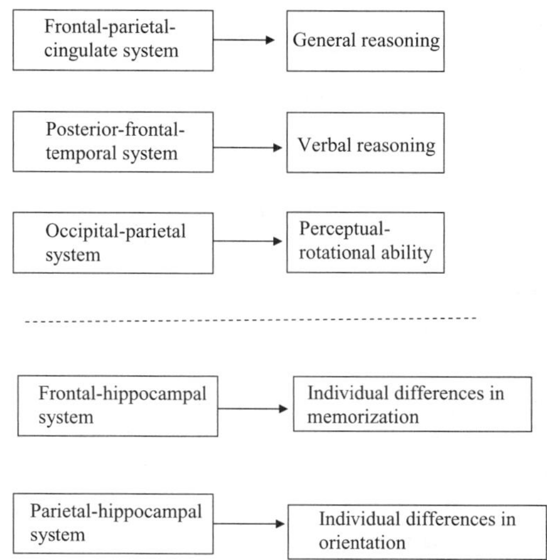

Figure 7.8. The relation between brain systems and broad (second-stratum) psychometric abilities. The boxes above the dotted line show relations between brain systems and the broad abilities identified in the VPR model of intelligence. The boxes below the dotted line show the relations between brain systems and cognitive skills that show strong individual differences, but that are not typically evaluated in psychometric studies due to limitations in the conventional testing paradigm.

Three of these systems map closely onto the dimensions identified in Johnson and Bouchard's VPR model of psychometric studies of intelligence.[55] The relationship is shown, in block diagram, in the region above the dotted line in Figure 7.8. The frontal-parietal-cingulate gyrus system supports general reasoning, with some hemispheric specialization for the modality involved, typically verbal versus spatial-visual reasoning. The system connecting the occipital and parietal cortex supports spatial-visual reasoning, while systems in the posterior frontal and temporal cortex are essential for verbal reasoning.

The systems approach is consistent with several findings showing that the densities of both gray matter and white matter correlate with intelligence test scores. This includes

---

54 Shaw et al., 2006.

55 Johnson & Bouchard, 2005a.

both general scores, such as the Full Scale IQ on the WAIS or the g composite on battery-type intelligence tests, and scores on specialized tests of verbal and nonverbal reasoning. The density of gray matter probably reflects the computing capacity within various specialized computation centers in the brain, while the white matter reflects the quality of the connections between them.

The part of the diagram below the dotted line in Figure 7.8 shows relationships between identifiable brain systems and functions that are clearly cognitive but are outside the VPR model, even though there are strong individual differences in them. The deficit is not unique to the VPR model; it is shared by all models of intelligence that are restricted to an analysis of psychometric data. Learning and orientation are certainly part of the conceptual meaning of intelligence. Their evaluation has been excluded from conventional testing simply because the necessary behavioral evaluations do not fit into the testing paradigm. This is a logistical rather than a scientific consideration, and ought not constrain our thinking about intelligence.

7.7.1. *Intelligence Emerges from the Interaction between Brain Systems*

Terms like "general reasoning capacity" and "verbal reasoning" refer to broad dimensions of intelligence, Carroll's[56] second-stratum abilities. These, by definition, can be applied in many situations.

The broad dimensions can be broken down further. This is essentially what studies of individual differences in information processing do. Figure 7.9 illustrates this, by showing a possible further breakdown of general reasoning ability. This diagram is not to be understood as a seriously proposed model, although it has some support. What it is intended to show is that concepts such as g and *working memory* refer to properties that emerge from the interaction between components that can be defined

at the information-processing level, and are supported by separate neural mechanisms. Similar diagrams could be drawn for verbal reasoning or for spatial-visual reasoning. Because broad abilities emerge from the interaction between components, attempts to connect broad intellectual abilities with brain-level and information-processing concepts should also deal with broad concepts, such as the neural circuits supporting the working memory and attention complex as a whole. Attempts to relate a widespread trait, such as g, to a component of the brain's functional networks, such as looking for the neural locus of intelligence in some small part of the frontal cortex, are not likely to work out very well. It is probably a good idea to remain at the appropriate system level, as shown in Figure 7.8, rather than trying to break the system into additive components.

This leaves us with the problem of explaining the nature of the general intelligence factor, g. Arthur Jensen has said that g is "a source of variance in performance associated with individual differences in the speed or efficiency of the neural processes that affect the kinds of behavior called mental abilities."[57] This leaves open the questions of "what neural processes?" and "what behaviors?" for different cognitive actions are supported by different brain systems.

Behaviorally, g is virtually synonymous with general reasoning ability, which in turn is synonymous with individual differences in working memory. By this argument the seat of g is in the frontal-parietal-cingulate cortex system. However, this raises some problems. Vocabulary tests are highly g loaded, but tests involving syntactical and semantic analyses of single words do not activate the entire frontal-parietal-cingulate system, and do activate areas outside of this system, notably in the temporal lobe.[58] The source of g seems to jump around as the task changes. Why?

56 Carroll, 1993.

57 Jensen, 1998, p. 74.
58 See Figure 7.5. For a typical study, see Friederici, Opitz, & von Croman, 2000.

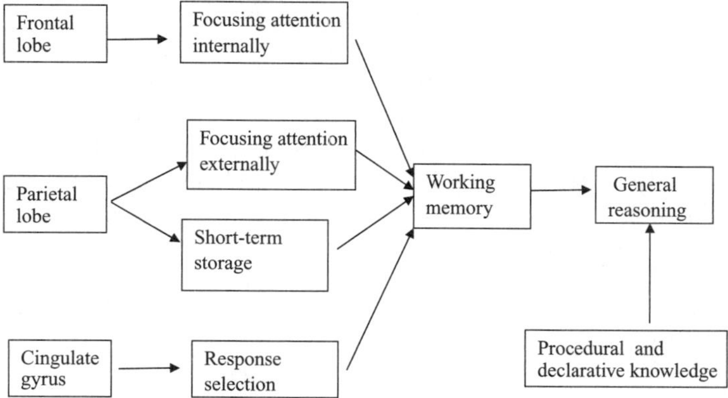

Figure 7.9. Hypothetical relationships between brain systems, narrowly defined information-processing functions, working memory, and general reasoning ability (*g*). This diagram is not proposed as a model, but rather to show the complexity of the issue, and the need to deal with broadly defined abilities, such as *g*, as emerging from a system of interacting components, rather than being a thing in itself.

7.7.2. *What More Do We Need to Know (and What Has Not Been Shown)?*

Investigations of the neural basis of intelligence are often more compelling than behavioral studies. The chance to look at the brains of intelligent and not-so-intelligent people seems to many to be far more exciting than poring through analyses of correlation matrices. There certainly is more to the neuroscience approach than just an increase in excitement. The imaging and enhanced electrophysiological technologies available today provide researchers on intelligence with a new source of data. They can rightly behave like nineteenth-century gold miners, who rushed from California to Australia to the Klondike in an effort to strike it rich in new fields. While a great many nuggets of information have been mined, there is no reason to believe that the neuroscience gold field is about to pan out. It does have its limitations.

Clearly overall brain size is correlated with intelligence test scores. The correlation appears to be in the .3 range, which is not everything, but is not to be dismissed. I doubt that there will be any great effort to develop this finding any more, because of the findings on the differential impor-

tance of various regions of the brain. These findings, and the multivariate nature of intelligence itself, make it clear that looking at something as gross as the relation between overall brain size and an omnibus intelligence score, such as the IQs derived from batteries of subtests, as in the WAIS, has gone about as far as it can go.

This chapter opened with an analogy between the way the brain produces thought and the way an orchestra produces music. The cognitive orchestra contains several functional players: working and long-term memory, verbal reasoning, visual-spatial reasoning, orientation ability, and numerous subdivisions within each of these functions. We now have a reasonably good idea where each of these players sits in the brain, although there are certainly details to fill in. We also know that intelligence is associated with slight structural changes and a marked shift in the efficiency with which the brain utilizes the players.

What we do not know is how the different players in the brain work. Most crucially, we do not know how the conductor works. It is certainly an advance in knowledge to move from saying "intelligence is associated with big brains" to talking about the locus of reasoning and executive control functions in the frontal, parietal, and cingulate gyrus. Nevertheless, such statements are maps of where an activity is, not explanations of what it is. It is one thing to say that the conductor is the person standing on the podium at the front of the orchestra. It is another to say that the conductor maintains the tempo and signals emphasis for the various orchestral sections. It is still another thing to say how the conductor maintains tempo, and so forth. We cannot stop by saying there is a conductor in, say, the system specified by the P-FIT model. That is like explaining the conductor by pointing to the podium. We have to explain how the various pieces of brain anatomy achieve their functions. This remains a mystery.

The second mystery has to do with the flexibility of the brain. To what extent is the brain's development under the control of a genetic program? How, and how much of this development can be altered by experience? Suppose we grant, for the minute, that the unusual size of Einstein's parietal cortex was associated with his undoubtedly superior mathematical talent. Was Einstein able to do mathematics because his parietal cortex was large? Or did Einstein's parietal cortex become large because he spent a lifetime thinking mathematical thoughts? On a more prosaic level, we know that experienced London taxicab drivers have large hippocampi and a superior sense of orientation along London's streets. Is this because their hippocampi enlarged as they acquired experience with London, or is it because novice taxicab drivers with smaller hippocampi could not develop the necessary cognitive map, and had to find new employment? We do not know.

Humans are provided, at conception, with the potential for a brain. The potential varies among individuals. Both *in utero* and throughout their life individuals are exposed to physical and social environments that affect the development of the brain. In the next two chapters we consider how that development takes place.

CHAPTER 8

The Genetic Basis of Intelligence

Darwinian man, although well behaved
At best is a monkey shaved.

W. S. Gilbert

8.1. Introduction

The epigraph, taken from the 1909 Gilbert and Sullivan operetta *Princess Ida*, almost gets the scientific facts right. In the interest of scientific accuracy the lines should read

Darwinian man, though well behaved
Is only an ape who's shaved.

for there are some key genetic differences between apes and monkeys. We and our other ape cousins have lost those elegant monkey tails, developed a different limb structure, and have bigger brains. The ape-monkey genetic changes took place twenty million years ago; five millions years ago more genetic changes produced the hominids. Somewhere around 100,000 years ago our own species, *Homo sapiens*, a very big-brained species with a limb structure that is fine for walking but terrible for climbing trees, began to spread from our place of origin in Africa, and by somewhat less than 15,000 years ago (the date is still debated) had reached the southern tip of South America, thus populating all the continents except Antarctica.

Genetic change did not stop as humans wandered across the globe. A very large majority of the genes that define humanity are shared by all humans, but there are significant genetic differences between populations. Swedes, Tanzanians, Chinese, and the Quechua Amerindians who live in the Andes differ in their appearance – within the range of human differences – and they differ in other ways as well. These include sensitivity to sunlight, the ability to metabolize milk and milk products, and susceptibility to a number of diseases. So it is reasonable to believe that there may be genetic differences in intelligence as well, and in Chapter 11 we will review the evidence that there are.

But, and it is a very big but, one of the reasons that humans were able to settle all over the globe, in very different ecological systems, is that their big brains and enhanced capabilities for learning allowed them to develop different cultures, to adapt to different environments. Then these cultures took on a life of their own, as they were socially transmitted from generation to generation. So it is reasonable to believe that there may be sociocultural differences in intelligence. And there are.

Theodosious Dobzhansky, one of the great geneticists of the twentieth century, said

> *Nothing in biology makes sense except in the light of evolution.*
> *Theodosius Dobzhansky*
> (The American Biology Teacher,
> *March 1973, p. 129)*

He was right, but when it comes to human intelligence we have to consider both biological and social evolution. Is intelligence something you inherit, genetically, or acquire through experience? The short answer is "both." The long answer is a lot more complicated.

The bad news is clear. There are genetically determined conditions that virtually guarantee mental disability. Mental disability can also be produced by environmental conditions, notably any event that results in brain damage. In other cases genetic configurations raise the risk of mental disability, but the degree of disability depends upon environmental conditions.

The good news is not so clear. Lots of things influence intelligence in the normal range, roughly from IQ 70 upward. Test scores are not as accurate in predicting cognitive competence, intelligence in the conceptual sense, in the upper range as they are in predicting mental deficiencies. Many mental disabilities are caused by one or a few genetic anomalies, or by catastrophic environmental events that produce brain damage. Variations in intelligence within the normal range are seldom caused by single events. They result from the cumulative effect of many genetic and environmental factors, with each factor having only a small effect. Therefore, the effects may be evident only on a population basis, and can be documented only by statistical analyses.

This chapter focuses on the genetic basis of intelligence. The next discusses environmental factors. No smoking guns will be revealed, for there are none. On a population basis, the effects of both genetic inheritance and environmental circumstances are measurable. Except in the case of mental disability, assigning a particular person's intelligence to genetics or environment is virtually impossible.

The chapter is divided into four sections. The first is a quick overview of basic genetic theory. The second discusses quantitative behavior genetics, a discipline that is concerned with the extent to which various human traits are inherited. We then look at molecular genetics, which deals with the mechanisms of genetic inheritance. The chapter closes with a summarization, and a discussion of some of the controversies that have surrounded studies of intelligence and genetics.

8.2. A Quick Introduction to Genetics

This section is a brief introduction to basic concepts in genetics. Hopefully it will provide an adequate introduction for readers who have not studied genetics, and a useful refresher for those who had a course some time ago.

The genetic model of inheritance was established in the mid nineteenth century by the Austrian monk Gregor Mendel (1822–1884). Today it seems that a monk would be an unlikely person to make a scientific contribution, but in Mendel's time a monk with a scientific career was not that unusual. Mendel spent a considerable portion of his professional life at the University of Vienna, and lectured at other institutions as well.

Mendel studied the inheritance of easily recognizable traits in plants, such as the color of pea plants. He discovered that a plant had a genetic potential, derived from its parent plants, for producing a trait, such as leaf color or form. Mendel established that

(a) The genetic potential of both parents is passed on to the offspring.

(b) Traits fall into two types. A *dominant* trait will be expressed in an offspring if it has inherited the potential for the trait from either parent. A *recessive* trait is expressed only if it is inherited from both parents.

(c) Therefore, we have to distinguish between the observable characteristics of an individual, the *phenotype*, and the genetic configuration, the *genotype*.

In modern terms, Mendel had inferred the existence of a *gene*. He also concluded that a gene could have two or more different forms, now called *alleles*, that might cause a characteristic to be expressed in different ways. For instance, a pea's pod cover can be either rough or smooth.

Imagine a plant that produces either a white or a red flower, and that the white color is dominant. Write C for the allele that produces white, and c for the allele that produces red. Furthermore, let the first term written be the gene inherited from the "alpha" parent (which in plant crossings is arbitrary) and the second the gene inherited from the "beta" parent. We have the following possibilities, using the terms *homozygous* to refer to an individual whose genetic makeup consists of two genes with the same allele, and *heterozygous* to refer to an individual whose genotype contains two different alleles.

Genotype	Phenotype	Term
CC	White	Homozygous
Cc	White	Heterozygous
cC	White	Heterozygous
cc	Red	Homozygous

Ignoring whether an allele came from the alpha or beta parent, there are three possible genotypes, CC, Cc, and cc, but only two possible phenotypes, white and red. The genotype implies the phenotype; if we know the genotype of a plant, we know the phenotype. The converse is not always true, for the phenotype "white flower" could be produced by either a CC or a cC genotype.

In simple cases genotypes can be inferred by combining the information from phenotypes of two or more generations of related individuals. This is called a *pedigree study*. In the example, a plant breeder could conduct a pedigree study by reasoning as follows:

"If I cross red with red, I will always get red."

"Suppose I cross red with white and, unknown to me, the white flower has genotype CC. All offspring will have genotype Cc, and thus I will get only white in the offspring generation. Let's call this batch of flowers 2A."

This situation is shown in Figure 8.1(a).

"But suppose that the white flower has genotype Cc. Then all the next generation will inherit a c from one parent and, equally likely, either a C or a c from the other parent. Call this batch of flowers 2B. In the 2B population all offspring will have either genotype Cc or cc, and I expect to have an equal number of them."

The resulting distribution of genotypes and phenotypes will be

Genotype	Probability	Phenotype
Cc	$\frac{1}{2}$	White
cc	$\frac{1}{2}$	Red.

The situation is shown in Figure 8.1(b).

The frequencies are statistical expectations, rather than determined values. Therefore, the breeder cannot expect batch 2B to be made up of an exactly equal number of red and white flowers. However, if just one red is seen, that is evidence that the white flower in the first generation could not have been CC. Therefore, the breeder can be "statistically certain" that the first generation white was CC only if the second generation is large enough that the probability of *not* generating a red from a first generation Cc white is very low.

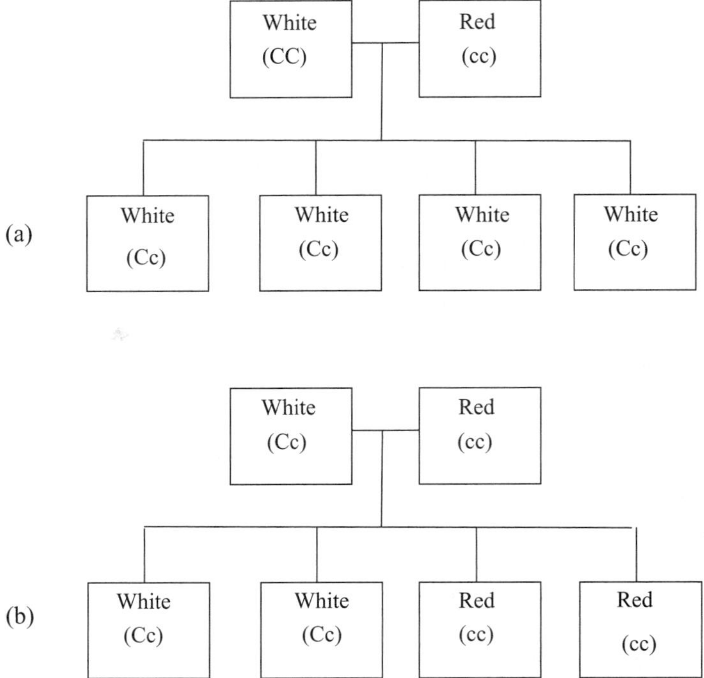

Figure 8.1. A simple illustration of Mendelian genetics. The situations shown are the "pedigrees" that might be derived from hybridization between two plants bearing a gene that has either a "white" allele (C), which results in white flowers, or a "red" allele (c), which results in red flowers. The upper figure, (a), shows the results that would be expected if a white plant with dominant genes only (phenotype = white, genotype = CC) is crossed with a plant carrying recessive genes only (phenotype = red, genotype = cc). The lower figure shows a similar pedigree assuming that the white "parent" had genotype Cc (heterozygous).

Pedigree studies provide a way of inferring genotypes from phenotypes, based on the pattern of inheritance. The idea works very well in plants, in situations where the expression of a phenotype is completely dictated by the genotype. However, it may take several generations before the pattern becomes apparent. This is no problem if we are dealing with plants that have discrete phenotypes, such as color or roughness, and where we know the ancestory of each individual. When it comes to people and intelligence, neither condition holds. We are dealing with a continuous trait, so the notion of discrete phenotypes is blurred. We are dealing with a relatively slow-breeding population; a human generation is a little over thirty years long. In addition, as will be illustrated, some traits may not reveal themselves until adulthood or even old age. We certainly cannot control mating, so we have no way of creating individuals with informative pedigrees, as a plant or animal breeder can. Therefore, while pedigree studies are sometimes useful in human genetics, it is more often the case that we have to look at statistics across populations. That turns out to be an advantage, rather than a defect, for such studies link genetics to evolution.

8.2.1. Mendel's Model Applied to Populations

In the 1930s Theodosius Dobzhansky (1900–1975), a Russian-born biologist who immigrated to the United States in 1927, developed techniques for studying genetics at the population level, without regard for individual pedigrees.[1] In addition to this insight, Dobzhansky's work provided the essential link between genetics and evolution. This section will consider only simple cases. Further complications are discussed in subsequent sections.

Dobzhansky worked with the common fruit fly, *Drosophila melanogaster*. From a genetic view, *Drosophilia* has three attractive characteristics: it is cheap; it breeds rapidly; and it has a number of traits that are controlled by single genes with only two alleles, as in the examples mentioned earlier. Dobzhansky used Mendel's principles to develop mathematical models of the distribution of traits in successive generations of a population of fruit flies.

To illustrate, let W and w be the alleles of the gene controlling the fly's body color. The normal ("wild type") body color in fruit flies is grayish, but there are shiny black (ebony) colored fruit flies. Imagine that a laboratory has available two large populations, one of wild type flies and another of ebony flies. At this point we do not know the genetic makeup of either population, because we do not know if a heterozygous (Ww) fly is grayish or ebony.

We then conduct an experiment in which we create a mixed population, containing 70% wild type flies and 30% ebony flies. In flies it is reasonable to assume random mating. The following combinations of parentages can be expected

Wild with wild: .70 × .70 = .49, just under half of the flies in the next generation.

Wild male with ebony female: .70 × .30 = .21, just over one-fifth of the flies.

Wild female with ebony male: .30 × .70 = .21, just over one-fifth of the flies.

Ebony male with ebony female: .30 × .30 = .09, just under one-tenth of the flies.

Now suppose that, unknown to us, all wild flies have genotype WW, all ebony flies have genotype ww, and W is dominant. If

these assumptions are correct, 91% (49% + 21% + 21% = 91%) of the flies in the offspring generation should have the gray, wild type phenotype, and 9% should have the ebony phenotype. The mathematics is a bit more complicated for the second generation – the offspring of the offspring – but the same principle applies. If we start with a mix of WW and ww populations, then the proportion of different genotypes, and by implication the proportion of phenotypes, is determined for all future generations. Statistical techniques (trust me!) can be used to determine the most likely starting configuration, given the distribution of phenotypes in later generations.

Similar models can be applied for genes with more than two alleles and for situations in which heterozygous genotypes (Cc or Ww in the examples) display a phenotype that is a mix between the two homozygous forms. Although the models are more complicated than the example, the principles are the same.

In order to link genetics to evolution we need the concept of *selective pressure*. This can be illustrated by continuing the example, including the assumption about the parent population containing 70% WW and 30% ww genotypes. The distribution of fertilized fly eggs, not mature flies, will have the following distribution of genotypes:

Phenotype	Genotype	Fraction
Wild	WW	.49
Wild	Ww	.42
Ebony	ww	.09

It is not immediately obvious, but can be proven, that if there is random mating within a population, the relative frequencies of the genotypes will be maintained. This is called *Hardy-Weinberg equilibrium*. In our example, if all three phenotypes were equally likely to survive to reproductive maturity, the fractions would be maintained in all subsequent generations. If we were to look ten generations ahead, the fractions would still be (.49, .42, .09).

---

1 Dobzhansky's major work, *Evolution and the Origin of the Species*, was first published in 1937. Two later revisions were published, the last in 1951.

This is where evolution comes in. Suppose that not all phenotypes are likely to survive at all, or to produce an equal number of offspring. In the example, it might be that ebony-type flies are easier to see, and thus more subject to predation, than the wild-type flies. The mechanism of selection does not matter; the numbers do.

Suppose that the gray-bodied phenotypes, all flies with the wild appearance, have a 90% chance of reaching sexual maturity (and hence reproducing themselves), while animals with an ebony-body phenotype have only an 80% chance. This is called a *selection pressure;* some genotypes are more likely to reproduce successfully than are other genotypes. Selective pressure will distort the population frequencies in the breeding population of the next generation. In this example, the distribution of genotypes in the breeding population of the first, second, and third generations would be:

Generation	WW	Ww	ww
1	.495	.424	.081
2	.505	.418	.077
3	.515	.413	.073
10	.574	.372	.054.

There is a drift toward domination by more viable phenotypes (genotypes WW and Ww), which comprise just under .92 of the genotypes in generation 1, rising to .946 after ten generations. After 100 generations the frequencies would be WW = .851, Ww = .143, ww = .005, with a .001 rounding error. The evolutionary pressure favoring a particular phenotype exerts a pressure that changes the genotypical distribution in the population. However, the unfavorable ww geneotype never quite dies out. Why not? The w alleles hide out, in the Ww genotype, which has a nonpathological phenotype. The ww form can reoccur when two Ww genotypes mate. Such matings account for 99% of the ww (pathological) genotypes at fifty generations.

Let's tie this back to human intelligence. The .9 figure for producing an offspring who also lives to reproductive age is far more characteristic of human populations than of fly populations.[2] As the example shows, selective pressures operate to reduce the frequency of genes associated with phenotypes that have low reproductive rates. However, it may take a long time for the less favorable genotypes to disappear from the population. This is illustrated in Figure 8.2, in which the example has been changed so that the two phenotypes have reproductive rates of .9 and .5. The figure shows the resulting frequencies of genotypes WW, Ww, and ww, extended over fifty generations. We could conduct the experiment in flies in about three months. An analogous experiment in humans would take over 1,500 years.

While one should always treat hypothetical examples with reservation, it is interesting to consider what this implies in social terms. Typically people know their phenotype, but not their genotype. Imagine a man and a woman, both of whom are of genotype Ww. As population figures approach stability, six out of every thousand couples would fall into this category. Neither would have any reason to suspect that they were carriers of the w allele, yet there would be one chance out of four that their child would be a ww, and hence exhibit the pathological phenotype.

Nevertheless, evolution has made things better. At the start of our hypothetical evolutionary cycle approximately one in six couples would have been in this situation. That is a lot worse than six out of a thousand in the evolved population.

Could situations like this actually occur in modern human populations? They can, and they do. Panel 8.1 presents an example, *Huntington's Disease,* and describes a famous case.

2 The *replacement rate* is the average number of offspring per woman required to maintain a stable population. In developed countries this is approximately 2.2, which implies that the probability that an individual offspring will live to reproduce is .909.

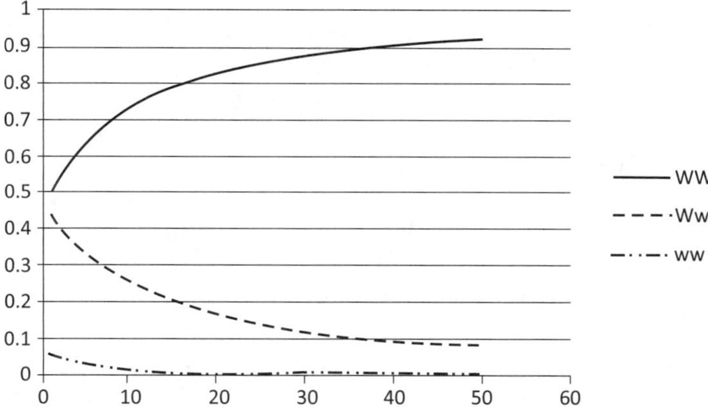

Figure 8.2. The effect of evolutionary selection on the distribution of genotypes. The relative frequency of three genotypes (ordinate) is plotted as a function of the number of generations (abscissa). The probability that a WW or Ww genotype will live to reproduce is assumed to be .9. The probability that a ww genotype (leading to a pathological phenotype) will live to reproduce has been set at .5. Initially the ww genotype had a frequency of about .05 (one in twenty cases in the population). By ten generations it had dropped to .01 (1 in 100). The change from thirty generations (.002) to fifty generations (.001, 1 in 1,000) was very small.

8.2.2. *On beyond Mendel: Complications when Dealing with Continuous Traits (like Intelligence)*

The single-gene model does a good job of explaining the inheritance of traits like the colors and surfaces of pea pods, eye and body color in fruit flies, and a surprising number of severe pathologies of human intelligence, such as Huntington's disease. Things rapidly become more complicated for continuous traits, and for traits that are influenced by more than one gene. Mendel thought of some of these complications; others he had no way of anticipating.

Multiple alleles. A gene can have more than two alleles. There is an important case, *Alzheimer's dementia*, in which this is a factor.

Additive genetic potentials for continuous traits. Alleles do not always fall neatly into "dominant" and "recessive" categories. The heterozygous form may have a phenotype that is intermediate between the phenotypes of the two homozygous forms. As a hypo-thetical example, suppose that the height of a plant is determined by a single gene, with two alleles. Represent these by A and a. If the heterozygous (Aa) genotype has a potential that is an additive mixture of the two phenotypes, then we might have the following situation:

Genotype	Phenotype	Expected Height
AA	HIGH	20 cm
Aa	MEDIUM	15 cm
Aa	LOW	10 cm

Environmental factors complicate the observation of genetic and phenotypic variation. A genotype is associated with the potential for expression of a trait. Environmental factors may cause the observed value to vary around the expected value. In the height example, suppose that the frequencies of the A and a forms of the gene were both .5 and that environmental factors produce deviations from the genetic expectation that are normally

Panel 8.1. Huntington's Disease: Woody Guthrie and His Family

Huntington's disease: Huntingon's disease is a severe form of mental and physical disability with an incidence of approximately 1 case in 30,000 people. Symptoms usually appear somewhere between thirty-five and fifty years of age, although symptoms in adolescence are not unknown. The initial symptoms are loss of short-term memory, then tremors and progressive failure of cognition. Abnormal irritation and aggressive behaviors have also been reported. Loss of muscular control follows, and then death.

The disease is caused by a dominant allele, so affected individuals need have only one copy of the gene. If a child of a Huntington's disease patient carries the allele, he or she is at risk of developing symptoms earlier than the parent did.

The singer Woodrow Wilson (Woody) Guthrie (1912–1965) was a prototypical example of the inheritance of Huntington's disease.

Guthrie was born to poor parents in Oklahoma shortly before World War I. His mother, who died in an Oklahoma mental institution, is now believed to have suffered from Huntington's disease. Guthrie's early adult life was marked by spectacular success as a folk and social protest singer in the 1930–40 depression era. His "This Land is Your Land" is considered a classic of the genre. In middle age Guthrie developed severe memory loss, progressive dementia, and other signs of deterioration typical of the syndrome. He died of the disease at age fifty-five.

Guthrie fathered eight children. Three of them died (two in auto accidents) at age twenty-one or younger, earlier than one would expect the disease to express itself. Therefore, we do not know if they were carriers of the gene for Huntington's disease. Two of the surviving children developed Huntington's disease. Both died at forty-one, younger than their father at the time of his death. The remaining three, including the contemporary folk singer Arlo Guthrie (1947–), are apparently not carriers.[*]

[*] Information from a website supporting a Public Broadcasting System tribute to Woody Guthrie, Wikipedia, and several biographical articles.

---

distributed with a mean of zero and a standard deviation of 2 cm. Figure 8.3(a) shows the distribution of heights that would result for each genotype. Figure 8.3(b) shows the distribution of phenotypes, that is, the distribution of observed height. This distribution was obtained by summing the distributions for each genotype, weighted by the probability of the genotype's occurrence.

Selection pressure complicates the situation. In the example of Figure 8.3, I assumed that there was no selection pressure. As the argument that led to Figure 8.2 showed, differences in probabilities of reproduction due to selection pressure will affect both genotype and phenotype frequencies over time. In the simplest case, which was illustrated in Figure 8.2, there is a "favorable" and an "unfavorable" allele, and the heterozygous genotype produces the phenotype, and therefore the reproductive success, associated with the dominant allele. There are cases in which the phenotype associated with the heterozygous genotype may have a reproductive success rate above, intermediate to, or below the success rates of the phenotypes associated with either homozygous genotype. Panel 8.2 describes one such case.

Dominance effects. Dominance refers to the extent to which one of the alleles in a heterozygotic pair dominates the other allele. Introductory examples of Mendel's laws usually present examples of complete dominance, in which the phenotype for the heterozygotic (Aa) form is the phenotype

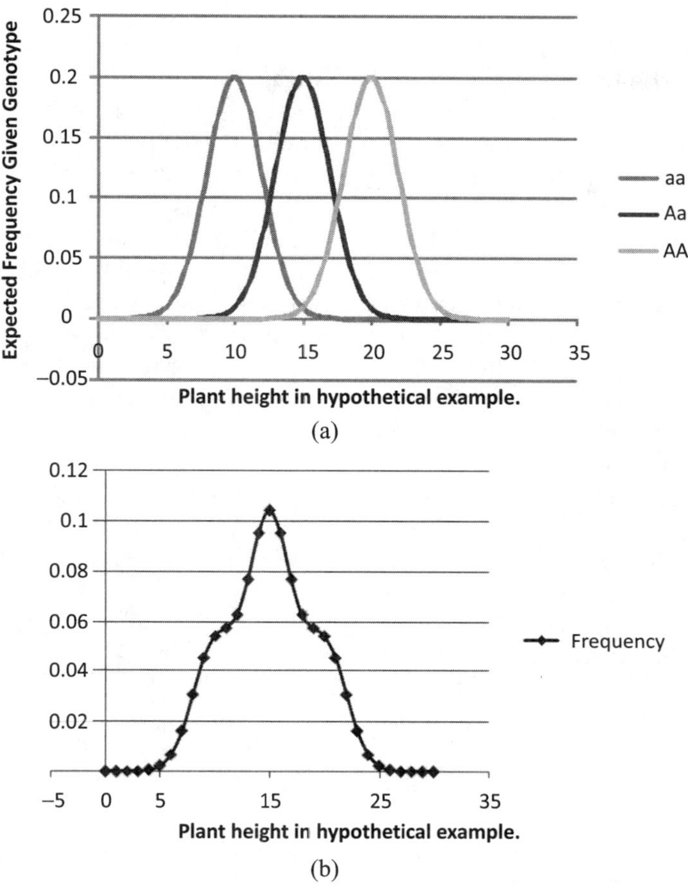

Figure 8.3. The distribution of phenotypes with independent environmental effects. This example shows the effects expected with three different genotypes, aa, Aa, and AA, with uniform environmental effects that are independent of the genotypical potential. See text for details. Figure (a) shows the conditional distribution of phenotypical values, given the genotype. Figure (b) shows the overall distribution of the phenotypical values, given equal frequency of the two alleles.

of the dominant (AA) allele, thus making a sharp distinction between dominant and recessive alleles. When the phenotypical trait is continuous, as in the case of intelligence, the heterozygotic phenotype can be a compromise between the phenotypes of the two homozygotic genotypes. That was the case for the hypothetical plant height illustration given earlier. In that illustration the heterozygotic phenotypical height was midway between the height associated with the two dominant genotypes. This is not necessarily the case. For instance, in the plant height example the Aa genotype might have

been associated with a genotypical height of 18 cm, closer to the 20 cm phenotypical height of the AA form.

In statistical analyses dominance effects appear as interactions, for the phenotypic effects of the two forms of the allele are not additive.

Probabilistic display of a phenotypical characteristic. In some cases genetic makeup influences the probability of displaying a trait, rather than the form that the trait has. This is particularly true of behavioral traits that depend upon interactions between the individual and the environment.

Panel 8.2. Sickle-Cell Anemia, Malaria, and the HBB Gene

The HBB gene influences the development of hemoglobin in the blood. Let H be the dominant form and h the recessive form. People who have the hh genotype suffer from *sickle-cell anemia*. Untreated, people with sickle-cell anemia usually die in their twenties. Treated patients now live into their thirties and forties.

People who are heterozygous (Hh) for the HBB gene have *sickle-cell trait*. The symptoms of sickle-cell anemia are generally not present. However, 25% of the children of parents with sickle-cell trait will be homozygous (hh), and therefore will have sickle-cell anemia. Since there is a good chance that a child with sickle-cell anemia will not live to reproductive age, especially if not treated, the reproductive success of the heterozygous parents is reduced.

To make things more complicated, the h allele confers some protection against malaria, a mosquito-borne disease. Worldwide, malaria is a major disease, especially in developing countries. There are 355 million to 500 million cases and about one million deaths each year, mostly when young children contract the disease. The disease has been virtually eradicated in developed countries, largely due to aggressive measures to control the mosquito population.

If malaria is prevalent, the order of reproductive success for the three genotypes is Hh, HH, hh. If malaria is not present, however, the order of reproductive success is HH, Hh, hh.*

---

* Information on sickle-cell anemia retrieved from www.nlm.nih.gov/medlineplus/ency/article/000527.htm. Information on malaria retrieved from www.nlm.nih.gov/medlineplus/ency/article/000621.htm, August 28, 2008.

Alcoholism, smoking, and other addictions illustrate such behaviors. People whose relatives are addicts are not necessarily slightly addicted, but the probability that they will become addicts is increased.

Genes are packaged on chromosomes. Genes are inherited in packages, rather than being inherited individually. Every cell in the body of every living creature contains structures called chromosomes, which bear the genes for that individual. The chromosomes come in two types, the *autosomes* and the *sex chromosomes*. In mammals the autosomes are paired, so that each member of a pair contains one of the alleles of a gene pair. The number of chromosome pairs varies with the species. Humans have twenty-two autosomes, referred to somewhat unimaginatively as chromosomes 1-22. An individual inherits one chromosome in each pair from the mother and the other from the father.

There are two types of sex chromosomes, X and Y. All normal human females have two X chromosomes, one inherited from each parent. Genetic transmission for females is thus the same on all twenty-three chromosome pairs. All normal males have an X chromosome inherited from the mother and a Y chromosome inherited from the father. The two chromosomes contain different genes. Probabilities of inheritance have to be modified accordingly. This is shown in the case described in panel 8.3.

We now turn to the case of inheritance controlled by several genes, the *polygenetic* situation.

8.2.3. *The Effect of Multiple Genes (the Polygenic Model)*

Suppose that there are two independently distributed genes, A and B, each with two equally likely alleles (A,a and B,b), and let the favorable alleles (A or B) each add five IQ points above the mean of 100 and the unfavorable alleles (a or b) each subtract five IQ points from the mean. There are

Panel 8.3. Male Pattern Baldness

Male pattern baldness (loss of hair spreading from just above the temples) is a sex-linked genetic trait. Male pattern baldness is not itself a cognitive trait, nor has it been linked to any variation in intelligence. The reason for discussing it here is that it is largely under the control of genes on the X chromosome. This also appears to be the case for many cognitive deficiencies. The ancestral relationships in male pattern baldness provide an easily observed analog to ancestral relationships that may be involved in the inheritance of some aspects of intelligence. Imagine a young man concerned over future hair loss. His father is not bald, but his two grandfathers both display male pattern baldness. Should the young man be worried?

Yes. The risk for male pattern baldness depends on an allele of the AR gene, located on the X chromosome.* Because the young man inherited a Y chromosome, but not an X chromosome, from his father, the father's hair pattern is irrelevant. By the same token, the father's father (the young man's paternal grandfather) is also irrelevant.

The maternal grandfather is another matter. The young man inherited his X chromosome from his mother. Mother had two X chromosomes, one from the man's maternal grandfather and one from the maternal grandmother. Because the maternal grandfather has male pattern baldness, the maternal grandfather probably carries the AR allele on his X chromosome. (There are other causes of baldness, but we disregard them for simplicity.) There is a 50% chance that the maternal grandfather's gene was carried forward to the young man, via his mother. Thus the probability is at least .5 that the young man carries the AR allele, putting him at risk for baldness.

Why do I say "at least"? There is also a chance that the AR allele was carried on the X chromosome that his mother inherited from her mother (the maternal grandmother). More generally, if there is a man with male pattern baldness somewhere in the maternal line beyond the grandparents, there is a chance that the baldness genotype will be carried forward, unexpressed, through the females of that line, until it reaches a male. The chances of this happening grow smaller and smaller with each generation, but the chance of inherited baldness never vanishes.

---

* Information on male pattern baldness retrieved from the National Institute of Health website ghr.nlm.nih.gov, March 29, 2008.

---

now nine possible genotypes with associated probabilities and phenotypical intelligence, which for simplicity I will denote IQ. The values are shown in Table 8.1.

Several of the genotypes in Table 8.1 produce the same phenotype, the same potential for an IQ score. Figure 8.4(a) rearranges the data to show the probability of different IQ potentials (phenotypes) regardless of the genotype. Figure 8.4(b) does the same thing for a more complicated case in which, instead of dealing with two genes, each of which contributes ± ten IQ points, we consider a situation in which there are ten genes, each with two alleles, and each allele either adds or subtracts .3 points of potential from the mean of 100. As the number of genes increases, the distribution of IQ potentials approaches the normal distribution.

8.2.4. *A Simple Polygenic Model of Intelligence*

Suppose that genetic and environmental effects are additive and independent. The phenotype, the observable score on a test, should be predictable by combining

Table 8.1. Genotypes and associated IQ potentials for the (artificially simple) case of two genes affecting intelligence. The assumptions are that each gene has two equally probable alleles, that a favorable allele contributes 5 points above a mean potential of 100, and that an unfavorable allele contributes 5 points below the mean potential. The genes are assumed to be independently distributed.

Genotype	*aa bb*	*aa Bb*	*Aa bb*	*aa BB*	*Aa Bb*	*AA bb*	*Aa BB*	*AA Bb*	*AA BB*
Probability	0.0625	0.1250	0.1250	0.0625	0.2500	0.0625	0.1250	0.1250	0.0625
Expected IQ	80	90	90	100	100	100	110	110	120

genetic and environmental influences, in the equation

$$X = G + E + e, \qquad (8.1)$$

where X is the score, G and E are the genetic and environmental contributions to the score, and e is a residual term due to test unreliability.

Equation 8.1 refers to statistical expectations and predictions. No one ever achieved an IQ score because they had such-and-such genetic inheritance and environmental experience. They achieved the score because of how they behaved on the test,

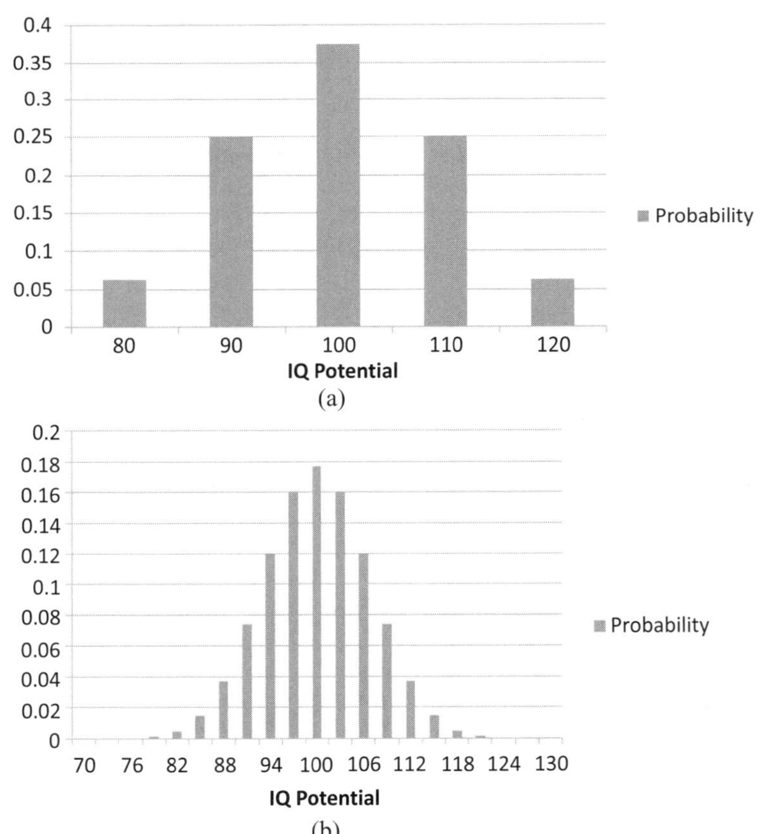

Figure 8.4. Probabilities for IQ potential (ordinate) as a function of the value of the genotypic potential. Calculations are for a two-gene model (a) and a ten-gene model (b). See text for further details.

which was determined by the state of their brain (and hence mind, for the brain has a mind of its own) at the moment of testing. The brain came to be in the state it was because of the combined influences of genetic heritage and environmental experience. These are *distal* causes of an IQ score. The behavior was the *proximal* cause. When we start to consider the relative influence of genetic and environmental influence on intelligence, the distal-proximal distinction becomes quite important.

Equation 8.1 cannot be used to break down the score of any individual into genetic and environmental components, for we would be explaining one observable in terms of two unknowns. The equation does imply the distribution of scores (and hence correlations) across individuals of different degrees of genetic relatedness. Therefore, we can untangle genetic and environmental influences by examining variations in IQ scores (or other variables) across individuals.

The variation in a set of scores is measured by the standard deviation; the larger the standard deviation, the more variable the trait underlying the score. The variance is the square of the standard deviation. The covariance measures the extent to which two scores vary together. Equation 8.1 implies that

$$Var(X) = Var(G) + Var(E)$$
$$+ 2\,Cov(G, E), \qquad (8.2)$$

where *Var* indicates variance and *Cov* indicates covariance. The term on the left, (*VarX*), is the variation of the observed test scores. The first term on the right, (*VarG*), measures the variation in the genetic makeup of the population; (*VarE*) is an index of the variation in the environment; and the third term, 2*Cov*(*G*, *E*), reflects the extent to which genetic and environmental contributions are correlated.

The extent to which a trait is heritable is defined as the proportion of variance in the trait that is due to variance in genetic

contribution. This is referred to as *broad sense heritability,*

$$h^2 = \frac{Var(G)}{Var(X)} \qquad (8.3)$$
$$h^2 = \frac{Var(G)}{Var(G) + Var(E) + 2Cov(G, E)}$$

This coefficient is the "statistic of choice" in many discussions of genetic influences on intelligence.

Heritability is the proportion of phenotypic variance associated with genotypic variance. It is important to remember (a) that variance is a measure defined on populations, but not on individuals in that population and (b) that variance is independent of the value of the expected (mean) value. These two conclusions also apply to h^2. It is a useful statistic, if we keep certain restrictions in mind.

(a) Unless h^2 is zero or one we do not know the extent to which any individual's intelligence, or any other phenotypic trait, has been determined by heredity or environment. For instance, modern studies of h^2 in European and North American samples usually result in an estimated h^2 of from .5 to .8, depending on certain characteristics of the sample, such as age. It does not follow that there is any person in the sample whose personal intelligence is 50–80% due to genetic inheritance.

(b) Because the variance is independent of the mean, an environmental variable can change the average level of a trait in that population without influencing the heritability. A good example is the height of Japanese-Americans. Height is a highly heritable trait. In addition, adult height is strongly dependent on the quality of infant nutrition. At the time of the major Japanese immigration to the United States, in the late nineteenth century, infant nutrition in Japan was poor by modern standards. A century later Japanese-Americans who are entirely descendants of the early immigrants (i.e., who have no non-Japanese ancestors) are substantially taller than their forbearers, even though they come from the same gene pool.

Could the same thing happen with intelligence? There are indications that it has. In the twentieth century there was a marked rise in the IQ scores of people in the developed nations. This change, over only three human generations, occurred far too quickly to have been due to genetic changes.

(c) The heritability coefficient is influenced by three things: the extent of genetic variation in the population; the *penetrance*, which is the extent to which the value of the phenotypic trait is determined by the genome; and the extent of relevant environmental variation in the population. If a population consists of genetically diverse individuals, the heritability coefficient will go up; to the extent that the population consists of genetically homogeneous individuals, the heritability coefficient will go down. Conversely, if relevant environmental variation goes up, the heritability coefficient goes down, and vice versa.

Point (c) is obvious when you inspect equation 8.3, because the term for genetic variance appears in both the numerator and the denominator, while the term for environmental variance appears only in the denominator. However, people do not always think mathematically, especially when the discussion of the genetics of intelligence becomes heated, so let us examine a few cases.

In the extreme, an army of clones (as in the science fiction *Star Wars* films) would have no genetic variability, and hence the heritability coefficient would be zero. This extreme is never reached in human populations, but different populations do vary a good deal in the extent of their genetic variability. Sub-Saharan African populations display considerably greater genetic variation than other populations. The genetic variability in sub-Saharan Africa should drive the heritability coefficient upward compared to genetic variability in other large populations.

Small, isolated populations generally show low genetic variability. The inhabitants of Norfolk Island in the Pacific Ocean provide a historically interesting case. Virtually all the modern inhabitants of Norfolk Island are descended from nine British sailors and twelve Polynesian women who fled to nearby Pitcairn Island after the famous *Bounty* mutiny in 1789. (Their descendents moved to richer, and then uninhabited, Norfolk Island in 1856.) We would expect the heritability coefficient to be low in the present-day Norfolk Islanders, due to low genetic variability.

Heritability also depends upon the extent to which there is environmental variation relevant to intelligence. Increases in relevant environmental variation decrease heritability; decreases in relevant environmental variation increase heritability. To illustrate the point I offer a thought experiment.

I conjecture that h^2 in the population of England has gone up since the nineteenth century, Galton's time. Why? For simplicity, let us disregard immigration, and assume that all present English citizens are descended from the English population of the nineteenth century. As a first approximation, assume that the variance in the genetic contribution to intelligence, $Var(G)$, is the same today as it was in the nineteenth century. As Dickens's novels so graphically portray, in the nineteenth century the economic, educational, and health differences between the rich and poor were stark. In the England of today reasonable health care, education, and nutrition are available to nearly everyone. In terms of equation 8.3, the variance in the environmental influence on intelligence, in the denominator of the equation, has decreased. Therefore, if the genetic variation is constant the heritability measure, h^2, will have gone up.

My idea about heritability in nineteenth-century England was labeled a conjecture because I do not have measures of either genetic or environmental variation in nineteenth-century England. However, a modern study, that had half the data, supports the conjecture.

In modern European–North American industrial and post-industrial populations, estimates of h^2 fall in the range $.40 < h^2 < .60$. This value may not hold in subpopulations. Studies in the United States have found h^2 values in the .5–.6 range for school-age children whose parents are of middle to high socioeconomic status (SES), but values of less than .40 for the children of low SES parents.[3] The investigators suggested that this is because variations in environment above a threshold quality, which most middle and high SES families exceed, have relatively little effect on intelligence. However, variations in environmental quality below this threshold, which may occur in many low SES families, have a substantial effect on intelligence. This is a reasonable explanation of the findings, and there is some evidence, based upon direct observation of the differences in children's environments in high and low SES homes, that the hypothesized environmental differences do exist.[4]

Gene x environment correlations are expressed by the $Cov(G, E)$ term in equation 8.2. It is possible that there are genetic and environmental influences that, causally, have separate influences on a phenotypic trait, including intelligence, and whose distributions are correlated in the population. Because the $Cov(G, E)$ term is in the denominator in equation 8.3, if the correlation between genetic and environmental effects goes up, h^2 will come down. That is simple algebra. The causal relations are more interesting, for at times discussions of the inheritance of intelligence have been faulted by a failure to consider gene x environment correlations. The issue has been particularly important when conclusions are based upon an observation of a correlation between a person's intelligence and parental SES.

Galton's *Hereditary Genius*, one of the seminal nineteenth-century books on intelligence, is almost a prototypical example of a failure to consider gene-environment correlations. Galton examined historical records of "eminent men," ranging from members of Parliament to war heroes, and found that they came from a relatively few families. He concluded:

> *The direct result of this inquiry is to make manifest the great and measurable differences between the mental and bodily facilities of individuals, and to prove that the laws of heredity are as applicable to the former as the latter. Its indirect result is to show that a vast but unused power is vested in each generation over the very nature of their successors–that is, over their inborn facilities and dispositions.*
>
> Francis Galton, Hereditary Genius, *Introduction to the 1892 reprinting*

Galton ignored the possibility that great families have social and economic resources that further their children's careers in ways that have nothing to do with biology. Could this happen today? What do you think? To assist you, panel 8.4 provides an American example that may be food for thought.

Galton leaped to a genetic conclusion, ignoring the effects of gene x environment correlations. Let us look at a contemporary error, but in the opposite direction.

One of the charges made against the use of the SAT as a college entrance requirement is that because examinees from high SES families obtain high test scores, the SAT perpetuates the "unfair" advantage that these examinees have because of their social background.[5] This argument turns Galton's conclusion on its head; the observation that there is a correlation between parental SES and SAT scores is taken as proof that children from well-to-do families have an unfair advantage because family wealth has been used to construct good environments for learning, including coaching on how to take the test. Therefore, the critics aver, the SAT should not be used to screen applicants to

---

3 Harden, Turkheimer, & Loehlin, 2007; Turkheimer et al., 2003.

4 See Nisbett, 2009, for a review of this evidence.

5 Lemann, 1999.

> ### Panel 8.4. Has Anyone Ever Inherited the American Presidency?
>
> As of 2010 the United States had had forty-five presidents. Four American families contributed two presidents apiece: two father-son combinations (John and John Quincy Adams, George H. W. and George W. Bush), one grandfather-grandson combination (William and Benjamin Harrison), and two distant cousins (Theodore and Franklin Roosevelt). The probability of this occurring by chance is miniscule; even in the Adams' time the population of the United States numbered in the millions. Does this mean that the United States never completely shook off the genetic determinism exemplified by the British royal family?
>
> We should not arbitrarily rule out the possibility that genetics contributed to these men's ability to behave in a way that would ultimately bring them to the presidency. But let us consider some gene by environment correlations. It is well documented that the elder Adams and Bush assisted their sons in their early careers. (An unfriendly newspaper columnist described George W. Bush as having been born with a silver shoe in his mouth.) Theodore and Franklin Roosevelt were born to separate branches of the very rich Roosevelt family. They both suffered severe illnesses (Theodore in childhood, Franklin as an adult) that, in less affluent individuals, would have severely restricted their career prospects. Each Roosevelt received the best treatment that the medical science of the day could offer, and price was not an issue.
>
> So was ascension to the presidency dominated by genetics or environment? It is impossible to say.

college, because doing so will solidify class lines.[6] This conclusion could be right, but it could be that relatively wealthy, highly educated parents pass on a genetic advantage to their children. If this is the reason that children from higher SES families get better SAT scores, then a different argument has to be made about the use or nonuse of the test.

In fairness to the many investigators who have conducted research in this area, I hasten to add that it is not easy to measure gene × environment correlations. The conceptual issue is easy to grasp. In practice, though, we have a model for calculating genetic resemblances, but we do not have any such model for calculating environmental resemblances. Here is the problem.

Mendelian genetics provides a model for the genotypic resemblance between two individuals with specified family relationships. You obtain half your genetic material from your mother and half from your father; going back a bit, you obtain a quarter of your genetic material from each grandparent. We do not have any such model to specify environmental relationships. The difference in genetic distance between grandparents, parents, and self is clear. The difference in environmental distance between generations is not clear at all.

As a result, investigators either treat environmental effects as an unmeasured residual – that is, a "left over" effect – or they try to measure environmental resemblances by determining the correlations between cognitive measures and proxy measures of the environment, such as parental education, income, or, in one case I have seen, government ratings of a neighborhood as being "poor," "middle-class," "upper middle-class," or "rich." In many studies only one such variable (e.g., parental education) is measured. There is a good chance that some crucial part of the environment will be overlooked. The size of the effect associated with the missing part can be measured, but the nature of the effect remains unknown.

6   Atkinson, 2005.

8.2.5. *Looking inside Genetic Effects*

Equations 8.1–8.3 treated genetic effects as a single package, G. Conceptually, G is the sum of four components;

$$G = A + D + I + (G : E) \qquad (8.4)$$

where A refers to additive genetic effects, D refers to dominance effects, I refers to a phenomenon called *epistasis*, and $(G : E)$ refers to gene-environment interactions. Let us take each of these in turn.

A is the sum of the independent effects of the genes. The D term adjusts for dominance, the fact that the influence of two alleles of the same gene may not be strictly additive. In a gene with two alleles, dominance occurs if the trait expressed by the heterozygotic case does not represent an average of the expressions of the two homozygotic cases.

Epistasis, the I term, refers to interactive effects between different genes.[7] Epistasis occurs if the expression of one gene depends upon alleles present in another gene. To take an oversimplified example from evolution, the presence of feathers does not guarantee flight, nor does the presence of light bone structure in the forelimbs. If you combine them, and make a few other adjustments to the limb structure, none of which alone permits flight, you have a bird!

As this example illustrates, on the evolutionary scale epistatic effects have been spectacular. Within the field of human intelligence, though, epistatic effects have virtually been ignored. This may be a mistake, for as we gain a better idea of how the genes work we are seeing more and more cases in which one part of the genome regulates the expression of another part. At present, though, we are only beginning to identify the genes involved in intelligence. When these are known, epistatic effects may come to play a greater part in our thinking about intelligence than they do now.

The $(G : E)$[8] term refers to *gene-environment* interactions. A gene-environment interaction occurs when an environmental variable alters the expression of a genetic potential, or when the genetic characteristic changes the influence of an environmental variable. Alcoholism is a good example. Protracted alcoholism can have disastrous effects on cognition. Susceptibility to alcoholism has a substantial genetic component.[9] In societies in which alcohol is widely used as a recreational drug, a person who has an inherited susceptibility to alcohol is at risk for cognitive deficit. There is no genetic risk in a society that does not use alcohol.

Gene-environment interactions are not the same as gene-environment correlations. A gene-environment correlation occurs when genetic and environmental influences make contributions to a trait that are independent within an individual, but have correlated distributions across the population. For instance, the argument against Galton's conclusion about genius, and the extent to which parental SES contributes to a person's SAT score, are examples of gene-environment correlations.

With a few exceptions (notably in the work of Urie Bronfrenbrenner and Stephen Ceci of Cornell University),[10] gene-environment interactions relevant to intelligence have not received very much attention. Part of the problem is a technical one. It is difficult to separate gene-environment interactions and gene-environment correlations by statistical analysis. Hopefully this will change as better models are developed.[11] There is also the continuing problem of deciding what environmental variables to measure. In some cases, though, the problem is conceptual. The alcoholism example was clear-cut. But what happens when the

---

7 Plomin et al., 2008, p. 377.

8 This term is often written G × E. I have chosen a different notation to avoid confusion between the genetic concept of interaction and the statistical concept, which depends upon the multiplication operation.

9 Plomin et al., 2008, pp. 270–277.

10 Bronfrenbrenner & Ceci, 1994; Ceci, 1990.

11 Johnson (2007) provides a good candidate for such a model.

interaction is social? Consider the case of children's intelligence.

Children's IQ scores are correlated with parental SES, with values in the .3–.4 range. Why? One possibility is that the effect is entirely environmental. Higher SES parents spend more time interacting with their children in ways that develop cognition than do lower SES parents.[12] For instance, the high SES parent is more likely to encourage children to solve problems on their own than is the low SES parent. The physical environment is also better in the high SES home; the high SES home provides more books and creative toys. It could be argued that this is an example of a gene-environment correlation; the lower SES children would have higher IQs if they had the home advantages of the high SES children. It may be, though, that there are genetic influences. High SES parents may be genetically predisposed to interact with their children in particular manners, and the high SES child may have inherited a genetic potential to be receptive to these interactions.

This example shows how difficult it is to untangle interaction effects when we are comparing a distal and a proximal influence. The genotype does not influence IQ scores in the same sense that it influences eye color. The IQ score is determined by the examinee's behavior in a testing situation, which is in turn determined by the examinee's experiences and ability to learn from them. However, people influence the way others react to them. Therefore, the genotype exerts a distal influence on IQ scores, while experiences exert proximal influences. Add to this the fact that there are correlations between environmental opportunity and genetic constitution, and it is easy to see why sophisticated statistical models are needed to separate main effects, interactions, and correlations.

8.2.6. *Calculating Genetic Variance*

Quantitative behavior genetics (QBG) attempts to identify the extent to which

variations in human traits are associated with genetic or environmental influences. In this section I will try to explain how this is done. I will start with a simplified model that illustrates the basic principles, and then explain the more realistic *ACE* model. First a few words are in order about the QBG approach itself.

QBG deals with statistical associations between variation in genetic and environmental makeup and variation in displays of intelligence, usually test scores. This is necessary because it is impossible to test causal hypotheses by controlling either genetic makeup or environmental conditions in humans, in the way that might be done in studies of plants or nonhuman animals.

Probably the easiest examples of QBG to understand are analyses of similarities and differences between monozygotic (MZ, "identical") and dizygotic (DZ, "fraternal") twins. Monozygotic (MZ) twins result from the splitting of a single fertilized ovum into two genetically identical ova, while dizygotic (DZ) twins result from the fertilization of two ova during a single act of sexual intercourse. This provides a "natural experiment," in which the MZ twins are genetically identical, while the DZ twins, like siblings (SS), share half of the permissible human variation in genetic material.[13] The difference is important.

The correlation between scholastic achievement test scores of ten-year-old identical (monozygotic, MZ) twins is about .78, varying a little with the academic topic. The correlation for fraternal (dizygotic, DZ) twins is about .50.[14] Intuitively the higher correlation in MZ twins suggests that genetic similarity is associated with similar academic accomplishments.

---

12 Nisbett (2009) presents this argument in detail.

13 Statements that two individuals share a certain percentage of their genes are a bit misleading. Most of the genes in the human genome are shared with all animals, and many are shared with plants. Other genes are invariant over all people. These are the genes that define the species. The statement that two individuals share x% of their genes refers to the extent to which the genotypes of two individuals covary over those genes that can vary in humans.

14 Plomin et al., 2008, Table 9.5.

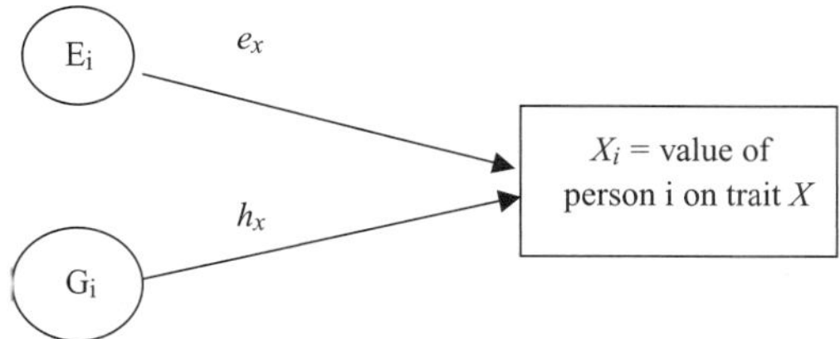

Figure 8.5. The relationship between genetic and environmental contributions in a single individual.

To go further, we need a more precise model of how the observed correlations are produced. Modern QBG relies heavily on a statistical technique called *path analysis* or, somewhat more frequently, *structural equation modeling*. The factor analytic techniques used in psychometrics (Chapter 4) are special cases of structural equation modeling. Historically, though, the factor analytic techniques were developed first.

Here is an illustrative simple model. Suppose that the genetic and environmental components are independent of each other. The phenotype for person i can be expressed as

$$X_i = h_x G_i + e_x E_i, \qquad (8.5)$$

where X_i is person i's score on test x (or any other record of a trait), G_i is i's genetic potential, and E_i refers to environmental effects that are statistically independent of, and hence unpredictable by, genetic potential. This model is shown in Figure 8.5.

The goal of the analysis is to determine the values of h and e, the coefficients representing the strength of the genetic and environmental influences. These are called the *path coefficients*. We cannot measure anything but X directly, so we cannot compute a simple regression of X on G and E. What we can observe, however, are the correlations (covariances) between the X values for people of known relationship. The variance in a trait can be broken down into its components;

$$Var(X) = h^2 Var(G) + e^2 Var(E)$$
$$+ 2he Cov(G, E) \qquad (8.6)$$

where *Var* indicates a variance and *Cov* a covariance. In words, equation 8.6 says that the variance in test scores is equal to the variance in genetic potential, weighted by the square of the genetic path coefficient, plus the variance in the environmental potential, weighted by the square of the environmental path coefficient, plus a term that depends upon the two path coefficients and the covariance between the genetic and environmental potentials.

Since the scales of all variables are arbitrary, we can deal with standardized variables, all of which have a mean of zero and a standard deviation of 1. Equation 8.6 becomes

$$1 = h^2 + e^2 + 2her(G, E), \qquad (8.7)$$

where $r(G, E)$ refers to the correlation between genetic and environmental potentials.

If we assume that there are no gene-environment correlations, $r(G, E) = 0$, equation 8.7 becomes

$$1 = h^2 + e^2. \qquad (8.8)$$

The parameter h^2 can be interpreted as the percent of variance in the phenotypical trait (X) that is associated with additive genetic effects. In general, a path coefficient is associated with every arc in the graphic version of the structural equation model. If there is no arc between two entities, as is the case for the G and E entities in Figure 8.5, a path coefficient of 0 is implied.

The next step is to make use of the fact that we know the degree of genetic relationship between any pair of relatives – for example, between siblings or between children and grandchildren. This lets us expand the basic model, as shown graphically in Figure 8.6. Instead of considering a single person, i, we consider two people, i *and* i', who stand in some known relation to each other – for example, MZ or DZ twins. Obviously there are equivalent equations and diagrams for each person individually. Figure 8.6 puts the two figures together, as indicated by the double-headed arrows,

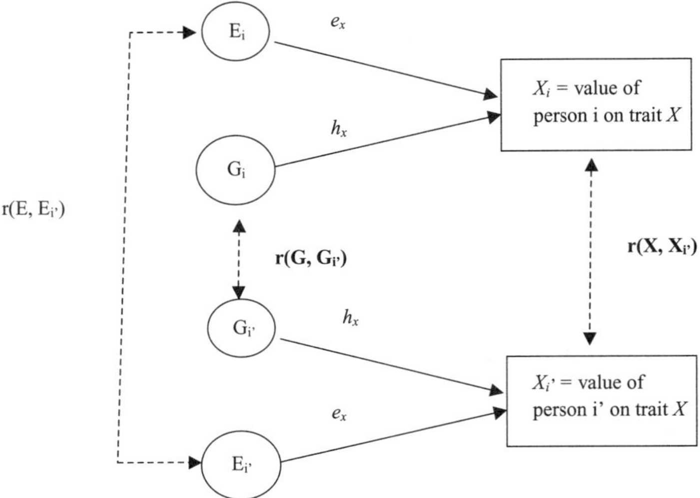

Figure 8.6. A model of the relation between genetic and environmental effects in two individuals, i and i'. Known path parameters are shown in boldface. If the kinship relation between the individuals is known (sibs, first cousins, etc.), the genetic correlation, **r(G_i, G_i')**, is known from genetic theory. The correlation between scores on trait X, **r(X_i, X_i')**, can be observed. Other parameters must be estimated. If one can assume that the environments are independent, then the environmental correlation r(E_i, E_i') can be set to zero.

which denote correlations between the two people's environments, $r(E_i, E_i')$, genetic constitutions, $r(G_i, G_i')$, and scores on the trait in question, e.g. IQ scores, $r(X_i, X_i')$.

The path coefficients and correlations, collectively, constitute the *observables* and the *parameters* of the model. The observable, shown in boldface in Figure 8.6, is the correlation between test scores. The parameters are either *fixed* or *free*. Fixed parameters (also shown in boldface in the figure) are parameters that are not directly observable, but are fixed by theoretical considerations. This is the point where QBG uses genetic theory. The correlation between genetic potentials is a fixed parameter, because genetic theory specifies the fraction of genetic variation shared by two related people. This can vary from 1, for monozygotic (MZ) twins, to 0 for genetically unrelated individuals. The h and e coefficients, which represent the effects of heredity and environment, are free parameters. Path analysis is used to find values for the free parameters that, when combined with the fixed parameters, reconstruct the correlations between observables as closely as possible.

It can be proven, although I will not do so here,[15] that the correlation between two observable variables will be equal to the sum of the products of the coefficients along each of the paths linking them in the diagram. Therefore, in this model the correlation between the X and X' scores is calculated across pairs of people of a given degree of relationship, such as all MZ or all DZ twin pairs.

$$r(X, X') = h_x r(G, G') h_x + e_x r(E, E') e_x$$
$$r(X, X') = h_x^2 r(G, G') + e_x^2 r(E, E')$$

$$(8.9)$$

Equation 8.9 expresses one observable, $r(X, X')$ in terms of four values on the

15 See Bollen, 1989, or Loehlin, 2004, for discussions.

right-hand side. Such equations are mathematically indeterminate, because more than one value for the right-hand side variables could be chosen to satisfy the equation. (This is generally the case whenever there are more values to be calculated than observables.) The solution to the problem is to consider different degrees of genetic and environmental relationships simultaneously.

As an example, suppose that we study two samples – one of same-sex siblings raised in their parents' home, and one of same-sex siblings in which each sibling is adopted into a different home. We make the following assumptions:

1. The adoptions occur very early in the children's life, ideally shortly after birth.
2. The adoption agency does not practice selective placement. There was no attempt to match the characteristics of the adoptive and biological parents.

Under these assumptions it is reasonable to assume that the environmental correlation between the adopted siblings, $r(E, E')$, is zero.[16] The equation for the correlation between two individuals adopted into different homes, equation (8.9), simplifies to

$$r_{apart}(X, X') = h_x^2 r(G, G').\qquad(8.10)$$

At this point QBG introduces genetic theory. Genetic theory tells us that for DZ twins and same-sex siblings, $r(G, G') = .5$.

The next step is to introduce observables. As quite a few studies of siblings raised together and apart have been conducted, we have a good idea of the value of the correlation between test scores, $r(X, X')$, for siblings raised together or apart – raised together .47, raised apart .24.[17]

Therefore, for the siblings raised apart

$$r_{apart}(X, X') = h_x^2(.5)\qquad(8.11)$$
$$h_x^2 = \frac{r_{apart}(X, X')}{.5}$$
$$h_x^2 = .48.$$

For siblings raised together there will be some unknown but possibly nonzero environmental correlation, $r(E, E')$, reflecting the fact that two children raised in the same family are likely to have similar environments:

$$r_{together}(X, X') = h_x^2(.5) + e^2 r(E, E').$$
$$(8.12)$$

Making appropriate substitutions for observed and theoretically established values,

$$h_x^2\,(.5) = .24 \text{ from equation 8.11}$$
$$e^2 = 1 - h^2 \text{ from equation 8.8}\qquad(8.13)$$
$$h_x^2\,(.5) + e^2 r(E, E') \text{ from equation 8.12.}$$

This is a system of three linear equations in three variables, and hence has a unique solution. Rearranging the first line establishes that $h^2 = .48$. Substituting this value into the second line, $e^2 = .52$. Using these values to solve for the remaining equation, we have $r(E, E') = .44$.

Conceptually, the model tells us that *if our assumptions are correct* the variance in the test scores is approximately equally associated with genetic variance and variance in the environment that is statistically independent of genetic variance, and that siblings raised together experience statistically related, but not identical, environmental influences.

But how do we tell if our assumptions are correct?

8.2.7. *Fitting Models to Data*

The example just presented illustrates a *saturated* model. In saturated models only

16 This assumption is widely made. However, it can be challenged. Nisbett (2009) has speculated that the very fact that two families are willing to adopt may make home environments similar in ways that are important to cognition.
17 Plomin et al., 2008, Figure 8.7.

one set of parameters will satisfy the data, and these parameters can be used to reconstruct the observed matrix of correlations or covariances perfectly. While studying saturated models can be informative, the fact that the parameters inevitably reconstruct the observations means that there has been no reduction in the complexity of our explanation. To illustrate, in the example just given only two parameters, h^2 and $r(E, E')$, were estimated from the data, because the value of e^2 was dictated once h^2 was determined. Therefore, we explained two observations, $r_{together}(X, X')$ and $r_{apart}(X, X')$, in terms of two estimated parameters. What we would like to do is to provide an explanation that is less complex than the original observations, by deriving K parameters to explain M observations, where K is (substantially) less than M. In order to do this we have to relax our requirement that the parameters reconstruct the observations exactly. Instead, we try to find parameters that can be used to derive *expected* observations that can be compared to the observed values.

This is done using complicated statistical estimation methods that are far beyond the scope of this book. However, a simple illustration can be used to show the spirit of model fitting, without going into computational details.

Suppose that we add to the previous example the case of dizygotic (DZ) twins raised together and apart. In theory, this should not make any difference, because DZ twins share the same amount of genetic material as do biological same-sex siblings (SS). In fact, though, the correlations are raised; $r_{DZ(together)}(X, X') = .55$ compared to $r_{SS(together)}(X, X') = .47$, and $r_{DX(apart)}(X, X') = .35$ compared to $r_{SS(apart)}(X, X') = .24$.

If we repeat the analysis of equations 8–13, using DZ correlations instead of SS correlations, our estimates become $h^2 = .70, e^2 = .30$, and $r(E, E') = .67$ (actually 2/3). These numbers reconstruct the DZ twins data, but do not reconstruct the data for siblings. What we want are parameter estimates that can be used to approximate both the SS and the DZ data. We could average the values of the estimates obtained from SS and DZ cases, so that

$$h^2 = \frac{.70 + .48}{2} = .59$$

$$r(E, E') = \frac{.67 + .44}{2} = .555.$$

The observed values of the correlations between test scores now differ from their predicted values:

Correlation	Predicted Value	Observed Value
$r_{SSapart}$	.295	.24
$r_{SStogether}$	.522	.47
$r_{DZapart}$	.295	.35
$r_{DZtogether}$	.522	.55

We have obtained greater parsimony, by reconstructing four observations from two estimated parameters, at the expense of accuracy.

At this point a certain amount of judgment is used. One could argue that genetics and environment must work the same way in both DZ and SS pairs, but because DZ pairs are the same age, their environments may be more similar than the environments of SS pairs. This is not an entirely ad hoc argument, for SS pairs are, by definition, made up of an older and a younger sibling, and just being the elder or the younger may have different influences on development. If you accept this argument, you should require that h^2 have the same value for DZ and SS pairs, but you allow for separate values for $r_{SS}(E, E')$ and $r_{DZ}(E, E')$. This changes the predicted-observed comparison to

Correlation	Predicted Value	Observed Value
$r_{SSapart}$	.295	.24
$r_{SStogether}$	.476	.47
$r_{DZapart}$	.295	.35
$r_{DZtogether}$	.568	.55

The predicted and observed values are now closer to each other than before, but some parsimony has been lost, because four observations are being derived from three estimates.

This example mirrors the use of structural equation modeling in modern QBG and, for that matter, in other fields in the behavioral and social sciences. The only major difference between what has been shown and what is done in practice is in the way the parameters are estimated. The averaging method was used solely because it is easy to understand. In practice scientists use computer-intensive techniques of parameter estimation, which we need not discuss. The important thing is to understand the principles behind model fitting, rather than the computational details.

8.2.8. *A Rough-and-Ready Method for Estimating* h^2

Prior to the development of structural equation modeling QBG relied heavily on "rough and ready" methods for calculating h^2. This often forced researchers to rely on questionable assumptions. Here are three commonly offered comparisons

One estimation method is based on comparisons of the correlations between scores of MZ and DZ twins. If the twins are raised in the same family,

$$r_{MZ} = h^2 + e^2 r(E, E')$$
$$r_{DZ} = \tfrac{1}{2}h^2 + e^2 r(E, E')$$
$$h^2 = 2(r_{MZ} - r_{DZ}).$$

(8.14)

This contrast is valid if the correlation between environmental influences is the same for pairs of MZ and (same-sex) DZ twins. If MZ twins live in more similar environments than DZ twins, the approximation in equation 8.14 will overestimate the heritability coefficient.

A similar logic can be used to contrast the MZ twin correlations to (same-sex) sibling correlations, or to parent-child correlations. In both cases the assumption that the same environmental correlation applies across types of relationship is suspect.

Another contrast is based on the test scores of MZ and DZ twin pairs when both

twin pairs have been raised apart. Such situations are unusual, but they do occur. If it can be assumed that the adoption process itself does not introduce a correlation between environments, the environmental correlation, $r(E, E')$, will be zero for both MZ and DZ twins. Therefore,

$$r_{MZ}(X, X') = h^2$$
$$r_{DZ}(X, X') = \tfrac{1}{2}h^2.$$

(8.15)

8.2.9. *The ACE Model*

We now examine a realistic, widely used model in QBG research on intelligence, the *ACE model*. This model assumes three sources of variation in test scores or similar indices:

A: Additive genetic effects. The sum of the effects of different genes, without considering dominance and epistatic effects.

C: Shared environmental effects. "Shared" here refers to shared variation. Recall that QBG models operate on pairs of individuals, such as siblings or twins, who stand in some relation to each other. Shared environmental effects refer to variations in the environment that vary across pairs, but are shared within a pair. For siblings, the clearest example of nonshared environment effects is a difference in the family environment. Even if both members of a sibling pair grow up in the same family, one will be older than the other, so the older and younger sib have different family environments.

E: Nonshared environmental effects. These are effects of the environment that differ both across pairs and within a pair. Continuing with the sibling example, each sibling is part of the other sibling's environment. An environmental effect associated with being an older or younger sibling – and there are such effects, as we shall see in Chapter 9 – would be a nonshared environmental effect.

The causal equation for the ACE model is

$$X = A + C + E,$$

(8.16)

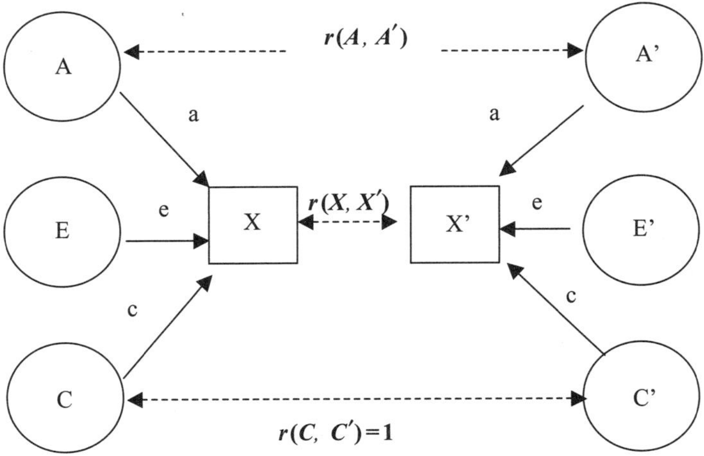

Figure 8.7. The ACE model. The path coefficient $r(A, A')$ is determined by genetic theory. The path coefficient $r(C, C')$ is set to 1, by the definition of shared environmental effects that act on each member of a pair. By a similar definition, $r(E, E')$ must be zero, and therefore is not contained in the model. The correlation between observable traits, $r(X, X')$, is determined by the data. Genetic and environmental coefficients a, c, e are estimated by fitting the model to the data for three or more types of pairs (e.g., MZ and DZ twins and siblings).

where X is a phenotypical trait score, A refers to additive genetic effects, C refers to shared environmental effects, and E refers to nonshared environmental effects. The path diagram for the ACE model is shown in Figure 8.7. As in Figure 8.6, observable correlations and theoretically dictated parameters are shown in boldface, and free parameters are shown in open type. The model permits estimation of heritability coefficients (h^2) and separate environmental coefficients for shared (c^2) and nonshared (e^2) environmental influences.

The ACE model is the model of choice for many of today's QBG studies of cognitive and personality traits. It has been criticized for failing to allow for gene-by-environment interactions and correlations. If these are present they will be erroneously assigned either to environmental or genetic main effects. Alternative models that do permit measurement of interactions have recently been developed,[18] but they require more observed correlations than the ACE model requires.

8.3. Observed Estimates of Heritability

Table 8.2 summarizes the results of over 200 studies of the heritability of intelligence, conducted up to 2000. I know of no studies since then that would substantially alter these results. Most of these studies involved European or North American, usually White, participants, with sampling somewhat but not markedly biased against the inclusion of low SES participants. In theory, studies in other populations could produce different results. However, studies done in both urban and rural India and in Japan have produced comparable correlations.[19]

---

18 Johnson, 2007.

19 These studies all rely on a comparison of the correlations between monozygotic and dyzygotic twins reared together. The Indian estimates, based on two small studies, report MZ correlations in the .9 range, which is exceptionally high for this sort of study. The DZ correlations were slightly less than .50. The resulting heritability estimate was in the .80 range (Nathawat & Puri, 1995; Pal, Shyam, & Singh, 1997). The Japanese study (Lynn & Hattori, 1990) produced a heritability estimate of approximately .60. Indian results are close to the highest values reported for studies using a contrast between MZ and DZ twins, but they are not entirely out of

Table 8.2. Correlations and heritability estimates for pairs of individuals of various degrees of relationship. The right-hand column shows the heritability coefficients calculated using the simple model of Figure 8.5, which assumes that environmental correlations are zero for individuals not raised in the same home.

Relationship	Raised in Same Home?	Degree of Genetic Relationship	Correlation of Test Scores	h^2 Estimate	Comparison Used to Make Estimate
MZ twins	Yes	1	.86	*	
MZ twins	No	1	.76	.76	MZ apart
DZ twins	Yes	.5	.55	.60	2 (MZ together–DZ together)
DZ twins	No	.5	.35	(1), 82, (2).70	(1) 2 (MZ apart–DZ apart), (2) 2 (DZ apart)
Siblings (SS) raised together	Yes	.5	.47	.78	2 (MZ together–sibling together)
Siblings (SS) raised apart	No	.5	.24	.48	2 (SS apart)
Unrelated individuals of different ages, raised in same homes; Intelligence measured in childhood	Yes	0	.25	0	*
"Virtual twins" measured in childhood	Yes	0	.26	*	*
Unrelated individuals of different age, raised in same homes; Intelligence measured in adulthood	Yes	0	.02	*	*
Parent-child	Yes	.5	.42	*	*
Parent-child	No	.5	.24	.48	2 (Parent-child apart)

Note: The data is based on summaries by Scarr, McGue et al., and by Plomin et al. and virtual twin studies by N. Segal and her colleagues (McGue et al., 1993; Plomin et al., 1997, p. 140; Scarr, 1997, p. 28). Unless specified otherwise the studies summarized were based on scores obtained when the offspring were in childhood and adolescence.

The right-hand column of Table 8.2 is the estimate of heritability obtained using the simple model presented in Figure 8.5, which assumes independent and additive environmental and genetic effects. Granted that the model is simplified, let us consider the important trends.

Heritability estimates lie in the .5–.8 range.

line. The Japanese study is in agreement with estimates of heritability obtained in Western industrialized nations.

There are environmental effects. For all four nonzero biological relationships the correlation between pairs is from .10 to .20 points higher when the pairs are raised in the same home. This increase is in the correlation coefficient, and is not affected by changes in the level of scores. We will deal with this in Chapter 9, where adoption effects are discussed.

The three rows labeled "unrelated individuals raised in the same household" and "virtual twins" are of special interest. "Same household" correlations refer either to children and adopted children in the same family, or to unrelated individuals who have been adopted into the same family. "Virtual twins" are a subset of the "same household" group in which the individuals are within nine months of age of each other, and have lived in the same household since before their first birthday. The correlation between cognitive test scores of virtual twins is .26 when taken in childhood. It would be of considerable interest to know if this correlation changes over the life span, but as of this writing the necessary research has not been done.

While there is considerable variability in the estimates, the variability is systematic. Heritability estimates involving twins are higher than heritability estimates that do not involve twins. This seems to be a fairly consistent finding over the studies I have examined. The correlation between the scores of DZ twins raised apart is substantially higher than the correlation between the scores of siblings raised apart, even though their genetic relationships are identical. Why? We do not know, but can consider some possibilities.

The method of estimation assumed that there were no gene-by-environment interactions. To the extent that a person's genetic makeup is important in shaping the environment, omitting this factor would inflate the correlation between MZ twins. A similar factor could influence the contrast between DZ twins and siblings. DZ and SS pairs are equal in the extent to which they share genetic makeup. However, DZ twins share the same prenatal environment, while SS pairs do not. Once they are born, any time-locked phenomenon that might influence cognition, such as exposure to measles or hepatitis, will influence DZ twins at the same age (which in some cases is an index of vulnerability), while SS pairs, being of different ages, will have different degrees of vulnerability. In the case of children raised together, SS pairs exert asymmetric influences on each other's environment, because one will be older than the other.

The rough and ready estimates of heritability presented in Table 8.2 cannot be disregarded. However, the exact values should not be regarded as set in stone, due to the failure to consider gene-by-environment interactions and correlations.

8.3.1. *Adoption Studies*

Adoption studies provide a way of separating environmental and genetic influences on intelligence. Environmental effects are indicated by correlations between an adoptee and members of his or her adoptive family, genetic influences by correlations between the intelligence of an adoptee and the biological parents. In the ideal adoption study the children will have been adopted very early in life, data will be available on the intelligence of both biological parents, and the adoptees will be followed until adulthood, to allow for dissipation of environmental effects and the effect of genetic traits that become apparent during adolescence, adulthood, and possibly old age. Such an ideal study has not been done, but several have come close. Four adoption studies are described in panel 8.5.

The results of virtually all adoption studies are consistent with the simple environment + genetic model described in Figures 8.5 and 8.6. As one reviewer put it,

The heritability of cognitive ability is around .50 when collapsing across all studies. However heritability appears to vary with age, with $h^2 = .40$ in early childhood, rising to .60 in early adulthood, finally rising to $h^2 = .80$ in later life.

Petrill, 2002, p. 284

Panel 8.5. Adoption Projects

Studies comparing adopted children to children living with their biological parents provide an opportunity to compare the effects of genetic inheritance and environmental influences on intelligence. The analysis is not simple.

At first glance, it might seem that any influence on an adoptee's intelligence that was associated with the adoptive family would be independent of the adoptee's genotype. This is not correct, for to a considerable extent people make their own environments. This can be apparent at a very young age. Children's reactivity has a partially genetic basis, and reactivity will influence how adults and other children interact with the adoptee. Such effects cannot be captured by a statistical model that assumes the non-existence of gene-by-environment interactions. Unfortunately, while it is easy to conceptualize a model that includes gene-by-environment interactions, it can be very difficult to obtain sufficient measurements to evaluate such a model.

Then we come to the practical reasons. In order to achieve adequate statistical reliability, and in order to allow for drop-outs, a good study should involve at least 200 people, and preferably more. The studies are of most value if the children can be followed to maturity. Because of the difficulty of following people for that long, it is desirable to take as many measures as possible. (While we will concentrate on measures of intelligence, many adoption studies also involve detailed studies of personality characteristics.) Large-scale studies that take place over an extended period of time require substantial amounts of long-term funding, which is difficult to obtain.

From the point of view of a study designer, adoption should occur as soon after birth as possible, in order to minimize the exposure that adoptees have to an environment related to the biological parents. The study designer wants placements to be random, so that there is no correlation between genetic and environmental potential. In practice, this may not happen, especially if the adoption agency attempts to match characteristics of the biological parents (or, more likely, the biological mother) with characteristics of the adopting family. Such a policy would produce a gene-environment correlation that would be hard to evaluate.

Generalization is a problem. Children put up for adoption and the families who wish to adopt them are not representative of the general population. Parents who wish to adopt a child tend to be wealthier and better-educated than parents who put their children up for adoption. There is further self-selection in transracial adoptions and in adoptions of foreign children. Adoption agencies, quite reasonably, try to ensure that the child will be raised in a socially and economically healthy environment. This is a reasonable policy, but it does restrict the range of environments to which adopted children are exposed. The very fact that families are willing to adopt children indicates that, as a group, they place considerable value on raising children. All these effects act to reduce the variance in the environment of adopting families, compared to the range of environmental variables in the general population. Therefore, adoption studies may underestimate the extent to which environmental variables influence the development of intelligence in the population at large.*

This panel describes four adoption studies carried out in the United States. They are somewhat different, but the findings are generally compatible. Taken together, they provide valuable information about the relative influences of genetic inheritance and environment upon intelligence.

(continued)

Panel 8.5 *(continued)*

The Texas Adoption Project

The Texas Adoption Project[†] began in the early 1960s. It focused on 300 adoptees from a church-affiliated adoption home for unwed mothers. Both the biological mothers and the adoptive parents were, for the most part, white and middle-class. This probably reflects the social mores of the day. A woman who was a single parent faced greater social disapproval in the 1960s than she would today, and as a result there was more pressure to give up a baby for adoption.

The adoptees, their biological mothers, adopting parents, and the biological children of adopting-parents were given intelligence tests. Either the WAIS or a nonverbal test was given, partly because of the varying ages of the children involved and also, in the case of the biological mothers, because of administrative conditions in the adoption home. The biological parents had an average IQ score of 100, but there was less variability in test scores than would be the case in the general population. The adoptive parents' IQs were slightly higher than those of the biological parents IQs – 100–101 for mothers, depending on the test used, and 104 or 105 for fathers. The mean IQ scores of the natural and adopted children were in the 104–105 range, again depending on what test was used. The restriction in range in all groups would have the effect of reducing correlations between the test scores of various classes of individuals, compared to the equivalent correlations in a representative population. The study is also different from several other studies in that the biological mothers and the adoptive parents had roughly equivalent SES. This contrasts with many other studies where adoptive parents tend to

be both better-educated and economically better-off (and hence better able to afford to raise a child) than the biological mothers.

There were two waves of testing, an initial wave when the adopted children were eight years old, on the average (with a considerable range), and a follow-up of about 50% of the original sample ten years later. A variety of cognitive, personality, and health measures were taken. Twenty years after the initiation of the study, a postal questionnaire was sent to all adoptees and biological children of participants and to the adoptive parents. The questionnaire covered various aspects of life adjustment, such as occupational and marital status.

Genetic influences were substantially larger than environmental influences. The correlations between cognitive test scores of the birth mother and the adopted child's scores ranged from .23 to .36 in the initial study, depending upon the intelligence test used, and from .26 to .78 (only a small number of cases) at the ten-year follow-up. The change over time illustrates Petrill's comment that the heritability coefficient increases with time. The correlations between scores of biologically unrelated individuals – adoptive mothers and fathers, and adopted children – ranged from .19 to .08 (again, depending on the test used and whether the mother or father's score is being considered) at the original testing, and from .15 to −.02 in the follow-up.

The postal survey twenty years later showed that the biological children of the adopting parents were doing slightly better than the adopted children, at least in terms of conventional, self-reported social adjustment. Adopting-parent characteristics were better predictors of the social adjustment of their biological than of their adopted children.

The Colorado Adoption Study

The Colorado Adoption Study, begun in the 1970s, was a twenty-year study of children recruited from two adoption agencies in Denver, Colorado.[‡] As was the case for the Texas study, the participants were largely White and middle-class. In addition to studying the development of adopted children, the experiment included a comparison group of over 200 families consisting of biological parents and children. Cognitive tests were conducted when the children were one, two, three, four, seven, twelve, and sixteen years of age. This made it possible to compare stability of intelligence, in the sense of the relative standing of a person compared to others of the same age, from infancy to adolescence.

The correlations between the test scores of adoptees and their adoptive parents were near zero at all ages. The correlations between the biological mothers' scores and the adoptees' scores increased from .18 in early and middle childhood to .38 at age sixteen. Factor analyses of the test scores showed that general intelligence, as indicated by the first factor on the cognitive tests, g, was responsible for the consistency in individual performance, and that this factor had a substantial genetic load. Instabilities in test scores over time appeared to be related to differences in nonshared, within-family, environmental influences.

The University of Minnesota Studies

The next two studies were both done at the University of Minnesota.[§] The transracial adoption study (TRA) dealt with African American children adopted by White families. Unlike the Texas and Colorado studies, in the TRA there was a substantial disparity between the socioeconomic status (and concomitant educational levels and intelligence test scores) of the biological mother and the adoptive parents. This difference was central to the study, which was motivated by a desire to see what the effects of improved environmental conditions would be on the adopted children. The issues involving racial differences in intelligence will be discussed in Chapter 11. The correlation between scores for adoptive parents and adopted children was .29, while the correlation for biological mothers and adopted children was .43. These correlations are somewhat higher but not out of line with the general trends reported in Table 8.2.

The adolescent adoption (AA) study was a study of people ranging in age from sixteen to twenty-two. The investigators tested a group of adoptees who had spent an average of eighteen years in their adopted homes. The correlation between scores of biologically related siblings was .35, while the correlation between adoptees and unrelated siblings, raised in the same home for an average of eighteen years, was zero!

Virtually all adoption studies in North America and Europe produce similar results. The pattern of correlations indicates that h^2 for general intelligence is at least .50. Environmental effects due to differences between families can be substantial early in childhood, but decrease in adolescence and almost vanish in adulthood. This suggests a dissipation in the effects of the adopting home over a person's lifetime, which is certainly reasonable. The genetic inheritance is retained throughout life.

---

[*] Nisbett, 2009.
[†] Loehlin, Horn, & Willerman, 1997; Loehlin, Horn, & Ernst, 2007.
[‡] Petrill et al., 2004; Plomin et al., 1997.
[§] Scarr & Weinberg, 1983.

Petrill's summary, and others like it, are statements about the effect of adoption upon variation in measures of cognition. They say nothing about the effect of adoption upon the mean scores of adopted children, that is, about any benefit or general cost of adoption. Such effects are found. There is generally a temporary elevation of cognitive skills, as indicated by test scores, through the school years, but this dissipates in adolescence and adulthood. This does not mean that adoption does no good, for an increase in cognitive abilities during the school years can itself be important to development later in life.

The second qualification has to do with generalization. Can heritability coefficients from studies of adopted children be extrapolated to people in general? A case can be made that they cannot, on the grounds that adults who adopt children are less variable, within their own population, than parents in general. For example, the median age of women who adopt children is thirty. This is higher than the median age of birth for women who raise their own children. Adults who adopt tend to be of higher SES and to have more education than typical parents. These tendencies work to reduce the environmental variability among adopting families to a lower value than population variability. As pointed out earlier, if environmental variance is reduced, heritability coefficients will go up.[20] The extent of the upward bias in heritability introduced by the homogeneity of adopting families is hard to estimate, but the fact that there is some bias should be kept in mind.

8.3.2. *Twin Studies*

The study of twins is of great interest in QBG, because the contrast between MZ and DZ twins shows the effects associated with a clearly established degree of genetic difference, between people of the same age, raised in either the same or different environments. Doing such studies is difficult, but not impossible, due to the relative scarcity of twins. DZ twins occur about once in 100 births, MZ twins once in 250 births.[21]

The results from different studies are consistent.[22] The MZ correlations are about .8, regardless of the twins' age. The correlations between DZ twins are about .6 until adulthood, at which point they drop to .4. This implies that the relative importance of genetic influences on intelligence *increases* in adulthood. The extent of the increase is illustrated in Figure 8.8, which shows the results of a large study in the Netherlands, which is typical of other findings.[23] The heritability coefficient was modest in early childhood, but increased to a staggering .85 in late adulthood. The result is similar to results found in a US study of twins.[24]

While the findings from these studies are consistent among themselves, recent studies have questioned the generality of their conclusions. Most of the twin studies rely on voluntary participation, sometimes over a considerable period of time. This introduces a bias toward the participation of better-educated, higher socioeconomic status children. Two recent studies of very large samples, taken over a wider range of the population, illustrate how this bias may affect estimates of the heritability of cognitive ability. One of these studies utilized WISC scores for seven-year-old children, obtained as part of a national study of children's health. The overall sample of over 300 twin pairs was split into a low SES group (one-third of the mothers in this group were on welfare) and a high SES group. The differences were dramatic. The heritability coefficient, h^2, was .72 in the high SES group and only .10 in the low SES group. A second study found a similar pattern in seventeen-year-olds.[25]

A similar study from the Netherlands found little, if any, difference in the

---

20 Stoolmiller, 1999.

21 The figures are given for natural births for Whites in the United States. African-Americans give birth to more twins, and Asian-Americans to fewer.

22 McGue et al., 1993, p. 63. See also Boomsma, Busjahn, & Peltonen, 2002.

23 Posthuma, De Geus, & Boomsma, 2004.

24 McGue et al., 1993, p. 72.

25 Turkheimer et al., 2003; Harden et al., 2007.

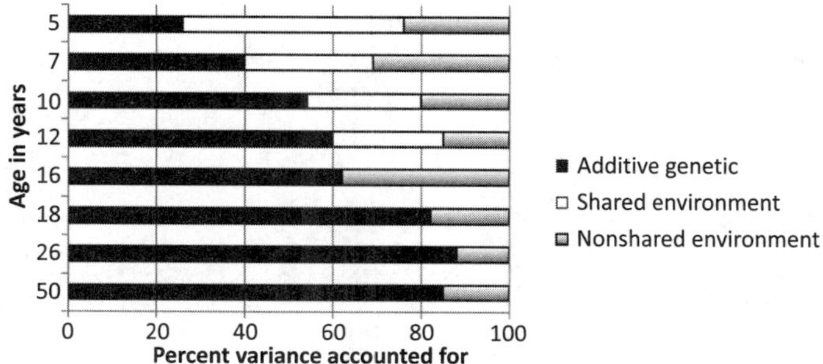

Figure 8.8. Percentage of the variance in intelligence test score account for by additive genetic influence, shared environmental influence, and nonshared environmental influence. Based on selected data from the Dutch Twins Study; Posthuma, De Geus, & Boomsma, 2004, Figure 9.1.

heritability of adult intelligence as a function of various socioeconomic indicators.[26] The authors of that study suggest that the expression of intelligence in children may be more sensitive to variations in the environment than is the expression of intelligence in adults. The authors also point out that studies of variation, which is typically the target of a QBG analysis, do not evaluate differences in means across groups. The study authors found a positive association between SES and adult intelligence test scores apart from the influence of heritability.

With a few exceptions, the twins studied in the research just described were raised in the same home, by their biological parents. Conceptually, the almost-perfect study of the heritability of IQ is the study of the intelligence of MZ and DZ twins raised in different households by adoptive parents, preferably without any interaction between the two twins. Pragmatically, such a study is hard to achieve. Twins are rare enough, and only a small fraction of all twins are adopted apart. The first study of similarities in MZ twins raised apart was a case study of a single pair, in 1922. There were only three reputable studies, with twelve, nineteen, and thirty-eight pairs of twins, in the next forty years.[27] In spite of the small sample sizes these studies produced consistent results. The correlations between test scores

for MZ twins raised apart (r_{MZA}) were, for each study, .71, .69, and .75.

There was also a larger, highly publicized study that reported $r_{MZA} = .77$. Unfortunately, in one of the more embarrassing moments in the history of Psychology, it was subsequently found that the data was not credible. Whether this was due to fraud or to unacceptably careless record keeping is still debated. The incident is described in panel 8.6.

The situation today is much better. Beginning in the 1970s, Thomas Bouchard, Jr., and his colleagues at the University of Minnesota began the Minnesota Study of Twins Raised Apart (MISTRA). Details of MISTRA are provided in panel 8.7. When enrollment ceased, in 2000, the MISTRA researchers had evaluated 139 twin pairs, in addition to evaluating the twins' spouses, partners, and some adoptive and biological relatives. The evaluations included personality testing and collection of biographical and anthropometric data. In the intelligence part of the evaluation participants took three previously developed batteries of cognitive tests, totaling forty-two tests of cognitive skills.[28]

About the same time that MISTRA began, a group of Swedish researchers initiated an extensive study of twins, raised together and raised apart.[29] Sweden, like

26 Van der Sluis, Willemsen, et al., 2008.
27 Bouchard, 1997, Table 5.1 and accompanying text.

28 See Johnson et al., 2007a, or Johnson & Bouchard, 2005, for a detailed listing of the tests.
29 Finkel & Pedersen, 2004.

Panel 8.6. The History of Studies of Twins Adopted Apart: I. Sir Cyril Burt

This panel describes one of the fascinating stories in the history of psychology, complete with intrigue and, perhaps, a villain.

Cyril Burt (1883–1971) was an extremely influential British psychologist. He was an early factor analyst, claiming credit for some of the major advances in the field. He held important posts in educational policy and research and conducted important research on juvenile delinquency. In 1932 Burt succeeded Spearman as Professor of Psychology at University College, London. A Professorship was then equivalent to a lifetime appointment as a Department Chair. The appointment carried with it much more authority and prestige than do such positions today. He appears to have discharged his duties in an intellectually impressive but socially imperious manner.

Burt retired in 1950 but continued to publish until his death in 1971. Among his other honors Burt was knighted and received a gold medal for distinguished lifetime contribution from the American Psychological Association.

Sometime before World War II, Burt began collecting data on twins. He published a variety of papers on the topic in the interval between 1943 and 1966. An additional paper was published posthumously in 1972. The most noted of these papers dealt with MZ twins raised apart. Some of the correlations reported were in the high .8's and even .9's, indicating almost complete heritability of intelligence. Related papers confirming Burt's results were published by a "Miss Conway" and a "Miss Howard."

In 1974, three years after Burt's death, Leon Kamin, a professor at Princeton and an ardent opponent of the idea that intelligence is determined genetically, observed that some of Burt's correlations, which were purportedly on different data sets, were identical to the third decimal point. The probability of this happening by chance is miniscule. Subsequently, Arthur Jensen, who is an advocate of genetic theories of intelligence, made a searching reexamination of Burt's data, and found additional suspicious entries.* Jensen pointed out that the results could either have been fraudulent or perhaps the result of confusion, as Burt was elderly at the time the papers were written. The plot thickened when a biographer of Burt's, Leslie Hearnshaw, found papers that suggested both that some of Burt's data was fraudulent and that the papers by Conway and Howard had in fact been written by Burt himself.† There appear to be few, if any, records that unambiguously document Conway's or Howard's career. Since Jensen's paper, in 1974, no knowledgeable scientist cites Burt's data.

I do not think we will ever know whether Burt was intentionally fraudulent or unacceptably careless in his later years. The cases for and against him rest largely on circumstantial evidence. But the issue is not whether Burt was a fraud or a good scientist gone bad as he aged. It is whether or not he hindered the advancement of knowledge.

The correlations Burt reported are only slightly higher than those reported, with far better data and no hint of fraud, by several contemporary studies of twins raised apart. So in the narrow sense Burt did not harm science. His claims did not lead scientists up a garden path, chasing a false result.

In a broader sense, Burt did profound harm to science in general, to Psychology, and in particular to Behavior Genetics.

In the 1960s and 1970s psychologists and educators emphasized the role of learning and social opportunity as agents for the development of cognitive skills. In the United States these beliefs were closely tied to social and moral issues, for there were great hopes that the end of segregated schooling would quickly result in economic and social equality between African Americans and Whites. Similar feelings were also strongly held in Europe. However, progress toward equality following desegregation proved to be much slower than had been anticipated.

In 1969 Jensen published a highly controversial paper in the *Harvard Educational Review* in which he pointed out that Black-White differences in academic achievement could be due in part to genetic differences between the races.[‡] Jensen cited ten of Burt's papers in support of his argument. Jensen's article elicited a furious counter-argument. The subsequent revelation that Burt's data was, at best, incompetent and, at worst, fraudulent led not only to a rejection of Jensen's argument but also to a general, albeit unjustified, condemnation of genetic studies of intelligence. This hurt the field in a variety of ways, not the least of which was a drying up of funds for research.

Science ought to inform policy makers wrestling with political and social issues. The only claim that scientists can make to a privileged status in such a discussion is their commitment to supporting their arguments with objectively collected data and thoughtful analysis, rather than moral suasion. When a scientist offers an opinion based on indefensible data it hurts us all.[§]

My comments are based on a book on Burt edited by Macintosh (1995) that includes papers by two who had known Burt personally, Arthur Jensen and Hans Eysenck.

[*] Jensen, 1974.

[†] Hearnshaw, 1979.

[‡] Jensen, 1969.

[§] See Hunt & Carlson, 2007a,b, for elaborations on this point.

many European countries, maintains government records of the health of its citizens. In 1978 some researchers noticed that a substantial number of twins born prior to 1945 indicated that they had been raised separately as children.[30] The investigators contacted all twins who were age fifty or older, and many of them agreed to interviews and fairly extensive psychological testing, although far short of the testing involved in the MISTRA project.

The Swedish and MISTRA studies complement each other. MISTRA dealt with twins aged eighteen upward into their sixties and seventies, in a single testing, using a cross-sectional design. The Swedish study tested participants on four different occasions, spanning a thirteen-year period. Comparing the studies, the MISTRA study covered a wider age range, while the Swedish study had relatively more participants in the fifty-plus age range. The MISTRA study had considerably more data on any one individual than did the Swedish study. Because of its longitudinal design, the Swedish study provided an opportunity to look at changes in cognition at the time of life when some people show marked cognitive decline.

The MISTRA data has been analyzed using Johnson and Bouchard's *g*-VPR model,[31] producing heritability estimates for *g* and the lower-stratum abilities, including the broad VPR factors. In addition, the MISTRA investigators were able to determine whether or not the different abilities are influenced by the same genetic factors. This is determined by calculating the *genetic correlation*, which can be thought of as an estimate of the correlation between the genetic influences on each of the two abilities being compared. The idea is shown, in diagrammatic form, in Figure 8.9.

30 These twins would have been at least thirty-three years old. They all would have been born either during the worldwide depression or during World War II. Sweden was neutral in the war, and received substantial numbers of refugee children from neighboring countries.

31 Johnson et al., 2007.

Panel 8.7. Studies of Twins Adopted Apart: II. The Minnesota Study of Twins Raised Apart (MISTRA)

Cyril Burt's emphasis on the study of MZ and DZ twins reared apart (panel 8.6) was a good idea, whatever the demerits of his own research. Both before and since Burt's time several studies of MZ and DZ twins have been attempted, but only a few of them have involved a substantial number of twins reared apart. The reason is simple: when one combines the criterion "being an MZ twin" and "being adopted away from your birth partner" you do not have very many people left.

In 1979 a group at the University of Minnesota, under the general leadership of Thomas Bouchard, Jr., embarked on an attempt to find as many twins raised apart as they possibly could. Recruitment was by advertising and word-of-mouth. By the time recruitment was terminated, in 2000, 139 twin pairs had been enrolled. In addition to the twins, Bouchard and his group interviewed and tested as many related people, including spouses, as they could find. Eventually over 400 people participated. The testing took approximately fifty hours, over a week-long visit to Minneapolis, and included personality tests, physical measurements, and collection of biographic data as well as extensive intelligence testing. The result has been the compilation of one of the most important and extensive databases on twins raised apart that exists.

Bouchard and his colleagues deserve great credit for their perseverance. Especially in the early years, government grant money for this important research was hard to come by, in no small part because of the political reaction against the idea that there are genetic influences on intelligence (see panel 8.6). The situation was not helped by the questionable status of Burt's widely discussed studies, but I think that the reaction would have occurred anyway, due to deeply held political/social beliefs that disparities in education and socioeconomic status in the United States are almost entirely due to environmental causes, often associated with past prejudice and privilege. Obviously I cannot prove this. Bouchard has expressed similar concerns.*

In addition to the investigators, the University of Minnesota deserves credit for its willingness to support Bouchard and his group in this important, extended research effort.

* Bouchard, 1997, pp. 126–127.

Figure 8.10 shows heritabilities (h^2) calculated for the latent traits at each stratum. The figure shows the division between genetic and environmental associations within each of the latent traits at each level – that is, the g level, the three VPR dimensions at the third level, and the narrower cognitive skills at the second level. With the exception of the perceptual trait, every third- and fourth-level trait has a heritability greater than .40. General intelligence (g) has a heritability value of more than .70. The genetic correlations between traits were substantial, showing that related genetic influences contribute to all abilities.

Similar results were found in the Swedish study, where the investigators used the scores provided by the WAIS rather than the g-VPR model. The heritability estimate for the g factor was .91! This is the highest heritability estimate for intelligence that I have seen, in any substantial study.[32]

8.3.3. *The Unfolding of Cognitive Abilities*

Turning back to Figure 8.8, we can see that in the Dutch study there was a regular increase in the heritability coefficient from childhood to age fifty. We see the same trend across

32 Reynolds et al., 2005, Table 5.

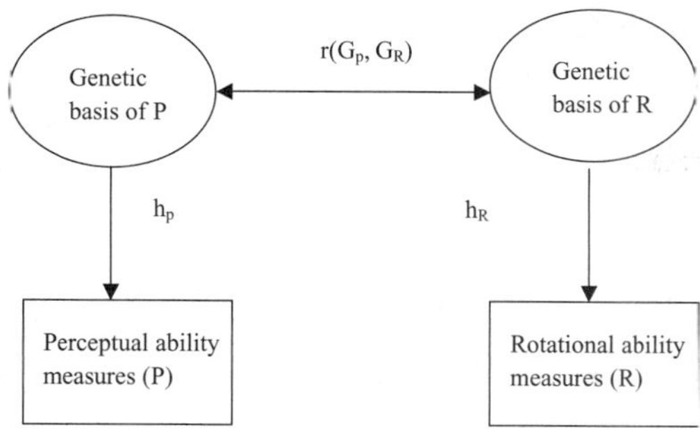

Figure 8.9. A schematic of genetic correlations involving the P and R factors in the VPR model of intelligence. The genetic correlation, $r(G_p, G_r)$, is a measure of the extent to which the genes responsible for each trait covary with each other. Genetic correlations can vary independently of the genetic loadings. Therefore, two traits might have high heritability and a low genetic correlation, or a low (but nonzero) heritability and a high genetic correlation.

studies. In the Colorado Adoption Study the heritability coefficient was .56 at age sixteen;[33] in the Swedish study it was .91 for people age fifty and older. At first this defies logic, for, as Bouchard put it to me in private correspondence, one would think that the slings and arrows of outrageous fortune would accumulate, producing environmental differences over the years. Are there clues in the data indicating why this result might occur?

I am struck by two pieces of evidence. The first is that the heritability estimate is influenced by the difference between twin correlations in MZ and DZ twins; the larger the difference, the larger the heritability estimate. In a review of the data available up to 1989,[34] it was clear that the increase in the heritability estimates was due to a decrease in the DZ correlation from .6 (childhood) to .4 (adult) while the MZ correlations stayed constant at slightly above .8. The second piece of evidence comes from the Swedish study of twins over fifty. Recall that in that study cognitive abilities were measured several times, making it possible to assess

both the overall cognitive level of participants over the fifty-to-eighty interval and the change in cognitive abilities over that interval. As would be expected, there was a general decrease in cognition as the participants moved into their sixties and seventies. Structural equation modeling showed that this decrease was largely due to nonshared environmental differences, the differences between twins, rather than the environmental differences across twin pairs. Note that "nonshared environmental differences" has a rather different interpretation when the comparison is based on adults living apart, rather than on children living in the same household.

I suggest that there are two processes going on. One is that some genetically influenced biological processes present themselves only during adulthood and, especially, old age. Huntington's disease (panel 8.1) and incipient signs of Alzheimer's Dementia, are examples. Among the healthy elderly, genetically influenced limitations on information-processing capacities may become more constraining as we grow older. These phenomena may account for a substantial part of the increase in heritability.

This sort of genetic limit would not be surprising from an evolutionary point of view. Genetic weaknesses that are not expressed until after the reproductive years do not affect a person's reproductive fitness, so there would be no selective pressure on the genes involved.

The second process is quite different. It is suggested to me by the constancy of the MZ correlations as the DZ correlations fall. To a substantial degree, people make their own environments. Genetic influences, acting as distal causes, influence exposure to environments that, acting as proximal causes, differentially accelerate or decelerate cognitive change. DZ twins, being genetically more distinct than MZ twins, will select environments that differ more than the environments selected by MZ twins, and, as a result, the DZ correlations will go down over time, due to nonshared (between twins) environmental differences being greater in the DZ than in the MZ twins.

33 Plomin et al., 1997.
34 McGue et al., 1993, Figure 1.

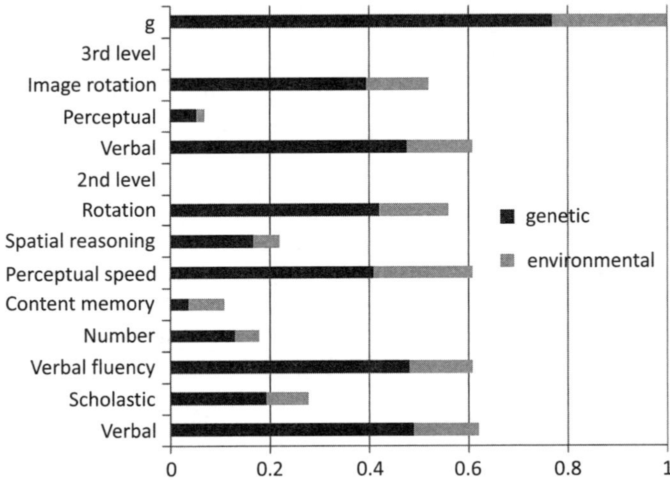

Figure 8.10. The relative proportions of variance associated with genetic and environmental variance in the factors defined for the *g*-VPR model. Data based on Johnson et al., 2007, Table 5.

This analysis is a conjecture. Proof will have to wait for further research.

8.3.4. *The Heritability of Information-processing Traits*

While there have been studies of the genetic basis of a large number of information-processing traits, our interest centers on the two information-processing functions shown to be most closely related to intelligence (Chapter 6), speed of processing and working memory. For the reasons given in Chapter 6, I will be concerned with working memory, overall, and will not attempt to fractionate it into finer components.

Both working memory and processing speed show substantial genetic heritability. The genetic correlations indicate that the genetic basis of the information-processing components is the same or nearly the same as the genetic basis of general intelligence. Most of our knowledge of this comes from studies of twins. Four such studies will be described. They have been selected to make a point about consistency of results.

The first of the studies was of Dutch twins, born in the early 1990s and evaluated at five and twelve years of age.[35] Siblings

were also studied. Participants took a comprehensive battery of markers for psychometric *g* and tasks evaluating the speed and capacity of working memory. Heritability estimates for both speed of processing and the capacity of working memory were in the .5–.6 range, increasing slightly from age five to age twelve. Stability, in the sense of the extent to which scores at age five could predict subsequent scores, appeared to be largely mediated by genetic influences. The authors point out that this is impressive, because the brain undergoes substantial development from five to twelve years of age.

An Australian study[36] evaluated genetic contributions to information processing and intelligence test scores in sixteen-year-old twins and their siblings. Heritability estimates for choice reaction time tasks varied from .7 to .5, with heritability increasing as the number of choices increased. A delayed reaction time task was used to evaluate working memory. It had a heritability estimate of .48.

In Japan a study was conducted of young adult twins (aged fourteen to twenty-nine, mean age twenty). The twins were given an intelligence test and both verbal and spatial-visual working memory tasks. The

---

35 Polderman et al., 2006, 2007. See Polderman et al., 2007, for a discussion of previous work on this topic.

36 Luciano, Wright, et al., 2001.

heritability coefficients for the working memory tasks ranged from .43 to .48, depending on the task.[37]

In the United States a twin study was conducted utilizing records maintained by the US Department of Veterans' Affairs (VA), which is responsible for ongoing studies of the health of military veterans.[38] Just under 350 pairs of male twins, ranging in age from forty-one to fifty-eight, were given the reading span measure of working memory (see Chapter 6). The estimate of h^2 based on the difference in correlations between MZ and DZ twins was .58. This was reduced slightly by more sophisticated modeling, but it was clear that the estimate should be in the .5–.6 range. Further analyses indicated that the correlation between the reading span measure and measures of reading skill were mediated genetically.

These four studies, done with participants of different ages and conducted by different laboratories in different countries, have produced consistent results. Working memory, one of the key information-processing underpinnings of intelligence, is subject to substantial genetic influence. However, the influence seems to be somewhat smaller than the genetic influence on measures of g.

Establishing the genetic basis for speed of cognitive processing is a bit complicated. Speed of cognitive processing has been shown to be a component of intelligence apart from the storage and attentional control components of working memory (Chapter 6). However, in above-average young adults (usually college students) the contribution of processing speed to conventional psychometric measures of intelligence is considerably smaller than the contribution of the working memory functions. By contrast, the decline in measures of psychometric intelligence from middle age onward is very largely associated with declines in speed of processing. This leads us to suspect that studies of college students may not tell us all that we need to know about the importance of speed of processing in the population at large.

There are many ways to measure speed of cognitive processing. Most conventional intelligence tests use pencil-and-paper methods, where the dependent measure is how many easy tasks can be accomplished in a fixed time period (e.g., simple additions). Researchers, especially those who have dealt with information-processing measures in contexts other than studies of individual difference, prefer the tighter control afforded by computer-controlled tasks, such as the choice reaction time (CRT) and inspection time (IT) measures. Within each of these broad paradigms, and especially within the information-processing paradigm, there are many variations in procedure.

In spite of these difficulties, studies of the genetic basis of speed of cognitive processing have been remarkably successful. A meta-analysis of several studies concluded that heritability was about .18 for easy timed tasks (which do not have high correlations with test scores) and .52 for hard tasks.[39] Looking at the details of a few of the studies is informative.

In the study of Dutch twins referred to earlier, the investigators found that, depending on the particular speed-of-processing task, heritability coefficients ranged in the .4–.5 range.[40] Moving to adolescents, investigators in the Colorado adoption study (panel 8.4) studied the genetics of speed of processing in sixteen-year-olds, using pencil-and-paper tasks. This study found a speed of processing heritability of .48.[41] Literally on the other side of the world, the estimated heritability of inspection time was .80 in the Australian study of sixteen-year-old twins.[42] This is the highest reported value of heritability that I know of.

One of the studies associated with the Dutch Twin Registry examined heritability in two cohorts, one aged twenty to thirty at the time of the examination and another

37 Ando, Ono, & Wright, 2001.
38 Kremen et al., 2007.

39 Beaujean, 2005. See also Jensen, 2006, p. 130 ff., for some brief notes concerning other studies.
40 Polderman et al., 2006.
41 Alarcon et al., 1999.
42 Luciano, Smith, et al., 2001.

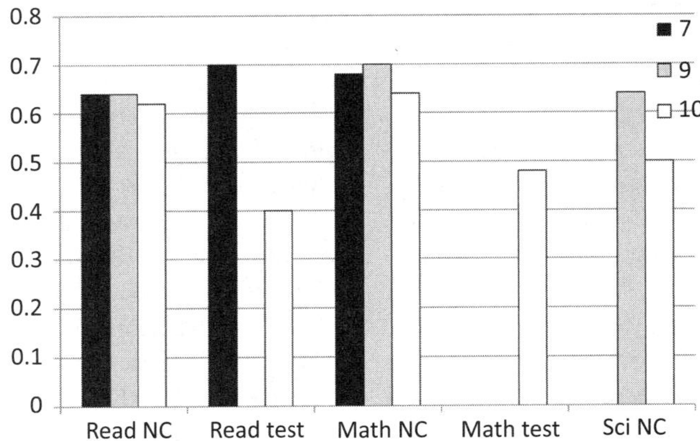

Figure 8.11. Heritability estimates for three academic skills, based on data from the TEDS study (Chapter II). NC refers to teachers' ratings of student progress on the United Kingdom national curriculum in reading or mathematics.

aged forty to fifty-five. The heritability estimate for the inspection time measure was .46, and did not differ across cohorts.[43]

The Swedish study of twins raised apart[44] contained participants from fifty to eighty years old. The study included pencil-and-paper measures of perceptual speed. Because this was a repeated-measures study it was possible to estimate the extent of heritability and environmental influences on both overall perceptual speed (as evaluated by pencil-and-paper testing) and changes in perceptual speed. The heritability coefficient was around .8 for overall speed (depending slightly on which of two tests was used to measure speed), but the major influence on change was the nonshared environmental difference.

8.3.5. *QBG Analyses of Academic Skills*

Conventional intelligence tests evaluate important cognitive traits, but any reasonable theory of intelligence has to include cognitive traits that are not evaluated by the tests, and quite possibly cannot be evaluated in the context of the time-limited "Drop in from the Sky" testing session. When discussing the genetics of intelligence it makes sense to ask what contribution genetic inher-

itance makes to cognitive skills that are important in the world, but lie outside the conventional testing realm. Among the most important of these are skills in reading and elementary mathematics, because of their central role in school and the workplace.

The largest study of genetics and academic achievement today, and probably the largest that will be conducted for some time, is the Twins Early Development Study (TEDS), a United Kingdom study of twins involving 12,000 participating families.[45] The study is described in panel 8.8. Testing was carried out in infancy, where the evaluation emphasized language development, and again at seven, nine, and ten years of age. At each year age-appropriate evaluations were made of children's progress in English-language studies, mathematics, and science. These evaluations were supplemented by teachers' ratings of student progress.

Figure 8.11 shows the estimated heritability for two classes of variables: teacher ratings and tests of children's mathematics, reading, and science levels at three different ages. The estimates range from a minimum of .4 to a maximum of .7. In all cases the heritability estimate exceeded the estimate for percentages of variance associated with either shared or nonshared environments,

43 Posthuma, de Geuss, & Boomsma, 2001.
44 Finkel & Pedersen, 2004; Reynolds et al., 2005.   45 Kovas et al., 2007.

Panel 8.8. The Twins Early Development Study (TEDS)

TEDS was a study of over 12,000 families, recruited from some 25,000 families who had twin births in the 1994–96 period, according to the United Kingdom (UK) National Health database. The children were tested when they were seven, nine, and ten years of age as, according to the UK's curriculum plan, these represent critical ages in cognitive development.

In-person testing was generally not possible. Therefore, the investigators relied on two sources of data: teachers' ratings of how well the students were doing in Reading, Mathematics, and Science, and some cleverly designed "distance tests" that could be administered (with parental cooperation) over the telephone or, for older children, over the World Wide Web. Verification studies involving in-person testing were conducted in order to check on the accuracy of the distance tests. Teacher ratings and the test results told basically the same story. Heritability was the largest single factor determining variation in all skills. Nonshared (basically within-family) environment was the second-largest factor.

The conclusions of the TEDS study that relate to our understanding of intelligence are presented in the main text. Here I will consider two further aspects of this large, important study: how widely its results can be generalized, and what these results mean for education, especially special education programs for children who are not doing well.

TEDS found that in a broad sense genetic heritability was the single largest influence on test scores. There was no evidence that very poor performance, in the bottom 5% or 15% of the population, was due to some special condition (e.g., a genetic condition that impacted ability to acquire language skills). Putting this somewhat colloquially, according to the TEDS results many of the children who, in the US, would qualify for special education in reading and mathematics aren't really special; they are just at the lower end of the distribution of reading and mathematics skills. Against this, we have to remember that there are specific genetic bases for a number of moderate mental disabilities, including reading disabilities. By lumping together all children below a certain ability level, the TEDS investigators may have developed a picture of disability that is accurate at a large scale, but that overlooks some important, albeit uncommon, specific disabilities.

Environmental effects upon the means of affected groups are well established. For instance (as is documented in the next chapter), intensive preschool educational programs can improve the academic readiness of children from very low SES groups. This indicates that better school environments can help, a point that has been amply demonstrated in a variety of settings.* Whether these programs will do anything to diminish the variation in performance between children is another matter.

The fact that genetic influences are so strong suggests that genetic analysis could serve as an early warning signal for identifying children who might have difficulty acquiring language and mathematical skills. The genetic analysis could be as simple as identifying a child whose relatives have had trouble with academics in the past, or it could be as complex as actually identifying the child's genome. We are not quite ready for the latter sort of testing. Leaving aside the costs of such a program, which are dropping rapidly, we do not know, yet, just what genes and alleles to look for! In addition, using genetic indicators as guides for educational decisions raises social policy issues that are quite beyond the scope of this book.

The TEDS analyses of children at the low end of mathematics, reading, and

(continued)

Panel 8.8 *(continued)*

science competency indicate that, in the vast majority of cases, these children represent the low end of normalcy rather than specific genetic or environmental defects. This has no implications at all for policy. Setting the level at which schoolchildren are considered for special education, in any field, has to be determined by two things: the level of competency the child requires in order to function in the society, and the money available to enroll students in special education programs.

Why a particular child falls into the defined class is of interest only if it serves as a guide to treatment, to tell the teacher how to fix the problem. The finding that the special class is actually the low end of the normal distribution is encouraging, because it indicates that the special education class will be reasonably homogeneous, so that uniform teaching methods may apply widely. What those methods should be is a topic beyond the current discussion.

* Nisbett, 2009, provides an extensive list of examples and discusses the difficulty of implementation.

and heritability often exceeded total environmental influences.

Genetic correlations were high, indicating that substantially the same genetic influences were being expressed in all topics. This is consistent with QBG analyses of psychometric tests (as discussed earlier); genetic influences appear to express themselves more on g than on specific cognitive skills. The environmental influences appeared to be unique to each of the three skills – reading, math, and science. Environmental effects appeared to control deviations from a genetically related stable path, either upward or downward, rather than individual differences in the average performance of a child, across time. As has been the case with studies of genetic influence on intelligence test scores, the environmental contribution was largely due to nonshared environmental differences, environmental differences between twins or siblings, rather than across families.

Educators (and parents) have long debated whether particularly poor school performance is an indication that a child has a specific genetic anomaly or whether children toward the bottom end of the performance scale have general educational deficits. To shed light on this question the TEDS researchers asked whether the models that applied to all children in the study

also applied to those in the lowest fifth or fifteenth percentiles. In the American context, low-performing children are often assigned to "special education" classes. The reduced samples still contained several hundred cases. In general, the same models that applied to the entire sample applied to the reduced samples.

This suggests that poor academic performance is generally the result of an overall cognitive deficit, rather than a specific problem. It is true that some cases of impaired learning skills have been identified with certain genomes.[46] However, the known specific disabilities account for only a small fraction of cases of poor reading or mathematics performance.

8.3.6. *Summary Comments on Quantitative Behavior Genetics*

Anyone familiar with the "now you find it, now you don't" phenomena that plague the social sciences has to be struck by the

46 Willcut et al., 2004. An example of such specific genetic anomalies is the FOXP2 gene, which was associated with very poor linguistic performance in a pedigree study of a single British family (Lai et al., 2001). The relevant allele was not found in any of the 270 cases of poor language performance in the TEDS study (Kovas et al., 2007, p. 108).

consistency of the behavior genetic findings. To review briefly:

1. Additive genetic heritability accounts for 40–80% of the variance in virtually all cognitive traits.
2. Somewhere around half of the variance is common to all traits. This strongly suggests that there are generalist genes that influence brain structures underlying virtually all cognitive performance.
3. Environmental effects (including the prenatal environment) are strongest in early childhood. They diminish thereafter.
4. Childhood environmental effects are primarily due to within-family differences – the way a child interacts with his or her familial environment – rather than being due to between-family environmental differences. Nonshared environmental influences are also the largest environmental influences in adults, but this now refers to life experiences that differentiate twins and siblings, rather than (in most cases) to family environments.
5. While genetic influences are strong in establishing the trajectory of a person's cognitive development and the later reduction of cognitive ability in old age, variations from that trajectory are influenced by environmental factors.

There are a few caveats that must be kept in mind. I will present them in inverse order of their importance, from least serious to most serious.

Twin studies loom large in the QBG study of intelligence. Heritability estimates from such studies are heavily influenced (and in some cases dictated) by the contrast between DZ and MZ twins. The rough and ready method of estimating the heritability of trait X as $2\,(r_{MZ}(X, X') - r_{DX}(X, X'))$ is a good example. This contrast is based on the assumption that MZ twins have identical geneotypes, which they do, and that DZ twins have half of the permissible human variation: $r_{MZ}(G, G') = 1$ and $r_{DZ}(G, G') = \frac{1}{2}$. The assumption about MZ twins is unarguable. The assumption about DZ twins

depends on the further assumption that the parental genetic correlations are zero; there is no tendency for males and females to select mates of similar genetic background. This may be true in fruit flies and fish, but it is not in humans. The correlation between cognitive test scores for spouses generally runs in the .2–.3 range. This tendency is called *assortative mating*.

As yet, we do not have a good idea of the extent to which assortative mating has to be considered. The topic is a difficult one to study, because the analysis requires test scores from both parents and children. Nevertheless, some studies are being done, and hopefully more will occur in the future.[47]

Most of the analyses used to determine heritability do not allow for gene-environment interactions or correlations. The failure to allow for interactions is a major deficiency of present QBG approaches. Why is it a problem, and why haven't QBG analyses allowed for it?

We know gene-environment interactions exist, for we can point to some. Many genetically influenced traits, such as alcoholism, involve a potential for a pathology that is released by environmental agents. As we get a better understanding of gene-environment interactions they are likely to play a larger role in our understanding of the inheritance of intelligence. Gene by environment correlations may also be very important. Several studies have reported higher heritability coefficients in middle and upper SES populations than for lower SES populations.[48] This is in itself an interaction in the statistical sense. But why would this occur? Several mechanisms have been postulated.

One argument is that harsh social environments will restrict the expression of genetic potential, and that therefore genetic variation can express itself only in an environment that nurtures cognition.[49] There is an analogy to weight: in a famine-stricken town everyone is emaciated; when food is

47 See Colom, Aluja-Fabregat, & Garcia-Lopez, 2002; Reynolds, Baker, & Pederson, 2000; van Leeuwen, Van den Berg, & Boomsma, 2008.
48 Harden, Turkheimer, & Loehlin, 2007; Rowe, 2004; Turkheimer et al., 2003.
49 Bronfenbrenner & Ceci, 1994.

available genetic tendencies toward obesity can express themselves. Substitute "getting something out of education" for weight and "bad schools" for famine and you have the idea.

A second argument is that society contains a number of positive feedback mechanisms that serve to increase variation, especially in the high range of the scale. Jim Flynn, a professor of political science at the University of Otago, New Zealand has been a particularly strong advocate of this hypothesis.[50] One of his frequently used analogies is to basketball. Initially a tall, strong young person may be singled out for special playing and coaching opportunities. The better the player, the more coaching the player gets, thus increasing the variance in skill between the initially mediocre and initially somewhat better players. Applied to cognitive skills, this suggests that if a school system practices "streaming" talented and untalented students onto different tracks, with different qualities of instruction, one can anticipate a rich-get-richer, poor-get-poorer phenomenon, in both basketball and intelligence. Initial, genetically produced talent is nurtured by the environment.

Both these explanations of the observed changes in h^2 with environment rest on interactions between initial talent and opportunities to develop talent. There is a third argument that is equally reasonable but has an entirely different basis. The issue may not be that higher SES environments permit the expression of greater genetic effects; it may be that lower SES environments have greater environmental ranges in variables that are relevant to intelligence. To put things graphically, the cognitive benefits of sending a child to a good, average middle class preschool, or even of not sending the child to preschool at all, but spending a lot of time interacting with the child at home, may not be very far behind the benefits of sending a child to an exceptionally expensive preschool. The differences between keeping children in a chaotic atmosphere, with very little encouragement to explore or express themselves, compared to sending the same

children to a modestly funded preschool three or four days a week may be profound. This sort of effect is *not* a gene-environment interaction. The effect is due to greater environmental variation in the lower SES environment compared to the higher SES environment.

I find these arguments for gene-environment interactions and correlations compelling. However, I see very little hope of untangling the effects by the use of structural equation models that make gross assumptions about how the environment covaries between people of different degrees of genetic relatedness. We need direct measures of the environmental variables that influence cognition. Without a theory of environmental action it is hard to know where to begin.

And that is the rub. In an article defending much of the research on twin studies and, by implication, most other QBG studies of intelligence, Bouchard[51] pointed out that most of the claims that additive heritability coefficients are due to hidden gene-environment interactive effects are arguments about what might be the case. The arguments are sometimes accompanied by analogies to gene-environment interactions in plants, but seldom if ever by an example involving human intelligence. In this respect, Flynn's apocryphal basketball example is interesting, but an actual example involving human intelligence would have been more convincing.

Bouchard made two arguments to counter the interactionists. Both have to do with the strategy one follows in scientific research. First, he observed that many of the arguments appealed to what ought to have been measured in various studies. My own concerns, as just expressed, are of this nature. Any result can be explained by appeal to unmeasured variables.[52] Second, scientists generally accept a principle known as *Occam's razor*. Given two equally accurate explanations of the same phenomenon, one should always prefer the simpler one.

50 Dickens & Flynn, 2001; Flynn, 2007.

51 Bouchard, 1997.
52 I wish I could take credit for this statement, but I cannot. I heard Bouchard say it in a public meeting.

QBG studies have shown that the assumption of substantial additive genetic variance can account for a great deal of data on the covariation of intelligence across people of different degrees of genetic relatedness. Therefore, the simple additive model deserves to be number one in a competition between theories. Until someone comes along with data to back up the more complicated interaction models.

QBG tells us how much heritability there is for intelligence within a given population. The only thing it says about the mechanism of inheritance is an appeal to the abstract Mendelian concept of a gene. To go further we have to ask what a gene is and how it influences the development of the brain.

8.4. The Molecular Genetics of Intelligence

Mendel established the logical basis of genetic inheritance, but knew nothing of its physical mechanism. That is the topic of *molecular genetics*, a field that started at the beginning of the twentieth century with the discovery that the chromosomes were the bearers of the genetic material. Discovery after discovery followed (along with several Nobel Prizes), the key one being James Watson and Francis Crick's discovery of the structure of the genetic material, deoxyribose nucleic acid (DNA), in 1953.[53] Genetic inheritance turns out to be a very complicated process. Fortunately a simplified model of the process is sufficient for our purposes.[54]

The material in the chromosome is a DNA molecule, which has the structure of a double helix, two strands of material twisted around each other. The strands are made up of four structures called bases. The four bases are adenine (A), thymine (T), guanine (G), and cytosine (C). The strands of the helix are bound together because the bases bind to each other, forming units called *base pairs*. The binding is unique. An A always pairs with a T, and a C with a G. Logically the DNA molecule can be thought of as a sequence disregarding its helical structure. The sequence constitutes a person's *genome*. This is why the term "sequencing the genome" is sometimes used to refer to the process of identifying a genome.

The bases form triplets, sequences of three bases. As there are four possible bases, there are sixty-four possible triplets. These are called *codons*. Each of the sixty-four possible codons either marks the starting and stopping points of the codon sequence that makes up a gene, or specifies the creation of one of twenty amino acids, which are the building blocks of enzymes and proteins out of which cells, and hence life, are constructed. Therefore, a protein-encoding gene is, physically, the sequence of codons between a "starting" and "stopping" codon. The sequence of bases within this interval provide the program for cellular mechanisms that initiate the construction of one or more proteins, just as the magnetic charges on a digital video disk (DVD) provide the program that initiates the display of pictures and playing of music on a modern television set. Since Watson and Crick's discovery, one of the major tasks of behavior genetics has been to find out how this program is read to produce proteins, then cells, and eventually an organism.

Variations in the sequence of bases within a gene define *alleles*, and hence variations in the program for building the organism. This provides the variation that evolution requires.

Figure 8.12 shows how genes are passed on from one generation to the next. The figure illustrates *meiosis*, the process of constructing a chromosome carried by a gamete (sperm cell in males, ovum in females). Recall that (for autosomes) there are two chromosomes. The two chromosomes link at a connecting point. A new chromosome is formed, containing a segment from each of the parental chromosomes. Therefore, base pairs that are located close to each other on a chromosome tend to be inherited together. In fertilization the chromosomes in the sperm and ovum unite, so that the

53 Watson & Crick, 1953.
54 Watson (2003) presents a well-written history and discussion of the twentieth-century discoveries.

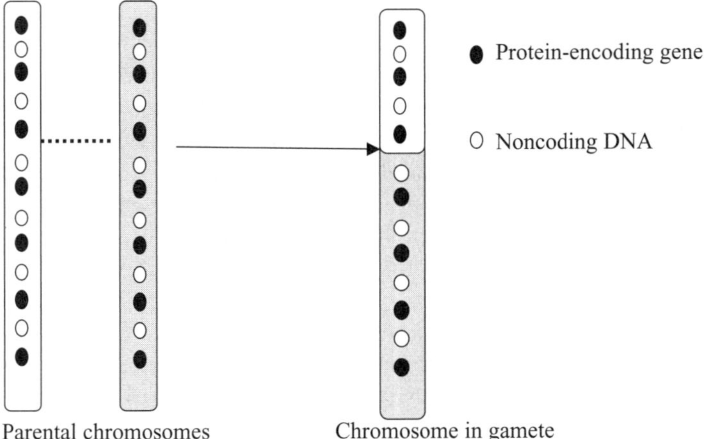

Figure 8.12. The reshuffling of genetic material in meiosis. Each chromosome in a chromosome pair can be thought of as a sequence of base pairs. In meiosis the two chromosomes link together at some midpoint, and then a new chromosome is constructed from one segment of each of the parental chromosomes. Therefore, base pairs that are close to each other on a chromosome will tend to be inherited together.

chromosome pair in the offspring contains one chromosome from each parent.

The process is somewhat different in the sex chromosomes. In females, who have two X chromosomes, the shuffling takes place as in the autosomes. In males, who have an X and Y chromosome pair, either the X or Y chromosome is carried over into a sperm cell. Accordingly, female zygotes contain two X chromosomes, one from each parent, but male zygotes contain a maternal X and a paternal Y chromosome. The Y chromosome represents a direct transfer of genetic material along the patrilineal line. While a male's X chromosome is always inherited from the mother, that chromosome might have come from either maternal grandparent, so an analogous continuous transfer of genes through the female line is not possible.[55]

The white and black dots in Figure 8.12 indicate base sequences. The black dots indicate sequences that make up the protein-encoding genes. The white dots indicate base sequences outside of the genes. The totality of the base sequences, across all chromosomes, constitutes the genome.

About 90% of the genome consists of sequences of bases that lie outside of the protein-encoding genes. There are also sequences of bases within the protein-encoding genes that do not code for proteins. At one time these sequences were thought to be inert and were referred to as "junk DNA." We now know that at least some of the sequences are active, because they regulate the expression of the protein-encoding genes. In addition, some genes regulate the expression of other genes.

There are many statements like "We share 50% of our genes with each of our parents." These statements are a bit misleading. The 50% figure refers to variation in the sequence of base pairs that can differ across human beings, and still produce a person. That is a small percentage of the total genome; roughly 99.9% of the genome is identical across humans, and we share 96% of the genome with our evolutionary cousin, the chimpanzee.

Nevertheless, there are differences. A difference that occurs at a base pair in

55 There is a way to trace female lineage. *Mitochondria* are organelles within a cell, but outside the nucleus. They contain their own DNA, mtDNA, for a total of thirty-seven genes, plus segments of noncoding DNA. MtDNA is inherited from the mother, so analysis of mtDNA provides a genetic record of female lineage.

Panel 8.9. A Few Stray Facts About the Genome

Here are a few facts about the genome.

1. There are approximately three billion (3,000,000,000) base pairs in the human genome. However, the number of protein-encoding genes is much smaller. The current (2010) estimate is between 25,000 and 30,000. This estimate is well below the estimates of 100,000 or more that were common as late as the year 2000.

2. Each gene specifies an average of three proteins. Different proteins may be expressed in different parts of the body. It has been estimated that about one-third of human genes have some expression in the brain.

3. A *mutation* occurs when a new allele arises. Some mutations arise due to errors in the process of DNA replication. Mutations can also be triggered by environmental hazards. These include nuclear radiation, ultraviolet light, and exposure to certain chemicals. Discouragingly, some of the hazardous chemicals are used in industrial processes. Finally, some mutations appear to occur "by chance," which simply means that we do not know what the causative process is.

4. Mutations are probably more frequent than we realize, for a great deal of the genome's programming specifies basic processes in the cell. In such cases pregnancy either does not begin or is terminated without detection. In other cases termination occurs later, with a detectable pregnancy, or a stillbirth occurs. Some mutations are viable, and can even produce superior individuals in some environments. That is how evolution works!

5. Some genes regulate the expression of other genes in the body. In addition, some of the (formerly believed to be) junk DNA lying outside the boundaries of protein-encoding genes serve as regulators of genetic expression. Microenvironmental factors within the cell can also control genetic expression.

6. A genetic influence may not be expressed for some time after birth, or in some cases may be suppressed throughout the individual's life.

---

at least 1% of the population is called a single nucleotide polymorphism (SNP or "snip"). There are about ten million SNPs in humans. Blocks of SNPs that are close together on the same chromosome, and so tend to be inherited together, are called *haploids*. The SNPs themselves may be in a protein-encoding gene, in a region between genes, or may be part of the nonencoding portion of a gene. One of the major steps in research on genetic differences involves locating haploids that differ between two or more populations of interest, such as individuals who do or do not have a particular form of mental disability.

Panel 8.9 presents a few more facts about the genome. The next two sections discuss some of the many genetic disorders of cognition.

8.4.1. *Genetic Pathologies of Intelligence*

A person is considered to be mentally disabled if his or her intelligence, as measured by standard tests, falls below an IQ of 70. This is obviously an arbitrary standard, for a great many people who are considered to have a mental disability have IQ scores in the 70–80 range. From the behavior genetics viewpoint, the mentally disabled fall into three distinct groups.

One group consists of people who have a cognitive deficiency with a known genetic cause. The mental deficiency is often only part of the syndrome, which may often include other organic problems. There are approximately 300 such syndromes known at present, and no doubt more will be discovered. In some cases there is a general mental deficiency; in others deficiencies may be unevenly distributed, although some general deficiency is usually found. The genes that have been identified as causes for these deficiencies are found on several different chromosomes. However, the rate of occurrence on the X chromosome is higher than would be expected by chance.[56]

Most of the genes associated with severe mental retardation are recessive. Accordingly, a man can suffer ill effects if he inherits a single copy of the allele associated with the pathology. Women, with two X chromosomes, have to inherit two copies of the allele in order to be affected.

The following examples of known genetic disorders have been chosen to illustrate the variety of syndromes that can occur. One of the examples is expressed in infancy, one in infancy and childhood, another in middle age, and the last is usually not expressed until old age. In the first three examples the genetic anomaly is both sufficient and necessary for the disorder to occur. In the fourth example the genetic anomaly increases the risk of the cognitive disorder, but is neither a sufficient nor a necessary condition for the disorder.

Phenylketonuria (PKU). This is one of the best understood of the genetic mental deficiencies. PKU is due to a mutation in the PAH gene located on chromosome 12. PAH codes for synthesis of *phenylalanine hydroxylase*, an enzyme that is important in the metabolism of *phenylalanine*, a substance that is found in certain foods, including artificial sweeteners. Untreated PKU can result in severe mental retardation. Fortunately the condition leading to PKU can be detected at birth, by an inexpensive blood test. Affected individuals have to maintain a restricted diet for a number of years. There are some indications that older children and adults who cease to follow the diet may be at risk for mild mental retardation, or at least a lower tested intelligence level than would be expected otherwise. In the extreme case a pregnant woman who is a carrier of the mutation may affect her child, not necessarily by passing on the gene, but by the harmful effects of a buildup of phenylalanine in her body during pregnancy.

Estimates of the frequency of PKU range from 1 per 13,500 to 1 per 19,000 births, varying across ethnic groups. Screening and treatment for PKU has been widespread since the 1960s, so the clinical form of the condition is now fairly rare in the industrially developed countries. This makes PKU a prototypical example of a gene-environment interaction. It is a disaster for children born without access to modern health care, but a treatable problem for children who have access to health care.

Fragile X syndrome. People suffering from fragile X syndrome display impulsiveness, difficulties in concentration, and, possibly concomitantly, some degree of mental retardation. The condition affects 1 in 4,000 men and 1 in 8,000 women. It is due to a mutation in the FRM1 gene on the X chromosome. This gene is involved in production of a protein that is important in, among other things, nerve synthesis.

Molecular geneticists have been able to go inside the gene, pointing to the manner of mutation that influences the gene's expression. In normal individuals the CGG codon occurs in a block of from ten to forty repetitions within the FRM1 gene. In affected individuals the block may contain from 200 to 1,000 repetitions. The repetitions block the gene's normal production of the protein.

Huntington's disease. Huntington's disease was discussed earlier as an illustration of a pathological gene that does not express itself until after a person reaches or passes reproductive age. See the discussion of Woody Guthrie and his family, presented in panel 8.1. The syndrome is caused by a dominant allele on chromosome 4, so affected individuals need have only one copy of the gene in order to express symptoms.

In general, if a pathological allele is dominant it quickly disappears from the

56 Inlow & Restifo, 2004.

population. Huntington's disease represents an insidious situation. The pathology does not manifest itself until after the affected individual is well into his or her reproductive period. Therefore, the disease gene can be passed on to the next generation before the illness appears.

As is the case with fragile X syndrome, the pathological allele has an abnormal number of repeats of a codon. Increasing numbers of repeats are associated with earlier onset of the syndrome. There is also evidence that the length of the repeat increases over generations, so if a child of a person with Huntington's disease carries the allele he or she is at risk for developing symptoms earlier than the parent did.

Alzheimer's disease.[57] Alzheimer's disease is a common and feared disease of the elderly. As of 2008, estimates of the number of people suffering from Alzheimer's dementia in the United States ranged from 4.5 to 7 million, out of a total population of just over 300 million – about 2% of the population. As the age distribution shifts toward higher percentages of elderly people, the incidence of Alzheimer's dementia will increase. If present incidence rates continue there will be eleven to sixteen million cases of the disease in the United States by 2050. Progress toward effective treatment or prevention has been disappointingly slow. Research on this economically and socially devastating disease is being given very high priority.

The disease comes in two forms. *Early onset* Alzheimer's is defined as Alzheimer's disease that manifests itself prior to age 65. Cases have occurred as early as the mid forties. The more common variety, *late onset* Alzheimer's disease, appears after age sixty-five. The initial symptoms are failures of short-term memory and attention, progressing to profound loss of long-term memory, including loss of the ability to recognize spouses and relatives known for fifty years or

more, loss of speech, and eventually death. Because intensive care may be required for a period of years the financial and emotional impact on caregivers can be very high.

The proximal cause of the memory loss is widespread deterioration of the nerve cells in the brain, beginning with the frontal cortex and the hippocampus. This is not surprising, as these structures are important for the development of new memories. Neural deterioration is accompanied by the formation of beta amaloid protein plaques in the brain.

Three genes have been identified as increasing the risk of early onset Alzheimer's, but they are not sufficient to account for all cases of the disease.

Late onset Alzheimer's has been associated with several genes, among them the Apolipoprotein E (APOE) gene on chromosome 19. The gene has three alleles, APOE2, APOE3, and APOE4. About half the population carries the APOE2 allele. The high-risk form of the allele, APOE4, is relatively common (15% of the European-derived population in the United States). About 50% of diagnosed Alzheimer's patients carry the APOE4 form, but less than half of the people who carry APOE4 express the disease. For those who are affected, the age of onset is related to the genetic load. Patients with genotype E4/E4 have a mean onset of sixty-eight years of age, patients carrying one E4 allele have a mean onset of seventy-five years, and patients with no E4 alleles have a mean onset of eighty-four years.

None of the genes linked with either type of Alzheimer's disease has a strong enough association to be considered the sole, or even a necessary, cause of the disease. Identifying a person's genotype makes it possible to assess the risk of developing the dementia, but we cannot say "for certain" that the dementia will or will not occur.

A number of environmental factors have been linked (somewhat tenuously) to Alzheimer's disease. These include severe inflammations of the brain and head injury. It has been suggested that industrial air and water pollutants may increase the risk of the disease. This has yet to be proven.

---

57 Information on symptoms, causation, and incidence downloaded from the Alzheimer's Association website and the National Institute of Aging website, March 2008.

Such a multiplicity of possible causes is not surprising. The proximal mechanism of deterioration is neural degeneration, possibly due to the development of protein plaques in the brain, degeneration of the synapses, and other insults to the brain itself. The deterioration can probably be initiated by several environmental and genetic hazards, which would act as distal causes.

Alzheimer's disease represents a common situation, in which both genetic and environmental factors increase the risk of expression of a pathology, but there does not appear to be any one factor that is either sufficient or necessary for the expression.

8.4.2. *Mental Pathologies Related to Chromosomal Abnormalities*

Several mental disabilities are caused by anomalies in the duplication of chromosomes, rather than by variations in genes.

Down's syndrome: Down's syndrome is characterized by poor physical development, mild to moderate mental retardation, and facial features that include elliptically shaped eyelids. It is fairly common, occurring in approximately 1 of every 800 births. The syndrome is caused by the presence of an extra chromosome 21. Down's syndrome sufferers usually die at a fairly early age, as the syndrome includes defects in the cardiovascular system as well as cognitive problems. Adult Down's syndrome patients display premature aging, including the physical deteriorations associated with advanced age and early Alzheimer's disease.

Relatives of a person with Down's syndrome are at risk of producing a Down's syndrome child. The risk is strongly related to the mother's age at birth. The risk rises from less than 1 in 1,000 births to women under thirty years old to 1 in 100 for women over forty.

Turner's syndrome.[58] Turner's syndrome is a condition that affects women born with a single X chromosome. Turner's patients display poor spatial-perceptual reasoning, the P and R components of the VPR model.

Verbal reasoning is unaffected. Affected women may also display difficulties with tasks that place high demands on the complex of working memory and attentional control, the behaviors labeled "executive functioning." Physical signs may appear. These include short stature, in some cases markedly thickened necks, and late and sometimes incomplete development of sexual characteristics. The women are also at risk for cardiovascular problems. All of these remarks have to be qualified by the fact of individual variation.

Turner's syndrome cases vary greatly. Some of these differences are tied to environmental variables. Girls who receive both growth hormone and estrogen replacement therapy may reach heights in the normal range and may be free of the physical signs associated with the syndrome. Supportive within-family social environments are important. Estrogen therapy appears to be effective in countering deficiencies in executive control functions, although it does not counter the deficiency in spatial-perceptual reasoning. This is interesting, because different brain structures are involved in executive control and spatial-visual reasoning. Clinically, the result is encouraging because a great many of our everyday spatial-perceptual tasks can also be accomplished using verbal strategies.

Turner's syndrome is, like PKU, an example of a gene-environment interaction. A baby girl born today with Turner's syndrome has a far better outlook than she would have had one hundred years ago, providing that she has been born into a social environment that can provide the necessary support.

XYY syndrome. Some males are born with two Y chromosomes. The genotype is associated with mild mental retardation. XYY males are typically large and fairly robust. During the 1960s it was suggested that XYY males are overly aggressive, to the point of exhibiting dangerous criminal behavior. The evidence for this was that there is an elevated incidence of XYY men among criminal populations.[59] However, it does not

---

58 Ross, Zinn, & McAuley, 2000.

59 Jarvik, Klodin, & Matsuyama, 1973.

follow from this observation that XYY men are likely to become criminals. Studies of XYY's in prison populations can establish the conditional probability of being XYY, given that the individual is known to be a (tall) criminal, $Pr(XYY|crime)$, but that is not the same thing as establishing the probability of being a criminal, given that the individual is known to be an XYY. The latter figure, $Pr(crime|XYY)$, is the statistic that would have to be high in order to justify proactive monitoring of XYY cases. This is difficult to establish, as the condition occurs only in approximately 1 in 1,000 male births.

Two small prospective studies have been done in which XYY's were identified and then followed for some time.[60] In both studies the incidence of criminality among XYY men was elevated above the general population but not above the population of men of comparable IQ. An analysis of the types of crimes committed indicated that that elevated criminality may be mediated by low intelligence levels, rather than heightened aggression.

Klinefelter's syndrome. Klinefelter's cases are men who have genotype XXY. Klinefelter's syndrome cases are fairly large men, although they are not unusually robust. The commonest cognitive characteristic is poor language development, along with an elevated incidence of mild to moderate mental retardation. This is consistent with an fMRI study that revealed decreased hemispheric specialization during language processing among Kleinfelter's patients, as compared to control groups.[61] Sexual development is retarded. There is some indication that hormone replacement therapy can ameliorate the symptoms of this condition.[62]

Various types of mental retardation affect slightly under 3% of the population. This estimate excludes people with Alzheimer's disease, which is usually considered a problem associated with old age rather than a mental disability. The mentally disabled impose a substantial burden on our social support systems. Finding techniques for ameliorating or effectively eliminating the consequences of these genetic anomalies, as we have with *PKU*, would have major moral, social, and economic rewards.

8.4.3. *The Genetic Basis of Normal Variability in Intelligence*

The molecular genetic analysis of normal variation in intelligence presents a very different picture than the analysis of pathological conditions. The first thing to say, and to say loudly, is that there is no one gene, or even a small number of genes, responsible for normal variations in intelligence. If there were one, we would have found it by now, for the techniques that have been used are quite adequate to identify any gene that accounted for 30% or more of the variation in intelligence within the normal range. No such gene has been found, so we may be pretty sure that it is not there.

We are clearly dealing with a polygenic inheritance model; lots of genes have their influence, but no one of them is the key gene. One of the most prominent researchers in the field, Robert Plomin, has speculated that variation in any one gene will control at most .5% of the variance in intelligence, as expressed in test scores.[63] This may be a bit pessimistic, for researchers have found at least two genes, the CHRM2 gene on chromosome 2 and the SNAP-25 gene on chromosome 20, where variations in alleles may account for as much as 3–4% of phenotypic variation.[64] However, such findings have to be replicated. And here is why.

Population-wide studies of genetics assess covariances between allele frequencies and phenotypical variations simultaneously, across many polymorphisms in the genotype. Because very many polymorphisms are being studied simultaneously, there is a substantial chance of finding polymorphisms that, by chance, happen to covary with the phenotypical measure in the sample,

60 Gotz, Johnstone, & Ratcliffe, 1999; Witkin et al., 1976.
61 Van Rijn et al., 2008.
62 Hazlett, 2005.
63 Plomin, Kennedy, & Craig, 2006.
64 Dick et al., 2007; Gosso et al., 2006.

even though there is no covariation between the allele frequencies and the phenotypical measure in the population. Such a finding is called a *false positive*.

The converse problem is *false negatives*. Suppose that Plomin's conjecture is right, that the covariation between allele frequencies in any one gene and intelligence test scores accounts for less than 1% of the total variation in test scores. Unless the sample is very large the chances of detecting a small covariation are not good.

The false positive and false negative effects play off against each other. Any widespread screening study maximizes the chances of finding false positives. When it comes to replication, though, a small effect can dip below the level of detectability in the replication sample. This makes the business of gene locating both time-consuming and expensive. That is the way it is.

8.4.4. *Techniques for Identifying Genes Associated with Normal Intelligence*

Several techniques have been used to identify genetic contributions to intelligence. Some of the technologies are described in panel 8.10. Here I look at the logic rather than the mechanics of any one method.

In a "bottom up" technique a gene is identified that is known to be associated with some physiological function that might, reasonably, be linked to intelligence. A study is then initiated in which people are given some form of intelligence test and have their genotypes determined. This was the method used to identify the CHRM and SNAP genes. Both are believed to be linked to the development of an efficient neural system.

Sometimes this method works out. But sometimes it does not. For instance, we know that brain volume is related to intelligence, and that the connection is very largely genetic.[65] Accordingly, it is not surprising that there was considerable excitement when it was found that variations in the allele frequencies of two genes,

MICROCEPHALIN (chromosome 8) and ASPM (chromosome 1), both known to be involved in pathological failures of the development of brain size, exhibit evidence of strong evolutionary pressures and, in addition, have a worldwide distribution suggesting that the pressure occurred about the times of the migration of *Homo sapiens* out of Africa and, much later, the development of agriculture.[66] However subsequent research showed that allele variations in these genes were not reliably associated with intelligence, within the normal range, or, for that matter, with head size and brain volume within the normal range.[67]

Failures to replicate or to show hypothesized correlations do not uncover bad science in the original studies. Given the statistical issues involved, the only way for the field to proceed is for scientists to publish their findings, and then call for replication.

An alternative strategy for finding the genetic basis of intelligence is to start from the "top down," by identifying individuals who differ in intelligence and then contrasting their genotypes. This is called *genome-wide association*. One such study compared DNA from children who had been identified as showing a very high level of mathematical ability to DNA from a normal control group. The two groups differed in the frequency of an allele of a gene associated with the synthesis of insulin.[68]

Because many DNA sequences are being screened at once, genome-wide association is prone to picking up false positives. The only feasible way to counteract this is to replicate findings. And, alas, when this particular study was replicated the allele-intelligence correlation was not found.[69]

Linkage analysis is usually applied in conjunction with the study of related individuals – the pedigree method applied to people rather than to plants. Linkage analyses can identify segments of DNA where polymorphisms are correlated with some measure

65 Posthuma, De Geus, & Boomsma, 2004.

66 Evans et al., 2005; Mekel-Bobrov et al., 2005.
67 Mekel-Bobrov et al., 2007; Rushton, Vernon, & Bons, 2007; Woods et al., 2006.
68 Chorney et al., 1998.
69 Hill et al., 2002.

Panel 8.10. Methods for Screening for Genetic Effects

This panel describes designs used to establish a correlation between variations in alleles (*polymorphisms*) and variations in a phenotypic trait, such as intelligence.

Differences between individual genomes (*polymorphisms*) occur when the sequence of nucleotides differs at one or more positions, as in the sequence A C G T A A compared to A C C T A A, where there is a difference between G and C in the third position. As the text explains, a variation such as this is called a *single nucleotide polymorphism* (SNP, "snip"). A SNP can occur inside or outside the boundaries of protein-encoding genes. Segments of DNA that contain one or more SNPs are referred to as *alleles* of that segment, a generalization of the idea that an allele is a variant of a gene to the idea that an allele is a variant of a SNP. SNPs occur roughly every 100 to 300 base positions along the genetic code.

A *genetic marker* is an identifiable segment of the sequence of bases in the genome. Genetic markers are used to identify segments of the genome within each chromosome. To take an oversimplified example, suppose that two markers, M_1 and M_2, have been identified, and that in one person the sequence of DNA between markers is M_1 A C G T A A M_2 and in the other the sequence is A C C T A A. There is a SNP at the third position. This means that there are at least two alleles of the genetic sequence between M_1 and M_2.

Participants in a study donate DNA samples and are measured on the phenotypic trait, perhaps by being given an intelligence test. The DNA samples are then broken up into segments between genetic markers. The data is examined for correlations between the presence of alleles and the values of the phenotypic trait. For instance, if one allele is statistically associated with high IQ scores and another with low scores, then a genetic association with IQ has been located.

The technique works best if the participants differ in their genotypes in some systematic way. Therefore *linkage analyses* are done using samples of related individuals. For instance, registrants in the Dutch twin registry and their relatives have participated in linkage analyses.

Linkage analysis is highly useful for tracing the genetic basis of discrete traits, with restricted reaction ranges, such as eye color. It can be applied to continuously measured traits, such as intelligence, but there may not be enough reliability in measuring the phenotypic trait to make the technique precise. This is especially true if, as is the case for cognitive measures, expression of the trait is affected by environmental as well as genetic factors. We know that this is the case for intelligence, for MZ twins, with identical genotypes, do not necessarily have the same test scores. Therefore, another method, *genome-wide analysis*, is used with continuous traits.

Genome-wide analysis depends on a technology for the detection of genetic expression by microarrays. A microarray is a small chip that is divided into cells, or "dots." In the screening application each dot contains a sequence of DNA located around one of the values of a previously identified SNP. Therefore, the segment of DNA in each dot is essentially a fragment of the allele of a SNP carried by one individual in the sample. Chips capable of evaluating a million SNPs have become available.

DNA samples are taken from individuals from one or more populations that vary on the trait in question. The genetic material from all individuals is pooled, to create a solution of DNA and other material. (The process, which is rather complicated, will not be further described.)

(continued)

> **Panel 8.10** *(continued)*
>
> The microarray chip is then immersed in the DNA. Because complementary DNA strands will bind to each other, DNA that matches the DNA at a dot on the chip will bind to that location. The amount of binding at each spot is then compared across groups, to see if differences in binding can be related to group membership. A case of this sort is described in the text.

of cognitive competence, usually intelligence test scores. (The technique would work just as well with measures of working memory, attention, or any other measurable trait, including such things as height and eye color.) The reason for using related individuals is that the occurrence of the polymorphism can be traced over generations and across different relationships, in order to establish a correlation between the polymorphism and the trait of interest. To date, segments of DNA that covary with intelligence test scores have been located on chromosomes 2 and 6.[70] However, we have to wait for replication to solidify these results. Once this is done, further studies can be initiated to locate the genes within or near the segment, including non-protein-encoding DNA regulator sequences, and to find out what they do.

Progress toward identifying the genes associated with normal variations in cognition has been slow. In a review of progress as of 2006, Robert Plomin, Kennedy, and Craig pointed out that discoveries in the field have followed a discouraging pattern. Initially genes emerge as reasonable candidates for the "intelligence gene" because of their involvement with neural efficiency, brain development, or some other key function that ought to be related to intelligence. Interesting associations are found at first, but the associations do not appear on replication. The fact that this pattern has appeared so frequently is what led Plomin to speculate that no gene, alone, accounts for more than .5% of the variance in intelligence.[71]

However, from quantitative genetic studies we know that in the populations studied at least half, and possibly more, of the variation in intelligence is due to genetic variation. It seems clear that we are dealing with a very large number of genes, each of which has a small effect. Smoking slingshots, not smoking guns!

The search for the genes for intelligence is not a hopeless project. Solid results from quantitative behavior genetics show that the target genes exist. The technology for associating genes with traits is getting better and better. Ultimately, we will locate the genes for intelligence and will understand their modes of action. This will be a huge step forward in understanding the biological basis of intelligence. Unless there is a spectacular breakthrough in technology, the search is going to take a lot longer than people thought it would at the start of the twenty-first century.

But be of (some) good cheer. The last fifty years of the twentieth century and the first decade of the twenty-first *did* see spectacular breakthroughs in the technology dealing with molecular genetics. Who knows what is to come?

8.5. Reprise and Commentary

The facts are incontrovertible. Human intelligence is heavily influenced by genetics. Specific genetic anomalies are clearly associated with identifiable mental abilities, and on a statistical basis substantial heritability coefficients have repeatedly been found in studies throughout industrial and post-industrial societies. The exact value for the heritability coefficient, h^2, may vary somewhat from study to study, but that is to

---

70 Luciano et al., 2006; Posthuma et al., 2005.

71 Plomin, Kennedy, & Craig, 2006. Plomin reiterated this theme in an address to the International Society for Intelligence Research, Amsterdam, December 2007.

be expected. It is never zero, and it is never one.

Hopefully, future studies will shift from trying to find a "true value" for this coefficient to determining what characteristics of a population determine the relative importance of genetic and environmental influences on intelligence. The heredity-environment debate has too often been posed as a contest. It is not. We need to find mechanisms for both. An unacknowledged problem that has hampered the field is that while we have an excellent theory of genetic variation, we do not have a comparable theory of environmental variation. It is easy to point to good and bad environments for the development of cognitive power. It is much harder to provide some sort of metric to say how good or how bad a particular environment is.

The current frontier in behavior genetics has shifted from trying to show that intelligence is inherited to trying to find the mechanism of inheritance. A good deal of success has been obtained in tracing the genetic causes of serious cognitive deficiencies, such as Huntington's disease and PKU. We have had much less success in identifying the genes associated with variations in normal intelligence. Why? The answer is simple: this is a harder problem. It may turn out that the strategy of looking for gene-intelligence correlations directly is the wrong approach. An alternate approach would be to look for the brain mechanisms that are associated with intelligence, and then try to find the genes that influence the development of these mechanisms.

The lay public has displayed an ambiguous attitude toward findings on the genetics of intelligence. I will revisit this topic in the final chapter of the book, where I look at social controversies more generally. Here I make only a few brief remarks.

Public opinion has accepted an analogy between physical defects and extreme mental deficiencies, especially when accompanied by physical stigmata. The lay person believes that it is reasonable to look for a physical cause for an extreme mental deficiency, just as it is sensible to look for a physical cause for, say, high cholesterol, which does have a genetic component. Such research has received strong public, political, and financial support. There is considerably more ambiguity about efforts to identify a genetic basis for intelligence, in the normal range. There are several reasons for this.

Modern Western society distrusts hereditary elites. The Age of Kings is definitely over. On the other hand, it is demonstrably the case that health, wealth, and opportunity for education, the trappings of high socioeconomic status, do pass on from one generation to the next. In the nineteenth century Galton concluded that this was largely a reflection of genetically endowed merit. Today that view is decidedly unpopular. Any suggestion that cognitive competence is largely inherited is seen as denying a popular legend – that you can be what you want to be, if you work hard enough.

The view that Behavioral Genetics denies the importance of individual opportunity and effort is frustrating to those who believe in the importance of the partial genetic inheritance of intelligence, because no competent behavioral geneticist argues that mental competence is completely inherited. Behavior geneticists agree with educators that socially important cognitive skills, which are far more important than test scores, can, within broad genetic limits, be acquired by a combination of education, experience, and effort. An argument for an inherited component of intelligence is *not* necessarily an argument against the value of education and effort. This point is often not appreciated by those who attack genetic models of intelligence.

Discussion of the evidence for a genetic basis for intelligence has been confounded with discussions of differences in cognitive competence between racial and ethnic groups. Again the facts are quite clear; in the world today certain ethnic groups, notably African-derived populations, are getting a smaller share of the economic/social pie than European-derived populations. This has been going on for a long time. Claims of genetic influences on intelligence are seen by some as tantamount to a sort of Darwinian justification of present economic and social inequalities.

In fact, these are separate issues. The vast majority of current studies in behavioral genetics have no direct implications, whatsoever, for issues surrounding racial and ethnic differences in intelligence, simply because they are studies of the variation of genes and intelligence within rather than across racial/ethnic groups, and generally within just one ethnic group, European-derived populations. The causes of within-group variation are not necessarily the same as the causes of between-group variation. Unfortunately this has not stopped people from speculating, on both sides of the issue. This issue is discussed in some detail in Chapter 11.

Now let us look at some environmental influences on intelligence.

CHAPTER 9

Environmental Effects on Intelligence

More of your conversation would infect my brain.

Shakespeare, *Coriolanus*, act 2, scene 1

Shakespeare was right (again). Every experience we have leaves an imprint on our brains, and from it, on our minds. Clearly physical experiences can change the brain. It has been claimed that early species of *Homo* got a leg up on the evolutionary ladder when they began to eat fish.[1] In modern days, *lecithin*, a substance found in a number of foods, including fish and eggs, has been studied to see if it can enhance learning. (The results are mixed.) We do not stop there; we concern ourselves with the social environment. If we do not believe that social experiences can affect the brains of children, why do we have decency ratings for movies and television programs? And why would it be possible to sell video programs for infants with names like *Baby Einstein*?[2] How might we manipulate the environment to improve intelligence?

There are two ways this question can be interpreted. The less interesting interpretation is "Can the environment be manipulated to improve test scores?" A more interesting question is "Can the environment be manipulated to improve general mental competence?" The answer to both questions is "yes."

Environment is a catch-all term. In discussing environmental effects on intelligence it is useful to make a distinction between the physical environment and the social environment. The physical environment involves things like nutrition, air pollutants, and disease – anything that makes itself felt by direct physical action. The social environment involves things like education, social actions that enhance or threaten security, and opportunities for self-development of cognitive skills. Both the social and the physical environment alter the brain's activity and, as Shakespeare said, infect (leave a physical trace on) the brain. It does not always pay to go to this level of analysis. A teacher in an elementary school does not

---

[1]   Broadhurst, Cunnane, & Crawford, 1998.
[2]   © The Disney Corporation.

care whether a vocabulary-learning exercise will move brain activity related to word recognition from the frontal cortex to the posterior temporal cortex. The teacher wants to know if the exercise will improve the way the students use words. It is important to keep our discussions at the appropriate level of analysis – Brunswikian symmetry again!

9.1. Three Key Issues in the Study of Environmental Effects

In much of the literature environmental effects are contrasted to genetic effects. This is best exemplified by the continuing arguments over genetic versus environmental causes of intelligence. A more sophisticated way of looking at this debate is to determine the extent to which genetic and environmental constraints limit behavioral potential. This is not a simple task. Three issues have to be kept in mind. They are the concepts of *reaction range*; the *distal-proximal distinction*, and the problem of *collinearity*. While these issues have been discussed before, they assume special importance in the study of environmental effects.

9.1.1. *Reaction Range*

The concept of reaction range was introduced in Chapter 1, section 1.5. To review briefly, genetics determines a potential for the expression of a trait, but in most situations the extent to which the trait is actually expressed (if at all) is influenced by the environment. At one extreme we have eye color, for which there is virtually no reaction range; at the other extreme are traits like alcoholism and Alzheimer's dementia, where a person inherits a risk that can be triggered by environmental events. Intelligence is decidedly the latter type of trait.

We can think of the environment as determining where a given person will operate, within his or her genetically specified reaction range. Because different people will operate within different environments, variations in behavior will be determined both by differences between people in reaction range and differences in environmental influences. This is the reason that h^2 varies in different situations; it reflects the relative importance of differences in reaction ranges and differences in environmental conditions that operate within the potential afforded by reaction ranges.

Environmental effects are often illustrated by experiments in which two relatively extreme environments are contrasted with each other. Such an experiment shows what might happen under certain extreme conditions. While this information can be important, it does not tell us what is likely to happen under normal conditions of environmental variation. At this point we have to deal with a measurement issue. In order to define the extent of environmental variation we have to have a metric specifing how close two environments are to each other. At present no such metric exists, largely because we do not have a good theory of environmental variation. In fact, we have hardly any such theory at all.

9.1.2. *Proximal and Distal Causation*

As any parent of two or more children knows, people exert a lot of influence over their own environments. Where one person has experiences, another will gain knowledge. Recall Ackerman's emphasis on the importance of intellectual engagement upon the development of intelligence in adulthood (Chapter 4). On the other hand, environments vary in the extent to which they encourage the acquisition of skills and knowledge. For instance, it is well established that parents in the higher socioeconomic status (SES) range are more likely to encourage their children to engage in exploratory and problem-solving activities than are parents in the lower SES ranges.[3] Suppose that variations in the initial tendency to explore an environment have a partially genetic basis. How are we to interpret a study that demonstrates that children show greater cognitive development if they

---

3 Nisbett, 2009.

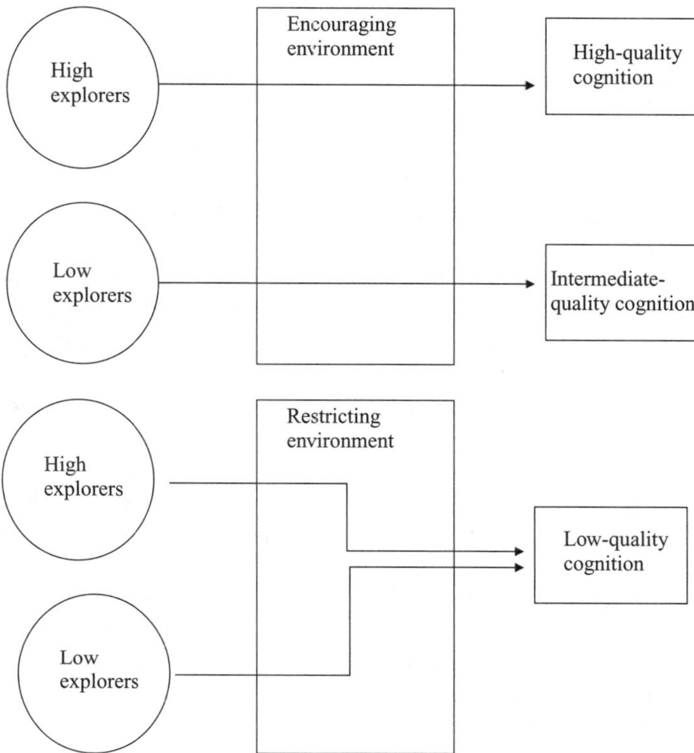

Figure 9.1. The design of a hypothetical experiment demonstrating how the development of cognition may depend on environments that encourage exploration. The environment acts as a proximal cause of the level of cognition. Unknown to the experimenter, the participating children are genetically divided into high and low explorers. Exploration tendency acts as a distal variable, producing variation in cognitive development within one environment but not within the other.

are exposed to enriched environments that encourage exploration? Would this be a distal genetic or proximal behavioral effect?

In fact, many such studies have been conducted. Figure 9.1 shows a widely used design. Children (of unknown genetic potential for exploration) are randomly assigned to an environment that either encourages or restricts cognitive development. We suppose that, unknown to the experimenter, the children vary in their genetic tendency to explore. To take an extreme, assume that there are genetically determined "high" and "low" explorers. Following the convention introduced in Chapter 1, the distinction is shown in ellipsoids, to designate an unobserved quantity. The experimenter can observe the sort of environment that the children are exposed to (center rectangles) and their cognitive performance (right-hand rectangles). If cognitive performance is better in the encouraging than in the restricting environment, the experimenter is justified in concluding that the environments influenced cognition, acting as proximal variables. However, genetic potential has also had an influence, as a distal variable. The restrictive environment does not permit genetic influences to act; the encouraging environment does; and the high explorers take more advantage of this opportunity than do the low explorers.

Figure 9.1 presents the proximal-distal distinction as it might occur in an experiment, where the distinction is clear-cut. The situation can be much more confusing in the natural world. The extent to which children are raised in an environment that encourages exploration varies with socio-economic status (SES). Generally, low SES children are raised in more restrictive environments than are the children of upper and middle SES families. Upper and middle SES children also, on the average, have higher IQ scores than lower SES children. But it may be that the children in upper- and middle-class SES families are more likely to be genetically predisposed to explore than are lower SES children. It might be that the upper- and middle-class SES parents are genetically predisposed to interact with children in a way that encourages exploration. And there are other possibilities. It could be that higher SES families are subject to fewer social stresses, and therefore are better able to create an encouraging environment. Outside of the laboratory proximal and distal variables are often thoroughly mixed up. In interpreting studies of the causes of intelligence this caution should be kept in mind.

9.1.3. *Collinearity*

Collinearity refers to a situation in which several possible causes of a phenomenon are themselves correlated. Collinearity presents serious difficulties for anyone interested in determining environmental influences on cognition. To illustrate, there is a negative correlation between family income and children's test scores. Nisbett has suggested a simple economic solution to the problem: providing poor people with subsidies to improve their and their children's life situation.[4] However, he has also pointed out that this would not help immediately, for family income is correlated with a number of other potential restrictions on children's development, including nutrition and child-rearing practices. Nisbett does not stress the point, but SES, which includes education and income, is also correlated with genetic inheritance, for people tend to marry people of their own general social class, especially

with respect to education.[5] Providing poor people with a subsidized income for child rearing might improve nutrition and certain other aspects of the environment immediately, might improve child-rearing practices over generations (a point Nisbett stresses), and would probably have little effect on genetic makeup.

The same thing happens on an international basis. Across nations, poor nutrition is associated with low test scores. Poor nutrition is most likely to occur in countries that have poor school systems, and to attack children whose parents have low IQ scores. So what is causing what?

Look at the issue symbolically. Let I be intelligence and $C_1 \dots C_k$ be a set of possible causes of intelligence. We observe a correlation between I and C_1. But C_1 is correlated with many of the other possible causes, $C_2 \dots C_k$, so the observed I, C_1 correlation might be due to any of the other possible causes. And to make things just a little harder, we have to consider possible feedback mechanisms. By any conceptual definition, intelligence is adaptive behavior. People with high intelligence are, in general, able to cope with unfavorable physical and social environments more effectively than people of low intelligence. To take a not unrealistic example, driving while intoxicated puts you at risk of severe head injury, which cannot be a good thing for your intelligence. But if you are intelligent, you are less likely to drive while intoxicated, compared to an unintelligent person.

The problem of collinearity is not unique to studies of intelligence. However, it is unusually severe in this field. For ethical and practical reasons, it is seldom possible to avoid the collinearity problem by conducting controlled experiments, where the levels of various causes are manipulated by an experimenter. It situations where controlled experiments can be conducted, there is often reason to question whether the laboratory results can be extrapolated to the day-to-day situation. The same criticism can

---

4 Nisbett, 2009, p. 192.

5 Blackwell & Lichter, 2000.

be levied against simple regression models, where one variable is "held constant" by statistical means. In these studies investigators determine the influence of causal variable C_i on the residual variance in intelligence (I) after removing variation in I due to all other causal variables of interest. This technique is a useful way of determining how much of the variation in the intelligence test scores can be associated with each of the predictors. We have to remember that the statistical model implies that each causal variable can be manipulated independently. In practice this may not be possible. Modern studies rely heavily on a structural equation-modeling technique similar to those used in quantitative behavior genetics, as described in the last chapter. This can go a long way toward disambiguating collinearities. Unfortunately, the resulting models become complex.

Given all these analytical problems, understanding environmental effects on intelligence is going to be hard work. Will the results be worth the effort? Only if environmental effects are very large. The next section shows that they can be.

9.2. How Much Can Environments Matter? The Cohort (Flynn) Effect

In Chapter 8 we saw that the existence of substantial heritability coefficients, h^2, showed that there are genetic influences on intelligence, without revealing anything about how the genetic influences operate. There is an analogous situation with regard to the environment. People are growing smarter at a rate that is far greater than can be accounted for by genetic/evolutionary effects. Senior citizens may find this hard to believe (unless they are talking about their grandchildren), but intelligence test scores rose throughout the twentieth century. This is called a *cohort* difference, where a cohort refers to the group of individuals born at a particular time – for example, the cohort of people born in 1970. Throughout most of the twentieth century each successive cohort was more intelligent than its predecessors.

The beginnings of studies of the cohort effect are interesting, because it appears the researchers expected to find something quite different from what they found.

9.2.1. *The Cohort Effect*

In the 1940s Read Tuddenham, a professor at the University of California, compared intelligence test scores for White men who had enlisted in the US Army during World Wars I and II.[6] Tuddenham wanted to test R. B. Cattell's conjecture that intelligence should drop over time, because people with high intelligence test scores have fewer children than people with low test scores.[7] Tuddenham found just the opposite. During the twenty-five year period between World War I (American participation 1917–18) and World War II (American participation 1941–45), the mean intelligence test score of young White males in the United States increased by approximately one standard deviation unit. See panel 9.1 for more details of Tuddenham's work.

In the 1950s K. Warner Schaie, who had worked with Tuddenham as an undergraduate, began graduate studies at the University of Washington. His thesis advisor was Charles R. Strother, a well-known clinical psychologist interested in aging. At the time a puzzling anomaly had been noticed. Studies of aging used one of two designs. In a *cross-sectional* design people of different ages are tested at the same time. Thus a study in, say, 1955 might involve people who were in their twenties, thirties, forties, and so on. In a *longitudinal* study a group of people of more or less the same age is followed for some period of time. For instance, an investigator might begin a study in 1955, with participants in their twenties, and follow them as they aged over the next twenty to thirty years. Cross-sectional studies led to the conclusion that cognitive functions begin to decline after a peak in the late twenties, with some differences in timing for different functions. Studies using

[6] Tuddenham, 1948.
[7] Cattell, 1940.

Panel 9.1. The Tuddenham Study

In 1917 the United States Army developed the Army Alpha Test as a device for screening recruits. In World War II (American participation 1941–45) the Army used a successor test, the Army General Classification Test. In order to compare the two tests the Army gave a version of the World War I test to 768 World War II soldiers, selected to represent the demographics of World War II enlistees. The median score of the World War II soldiers was approximately one standard deviation higher (using World War I norms) than the median score for the World War I soldiers.

Tuddenham pointed to several possible causes of the discrepancy. He felt that the most important of these was that the 1945 soldiers had, on the average, much more education than the 1917–18 soldiers. He reinforced this conclusion by showing that those World War I soldiers who were literate had test scores reasonably close to the scores of the World War II soldiers. Figure 9.2 shows both the general effect and the effect of introducing literacy as a covariate. In many ways Tuddenham's study anticipated discussions of the cohort effect that were to emerge over the next fifty years.

longitudinal designs found that declines did not begin until people were in their fifties or sixties.

Schaie and Strother realized that both cross-sectional and longitudinal studies are confounded with cohort effects, but in different ways.[8] A cross-sectional study completely confounds age with cohort; if people are tested in, say, 2000, then all the thirty-year-olds will have been born in 1970, the forty-year-olds in 1960, and so forth. A longitudinal study is conducted within a single cohort; if people are followed from twenty to fifty, beginning in 1980, all participants will have been born in 1960. Schaie and Strother offered an elegant solution to the design issue, the *cohort-sequential design.*

In a cohort-sequential design a cross-sectional sample of people of varying ages (and birth cohorts) is collected at time 1. Then, after a period of time (in Schaie and Strother's case, seven years) a second cross-sectional design is conducted, drawing a sample from the same population, at time 2. In addition, the first sample is contacted again, and as many people as possible are retested in a second wave. The procedure is repeated over as many testing waves as

possible. Cohort and age studies can now be analyzed separately.

Suppose that two test waves have been conducted, in 1956 and 1963 (the actual test dates of Schaie and Strother's first two waves). Consider the following four participants:

Person A	*born 1936*	*Tested in 1956 at age twenty and in 1963 at age twenty-seven*
Person B	*born 1916*	*Tested in 1956 at age forty and in 1963 at age forty-seven*
Person C	*born 1943*	*Tested . . . . in 1963 at age twenty*
Person D	*born 1923*	*Tested . . . . in 1963 at age forty*

There are two longitudinal contrasts: between person A in 1956 and 1963, covering the age span twenty to twenty-seven, and between person B in 1956 and 1963, covering the age span forty to forty-seven. There are three cross sectional contrasts. They are between person A and B, tested in 1956, at ages twenty and forty; between persons A and B, tested in 1965, at ages twenty-seven and forty-seven, and between persons C and D, tested in 1963, at ages twenty and forty. There are two *cohort* contrasts: between person A, tested in 1956, and person C, tested in

---

[8] Schaie & Strother, 1968.

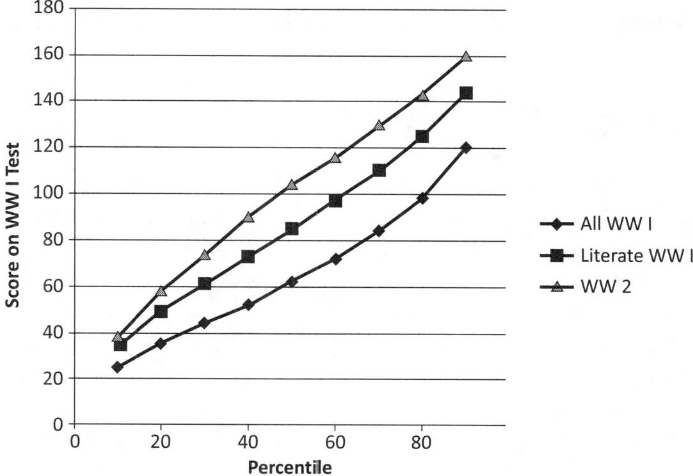

Figure 9.2. Scores on the Army Alpha Test obtained by World War I soldiers, World War II soldiers, and literate World War I soldiers. Scores are shown by increasing deciles – that is, the scores on the far left are for the tenth decile of each group, and so forth. Data from Tuddenham, 1948.

1963, both at age twenty at the time of testing, and between person B, tested in 1956, and person D, tested in 1963, both at age forty at time of testing.

The cross-sequential design makes it possible to determine longitudinal, cross-sectional, and cohort effects. It does confound date of testing with other effects, but I have never heard of any reason that date of testing, alone, should have an influence on test scores.

In addition to its design aspects, Schaie and Strother's study was noteworthy for its sophisticated measurements. Instead of relying on a single test score, Schaie and Strother used numerous tests to evaluate different aspects of intelligence. For our purposes the most interesting are their measures of inductive reasoning, verbal comprehension, and spatial reasoning. These measures correspond well to the modern *g*-VPR theory: inductive reasoning maps onto *g*; verbal comprehension maps onto the verbal dimension; and the spatial reasoning task they used appears to me to be a mix of the perceptual and rotational dimensions in Johnson and Bouchard's VPR model.[9]

The 1968 article reported large cohort differences in all three types of reasoning. They were invariably in favor of later-born cohorts, which is consistent with Tuddenham's results. Schaie and Strother concluded that the rapid drop in intelligence after early middle age (thirty to forty) that had been observed in cross-sectional studies was very largely a cohort rather than an aging effect.

Schaie has continued and expanded the study, using the cross-sequential design, collecting data every seven years for over forty years! The study, which is now known as the *Seattle Longitudinal Study*, is described in panel 9.2.

Figure 9.3 shows the effect of cohort changes since the birth cohort of 1903 (who were fifty-three at the time of the first testing) until the last testing in 1998. The results are typical of what is found in this field. Compared to the birth cohort of 1903, all subsequent birth cohorts showed a steady increase in reasoning. The increase in spatial orientation ability was somewhat more uneven, but still marked. The ability to extract verbal meaning increased until the birth cohort of 1952, and subsequently decreased.

---

9 Johnson & Bouchard, 2005.

Panel 9.2. The Seattle Longitudinal Study

The Seattle Longitudinal Study grew out of a fortuitous combination of interests, combined with K. Warner Schaie's tenacious pursuit of a good idea. Following his undergraduate work with Read Tuddenham at the University of California, Berkeley, Schaie moved to the University of Washington to begin studies for his Ph.D. with Charles R. Strother, a senior professor in clinical psychology who was very interested in public health issues.

Strother had helped found the Seattle Group Health Program, one of the first large, open-access health maintenance organizations (HMOs) in the United States. (Previous HMOs had been associated with certain industries or institutions.) He and Schaie realized that the people enrolled in the program constituted a group that could be approached over time. With the cooperation of the Group Health organization, Schaie has managed to collect data over seven consecutive waves, extending until the latest wave in 2005. This has been an impressive feat of scientific management and persistence.

The project has measured intelligence using tests based on Thurstone's Primary Mental Abilities model, which includes separate factors for verbal reasoning, nonverbal reasoning, induction, and numerical/arithmetic reasoning. Data has also been gathered on personality factors, health, and lifestyle. Related studies have been conducted on interventions designed to ameliorate cognitive deterioration in old age. The results have been reported in two books* and numerous research papers.

* Schaie, 1996, 2005.

To make these numbers a bit less abstract, here is a hypothetical example. Since the measures of reasoning are closest to what would be considered measures of *g* in modern theories, the comparisons will be made for the reasoning test, converted from standard deviation units to IQ points.

Consider two people of age thirty, born in 1903 and tested in 1933. We select them so that one is at the median level of intelligence in his or her 1903 birth cohort and the other is at the eighty-fifth percentile. By definition, the first person will have an IQ of 100 and the second an IQ of 115, by 1933 standards.

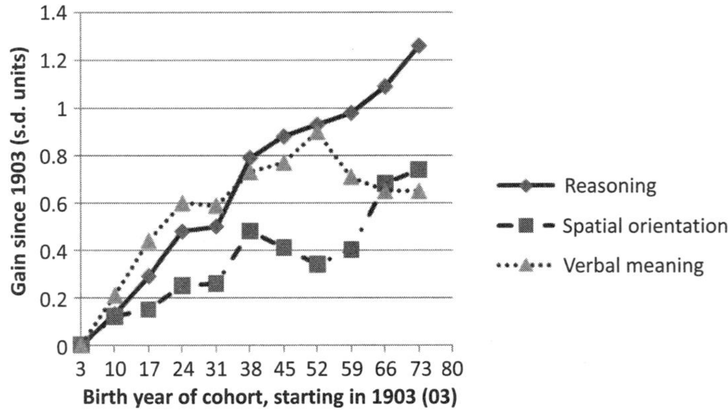

Figure 9.3. The increase in three dimensions of intelligence over cohorts, using the 1903 birth cohort as a base. Data from Schaie, 2005, p. 135; converted to standard scores.

We now take two more people, age thirty, but born in 1973, who are tested in 2003, and who are at the fiftieth and eighty-fifth percentile by 2003 standards. They would have, respectively, IQs of 115 and 130 by 1933 standards! People are getting smarter.

9.2.2. *The Cohort Effect Goes International! The Flynn Effect*

Early in the 1980s Jim Flynn, a political philosopher at the University of Otago, in New Zealand, became interested in changes in the difficulty of standardized tests of intelligence, such as the Wechsler tests and the Stanford-Binet tests. Flynn located seventy-three different studies, covering eighteen pairings in which the same people had been given both a current test and a test standardized at some earlier time (e.g., the original Wechsler test, standardized in 1935–37, and the second version, standardized in 1953–54). In seventeen of the eighteen comparisons people scored higher on the earlier version of the test than on the later version.[10] For instance, in the comparisons of the original and second Wechsler tests there was a difference of 4.69 IQ points, approximately one-third of a standard deviation unit, over a period of seventeen years. Flynn concluded that whatever trait the Wechsler tests measure had increased steadily in the US population.[11]

Flynn then examined test scores in standardization studies conducted in fourteen different industrialized nations.[12] All of them showed cohort effects, ranging from a high of twenty-five IQ points (France, 1949–74) to a low of six points (United States, 1954–78).

In subsequent studies Flynn found that the increase in scores over time was markedly larger for nonverbal, culture-reduced tests than it was for verbal tests. This is consistent with results from the Seattle longitudinal study, where the cohort effects on a nonverbal reasoning test were greater than those on a verbal comprehension test (Figure 9.3). Flynn also contrasted the increase in US intelligence test scores with decreases in SAT scores over the period since World War II.[13] He concluded that, at a descriptive level, there had been substantial gains in IQ scores, intelligence in the narrow sense, over the first three quarters of the twentieth century, and that they were concentrated in abstract reasoning tests. He also expressed considerable skepticism about whether intelligence in the conceptual sense had similarly increased, for he did not believe that people today are markedly smarter than their ancestors.

9.2.3. *Further Documentation of Flynn's Observations*

Flynn's research caught the public eye. Herrnstein and Murray coined the term "Flynn effect" in 1994.[14] In 1996 the American Psychological Association sponsored a symposium on possible causes of the effect.[15] Flynn himself published a book in which he considered further studies and their implications in 2007.[16] Many articles by other writers have commented on the effect. Surprisingly, only minimal references have been made to Schaie's work, even though it was very well known to gerontologists.

Research on the Flynn version of the cohort effect has been greatly helped by a social phenomenon. Although only a few

---

[10] The one negative finding involved comparisons of tests intended for populations of different ages.

[11] Flynn, 1984.

[12] Flynn, 1987. The nations involved were Austria, Australia, Belgium, Canada, France, German Democratic Republic (now part of Germany), German Federal Republic (now part of Germany), Great Britain, Japan, the Netherlands, New Zealand, Norway, Switzerland, and the United States of America.

[13] The drop in scores was dramatic, especially over the period 1970–92. However, the contrast over cohorts is problematical. The SAT is taken by a self-selected population, people intending to enter college. During the 1950–2000 period there was a considerable increase in the percentage of high school students who took the test. Therefore, it is hard to draw conclusions about changes in the cognitive competence of the US population, in general, from changes in SAT scores over time.

[14] Herrnstein & Murray, 1994.

[15] Neisser, 1998.

[16] Flynn, 2007.

developed countries currently have compulsory military service, several European countries require that young men register for possible conscription in case of national emergency. When they enroll the registrants are given medical and psychological examinations, including a test of cognitive skills.[17] Raven's Standard Progressive Matrices or similar tests are used by some countries. As a result, it is possible to compare scores of virtually the entire population of eighteen-year-old men, on the same test, over the years.

Figure 9.4 shows the test scores for Danish registrants, as a function of time of testing.[18] This figure, which is typical of data obtained in other studies, shows three important features of the Flynn effect. The first is that the effect is certainly there; test scores increased markedly in the thirty-year period from 1958 until 1988. The second is that the effect is greatest at the lowest level of scores. The two top levels, the ninetieth and seventy-fifth percentiles, show very little effect.[19] The third is that there is some indication that the effect is slowing over time. Studies using data obtained since 1990 show considerably smaller increases, and some have even suggested decreases in the 1980s and 1990s birth cohorts.[20]

9.2.4. *What Does the Cohort Effect Tell Us?*

Does the cohort effect exist? Objections can be raised to the design of many of the studies of the effect, individually. Some of the problems are discussed in panel 9.3. These problems raise potential objections, rather than disproving the findings. Also, the nature of

the objections varies from study to study. This does not seem to matter; the results are surprisingly robust. Test scores rose substantially from the 1920s until the late 1980s, and then either leveled off or, possibly, dropped. The facts are clear. What to make of them is not.

Are people really getting smarter? If the correlations between intelligence test scores and measures of socially important cognitive achievements, such as school grades and income, were close to one, the answer would have to be "yes." If the correlations were close to zero, changes in test scores would be irrelevant to discussions of cognition in everyday life. In fact, the correlations are in the .4–.6 range; certainly not one, but high enough to show that test scores have to be taken seriously. (More details are given in Chapter 10.) As was pointed out in Chapter 1, what correlations in this range show is that intelligence tests evaluate "life-relevant" cognitive skills and some skills that are unique to the testing situation. Is the cohort effect due to changes in the life-relevant skills or the test-unique skills?

The *test sophistication* argument asserts that the cohort effect is due to an increase in test-unique skills, because over the years cognitive testing has become more a part of everyday experience. I do not think that this argument can be maintained. If test scores increasingly reflected test-taking skills, then the correlation between test scores and other measures of cognitive achievement should have fallen over time. There is no evidence that this is the case. Also, American test scores continued to rise in the 1960–80 period, which is well after the widespread introduction of testing in the United States. The rise in test scores almost certainly represents a rise in cognitive skills across the developed world.

The cohort effect varies with the type of test. By far the greatest rise is found in nonverbal, *g*-loaded tests, such as progressive matrix tests. Flynn[21] contrasts this rise to the stability in performance on

---

[17] The United States currently requires registration but does not do any testing.

[18] Teasdale & Owen, 2000.

[19] It has been claimed that the lack of effect at the top is due to an artifact in scoring called the "ceiling effect." If a substantial number of people score at the top, their scores cannot increase (J. Raven, 2000). This argument applies only to the highest percentile considered, here the ninetieth percentile. As the figure shows, there is clearly a trend to smaller and smaller cohort effects as the percentile increases.

[20] See Teasdale & Owen, 2008, for data and further references.

[21] Flynn, 1987; 2007, Chapter 2.

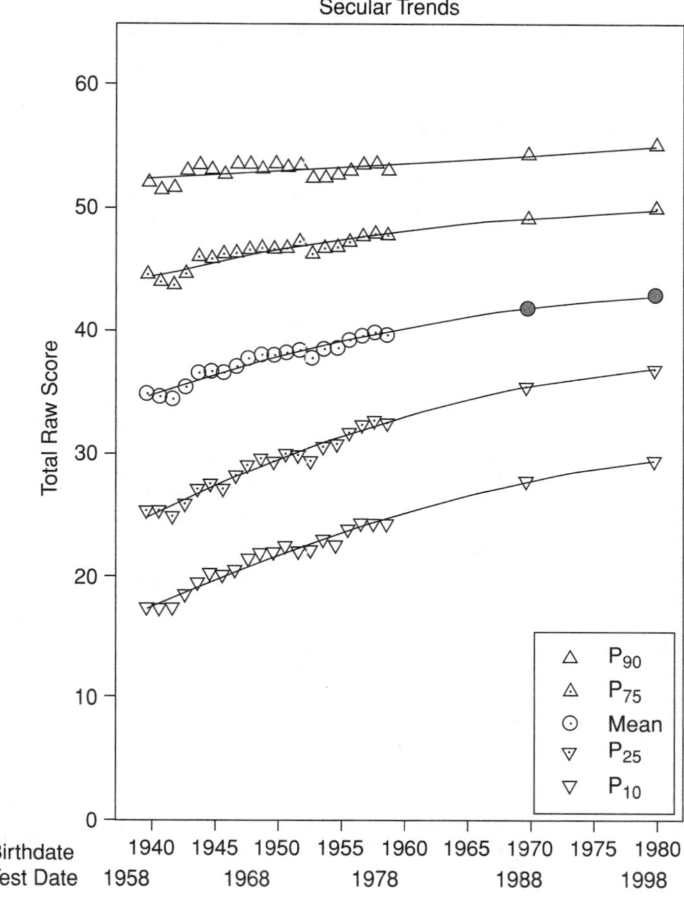

Figure 9.4. Progressive matrix test scores for Danish eighteen-year-old men registering for military enlistment, 1958–98. From Teasdale & Owen, 2000, with permission from Elsevier.

assessments of explicitly taught school subjects. IQ test scores rose from 1971 to 2002, especially on tests requiring abstract reasoning. The twelfth-grade achievement scores for the National Assessments of Educational Progress (NAEP) tests, which focus on school subjects, did not rise. Flynn concluded that there has been an increase in abstract reasoning skills without a concomitant increase in academic knowledge. In terms of the three-stratum model, Gf is up while Gc is flat. Why?

As Flynn and others have pointed out, any discussion of the cohort effect has to deal with a paradox. Flynn estimated that there has been a rise of .3 IQ point per year. If we project this backward, to calculate the intelligence of past cohorts, we find that the mean IQ score for young male adults in 1942 was equivalent to 80 by 2008 standards. If we accept this finding at face value, it leads to the conclusion that almost half of the soldiers who fought in World War II, the group that have been called "The Greatest Generation,"[22] would not meet the mental requirements for enlistment into today's army. This conclusion is ridiculous. But what has happened?

To answer that question we have to ask what might cause the cohort effect in the first place. The cohort effect cannot be due to genotypical changes. There is a negative

---

[22] Brokaw, 1998.

Panel 9.3. Design Issues in the Study of Cohort Effects

Studies of the cohort effect have taken two forms. The first, which is typified by the Tuddenham study, some aspects of the Seattle Longitudinal Study, the normalization comparisons for Raven's Standard Progressive Matrices, and the various European studies of enlistees, compares the scores obtained on the same test by people of the same age, but from different cohorts – for example, registrants for the military in Denmark in 1958, and then again in 1978. A generalization is then drawn to some larger population. I will call this *the same-test, different-cohorts* paradigm. Drawing conclusions from this design requires two assumptions.

The first is that the test is a meaningful way to evaluate cognition in different cohorts. This seems a reasonable assumption for "culture-reduced" tests, such as progressive matrix tests, given to the same overall population – for instance, the population of the United States in 1933 compared to the population in 1983. It is also reasonable if the cohorts are not far apart in years, for cultures do not change that quickly.

There are situations where this assumption would not be reasonable. For instance, if the tests were to be conducted in a developing country it might be the case that proportionately more people in the more recent cohort would be accustomed to the testing paradigm, due to dramatic increases in schooling, and with it, testing. Such an argument is much less tenable for a comparison of cohorts in an industrially developed country.

Tests of verbal behavior and general knowledge have to be modified for the cohort involved. To take an extreme, albeit slightly frivolous, example, in 1938 the term *gay bachelor* referred to an unmarried man who enjoys the company of women. By 2008 the term had come to acquire a rather different meaning. Any test involving cultural knowledge also faces the danger of being frozen in time or restricted to a particular cultural group. In order to maintain widespread applicability, commercial tests that evaluate crystallized knowledge (Gc) tend to evaluate "least common denominators," knowledge that is held widely through the society. Common knowledge changes over cohorts. The tests have to be changed accordingly.

The second assumption is that the cohorts are similar samples of a larger population. Findings on the cohort effect have been unhesitatingly generalized to entire populations. In fact, few studies utilize a random sample of the population for which generalization is intended. For instance, the 1992 United States standardization sample for the widely used Raven's Standard Progressive Matrices test was entirely drawn from Des Moines, Iowa. To what extent, then, can we generalize to the population of the United States?* Tuddenham compared US military recruits from World War I to recruits from World War II. Recruitment procedures were not the same in the two wars, so is it valid to make an inference about changes in population IQ? The Seattle Longitudinal Study drew from a population of enrollees in a health care program. To what extent is this population representative of the US population in general? Also, to what extent did the nature of the enrollees in the health care program change over the almost half-century lifetime of the project?

Because of questions like these the European military registration studies are particularly valuable. They involve repeated sampling of the same subpopulation, young men eligible for military service, over fairly brief time intervals. The fact that a cohort effect appears in several European studies of this group is an important confirmation of other same-test, different-cohort designs.

Flynn relied on a second paradigm, in which two tests, with norms established at different times, were given to the same sample. Call this the *two-test, one-cohort* design, and refer to the test with the earlier norms as Test 1 and the second test as Test 2. Suppose that scores are higher, in terms of percentiles defined by the original standardization, on Test 1 than on Test 2. This implies that the standardization sample for Test 1 had lower abilities than the standardization sample for Test 2.

The argument depends on the two standardization samples being equally representative of the general population at the time that the standardization is done. Considerable care is taken in standardizing tests such as the Stanford-Binet and Wechsler tests, as these tests are widely used in clinical practice, and to establish legal competency and/or qualification for special education programs. The cohort effect can be illustrated with these tests.

* Raven, 2000. Des Moines was chosen because, on some statistical criteria, such as age distribution and distribution of ethnic groups, the city was claimed to have matched the United States as a whole. The same logic was used for the British standardization, where the sample was drawn from Dumfries, Scotland. The problem with this approach is that the matching is solely on those variables that the investigator thinks are appropriate, and leaves any other measures free to vary. For instance, in the United States educational standards vary widely across states and even across school districts within states. Was the quality of education in Des Moines equivalent to the typical quality of education in the United States at the time? Random sampling avoids such problems by equating statistical expectations for all covariates, not just for those felt to be important by the investigator.

correlation between IQ scores and fertility (number of live births per woman).[23] Because of this, some investigators have argued that on a population basis the genetic potential for intelligence has dropped, even though IQ scores have risen.[24]

While this argument has a certain amount of merit, it is not completely compelling. Differential fertility, alone, does not guarantee a "dysgenic effect," lowering the mean intelligence of the population by lowering the genetic potential. This result would depend upon a number of other things, including the initial relative frequencies of various genetic potentials and the mating practices in the society.[25] One could create a situation in which the genetic potential of a population increased, even though there was a negative correlation between intelligence and fertility. However, this can happen only if the society follows mating practices that are not found in any of the industrialized nations where the cohort effect has been observed.[26] The cohort effect is environmental.

There is an analogy between the cohort effect and the finding that the heritability coefficient is .50 or higher (Chapter 8). The heritability finding shows that genetics is important, but it does not identify the relevant genes. The cohort effect does the same thing for environmental influences. It shows that environmental influences are important, but does not identify the influences. If we look at any time-linked phenomenon extending over a period of seventy to one hundred years, we find that there have been

[23] Herrnstein & Murray, 1994.
[24] Herrnstein & Murray, 1994, pp. 348–352; Lynn, 1998.
[25] Loehlin, 1998; Preston, 1998.

[26] This situation could arise if males with high genetic potential had more offspring than males with lower genetic potential. The discrepancy would have to be large enough to overcome the negative correlation between intelligence and female fertility. This could happen in a polygamous society, if the males with high genetic potential had more access to women than males with low genetic potential. There may be one spectacular case. Genetic analyses indicate that 8% of the men living in Central Asia (approximately .5% of the world's men) are descended from one individual who lived approximately a thousand years ago. If we combine this observation with historical records, suspicion falls on Genghis Khan, the founder of the Mongol Empire (Zerjal et al., 2003).

so many, highly collinear social changes that it is virtually impossible to single out any one of them and say "That's it."

The analogy goes further. Behavioral geneticists and biomedical scientists have found some genes that are very bad for intelligence, but have not been able to isolate the genes that produce high intelligence. We can identify environments that are very bad for intelligence, but have not been able to identify environments that are very good for it.

9.3. The Physical Environment

Several features of the physical environment are associated with low intelligence test scores. These include poor health practices, frequent or severe injuries, substance abuse, poor nutrition (especially in infancy), and exposure to atmospheric pollutants. In some cases the direction of causality is clear-cut. Any physical agent that damages the structure of the brain or interferes with brain processing may reduce intelligence, on either a temporary or a permanent basis. That is simply common sense. In other cases there is a statistically reliable association between intelligence and some potentially harmful agent, but causality is difficult to determine.

One of the reasons for this is a sort of chicken-and-egg problem: which came first, reduced intelligence or exposure to the agent? Linda Gottfredson, who has written widely on the social implications of intelligence, has pointed out that the task of following health and safety regimens is itself cognitively challenging.[27] To take a specific case, intelligence test scores are predictors of involvement in motor vehicle accidents, and such accidents are one of the commonest causes of head injury.[28] Granted that individuals who have suffered head injuries behave unintelligently at times, how likely were they to behave unintelligently prior to the accident?

Collinearity makes it hard to determine causality. Exposure to dangerous conditions

[27] Gottfredson, 2007b.
[28] O'Toole, 1990; Smith & Kirkham, 1982.

and low intelligence test scores are correlated with many other variables, such as socioeconomic status (SES), low parental intelligence, and inadequate access to good schools, that could themselves adversely affect intelligence. Picking out just one of these factors as the cause of low intelligence becomes hard to justify.

In order to assert that a particular incident or environmental condition has affected intelligence it is necessary to show (a) that low intelligence did not contribute to the incident or condition, and (b) that other possibly relevant conditions have been measured or controlled experimentally. In the ideal case *pre-morbid* measures of intelligence, taken before the incident or exposure, are compared to measures taken after the fact.

9.3.1. *Direct Insults to the Brain*

Chapter 7 discussed the relationship between brain structures and intelligence. There it was pointed out that damage to certain areas of the brain will result in loss of intelligence and, if the injury is sufficiently discrete, may disrupt certain intellectual functions and not others. Damage to the forebrain-parietal system will disrupt the working memory–attentional control complex, thus damaging the functions underlying general reasoning (Gf or *g*). Damage in the medial temporal region, and especially to the hippocampus, will disrupt the ability to form new memories (*anterograde amnesia*). The disability can be severe enough that the affected person has to be in custodial care for life. Paradoxically, some writers have claimed that this does not affect intelligence, on the ground that IQ test scores many not be lowered. Because any reasonable definition of intelligence has to include the ability to learn from experience, the fact that profound anterograde amnesia does not influence IQ test scores simply shows that test scores are only partial indices of intelligence.

Less dramatic, but important, losses of cognitive functions can occur when the brain is subjected to apparently minor physical damage. Closed head injury, *concussion*, is of special interest because of its prevalence; there are more than a million cases annually in the United States.[29] Closed head injuries are often followed by a period of disorientation that is obvious both to the individual and to others. In most cases this subsides. When conventional intelligence tests are given, a year or more later, effects are often *not* found. When effects are found they are usually on abstract, nonverbal reasoning. Tests that emphasize verbal cognition (or Gc, if you wish to use the Gf-Gc model) appear to be much less sensitive to the aftermath of severe concussions. So, if we were to restrict ourselves to the intelligence test data alone, we might conclude that "a knock on the head" is not all that serious. A closer look shows that that is not the case.

When patients are tested using laboratory tasks evaluating working memory functions, effects will be found. However, the laboratory tests are considerably more searching than the memory evaluations included in an intelligence test. The people who have been injured often do not report problems in everyday life, even though they have trouble with the laboratory tests. We might then conclude that the residual effects of concussion are not serious enough to be of concern. But that is not the case.

Investigators at the United Kingdom's Applied Psychology Unit (Cambridge) went a step further. They asked the living partners of people who had suffered concussions whether or not there had been any long-term effects. The partners replied that there had been, and furthermore, the severity of the deficit, as reported by the partner but not the affected individual, was correlated with the difficulty the affected person had in dealing with the laboratory tasks.[30] In addition to being interesting in itself, this study showed the importance of obtaining information about a person's everyday performance, as well as observing performance

during an out-of-context situation, such as a laboratory study or a conventional testing session.

A second study shows how concussion can act as a distal influence that increases the risk of incurring a condition that acts as a proximal influence on intelligence. The people studied were elderly (sixty-plus) pairs of twins, where one twin suffered from Parkinson's disease, which results in a loss of intelligence in its latter stages, and the other did not. The risk of incurring Parkinson's disease tripled for those who had experienced head injuries, even though the head injuries had occurred, on average, thirty-seven years before the study was conducted.[31]

As these two studies illustrate, long-term damage to intelligence can result from what are, at the time, apparently recoverable injuries to the brain. Stories of punch-drunk boxers are not just legend.[32]

9.3.2. *Prenatal and Infant Health Issues*

A great deal of attention has been devoted to prenatal and infant development, because this is when the foundations of cognition are laid down. In their first year infants acquire a great deal of information about their language and about social interactions.[33] To what extent do individual differences in cognitive function in infancy predict later indices of intelligence? Infancy is also a period of high physiological vulnerability. To what extent are these early indicators sensitive to environmental variables?

Infant development is often measured by the Bayley scales of development, developed originally by Nancy Bayley and her colleagues at the University of California, Berkeley, and updated periodically.[34] These scales document the age of normal occurrence of a variety of behaviors, such as

---

[29] Information downloaded from www.healthline.com/adamcontent/concussion, June 2009.

[30] Sunderland, Harris, & Baddeley, 1983.

[31] Goldman et al., 2006.

[32] Nor do we need to rely on legend. Survey results have shown that the incidence of memory problems is markedly elevated among retired professional football players (*New York Times*, Sept. 30, 2009, p. A1).

[33] Gopnick, Meltzoff, & Kuhl, 1999.

[34] Bayley, 2005.

crawling, toddling, vocalization, and reactivity. Contemporary middle- and upper-class parents are notoriously concerned that their children be on schedule. This concern may be a bit overdone. The correlation between scores on developmental scales that are based on activity and vocalization over the first thirty-six months of life, and scores on adult intelligence tests is nearly zero.[35] However, this does not mean that the development of information-processing and verbal measures can be disregarded. By the age of three, tests that involve vocabulary correlate in the .5–.7 range with IQ scores for young adults.

One of the most important things an infant has to do is to recognize stability and change in the environment. The infant's ability to do this can be evaluated by measuring *habituation*, the ability to discriminate between novel and repeated stimuli.[36] Let us take a closer look at the procedure used.

Joseph Fagan, a professor at Case University, and his colleagues have measured habituation by showing infants an "interesting" picture, often a picture of another infant. After the infant has viewed one picture it is removed, and then presented again, along with a new picture. The measure of habituation is the extent to which the infant looks at the new picture. This simple test for six- to twelve-month-old infants has a correlation of .32 (corrected for reliability, .59) with measures of adult intelligence at twenty-one years of age.[37]

Birth weight, one of the most commonly used indices of prenatal health, is correlated with intelligence, for both premature and normal term infants. One study estimated that there is an increase of between .3 to .5 IQ points for every 100 grams of birth weight over 2,500 grams (about 5.5 pounds).[38] This finding, standing alone, is ambiguous, because maternal IQ is positively correlated with the birth weight of the child. Collinearity again! When maternal IQ is controlled statistically, the relationship between IQ and birth weight drops but does not disappear.[39] The finding is not confined to cases of abnormally low birth weight. Differences in intelligence between heavier and lighter babies in the normal range (2,000 grams and above) have been reported in studies in a variety of North American and European countries, and in both white and African American populations in the United States.[40]

The relationship does not solely reflect any tendency for bright mothers to have children that are both heavier and have a higher genetic potential for intelligence, as separate effects. This was shown in an elegant study of two large samples, one in New Zealand and one in the United Kingdom.[41] Because of the size of the samples it was possible to compare birth weights and IQ scores in monozygotic (MZ) twins, thus controlling for genetic influences. The heavier twins had higher IQ scores, demonstrating the importance of the prenatal environment independent of genotype.

We can take the comparison to an extreme by looking at "preemies," newborns with a gestational age of less than thirty-two weeks, many of whom have birth weights well below 2,000 grams. These children, on the average, have IQ scores almost one standard deviation unit below a control group.[42] In general, nonverbal functioning and abstract reasoning are more affected than verbal functioning. Considering the links between information processing and *g*, it is not surprising to find that premature infants do poorly in childhood (eight to twelve years) on tests of working memory and attentional control.[43]

Because birth weight predicts future intelligence, it is of interest to know what variables may lead to low birth weight. By far the largest risk factor is premature birth,

35 Bayley, 1968.
36 Brody, 1992, p. 232; Fagan, Holland, & Wheeler, 2007.
37 Fagan, Holland, & Wheeler, 2007. See also the references therein for citations to earlier studies.
38 Matte et al., 2001.
39 Deary, Der, & Shenkin, 2005.
40 Dombrowski, Noonan, & Martin, 2007.
41 Newcombe et al., 2007.
42 Esbjorn et al., 2006.
43 Bayless & Stevenson, 2007.

Panel 9.4. Fetal Alcohol Syndrome

Fetal alcohol syndrome (FAS) is a defect in intelligence occuring in children whose mothers drank heavily (more than four drinks per occasion) during pregnancy. Prevalence in the US is somewhat less than one case per thousand births. Prevalence is higher in social groups that have high rates of alcohol abuse. The problem is particularly acute in the Native American population, where the incidence of FAS has been estimated to be from 1.5 to 2.5 cases per thousand births.

The effects can be devastating. FAS is characterized by facial malformation (short noses, small eye openings, thin upper lips, and skin folds over the eyes, among other features) and severe cognitive retardation. A broader term, fetal alcohol spectrum disorder (FASD), is used to refer to prenatal alcohol damage that includes all damage due to alcohol consumption during pregnancy.

The National Institute of Health guidelines advocate complete abstinence during pregnancy. Damage can be inflicted early in the first trimester of pregnancy, so a woman might damage the fetus before becoming aware that she is pregnant.

The fetus can be put at risk by drinking in the social range, below the level of intoxication. Anne Streissguth and her group at the University of Washington Medical School have conducted longitudinal studies of the children of women who either abstained completely or were social drinkers during their pregnancies. Among the latter, small but clear indications of impulsive decision making and difficulties with attentional control were detected in their children when they were fourteen years old. The degree of impulsivity varied with the amount drunk during pregnancy, even though none of the mothers would be considered to have been alcoholics.*

General information on fetal alcohol syndrome was downloaded from www.nlm.nih.gov/medlineplus/ fetalalcoholsyndrome.html#cat1, June 2008, and links derived from this page.
* Sampson et al., 1997; Connor et al., 2001.

although a myriad of other causes can also affect maternal and fetal health. The optimal age for childbearing, at least as far as the risk of low birth weight is concerned, is from twenty-five to thirty-two; women outside this age range are at heightened risk for premature birth and for having a low birth weight child.

Not surprisingly, expectant mothers are strongly advised to avoid ingesting any substance that is toxic to neural development. In our own society perhaps the commonest such substance is alcohol. Social drinking can have an effect, and maternal drinking to the point of serious intoxication can have devastating influences on fetal intellectual development. This is discussed in more detail in panel 9.4.

We seem to be close to the situation we encountered with respect to molecular genetics; we know neonatal-infant environmental effects that can harm intelligence. Is there any way to improve intelligence, within the normal range? Some interesting things have been tried, but there is little objective evidence that various diets, exercise regimens, or even having the expectant mother listen to classical music (see panel 9.5) does very much good. The way to make sure children are born highly intelligent still eludes us.

9.3.3. *Nutrition*

Nutrition, in the broadest sense, refers to anything that people ingest as food or drink. This excludes certain substances that are ingested but not for the purpose of fueling metabolism, such as the ingestion of a psychoactive drug. There are a few cases of

Panel 9.5. The Mozart Effect

There has been a good deal of interest in the possibility that listening to music – and for some reason, listening to the works of Mozart – might improve spatial-visual reasoning.[*] The claim has even been made that the effect can be observed in rats! The phenomenon has been dubbed the "Mozart effect."

The first reports of the effect led to a crescendo of replications, and an exchange of letters on the topic in *Nature* in 1999.[†] My own belief is that the effects, if any, are small and transient, and are probably due to structured music temporarily stimulating some of the brain regions used to solve spatial-visual problems. It seems unlikely but not impossible that a permanent enhancement of spatial-visual reasoning results. Edward Zigler, a highly respected specialist in developmental psychology, has criticized the fascination with the (alleged) effect as yet another search for a "quick fix" in early childhood education and support. Zigler worries that the attention focused on such fads distracts public attention from the development of less dramatic, more expensive, high-quality infant care and pre-school programs.[‡]

[*]   Rauscher, Shaw, & Ky, 1993.
[†]   Chabris, 1999.
[‡]   Jones & Zigler, 2002.

---

substances that have been ingested for nutritional purposes, but that contain pathogens that can produce a loss of intelligence. Panel 9.6 describes two such cases.

Intuitively, it makes good sense to think that nutrition will influence intelligence, especially during periods of neural growth. It turns out to be difficult to prove this, for several reasons. We want to distinguish between temporary effects, during a period of malnutrition, and permanent effects, exhibited following recovery from malnutrition. It is also necessary to distinguish between the effects of brief periods of malnutrition (and when, in development, these periods take place) and the effects of chronic malnutrition. The type of malnutrition is also an issue. A diet may have adequate caloric intake and still be deficient in protein, iron, or other substances important for neural development. There is also the problem of distinguishing between cognitive and temporary attentional effects. Malnourished people are physically weak and have trouble concentrating. This may lead to underperformance both in a testing session and, more importantly, in any situation involving cognitive demands over a long period of time.

These are conceptual problems. There are also some major practical problems.

It would not be ethical to subject people to malnutrition in a controlled study, so correlational and epidemiologic studies are necessary. Reliable records of nutritional intake may not be available. Collinearity is an issue. Malnutrition to a level that would influence neural development, and hence intelligence, is rare in the industrially developed countries. When it does occur it is likely to be accompanied by poor general parenting practices and a lack of social support for mother and child. In the developing countries malnutrition does occur, but it tends to occur in the poorest areas of the country, those with the least access to schools and medical facilities. In general, more intelligent, better-educated mothers provide better nutritional environments for their children.[44] Genetic and social effects on the child's intelligence can appear to be due to nutrition unless care is taken to measure the appropriate covariates.

Nonetheless, the problem is an important one, so researchers have persevered. We

[44]   For example, a study of Egyptian mothers by Wachs & McCabe, 2001.

Panel 9.6. Two Cases of Very Bad Dietary Practices

In America and Europe today a great deal of publicity is given to dietary practices. Most of that concern is directed toward obesity and cardiovascular health. There are some cases, though, in which the concern is overingestion of foods containing pathogens that may influence the brain. The famous Salem Witch Trials in seventeenth-century Massachusetts were a response to bizarre behavior by children. A case has been made that the behavior may have been due to a neurotoxic fungus in bread that the children ate.[*] But this is only speculation. Here are two better-documented examples. One involves an exotic social practice that, thankfully, is no longer with us. The other illustrates the dangers that can result when a pathogen gets into the vast, almost unseen food chain in industrially developed nations.

Kuru is a disease that attacks the brain and central nervous system. It is caused by a slowly acting agent called a *prion* that destroys neural structures.[†] In the 1950–60 period kuru broke out in the highlands of New Guinea, then one of the world's most primitive areas. The outbreak was due to cannibalism; people became infected by eating the brains of people who were already infected with kuru. The connection was not immediately obvious because of the long period of time that typically elapses between infection and the manifestation of the disease. Today kuru has virtually disappeared because of the modern Papua New Guinea government's policy of strongly discouraging the practice of cannibalism.[‡]

A related brain disorder, Creutzfeldt-Jakob disease, can be acquired by ingestion of infected tissue from meat. (The risk of acquiring the disease is also partially under genetic influence.) The purity of meat is regulated by social practices, especially the screening of cattle for the presence of a bovine form of the disease ("mad cow" disease) prior to slaughter and rendering into commercial beef.[§] The fact that infected meat could produce Creutzfeldt-Jakob disease was first discovered in Britain in 1996, following a sharp rise in the incidence of the disease. Since then screening of cattle has greatly increased. Nevertheless, in 2008 there were major political protests when the government of the Republic of Korea decided to permit importation of US beef although mad cow disease had been detected in the US herd.

[*] Caporael, 1976.
[†] Gajdusek & Zivas, 1957. Gajdusek received the Nobel Prize in Medicine in 1976 for the discovery of slow-acting prions.
[‡] Information recovered from www.ninds.nih.gov/disorders/kuru/kuru.htm, June 2008.
[§] Information recovered from www.ninds.nih.gov/disorders/cjd/detail_cjd.htm, June 2008.

will look at a few key studies. Most of these have involved infants or young children, as they are perceived to be most vulnerable to the effects of malnutrition. There are a few studies of the relation between nutrition and adult cognition.

Brief periods of malnutrition do not appear to leave permanent effects, even when the malnutrition occurs *in utero* or in infancy. The evidence for this comes from a large, quasi-experimental study that occurred in the Netherlands as a byproduct of the battles in Western Europe during World War II. The events and the study are described in panel 9.7. The gist of the findings was that male children exposed to a few months of intense starvation during their infancy did not show any effect of that experience on cognition, when they were tested nineteen years later. Apparently the effects of severe short-term malnutrition are reversible.

Panel 9.7. The Hunger Winter Study

A dramatic and tragic incident in World War II provided one of the best demonstrations that temporary malnourishment does not have a permanent effect on cognition.

At the beginning of 1944 Western Europe was occupied by Nazi German forces. In June 1944 American and British troops, together with smaller Allied contingents, landed in France and began a steady march eastward toward Germany. In September 1944 British paratroopers attempted to seize bridges on the Rhine at Arnhem in the Netherlands. The plan was for the paratroopers to link up with British ground forces advancing from the southwest. The combined forces would then cross the bridges into Germany.

The Dutch railway workers went on strike, hoping to cut off supplies to the Germans. However, the British ground forces were unable to advance, and the paratroopers were overrun. To retaliate against the Dutch the Nazis imposed a transportation embargo on the northern Dutch cities under their control. Starvation ensued. At one point the estimated caloric content of rations was down to 640 calories per adult per day.

(Depending on age and size, the recommended US daily caloric intake is somewhat over 2,000 calories.) Meanwhile the southern Dutch cities, under Allied control, received adequate food. The starvation period lasted from September until March, when American troops seized a bridge across the Rhine at Remagen. Allied forces crossed rapidly into Germany, and the Dutch cities were relieved and supplied. The war in Europe ended shortly thereafter.

In the Netherlands men register for military service at age nineteen. Registrants are given a progressive matrix test. Zena Stein and her colleagues from Columbia University compared the scores of men who were either *in utero* or neonates during the four months of the starvation period to the scores of men who had been born at the same time, but in the cities under Allied control. Other records of mental capabilities, such as the frequency of mental retardation, were also compared across the two populations. There was no difference in any indicator of mental competence. This study of over 125,000 men provides striking evidence of the resilience of human cognition.*

* Stein et al., 1972.

Chronic, prolonged malnutrition is something else. Numerous studies in developing nations have provided evidence that prolonged malnutrition is associated with low test scores, particularly on nonverbal tests. A closer look reveals an interesting pattern of defects. Malnourished children are described as less attentive, impulsive, and easily distracted. Researchers primarily interested in nutrition describe this as a confounding variable, saying that it is unclear whether the effects of malnutrition are on intelligence, or whether they are on attention.[45] If we consider these observations in the light of studies of the role of basic information processing in intelligence, we reach a somewhat different conclusion.

The behaviors that characterize malnourished children are indications of lack of attentional control, which is a vital part of the working memory complex. Individual differences in working memory and the control of attention are highly related to intelligence, especially measures of g and Gf. Prolonged malnutrition also influences habituation, which, as we have seen, is an indicator of infant intelligence.

Viewed in this light, malnutrition directly influences intelligence test scores, because

[45] Sigman & Whaley, 1998.

the act of taking the test requires exercise of the working memory complex. The same deficiencies in information processing influence young children's school performance. This produces a deficiency in the knowledge-based aspects of intelligence. A physical agent, malnutrition, results in an inability to benefit from environmental supports that improve cognition.

This conclusion is reinforced by studies of the beneficial effects of intervention. Two sources of intervention have been tried: improvements in general nutrition and improvements in intake of specific nutrients, primarily iron and protein. Iron is important because iron-deficiency anemia leads to general listlessness and, once again, inability to focus attention. Proteins are considered necessary for development of the neural system.

The results of a study conducted in rural Guatemala are particularly informative. Protein supplementation was provided for some children, while a nonprotein supplement was offered to others. Protein supplementation improved various measures of cognitive performance. In addition, there was an important interaction. The greatest gains occurred when protein supplementation was combined with school attendance.[46] This is consistent with the argument that appropriate nutrition will benefit working memory and related attentional processes. These then make it possible to take advantage of an environment that supports the development of cognitive skills. For optimal effect a program to help children recover from malnutrition should be combined with an educational program.

The sorts of serious malnutrition that lead to cognitive deficits are generally not found in the industrially developed countries. In these countries excess caloric input, which can lead to a quite different set of problems, is more of an issue. When severe malnutrition occurs in the developing countries, it is usually because of a situation over which the individual family has little control – war, famine, or drought. The next physical environmental effect that we look at, alcoholism,

is a matter of lifestyle, and is found widely in Europe, the Americas, and in industrial Asia.

9.3.4. *Alcohol Abuse*

Alcohol is the commonest, and most abused, recreational drug in the world. We have already discussed the effects of maternal alcohol consumption on the fetus (panel 9.5). Here we concentrate on the effects on the consuming adult.

While definitions of abuse have shifted over time and place, present psychiatric criteria distinguish two forms of alcoholism: *alcohol dependence*, in which the affected person can scarcely go without a drink, and *alcohol abuse*, which refers to people who consume alcohol frequently, and heavily, but can go for periods of time without drinking. According to the US National Institutes of Health (NIH) statistics for 2001–02, 75 of every 1,000 adults over the age of eighteen, or 7.5%, fell into one of these two categories. (The figure includes "recovering alcoholics," who are not currently drinking.) For reference, the incidence of heart disease, the commonest cause of death in the US, is slightly greater than 8%. There is a genetic component to alcoholism; the close relatives of alcoholics are at heightened risk for alcoholism.[47] However, the genetic component is by no means a determiner.

Alcoholism is diagnosed using four behavioral criteria. They are:

Craving: A strong compulsion to drink. This goes well beyond thinking it would be nice to have wine with your meal.

Loss of control: The inability to cease drinking once drinking is begun.

Withdrawl symptoms: Nausea, sweating, shakiness, and anxiety when alcohol use is stopped.

Tolerance: The need to drink ever greater amounts of alcohol in order to experience symptoms of intoxication, including relaxation and euphoria.

---

[46] Pollitt et al., 1993.

[47] McGue, 1999.

Brain imaging studies of alcohol abusers, compared to age-matched controls, have shown something that had long been suspected on behavioral grounds.[48] Prolonged alcoholism damages the frontal lobes.[49] This is accompanied by decrements in abstract reasoning and in visual-spatial reasoning, the sorts of behaviors that one associates with decreased working memory, loss of the ability to plan actions, and diminished attentional control.[50] Extremely heavy, prolonged drinking can produce damage to the limbic system, with an associated loss of the ability to store new memories (*Korsakoff's syndrome*). Korsakoff's syndrome patients are unable to function in society, and hence must be hospitalized.

The results are clearly due to alcohol abuse, and not to pre-existing genetic or familial conditions, because the effects of excess use of alcohol can be demonstrated in twins, where one twin is an abuser and the other is not.[51]

The issue with regard to social drinking is less clear. Surveys of social drinkers indicate that there is a small negative association between moderate social drinking and cognitive test scores. Not surprisingly, the effect is most marked among those who consume alcohol more than four times a week, and who regularly consume more than 40–50 ml of alcohol per occasion. This is roughly equivalent to three or four drinks of hard liquor, glasses of wine, or bottles of beer. There are marked individual differences in tolerance. The critical amount varies with weight and with sex, women generally being more sensitive. In terms of psychometric models, the effects appear to be on g or Gf, depending upon whether the g-VPR or three-stratum model is used to describe the results. There is not enough data to make a clear statement about the effects of social drinking upon visual-perceptual reasoning.[52]

Collinearity makes it hard to define causality. The extent of social drinking varies greatly among different racial, ethnic, and demographic groups. In some circles social drinking is an accepted and (almost) expected practice. In others any use of alcohol is frowned upon. It is difficult to disentangle the effects of social drinking from inherited intellectual potential, health practices, and other lifestyle variables. There is also a chicken-and-egg problem: does heavy social drinking reduce intelligence, or is it the case that the intelligent person does not drink heavily?

This is hard to say, because there is data indicating that childhood intelligence tests (i.e., measures of cognitive power taken before people begin to drink) predict drinking patterns. People with higher test scores are less likely to drink to the point of having a hangover, surely an intelligent thing to do, and are more likely to consume wine, which is generally drunk more slowly and more likely to be drunk with meals, than whiskey or beer.[53] This distinction is important, because the toxic effects of alcohol are related to a buildup of alcohol metabolites in the bloodstream. This occurs when alcohol is taken in at a faster rate than it can be processed through the liver. When alcohol is taken with food, the rate of absorption from the stomach to the bloodstream is reduced, thus lessening the influence of the drug.

While admitting that the issue is not clear, the evidence favors the hypothesis that repeated heavy drinking, to the point of feeling somewhat "high," although not necessarily to the point of losing consciousness or marked motor control, does lead to cognitive deficit.

The effects of alcohol on intelligence are extremely important on a population basis. According to a Center for Disease Control

---

[48] There are many studies showing deficiencies in reasoning and intelligence associated with alcohol abuse. Clarke & Haughton, 1975, and Leckliter & Matarazzo, 1989, are typical examples.

[49] Moshelhy, Georgiou, & Kahn, 2001.

[50] See Schottenbauer et al., 2007, for a recent example of such a study and note how these results, using imaging technology, expand but do not alter the conclusions of a study by Jones (1971) thirty-five years earlier.

[51] Toomey et al., 2003.

[52] See Parker, Parker, & Harford, 1991, for a review and discussion of this research.

[53] Batty, Deary, & McIntyre, 2006; Mortensen, Sorensen, & Gronbaek, 2005.

survey taken in 2006, slightly more than 60% of US adults twelve or over described themselves as current drinkers. About 22% of the adults surveyed reported at least one incident of binge drinking, which was defined as five drinks or more per occasion. This is well over the danger level suggested by the literature. Binge drinking was heaviest among people eighteen to twenty-five (43% of the group), and within this group heaviest among college students. The famed (or infamous) weekend fraternity bash is the most dangerous mode of consumption a social drinker can engage in.

We now turn our attention from what we put into our mouths to what we breathe in from the air.

9.3.5. *Atmospheric Lead*

Modern environmentalists worry a great deal about industrial pollutants in the air, water, and soil. The problem is not new. Mercury nitrate, a neurotoxin, was used in hat making until the twentieth century. A century earlier the phrase "mad as a hatter" was in common use, for hat makers were thought to have delusions and poor motor control. Today mercury's dangers are well known, and industrial exposure is tightly regulated. There is considerable concern over the presence of trace amounts of mercury in the food chain, especially in certain fish. A much commoner pollutant, lead, presents a larger problem, worldwide.

Lead was one of the first metals to be mined, for reasons ranging from its malleability to its taste (!).[54] Analyses of human remains show that prior to the beginning of metallurgy, about 4000 BCE, the concentration of lead in the human body was .0016 micrograms per deciliter (μg/dL). In 1975–80 the concentration in American children was estimated to be 15 μg/dL, over 1,000 times the natural level. The concentration has fallen markedly since then, due largely to the banning of tetraethyl ("lead added") gasoline.[55]

The controversy over, and eventual banning of, lead additives in gasoline did not represent a newfound concern over lead. Debates over the costs and benefits of using the metal can be traced back to the time of the Roman Empire. Panel 9.8 presents some of the history. It shows the difficulty of striking a balance between the undeniable economic benefits of an activity and the equally undeniable cost of risks to public health.

The earlier controversies were over the effects of the levels of exposure that might be experienced in an industrial operation using lead. Today's concerns are over the cumulative effects of exposures to much lower concentrations of atmospheric lead, and in particular the effects upon children. These concerns were heightened by results reported by Herbert Needleman of the University of Pittsburgh in 1979.[56] Needleman realized that a large-scale epidemiological survey of lead concentrations in children's bodies could be conducted, in a highly noninvasive manner, by collecting young schoolchildren's "baby teeth" after they fell out and analyzing them for lead content. He then contrasted the Wechsler test (WISC-R) performance of first and second grade children with high and low concentrations of lead in their teeth. Higher concentrations were associated with low IQ scores. In a second study the level of lead in the body was positive correlated with teachers' reports of children's impulsive behavior. The researchers allowed for the effects of a number of control variables, including parental SES. On its face this was an impressive study of over 2,000 children.

Needleman made the dramatic claim that lead concentrations could be responsible for a six- to seven-point IQ drop in children. Given the substantial economic implications of this assertion, it is hardly surprising that his work was challenged. Some of these challenges amounted to accusations of improper manipulation of data. These charges were investigated, and Needleman was exonerated of any wrongdoing.

---

[54] The Romans used lead sulfate to sweeten wines.

[55] Hubbs-Tait et al., 2005.

[56] Needleman et al., 1979.

Panel 9.8. The History of Concerns over Lead Poisoning

Lead has been used since antiquity. Its widespread use was accompanied by unheeded warnings.

The Romans used lead in dishes and in water pipes, in spite of the architectural engineer Vitruvius's warning that lead could "rob the limbs of the virtues of the blood." Seventeen hundred years later Benjamin Franklin gave a similar warning. Franklin, a shrewd observer of both physical and social realities, said that his warning would be ignored because of the economic benefits of using the metal. In the early twentieth century Alice Hamilton, M.D., the first woman admitted to the Harvard faculty, documented over 500 cases of lead poisoning. She observed that her findings were consistent with those of French authorities one hundred years earlier. The public health problem became acute with the advent of the automobile.

Tetraethyl lead in gasoline is a cost-effective anti-knock agent. The first refineries for leaded gasoline were developed after World War I by a cooperative effort of General Motors, Standard Oil Company (now Exxon), and DuPont. In 1924 there were outbreaks of insanity, illness, and death in two of the new refineries. Various controversies, investigations, and court cases occurred from the 1920s through the 1940s. The automobile industry avoided being regulated, although the evidence against lead mounted and mounted. The debate was bitter. Alice Hamilton personally confronted Charles Kettering, General Motors vice president for research (and a famous automotive engineer), and called him a murderer!

In the 1970s legislation was passed to remove lead from gasoline, due to the perceived public health hazards. This decision cost the automotive industry billions of dollars, a cost that was promptly passed along throughout the economy. This did not clear the air, for the lead produced by automobile combustion is only part of the problem. Many industrial processes produce atmospheric lead as a by-product. Removal costs can run into millions of dollars. Therefore, there was further debate over whether other processes, including lead smelting, produced a sufficient health hazard to justify the economic costs of controlling emissions. The consensus now is that they do, and in the developed industrial countries the emission of lead into the atmosphere and the use of lead in home products are both strictly regulated.

Nevertheless, many products used in the home are sources of lead. These include paints (especially older versions, still found in many homes), polyethylene plastic bags, and even candy wrappers. In November of 2007 some Chinese-made toys intended for the US Christmas market were found to contain unacceptable levels of lead. Senator (later President) Barack Obama, then involved in a tight race for the Democratic nomination for president, made the sweeping statement that if elected he would bar the importation of toys from China. Obama subsequently retreated from this promise, possibly because 80% of US toys are made in China.

The laws regulating lead present costs to industry that may reach into the billions of dollars. On the other side of the coin, the CDC has estimated that in the early 2000s 1.1% of US children under the age of five had blood lead concentrations higher than the current allowable level of $10\mu l/dl$. As of 2007, the Census Bureau estimated that there were 20.75 million children in this age bracket. That comes to 228,250 children who may be building up dangerous concentrations of lead. This is a significant health risk. The problem is confounded by the fact that lead sources tend to be located in poorer residential areas, close to industrial operations.

It would be impossible, and inappropriate, for a book on intelligence to attempt to weigh the relative costs and benefits of lead use, or to comment on the costs and benefits of similar industrial–public health trade-offs. What we can do is examine the research that has caused us to be concerned.

The information in this summary comes from Hubbs-Tait et al., 2005, and Kovarik, 2005.

Collinearity posed a more difficult problem in interpretation. Was the poor test performance of children with higher lead concentrations caused by the concentration of lead, or did they perform poorly because they tended to come from poorer homes and/or to be minority group members, and therefore would be expected, on statistical grounds, to have lower scores on intelligence tests? The best way to investigate this issue is by replication of a result, in situations where the collinearity problems plaguing the original finding do not occur.

Several such replications have been conducted. One is a longitudinal study of children living near industrial operations in Port Pirie, Australia.[57] A second longitudinal study following up children from two to seven was carried out in Kosovo in the 1990s.[58] In both these studies investigators obtained maternal IQ scores and took extensive measures of the home environment. In the Kosovo study two separate populations were studied, children living in a relatively large town near a lead smelter and children in a similar town, twenty-five miles away, where the atmospheric lead exposure level was much lower. Pregnant mothers were enrolled, prenatal lead concentrations were estimated, and children were followed up until they were seven in order to assess the effects of a buildup of lead in the body. Both prenatal levels of lead and postnatal increases were associated with drops of intelligence after all other variables were considered. There was no evidence of threshold effects, which provides an argument against maintaining a permissible concentration level of 10 μm/dl, as is now done.

Lead concentrations were statistically associated with just over 4% of the variance in children's IQ test scores. Similar results have been obtained in other studies in the US and in South America, so we have a highly generalizable finding.[59]

In 2005 a consortium of researchers involved in these studies published an analysis of the international findings.[60] They concluded that there is a non-linear relationship between intelligence test (IQ) scores and the level of lead in the blood. Their guide was

Increment in lead in blood	Expected loss in IQ points
2.4 to 10 μ/dL	3.9
10 to 20 μ/dL	1.9
20 to 30 μ/dL	1.1.

The losses are cumulative, so the expected loss for a child with a 30 μ/dL concentration of lead in the blood would be 6.9 IQ points, Needleman's original estimate.

A drop of five to seven IQ points is not serious on an individual basis. We would not expect to find a great deal of difference in the cognitive capabilities of two children, one with an IQ of 100 and the other with an IQ of 95. On a population basis, though, this would be a serious issue, because of changes

---

57 Baghurst et al., 1992.
58 Wasserman et al., 2000. The study was carried out at a time when Kosovo was part of Serbia, and was not disrupted by war.

59 Wasserman et al., 2000, p. 815. See related work in the United States by Chiodo et al. (2007) and in South America by Counter, Buchanan, & Ortega (2005).
60 Lanphear et al., 2005.

Table 9.1. Levels of blood lead concentration in children, together with recommended actions

Class	Blood Lead Concentration (µg/dl)	Comment
I	Less than 10	Not lead poisoned.
IIA	10–14	Children in Class IIA should be screened frequently. If many children in a community test in this range, community-wide preventive measures should be taken.
IIB	15–19	A child in Class IIB should receive nutritional and educational interventions and more frequent screening. Environmental investigations and interventions should be initiated.
III	20–44	A child in Class III should receive a medical evaluation. The child may require pharmacological treatment for lead poisoning. Environmental evaluation and remediation is called for.
IV	45–69	A child in Class IV requires medical and environmental intervention, including chelation therapy (a technique for removing lead from the body).
V	70 or above	The child is suffering from lead poisoning. This is a medical emergency. Medical intervention and environmental management must begin immediately.

Note: Information provided by the US Center for Disease Control brochure "Preventing Lead Poisoning in Young Children," published in October 1991. The commentary has been paraphrased from comments in the brochure.

in the frequency of exceptionally high and low levels of intelligence. Consider a population of a thousand children. If the mean IQ in the population were 100, we would expect to find approximately fifty children with IQs below 70, which is often considered an indication for enrollment in a special education program, and an equal number of children with IQs above 130, in some programs a marker for entry into a gifted education curriculum. If the mean of the population dropped to 95, we would expect to find about one hundred children with IQs below 70, and only twenty-five with IQs above 130. In other words, a drop of five IQ points in the population average would be associated with a doubling of the number of children in the special education program, while the number of children eligible for the gifted program would drop by a half.

These research findings have had an effect on public policy, at least in the industrial and postindustrial countries. In 1960 the border between safe and unsafe exposure levels was 60 µ/dL, twice the level used as a point of concern in the 2005 comprehensive review. Table 9.1 shows the current guidelines from the US Center for Disease Control (CDC). Actions to reduce lead concentrations are now recommended when children's blood levels exceed 10 µ/dL, and a blood level above 45 µ/dL is seen as a medical emergency. An advisory committee report publicized by the CDC has indicated that concentrations higher than 10 µ/dL can warrant actions to reduce the levels of lead in the home or near schools.[61]

Unfortunately, significantly higher levels of atmospheric lead are found in some developing countries. For instance, in the industrial port of Callao, near Lima, Peru, lead storage areas are located near one of the

[61] CDC Advisory Committee, 2007.

poorest residential areas of the city. A survey found that approximately half of the early elementary school children had blood lead levels of 20 μ/dL or higher.[62]

Lead in the atmosphere clearly represents one of the major threats to the development of intelligence in some areas of the world today.

9.4. The Social Environment

The social environment is an important determiner of cognitive power. Charles Murray has called the development of certain ways of thinking "meta-inventions," because societies and individuals who use these ways of thinking have a huge advantage over those who do not.[63] Literacy is probably the most important of the meta inventions, because it fosters abstract thinking and provides continuity with the past. Mathematical reasoning and scientific approaches to problem solving also improve thinking. In our society the intelligent person is one who has a good grasp of these tools of thought.

Americans spend a good deal of time and effort trying to ensure that their children become familiar with the tools of intelligence. The effort literally begins at home. The Disney Corporation's *Baby Einstein* DVD programs for three-month- to three-year-olds are supposed to enhance intelligence in toddlers. Whether they do so is questionable.[64] However, viewing quality children's television programs, such as the *Sesame Street* series, does improve cognitive skills in pre-schoolers.[65] The United States spends more money per student on K-12 education than any other country. Nevertheless, panels of business and government leaders regularly decry the (alleged) fact that American schools are failing to produce people who can solve problems and face new cog-

nitive challenges – the very definition of fluid intelligence.

The problem is not to show that the social environment influences the development of intelligence, the problem is to find out how it does so. This is not easy.

Social variables are easy to name, but hard to define. "Good parenting" is something we all applaud, but just exactly what is a good parent? Socioeconomic status (SES) is real. But how do you measure it? Income is often used as a proxy. In 2008 the Chief Justice of the United States, John Roberts, had a salary of $217,000. Alex Rodriguez, third baseman for the New York Yankees baseball team, had a salary of $28,000,000. Who had higher socioeconomic status, the chief justice or the third baseman?

Measurement is not the only problem. As has been pointed out earlier, we do not have a theory of the social environment that approaches the clarity of Mendel's theory of genetic inheritance. Nor do we have any broad theoretical approach to environmental issues that can play a role similar to the role that Darwin's theory of evolution has in biology. Lack of a comprehensive theory of the environment has resulted in a great many ad hoc studies without a great deal of accumulated knowledge. The lack of an adequate theory has also made it hard to understand the relations that we do observe. Social variables are highly collinear with each other, with genetic measurements, and with measurements of the physical environment. Nutrition is linked to socioeconomic status, especially in the developing world. Parents who produce favorable home environments for their children are likely to seek out the best school environments. In modern developed countries (and in urban districts worldwide) residence is closely tied to SES and sometimes to ethnic status. This constrains the composition of children's play groups. Without a theory it is difficult to develop models that can guide the selection of variables to study.

These are real problems. Nevertheless, psychologists and educators have learned something about social environments that nurture or restrict intelligence.

---

[62] Guerrero, 2009, Table 02.
[63] Murray, 2003.
[64] Zimmerman, Christakis, & Meltzoff, 2007.
[65] Anderson, 1998.

9.4.1. *Socioeconomic Status and Intelligence*

Socioeconomic status (SES) refers to the obvious, but nebulous, concept that there are classes. There is no generally agreed-upon definition of what a class is, so the idea is clearly a fuzzy one. The commonest practice is to define anywhere from three to six different classes, based upon combinations of income, education, and occupational prestige. It is not unusual to find studies in which a single variable, such as income or education, is used as a proxy for SES. Given the variety of definitions, it is a bit surprising to find that SES is correlated in the .30–.40 range with performance on such diverse variables as the WAIS tests, the SAT, and Raven's progressive matrix tests.[66] However, the direction of causality is far from clear, and it is probably bidirectional. There is a correlation of slightly over .40 between parental SES and SAT scores.[67] The same thing is true for other measures of intelligence, such as IQ tests and academic performance.[68] These findings suggest that SES is causal to intelligence. At the same time, test scores obtained in adolescence correlate with a person's own SES roughly twenty years later, which is consistent with the argument that intelligence causes SES.[69] As a further complication, test scores and SES are both correlated with parental advantages of various sorts, including parental, and hence one's own, genetic constitution. Parental advantage, carried forward across the generations, could, at least in theory, be a cause for one's own socioeconomic success. And just to make things even more confusing, cognitive tests such as the SAT are used as screening devices in education, raising the possibility that measures of intelligence act as a gatekeeper for access to resources that determine social success, but that intelligence itself has little causal influence.

The problem is that SES is too global a measure of either parental influence or one's own success in life. In order to understand the influence of social class upon intelligence we have to take a finer look at phenomena that underlie the correlation. Three classes of studies have been used to evaluate the effects of the social environment: adoption studies, studies involving social interventions, and multivariate analyses of specific features in the environment. We consider each of them in turn.

9.4.2. *Adoption*

As we saw in Chapter 8, adoption studies are frequently cited as supporting a genetic cause for intelligence, on the grounds that correlations between measures of cognition in adoptees and their biological parents are higher, and usually substantially higher, than the correlations between adoptees and their adoptive parents. A different statistic, the mean intelligence test scores of adoptees, can be cited in support of environmental influences.

An early, much-cited British study in the 1930s produced what turned out to be fairly typical results.[70] The biological parents were all "working-class," as defined in Britain at that time. The mothers, as a group, had an estimated mean IQ of 86. The adopting parents were all described as well educated. Given this information, one would expect the adoptees to have IQ scores in the 90s, somewhat higher than the mothers' IQs, but still below the population mean of 100.[71] This is not what happened. The mean IQs were 117 at age two, and 108 at thirteen. This is evidence for an effect of the childhood home environment. However, the correlations between the biological mother's level of education and adoptee's IQ scores were

---

[66] Ceci & Williams, 1997; Raven, 1989.

[67] Sackett et al., 2009.

[68] Teasdale & Owen, 1986; Zwick & Green, 2007.

[69] Herrnstein & Murray, 1994.

[70] Skodak & Skeels, 1949.

[71] The reason for this is a statistical phenomenon known as "regression toward the mean." Whenever an extreme score is observed on a test of less-than-perfect reliability, the best estimate of the score that would be obtained upon retesting, under exactly the same conditions, would be a score between the original extreme score and the population mean.

Table 9.2. Mean IQ scores of adopted children as pre-schoolers and as adolescents, compared to scores by biological children of the adopting family

Group	Time 1 (~ 1976)	Time 2 (~1986)
Biological children	116.4	109.4
Adopted African American	106.1	98.1
Adopted White	117.6	105.6

Source: Data excerpted from Weinberg, Scarr, & Waldman, 1992, Table 2.

.04 at age two and .31 at age thirteen, reflecting what was to be a typical finding in later studies: measures of genetic influences upon intelligence rise as children grow older.

At this point, it may be helpful to look back to Figure 9.1. If we substitute "adoptive home" and "biological home" for "encouraging environment" and "restricting environment," the figure illustrates how an environmental effect upon mean scores could occur along with a correlation between test scores and measures of genetic potential.

We then "fast forward" almost forty years, to the Minnesota Trans-Racial Adoption (MTRA) study conducted in the 1970s in the American Midwest. The MTRA study contrasted the test scores of African American and White children who had been adopted into upper-middle-class White homes. Both adoptees and biological children of the adoptive family were tested, first when the adoptees were pre-schoolers and then ten years later, when the adoptees were adolescents.[72] Table 9.2 shows the results. Biological children consistently outscored adopted children in the transracial but not in the intraracial groups. All test scores declined somewhat from childhood to adolescence. This could be caused by a variety of factors, including the fact that the tests used differed somewhat over time. The African American adoptees had an average score near or above 100 (the putative national mean) and well above the score of 85 typically found in African American populations on this type of test.

The practice of comparing the adoptees' obtained scores to maternal scores or to population expectations can be criticized. Suppose that the birth mother's IQ is 90. This does not mean that a child would be expected to have an IQ of 90, for two reasons. No allowance has been made for father's intelligence, which is typically unknown. In addition, regression to the mean (see footnote 71) implies that the child's IQ will be closer to the appropriate population mean than is the mid-parent IQ. But what is the appropriate mean? Mothers who give up their children for adoption are hardly a randomly selected group of all women, or even of all women in the appropriate racial, ethnic, or educational group. A better way is needed to estimate the expected IQ of adopted children.

One way of doing this is to compare the cognitive performance of adoptees to the cognitive performance of children who have not been adopted, but who might have been. The test scores of adopted children can be compared either to those of unadopted siblings or to unrelated, unadopted children in the same pool of potential adoptees. When this is done the results show a positive adoption effect of slightly less than one standard deviation unit, both for test results and for measures of school performance.[73] This is probably an overestimate of the adoption effect, because the comparison includes the effects of any tendency leading to adoption of apparently more favorable children. However, given that most children are adopted as infants, and that standard

---

[72] Scarr & Weinberg, 1976; Weinberg, Scarr, & Waldman, 1992.

[73] Van Ijzendoorn, Juffer, & Poelhuis, 2005.

Table 9.3. Mean WISC-R scores as a function of SES of birth and adopting parents. The number in parentheses is the number of cases.

	Adopting Parents High SES	Adopting Parents Low SES	Average
Birth parents high SES	119.6 (10)	107.5 (8)	114.2
Birth parents low SES	103.6 (10)	92.4 (10)	98.0
Average	111.6	99.1	

Source: Based on data reported by Capron & Duyme, 1989.

developmental inventories do not do a good job of predicting later intelligence, this effect is likely to be small. Except for pathological cases, adoption agencies would have a difficult time identifying infants who were going to be bright or dull fifteen years later.

Understandably, most studies stress the positive effects of adoption. Negative effects are conceivable. It should be possible to move intelligence upward or downward by adoption, depending upon the relative SES of the biological and adopting parents. Such an analysis requires an unusual situation, for high SES parents are less likely to give up their children than are low SES parents, and adoption agencies are more likely to place adoptees with high rather than low SES families. However, the unusual does occur. French researchers were able to locate a relatively small number of young children (eight to ten per cell) in a study that did fit the appropriate design.[74] Table 9.3 shows the IQ scores achieved on the Wechsler Intelligence Scale for Children (Revised) at an average age of fourteen years.

Taken at face value, the data in Table 9.3 indicates a high birth SES–low birth SES effect of about 16 IQ points, and a high adopting SES–low adopting SES effect of 12.5 points. In other words, the data is consistent with both hereditarian and environmental effects on intelligence, and makes the important point that the two causes are not mutually exclusive. I think it would be unwise to go much beyond this, for the size of the effects certainly should not be generalized. The study is a small one, and it is not

clear that the difference between the adoptive high and low SES groups was equivalent to the difference between the high and low SES birth parents.

The results of adoption studies have been used to argue for both environmental and genetic influences on intelligence. People who want to emphasize genetic causes cite the fact that indices of adoptees' cognitive competence are better predicted by biological parent's competence than by adoptive parent's competence as evidence for the importance of genetics. People who want to emphasize environmental causes cite gains in intelligence achieved by adoptees. The debate over how to interpret these findings can be heated. In some of the studies put forward to support the genetic position the authors do not report changes in mean scores, while in studies put forward to support the environmental positions the authors do not report parent-adoptee correlations. This practice more resembles the behavior of a lawyer presenting the evidence for a client than the behavior of a scientist reporting data to be considered in evaluating theories.

In fact, there is no conflict between the results. Erik Turkheimer, of the University of Virginia, offered an analysis that brings both these results into the same framework.[75] His analysis was based upon the concept of reaction range, as discussed in Chapter 1, section 5, and illustrated in Figure 9.1 of this chapter. Turkheimer developed a mathematical model that separates the genetic and environmental effects in circumstances such as those illustrated in the

---

[74] Capron & Duyme, 1989, 1996.

[75] Turkheimer, 1991.

figure, and used it to reanalyze a study contrasting adopted and nonadopted siblings.[76] The original authors had concluded that there was a major effect of social class, on the grounds that adoptees had higher intelligence scores than their nonadopted siblings, and that the adopting parents had higher occupational status than the biological parents. According to Turkheimer's analysis, which treated the within-group and between-group effects in a single framework, there was no reliable effect of a direct measure of adoptive SES – father's occupational status – but there was still a large (and unexplained) effect in favor of the adopted children. How could this occur?

While various explanations of this finding have been offered, I believe that the ambiguities in studies like this will not be cleared up until we take a finer look at environmental measures. Variables like "adoption," "socioeconomic status," and even paternal intelligence and occupation are *distal* variables with respect to the development of intelligence. Nutrition, schooling, and parenting practices are *proximal* variables, acting directly upon intellectual development. What we need to do is to look at some proximal effects.

9.4.3. *The Home Environment*

Parenting practices are evaluated by rating homes on such things as the general orderliness of the home, the amount of reading or other explicitly educational material available, the number and quality of interactions between parents and children, and the extent to which children are encouraged to work out the answers to questions and puzzles, as opposed to being told how to do so. It appears that the best environment for intellectual development is one in which the child is encouraged to work out problems with guidance and support from parents, as opposed to an authoritarian setting in which the parent tells the child what to do, or a laissez-faire setting in which the child is pretty well left on his or her own. Parenting

styles, and especially substandard parenting practices, are statistically associated with indices of socioeconomic status and family solidarity, such as income and whether the child is in a one-parent, father-absent, or conventional mother-father home.[77] These variables are important, for the home environment has a great deal to do with intellectual development in young children. This has been shown by two interesting lines of research.

The first line involves observation of the influence of the home environment upon measures of children's intelligence, including but not limited to test performance. In one such study Victoria Molfese and her colleagues at Southern Illinois University followed 121 children, none of whom had experienced extreme neonatal or birth risks, from age three to age five.[78] The children were given intelligence tests annually. Family SES was determined by combining indices of education, occupation, and income. The home environment was determined by observation and rating, using the widely accepted Home Observation for Measurement of the Environment (HOME) scale, which requires observation of the child's home, including the provision and use of reading material for children and reports of the manner in which adults interact with the child.[79] Figure 9.5 shows the combined and independent contributions of SES and HOME ratings to the prediction of children's WISC scores. While there are some irregularities, there is a trend toward a decreasing influence of home environment and increasing influence of SES as the children aged. This is consistent with behavior genetic studies that show generally increasing influences of genetic heritage and lowered influence of home environment

---

76 Schiff & Lewontin, 1986.

77 Kotchick & Forehand, 2002. Kotchick and Forehand make the interesting point that if a family lives in a potentially threatening environment, an authoritarian, controlling style of raising young children may be adaptive, even though it does not foster intellectual development, because of the need to protect the child.

78 Molfese, DiLalla, & Bunce, 1997. This article also contains references to a number of related reports.

79 Bradley, 1993.

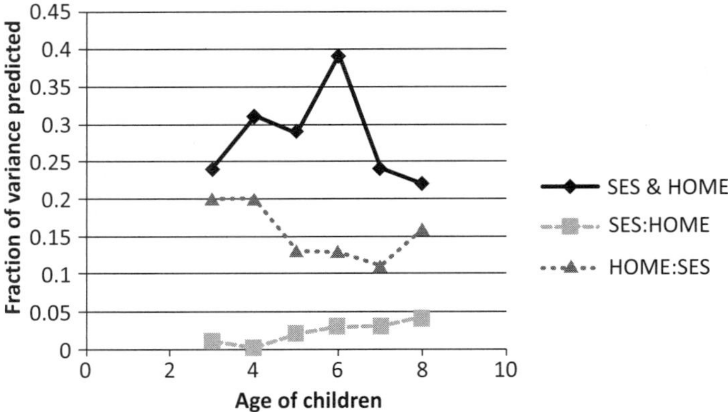

Figure 9.5. The fraction of variance in WISC scores predictable from measures of SES and home environment. For reference, a fraction of .04 is equivalent to a correlation of .2. Calculations based on data in Molfese, DiLalla, & Bunce, 1997, Table 2.

upon intelligence as people age, albeit over a much greater time span than was the case in the Molfese and colleagues study.

Two more studies illustrate the widespread influence of the home environment during the early years. Both results come from studies previously cited to make points about the physical environment: observations of rural Filipino children and observation of children growing up in Kosovo, in the Balkans. In the Philippine study, used earlier to indicate the relation between nutritional status and intelligence, ratings of home environments similar to the HOME scale added to the prediction of a child's intelligence, after allowance for a variety of other variables, including maternal intelligence test score, paternal education, and physical environmental variables.[80] In the Kosovo study of atmospheric lead, the HOME score had the highest correlation with children's intelligence test scores of all the variables considered, which included measures of maternal intelligence (Raven matrix score) and maternal education.[81]

The American Midwest, the rural Philippines, and the Balkans are very different places. When relations between any variable and intelligence are consistently related over such diverse settings, one has to pay attention. The microenvironment of the home has a substantial influence on intelligence during the early childhood years. A good home environment gives a child a leg up as he or she enters school. And, as will be shown shortly, schooling counts as well. Things mount up.

9.4.4. *Early Childhood Interventions in "at Risk" Populations*

There have been substantial attempts to improve the environments of children who are thought to be "at risk" for showing poor cognitive development. Since the 1960s the US Government has funded *Head Start* programs for pre-schoolers from low SES families. Head Start was motivated by a concern that low SES, and particularly African American, children entered primary school lacking a number of cognitive and social skills that were thought to be important in children's adjustment to the school experience. These programs typically involve pre-school training for a half-day, five days a week, for the year prior to entering school. Many Head Start programs also include some form of parental education, as it is felt that inadequate parental support may be a factor leading to the children's poor performance in schools.

[80] Church & Katigbak, 1991, Table 6.
[81] Wasserman, 2000.

Progress toward the goal of improving cognition has been spotty, at best. In 1969 Arthur Jensen, a Professor of Education at the University of California, Berkeley, published a controversial paper in the *Harvard Educational Review*. He began

> *Compensatory education has been tried and apparently it has failed.*
>
> *Jensen, 1969, p. 2*

Later in the article he said

> *The evidence so far suggests the tentative conclusion that the payoff of preschool and compensatory programs in terms of IQ gains is small.*

And further down on the same page:

> *The techniques of raising intelligence per se in the sense of g, probably lie more in the province of the biological sciences than in psychology and education.*
>
> *Jensen, 1969, p. 108*

Jensen maintained this position, virtually without change, in an important book on intelligence published almost thirty years after the *Harvard Educational Review* article.[82]

A similar conclusion was echoed in 1994 by Herrnstein and Murray, in a book that was received as contentiously as Jensen's earlier conclusions had been.[83]

> *The school is not a promising place to try to raise intelligence or to reduce intellectual differences, given the constraints on school budgets and the state of educational science.*
>
> *Herrnstein and Murray, 1995, p. 414*

Quite a different view has been expressed by Edward Zigler, a Yale Professor who, as a government official, became famous as the "Father of Head Start." Zigler observed that a variety of behaviors are improved by Head Start programs. These include good study habits, cooperative work skills, and improved parental support. Improving these characteristics was, according to Zigler, at

least as important as improving the cognitive skills measured by test scores.[84]

The debate over Head Start is more nuanced than it appears when people simply recite mantras that Head Start programs do (or don't) work. Critics like Jensen and Herrnstein and Murray generally focus on IQ and similar tests as essentially complete measures of intelligence, while the supporters have a more expanded view of intelligence, to include things like knowing how to manage time and how to learn arbitrary material – "associative learning," in Jensen's terms. The supporters also stress improvement in the child's general social situation, as Zigler's comment about parenting skills indicates. Such concerns, which strike me as being quite legitimate criteria by which to evaluate a pre-school program, are not considered in the criticisms raised by Jensen and Herrnstein and Murray.

There is another qualification. Jensen and Herrnstein and Murray did not say that preschool programs will not work; they said that those programs that were economically realistic did not work. That is an important distinction. "What early childhood programs improve intelligence?" is a question for educational psychologists. "What could work at a cost of x dollars per child?" is an important question for educational policy makers. The two viewpoints are not the same. In his book on the improvement of intelligence, Nisbett concluded that

> *Several early childhood education programs actually do produce large immediate gains in IQ, as well as long term gains in IQ or academic achievement, or both.*
>
> *Nisbett, 2009, p. 120*

Two meta-analytic reviews[85] show that the picture is not as bleak as Jensen painted it, but that Nisbett's statement may be a bit optimistic.

There is a great deal of variation among pre-school intervention programs. Expenditures cover an eight-to-one ratio. At the low end we have minimal head-start programs,

---

[82] Jensen, 1998.
[83] Herrnstein & Murray, 1994.

[84] Zigler & Styfco, 1997.
[85] Barnett, 1998; Gorey, 2001.

in which children attend reasonably well-run pre-school programs with educational components from two to five times a week for one or two years. At the high end some intense programs have included staff/client ratios as high as one well-trained teacher for every three students, parental counseling, and interventions for five years or more. In general, the meta-analyses show that the less intense programs have short-term results, but that these results (in terms of IQ scores and school accomplishment) fade away quickly. By contrast, the more intense programs have results that last for years, in terms of both intelligence test scores and, more importantly, school achievement. One meta-analysis reports an improvement of nine IQ points for the intensive programs, five years after the programs ended. This would be somewhere toward the end of elementary school for most participants. Only a few studies have followed students as far as high school, although two very intense intervention studies traced participants into adulthood. These studies report substantial positive effects on social behaviors, such as encounters with the law, and smaller effects on IQ scores more than ten years after pre-school participation.

Possibly the most intensive program, the ABCDerian project, was aimed at a deeply impoverished group of students in North Carolina. This study has reported positive results, compared to a control group, at age twenty-one.[86] Because this is generally conceded to be one of the most effective (and expensive) of the pre-school programs, it is worth looking at the study in more detail.

The participants were children from low SES families in North Carolina. Virtually all the children were African American. Slightly over one hundred children were assigned to the special program or to a control group. The intervention began at an average age of 4.4 *months* and continued until the children entered kindergarten. Depending upon the period, there was one instructor for every three to six children. In addition to instruction and supervision, a nutritional program was developed and offered to both the experimental and control group. The pre-school lasted virtually the entire day, five days a week. Participants were followed until they were twenty-one.

When the program ended, at age five, the children took the Wechsler Preschool Intelligence test. The experimental group had a mean IQ of 100 and the control group a mean IQ of 94. (Both scores are somewhat above what would be predicted from demographic data.) Figure 9.6 shows the results of subsequent testing. There are two striking features of the graph. Both groups showed a steady decline in test scores over the years after leaving the project. At the same time, the experimental group maintained a roughly five IQ points ($d = .3$) advantage over the control group throughout. How could this come about?

The decline is not surprising. IQ tests for children below the age of five are at best moderately predictive of scores at a later age. This could be because the tests for very young children are tests of cognitive functions different from those evaluated by later tests, or it could be because the cognitive systems important for test performance (e.g., working memory) are only slightly developed in young children. (Recall that heritability coefficients are lowest for very young children, suggesting that maturing of the cognitive system is a serious possibility.) Several studies, to be discussed in Chapter 11, have shown that African American children obtain test scores in the 100 range (equivalent to Whites) in the early school years. African American scores decline to a mean of roughly 85 by adulthood. The control group appears to be doing this. The experimental group also showed a regression effect, but maintained its advantage over the control group into adulthood.

The picture for academic achievement, which is of more social importantce than doing well on a test, is more encouraging. One meta-analysis[87] determined that 80% of the children who participated in intensive programs had a higher level of achievement

[86] Campbell et al., 2001.

[87] Barnett, 1998.

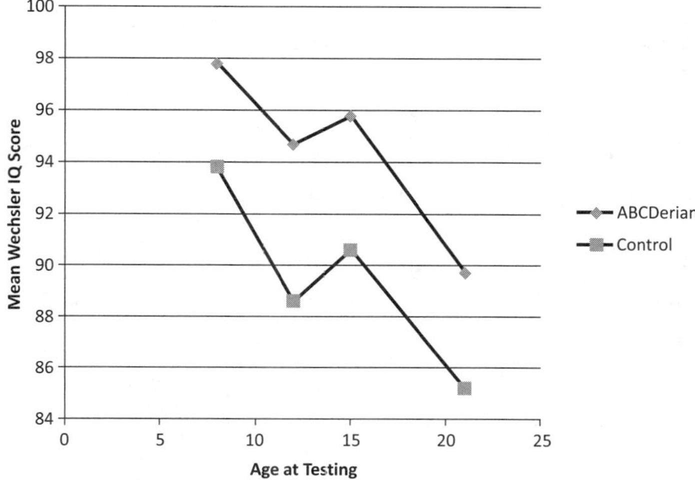

Figure 9.6. Mean IQ scores obtained by the participants in the ABCDerian project and in a randomly chosen control group. The intervention ended when the children entered school, at approximately age six. Data from Campbell et al., 2001, Table 1.

than that of the median participant in the control group, five years or more after the intervention ended. Participants also experienced fewer social and behavioral problems. Entry to college was also higher in participants of these programs, compared to control groups.

So what does the scoreboard say? Statements like "Head Start is a (failure) (success)" mask agreement over the facts, and disgreement over how to describe them. If you believe that the role of early childhood intervention and special education is to improve intelligence, as measured by test scores, the critics are right that at best marginal improvements can be made.[88] However, the programs do improve a number of academically relevant behaviors, ranging from study skills to improvement in interacting with students and teachers. Such behavior leads to improved learning in formal educational settings. These are not negligible benefits.

Scaling up a project like the ABCDerian project to cover a substantial portion of low SES children would require a huge financial investment and pose a tremendous problem of staffing. One can argue over the relative values of the costs and benefits, and how they should be assessed. These are educational policy issues, not issues in the study of intelligence.

9.4.5. *The Home Environment: Competition for Resources*

The behavior genetic studies reviewed in Chapter 8 have consistently found that 'nonshared environmental influences,' which refers to environmental influences that differ between family members, are a substantial source of environmental effects on intelligence.[89] As many autobiographical accounts make clear, one of the biggest differences in a child's early life is simply whether he or she is raised in a large family. The extreme, I suppose, would be a medieval royal family, where early-born children, as potential heirs to the throne, received very different treatment than did later-born children. As anyone who has either raised or been raised in a large family will attest, having several brothers and sisters is not like being an only child.

Children raised in large families tend, on the average, to have lower test scores than

---

[88] Detterman & Thompson, 1997; Herrnstein & Murray, 1994; Jensen, 1998.

[89] Jensen, 1997.

Panel 9.9. The National Longitudinal Studies

The National Longitudinal Studies are studies carried out by the US Department of Labor in order to obtain an accurate picture of the demographics, social structure, and economics of the United States. Such information is needed by policy makers. The surveys also provide valuable sources of data for economists, sociologists, educational researchers, and increasingly for psychologists. In general, the surveys utilize a random sample of US citizens relevant to the purpose of the survey. On occasion certain subgroups of interest are intentionally oversampled, in order to provide more accurate information about them.

The National Longitudinal Study of Youth 1979 (NLSY79) was a survey of over 10,000 young men and women, aged fourteen to twenty-two when the survey was initiated in 1979. This sample has been followed up periodically. Information on health, economics, and social status has been obtained. At the time of the first survey a fortuitous event occurred. The Department of Defense needed to update its normative sample of the Armed Services Vocational Aptitude Battery (ASVAB) and the associated Armed Forces Qualification Test (AFQT). Accordingly, a large percentage of the NLSY79 participants took the ASVAB. The result was an important prospective study of intelligence, for the ASVAB scores of the fourteen- to twenty-two-year-old participants can be related to their subsequent progress through life. Herrnstein and Murray made extensive use of the NLSY79 database in their provocative 1994 book.

The NLSY has "spawned" (in a somewhat literal sense) a second survey, the NLSY Children and Young Adults study, in which data is gathered on children of the NLSY79 participants. This provides social scientists with valuable data on changes in the population over generations.

The NLSY97 survey is something of a repeat of the 1979 survey. Over 9,000 young men and women born in the 1980–84 period were enrolled, and are interviewed on an annual basis. The purpose is to track social issues concerned with the transition from youth to adulthood. Comparisons to the NLSY79 data, when possible, provide a way of comparing cohorts as they transit from youth to adult life.

---

children raised in small families. This trend is shown in Figure 9.7, which presents data from the National Longitudinal Study of Youth 1979 study (described in panel 9.9). Similar findings have been obtained in many other studies. There is a correlation somewhere between −.15 and −.20 between family size and children's intelligence test scores.[90]

While the fact is clear, the reason for the fact is definitely not clear. Most debates stress either genetic or environmental influences. Galton worried that because large families seemed to produce less intelligent people the intelligence of the society, as a whole, must fall. Essentially the same concern over a "dysgenic effect" was voiced by Cattell in the mid twentieth century,[91] and by Richard Lynn more than fifty years later.[92] A key point in their argument is that family size increases as maternal intelligence drops, as is shown in Figure 9.8. The data shown are typical of numerous similar findings.

Those who worry about dysgenics, from Galton to Lynn, appear to assume that graphs such as these represent a proximal genetic effect; unintelligent mothers have

[90] Anastasi, 1956; Herrnstein & Murray, 1994; Lynn, 1998; Lynn & Harvey, 2008; Lynn & Van Court, 2004.

[91] Cattell, 1940.
[92] Lynn, 1998.

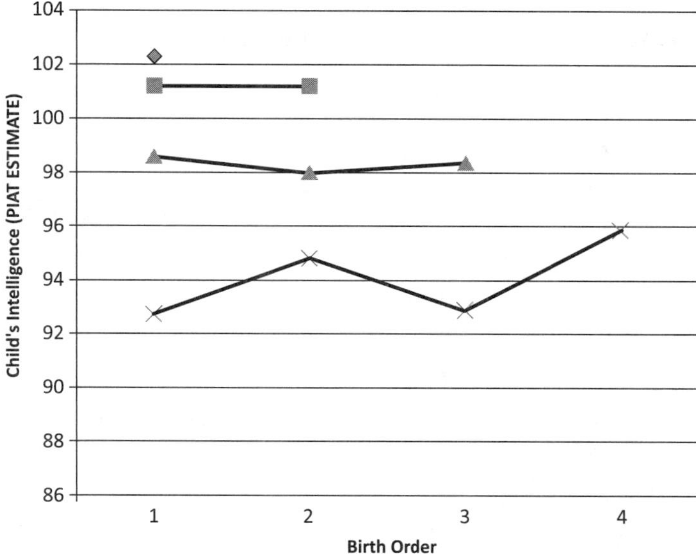

Figure 9.7. Mean intelligence estimates of young children born to mothers who were in the NLSY79 survey. The estimate is based on the Peabody Test, which is suitable for children in the pre-school and elementary school age range. Based on Rodgers et al., 2001, Table 4.

children who are genetically unintelligent, and have lots of them. Before we accept this argument a third phenomenon has to be considered, the birth-order effect.

Intelligence test scores are related to birth order; firstborns, on the average, have higher scores than second-borns, and so on. Figure 9.9 shows the results of a study from Norway, in which birth-order effects were shown in the intelligence test scores obtained by Norwegian young men when they registered for military service.[93] The birth-order effect is clearly social. If an older sibling dies, the next sibling in line assumes the "benefits" of the older sibling's place. Evidently acquiring intelligence is a bit like the medieval rules for acquiring a kingship: oldest surviving child gets the crown and the IQ points.

Birth-order effects are not apparent in the NLSY data set (Figure 9.7). This is not a contradiction of the evidence for birth-order effects, for the children of NLSY participants were tested before they were ten. If

birth-order effects are based on a competition for resources, the effect may accumulate over time, rather than being apparent early in the child's life. At the same time, the birth-order effect cannot be the sole cause of the family-size effect, for, as Figure 9.7 shows, the family-size effect can be obtained in a situation where there is no birth-order effect.

Robert Zajonc, a professor at the University of Michigan, and his colleagues have developed a model of family dynamics that they refer to as the *confluence model*.[94] Zajonc argues that a child's intelligence will be stimulated by an intellectually challenging environment, and that the mean age of the family is an indicator of the intellectual challenge in the home environment. To illustrate, a seven-year-old only child whose father and mother are both thirty will be in a family where the mean age of family members is $(30 + 30 + 7)/3$, or 22 1/3. For a seven-year-old with a three-year-old sibling, the mean age of family members is $(30 + 30 + 7 + 3)/4$, or 17 ½. This accounts for the

[93] Bjerkedal et al., 2007; Kristensen & Bjerkedal, 2007.

[94] Zajonc, 1983; Zajonc, Markus, & Markus, 1979.

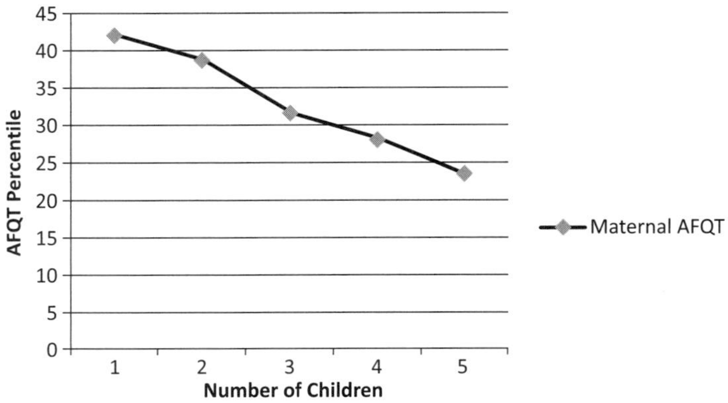

Figure 9.8. The relation between number of children and maternal intelligence score (AFQT percentile score) in the NLSY79 data set. *Source:* Rodgers et al., 2001, Table 6.

family effect; large families will have lower mean ages of the members.

The general tone of Zajonc's argument, that large families do not provide good environments for the development of intelligence, has been widely accepted. It has even led to "popular psychology" advice against having large families, on the grounds that the social environment of a large family will work against the development of children's intelligence.[95]

The facts are clear; the explanation is not. Here are three alternatives.

1. A proximal dysgenic hypothesis: Mothers' test scores indicate their genetic potential (probably in part correct), and they pass on this potential to their offspring (certainly true). The offsprings' test scores reflect the offsprings' genetic potential (probably in part correct). Genetic potential acts as a proximal influence on intelligence, thus producing the family-size effect.

2. A distal genetic hypothesis: Low maternal intelligence results in poorer parenting practices, including a tendency to begin child bearing at an earlier age. This practice may itself be partially due to genetic influences. The environment in large families tends to restrict the development of intelligence. Genet-

ics acts as a distal variable, leading to environmental practices that, as proximal variables, directly influence the intelligence of offspring.

3. An environmental explanation: The following argument is based on Nisbett's stress that culture matters in the development of intelligence.[96] Maternal intelligence test scores are negatively correlated with SES, and are also correlated with membership in low-status racial and ethnic groups. These groups have reduced access to resources in time and money that could improve parenting practices. In addition, there is a tendency for them to follow cultural practices that lead to childbearing at a younger age, and therefore to produce large families in which children have to compete for resources.

An argument based on proximal genetic influences, alone, cannot be maintained because it cannot account for the birth-order effect. It also cannot account for the worldwide trend toward reduced family sizes as people move into urban settings.[97]

Either the distal genetic or environmental explanations could account for all three effects: family-size, maternal intelligence, and birth order. As is often the case with social and behavioral phenomena, multiple

---

[95] See, e.g., Brothers, 1981.

[96] Nisbett, 2009.
[97] Mace, 2008.

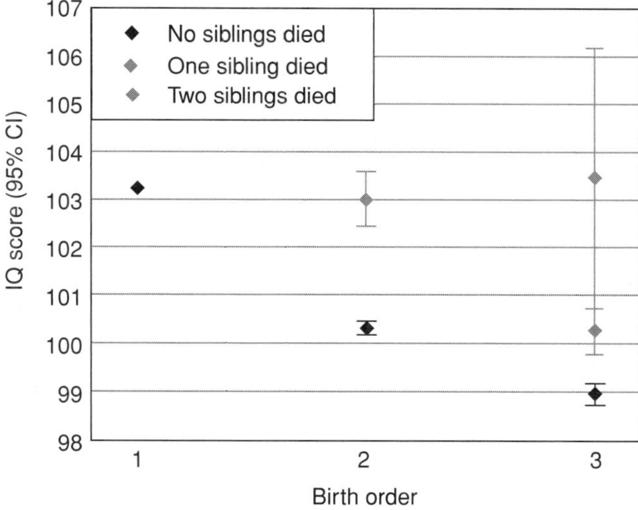

Figure 9.9. The birth order effect appears in families where a child becomes the oldest due to the death of an elder sibling. Scores have been adjusted to allow for parental education level, maternal age at birth, birth weight, and cohort effects. Bars show 95% confidence intervals. From Kristensen, P., & Bjerkedal, T. (2007) Explaining the relation between birth order and intelligence. *Science*, 316 (5832), 1717, Figure 1. Reprinted with permission from AAAS.

explanations are possible, and they are often not mutually exclusive.

Family-size effects, along with the cohort effect and the repeated findings of large heritability coefficients, represent well-documented phenomena with unclear explanations. Psychological research has established what happens, but not why it happens.

9.4.6. *Summary and a Value Judgment*

Family environments clearly do exert an effect on children's development of intelligence. Within the range of normal family environments in the developed nations, roughly within the top two-thirds of the socioeconomic spectrum, these effects appear to be modest and ephemeral. They virtually disappear in adulthood. The situation is quite different when we look at extreme environments, such as the homes of the children at risk for lowered cognitive development – for example, those who participated in the ABCDerian project.

Unfortunately, though, this does not get us very far, for SES is a composite, abstract variable that covaries with many other variables. It is difficult to disentangle the effects of family social practices – such as failure to encourage children's problem solving, authoritarian styles of adult-child interaction, and other practices considered bad parenting – from concomitant deficiencies in the physical environment and genetic inheritance. We cannot unambiguously assign damaging SES effects either to heredity, or to social or physical variables. Just as there may be many genes affecting intelligence, each one individually making a small contribution, there may be many familial variables affecting intelligence, each one individually making a small contribution.

High-cost intervention projects have produced improved cognitive performance. Unfortunately, the effects are far less than most social engineers would like to see. Many less expensive projects, such as the typical Head Start program, show very little effect on test scores, or on other purely cognitive behavior, beyond the early school years. However, there are indications that these programs do prepare at risk children for the social experience of school, and that this may facilitate later school development.

The last point is very important. In industrial and post-industrial societies schooling is a major factor in determining a person's contribution to the general society. In 2006 it was estimated that in the United States a person without a high school diploma earned only two-thirds as much a someone with one.[98] Other social problems, such as poor health and criminal convictions, also are negatively correlated with the possession of a diploma. Any program that increases the likelihood that children in at risk situations will complete schooling is a socially valuable program. It has also been estimated that even the more expensive programs are cost-effective, when the total cost to society over a long period of time is considered.[99] I must admit, though, that these projections are based upon a number of assumptions that I, for one, find suspect.

I close this section with a comment that is avowedly, and openly, a statement of social beliefs.

I once heard an address by Sandra Scarr, herself a major contributor to the literature on genetic and environmental effects on intelligence, and by no means a person who denies the importance of genetics. I regret that I have no reference except my memory. Scarr pointed out that a child born to a poor family, with limited resources, is often in a bleak environment. It is a good thing, in itself, to provide programs offering such children better nutrition, a safe place to interact with adults and other children, and an interesting, challenging environment. If the resulting program also improves their cognitive abilities, their intelligence in the important, conceptual sense, then that is a very nice benefit of having done a good thing. If the program just improves test scores, but does not improve cognitive

abilities in the more general sense, then that is just a curiosity. Whatever the outcome, society should provide as good a social environment as can be arranged. You do not need a reason to do a good thing, you should just do it.

I find Scarr's reasoning compelling. Providing aid to disadvantaged children is a duty owed to the children. Costs and benefits are relevant when comparing programs; there is no sense in spending more than you have to. However, I believe that society has a duty to provide such programs, just as much as it has a duty to provide military defense and security for the aged.

9.5. Education

The cohort effect shows that changes in the environment can result in major changes in intelligence, on a population basis. Over the twentieth century the industrially developed countries saw improvements in nutrition, better health practices, smaller family sizes, and increases in the availability of pre-school programs. There have also been huge changes in education.

The US data, which mirrors that of other industrially developed countries, shows how strong the educational change has been. In 1900 the school enrollment rate for fifteen- to nineteen-year-olds was 50%; it rose to 75% by 1940, and has remained relatively stable at slightly above 90% since 1990. In 1910 the median number of years of education for people twenty-five years old or older was 8.1 years. In 1940, at the outset of World War II, it was only 8.6. In 2008 better than 85% of adults had twelve or more years of education.[100] In the first half of the twentieth century the big change in education was that more people gained basic skills in the traditional "reading, writing, and 'rithmetic'" than had been the case earlier. Illiteracy, arguably the most important single result of a lack of formal schooling, had fallen from 10.7% in 1900 to 2.9% in 1940. By 2000 the

---

[98] Retrieved from centerforpubliceducation.org, June 2008.

[99] Barnett, 1998.

[100] U.S. Census Bureau, 2010 Statistical Abstract, Table 224.

illiteracy rate was less than 1%. The second half of the twentieth century was characterized by marked increases in secondary and tertiary education, especially for women and minority group members. By 2007, 29% of the adults in the US had a college degree. Similar trends have been observed in other industrialized countries. It is not unreasonable to assume that all this education had an effect on cognitive skills, and hence, on intelligence. But just what?

Once again we have to be clear about our definitions. If we take the attitude that intelligence is essentially *g*, as indexed by a *g*-loaded nonverbal test, such as a progressive matrix test, education may not increase intelligence that much. Alternatively, if we accept the fluid intelligence–crystallized intelligence (Gf-Gc) distinction, we may find different effects of education on Gf and Gc. I will generally take this approach, as I believe that it offers a useful perspective for dealing with the effects of schooling. I will keep coming back to my point that the important components of intelligence are those skills that are useful in society. Test scores are of interest only to the extent that they indicate which examinees possess these skills.

We also have to be careful about what we mean when we talk about education. Do we mean any form of training? Do we include commercial programs that are intended to increase one's intelligence (many are advertised, few have been evaluated), or do we restrict our interest to programs of formal education, the familiar K-12 and college/university systems? I will consider two issues: the influence of the formal system and the (very few) attempts that have been made to teach general reasoning skills and that have been formally evaluated. And where do commercial programs to increase scores on tests like the SAT fall on this spectrum?

9.5.1. *What the Educational System Tries to Do*

The developed countries hand over a great deal of the task of educating the young to formal school systems. This is a marked contrast to the situation less than 300 years ago, when most children learned what they needed to know by some form of apprenticeship, augmented by a very small amount of formal training. Formal schools did exist in both pre-literate and ancient societies. The seafaring Polynesians had schools to teach navigators to guide canoes on ocean voyages of up to a thousand miles. As part of their training they learned to use sophisticated star charts.[101] In ancient Egypt scribes went to school to learn accounting, surveying, construction, mathematics, and engineering.[102] What is different about our society is the near-universality of formal schooling, not the concept itself.

Today's K-12 school systems are responsible for transmitting three classes of knowledge: the basic beliefs and traditions of the society, cognitive and motor skills useful in solving frequently encountered problems, and specific pieces of knowledge that will be required in utilizing these skills.[103] To illustrate, somewhat flippantly, for the United States circa 2010, this means, "God Bless America, learn to read, and a camel's a mammal."

Upwards of 50% of the citizens in the industrially developed nations receive some form of post-secondary education. While there are some discussions of the importance of a liberal education, most post-secondary instruction is oriented toward the training of specialists in fields ranging from welding to the law. The result has been a tremendous extension of the time between the end of childhood and the point at which a fully trained adult enters society. Alexander the Great was twenty-two when he led the Macedonian/Greek army into Asia. Napoleon was appointed brigadier general at twenty-four. In today's military they would both be lieutenants.

Richard Snow, an educational psychologist at Stanford University, has argued that schools are successful if they provide

---

[101] Hutchins, 1983.
[102] Information provided by the King Tutankhamen exhibit at the Field Museum, Chicago, 2006.
[103] Cole, 2005.

students with useful *aptitudes*, by which he meant skills that can be used to operate in the larger society and to guide further learning.[104] Snow divided the cognitive aptitudes into two classes: specific skills (e.g., reading, knowledge of history) used to solve certain classes of problems, and general reasoning skills used both to solve problems and to guide further learning. Snow's categorization of aptitudes mirrors the Cattell-Horn distinction between Gf and Gc, but was set in a broader context than that of the testing paradigm.

Snow pointed out that schools also taught skills in self-management and cooperative problem solving. While some may not wish to include such skills in the definition of intelligence, they are certainly relevant to the application of one's intelligence to problems outside of a school setting. These skills are often taught implicitly, by procedures that Snow referred to as a *metacurriculum*, encouraging independent inquiry and cooperative studies. This is certainly the approved practice in education today, although it is not always what actually happens. It represents a departure from the authoritarian, didactic methods that were common in all schools up to about 1950, and that are not unknown today.[105]

9.5.2. The Evidence for Educational Influences on Intelligence

The American President Theodore ("Teddy") Roosevelt is reputed to have said,

> *A man who has never gone to school may steal from a freight car; but if he has a university education, he may steal the whole railroad.*
> Attributed to Roosevelt by Laurence Peters (1977, p. 117)

Can you imagine a more ringing affirmation of the value of education?

I suspect that Roosevelt would have regarded the question "Does schooling increase intelligence" as trivial, because it is obvious that educated people are generally capable of solving problems that uneducated people cannot. Many of these problems are socially relevant. They range from reading and understanding newspapers to balancing checkbooks and comprehending the terms of mortgages. A substantial part of a person's intelligence, in the conceptual sense of being able to solve socially relevant problems, is clearly the product of education.

What about the effects of education upon intelligence in the much narrower sense of improving test scores? Today that is a fairly hard question to answer, because virtually everyone goes to school at least up to the point at which education shifts toward specialty training. However, this was not always true, so prior to World War II it was possible to conduct a study contrasting groups of children, of similar socioeconomic background, who either did or did not have access to formal schooling. This situation often occurred for reasons that had nothing to do with the personal traits of the students, such as the decision to locate a road, and with it a school, near one community and distant from another. The children who had access to schools had higher intelligence test scores than those who did not. The difference in test scores between groups increased with increases in the difference in the available schooling.[106]

In today's society there is a positive relation between a person's intelligence test score and his or her level of education. High school drop-outs have generally lower intelligence test scores than those who complete high school. The effect interacts with SES; low intelligence is more predictive of dropping out for students from low SES families than it is for students from moderate or high SES families.[107] But what is cause and what is effect? The correlation could come about because intelligence produces success in school, or because increasing amounts of schooling produce intelligence, or both.

---

[104] Snow, 1996.
[105] Bransford, Brown, & Cocking, 1999.

[106] Ceci, 1990; Bronfenbrenner et al., 1996; Ceci & Williams, 1997.
[107] Herrnstein & Murray, 1994, Chapter 6.

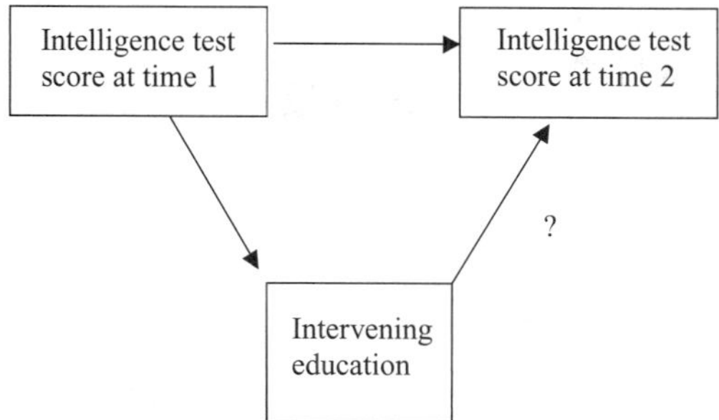

Figure 9.10. The path diagram for a study showing the influence of education on intelligence. It is necessary to show that education has an influence on intelligence at time 2 (the ? in the figure) in addition to the influence exerted by intelligence at time 1.

One way to disentangle the situation is to look at cases in which nonschool intelligence test measures are taken before some variable period of schooling, followed by a second intelligence test. The path diagram for this design is shown in Figure 9.10. The question is whether scores on the second intelligence test are influenced by schooling, after accounting for the relation between the first and second tests. Herrnstein and Murray analyzed scores for people in the NSLY79 for whom first test scores were available (see panel 9.9) and concluded that schooling had little, if any, effect. This result has been widely quoted. However, a detailed reanalysis of the same data by Christopher Winship (Harvard University) and Sandor Korenman (City University of New York)[108] questioned their conclusion. Winship and Korenman also reviewed a number of other studies using some variant of the design sketched in Figure 9.10. A Norwegian study was particularly important, because it provided an unusually good natural experiment.

Norwegian schoolchildren are given intelligence tests at age thirteen. At age eighteen all Norwegian men take an intelligence test as part of their registration for military service. The eighteen-year-old population contains some people who are still students, and others who have dropped out at various periods following completion of compulsory education. Those who continued as students tended to have higher test scores at age eighteen than did the registrants who dropped out of the educational system. This fact, alone, is not compelling evidence, because it could be because the more intelligent people stayed in school longer. However, the people who stayed in school had higher scores at age eighteen than would have been predicted from their scores at age thirteen, indicating a beneficial effect of schooling.

On the basis of their own analyses and the studies that they reviewed, Winship and Korenman estimated that an additional year of education (through the K-12 years) adds approximately 2.7 IQ points to a person's test score. Speculating a bit, suppose we combine this estimate with data on the increase in educational attainment in the United States. In 1946 the median of educational attainment for adults was 8.6 years. Today the median is "some college," which I arbitrarily (and conservatively) set at 13.1 years. Most of this increase has occurred since 1940. Taking the Winship and Korenman figures at face value, this implies that a $4.5 \times 2.7 = 12.15$ IQ point rise in test scores over the last half of the twentieth century could be accounted for by increases in education.[109]

What does education do to raise intelligence? We need to distinguish between aptitudes that are taught explicitly and those that are taught implicitly.

Explicitly, educational systems try to provide students with the knowledge and cognitive skills required to operate in their society. This is very close to the definition of Gc. Not surprisingly, all battery-type intelligence tests include tests that assess such knowledge and skills, either directly or indirectly. This is certainly true of the Armed Forces Qualifying Test (AFQT) described in Chapter 3 of this book, and treated by some researchers (including Herrnstein and Murray) as virtually synonymous with *g*.

---

[108] Winship & Korenman, 1997.

[109] Nancy Robinson, a developmental psychologist at the University of Washington, has pointed out to me that this argument does not explain why scores on young children's intelligence tests have also risen.

The AFQT is based on the Armed Services Vocational Aptitude Battery (ASVAB) subtests of word knowledge, arithmetic reasoning, paragraph comprehension, and mathematics knowledge – all subjects that are explicitly taught in school. As a result, the ASVAB, and of necessity the AFQT, evaluates Gc.[110]

Schools implicitly teach three other aptitudes that are important in modern society: problem solving removed from the immediate context of life, abstract conceptual thinking, and (more recently) the ability to detect patterns in stimuli. There is no claim that the teaching is perfect, or that schooling is the only way to develop reasoning skills. There are many illustrations showing that relatively unschooled people can exhibit sophisticated reasoning in the context of everyday problems.[111] These cautions do not detract from the main point. All that needs be maintained is that schooling increases the likelihood that children will acquire powerful, abstract problem-solving methods that can be applied to a variety of problems.

Literacy is probably the most powerful of these skills. Studies contrasting literate and nonliterate societies have shown that the possession of literacy increases willingness to think about hypothetical situations, and that literacy increases the tendency to use abstract classification systems based on object features, rather than classification based upon a concrete situation. Classification-based reasoning tasks are part of many intelligence tests. In addition, modern educational methods have stressed the importance of evaluating evidence by detecting patterns. This is particularly the case for instruction in science and mathematics. Spearman argued that this ability – "eduction," in his terms – is one of the most important components of intelligence.[112] An analysis of the techniques used in modern elementary school mathematics classes has shown not only that the schools teach "educ-

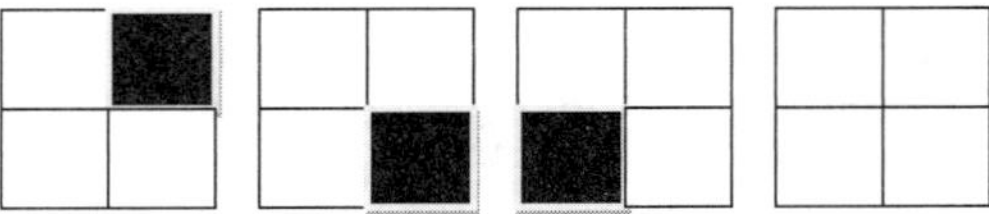

Figure 9.11. A problem similar to the problems presented in K-2 mathematics textbooks. The task is to complete the sequence of figures. Based on examples provided in Blair et al., 2005.

tion," but also that some of the exercises that they use to do so closely resemble the sorts of items that appear on intelligence tests of inductive ability.[113] An example is shown in Figure 9.11.

The relation between intelligence and schooling is interactive. Not everyone will gain exactly 2.5 IQ points from a year of education. There are strong feedback loops between intelligence and the effects of education; more intelligent people learn more, and often quite a bit more, from schooling than do less intelligent people. We go into this in some detail in Chapter 10. Nevertheless, the overall message is clear. Education does increase intelligence, both in the narrow sense of increasing IQ scores and in the far more important sense of increasing one's ability to solve life's problems.

Was Roosevelt's praise of university education justified? Although some university officials claim that the purpose of a (liberal) college education is to teach people to think, the claim has never been tested. This is due, in no small part, to university educators' failing to agree on just what the empirical definition of "being able to think" ought to be. Of course, we do know that colleges and universities do an excellent job of training high-level specialists such as engineers and physicians. And for a direct test of Roosevelt's claim?

In the first six months of 2009 two separate financial scandals were revealed. Quite independently of each other, Bernard Madoff and Allen Stanford, both university graduates, had bilked investors of tens of *billions* of dollars in sophisticated frauds. This makes Robin Hood look like a penny ante thief, and makes Roosevelt look prescient.

---

[110] Roberts et al., 2000.

[111] See Cole, 2005; Hunt & Minstrell, 1994, 1996; and Lave, 1988, for some examples.

[112] Spearman, 1923.

[113] Blair et al., 2005.

9.6. Training Intelligence

In this section we move from considering the effects of schooling to the effects of briefer training programs that are supposed to influence general reasoning skills. It is important to distinguish these programs from programs that are essentially adjuncts to the formal education program, in which they teach specific topics, for example, reading or mathematics. Some of the supplementary teaching programs are good, some are not, and there is no point in discussing them. Other commercial programs are marketed as ways to improve your thinking, which is a rather nebulous claim. I do not know of a single one of these programs that has ever offered acceptable scientific evidence of its effectiveness. The programs are marketed on the basis of endorsements by users, rather than by comparisons between experimental and control groups. A reviewer with scientific training will want to scream *uncontrolled placebo effects!*

There is a lively market in coaching programs intended to improve students' scores on socially important tests, such as a college entrance test. The SAT is a favored target. These programs do work. It is worth looking at their claim to have improved intelligence.

In principle, there is another way to improve intelligence through training. While we certainly do not know all about the basic cognitive processes that underlie intelligence, we do know a good deal (cf. Chapters 6 and 7). Could intelligence be improved by training basic information-processing functions, by analogy to the way in which athletic performance is improved by exercise? There has been some progress along this path.

9.6.1. *Coaching Programs that Raise Test Scores*

Suppose that I offered to sell you a training/coaching program that would improve your score on test X, where test X is any one of the commonly used tests related to intelligence, ranging from the SAT to a progressive matrix test. Should you buy it?

The question is not fanciful. Several coaching programs that improve scores on college entrance and similar examinations are available. These programs do increase test scores. But do they increase intelligence?

The distinction between crystallized and fluid intelligence is relevant. Gc, in its generalized sense of culturally useful knowledge, rather than in the more limited sense of questions about knowledge that find their way into an intelligence test, is certainly part of intelligence. Note that the generalized definition includes most of what Robert Sternberg has referred to as "practical intelligence."[114] Of course, such knowledge can be acquired by coaching, which then becomes an extension of formal education. If you are going to have to take an examination in Spanish, it makes sense to be trained in Spanish, and as you receive this training you will probably pick up some nonlinguistic but useful information about Spanish culture and society. Gc will be increased. It is not surprising that a coaching program would work, and if the price is right, buy it.

A coaching program might also increase scores by improving skills that are useful in test taking, but not useful for much else. An example is the strategy of improving your chances on a multiple choice test by ruling out obviously wrong alternative answers, and then guessing. It might be rational to purchase a coaching program that taught test-specific skills if passing the test were a goal in itself, but not if you were interested in improving the socially relevant mental abilities that the test measured.

Two psychologists at the Educational Testing Service, Samuel Messick and Ann Jungeblut, have shown that these distinctions apply to the coaching programs marketed as ways to prepare for the SAT.[115] These programs vary from a two- or three-hour session on "how to take a test" to intensive tutoring over a period of several months. Depending on the program, documented gains on the verbal and mathematical

---

[114] Sternberg, 2003; Sternberg et al., 2000.
[115] Messick & Jungeblut, 1981.

sections of the SAT ranged from 10 or 20 points per section (.10 in standard deviation units) to as much as 100 points (1 standard deviation unit), which is quite a lot. There was a correlation of .7 between the length of the coaching program and the size of the program's effect. Not surprisingly, the shorter coaching programs concentrated on test-taking skills, while the longer ones amounted to education, which translates into a real gain in Gc.

Many people would regard these remarks as simple statements of the obvious. When people talk about improving intelligence, or alternative terms, such as "reasoning" or "problem solving," I think they are generally talking about fluid intelligence – the ability to solve unexpected or unfamiliar problems. Can this be done?

Here we bump up against a problem of definition. It is easy enough to see whether a training program has developed a person's vocabulary, or his or her ability to do specific types of problem solving, in anything from carpentry to physics to the law. But how are we to know whether a person has been trained to think? A program to teach intelligence is successful to the extent that it raises some of the skills that constitute the general definition of intelligence. In order to measure the effect of a program we measure performance on a test of fluid intelligence. This alone is not enough. We have to show that improved test performance has been accompanied by improved performance in socially relevant tasks outside of the testing context. Otherwise we are open to the charge that what has been taught are test-specific skills. This is a real issue. Not surprisingly, if people take the same cognitive test twice, they get better scores the second time. This applies to tests as different as battery-type intelligence tests and progressive matrix tests. However, statistical analyses of the improved scores show that they are not related to the general reasoning factor (g). Test-specific skills have been improved by familiarity with the tests.[116]

What we would like to have is a demonstration that going through some form of training program that is very different from a test of g results in improvements on a g-loaded test. I know of very few such efforts. The next section discusses two such attempts, one that succeeded and one that failed. I then make some speculative remarks about the sorts of situations that can lead to success.

9.6.2. *Mixed Results from School-based Programs that Might Improve Gf*

The good news for the training of intelligence comes from an unlikely place – the Sudan. In 2007 a group of researchers lead by Paul Irwing, of the University of Manchester, and including Sudanese colleagues, conducted a study on the effects of training with the abacus, an ancient computing device that is still used in the Mideast and northern Africa. The experimenters compared schoolchildren's Raven Progressive Matrices performance, before and after the children had either completed a normal school curriculum or had had the same curriculum, plus sixty-eight hours of abacus instruction, two hours per week for several months. Both groups showed improvement on the progressive matrix test, which is not surprising because it was a second administration, and also because the children were now almost half a year older. The key point is whether the experimental groups showed more improvement than the control. Figure 9.12 shows that they did. This suggests that the training program did influence general reasoning skills.

The negative results come from my own laboratory. For a number of years my colleagues at the University of Washington and I, in cooperation with Jim Minstrell, an award-winning high school science teacher, worked on the development of educational programs to improve high school science instruction, largely by presenting challenging problems to be solved, and then emphasizing the reasoning involved.[117] In some of

---

[116] te Nijenhuis, van Vianen, & van der Flier, 2007.

[117] Hunt & Minstrell, 1994, 1996.

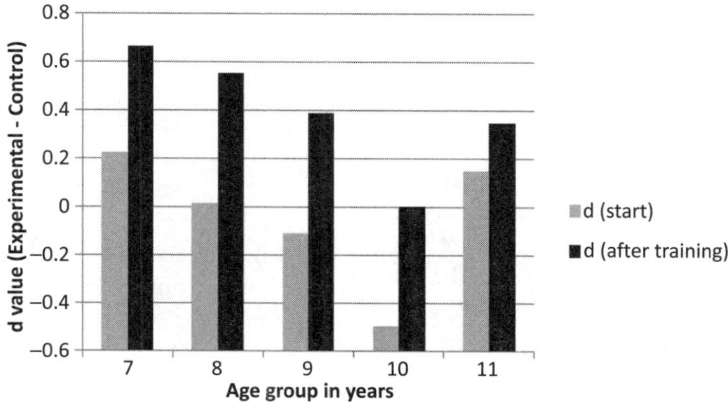

Figure 9.12. Abacus training improves intelligence test scores. The difference between the experimental and control groups, in *d* units, for Raven Standard Progressive Matrices scores obtained by Sudanese children, before and after the experimental group completed abacus training. The *d* values within age group are approximations, based on the data in Irwing et al., 2008, Table 2, on the assumption that there were approximately equal numbers in the experimental and control groups.

our studies we had students attempt progressive matrix problems before and after receiving up to a year's instruction. While the programs were quite successful in teaching reasoning about topics in introductory physics, we did not find any consistent gains on progressive matrix problems.[118]

There are so many differences between elementary schools in the Sudan and high school students from affluent American school districts that one hesitates to draw any conclusions at all. There is also a puzzling aspect to the study. The problems presented to the American students stressed reasoning, not (for the most part) detailed knowledge of the minutiae of physics. Doing arithmetic on the abacus does not require a great deal of problem solving, once you have grasped the basic principles of the device, but it does require concentration and an ability to hold intermediate calculations in one's head. Naively, one might think that solving physics problems would be more like solving progressive matrix problems than doing abacus arithmetic. So why did the results come out the way they did? Speculation about this is instructive, because it raises some general

considerations about interpretation of findings in this area of research.

The authors of the Sudanese study say that children in both the experimental and control group were following a standard curriculum, but provide no details about any differences in other education-relevant or environmental experiences that might have differed between the groups. They did not indicate whether experimental and control classes were chosen at random, something that is essential in evaluating educational research. My evaluation is that some environmental variable improved reasoning in the Sudanese children, and that it was probably associated with abacus training, but I would like to have more details.

A second reason that I *speculate* as being a cause of the discrepancy in results is that the participants in the study were operating at different levels of general reasoning. The Sudanese children were operating at the twelfth percentile of performance, in terms of the British standardization of the Raven Progressive Matrices test. A similar statistic is not available for the American teenagers, but they were in schools that served middle to high SES families, and were voluntarily taking high school physics, an optional

---

[118] Levidow, 1993.

course that students consider to be difficult. It is reasonable to assume that they were in roughly the upper third of general reasoning talent.

Recall the consistent finding that we know quite a few aspects of the environment that harm intelligence, and only a few that make much improvement at the top. The Sudanese children were probably operating toward the bottom of the scale and, compared to the American students, in quite unfavorable environments. If my conjecture is correct, their (low) reasoning scores would be relatively malleable. The American students were operating at a much higher level on the reasoning scale, so the changes that were made to the instruction, although beneficial in the narrow sense of teaching physics (the primary purpose of the intervention), made little if any difference in terms of general reasoning capabilities.

9.6.3. *Training Information-processing Capacities: Processing Speed and Automation*

Cognitive processing speed refers to the speed with which the brain can accomplish simple decision and recognition tasks. Intelligence theorists have tended to treat processing speed as a stable trait that has a correlation with intelligence test scores around .30 in college students.[119] The correlation increases if we expand our studies throughout the adult age range, because cognitive slowing is a general characteristic of aging. What apparently has not been realized (at least by most intelligence researchers) is how malleable processing speed is.

In the 1970s Walter Schneider (now at the University of Pittsburgh) and Richard Shiffrin (now at the University of Indiana) conducted a very important series of experiments on the influence of practice upon visual detection. In *visual detection* tasks an observer scans an array of stimuli to determine whether or not a target stimulus is present. To illustrate, is the letter K (the

target) present in the following array?

A	R	V	B
H	K	T	P
F	W	E	Q

Schneider and Shiffrin showed that under certain conditions training can decrease the time required to detect a familiar target by a factor of 10, from over 200 milliseconds to as few as 20 or 30 milliseconds. The training requires hundreds of trials in which observers always search for the same target.[120] Further research showed that the phenomenon is not restricted to visual detection. Similar, somewhat smaller reductions in detection time are found when observers search for exemplars of abstract categories, such as searching an array of words for an animal name.[121]

Schneider and Shiffrin presented their results as a demonstration of *automaticity*, the principle that if the same task is practiced over and over again it becomes very fast, and not subject to the control of the relatively slow working memory–attentional control system. Their explanation has been verified by imaging studies in which participants have their brains scanned as they practice tasks to the point of automation. There is a shift in activity from the forebrain regions involved in the working memory–attentional control system to task-specific regions of the brain.[122] This has implications for higher-order cognition.

Anders Ericsson, a professor at Florida State University who has conducted systematic studies of expert behavior, has shown that experts in many fields practice in such a way as to encourage the automatization of those components of a complex task that can be automated.[123] This allows the expert to concentrate his or her attention on those aspects of a task that require thought. To take an example from athletics, during a

---

[119] Jensen, 2006.

[120] Schneider & Shiffrin, 1977.
[121] Fisk & Schneider, 1983.
[122] Hill & Schneider, 2006.
[123] Ericsson, Krampe, & Tesch-Römer, 1993.

match a champion tennis player will concentrate on where to place the ball, not on how to hit it. That has already been drilled into the champion's brain, by hours and hours of practice.

We may illustrate the same thing with respect to tasks specifically studied in intelligence research. I offer an example from a study done in my own laboratory. Recall that in the g-VPR model of intelligence[124] the ability to mentally rotate a visual percept "in the mind's eye" is seen as a basic dimension of intelligence. An often-repeated finding is that mental rotation is faster in men than in women, and that it deteriorates over the adult years. With only five days of training, one hour a day, we trained middle-aged women to perform mental rotation tasks as quickly as they were performed by male undergraduate students when they walk into the laboratory. We did not destroy the age effect, for the undergraduates also got faster with practice. What we did show is that mental rotation, the prototypical task for assessing R in the g-VPR model, is not invariant over practice.[125]

Is automation relevant to everyday problem solving? The answer to this question is "yes, almost always a little bit, and sometimes a lot." We can think of automation as an increase in the speed with which people can recognize that certain responses are dictated by the situation. Tasks can be automated if there is a constant mapping between a stimulus and a response; for instance, you are always supposed to stop at a red traffic light, and $2 + 4$ always makes 6. Very few of the activities that we call "thinking" can be entirely automated. Almost all of them contain elements that can be automated. Here are two examples.

Mathematics is not the same as arithmetic, but mathematicians know their arithmetic very, very well. Alexander Aitken, a leading British mathematician in the mid twentieth century, was also a formidable mental calculator.[126] Schoolchildren are

drilled until they know their multiplication table, up to 10 × 10. Several mathematicians have been reported to know a good part of the multiplication table up to 100 × 100! It is important, though, to distinguish between arithmetical calculation and doing mathematics. Calculation is a tool for mathematics, distinct from any deep understanding of mathematics. It is hard to imagine a mathematician who could not calculate. On the other hand, there are numerous cases of calculating prodigies who had little mathematical talent.

What is going on? Mathematicians learn many arithmetical facts to the point that they are readily accessible from long-term memory. As is the case in many other areas of expertise, these facts are organized into coherent networks of relationships, so that they may be easily retrieved. There are specialized brain areas associated with calculation and simple mathematics, arithmetic and number representation. In both mathematicians and calculating prodigies the mental calculation areas simply run more efficiently than in most of us. Mathematicians utilize their efficient mental calculations in the service of deeper understanding of mathematics. The calculating prodigies stop at arithmetic.[127]

And then we have verbal comprehension. Here is a fragment of a poem written by Lewis Carroll, the author of *Alice in Wonderland*.

> *"The time has come," the walrus said*
> *"to talk of many things: Of shoes and*
> *ships – and sealing wax, – of cabbages*
> *and kings."*
> —*Lewis Carroll, "The Walrus and*
> *the Carpenter" (1872)*

Figuring out the meaning of this passage is hard enough without wasting time searching for the meanings of *walrus, shoes, ships, sealing wax, cabbages*, and *kings*. Automated word retrieval leaves time for the hard tasks.

An intelligent person will have reduced the processing time required to retrieve millions of items of information that are useful

[124] Johnson & Bouchard, 2005.
[125] Berg, Hertzog, & Hunt, 1982.
[126] Nickerson, 2010, pp. 159–162.

[127] Butterworth, 2006.

in everyday life. And how will automation be achieved? By practice.

9.6.4. *Training Working Memory*

The working memory–attentional control complex is a central part of the information-processing functions supporting intelligence. A demonstration that the efficiency of working memory can be improved is tantamount to a demonstration that intelligence can be improved. Why?

Working memory is illustrated by tasks that require participants to do several things at once, such as simultaneously monitoring visual and verbal input streams, or suppressing information from one input stream while processing information from another. Such tasks are not demonstrations of intelligence in themselves. They are measures of the functioning of an information-processing system in the brain, primarily in the frontal and parietal cortices and in the cingulate cortex, that provides capacities vital for solving complex problems.[128] The brain has considerable plasticity; it can reorganize itself as a result of experience. Two recent studies have shown that practice on tasks involving working memory and the control of attention will improve performance on intelligence tests.

One was a study by a joint University of Michigan–University of Bern (Switzerland) group that emphasized the storage component of the working memory complex.[129] The task used was an *n-back* task. In this task a stream of stimuli are presented, one at a time. The participant indicates when the current item is a repetition of the item presented a certain number of items back. To illustrate, in the stream

---

| X | X | Y | Z | Z | X | Y | X |

---

the third X is a repetition of the stimulus presented four items previously. In a four-back task the participant would be

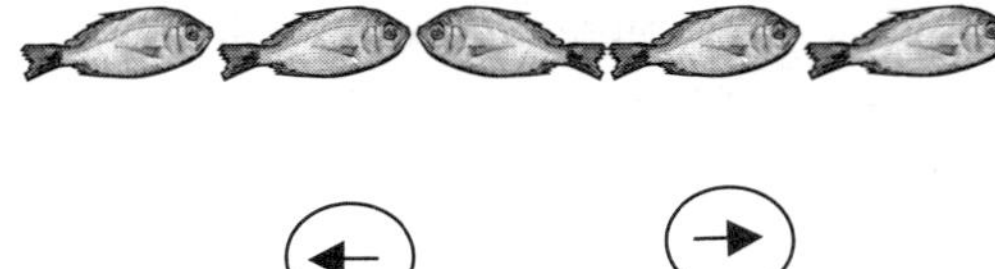

Figure 9.13. A cartoon rendition of Posner and Rothbart's attention-training task. The task is to press the key showing the direction of the center fish. The fish on the right and left of the center fish may point in the same or the opposite direction of the center fish.

asked to indicate the repetition. College students attempted a version of the task in which they were required to monitor two simultaneously presented streams of stimuli, one presented visually and one presented aurally. The students practiced for from one to nineteen days. They also took a variety of fluid intelligence tests before and after practicing the working memory tasks. Test scores increased after practice on the working memory tasks, and, most impressively, the amount of increase was directly related to the amount of practice.

The second study was done by Michael Posner and Mary Rothbart of the University of Oregon.[130] Young children were trained on a visual attention task intended to force them to focus on one part of a visual scene while ignoring others. The task itself is shown in Figure 9.13. Compared to a control group, the children trained on the visual attention task showed improved performance on the Kauffman children's test of cognitive ability.

The working memory–attention complex is not the only information-processing function that is both relevant to intelligence and trainable. Processing speed can also be trained. The mechanism for training is simple and ubiquitous in our society: action video games. It has been shown that adolescents and young adults who play action video games perform better on a variety of tests of general processing speed than do their contemporaries who do not play the games. This cannot be entirely a selection effect, for it is possible to take people

---

[128] See Chapter 5 for a discussion.
[129] Jaeggi et al., 2008.

[130] Posner & Rothbart, 2007.

who do not normally play games and have them practice playing; they then show superior performance on measures of cognitive processing speed outside of the gaming context.[131]

Results such as these illustrate how practice on tasks that themselves do not evaluate intelligence, in any usual sense of the word, can improve performance on the complex problems presented on intelligence tests. There is a close analogy to the finding that intelligence test performance can be improved by, in Posner and Rothbart's term, "training the brain," and the totally unsurprising, but important, finding that weight training can improve performance in athletics.

However, it is important not to overinterpret laboratory studies like these. They show how an environmental effect on intelligence could be produced, but they do not show that variations in intelligence are produced this way in the world outside the laboratory. Take, for example, the correlation between parental SES and children's intelligence. There are differences in the home environments of children in high and low SES homes, especially in the amount of exploratory activity permitted, parental encouragement of independent problem solving, and amount (and type) of TV watching. Do these differences translate into differences in opportunities to exercise the working memory–attention control complex? The question could be answered by a painstaking cognitive task analysis of children's environments. To my knowledge, no such analysis has been conducted.

9.7. The Challenge Hypothesis

The Challenge Hypothesis (Chapter 1) is a claim that people develop their intelligence when they rise to meet environmental challenges. Genetic inheritance establishes a reaction range, which determines the limits of development. The level of intelligence a person achieves within these limits depends upon both the environment and the way the person reacts to it. The following principles apply:

1. The physical environment constrains the reaction range. The constraints generally have the effect of driving intelligence downward, as in the case of alcoholism, poor nutrition, and atmospheric lead. Certain drugs related to the amphetamines can provide a temporary enhancement of alertness, and can produce transient improvement of some cognitive functions, but their long-term effects are not known, and could well be deleterious. More generally, within the range of the physical environments present in post-industrial societies, benefitting from the physical environment is largely a matter of avoiding things that will make you stupid.

2. Within a person's reaction range, realized intelligence is produced by interacting with the social environment. This includes the early home environment, the school, and in adult life, personal and professional experiences.

3. The extent to which a person benefits from environmental challenges depends upon how the person engages with them. Sternberg[132] has identified three strategies for engagement. *Adaption* is accepting the situation and changing your own behavior to meet it. Deciding to study for an examination is a prosaic example. *Shaping* is changing the situation to adjust to your abilities. This in itself can be a learning experience. *Selection* is finding a situation in which you can more easily prosper, given your current talents. When a student drops a tough class in favor of an easy one, he or she selects and, as the example shows, disengages. Each of these strategies makes sense in an appropriate situation, but only adaption and shaping are likely to lead to expanded intelligence.

---

[131] Dye, Green, & Bavelier, 2009.

[132] Sternberg, 2003b; Sternberg, Grigorenko, & Zhang, 2008.

I will now make some frankly speculative remarks about society and even civilizations.

Social environments vary in the extent to which they encourage the development of intelligence, because they vary in the extent to which they encourage engagement by adaption and shaping. A society that endorses the belief that intelligence is fixed inhibits the development of intelligence, because it encourages people to avoid challenging problems. Look at this rationally. If you encounter a problem that appears difficult, and if you believe that your own abilities are fixed, then the sensible thing to do is to select a new environment.

This is particularly the case if the costs of failure are high. And in the case of schoolchildren and adolescents, the cost of failure in front of the peer group is very high. A person who engages with intellectually challenging, and hence intelligence-developing, problems is going to make errors. The important thing is what happens next. There is an apocryphal saying that engineers analyze an accident in order to prevent the next one, while lawyers analyze an accident in order to find someone to blame. If we want people to develop intelligence, we have to encourage them to take an engineer's attitude, not a lawyer's.

Having established this attitude, society must provide the challenges. This is easy, providing that a society does not become fixed in a belief that the way it does things, now, is the only way to do them. This is a point where we can be optimistic about our society. The sociologist Carmi Schooler has pointed out that the rise in intelligence test scores across generations has been paralleled by a rise in the complexity of society.[133] Personal finance provides a good illustration of Schooler's point. It used to be that personal finance was simple for all but the very wealthy. If you had the money to buy something, you could; if you did not have the money, you could not. Today we have credit cards, adjustable rate mortgages, auto loans, student loans, and what have you. For most

of the citizenry cash is passé, and thinking about one's personal finances is challenging.

There are people who have argued that the same could be said of our much-condemned video games. Some of them contain elements of the techniques used to train visual-spatial reasoning, processing speed, and the working memory–attention complex![134]

A dynamic society challenges its members and, as it does so, redefines what it means to be intelligent. If a society is pervaded by a belief that the old ways are the best ways (or the only ways), both the development and the definition of intelligence are constrained. Since history does move on, the environmentally driven improvement in intelligence that we are seeing today has happened before, and probably in a more extensive way than could be documented by changes in performance on the intellectual puzzles we call "intelligence tests."

The present human species has been around for roughly 100,000 years. The last five thousand have seen the development of ideas that have profoundly changed human existence. These include the concept of agriculture, literacy, the use of formal laws to order social conduct, the development of mathematics and logic, and induction based on scientific reasoning. These ideas in turn made possible the spread of technologies that fostered further new ideas. Agriculture made economic specialization possible, which in turn led to urbanization, a need for formal laws, business transactions, surveying of land, and construction. Humanity was on the way toward literacy and mathematics.

People in technologically and intellectually demanding cultures respond to the challenge, and move toward the top of their reaction ranges – at least with respect to those aspects of cognition that their culture sees as important. The Sumerians were smarter than the nomads on the steppes, and the Roman soldiers who manned Hadrian's Wall were smarter than the Picts and Celts outside it.

---

[133] Schooler, 1998.

[134] See Greenfield, 1998, for some early examples, especially in the spatial-visual realm, and Dye, Green, & Bavelier, 2009, for more recent work.

Nobody, and no culture, thinks of everything. Charles Murray has coined the elegant term *metainvention* to describe ideas that have profound implications for society, such as logic and the rule of law.[135] He points out that virtually all metainventions have arisen along the Eurasian land mass, primarily in northern Europe, with a "recent" (since 1600 CE) rise in the Americas, following the European migrations to the New World. Why?

Galton and his colleagues in Victorian England would have said that this is because the northern Europeans are genetically superior, with respect to intelligence. There are scientists today who would agree with him, a topic that will be taken up in Chapter 11. The genetic hypothesis cannot be refuted on the basis of the geographic distribution of intellectual contributions. But there is an environmental explanation.

The ecologist Jared Diamond[136] has argued that great ideas and cultural innovations arise when societies meet, both to exchange and to challenge ideas. Diamond further believed that this psychological/sociological process interacted with geography. The East-West orientation of Eurasia permits migration, travel, and trade literally from the Atlantic to the Pacific. Such movements produce exchanges and development of ideas. The Americas and Africa are oriented North-South, so that ecological barriers such as the jungles of Panama and the Sahara Desert discourage travel along the major axes of the continents. A particularly telling example is in the New Guinea highlands, where Melanesian peoples developed agriculture independently of its appearance in the Middle East, but otherwise remained in the Neolithic Era. Diamond argues that this was not because of a genetic difference between Asians and Melanesians; it was because of the isolation of the New Guinea highlands.

Geographic isolation is not the only way to prevent the development of intelligence by engagement; social isolation works as well. The Chinese Empire in many ways failed to participate in the avalanche of ideas that started with the European Renaissance and the Age of Exploration. Why? At least in part because the conservative philosophy of Imperial China left the Chinese uninterested in other cultures.

At both levels, the society and the individual, intelligence increases when there is a combination of a challenge and a willingness to rise to it. Humans will never produce a society that makes intellectual demands beyond the human potential – by definition. How close individuals come to reaching their cognitive potential depends on how much thought their society demands from them.

9.8. Summary: What Produces the Cohort Effect?

Just as nonzero heritability coefficients show that genetic inheritance is an important determiner of intelligence, the rise in test scores throughout the twentieth century shows that environmental effects can be very powerful. These demonstrations, alone, do not tell us how genetic and environmental variables act upon intelligence. In Chapter 8 we saw that great progress has been made toward finding out which genes reduce human intelligence markedly, but that it has been much harder to find the genes that produce variation in the normal range.

Much the same can be said of the physical environment. We know that we should avoid poor nutrition, atmospheric lead, and other environmental hazards. Very little progress has been made toward identifying the positive aspects of the environment that further intellectual development, within the range of environments present in the industrially developed countries.

Schooling is clearly important. Over the course of the twentieth century the developed countries reached a goal of almost universal education. In addition to increasing the level of education of the average person, the developed societies made a huge effort to reduce the number of school drop-outs.

[135] Murray, 2003.
[136] Diamond, 1997.

This is almost certainly one reason that the cohort effect is largely driven by increases in the absolute level of test scores in the lower range of cognitive ability.

The effects of changes outside of formal schooling are harder to establish. While some very intense pre-school programs, such as the ABCDerian effort, have shown promising long-term results, projects of this intensity have affected only a few hundred students. This is not nearly enough to influence population-level IQ scores. More widespread programs, such as the American Head Start program, are probably not intensive enough to make permanent changes in cognitive capabilities.

Family sizes have dropped precipitously in the developed countries. Similar reductions in family size are now being seen worldwide. Even after allowance for parental intelligence is made, smaller families produce somewhat more intelligent children. However, these effects are too small to account entirely for the cohort effect.

Intelligence is statistically associated with a tendency to become intellectually engaged with challenging tasks. Although correlation does not mean causality, it is at least arguable that those people who engage in intellectually challenging activities improve their cognitive capacities – their intelligence in a far larger and more important sense than in the narrow sense of improving intelligence test scores. A plausible argument can also be made that throughout the twentieth century there was an increase in the cognitive complexity of the environment. People really were getting brighter, at least in the sense of greater acquisition of those cognitive skills evaluated by the tests.

Are these intelligent people benefitting from their capabilities? In the next chapter we consider what intelligence is worth in the post-industrial society.

CHAPTER 10

What Use Is Intelligence?

As of the end of the twentieth century, the United States is run by rules that are congenial to people with high IQ and that make life more difficult for everyone else.

Herrnstein & Murray, 1994, p. 541

The quotation from *The Bell Curve: Intelligence and Class Structure in American Life*, is a pretty strong statement about the importance of intelligence. When Herrnstein and Murray made it they were attacked as elitist and antidemocractic. Other people, with impeccable democratic credentials, had said similar things in a less contentious way. Just a few years before Herrnstein and Murray wrote, Robert Reich, a sociologist who had served as Secretary of Labor in the Clinton administration, wrote that work has shifted from emphasizing the manipulation of objects to the manipulation of abstract ideas, varying from programming a robot to analyzing a financial system.[1] It follows that skill in manipulating abstract concepts, intelligence, has become progressively more valuable over time. To what extent do cognitive tests predict such skill?

10.1. Problems in Investigating the Relationship between Intelligence and Success

This chapter examines the relation between intelligence and success in three broad regions; academics, the workplace, and personal life. These studies are not easy to do, for several reasons. First, we have to specify what we mean by success in each arena. Next, we have to select quantitative measures of success. Observable measures, such as grade point average or money earned, are frequently only partially satisfactory measures for our criteria. They often have undesirable statistical and measurement properties that hinder analysis and interpretation. Finally, there is the important problem of generality. We cannot study the totality of academia, the workplace, or, certainly, personal life. We have to study slices of them, where the necessary measures can be obtained. These slices are almost

---

1   Reich, 1991.

never random samples of the arenas, and in only a few cases can we obtain the ideal experimental group–control group contrast.

As is true in other areas of research on intelligence, we can learn something from imperfect studies. We just have to keep the imperfections in mind when we consider what has been learned. The rest of this section describes some of these imperfections. Do not lose sight of the magnificence of the forest because the trees have woodpecker holes in them! Quite a lot has been learned.

10.1.1. *The Conceptual Criterion Problem*

The biggest problem is defining success. In the academic arena a student is successful if he or she has learned. The commonest measure of academic success is a person's grade point average (GPA) across classes. However, grade point averages are not comparable across classes or institutions. A student with a GPA of 3.5 in English classes in a community college is not necessarily a better student than one with a GPA of 3.1 in Physics at Stanford. Merging gross measures of learning, such as GPA, across subjects or across schools introduces unwanted sources of variance. This will make the intelligence-GPA relation appear to be smaller than it is. But measuring the relation in one class or institution raises question about how the finding can be generalized.

An alternative measure of success is graduation or, in the K-12 system, its inverse, dropping out. Once again we have noncomparability across institutions; without naming names, not all our high schools, colleges, and universities are equivalent. Americans keep school records by district or state, not by a national register. If a student disappears from a K-12 system or fails to complete a postsecondary program, there is no record of where that student went. They may have dropped out, or they may have enrolled at another educational institution.

It is even harder to define success in the workplace. Within an industry or occupation income partially captures the idea of success, but incomes across occupations are hard to compare. Incomes are also often determined by variables unrelated to intelligence, such as seniority of employment. Some of our larger companies do keep records of periodic evaluations of employee performance, most commonly supervisors' ratings. Ratings are not reliable unless the raters are trained and the criteria for rating have been agreed upon. Objective measures of employee output are often hard to come by and generally capture only a part of a person's job. COSTCO, a giant warehouse sales company, tracks the number of check-outs per hour that each of their check-out clerks handles. It does not directly measure things like customers' reactions to a clerk's manner.

Defining success in life is even harder. We can measure extreme social adjustment, which can vary from achieving a civic prize to going to jail, but most people do neither. Success in life is a multifaceted thing. Informative studies have been conducted of the relation between intelligence and particular aspects of life success, such as health, but trying to relate intelligence, or virtually any other trait, to such a nebulous thing as "life success" is probably not a useful exercise.

Once we have defined our criteria we face the problem of actually getting the data. Several strategies have been followed. One is to conduct an experimental study, in which the investigator obtains measures of both intelligence and success from a selected set of participants. To take an example, one study related intelligence test scores to success as a race track gambler.[2] Such studies tend to be fairly small and to deal with unique situations. Because they are small, they can detect only large relationships. (Technically, they have *low statistical power*.) This brings us to a discussion of statistical issues.

10.1.2. *The Statistical Problems*

We measure the extent to which intelligence is related to some index of success by calculating *predictive validity*, which is defined as the correlation between a measure of

2 Ceci & Liker, 1986.

intelligence and the criterion measure. The process is sensitive to three statistical issues: reliability, range restriction, and generalization. In order to understand them we need a brief digression into statistical reasoning.

THE RELIABILITY ISSUE

Any measurement contains two elements, a "true value" and a residual term. While the residual term is frequently referred to as "error," it is not necessarily error in the sense of a mistake. It refers to the sum of all influences on the measured variable that are statistically independent of the true value. To take an example, consider the way in which weight is measured during the typical annual physical. Examinees are told to take off their shoes and stand on a scale. Measured weight is then shown on the scale. The measured weight has the following components:

Measured weight = actual body weight +
(weight of clothes + scale bias),

where *scale bias* refers to any tendency of the scale to weigh high or low. The terms in parentheses, here *weight of clothes* and *scale bias*, are residual effects, uncorrelated with the examinee's actual weight. If an examinee were to be weighed on a different scale, wearing different clothes, measured weight might change even though actual body weight remained the same. Measured weight is said to be *reliable* to the extent that the same measure is obtained across comparable conditions. This reasoning applies to intelligence testing.

An intelligence test score x is determined by the examinee's "real" intelligence and a residual term that is unique to the examination of that person at that time. Exactly the same thing can be said of an academic grade, y. The grade is determined in part by what the student really knows about, say, English Literature and in part by a residual term unique to the examination and the person. Symbolically,

$$x = x_t + e_x; \quad y = y_t + e_y, \qquad (10.1)$$

where the subscript t stands for "true" and e denotes the residual term. Now define the reliability of an intelligence test or a grade as the correlation between two measures, each assumed to be equally good, taken on the same person. Examples would be the correlation between two equivalent forms of the SAT, or the correlation between the grades assigned to the same set of English Literature examinations by two equally qualified graders.

What we can observe is the correlation between test scores and grades, r_{xy}. What we want to know is the correlation between intelligence and academic achievement, $r_{x_t y_t}$. This is

$$r_{x_t y_t} = \frac{r_{xy}}{\sqrt{r_{xx} r_{yy}}}. \qquad (10.2)$$

where r_{xx} and r_{yy} are the reliability correlations for the intelligence test, x, and the academic measure, y. The correlation $r_{x_t y_t}$ is sometimes referred to as the "true" correlation.

As reliability coefficients range between 0 and 1, the denominator, $\sqrt{r_{xx} r_{yy}}$, will also range between zero and one. Therefore, the correlation between the "true" variables, $r_{x_t y_t}$, will be at least as big, and generally larger, than the correlation between the observed variables, r_{xy}. Corrections for unreliability have to be treated with caution, as the reliabilities are themselves estimates, and if they are too low the estimated true correlation can exceed one, which is obviously not correct.

In both the academic and industrial cases the difference between the observed correlation and the (estimated) true correlation can be substantial. Professionally developed intelligence tests generally have reliabilities of .85 or above, but this is because of a great deal of careful item selection (Chapter 2). Large-scale academic achievement tests, such as those used in the United States to assess educational progress on a statewide basis,[3] have similar reliability

---

3 As of 2009 such tests were required by federal law – the No Child Left Behind Act.

coefficients. Within-class, teacher-assigned grades are quite another matter. I know of one case where thirty essays were graded, independently, by two university professors. The correlation between the two sets of grades was .3![4] Fortunately, this is an extreme. In most cases grades have reliabilities in the .6 to .8 range. This means that if a typical study of the relation between intelligence and grades within a class produces a value of r, that value should be multiplied by approximately 1.38 to estimate the true correlation between intelligence and academic achievement.[5] This substantial correction applies to studies of grades within a class. As the GPA is an average across classes, the reliability of the GPA is much higher than the reliability of a grade within a class, so the correction would be smaller.

Probably the most commonly used criterion for achievement in industrial settings is a supervisor's rating of performance. Unless these ratings are the result of carefully structured evaluations they are likely to have reliabilities in the .6 range or lower, considerably lower than the typical reliabilities of cognitive tests.

RESTRICTION OF RANGE

In most studies the variability of intelligence in the group actually studied will be smaller than the range in the population to which we wish to generalize. The problem of estimating intelligence-grade relations in elementary schools (K-5) illustrates the situation. Elementary schools generally draw students from the neighborhood immediately around them. In most industrially developed countries neighborhoods tend to have distinct socioeconomic and sometimes demographic characteristics. Therefore, the student demographics in a single elementary school will be more homogeneous than in the district or state. We say that the scores are subject to *range restriction*. In the case of the elementary schools, we would expect there to be less variability in a measure of intelligence within a school than across a state.

Range restriction influences the correlation coefficient. Let σ_s be the standard deviation of observed scores in the sample, and σ_p be the standard deviation in the population (in the school and in the district, in the elementary school illustration). The relation between the observed correlation in the sample, r_s, and the correlation to be estimated in the population, r_p, is

$$r_p = \frac{\frac{\sigma_p}{\sigma_s} r_s}{\sqrt{\left(\frac{\sigma_p}{\sigma_s}\right)^2 - 1\,)\, r_s + 1}}. \qquad (10.3)$$

In this equation r_p is greater than r_s if $\sigma_p > \sigma_s$. Note that this corrects only for attenuation on one of the two variables, either the intelligence variable or the criterion variable. Correction on both variables is also possible and often reasonable. For instance, suppose that a study were done in which we observed the correlation between intelligence test scores and scores on an achievement test in a school, and we wanted to estimate the correlation in the state. It would be appropriate to correct for range restriction on both the intelligence test and the achievement test.

Selection restriction is an important special case of range restriction. Selection restriction occurs whenever an applicant population takes a predictor test, here some sort of intelligence test, as part of application for a job or educational opportunity. All applicants above a given *cut score* are then accepted, and their performance on the job or in the school is recorded. For example, suppose a university uses an entrance examination, and admits the top 50% of the applicants. In order to validate the entrance examination, university officials would want to know if it was a good predictor of the grades that an applicant would obtain. However, grades are available only for the admitted students. Since, obviously, the top 50% of the applicants will have less variation in

---

4　The statement is based on personal observation.
5　This conclusion follows from the following argument. Assume that the reliability of the intelligence test is .88 and the reliability of the grade is .6. By application of equation 10.2, the observed correlation should be multiplied by $1/\sqrt{.528} = 1.38$.

examination scores than the entire group of applicants, the correlation between examination scores and grades in the applicant population can be estimated by computing the examination-grades correlation in the admitted group, and then correcting for range restriction.

Corrections for restriction in range can be substantial. A reasonable value for the hypothetical university example is $\sigma_s = .6\,\sigma_p$.[6] An observed correlation of .33 in the selected students would be corrected to .50 for the applicant population. As correlations are often squared and reinterpreted as representing "percentage of variance accounted for," this would change r_2 from 11% to 25%, a substantial change.

Because corrections for reliability and range restriction can be considerable, knowing when to use them is important. Here are some general rules.

1. Correction for reliability is appropriate when one's interest is in theoretical constructs underlying measures – for instance, whether intelligence as a concept is related to academic ability as a concept. The correction is not appropriate when one's interest is in whether one set of scores predicts the value of another set of scores – for instance, if you wanted to know whether the SAT predicts first-year college GPA.
2. Correction for selection restriction should be done whenever the purpose of the study is to determine the validity of a predictor, such as an entrance or hiring examination.
3. Correcting for range restriction is appropriate when the available observations are known to be a nonrandom sample in which scores are less variable than they are in the population. The case of using observations within a single school to estimate a population in the district is an example. However, in such cases

correcting for range restriction will be possible only if an estimate of the population standard deviation is available.

4. If the sample is a true random sample of the population, the correction for range restriction should *not* be used.
5. Any correction for range restriction carries with it the assumption that the same (linear) relation holds between scores in the sample and in the population. This is not a trivial assumption. To take one example, there is evidence that the relation between IQ test scores and adult age is nonlinear. Scores decline more sharply with age beyond sixty than before. Therefore, it would not be appropriate to apply range restriction to estimate the age-IQ relation in adults from a sample of adults age sixty and older.

Rule 5 leads to a discussion of our last statistical issue, power.

Statistical power. To explain these issues, we need a bit of notation and a review of introductory statistics.

By tradition, scientific results are said to be "statistically significant" if they would be obtained by chance only in fewer than 1 out of 20 studies ($p < .05$) or fewer than 1 out of 100 studies ($p < .01$), on the assumption that the variables being studied in a sample are actually unrelated in the population (the "null hypothesis"). In research on intelligence, "unrelated" means that in the population there is no correlation between the predictor (an intelligence test score) and the criterion, $r_p = 0$. However, r_p cannot be observed directly. Instead it is estimated by an observed correlation, r_s, in a sample of N observations.

Assuming that the sample can be regarded as being chosen randomly from the population, there will be some critical value of the observed correlation, r^*, such that if the observed correlation, r_s, exceeds that value ($r_s > r^*$) we reject the null hypothesis that $r_p = 0$ at some level, p, where p refers to the probability of observing $r_s > r^*$ if the null hypothesis is true. The value of r^* increases if we lower the significance level (typically

---

6 In the case of selection restriction the percentage of applicants accepted determines the relationship between the variances in the sample and the population. In other cases of range restriction this has to be estimated.

from $p = .05$ to $p = .01$) and decreases as the size of the sample, N, increases. To take some examples, at the $p < .05$ level the critical value, r^*, is .36 for a study with 30 observations ($N = 30$), and .20 for a study with $N = 100$. At the $p < .01$ level the values are .46 and .26.

This much is taught in elementary statistics. The second point is taught but often not stressed. Suppose that the sample correlation is less than the critical value, $r_s < r^*$. This means that we cannot *reject* the null hypothesis. "Not rejecting" is not the same as accepting. What we have is what, in law, would be called a verdict of "not proven."[7]

Suppose that the population correlation is some value other than zero. (For simplicity, consider only positive values.) There would still be some probability that the sample correlation fell below the critical value – that we observe $r_s < r^*$ even though $r_p > 0$. This probability depends upon what the population value is, so the probability has to be specified given a population value and the size of the study, $Pr(r_s < r^* | r_p = k, N)$. The *power* of a study is the complement of this,

$$Power(r_p = k, N)$$
$$= Pr(r_s \geq r^* | r_p = k, N). \qquad (10.4)$$

In words, this is the probability that a sample of size N, drawn from a population in which the population correlation has value k, will have a sample correlation above the critical value. Going back to the earlier example, suppose that the population correlation is .50. If we set the significance level at $p < .05$, the power of a study with a sample size of 25 is .84. This means that 16 out of 100 samples will *not* reach a value reliably greater than zero even though the population correlation is a substantial .50.

Power increases with sample size. In the example just given, if the sample is increased to 100, the power is greater than .995.

The power problem becomes critical when it is combined with the problem of

criterion reliability. Grades within a class and employer rating systems will often have a reliability of around .60, and intelligence tests will have a reliability of about .85. Suppose that the true correlation between intelligence and academic ability, the hypothetical variables underlying these measures, is .50 in the population. A bit of algebraic manipulation of equation 10.3 will show that the expected population correlation between test scores and grades is .26 after correction for attenuation. Setting the significance level at .05, the power of a study with 25 is participants is approximately .36.[8] About two out of three studies of this size would *not* provide strong enough evidence to reject the null hypothesis that $r_p = 0$, even though it is false. If the sample size were to be increased to 100, power would increase to about .75. In this case failure to reach statistical significance would be reasonable evidence against the hypothesis that a "true score" value of r_p was .50 or larger.

What these examples show is that power is produced by an interaction between the reliability of the measures and the size of the study. This interaction has to be taken into account in evaluating null results. Do people actually fail to do this? The answer is, stunningly, "yes." Panel 10.1 presents the case of a widely cited study in which no consideration was given to these issues.

10.1.3. *Drawing Conclusions in the Face of Statistical Uncertainties*

Given all these problems, can any conclusions at all be drawn? The answer is "yes," but only after careful consideration.

When evaluating empirical results we have to consider which statistic is appropriate. Are we interested in the observed correlation, or should the correlation be corrected for reliability and/or restriction in range? The rules given in the previous section apply.

We must be aware of power considerations. We need to be especially wary of

---

7 Such verdicts are not allowed in US courts, but they are allowed in some countries.

8 Power estimates are based on Table 3.3.2 in Cohen, 1988.

Panel 10.1. A Day at the Races: A Failure to Consider Power and Reliability

In 1986 two Cornell University psychologists, Stephen Ceci and J. K. Liker, published an eye-catching article entitled "A Day at the Races."[*] They reported a four-year study of the expertise of a group of thirty habitual bettors on harness racing. Ceci and Liker did not study the accuracy with which these bettors predicted winners because, as they said and as many horse racing fans know, the winners are often determined by unpredictable events. Instead they studied the accuracy with which the bettors were able to predict the favorite and top three favorites at post time (the start of the race), given the extensive information about each horse that was contained in the daily racing form, which is available to bettors prior to a race. Although secondary references often misinterpret this, what Ceci and Liker actually studied was their participants' ability to predict how other bettors would place their bets, not which horse would win.

Ceci and Liker found that the participants' decision was a mathematically complex function of the information contained on the racing form, and that the accuracy of the predictions had a correlation of $-.03$, essentially zero, with the participants' IQs scores on the short form of the WAIS.[†] Ceci and Liker drew the following strong conclusion:

(a) IQ is unrelated to performance at the racetrack but, more important (b) IQ is unrelated to real-world forms of cognitive complexity.

> *Ceci & Liker, 1986, p. 255*

These are strong words indeed. The null finding was claimed to be reliable, and the task, something that is related to but not the same as picking the winners in a race, was unhesitatingly generalized to the universe of complex tasks. Nowhere in the article was there any mention of reliability or power.

Douglas Detterman and his colleague Kathleen Spry wrote a detailed critique of the Ceci and Liker study.[‡] Among other things, they observed that Ceci and Liker's criterion, the ability to predict the odds at post time, had a reliability of at most .41. What does this mean? Suppose that the correlation between the underlying abilities, intelligence and skill at setting the odds, is 1. In terms of the text, $r_p = 1$. The reliability of the short form of the WAIS is known to be .85. Therefore, the expected value of the correlation in the sample would be $.85 \times .41 = .35$. If $N = 30$, the power of the Ceci and Liker study would be approximately .5, which means that a study like theirs should fail to reach the convention .05 level of statistical significance five out of ten times even if the underlying correlation was one.

Of course, nobody thinks that the correlation between intelligence and race track betting is identically one. Based on meta-analysis, a widely quoted estimate of the correlation between intelligence and performance on a cognitively complex task is $r_p = .5$.[§] To be generous, increase this to .6. Then, solely on the basis of reliability, the expected sample correlation would be $r_s = .21$. Using this estimation the power of the Ceci and Liker study was .20; studies like theirs should fail to reach the .05 level of significance four out of five times.

The Ceci and Liker study presents us with good news and bad news. The good news is that when a published study contains major flaws, other scientists point out the errors. The bad news is that almost no one notices the correction. The Ceci and Liker study has been cited ninety times, as evidence that intelligence, as measured by the IQ tests, is not related to real-world cognition. The Detterman and Spry study has been cited seven times.[**]

---

[*] Ceci & Liker, 1986.

[†] This figure is a correction to the original value, provided in Ceci & Liker, 1987.

[‡] Detterman & Spry, 1988. This much-neglected article contains several other strong criticisms of the Ceci and Liker work.

[§] Schmidt & Hunter, 1998.

[**] Data collected from an ISI Web of Knowledge citation search, July 2, 2009.

concluding that there is no relation between intelligence and some other variable when the study involved is small or uses a measure of unproven reliability.

One way to address the power issue is to do studies with a very large number of participants. The extreme case is to utilize large surveys, such as the Department of Labor longitudinal studies of US citizens described in panel 9.9. Sometimes surveys are "constructed" by analyzing records of intelligence, health, educational accomplishment, and occupational status that have been collected for other purposes.

Obviously, though, the larger the study and the more time required of the participants, the more costly the experiment or survey. In many cases the investigator has to accept less-than-ideal measures, such as using a brief vocabulary test as a proxy for a measurement of intelligence, or using place of residence as the sole measure of a participant's socioeconomic status. Such compromises are not fatal errors; they are things that have to be considered when evaluating results.

Another way to address the power problem is to use a statistical technique called *meta-analysis* to draw conclusions from multiple studies.[9] Special statistical methods are used to identify trends that may not be clear from focusing on the details of any one study. This technique can be quite revealing. However, there are reservations.

As is the case for any statistical technique, generalizations based upon any unjustifiable assumptions of random sampling are suspect. For example, many studies have been conducted of the relation between scores on college entrance examinations and student grades. Meta-analysis can, and has, been applied to these studies. The participating institutions tend to be the larger institutions, with budgets sufficient to support internal research organizations. Therefore, the result of a meta-analysis of such studies is a useful descriptive statement, but any appeal based upon a claim of random selection of institutions is questionable.

The individual studies reviewed in a meta-analysis will, inevitably, vary in the quality of the measurements taken and the procedures used. These considerations are judgments that have to be made by considering the details of each study. They do not lend themselves to statistical treatment. All reviewers will agree, for instance, on the number of participants in a study, and the effect this has on statistical power. They may not agree on the appropriateness of the measures used, or the way in which the measures were taken. Some meta-analyses have attempted to deal with this problem by classifying studies by their perceived quality, and then analyzing high- and low-quality studies separately, to see if this makes any difference. A finding that only appeared in low quality studies would certainly be treated with suspicion.

10.1.4. *Problems Related to Research Design*

The final problems to be considered have to do with research design, rather than statistics and measurement.

The ideal research design is a *prospective* study, in which the investigator obtains data on the intelligence of people at some point in their lives, ideally before they enter an academic program or the workforce, and then determines how well they succeed. This is by far the easiest kind of study to interpret. However, it is possible only if the investigator has some way of testing a large number of people, and then following them for a reasonably long period. There are a few studies that have done this. The Seattle Longitudinal Study[10] (panel 9.2) and the National Longitudinal Studies (panel 9.9) are important examples. However, such studies are expensive, and so are few and far between.

Prospective studies can sometimes be conducted by examination of government records. Studies of this sort have been carried out in those European countries in which eighteen- to twenty-year-old men have to register and be tested for potential

9 Hunter & Schmidt, 1990.

10 Schaie, 2005.

military enlistment. (As far as I know, Israel is the only country that requires registration for both men and women.) Valuable information can be gained if some of the registrants can be reinterviewed later in life, to determine how well they have fared. In some countries this can be done without actually interviewing the individuals, because the government keeps extensive records of the health, education, and income of its citizens. Legal and ethical issues concerning access to such data have to be resolved, but the important point is that the studies often can be done.

The alternative to a prospective study of the relation between intelligence and success is a *retrospective* study. In a retrospective study a group of people are identified who have, or do not have, varying degrees of social success. The investigator then attempts to determine their intelligence, either by direct testing or by examination of relevant records. Studies of eminence or genius often fall into this category. The investigator identifies a group of individuals who meet some criterion for accomplishment and then tries to identify the common characteristics of the group. Possibly one of the most ambitious of these studies was Simonton's determination of the correlation between a measure of intellectual capacity, reconstructed from historical records, and historians' ratings of the performance of the forty-two US presidents, from George Washington through George Bush.[11] The correlation was .56.

Studies of the relation between intelligence and success are prone to collinearity problems. To illustrate, intelligence test scores during adolescence are positively correlated with subsequent income.[12] Does this mean that high intelligence causes a rise in income? Perhaps. But it is also true that children's test scores are positively correlated with parental socioeconomic status, although the correlation ($\sim$.40) is not as high as many people assume. Is current income due to intelligence, or is it a legacy of the privilege of having come from a wealthy (or poor) background, with concomitant opportunities (or lack of opportunities) to get a foothold on the economic ladder? Or both?

10.2. The Relation between Intelligence and Academic Achievement

Binet's motivation for constructing the original intelligence test was to identify children who were at risk for failing in the standard academic system. Subsequent test developers generalized the goal to predicting degrees of success at all levels of education. How well has this worked?

10.2.1. *Intelligence in the K-12 System*

In 1972 the American clinical psychologist Joseph Matarazzo reviewed the evidence, and concluded that IQ, as measured by the Wechsler tests, was a good predictor of high school graduation.[13] In 1994 Herrnstein and Murray addressed the same question using the AFQT and the NLSY79 data. Figure 10.1 shows their results for graduation rates in the 1980–85 period. The finding is clearly robust. Different tests were used at different times, and with different definitions of "failure to graduate." Nevertheless, both studies found the same positive relation between test scores and probability of graduation.

Matarazzo also said that, based on "thousands" of studies, it had been shown that intelligence test scores correlate .50 with grades in the K-12 system.[14] This estimate has been widely accepted by subsequent reviewers.[15] Later reviewers do qualify the estimate, by saying that the correlations tend to be higher in elementary than in middle school, and drop to perhaps .40 in high school. As psychological studies are notorious for failures to replicate findings, the agreement among reviewers, over a considerable time span, is reassuring.

11 Simonton, 2006.
12 Herrnstein and Murray, 1994.
13 Matarazzo, 1972.
14 Matarazzo, 1972, p. 283.
15 Brody, 1992, pp. 251–254; Jensen, 1998; Macintosh, 1998, Chapter 2; Neisser et al., 1996.

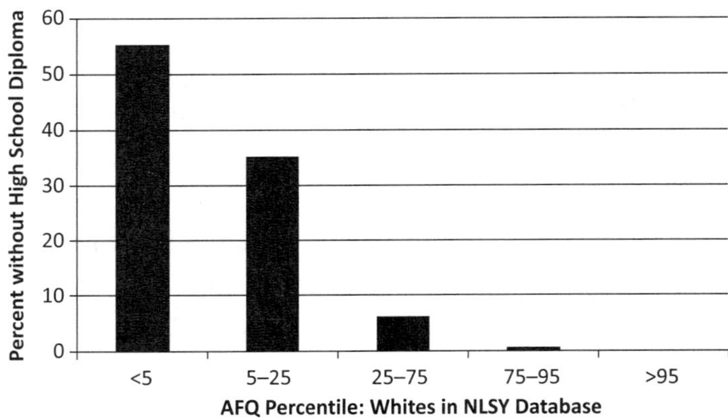

Figure 10.1. Percentage of White young adults in the NLSY79 survey who did not complete high school, plotted as a function of their percentile scores on the AFQT. Data from Herrnstein & Murray, 1994.

The .50 figure applies to measures of grades computed across classes, elementary, middle, or high school GPA. If the correlation is calculated for scores within a single class, it will drop due to range restriction and, often, due to the lowered reliability of locally produced tests. A study by researchers at the University of Pennsylvania found a correlation of just slightly over .30 between Otis-Lennon test scores (see Chapter 2) and academic achievement on tests at the end of the eighth grade.[16] This study was done in a "magnet" high school where the students had already been selected on the basis of test scores and previous grades, so range restriction was certainly a factor. Other studies confined to a single school or class have found correlations of about .5 between test scores and grade point averages in the early primary grades and in high school.[17]

Macintosh[18] has observed that although restriction of range is frequently appealed to as a mechanism that should reduce test-achievement correlations, the effect has never actually been observed, at least in studies of the K-12 system. Two large European studies come close to addressing Macintosh's concern.

The English system of education is much more centralized than the American. One year something over 78,000 students were given the Cognitive Abilities Test (CAT, described in Chapter 2). The test takers included almost all the eleven-year-olds in England, so range restriction is not relevant. At age sixteen all English students take nationwide examinations in a variety of subjects. The national examinations are subject to much more careful psychometric evaluation than is typically the case for locally generated (and certainly for teacher-generated) examinations, so reliability of the criterion variable was not a major concern.

Ian Deary and his colleagues[19] extracted a general intelligence (g) factor from the CAT scores and a general academic achievement factor, which I will call a, from the scholastic examination scores. The correlation between the two was $r_{ga} = .81$. This is a very high value. There was substantial variation between associations with the g factor and educational accomplishment within topics. Correlations ranged from a high of .77 for mathematics to .43 for Art and Design. In general, the topics usually considered the academic core courses – the Humanities, Mathematics, and the Sciences – had correlations in the .50–.75 range, while "practical" topics, such as Art and

16 Duckworth & Seligman, 2005.
17 Kaplan, 1996; Zwick & Green, 2007.
18 Macintosh, 1998.

19 Deary, Strand, et al., 2007.

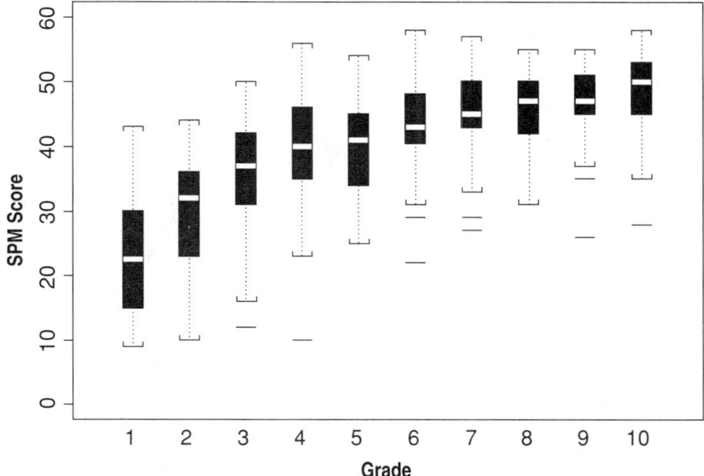

Figure 10.2. The distribution of RSPM scores across grades in a representative sample of 500 Icelandic schoolchildren. From Pind, Gunnarsdóttir, & Jóhannesson, 2003, Figure 1, with permission from Elsevier.

Design, Music, and Textiles, had correlations in the .4–.5 range. This very large study provides strong evidence for a robust relationship between intelligence, as assessed by a standard test, and general academic achievement.

Correlations between battery-type tests and academic achievement can be criticized on the grounds that some of the subtests in a test battery are close to a sample of academic tasks, so what we are measuring is the stability of academic aptitude, rather than a more general factor of intelligence. This interpretation cannot explain the fact that results somewhat similar to those in the English study have been obtained in Iceland, using Raven's Standard Progressive Matrices (RSPM), which is certainly not tied to the K-12 curriculum.[20] As was the case for the English study, this study used a very large sample, representative of the population of schoolchildren in Iceland. Figure 10.2 shows the results. Scores rise over the school-age years, agreeing with our intuition that children increase in their cognitive competence as they grow older. The RSPM scores within class levels were correlated with grades. At the seventh-grade level

the correlations were .75 for overall mathematics grades and .64 for overall Icelandic (language arts) grades.

The British and Icelandic studies agree with each other well, even though the particular tests of intelligence used were quite different. They answer Macintosh's legitimate concern. Range restriction effects do operate in small, localized studies, and therefore corrections for range restriction are appropriate. The correlation between intelligence test scores and academic achievement in the K-12 system, calculated across large units, such as districts, is at least .50 for the core academic courses, such as language arts, science, and mathematics, and somewhat lower for courses in vocational topics and in the arts. Within smaller units, such as a school or a class, the correlation will drop to around .30, due to restriction of range.

In the K-12 system cognitive test scores are used to identify students whose low scores indicate that they may need to be assigned to special education classes. Tests are also used to assign students to accelerated programs for the gifted. In both cases other factors are also considered. The majority of students fall somewhere between these extremes, and for them the test scores do not matter, for no

20 Pind, Gunnarsdottir, & Johanesson, 2003.

Table 10.1. Correlations between tests used for college/university selection, the ASVAB general factor or AFQT, and Raven's Advanced Progressive Matrices

Test	SAT	ACT	ASVAB
ACT	.87 (1)		
ASVAB	.87 (3), .92 (1)	.77 (4), .90 (1)	
Raven's Advanced Progressive Matrices	.71 (2)	.61 (3)	***

Source: Data sources are (1) Coyle & Pillow, 2008 (NLSY97 data); (2) Frey & Detterman, 2004; (3) Koenig, Frey, & Detterman, 2008.

decisions are made on the basis of these scores. In college and university entrance decisions test scores matter, a lot, across the entire range of scores.

10.2.2. *Intelligence in the Post-Secondary System*

Since World War II American colleges and universities have incorporated two major testing programs, the SAT and the American College Testing Program (ACT), into the admissions process. These tests are validated regularly, by correlating test scores with first-year grade point average (GPA1), cumulative grade point average (GPAC), or probability of graduation within a specified period of time after matriculation, usually four to six years. The use of the tests is not without controversies, a point that was made earlier (section 2.7.3). We concentrate on technical rather than policy issues here.

Recall, from the discussion in Chapter 2, that the first portion of the current SAT, referred to officially as the SAT-I, contains sections stressing verbal comprehension and logical reasoning. By tradition (and officially, in earlier versions), these two sections have been referred to as the SAT-V and SAT-M. I will continue this usage. Both tests represent attempts to evaluate comprehension and reasoning without tying questions to specific high school curricula.

The American College Testing program takes a different approach. It develops tests that are specifically tied to curricular material, such as history and mathematics. The idea is to predict what a student will learn in college by determining how much he or she has learned in high school. The second part of the SAT program, the SAT-II, does the same thing.

Although there have been arguments about which approach is better,[21] the tests could be interchanged in an academic selection program without changing acceptance and rejection decisions very much. Table 10.1 presents estimates of the correlations between the SAT, ACT (summary score), and the general factor derived from the ASVAB, which is closely approximated by the Armed Forces Qualifying Test (AFQT). The correlations with Raven's Advanced Progressive Matrices are also included, in order to show the relation between the educational tests and an avowed marker for general intelligence, *g*.

The correlations are quite high. The correlation between the SAT and the ACT approaches the reliabilities of the two tests. This suggests that the true correlation between the two tests is one! A study using NLSY97 data found that both academic aptitude tests had loadings of about .9 on a general factor derived from the ASVAB.[22] The finding is important because the ASVAB general factor is a measure of crystallized intelligence (Gc), rather than of Gf.[23]

The need to distinguish between Gf and Gc in college students is shown by the fact that the correlations between matrix tests and the SAT and the ACT are in the .6–.7 range.[24] This is about what one would

21 Lemann (1999) discusses the dispute in some detail. It has been carried forward to this day.
22 Coyle & Pillow, 2008.
23 Roberts et al., 2000.
24 Frey & Detterman, 2004; Koenig, Fry, & Detterman, 2008.

expect, because the fact that Gc and Gf are themselves correlated in the .5–.7 range, depending upon the sample. Because aspiring and attending college students represent roughly the upper two-thirds of the general population, in terms of cognitive skills, one expects the general factor to be somewhat weaker among this group than among the population at large. (See Chapter 3 for elaboration.)

Do the tests work? Several appropriately designed large studies of the SAT have produced consistent results. The correlation between SAT scores and GPA1 is approximately .35 in students who have been admitted, and who therefore have both SAT and GPA1's available.[25] This is the uncorrected correlation in the selected population, whereas what is needed is predictive correlation in the applicant population. An extensive study by Paul Sackett and his colleagues at the University of Minnesota, in which they conducted a meta-analysis of previous studies, shows quite clearly what the situation is.

Sackett and his colleagues analyzed data provided by the College Board for 41 colleges and universities where the SAT was used in 1995–97. Over 155,000 test takers were involved. The researchers calculated three SAT-grade correlations. They were:

1. r_s – the correlation between SAT and GPA1 in admitted students, calculated within institutions and then averaged. $r_s = .35$.
2. r_{p1} – r_s corrected for restriction of range within the applicant population for each institution, and then averaged. This is the predictive correlation that would be of interest to admission officers. $r_{p1} = .47$.
3. r_{p2} – r_s corrected for restriction of range of SAT scores across all institutions. This can be thought of as the predictive correlation to be used to determine the benefit of using the test across all participating institutions. $r_{p2} = .53$.

Freshman grade point averages indicate a student's initial reaction to college. What about predicting later performance or graduation? Beyond the first year there is great variation in the courses college students take, and there are also substantial differences in grading practices across disciplines. This muddies the situation.

There is a negative correlation between the SATs of students within an academic program and the mean grade point assigned by that program. This is because mathematics and science programs, which assign relatively low grades, tend to draw the students with the highest SATs, while humanities and education programs, which assign high grades, draw students with lower SATs. The effect is quite large. A study involving over 200,000 students from 38 public universities during the 1990s[26] found that the difference in SAT scores between the discipline with the highest entering scores, engineering, and the one with the lowest scores, education, was .92 standard deviation units.[27] The negative correlation between the rigorousness of grading within a discipline and the SATs of the entering students will reduce the correlation between overall GPAs and entering SATs, calculated over the institution as a whole.

The probability of graduation behaves much like, but not exactly like, GPA1. Herrnstein and Murray's analysis of the NLSY79 database showed that, as of the 1980s, approximately 70% of the survey participants in the top decile of AFQT scores obtained bachelor's degrees. This fell to 30% in the eighth decile, and to 10% in the fifth decile.[28] A detailed report from the College Board[29] found that graduation

25 Geiser & Studley, 2002; Kobrin et al., 2008; Sackett et al., 2009.

26 Kroc et al., 1997.

27 This is a conservative estimate, based on the assumption that the within-discipline standard deviation is equal to the population standard deviations. The assumption is very unlikely to be valid. The effect of interdisciplinary variation would be to reduce the variance (and hence the standard deviation) within disciplines. The upshot would be that *less than* 18% of the entering education students would be expected to have SAT scores above the engineering mean.

28 Herrnstein & Murray, 1994, p. 37.

29 Kroc et al., 1997.

rates are nonlinearly (logistic) related to an index composed of SAT, High School Grade Point Average (HSGPA), and several demographic variables, including gender and race. People with relatively low scores on the index generally were unlikely to graduate; people with high scores were highly likely to graduate; and the probability of graduation changed markedly between "low average" and "high average" scores.

As was the case for the K-12 system, the findings on the correlation between test scores and college/university success are strikingly consistent. The SAT, the most widely used test, has a predictive validity of about .5. This is probably an underestimate of the correlation between the SAT and an abstract measure of academic ability. Because students with high SAT scores are more likely to enroll in "tough-grading" courses than students with low SATs the SAT-GPA1 correlations will be depressed below what they would have been if all students took the same courses.

Are these correlations really enough to justify test use? Answering that question requires a brief discussion of the statistics of personnel selection.

10.2.3. *Cognitive Tests and Selection Decisions*

The college/university admissions process is an example of a personnel selection decision. How useful are entrance examinations, such as the SAT, in making such decisions? This raises the question of how high a correlation has to be in order to be useful in practice, whether or not it is "statistically significant." This depends upon how the correlation is to be used.

A widely cited way of evaluating the size of a correlation is to square it, and then to report it as the proportion of variance accounted for in either variable by predictions using the other variable. In the admissions case, r_{p1}^2 would be the proportion of variance in grades that could be associated with variance in an admissions test – approximately $.5^2 = .25$. Multiplied by 100, one

could say that 25% of the variance in grades is accounted for by variance in the examination. If, as is often (and erroneously) done, this logic is applied to the uncorrected correlation between grades and test scores, in the population of admitted students, $.35^2 = .11$, so 11% of the variance of grades is associated with variance in test scores – which does not seem high. However, that is misleading.

If the selector uses a screening examination, it is possible to predict aptitude (grades or workplace performance) and accept people in order of predicted performance. Unless prediction is perfect (predictive validity = 1) people with the same predicted performance usually turn out to have different actual performances. Students with identical SATs do not all have identical grades. In statistical terms, there is variance around the predicted performance level, and the greater the variance, the less accurate the prediction. However, variance around the predicted performance can never be greater than the variance in the applicant population. So variance in the *applicant* population can be used to scale the extent to which the prediction is *not* accurate. The ratio I = (variance around predicted value of aptitude)/(variance of aptitude in applicant population) represents an "inaccuracy" index, relative to the inaccuracy that would be achieved without using a selection examination. It follows that the complement of I, $1 - I$, is an index of accuracy. It can be interpreted as the relative reduction in inaccuracy achieved by using a predictor test. The I index is related to predictive validity, as defined in section 10.1, by the equation

$$r_{\mathrm{p}}^2 = 1 - I \qquad (10.5)$$

where $p = 1$ or 2, depending upon whether you are interested in within-institution or across-institution predictivity. Multiplied by 100, r_{p}^2 is the percent increase in efficiency achieved by using a screening examination. If, as is the case, $r_p = .5$, the increase in efficiency is 25%.

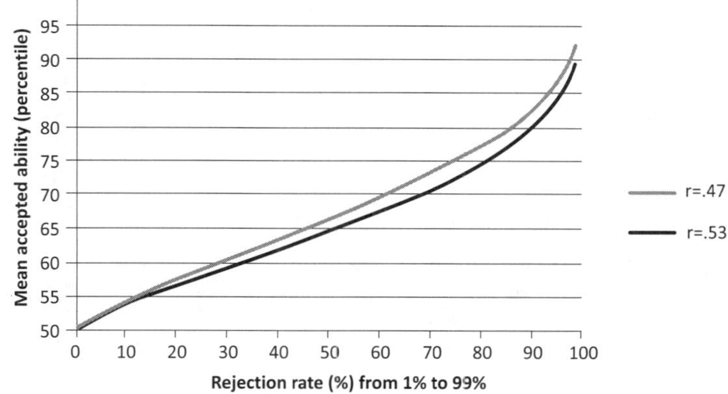

Figure 10.3. Test accuracy and rejection rate interact to produce quality acceptances. The expected value of aptitude for an accepted candidate (student or worker), measured in terms of the percentile of aptitude in the applicant population and shown as a function of the rejection rate and the predictive validity of a screening examination.

At this point we can see an argument brewing between the admissions committee and the rejected applicants. Suppose an applicant is rejected, and then learns that among accepted applicants (students) the correlation between SAT and grades is only .35. How dare the committee reject an applicant on the basis of a test that is only 11% better than chance?

The committee's first reply can be that the correlation is not really .35; it is .5. The applicant's rejoinder is that a 25% improvement over chance still is not good enough. But this is not the admissions committee's real argument.

The admissions committee is not interested in the accuracy of individual predictions; it is interested in selecting the best possible entering class. Suppose that the institution has room for only 10% of its applicants (a rejection rate of 90%). Insofar as is possible, the committee wants to select the top 10% of the applicants in terms of academic aptitude. However, the committee knows only the top 10% of the test scorers. If $r_p = 1$, the two "top ten percents" will be the same people; to the extent that r_p is less than 1, there will be some disagreement.

The success of the selection process will be determined by both the accuracy of the test, r_p, and the rejection rate. If the rejection rate is zero, everyone who wants to enter gets to enter. The accuracy of the test does not matter, because no decision is going to be made using the test score. At the other extreme, suppose there is just room for one person. The person accepted will be the one with the highest test score, and the probability of that person being the person with the highest aptitude in the applicant pool will depend upon the accuracy of the test.

Between these two extremes, the expected quality of accepted applicants is determined by an interaction between r_p and the rejection rate. The form of this interaction is shown in Figure 10.3, using Sackett's two estimates of the predictive correlation as examples. If the rejection rate is low, the value of the predictive correlation matters very little. If the rejection rate is high, it matters a lot. For example, if the rejection rate is 90%, as it is for some of our elite universities, the use of an entrance examination with a predictive correlation of .47 can improve the mean level of aptitude in the entering class from the fiftieth percentile of the aptitude in the applicant population (no test used) to about the seventy-seventh percentile.

Exactly the same reasoning applies to industrial hiring. If the rejection rate is high, a screening examination with predictive validity in the .4–.5 range can substantially

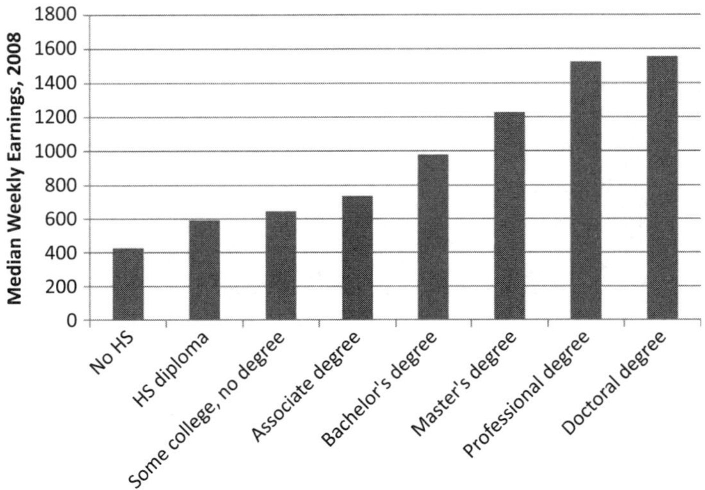

Figure 10.4. Median weekly earnings in 2008 as a function of level of education. *Source:* US Bureau of Labor Statistics. HS – high school diploma.

improve the selection process, as seen by the employer.

Note that quality has been defined in terms of the quality available in the applicant population. Personnel selection has to operate with this constraint; you cannot select people who do not apply. Any recruitment technique that improves or diminishes the distribution of aptitudes in the applicant population will affect the quality of the selected applicants – either the student body or the workforce. What this effect will be will depend upon the amount of change in applicant aptitude and upon the effect of added or reduced recruitment upon the rejection rate.

10.2.4. *Alternatives and Augmentations to the Use of Test Scores in College Entrance Decisions*

Chapter 9, section 5, contained a century-old quotation from Theodore Roosevelt about the economic value of education. Figure 10.4 shows income figures, as of 2008, as a function of level of education completed. Roosevelt's remark rings true. How we decide who gets to go to college makes a tremendous difference in who has economic and social opportunity. Therefore, it is understandable that college entrance

examinations such as the SAT and the ACT have received considerable scrutiny.

SAT scores are positively correlated with parental SES. This has led some to fear that using the SAT simply identifies applicants who have the social and financial resources to complete the undergraduate program. Giving these applicants preference in college admission will therefore exacerbate inherited social advantages, something that is generally not considered a good thing in a democracy. (Paradoxically, the SAT was originally designed to reduce these advantages! See the discussion of the SAT in Chapter 2.)

To what extent is this concern warranted? The way to investigate the question is to examine the partial correlation between grades and test scores, equating for SES. If the SAT is a proxy for SES, the partial correlation should approach zero. However, it does not. An analysis of the forty-one-institution data collected by the College Board found that the partial correlation, based on an analysis of over 155,000 students, is .44 – very little different from the predictive correlation without considering SES, .47. The analysis can be reversed, to see if SES is associated with first-year grades, after equating for test scores. When this is done the correlation between SES and

GPA1 drops from .31 to .05. Similar results were found in the meta-analysis of previous studies.[30]

These values are consistent with the assumption that parental SES does influence undergraduate performance, but that it does so as a distal variable. SES exerts its influence by influencing traits that are important for success as an undergraduate and that are measured by the SAT. Presumably these traits are what we mean by intelligence.

High school grade point average (HSGPA) has also been used as a predictor of GPA1 and college graduation. A study conducted in the University of California system found that, averaged over the incoming freshman classes of 1996–99, the SAT-I could predict 13% of the variance in GPA1 ($r = .36$), HSGPA could predict 15.4% ($r = .39$), and the two of them together could predict 20.8% of the variance ($R = .46$).[31] These correlations, which are consistent with the data from the forty-one-institution study, have not been corrected for range restriction. As far as accuracy of prediction is concerned, the appropriate thing to do is to combine the entrance examination and HSGPA into a single index.

As is true of all cognitive tests, the SAT has been designed to measure "can do" aspects of cognition. Cumulative indices of performance, such as HSGPA and GPA1, also tap "will do" aspects of performance, such as study habits and perseverance. We have seen this already for HSGPA; the same thing is true for GPA1.[32] The fact that HSGPA and the SAT, combined, do better than either alone is further support for an expanded definition of intelligence, to include skill in allocation of effort over the long haul, outside of the conventional testing paradigm.

We have been concerned here solely with the relation between intelligence and cognitive performance after matriculation. We need to remember that this is a limited view of only one aspect of the admissions decision. Admissions policy makers also consider other ways in which prospective students may contribute to the university. These vary from maintaining family ties to an institution (the "legacies" that produce endowments on which some universities rely) to a student's athletic abilities. Policy makers are also influenced by a desire to balance male-female ratios and to promote racial and ethnic diversity in the student body. Considering the appropriate role of these goals in student admissions would take us far beyond a discussion of the value of intelligence in education.

10.2.5. *Post-Graduate Education*

In 1837 a twenty-three-year-old named Edward Cree received a license to practice as an apothecary from the University of Edinburgh. Having a desire to go to sea, he was appointed a Surgeon in the Royal Navy. Ten years later he took some time off from the Navy to complete his M.D.[33] The same sort of thing happened in the United States. The *Greenfield Village* "living museum," part of the Henry Ford Museum, contains an account of a mid-nineteenth-century physician who "studied medicine awhile" at the University of Michigan and Case-Western Reserve University, decided he had learned all about medicine that he needed to know, and set up his practice on the northwestern frontier.

Today we are a bit more formal. We demand completion of programs for entry into many professions. No credit is given for attendance. The rewards for completion can be considerable. Just as there is a 50% increase in income for going from the High School degree to the Bachelor's, there is another 50% by going from the Bachelor's to the Doctorate (Figure 10.4).

A variety of cognitive tests are used as screening examinations for post-graduate educational programs. It is difficult to say anything comprehensive about their validity, for the importance of grades in graduate education varies tremendously with the

---

30 Sackett et al., 2009.
31 Geiser & Studley, 2002.
32 Credé & Kuncel, 2008.

33 Cree, 1982.

Table 10.2. Odds ratios comparing probability of graduation for the top and bottom halves of admission test scores in an entering population of post-graduate students

Test	Typical Manner of Use	Odds Ratio
Graduate Record Examination	Entrance into Ph.D. programs in many fields of study	2.3:1
Miller Analogies Test	Entrance into Ph.D. programs in many fields of study	2.2:1
Law School Admissions Test	Entrance into Law School	1.4:1
Graduate Management Admissions Test	Entrance into MBA programs in business and management	1.6:1
Medical College Admissions Test	Entrance into Medical School	1.7:1

Source: Data excerpted from the supporting online material for Kuncel & Hezlett, 2007, Table s1. Reprinted with permission from AAAS.

program. It is my impression (but no more than that) that grades are taken fairly seriously in professional programs such as Law, Business, and Medicine, and are regarded as incidental to research participation in most science programs. A validity measure that does not require equating grades across programs is the accuracy with which high scores predict program completion. This is measured by the *odds ratio* for program completion, which is defined as

$$\text{Odds Ratio} = \frac{\text{Completion rate for students whose entrance scores are in the top half}}{\text{Completion rate for students whose entrance scores are in the bottom half}}.$$

Table 10.2 shows the odds ratios for a variety of entrance examinations used as part of the screening examinations for entry into various graduate schools. The odds ratios vary from a low of 1.4 (for the Law School examination) to a high of 2.3 (Graduate Record Examination). Having a test score in the top half of applicants is associated with at least a 40% improvement in probability of graduation, compared to test scorers in the bottom half.

Although having a post-graduate degree clearly pays off, completing a post-graduate course often entails considerable financial and personal sacrifice in the short term. The information in Table 10.2 is of as much use to an accepted applicant, trying to decide whether to enter graduate school, as it is to an admissions officer.

10.3. The Workplace

Do tests of intelligence predict performance in the workplace? Here is a claim by three industrial-organizational psychologists.

Many laypeople, as well as social scientists, subscribe to the belief that the abilities required for success in the real world differ substantially from what is needed to achieve success in the classroom. Yet, this belief is not empirically or theoretically supported. A century of scientific research has shown that general cognitive ability, or g, predicts a broad spectrum of important life outcomes, behaviors, and performances.

Kuncel, Hezlett & Ones, 2004, p. 148

Putting Kuncel and colleagues' proposition more argumentatively, this is a case where the public (and many social scientists) have made up their mind, so please do not confuse them with facts.

Linda Gottfredson is ready to plunge ahead, whether she is believed or not:

In no realm of life g is all that matters, but neither does it seem irrelevant in any. In the vast toolkit of human abilities, none has been found as broadly useful – as general – as g.

Gottfredson, 2002, p. 332

Gottfredson is right, but Kuncel and colleagues are right to be concerned that the facts are a hard sell. Some of the reasons why are captured in a third quote, this time by J. Raven, the son of the J. C. Raven who developed progressive matrix testing and himself a prolific researcher on intelligence. Given his pedigree, one might expect J. Raven to take Gottfredson's position, but he is rather hesitant.

In the workplace and in the educational system numerous other qualities are important but remain invisible if one utilizes only tools developed within the traditional measurement paradigm, focuses mainly on conventional criteria of job performance, and accepts assumptions about the functionality of hierarchical organization of workplaces and society.

J. Raven, 2008c, p. 432

J. Raven further argues that the important things determining job performance are not general cognitive power, but rather the specific skills and the motivation that a person brings to work. He also points out that evaluations of both job performance and academic success take place in constrained situations. The constraints of the situation may be just as important as cognitive capabilities in determining behavior. Constraints on job performance vary widely across the workplace, while academic constraints are more uniform. This argument is worth developing.

In the academic setting there is a reasonably clear-cut criterion for success – how well does a student know the material stated in the curriculum? When implicit objectives like "teaching a student how to think" are introduced, agreement over the criteria for success vanishes.

10.3.1. *Some Evidence from Studies of Military Enlisted Performance*

In the 1980s the United States Department of Defense conducted extensive studies of the prediction and assessment of the job performance of enlisted personnel.[34] The predictive measurements taken included cognitive and personality tests and biographical statements of interests. Occupational assessments were similarly varied. They included examination of service record books (which contain job performance ratings) and records of promotions, commendations, and disciplinary actions. In addition, both pencil-and-paper and hands-on performance tests were given. Examinees had to demonstrate their general skills and knowledge as soldiers, sailors, marines, or airmen and their proficiency in their specific occupations. The occupations chosen varied from strictly military positions, such as infantrymen and artillerymen, to jobs with exact counterparts in the civilian world, such as automobile mechanics, clerks, and cooks.

Five dimensions of job performance were identified. Two, *general military proficiency* and *technical proficiency* in one's specialty, were "can do" measures. They evaluated how well a person could do his or her job, when they knew that they were being evaluated. The next three factors were "will do" measures. *Discipline* referred to whether or not the individual followed regulations and could be relied upon to be ready to do his or her job. *Leadership* referred to the ability to encourage others and to take initiative. *Fitness* referred to personal bearing, appearance, and physical fitness. With the possible exception of fitness these dimensions apply to both the military and civilian workplaces.

Figure 10.5 shows the relation between the five factors and measures of personality, biographical interests, and cognitive performance (including scores derived from the ASVAB). The cognitive measures were the best predictors, by far, of the two "can do"

34 Campbell & Knapp, 2001.

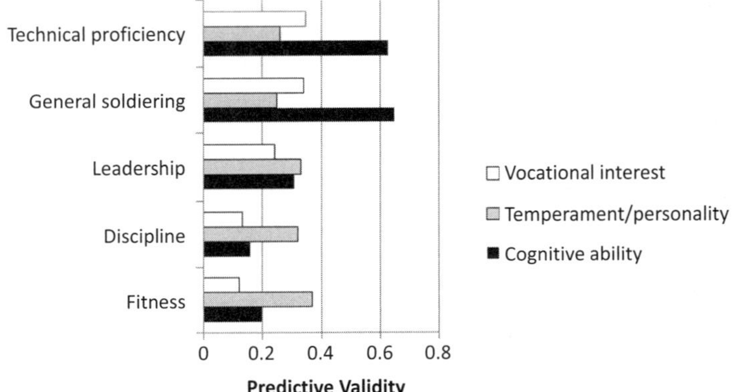

Figure 10.5. Correlations between predictors and criterion measures in the U.S. Army study of enlisted performance. Data from McHenry et al., 1990, Table 4.

factors. Interest and personality measures were the best predictors of the "will do" aspects of job performance.

Steven Hunt, an industrial and organizational psychologist, has pointed out that the first two steps in developing an assessment program in industry are to define the job that you expect employees to do and to determine how you are going to decide whether their performance measures up to these expectations.[35] It is not reasonable to expect anyone to excel in all aspects of performance. To the extent that the required job skills are themselves not correlated, it is impossible for one predictor to predict them all. The results shown in Figure 10.5 illustrate Steven Hunt's point. "Can do" is useless without "will do."

Job performance is highly dependent upon experience, because the more one practices something, the better one becomes at it. Expertise in complex tasks can take years to acquire.[36] Expertise implies the ability to learn from experience.

Further military studies showed that job performance was a joint function of experience on the job and intelligence. Soldiers at all intelligence levels took about eighteen months to approach their top levels of performance, with much slower improvement in the next two years. Soldiers with the highest cognitive scores (AFQT Level I and II)

performed better after six months on the job than soldiers with lower scores after forty-two months.[37]

The military provides a highly structured workplace, and the workforce is younger than the civilian workforce. What are the relationships between intelligence and performance in the civilian workplace?

10.3.2. *Evidence from the Civilian Workplace*

Literally hundreds of studies have been done of the relation between test scores and job performance in the civilian sector, using tests ranging from the ASVAB, which takes several hours, to the Wonderlic and the Raven tests. Two American industrial-organizational psychologists, John Hunter and Frank Schmidt, have conducted a number of widely cited meta-analyses of these results. Figure 10.6, taken from one of their best-known studies,[38] shows that in the blue-collar, clerical, and administrative occupations the predictive validity of general intelligence, averaged over all studies, is .51 (corrected for range restriction and unreliability in the job performance criterion). The validity coefficient can be increased by combining a measure of general mental ability with various other assessment methods. Predictive ability can be raised to its

35 S. Hunt, 2007, Chapter 5.
36 Ericsson, 2003.

37 Wigdor & Green, 1991.
38 Schmidt & Hunter, 1998.

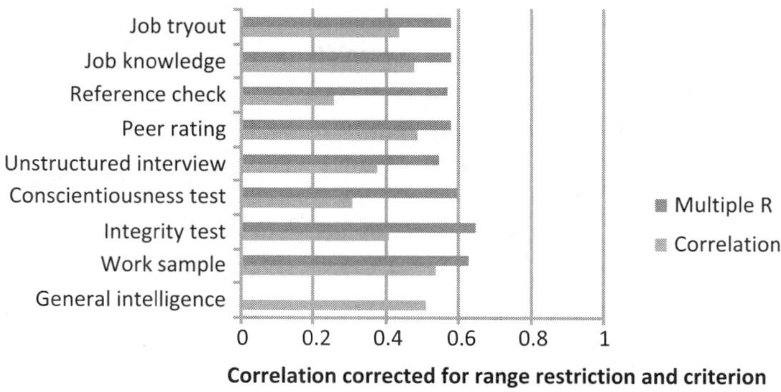

Figure 10.6. The correlations between measures of job performance, measures of general intelligence, and a variety of other assessment measures. The values shown are for the correlation between job performance and the assessment (Correlation) and the correlation between job performance and an optimum weighting of the assessment and the assessment of general intelligence (Multiple R). Data from Schmidt & Hunter, 1998, Table 1.

maximum validity, .65, by combining a measure of general intelligence with a test of integrity. (Conscientiousness is a close second, at .60.) This illustrates the combined importance of "can do" and "will do" traits.

The correspondence between the military and civilian data shows that the findings are robust over different situations and different methods of evaluation. The military data was gathered by direct observation of young adults; the civilian figures were based on a meta-analysis of dozens of small studies, covering all age ranges, but none as comprehensive or rigorous as the military studies.

The fact is clear. General intelligence has a predictive validity of about .50 in the workplace, just as it does in academia. No other method of assessment does any better. Nevertheless, people persist in using other techniques for predicting workplace performance. An examination of these alternatives is in order.

The only type of test with predictive ability greater than a test of general intelligence is a work sample (correlation of .54 compared to .51). This can be used in some situations. For instance, when musicians audition for places in major symphony orchestras they are often asked to play their instruments behind a curtain, so that the judges do not know who the candidate is.

Work samples have two highly desirable qualities: they are statistically valid, and they are easily justified when assessment methods are challenged. Their drawbacks are that they can be rather expensive and that they can be used only if the candidates for a job have already been trained to do the job.

Combining a work sample and a general intelligence measure increases predictive validity to .63. The increase is not surprising, for by combining a general intelligence measure with a work sample the employer is simultaneously informed about the prospective employee's general reasoning powers and specific job knowledge.

In personnel selection situations a test this accurate, combined with a high rejection rate, can greatly increase the quality of the employed workforce. Recall that if no screening test is used, the average person hired should have an ability level equal to the fiftieth percentile (median) of the applicant population, regardless of the rejection rate. If a predictive validity of .63 is combined with a rejection rate of 50% (half the applicants are hired), the average ability level of a person hired will be at the sixty-ninth percentile of the applicant population.

An *unstructured interview* is an interview in which the recruiter and the candidate "just chat," so that the recruiter can get a feel for the candidate. This is probably the most widely used selection procedure. The unstructured interview is not very good on its own (r = .38, corrected) and adds very little to the information gained in a test of general intelligence.

A *structured interview* (not shown in the figure, but included in Schmidt and Hunter's analyses) is an interview in which the recruiter has decided, beforehand, what topics are to be discussed in the interview, and what information must be provided. The technique requires a careful analysis of the requirements of the position to be filled, before searching for candidates. Structured interviews have good predictive validity, both on their own and when combined with a test of general intelligence (r = .51, R = .63).

Job knowledge is usually assessed by performance on a written test, where the questions are chosen to reflect what a job holder should know. This is a face-valid measure; we can reasonably expect bus drivers to know the rules of the road, and firefighters to know how to use various pieces of equipment. Job knowledge is not quite as good a predictor as is general intelligence, but it does add to predictive validity beyond that provided by a general intelligence score (r = .48, R = .58). In terms of the Gf-Gc model of intelligence, what a job knowledge test does is assess what the applicant knows about the particular situation in which he or she will be working. The same idea is captured by Robert Sternberg's emphasis on practical intelligence, which would include job knowledge. Sternberg and his colleagues have provided such tests, and they have on occasion shown some incremental validity.[39]

The practical intelligence tests Sternberg and his colleagues have described are very close to job knowledge tests. For instance, one practical intelligence test, designed for Alaskan hunters, asked what different pieces of evidence mean as indicators of coming weather.[40] Such questions measure crystallized intelligence (Gc) within a specialized context.[41]

10.3.3. *Upper-Level Managerial and Professional Positions*

The data presented so far is based largely on data from studies of blue-collar and white-collar jobs, up to the lower managerial level. In this population of occupations the correlation between general intelligence test scores and job performance generally rises with increasing job complexity.[42] Given this fact, it would be reasonable to expect the correlation to be still higher for high-level managerial, executive, and professional positions. However, there are reasons not to assume a straightforward extrapolation of the results to the managerial/professional class.

Many studies of high-level occupations report the observed correlation between test scores and measures of job performance, but cannot correct for selection restriction because there is no data on the applicant population. This is serious, because the selection effects are likely to be large. High-level positions are quite competitive, and are virtually always filled by people in the upper quartile of the intelligence range, IQ 110 and above. It is also difficult to find a measure of how well a professional or executive is doing, beyond gross judgments of satisfactory or unsatisfactory performance. As *Fortune* magazine repeatedly shows in its annual survey of executive salaries, the correlations between executive compensation and objective measures of company performance are close to zero. Physicians, attorneys, and other professionals are evaluated periodically, but the ratings are often limited to certification of competence without any further differentiation.

It is also often hard to acquire the required data on intelligence. People who

---

39 See Sternberg, 2003, for a general discussion, and Sternberg et al., 2000, for a compendium of many of the studies.

40 Grigorenko et al., 2004.
41 See Gottfredson, 2003a, and Hunt, 2008, for expansions on this point.
42 Gottfredson 1997, 2002.

occupy high-level positions are busy, and usually see no need to have their cognitive skills evaluated. As a substitute for direct observation, many studies look at professional training rather than on-the-job performance. As was shown in the section on post-graduate education, cognitive tests do surprisingly well in predicting completion of professional and managerial training.

There is also the problem of the multidimensionality of the criterion. People who occupy high-level positions are typically asked to do a number of different tasks. These range from high-level planning to public relations, face-to-face leadership, and negotiations. The relative importance of different tasks varies greatly across occupations and even from time to time within an occupation. It is not surprising that there has been a good deal of resistance to the idea that any unidimensional measure could predict performance at high levels. This has led to three different approaches.

In order to evaluate highly intelligent people using the conventional psychometric paradigm we have to have harder tests. Examples are the advanced version of the Raven tests, the Raven Advanced Progressive Matrices (RAMP), and the Miller Analogy Test (MAT), which contains difficult verbal analogy problems. These tests do predict job performance, with observed correlations in the .15–.30 range, depending upon the criterion used to evaluate performance, and with a predictive ability on the order of .40.[43] This is somewhat below the level of prediction obtained for higher-level skilled work, but still a reasonable figure.

It is somewhat more enlightening to look at a single large prospective study. During the 1960s the Bell Telephone System, at the time a near-monopoly covering telephone services in the United States, used the assessment center technique to select beginning managers. Management trainees spent several days in an assessment center, where they were rated for their ability to solve complicated problems both individually and in groups, and also given a cognitive test similar to the SAT reasoning tests, along with several personality tests. The results of these assessments were carefully shielded from their superiors in the company, so that the test scores could not influence supervisors' judgments or hiring decisions. (By contrast, in the US military a service person's scores on entry tests are part of his or her service record, and hence are available to commanders and promotion boards.) Twenty years later the assessment center results were validated by determining whether they predicted the level of management the candidate had achieved. The cognitive test ($r = .38$) was by far the best predictor.[44] As would be suggested by Schmidt and Hunter's analyses, personality tests had lower validity than cognitive tests, but did add substantially to predictivity.

Because high-level performance is said to be so multidimensional, some interesting alternatives to the conventional testing methods have been developed. One of the more popular of these is the *situational judgment test*. In this test an examinee is asked what he or she would do in a realistic, difficult situation. An example I particularly like, and that has appeared in a number of guises, is asking an applicant for a middle management position how they would inform their own supervisor that the supervisor's pet project was not working. As the example illustrates, an attempt is made to design situational judgment tests that draw on both cognitive skill narrowly defined and the examinee's social skills. Situational judgment tests add an additional .06 to the predictive validity that can be achieved by a cognitive test alone – not a large amount, but enough to be worthwhile in a large scale assessment program.[45] It is worth noting, though, that a situational judgment test asks the examinee what he or she would do in a hypothetical situation. It does not immediately follow that that is what the examinee would do, if placed in an actual, possibly emotional situation.

43 Kuncel, Hezlett, & Ones, 2004; Raven, 2008b.

44 Howard & Bray, 1988.
45 McDaniel et al., 2001.

To summarize, general cognitive ability is the best single predictor of executive/professional-level performance, just as it is of performance in the middle to high-end range of the general workforce. Prediction of executive/professional performance is somewhat less accurate than prediction of general workplace performance. There are several reasons why this might be so. They include difficulties in defining and obtaining measures of job performance, the extreme restriction in range of intelligence among applicants for high-level positions, and, possibly, the fact that general cognitive ability is a less dominating factor, compared to other dimensions of intelligence, in the upper ranges of cognitive competence than in the lower (see Chapter 4). Nevertheless, it is reassuring to know that among the movers and shakers in our society intelligence does count.

10.3.4. *The Rewards for Cognitive Skills in the Workplace*

The previous sections have shown that there is a positive relation between intelligence and workplace performance, within both military and civilian occupations. This is the sort of information employers want to have. From the viewpoint of an individual entering the workforce, the question is rather different. The individual wants to know what sort of economic niche he or she is likely to occupy, given a certain level of intelligence. As an ancillary question, what sort of rewards can the intelligent person look forward to, in terms of either money or occupational prestige?

Determining the statistical relationship between rewards and prestige is straightforward. You look at the correlation between test scores and some index of rewards. This can be done on an individual basis, or, as is sometimes easier to do, researchers can determine the typical level of intelligence of people in different occupations, and then look at the prestige and economic rewards offered by those occupations. However, as always, correlation does not necessarily mean causation.

In Chapter 1 I introduced the challenge hypothesis, the idea that within genetically prescribed limits people will increase their intelligence in response to a cognitively challenging environment. It has been shown, for instance, that there are qualitative differences in the reasoning skills of psychologists, physical scientists, and lawyers. Psychologists, who receive substantial training in statistics, are more sensitive to arguments based on probabilities than are people in the other two fields.[46] Were the psychologists, physical scientists, and lawyers attracted to their fields because the demands of the field matched their preferred styles of reasoning, or were the styles of reasoning determined by their experiences? The best way to answer this question is by a prospective study, where a person's intelligence is determined before he or she enters the workforce, and then related to the person's subsequent work history.

During World War II the United States Army Air Force (USAAF, the predecessor of today's Air Force, USAF) tested large numbers of young men who had applied to serve as aviation officers.[47] Two Columbia University psychologists, Robert Thorndike and Elizabeth Hagen, located approximately 10,000 of the men about twelve years after they had been tested.[48] At that time most of the men were in their early to mid-thirties.

Table 10.3 shows the mean test scores on general reasoning, verbal, and perceptual-motor scales of the original test, for men in selected occupations. These estimates were then converted to IQ ranges. The cadets who eventually entered those occupations that we consider more generally intellectually challenging, or that require a considerable amount of education, were also the cadets who had, at age twenty-one, scored high on the general reasoning tests. As we scan down the general reasoning scale we begin to encounter white-collar office jobs, and then various blue-collar jobs that, although they

46 Amsel, Langer, & Loutzenhiser, 1991.
47 Women were not accepted for aviation cadet training. Some women who had already qualified as aviators in the civilian sector did serve.
48 Thorndike & Hagen, 1959.

Table 10.3. Cognitive skills assessed in USAAF aviation cadets, shown by occupation followed after WW II. The far left-hand column shows estimated general intelligence measures using the conventional IQ scale. The estimate is based on a conversion of the general reasoning score, assuming that 0 on that scale corresponds to 105 on the IQ scale. Right-hand columns show mean scores achieved at approximately age twenty-one on three different composites of a testing battery. All three scales have a mean of 0 and a standard deviation of 100 in the sample of cadets.

Estimated IQ Range	Occupation	General Reasoning	Numerical	Visual-Perceptual
≥115	Chemical engineer	106	42	30
	Mechanical engineer	93	34	44
	Physical scientist	80	22	23
	College professor	75	38	38
	Civil engineer	75	31	56
	Electrical engineer	65	6	9
110≤ − <115	Physician	59	20	18
	Treasurer/comptroller	55	96	23
	Industrial engineer	44	31	34
	Lawyer	39	22	−7
	Personnel manager	33	18	13
	Pharmacist	29	39	−9
105≤ − <110	Dentist	28	20	15
	Accountant/auditor	28	54	−4
	Optometrist	14	34	−4
	Clergyman	13	1	−17
	Airplane pilot	13	10	−1
	Real estate salesman	6	17	6
100≤ − <105	Office manager	4	33	9
	Insurance underwriter	3	2	−9
	Veterinarian	−8	−2	−20
	Insurance claims adjuster	−13	−5	−9
	Bricklayer	−24	−5	−38
	Radio/TV repairman	−33	−37	21
95-<-<100	Hardware Salesman	−36	−12	−9
	Sales clerk	−40	−22	−28
	Plumber	−42	−21	−31
	Carpenter	−44	−17	−4
	Police detective	−50	−26	−20
	House painter	−63	−12	−24
<95	Crane operator	−66	−84	−37
	Vehicle mechanic	−72	−65	−7
	Assembler (in factories)	−83	−76	−40

Source: Data selected from Thorndike and Hagen, 1959.

may require considerable skill, are less intellectually demanding and can be learned on the job rather than via formal education.

Some pairwise comparisons are interesting. Cadets who became physicians had general reasoning skills similar to those of cadets who became treasurers/comptrollers (i.e., high-level financial managers), but the treasurer/comptrollers had higher numerical skills than the physicians. Cadets who became college professors had the same general reasoning skills as those who became civil engineers, but the engineers had higher perceptual skills. This illustrates the point

Table 10.4. Correlations between AFQT scores obtained at age sixteen to eighteen and measures of social outcomes when the participants were in their early thirties

Demographic Group	Educational Attainment	Square Root Income	Occupational Status Index
White men	.67	.39	.54
Black men	.48	.29	.45
White women	.59	.31	.45
Black women	.53	.44	.47

Source: Data from Scullin et al., 2000, Table 2.

that in many occupations general reasoning skills have to be augmented by more specific cognitive skills.

Other pairwise comparisons show that occupations can be the same in terms of the stress they put on different special abilities, but differ in the level of associated general reasoning skills. Treasurers and comptrollers (high-level financial officers) and accountants and auditors (financial technicians) were both characterized by high reasoning and numerical skills, but the cadets who became treasurer/comptrollers had higher levels of these skills.

While the Thorndike and Hagen study is certainly informative, there are some aspects that limit sweeping conclusions. The participants, aviation officers, were an intellectually select group, with an estimated mean IQ of 105. The occupations these young officers entered, following the war, were fairly high on the occupational scale. And the test battery was designed for aviation cadets. Accordingly, compared to the typical battery-type IQ test the aviation battery was biased toward the evaluation of visual-perceptual skills – so much so that verbal skills were incorporated within the general reasoning factor. Even given these limits, a coherent picture emerged: intelligence is worth quite a bit.

Thorndike and Hagen studied the workplace of the mid twentieth century. Compared to that workplace, today's workplace places much more emphasis on the manipulation of data and abstract representations, rather than things.[49] Have these changes in the workplace changed the requirements for cognitive skills?

To address that question we look at a second prospective study using the NLSY79 data (see panel 9.9). Recall that in this study a nationally representative sample of adolescents and young adults took the AFQT. In 2000 a research group at Cornell University investigated the occupational and income status, as of 1995–96, for over 2,400 of the panelists who had been born in 1963–64.[50] The men and women in this study were of approximately the same age as the former aviation cadets studied by Thorndike and Hagen, but in a cohort born roughly forty years later.

In general, the Cornell group found that there was a moderate positive correlation between AFQT score, educational attainment, income, and occupational prestige (SEI). The correlations are shown in Table 10.4, reported separately for four different demographic groups, White and Black men and women. Although the correlations are all positive, and never negligible, they do vary markedly across demographic groups. As a rough generalization, intelligence seems to be a more useful predictor of future success if you are a White man or a Black woman than if you are a White woman or a Black man.

Table 10.4 treats educational attainment as an outcome. Education can also be thought of as something to be achieved en route to further social and economic success, rather than as an end in itself.

49 Hunt, 1995; Reich, 1991; Zuboff, 1988.

50 Scullin et al., 2000.

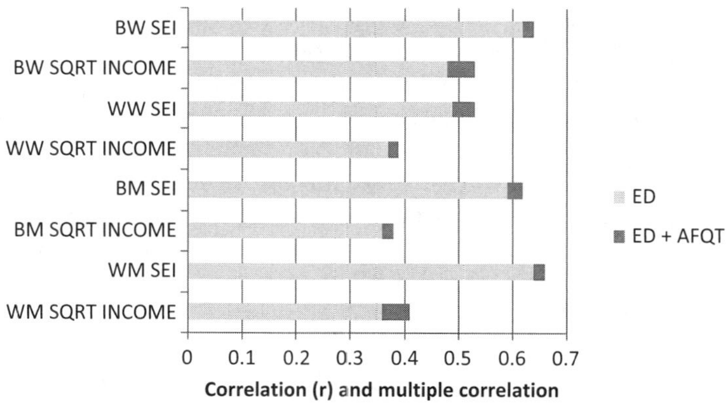

Figure 10.7. Predicting square root income (SQRT INCOME) and occupational prestige (SEI) in 1995 from educational attainment (in years) and AFQT score obtained in 1980. Respondents were sixteen to eighteen years old in 1980. Codes: WM – White men, BM – Black men, WW – White women, BW – Black women. Data for calculations from Scullin et al., 2000, Table 2.

Not surprisingly, educational attainment and AFQT score are substantially correlated in this sample, ranging from .67 (White men) to .48 (Black men). This is consistent with the data reported in section 10.2, relating intelligence to academic achievement. Figure 10.7 shows that there is little added predictive value of knowing a person's AFQT score, once his or her educational attainment is known.

There are three possible interpretations of this finding. One is that education is the proximal variable that determines socioeconomic outcome and income, while intelligence acts as a distal variable, determining education but then playing no further role. The other is that intelligence acts as a proximal variable, and that education serves as an additional statistical marker for intelligence beyond the AFQT score. These explanations can be discriminated by contrasting the partial correlations between AFQT and the outcome variable, occupational prestige or income, holding education constant, or between education and the outcome variable, holding AFQT score constant. I calculated these and found that for income the partial correlations for education are generally larger than for AFQT score, but that the differences are not great. The results for occupational prestige are striking. The partial correlations for education

given AFQT score are .43 for Blacks (both men and women), and .38 and .28 for White men and women, respectively. The corresponding values for AFQT given education range from .16 (White men) to .20 (White women). Evidently education and intelligence are collinear predictors of income. Intelligence acts as a distal variable, exerting its influence through education, which then permits entry into prestigious occupations. The educational effect seems to be stronger for Blacks than for Whites.

Another way to determine what the workplace is willing to pay for intelligence is to examine the test scores of people who apply for jobs in various occupations. This carries with it the defensible assumption that the applicants exert self-selection. People without college degrees generally do not apply for entry-level executive positions.

Gottfredson used a number of studies of intelligence test scores in job applicants to construct a "life's chances" chart for various occupations.[51] She associated IQ equivalents with five classes of occupation, ranging from what she regarded as "slow, supervised" work to "gathers own information." Table 10.5 lists occupations cited by Gottfredson, along with her estimates of the typical IQ score for an applicant.

51 Gottfredson, 1997.

Table 10.5. Gottfredson's examples of intelligence levels (on IQ scale) associated with different occupations and techniques of information processing. The columns to the right of Gottfredson's figures show the intelligence-level estimates obtained from Thorndike and Hagen's study of the careers of USAAF aviation cadets, approximately fifty years earlier (Table 10.4) and the range of Wonderlic scores of applicants reported in the Wonderlic Corporation's Normative Report (April 2007) for the WPT-R, revised in 2003. As occupations used in the norming for the WPT and WPT-R, a comparable profession to Gottfredson's "typical profession" was used. Wonderlic scores have been converted to IQ units using the conversion 2 * Wonderlic score + 60 (Dodrill, 1981; Dodrill & Warner, 1988).

Training and Qualification Method	Typical Position	Gottfredson's Estimated Typical IQ Score	Estimates Based on Thorndike & Hagen Data	WONDERLIC with Comparison Occupation
Explicit, hands-on training	Assembler	80–90	<95	88–104 Electro-mechanical assembler
Mastery learning, hands-on training	Police officer	95–105	95–100	100–114 Police and sheriff officer
College formal instruction	Accountant	110–120	105–110	102–120 Accountant
Graduate instruction, gathers own information	Attorney	120 +	110–115	110–124 Executive

The table also includes data for comparable occupations, based on the Thorndike and Hagen data, taken forty years earlier, and for the 2003 revision of the WONDER-LIC test, the WPT-R. There is a striking similarity between Gottfredson's estimates, the WONDERLIC estimates, and the estimates that Thorndike and Hagen had made forty years earlier. The data was gathered using different sampling methods, in different workplaces separated by over half a century, and the tests used were quite different.[52] Nevertheless, the estimates are basically the same. Comparing Tables 10.4 and 10.5, it appears that the role of intelligence in today's workplace is very much the

same as it was before the term "information technology" was invented.

A second retrospective study provides a more comprehensive look at general levels of occupational accomplishment, but does not provide data on individual occupations.

In the late 1980s the Center for Disease Control conducted a follow-up study of the health of people (primarily men) who had served in the military during the Vietnam War era (1967–76). A large number of veterans were contacted and asked to participate in extensive physical and mental testing. Helmut Nyborg, a Danish psychologist, and Arthur Jensen related the veterans' current occupational status to their educational attainment and to a measure of g extracted from their test scores, as of the late 1980s.[53] Figure 10.8 shows the results

52 Thorndike and Hagen's general reasoning factor was extracted from a battery of subtests that took several hours to complete. Gottfredson's estimates were based on data from the Wonderlic Personnel Test (WPT) The current Wonderlic estimates are based on the revised version, WPT-R, with data from 2003. See Chapter 2 for a description of the WPT.

53 Nyborg & Jensen, 2001.

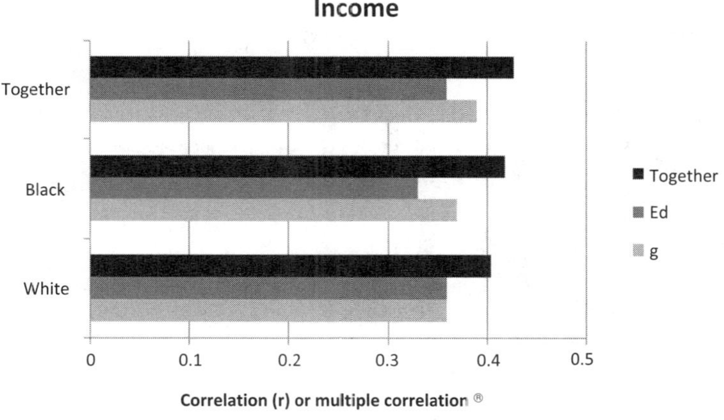

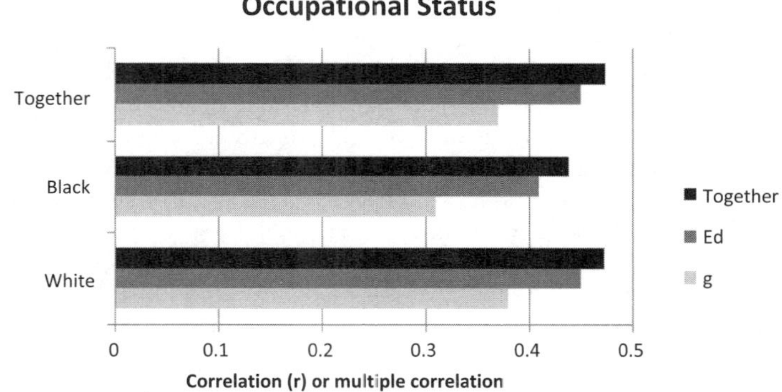

Figure 10.8. Correlations and multiple correlations between income (top) and occupational status (bottom) and general intelligence and educational level. The calculations are based on Table 3 of Nyborg & Jensen, 2001.

of Nyborg and Jensen's analysis. Data are shown separately for black and white veterans, as they differed on educational, intelligence, occupational, and income measures.

In this sample the intelligence test score was a slightly better predictor of income than was educational achievement, while the reverse was true for the NLSY data. It would be unwise to make very much of this. The samples were different, the tests were different, and the NLSY analysis attempted to predict future accomplishment from measures taken in adolescence, while Nyborg and Jensen related current test performance to current accomplishment. In any case, the similarities are far greater than the differences.

Both educational level and intelligence are substantial predictors of accomplishment in the workplace. The two are highly

correlated. This is hardly surprising. Both measures are based on the development and display of cognitive skills.

10.3.5. *What the Jobs Demand*

Another way of determining the value of intelligence in the workplace is to analyze the job requirements of a large number of occupations, and infer what this means in terms of the demands on intelligence. The first step is to make an analysis of the relative value of cognitive skills for different jobs.

The US Department of Labor (DOL) maintains an elaborate job counseling service, in which it describes over 12,000 jobs and rates the extent to which they require certain skills. The skills rated range from general reasoning ability to finger dexterity. The rating system was originally

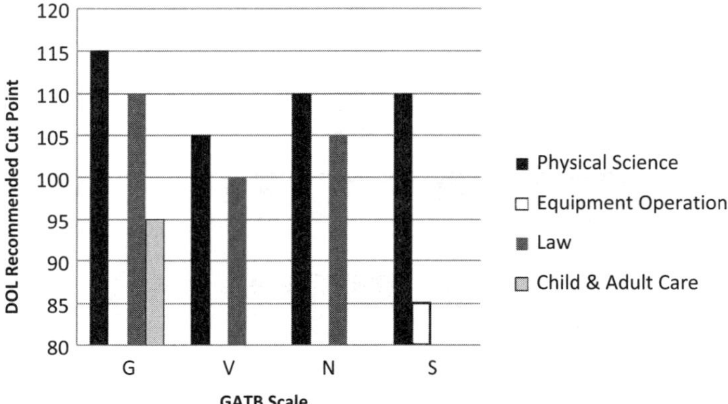

Figure 10.9. Recommended GATB cut points for four occupations, taken from high-status and lower-status patterns, within the class of occupations dealing with physical or with social relationships. GATB scales are G – general reasoning, V – verbal, N – numerical, and S – spatial. Data selected from Gottfredson, 1986, Table 2. In cases where no value is specified the DOL analysts had made the judgment that virtually anyone would have sufficient ability to do the job. For instance, there is no cut point for spatial reasoning required for the law, and no cut point for general reasoning required for heavy equipment operation.

incorporated into a descriptive volume called the *Dictionary of Occupational Titles* (DOT). The DOT has been superseded by an on-line, interactive system called O*NET. O*NET is a considerable expansion over the DOT, designed primarily to help job seekers. As a side benefit, it contains a massive amount of data available to researchers interested in issues involving workforce skills.

Gottfredson utilized the original DOT system to construct a "space" of jobs.[54] Her analysis coordinated job ratings with data on the test performance of people who had applied for, or were occupying, a variety of jobs. She identified five classes of occupations – those dealing with physical relations, social and economic relations, maintaining bureaucratic order, and performing. (She also had a small class of "leftover" occupational patterns that will not be dealt with further.) Within each of these classes she identified the patterns of aptitudes required. For example, within the class of occupations dealing with physical relations there was a cluster of occupations that dealt

with research and design (e.g., physicist, engineer) and a cluster that dealt with building, maintaining, or operating physical objects (e.g., equipment operators, craftsmen). Within the class dealing with social and economic systems one cluster dealt with research and design (including social research, law, and finance), while another dealt with providing service to individuals (including hospitality services, and child and adult care).

Individual jobs within a cluster could be associated with a pattern of abilities, as defined by the DOL's General Aptitude Test Battery (GATB), which was in use at the time. The DOL used these values to recommend minimum values (cut points) for a job along each of four GATB dimensions: general reasoning, verbal reasoning, numerical skills, and spatial skills. Figure 10.9 provides examples for four occupations, two from Gottfredsons's class of occupations dealing with physical relations and two from the class dealing with social relations. Within each class one occupation was selected from Gottfredson's high-status cluster, and the other from a lower-status cluster. Physical scientists and lawyers,

54 Gottfredson, 1986.

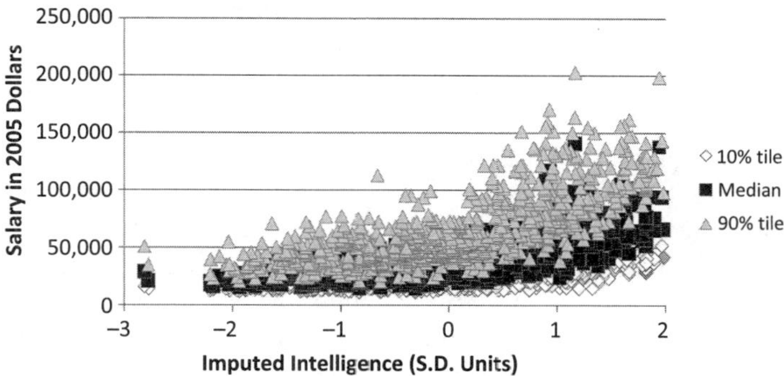

Figure 10.10. The ninetieth, fiftieth (median) and tenth decile of incomes in various occupations, plotted as a function of the imputed intelligence demands for the occupation. Data from US Census Bureau and from Hunt and Madhyastha's analysis of job demands.

high-status occupations from the physical relations and social relations clusters, have similar high-level patterns except that lawyers are not required to have spatial reasoning skills, and do not have quite as high scores on other scales as the physical scientists do. Equipment operators have to have a certain minimal level of spatial reasoning skills, while personal caretakers have to have a minimal level of general reasoning skills.

Gottfredson found that general intelligence was by far the biggest driver of variations in cognitive skills across occupations. Verbal, numerical, and spatial skills were important in some occupations, but they accounted for much less of the variation in the descriptions of occupational requirements than did differences in requirements for general reasoning.

Tara Madhyastha and I have analyzed the modern O*NET data (as of 2008) using different techniques than Gottfredson had used, but intended to answer basically the same questions. In general, our analysis of cognitive demands agreed well with Gottfredson's.[55] We found that the ratings of skills could be described by a two-dimensional space, where one dimension was a general reasoning factor and the other was a *bipolar* factor, indicating whether the job emphasized verbal or perceptual-motor

skills. We also found a smaller factor indicating the extent to which a job required numerical skills. The factors were not statistically independent, because most jobs that require a high degree of general reasoning also require fairly high verbal skills, just as Gottfredson had noticed. This is not surprising; people who hold intellectually demanding jobs usually have to communicate with other people. In spite of comic strip stereotypes, real computer programmers spend a great deal of time describing what their programs do, and how they fit into suites of programs developed by other people.

Our analysis also allowed us to relate the incomes associated with different occupations to the cognitive demands of those occupations. The relations to general intelligence are shown in Figure 10.10. The income associated with occupations increased as the occupations demanded higher levels of intelligence. However, there appeared to be a nonlinear increase; incomes are fairly flat over occupations that require slightly more than average intelligence. Incomes are more closely related to demands on intelligence if the occupation requires an IQ of more than about 105 ($g \geq .3$ on the standard deviation scale). What is even more striking is the range of incomes associated with a given level of cognitive demand. This is clearly shown in the figure. The range in annual income between the 10% best-paid and 10% worst-paid occupations with a cognitive demand of 100 (0 in standard deviation

55 Unfortunately it is not possible to compare our analysis to the data obtained by Gottfredson or by Thorndike and Hagen, because our analysis was at a much finer level of detail.

units) was about $65,000 (2005 dollars). The range for jobs with a cognitive demand of 116 (1 in standard deviation units) was roughly $140,000.

Figure 10.10 also shows that the distribution of income is markedly positively skewed at all levels of intelligence. The absolute difference between the median and the ninetieth percentile is always greater than the absolute difference between the median and the tenth percentile. The extent of the skew increases with increasing imputed intelligence, a trend that begins much sooner than the rise in median income as a function of imputed intelligence.

10.3.6. *Summary: The Role of Intelligence in the Workplace*

The quotations that began this section, from Gottfredson and from Kuncel and colleagues, were accurate. Intelligence predicts a person's job status and income better than any other trait that has been studied. This leaves us with two questions: why does the association exist, and why is it that the association is so widely denied by people who have not studied the topic?

The influence of intelligence is undoubtedly mediated in part by education. This is especially true across fields, for the vast majority of the more lucrative occupations have, as an entry requirement, at least a college education. The best-paid professional occupations require substantial graduate-level training. It is increasingly the case that the entry routes to skilled trades, such as auto mechanic, involve academic certification through community college or other professional training programs. Because educational attainment is strongly related to intelligence, any variable that is correlated with educational attainment will also correlate with intelligence.

In the case of the professions education is essential; no one wants to have a surgeon (or an airline pilot) who is learning basic skills on the job. To the extent that intelligence is required to get through a rigorous training program, intelligence and education are entwined.

Charles Murray has argued that in many cases education is not really needed for success in a field, but that education is used as a (socioeconomic?) screening device.[56] To the extent that this is true a spurious relation between intelligence and economic success could be created, via a real relationship between intelligence and educational attainment and a spurious one between educational attainment and economic success, calculated across occupations. However, this is not completely the case. Both intelligence and education are important, because there are nonzero partial correlations between indices of workplace success and either intelligence or education, after the other has been held constant.

The fact that intelligence is correlated with on-the-job performance in a wide range of military and civilian occupations, including ones that do not have high educational requirements, provides further evidence that intelligence is important in itself, not just as a facilitator of education.

10.4. The Social and Economic Prospects at the Ends of the Bell Curve

If intelligence is an important trait in our society, then the lifetime prospects of people on the two extremes of the distribution of intelligence should be very different. And they are. In this section we take a look at the careers of some people who are at the upper and lower ends of the intelligence distribution.

It is important to be clear that we will *not* be looking at people who are conventionally labeled "geniuses" or at people who are mentally handicapped to the point that they cannot function in our society without special help. There are reasons for avoiding these extremes.

The term "genius" is usually applied to people who have accomplished great things. The consensus of people who have studied genius is that extraordinary accomplishment in any field requires some talent, but

56 Murray, 2008.

also a great deal of motivation, and very hard work. The social support network must be right. Howard Gardner makes this point in his excellent study of extreme creators, in such varied fields as physics (Einstein), writing (T. S. Eliot), politics (Gandhi), and art (Picasso).[57] Gardner's subjects were geniuses in any sense of the word. They were all very bright. They also had a single-minded sense of purpose *and* a social network of people who were willing to support their single-minded efforts. In addition, the times must be right. An unknown Sumerian genius invented the wheel around 3500 BCE. His or her invention spread rapidly through the ancient world, for it greatly improved the utility of oxen and horses. Perhaps 2,500 years later, and completely independently, an equally unknown Aztec invented wheels for children's toys. The idea never went further, for the Aztecs had no beasts of burden. Cognitive traits undoubtedly are important in the creation of genius, so are noncognitive traits and features of the situation. Studying acknowledged geniuses is important in itself,[58] but it is not a good way to determine how high intelligence affects one's progress through life.

At the other end of the scale, there is little point in studying the lives of the extremely mentally disabled, who simply cannot cope with our society. Determining the sorts of social support these unfortunate individuals require is an important topic, but one that is far beyond the scope of this book. What we can do is to examine the lives of people who fall in the "low normal" range, roughly IQ scores of 70–85. Most of these individuals are productive members of society, but seldom maximally productive members.

Once again, we have to balance the relative costs and benefits of retrospective and prospective studies. There have been numerous retrospective studies of the characteristics of high achievers, ranging from artists to politicians.[59] There have been even more studies of various low-achieving groups, such as welfare recipients and criminals. In both cases it is possible to find some traits that seem to characterize the target group. However, as is almost always the case with retrospective studies, it is hard to interpret these findings. For instance, eighteen of the first forty-four presidents of the United States received earned degrees from one or more of just five colleges.[60] Does this mean that if you attend one of these colleges you have a good chance of becoming president? Hardly. Only a miniscule fraction of the graduates of these colleges attained the presidency.

At the other end of the social scale, it has been estimated that about one in every six homeless persons has either schizophrenia or manic-depressive psychosis. Does this mean that a person who suffers from either of these diseases has roughly one chance in six of becoming homeless? Hardly. Approximately 3% of the US population, roughly nine million people, suffers from one of these two diseases. Some 200,000 are both homeless and are either schizophrenic or suffer from bipolar disorder. The chances are roughly one in forty-five, not one in six, of a mentally ill person becoming homeless.

The best way to determine what happens to intellectually gifted or below-normal individuals is to start with a group of (gifted) (below-normal) persons and follow that group through some portion of their lives, in a prospective manner, rather than attempting a retrospective study of people who have had a particular life outcome.

We will look first at a study of the gifted, and then examine the low-normal group. In each case my discussion will use as illustration the results of one or two large studies.

57 Gardner, 1993b.
58 See, especially, Simonton, 1984.

59 See, Simonton, 1984, and Gardner, 1993b.
60 The colleges are Harvard (six), the College of William and Mary (four), Yale (four), Princeton and the US Military Academy (two each). The list includes George Washington, who received a surveyor's certificate from William and Mary. This was his only post-secondary education. I have assigned George W. Bush to Yale, where he received a B.A. He also received an MBA from Harvard.

Table 10.6. Percentages of men and women in the Terman study who attained various levels of education, compared to educational achievements of their cohort

Group	Men in Terman Study	Women in Terman Study	General Public, Men	General Public, Women
College graduates	70	67	10	6
Graduate studies given graduation from college	56	33	19	Unknown
Doctorates	14	4	2	2

Source: Data from Terman & Oden, 1959.

10.4.1. *The Gifted I: The Quiz Kids and the Termites*

During the 1940s and 1950s there was a popular radio program called *The Quiz Kids*. A panel of very knowledgeable six- to sixteen-year-old children answered questions that required anything from an ability to do rapid mental calculations to knowing rather obscure scientific and historical facts. Their performance was impressive. Some were said to have IQs of 200, but that was apparently a score based on the old mental age/chronological age calculation. A more realistic estimate is that the IQ scores ranged in the 140–160+ range, roughly the top one in one thousand.

About thirty years later one of the former Quiz Kids, who had become a professor, located a number of them to see how they were doing.[61] The commonest answer was generally quite well, thank you. An inordinate number of them had followed academic professions. The others were mostly in professional fields. One had received the Nobel Prize in Medicine and Physiology.[62] To be sure, not every one of the Quiz Kids had done well, and some had rather unhappy lives. But, on the whole, they were successes.

The Quiz Kids hardly represents a scientific study. Candidates were recruited rather informally from the general Chicago area. I am sure the selection of candidates depended on both the child's apparent intelligence and the radio show producers' judgment about how appealing the child would be on the radio stage. Fortunately, more formal studies have been done.

The Quiz Kid idea was a popularized version of a well-known study that had been (and was being) carried out by Louis Terman, the Stanford University professor who introduced the Binet tests into the United States. In the early 1920s Terman asked teachers in California schools to nominate exceptionally bright children for a long-term study. The children were then given IQ tests, and those who scored 140 or above (one in a thousand) were invited to participate. Eventually 1,528 students were enrolled. The study continued after Terman's death in 1956. Eventually the "termites," as they were sometimes called, were followed into their seventies.[63]

The results were clear in one way, and difficult to interpret in another. Terman's participants were born around 1910–20, so the cultural aspects of their time have to be kept in mind. In spite of living through a depression and a world war, they did exceptionally well. A few statistics from the last study in which Terman himself participated, at which time the "termites" were in their fifties, shows what had happened.[64]

By the 1950s virtually all of the people in the study had completed their education. Table 10.6 provides a comparison of their

61 Feldman, 1982.
62 James Watson, for the discovery of the structure of DNA.
63 Holahan & Sears, 1995.
64 Terman & Oden, 1959.

Table 10.7. Family income distribution of Terman study participants in the 1950s, compared to "urban white families" at that time. Income figures are in 1950s dollars. The study participants earned much more than the base rate established for similar families.

Group	"Urban White Families"	Terman Participants
Income > $15,000	1%	30%
$15,000 ≥ income > $5000	36%	64%
$5000 > income	63%	6%

Source: Data from Terman & Oden, 1959.

achievements compared to those born in roughly the same cohort. Clearly the gifted had much greater educational attainment than was typical of the time. The college graduation rate for the gifted, who went to college during the Great Depression, was higher than the general graduation rates at the start of the twenty-first century! This was true for both men and women.

Over 80% of the men in the study followed professional or business careers. As was typical of the times, many of the women became homemakers. Table 10.7 contrasts the family incomes of the study group to a group that Terman referred to as "urban white families." This was an appropriate comparison group, for the participants were themselves predominantly urban and white.

The final follow-up of this group, when they were in their seventies, reinforced the picture. The "termites" had achieved high educational levels and had had successful careers. They were healthy and satisfied. Their marriage rates were high, compared to their cohorts, and their divorce rates were low. The incidence of severe mental illnesses, alcoholism, and other types of social dysfunction was similarly low. The study gave no support whatsoever to the stereotype of the sickly, neurotic genius. Nor, I add, has any other study of the gifted.

To what extent was the success of the termites due to their intelligence? Here the answer is not so clear. Terman's work has been criticized on three grounds. The most serious is that reliance on teacher reports and personal contacts biased the study toward the selection of upper-middle-class urban Whites. The second is that Terman actively interfered in the lives of the participants, through interviews and mail contacts. The third is that the participants were not really geniuses.

Terman's selection methods were biased toward selecting children from high SES, White homes. On the average, although not in all cases, Terman's participants benefited from strong social support, such as having families who could support them during their college years, and having the social contacts that facilitated success. In hindsight, it would have been nice if Terman had also followed children from a comparable SES group who did not have unusually high IQ scores. This would have greatly increased the cost of the study. The disparity between success rates in Terman's group, compared to base rates in similar social groups, is so great that I do not think that the bias toward upper SES participants could have entirely accounted for the results.

Terman's selection methods were biased against identifying highly intelligent children in low SES families or in minority groups. The bias against minorities was a side effect of the bias toward selecting children from families with relatively high SES, because in California in the 1920s the difference in SES between Whites and Blacks or Latinos was much greater than it is today. There may have been many talented individuals who should have been in Terman's group but were not selected. However, Terman never set out to study all, or even a representative group, of gifted schoolchildren in California. His intention was to find some gifted students and follow them literally throughout life. He did this. What the distribution of gifted is in the general population is a different question.

Would the conclusions have been any different had there been an aggressive attempt to recruit bright Black and Latino children? We will never know.

10.4.2. *The Gifted II: The Study of Mathematically Precocious Youth and Related Studies*

We now turn to a more modern, much larger study that is every bit as ambitious as Terman's was, but has a more clearly defined recruitment procedure.

In 1971 Julian Stanley, a professor at Johns Hopkins University, began the Study of Mathematically Precocious Youth (SMPY).[65] Students in middle schools (then called "junior high schools") were urged to take the SAT when they were twelve or thirteen years old. Recall that the SAT is designed for students in the third or fourth year of high school, at age sixteen to eighteen. Stanley initially focused on mathematical precocity, but in 1973 he began to study verbal precocity as well.

A two-tiered selection procedure was used. The SMPY researchers identified those twelve- to thirteen-year-old students who had scored in the top 3% on standardized tests that had already been given, as part of their school's normal assessment program, and asked them to take the SAT. Students who scored 500 or higher on either the mathematics or verbal (SAT-M or SAT-V) portion of the test were asked to participate in the main study. This score would put a twelve- or thirteen-year-old student in the top half of seventeen-year-olds. Such a level of accomplishment on the SAT-M is an impressive accomplishment, because this test evaluates proficiency in mathematical topics that are often not covered until late middle or high school. The middle school students either had to have studied these topics outside of school or had to apply

general reasoning to solve the problems on the test. The researchers regarded the students who scored 500 or above to be in the top one-half of one percent (1 in 200) in their age group, while the students who scored 700 or higher were believed to be in the top one-hundredth of one percent (1 in 10,000). The design of the study thus permits comparison between the bright and the extremely bright.

Stanley died in 2005. The SMPY study has been carried on by Stanley's colleagues, Camilla Benbow and David Lubinski, at Vanderbilt University. Their intent is to make SMPY a fifty-year study of the careers of people identified as talented in their early adolescence. (Stanley's first participants were born in the late 1950s and early 1960s.) In addition to observing the behavior of talented students, Stanley and his colleagues were interested in the nurturing of exceptional talent, especially in mathematics. Therefore, the SMPY has included a teaching component, in which participants are enrolled in intensive summer programs.

The data that has been gathered at this time (2010), which roughly carries the participants through their thirties, provides insight into several aspects of the development of the gifted. These include reactions to academic environments, academic achievement, and accomplishments by early middle age.[66]

The students took to intensive academic instruction like ducks to water. The SMPY students could assimilate a year's high school course work in about three weeks of intensive study. This is consistent with other reports, indicating that when special instruction is offered it helps everyone, but it helps the talented students the most.[67] I would add a caveat to this. The statement is true unless the special instruction is highly structured and specifically developed for a low-ability group. In this case the high-ability group's accomplishments may

---

65 Stanley, 1996; Brody & Blackburn, 1996.

66 The data cited here is largely taken from Lubinski and Benbow's (2006) review of the status of the project thirty-five years after the initial enrollment of students.

67 Ceci & Papierno, 2005.

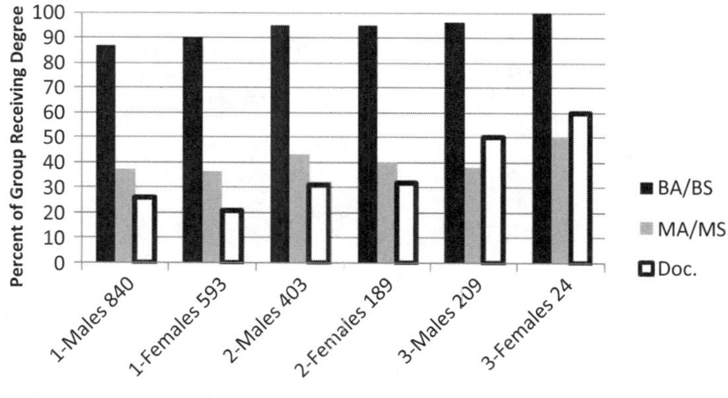

Figure 10.11. Educational attainment of participants in the SMPY, by age thirty-three. Members of cohorts 1 and 2 attained scores of 500 or better on the SAT-M by age thirteen. Members of cohort 3 attained scores of 700 or better. For reference, in the general population in the US as of 2004, 27% of the population twenty-five or older had received bachelor's degrees, 9% had master's degrees, and 3% held a doctorate of some type, including the Ph.D., M.D., L.L.D., and E.D. degrees. Data from Lubinski & Benbow, 2006.

actually deteriorate due to loss of interest and motivation.[68]

The academic achievements of the group are staggering. Figure 10.11 shows the level of academic achievement obtained by SMPY participants who had achieved scores of either 500 or greater or 700 or greater on the SAT-M. Lubinski and Benbow have pointed out that it is, to say the least, interesting that a two-hour test taken at age thirteen or younger can predict that the "risk," if you will, of obtaining a doctorate has risen from three in one hundred, the U.S. national rate, to one in two (cohort 3 in Figure 10.11).

What about on beyond schooling? At the time of this writing (2010) the SMPY participants are less than fifty years old. Nevertheless, their accomplishments are spectacular. Because many of the participants went into science, engineering, and related careers, a particularly compelling comparison contrasts the SMPY participants to graduate students of a similar age who had attended highly ranked university programs in science or engineering. Figure 10.12 shows

this comparison for a distinctly academic criterion, employment at highly ranked universities, and a distinctly nonacademic criterion, how much money the individual was making. By age thirty-three approximately 8% of the "over 700" men were earning more than $250,000 as individuals. In 2005 (the time of the survey) approximately 1.5% of all US *households* earned more than $250,000.

The SMPY was initially motivated by a desire to study the life histories of adolescents who showed exceptional promise in mathematics. As the study progressed it extended its reach to the evaluation of people with high SAT-V scores. This made it possible to study people whose talents were tilted toward either mathematical or verbal skills. It should be remembered, though, that people with very high verbal scores will probably have above-average mathematics scores, and vice versa.

The tilt definitely affected the type of contribution that was made. SMPY participants whose strongest test scores were on the SAT-V tended to major in the social sciences and humanities; those with high SAT-M scores chose the sciences and engineering fields. This difference held true both for

68 Snow, 1982, 1996.

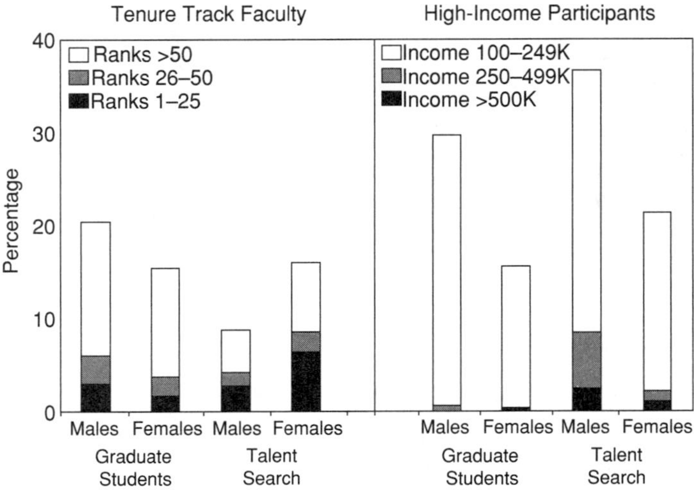

Figure 10.12. The SMPY participants compared to graduate students of the same age. A comparison of the accomplishments, by age thirty-three, of SMPY participants who had scored 700 or better on either the SAT-V or SAT-M, at age thirteen, to the accomplishments of graduate students from highly ranked U.S. university programs. From Lubinski and Benbow, 2006, Figure 3.

choice of major and for later professional work.[69]

The mathematically precocious youth did not rest on their laurels. They were willing to work more hours than the graduate students to whom they were compared – even though mathematics and science graduate students, all in highly rated programs, are a notoriously hard-working group. Somewhat more men than women qualified for the program. The disparity between men and women increased sharply as a function of the SAT-M score. This can be seen from an examination of Figure 10.11. The male/female ratio in cohorts I and II, which were in the top 1/200 group, is 1.6 to one. The male/female ratio in cohort III, the 1 in 10,000 group, was 8.7 to one.

The SMPY participants tended to come from small families of relatively high SES. Their parents were much more likely to have college degrees, including advanced degrees, than would be the case for randomly selected students. These two relationships are not independent, for family size is negatively correlated with SES.

Only about 1% of the SMPY participants were African American or Latino. This is comparable to the figure in Terman's study, although the percentage of African American and Latino students in the schools had increased markedly between the SMPY recruitment and Terman's recruitment, fifty years earlier.

Thirty-three percent of the participants in the SMPY and related programs are Asian.[70] Nationally, Asians constitute about 4% of the population. It has been claimed that Asians have a greater genetic potential for intelligence, and especially for mathematical reasoning. This claim is somewhat controversial.[71] However, genetic potential is unlikely to have been a cause for the overrepresentations of Asians. Eighty percent of the Asian participants had parents who had been born and educated outside of the United States. Were the contrast to be due to genetics, one would have expected a much higher percentage of Asians whose

69 Park, Lubinski, & Benbow, 2007.

70 Brody & Blackburn, 1996. Unfortunately these authors did not provide figures for the various Asian groups.

71 See Flynn, 1991. This topic is discussed in more detail in Chapter 11.

parents had been born in the US. Nor is the contrast likely to be due to some great deficiency in US schooling, for most of the non-Asian participants had been educated in the US school system. This strongly suggests that environmental factors influencing the home life of recent Asian immigrants were a major factor in the children's developing interests and skills in academic pursuits.

The Terman study and the SMPY are not the only studies of the gifted, but they are perhaps the largest, and their results are representative. People who do well on cognitive tests in their late childhood or early teens have quite bright prospects. High scorers tend to come from fairly high SES families, so some of their success may be due to the advantages of privilege. However, the accomplishments of the gifted are too substantial to support a claim that advantage is all they have. Their own ability counts for a great deal.

10.4.3. *Developing the Gifted*

A variety of acceleration programs have been developed to assist the gifted in reaching their potential. These vary from special summer courses, as in the case of the SMPY, to provision of accelerated tracks in public high schools and offering children as young as fourteen early admissions to universities. Gifted children perform very well in such programs. They also report enjoying them. There is little evidence for widespread social maladjustment, although participants in the early college entrance programs report preferring the company of their equally gifted age-mates to that of the considerably older college students. One particularly telling comment was made by Nancy Robinson, a professor at the University of Washington who, together with her husband, Halbert, developed an early entrance program at that university. She noted that gifted students who came from the public schools benefitted from a pretraining program that prepared them for the pace of instruction at a major university. Why? Because they needed to develop study

habits! They had been able to get by in their regular schools without exercising the discipline needed when they were thrown into the far less supportive atmosphere of university instruction.[72]

10.4.4. *A Comment on Criticisms of the Concept of the Gifted*

On occasion the results of the studies of the gifted have been criticized in ways that I think are unfair or irrelevant. For instance, I have heard the Terman study criticized for not having identified a Nobel laureate! There are also widespread, although as far as I know undocumented, stories that two men who did subsequently win Nobel Prizes in science were overlooked during the selection of participants. Such criticisms set an unrealistic standard, by asking the researchers to predict a one in a million event, while ignoring major trends in the data.

Another criticism is a claim that very high scores on cognitive tests do not predict anything. This belief is extremely widespread, even among psychologists.[73] It is false. In the SMPY there is a substantial difference between the accomplishments of the top 1 in 200 among test scorers and the accomplishments of the top 1 in 10,000. Similar findings were noticed by Terman for people with IQs over 170 as children.

10.4.5. *The Prospects for Individuals with Low Test Scores*

What about the other side of the coin, people in the low normal intelligence range, which I shall define as those whose IQs lie between 70 and 90?

People in the low intelligence range are not automatically candidates for assisted living or other institutional programs. However, more people in the low intelligence range are found in welfare and prison/jail

---

72 See Cronbach, 1996, and Robinson, 1996, for elaboration on these points.

73 See Muller et al., 2005, and Vasquez & Jones, 2006, for examples of such assertions.

populations than would be found if the welfare and prison/jail populations were selected randomly from the population. This does not mean that the majority of low intelligence individuals are headed for some form of institutional control. It simply means that they are at a greater risk of having these bad things happen than is the case for a randomly chosen member of the population.

As in the case of the gifted, the best way to understand the issues facing people in the low intelligence range is to examine prospective studies, in which individuals in the low intelligence range are first identified, and then, hopefully along with a control group of average and above-average individuals, are followed for some time. Here are three such studies.

In Herrnstein and Murray's "Bell Curve" study[74] of the NLSY79 panel, teenage men and women took the AFQT in their mid to late teens.[75] The Department of Defense uses these scores to classify people into categories I–V, with categories IV and V covering the range of scores below 90. About 45% of the NLSY79 men and women in categories IV and V failed to obtain either a high school diploma or a general education degree (GED). The base rate for the entire NLSY79 panel was 9%. Measures of workplace performance were similarly low. Herrnstein and Murray concluded from this that intelligence, as measured as a teenager, is a major predictor of income as a young adult. Other analyses of the same data[76] have agreed that intelligence is indeed a predictor of income, but that ethnic status, gender, and location in the country also have to be considered.

If we look at analyses of the intellectual demands of the workplace, this is not surprising. Look back to Figure 10.10, which plots wages against imputed intelligence requirements for over 800 jobs. Income is fairly flat over the wide range of occupations that have low imputed intelligence requirements. The figure also shows that there is

74 Herrnstein & Murray, 1994.
75 See Chapter 2 for a discussion of the ASVAB and
     the AFQT.
76 See, e.g. the analyses in Devlin et al., 1998.

a considerable spread between the mean and ninetieth percentile of earnings within occupations. To the extent that intelligence determines within-occupation earnings, as we have seen that it does (section 10.3), one would expect people with low scores to earn less. And they do.

The picture is somewhat bleaker with respect to welfare. In this case we have to make a distinction by ethnicity, for welfare rates vary markedly with ethnic status. Herrnstein and Murray found that the rate at which White women in the low intelligence range had received Aid for Dependent Children support was better than four times the rate in the NLSY79 sample as a whole.

A more detailed picture of what happens to the low intelligence group in the workplace can be obtained by examining a Department of Defense study of how low intelligence males fared in military service, in a setting where working conditions are more precisely defined and recorded than they are in the civilian workforce. The study, *Project 100,000*, conducted in the late 1960s at the behest of Secretary of Defense Robert McNamara, was motivated by an important policy issue.

The US military normally does not recruit Category V individuals, and is limited, by law, to recruiting a fixed percentage of Category IV soldiers. The argument for the policy is that it does not make sense to go to the added expense of training and supervising personnel who perform at a low level. On the other hand, the military forces have to have a certain number of recruits each year. If the category IV designation is a false indicator of military performance, excluding these men and women would amount to ignoring a potential recruiting population.

In Project 100,000 approximately 100,000 Category IV men (IQ range roughly 80–90) were enlisted outside of the normal channels. Their military careers were compared to those of a control group of enlisted servicemen who matched them in age and educational status prior to entry, and who had met normal recruitment standards. The control group underrepresented the higher levels of AFQT scores (I and II) compared to

Table 10.8. Attrition rates during basic training (percentages) for Project 100,000 participants and for the service as a whole, broken down by military branch.

Branch of Service	Project 100,000 Enlistees	Overall Service Rate
Army	3.7	2.0
Marines	11.1	4.4
Navy	8.6	2.8
Air Force	9.2	3.0

Note: Data from Sticht et al., 1987. Figures are for the 1969–72 period, during the Vietnam War.

the percentages found in the general population, for there were no officers in the study.[77] In civilian terms, Project 100,000 examined the workplace performance of people involved in blue-collar and lower-level white-collar occupations, excluding managerial positions above the foreman level, and excluding professional occupations.

In all military services the first thing that enlistees do is to go through recruit training or, as it is known in the Navy and Marines, boot camp. The ostensible goal of recruit training is to inform the enlistees about service customs and to provide them with a taste of the life they can expect in the future. This taste (and the service life that follows) varies greatly depending upon the service; the Army and Marines envisage a different life for recruits than do the Navy and the Air Force, and the Navy and Air Force differ from each other. Boot camp has a second, less announced purpose. It serves as a screening device to see which enlistees have the adaptability to change from civilian to a more disciplined military life.

Table 10.8 shows the attrition rate from boot camp during the period of the Project 100,000 study, roughly 1969–71. Attrition rates were higher for Project 100,000 than for the control group in every service. Attrition rates also varied considerably across services. This may be because of both differential recruitment by the services and differences in basic training itself. Basic military training, strictly construed, requires roughly a fourth-grade reading ability. Because the

Navy and the Air Force have more technical billets than the other services, higher reading and mathematics requirements may have been in force in those services. These requirements would be especially hard on the Project 100,000 servicemen, compared to members of the control group. By contrast, the Army and the Marines place more stress on determining a recruit's ability to follow instructions in physically demanding situations.

Looking at the other side of the coin, the vast majority of the Project 100,000 servicemen did complete basic training. From the viewpoint of the services, a rigid insistence on conventional standards would have excluded over 90,000 trainable enlistees. That would have been a serious loss.

Modern military services are a microcosm of society. They contain some positions, such as infantryman, that are clearly unique to warfare. They also contain many positions that either have exact civilian counterparts, such as clerk or electronic technician, or have close analogs in civilian life, especially outside of combat. We have already seen, from the analysis of civilian occupations in section 10.3, that occupations vary a good deal in their demands for intelligence. Where did the Project 100,000 servicemen wind up during their first term of service?

Figure 10.13 shows that Project 100,000 servicemen were much more likely to be assigned to nontechnical, nonspecialized jobs than were normally enlisted servicemen matched for pre-service education and ethnic status. However, the evidence that this is

77 Sticht et al., 1987.

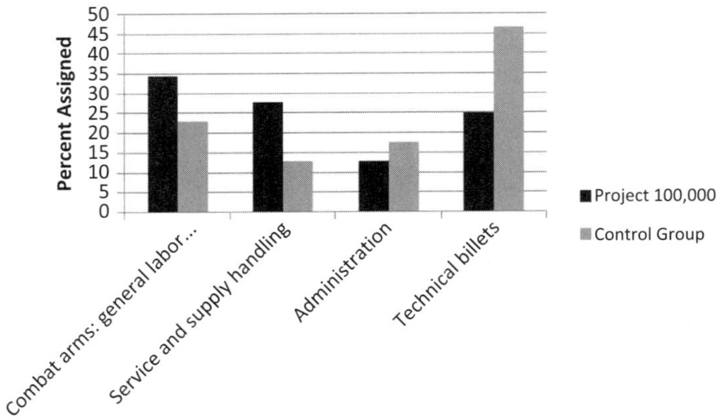

Figure 10.13. Assignment of Project 100,000 and a matched control group to different classes of military occupations during their first term of enlistment. Based on data reported by Sticht et al., 1987.

due to their demonstrated abilities (or lack of them) after testing is not as strong as it could be. Assignments to technical billets are made based partly upon observations and interviews during recruit training, and partly upon a serviceman's ASVAB scores, obtained prior to entry. This means that the low scores of the Project 100,000 servicemen may have influenced their assignment.

From the viewpoint of a scientific study, this was a flaw in the design. However, one can hardly fault the services for using the scores to make assignments in ways believed to minimize training costs.

As in the case of the data on attrition, one can see two different things in the data on occupations. On the one hand, it shows (not surprisingly) that low intelligence men tended not to be assigned to technical and administrative occupations. On the other, they filled roles that are vital to the military mission.

What happened after the servicemen completed recruit training? Figure 10.14 compares the career progress of Project 100,000 and control servicemen, in terms of rank attained through their first enlistment and, for those that stayed in the service, their status in 1983, which would have been from twelve to fourteen years after initial enlistment. The picture is similar to the earlier comparisons. The Project 100,000 servicemen were generally not "top of the line," rapidly promoted military personnel. On the

other hand, they did show progress in their careers.

Project 100,000 was replicated...accidentally. During the 1980s a technical mistake was made in determining the norms for a revised version of the ASVAB. Before the mistake was discovered several thousand normally unqualified Category IV soldiers were enlisted into the Army. The careers of these soldiers have been followed, and by and large the results are the same as those obtained in the better-controlled Project 100,000 study.[78] There would be little point in repeating the statistics. However, I will recount a hopefully informative anecdote to enliven the statistics.

While serving as a consultant to a research project studying the accidentally recruited Category IV soldiers, I interviewed a lieutenant colonel who had commanded an armored battalion containing a high percentage of Category IV soldiers. The colonel believed that category IV soldiers performed well when doing clearly defined tasks, even if they were quite detailed. He offered as an example the task of replacing the power unit on a tank. This task is done in over a dozen well-defined steps, always done in the same sequence. After training, Category IV soldiers could replace the power unit.

78 Sticht et al., 1987, discusses the renorming problem and the resulting performance of the soldiers involved in some detail.

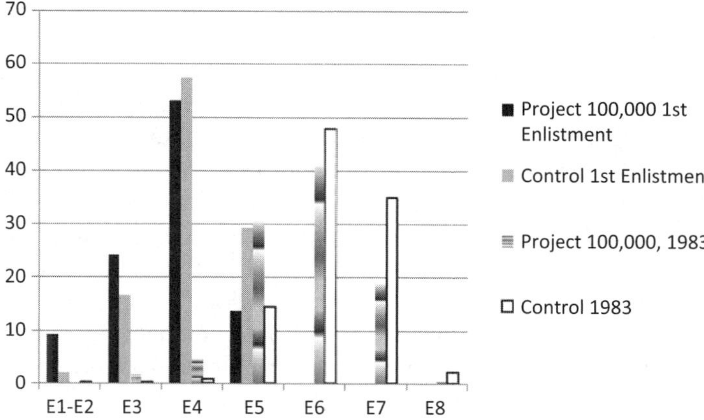

Figure 10.14. The advancement in rank of Project 100,000 personnel. The percentage of servicemen in the Project 100,000 and control groups who had reached different enlisted pay grades either during their first enlistment or after approximately thirteen years of service. Pay grades E1 and E2 were the grades typically assigned immediately upon completion of recruit service (e.g., private or private first class in the Army and Marines). Pay grade E4 (sergeant in the Army or Marines) was considered satisfactory service during the first enlistment. The higher pay grades represent staff noncommissioned officers (NCOs) or, in the Navy, Petty Officers. Grade E8, Master Sergeant or Chief Petty Officer, was a position with considerable prestige and responsibility.

More generally, the colonel believed that Category IV soldiers could be trained to do tasks where the instructions were "do this, then do that, then the other thing..."

The colonel thought that Category IV soldiers had trouble with tasks that are defined by the end to be accomplished, rather than by the steps to be taken. He offered as an example the task of recalibrating a gun sight that has been knocked out of alignment with the barrel of a tank's cannon. The instructions for this task began, "Find a way to fix the sight rigidly on the tank's hull." This instruction defines the goal to be accomplished and leaves it up to the soldier to find a way of accomplishing the goal.

If we place this in a more psychological framework – for the colonel certainly did not use such words – the Category IV soldier could learn what to do in a well-defined situation but had trouble anticipating what would happen if he took a particular sort of action in a more poorly defined situation. This sort of deficit appears to be characteristic of low intelligence people in schools, the military, and the civilian workplace. Depending upon whether you approach intelligence from the viewpoint of the psychometrician, the information-processing psychologist, or the cognitive neuroscientist, you can say that people with low intelligence have trouble with tasks that have a high demand for g, tasks that involve the working memory/executive function class of behaviors, or tasks that place demands on the forebrain–cingulate cortex circuit. All three statements amount to the same thing.

10.5. A Concluding Comment on Intelligence and the Workplace

Someone who says that intelligence, as assessed by standard cognitive tests, is irrelevant to performance in either academia or the workplace is simply wrong. So is someone who says that intelligence does not amount to very much, compared to a variety of personality characteristics. The data both within and across occupations show that measures of intelligence are among the best, and most often *the* best, predictors of academic and occupational success. On the other hand, no one has claimed that cognitive tests are perfect predictors. Predictive validity correlations are in the .4–.6 range, which is much better prediction than can be achieved with any personality measure, but is still far from perfect.

The same message can be extracted from studies of extremes. On the whole, people who have high intelligence test scores do quite well. *On the average* the gifted get better jobs and make more money. The Terman study, and all studies of the gifted afterward, gave the lie to the stereotype of a gifted person as a neurotic introvert with health problems. The contrast between the SMPY 1 in 200 and 1 in 10,000 groups shows that the tests have predictive power at very high levels, directly contradicting statements to the contrary by psychologists who do not, themselves, study individual differences.

Here are some documented statistics, but on a very small sample, so the report falls somewhere between a scientific fact and an anecdote. In the 1960s the National Aeronautic and Space Agency conducted an intensive screening of volunteers to become the first American astronauts, the MERCURY and GEMENI programs. The selected candidates had WAIS IQs averaging 135. Unselected candidates had IQs averaging 131. A control group of comparably aged aviators averaged 118. Being intelligent is part of having the right stuff.[79]

At the opposite end of the distribution, people in the low intelligence range generally have difficulty with school, especially if they are placed on an academic track, and usually take occupations that do not make high cognitive demands. They earn less than people in the normal-high intelligence ranges and are more likely to require some form of welfare assistance.

It cannot be stressed too strongly, though, that these are trends. Every study of the extremes comes up with exceptions. There are people who do quite well although they had modest test scores, and there are stunning examples of people with high scores who never live up to their promise.

Given these facts, why is there a widespread belief that intelligence does not count for very much in life? I think, but cannot prove, that several factors are involved.

One factor is a failure of unrealistic expectation. We may expect the gifted person to be a casual genius who can solve difficult problems without much care or effort. That is not the case. Two of the personality characteristics of the gifted are that they generally enjoy their work, and that they work very hard at it. The brilliant genius who, without training, knows at a glance the answer to difficult problems in mathematics, physics, or what have you is a very rare bird.[80]

People without statistical training have a hard time grasping the concept of something that increases the probability of an event but does not establish its certainty. Thus if we can think of examples of people with high test scores doing stupid things, or people with low test scores doing good things, that is taken as proof that the predictors do not work. In the newspaper business "Man bites dog" is news, "Dog bites man" is not. The unusual is publicized and sticks in our minds. The prosaic does not.

We may have an unrealistic idea about the extent to which personal characteristics determine success. Large-scale social and economic forces, and idiosyncratic impersonal events, can play a great part. The various reports of the Terman group stress how much these highly intelligent people were influenced by having come of age during the Great Depression and then, especially for the men, having had to deal with World War II. The SMPY group has grown up in times of relative peace and economic expansion, at least until 2010. Such things

---

79 Santy, 1994, p. 276.

80 It is possible that a very few such individuals exist. The best-documented case study is of the Indian mathematician Ramanujam, who made major contributions to mathematics even though he was self-taught. He also spent a great deal of time working on mathematical problems.

influence one's success, quite outside of personal traits. While it is true that we partly make our own environments, we are partly stuck with them.

People are heavily influenced by their personal experiences. Charles Murray has pointed out that we live in a society that is sharply stratified by intelligence.[81] College-educated people, by and large, deal with other college-educated people, and people with high school educations deal with each other. Within the restricted range of intelligence that people can observe directly, other variables may account for more variation in performance than intelligence does. It is only when we step back and look at the big picture that the importance of intelligence becomes clear.

My final speculation is that some people, for understandable reasons, do not want to find that intelligence has an effect upon success.

Many people in post-industrial society, and especially in post-industrial American society, hold a belief and have two attitudes that, combined, provide a motivation for rejecting intelligence as a (partial) explanation of workplace success. The belief is that intelligence is something that is more or less fixed for life. As was discussed in Chapter 9, and will be discussed further in the section on aging in Chapter 11, this is a false belief – especially about intelligence in the conceptual sense of the problems that people can solve, rather than in the narrower sense of a test score. But that is not what people think. When one combines a belief in the permanence of intelligence with an attitude of distrust of elites, it becomes almost necessary to argue that intelligence is of little relevance in life, for to do otherwise can be seen as an affirmation of the appropriateness of rewarding an elite class of thinkers.

The second attitude is quite different. It has to do with a sincere desire for equal opportunity for all.

There are marked differences in the typical cognitive test scores obtained by members of different racial and ethnic groups. There are much smaller, rather complex differences in test scores between men and women. Up to the middle of the twentieth century these differences were used to justify varying degrees of segregation of minority groups, in areas including admission to universities and the granting of specialized degrees, and to place less strict, but still important, restrictions on women's opportunities. Since that time overt discrimination has virtually stopped, but there are people who have used group differences in test scores as evidence for the proposition that group differences in educational and professional achievement are largely due to group differences in intelligence.[82] To the extent that this conclusion is correct, provision of equal opportunity for all groups in society will not produce an equal distribution of social and economic rewards across groups.

Many people who are deeply committed to social equality find such a conclusion offensive. It is difficult for them to argue about the fact of differential distribution of test scores. Therefore, they deny the relevance of scores to social outcomes. This denial cannot be maintained.

The discussion of racial and ethnic differences in intelligence, and male:female differences in intelligence, raises extremely complex issues. We take them up in the next chapter.

---

81 Murray, 2008.

82 See, for instance, Murray, 2005; Rushton & Jensen, 2005; and Lynn and Vanhanen, 2002, 2006.

CHAPTER 11

The Demography of Intelligence

By nature men are nearly alike. By practice they get to be far apart.

> – Confucius (attribution in *Bartlett's Familiar Quotations*, 15th ed., 1980)

People are not all the same. There are young people, old people, and people in between. Nevertheless, we do make distinctions, ranging from binary decisions about the right to vote to the minimum age at which one qualifies for a pension. Many of these distinctions are based on the underlying presumption that intelligence grows, and then declines. There are mandatory retirement age requirements for air traffic controllers and commercial aviators, largely because of our beliefs about changes in their cognitive capabilities. In the United States federal judges are appointed for life. Many of the individual states have mandatory age limits for judges.

There are men and women, a sharper biological distinction than young and old. Historically, many societies have assumed that men and women have different cognitive capacities. In contemporary post-industrial societies there is a presumption of equality. But does "equality" mean "identity?" Should we regard a low incidence of women in corporate law practice with suspicion? Should the acceptable percentage of women in corporate law practice be the same as the acceptable percentage of women working as helicopter pilots?

People are identified with, and self-identify with, various racial and ethnic groups. Do these groups differ in intelligence? To some people the answer is obvious – they do. Other people believe that even the suggestion of a difference is evidence that the speaker is prejudiced. Worldwide, we are organized into nations. Do the people of the world all have the same intelligence? Herodotus, the father of history, thought that easy climates produce people with soft minds and little resolve. Richard Lynn, a modern professor at the University of Ulster, has given new life to this argument.[1]

____

1   Lynn, 2006.

And identifying group differences is seldom enough. We want to know why differences occur.

This chapter describes the scientific evidence regarding the relation between intelligence and demographic variables: age, sex, race, and ethnicity. I shall try to present an objective discussion of these contentious issues.

11.1. The Issues Involved

I will not present any simple one-liner answers to any issue involving group differences. In my opinion none exists. A person who makes a sweeping assertion about the existence or cause of age, sex, racial/ethnic, or national differences should be regarded with extreme suspicion. Throughout I have tried to separate discussions of scientific fact from hypotheses and from discussions of policy. Maintaining the distinction between scientific findings and policy recommendations is very important. Psychologists can, for instance, inform lawmakers about the facts that reaction times increase and the ability to control attention drops as people age. Whether or not there should be upper age limits on automobile driving is a policy decision.

Because the study of group differences can be so contentious, it is a good idea to set the ground rules by discussing some problems of analysis and interpretation that keep coming up in this area of investigation. The rules fall into two categories: general principles and issues of interpretation. Panel 11.1 sets forth some general principles. The rest of this section focuses on issues of interpretation.

11.1.1. *Distinguishing between Cognitive and Noncognitive Effects*

Intelligence is a "can do" concept. The distinction between "can do" and "will do" is relevant to the study of group differences, because when group differences in performance are observed it may not be clear whether they are due to differences in intelligence or motivation.

The case of Asian-Americans in the United States provides a good example. As a group, Asian-Americans are represented in higher education far out of proportion to their frequency in the population. In autumn of 2008 Asians made up 35% of the student body at the University of California, Berkeley. Asians constitute just over 4% of the US population, and 12% of the population of California.[2] Some have attributed the overrepresentation of Asians in selective universities to Asian intelligence, for Asians as a group score slightly above the population mean on some *g*-loaded intelligence tests. This point is discussed in more detail in section 11.3. But is this because of a biological capacity? One also has to consider cultural traditions and expectations about the advantages of education that may provide Asian-Americans with more-than-average motivation to succeed in cognitive endeavors.[3]

A good deal has been made of the possibility that some people consistently score below their capabilities on cognitive tests and other measurements of achievement because they just do not try. The phenomenon is by no means limited to cognition; if people have a mindset to expect low achievement, they will not work hard to become high achievers in almost any field.[4] In the case of group differences, it has been claimed that a particular type of negative mindset, *stereotype threat*, may be one of the reasons that certain groups, including African Americans and women, tend not to do well on tests of mathematical reasoning. They believe that they are not the sort of people who do mathematics well, so they are willing to disengage from the hard work of problem solving required to obtain high scores on mathematics tests.[5]

---

2 Information provided by the University of California, Berkeley, at the website osr2.berkeley.edu/twiki/bin/view/Main/Fall2008EthnicDistribution, and by the 2000 US Census.
3 Flynn, 1991; Sue & Okazaki, 1990.
4 Dweck, 2006.
5 Steele & Aronson, 1995, 1998.

Panel 11.1. Some Principles for Guiding Research on Group Differences in Intelligence

The following rules are abridgments of suggestions about conducting research on group differences that my colleague Prof. Jerry Carlson, of the University of California, Riverside, and I made in an article in the journal *Perspectives on Psychological Science*.[*] Our ideas were attacked on the somewhat contradictory grounds that our guidelines would unduly restrict inquiry[†] and that they would encourage delving into questions that are not scientific and that we did not understand.[‡] We made a rejoinder.[§] I encourage readers interested in this issue to look at the original articles. Here I simply paraphrase the guidelines.

1. The measures must have construct validity, that is, it should be clear why they measure what they purport to measure.
2. Measurements must be valid in all groups involved. See the main text for a discussion of what this means.
3. The fact that a score can be changed by training is not evidence against an inherent group difference unless the altered score is as valid a measure as the original score.
4. Generalization to populations depends crucially upon the relation between the sample and the population. "Any old convenient sample" will not do. A generalization from observations of a group difference in college students, for instance, to a conclusion about group differences for people of all ages is not automatically valid.
5. Literature summations must be done carefully, with special attention to research results that do not conform to the reviewer's conclusions. Complete objectivity is impossible, but discussants in a scientific debate should strive for this ideal.
6. Alternative hypotheses and models should be considered.
7. The alternatives should duly represent the original authors' ideas. Straw models should not be set up in order to be knocked down. This has been a particular problem in the study of group differences. For instance, people sometimes attack the position that group differences are either entirely genetic or entirely environmental, whereas the real question is how much the environment or genetic inheritance influences the difference.
8. Heritability coefficients are measures of the relative size of genetic and environmental influence, and can vary across populations.
9. When a policy recommendation is made, one's policy model, including attitudes about desirable consequences, should be stated.
10. Be willing to say "We don't know." In many cases we do not know what causes a group difference. There are some cases, especially involving the evolution of cognition, where it is unlikely that we shall ever know. Be willing to acknowledge such situations. Acknowledging ambiguity is not a sign of weakness, it is a sign of intelligence!

[*]   Hunt & Carlson, 2007a,c.
[†]   Gottfredson, 2007a.
[‡]   Sternberg & Grigorenko, 2007.
[§]   Hunt & Carlson, 2007b.

There is no doubt that stereotype threat exists. The effect has been demonstrated in laboratory studies involving racial/ethnic groups, men and women, and aging participants. There is considerable controversy over whether the phenomenon occurs when students take a high stakes test, such as a college entrance examination, because when the stakes are high external motivating factors may override any internal willingness to give up. The evidence for and against stereotype threat effects will be discussed later. Here I bring up the problem as an example of how behavior will depend upon both "can do" and "will do." Before we can use a difference between two groups in test scores, or any other cognitive achievement, as evidence of a difference in underlying intelligence, we must be sure that motivation was equivalent in each group.

11.1.2. *Recruitment Effects*

It is probably true that more studies have been carried out on college students than on any other population. For instance, a great deal of our information about the differences in cognitive abilities of men and women is based on observed differences between male and female college students. Such studies are subject to *recruitment effects* that limit their generality. Let us look at such situations abstractly.

In the typical study of group differences an investigator identifies some *accessible* population (e.g., college students) that contains members of the groups of interest. Obviously, there are male and female college students. Participants are selected from the groups of interest within the accessible population. Group differences are then observed. Assuming a random selection from the accessible population, conventional statistical methods can be used to justify making a general statement about the accessible population. But what about conclusions about group differences in the population at large? The validity of generalization depends upon how group members are recruited into the accessible population.

Here is a concrete example. Two Canadian psychologists, Douglas Jackson and J. Phillipe Rushton, found that in the population of people who had taken the SAT, men had higher scores than women.[6] Does this mean that men in their late teens (the age at which the SAT is usually taken) are

generally more intelligent, as assessed by the SAT, than women of the same age? The conclusion would be valid if young men and women, in the population at large, were equally likely to take the SAT. But they are not. Since 1980 the majority of college students have been women. It may be that the most intelligent 60% of women attempt to go to college, compared to the most intelligent 40% of men. If this is so, the recruitment process is different for men and women.

In such a case comparison of the SAT scores would give a false picture of the population difference. If there are no male-female differences in intelligence in the general population, the top 60% of the female population would be expected to score lower, on the average, than the top 40% of the male population. Of course, this is an oversimplification. A more sophisticated model of male-female differences in the recruitment process for taking the SAT has been verified. Applying it, my colleague Tara Madhyastha and I found that Jackson and Rushton's results could not be used to argue that there are differences in intelligence between men and women in general, although they could be used to argue that there are differences in intelligence within the college population.[7]

Recruitment effects can be very large. They affect all types of group differences that we will consider: age differences, male-female differences, racial/ethnic differences, and international comparisons.

11.1.3. *Establishing Causation*

Students in the social sciences learn to recite, almost as a mantra, "Correlation does not mean causation." The rooster may crow before dawn, but we do not conclude that the rooster's crowing makes the sun rise. In laboratory situations we avoid confusing correlation with causation by conducting controlled experiments, where one possible causal factor is systematically changed as other factors are held constant, or by assigning participants randomly to experimental

---

6 Jackson & Rushton, 2006.

7 Hunt and Madhyastha, 2008.

and control groups. This does not work for the study of group differences. We cannot assign people randomly to be young or old, male or female, Black or White, American or British. They come as they are. And when they do, they typically come with many differences besides their group membership. This makes understanding some differences extremely difficult.

There are collinearities between group membership and a host of variables. Consider the relation between intelligence and national wealth. (We will go into this in considerable detail in section 11.5.) There is a fairly high correlation between national wealth, measured by gross domestic product per person (GDP/c), and national average scores on intelligence tests. There is also a high correlation between mean intelligence test scores and indices of physical health, intelligence, scholastic achievement, and GDP/c. What are the causal relations? One could argue that intelligence causes wealth, or that school achievement causes wealth, or that wealth makes possible good schools, which in turn cause intelligence to rise.

Unfortunately, there have been studies in which investigators simply ignore the problem. They seize upon a single causal variable, establish that it has a correlation with, say, intelligence, and spin a plausible tale about why this is so. Historically, this is the sort of reasoning that led people to believe that malaria (Latin, *mal aria* = bad air) was due to dank, hot air because there was a correlation between humid conditions and outbreaks of the disease. We now know that the disease is borne by mosquitoes. Emphasizing isolated correlations might have been justified in the days before the technologies for multivariate statistical analyses had been developed. They are not justifiable today.

Collinearity issues are partly addressed in *quasi-experimental designs*, in which we find two groups that appear to be equal on all the variables that we believe are relevant, except one, which may or may not be an experimental manipulation. This is the sort of design used when teaching methods are contrasted in comparable school districts, with

one method being used in one district and another method in another. Similar cases appear in the literature on intelligence. For instance, one of the pieces of evidence used to argue that schooling influences general reasoning is that in the early twentieth century children's IQ test scores were higher in isolated rural communities that had schools, compared to the scores of children who did not have access to schools.[8] The argument is valid to the extent that the different communities really were equated on variables, such as nutrition and health, that could also influence test scores.

Collinearity issues can be addressed by means of a statistical technique known as *causal modeling*, which is used to determine which of several explanations best fits the data. For instance, the previous chapter reported an investigation of the relation between socioeconomic status (SES), intelligence (as indexed by the SAT) and academic achievement.[9] Three causal models were considered: one in which intelligence and SES had independent influences on academic achievement, one in which intelligence had an influence only as a proxy for SES, and one in which SES had no direct influence on academic achievement, beyond any influence that it had on intelligence. The third model was shown to be the most accurate. Note that the question has shifted from finding a statistically significant relationship to the more sophisticated issue of selecting the best model.

Causal modeling is a powerful technique but is not perfect. When all is said and done, causal models are based on correlations, and correlation is still not causation. Causal modeling does not establish what the truth is. The technique gains its power by rejecting initially plausible models for better ones, not by rejecting the null hypothesis, which almost no one believes in anyway.

Numerous studies have been done using what at first appears to be a classic experimental design. Members of different groups

8 Ceci & Williams, 1997.
9 Sackett et al., 2009.

are recruited; within each group participants are randomly assigned to experimental and control conditions, and the result of the experiment-control contrast is compared across groups. Stereotype threat has been investigated in this way. People in an affected group (women, African Americans, etc.) are either reminded of their group identity or not reminded of it, and then given a test on which members of the group are said to do poorly. The same logic could be used to compare test scores obtained by people who had been given either a newly invented "IQ pill" or a placebo. In an extension of this design, the same experimental-control contrast is applied within different groups, for instance, in an investigation contrasting two teaching methods in groups of Black and White students.

Studies of this sort are excellent ways of demonstrating that a particular manipulation can (or cannot) have an effect on test scores. They do not show whether the effect actually occurs, or how large it is compared to other effects, in the world outside the laboratory.

No method for investigating group differences in intelligence is perfect. They all have something to contribute. The strengths and weaknesses of the various designs have to be kept in mind as we consider the many results that have been obtained in the study of group differences in intelligence.

11.1.4. *Statistical and Measurement Issues*

In evaluating studies of group differences two statistical issues are of importance. They deal with measurements of the size of a group difference and the appropriateness of using tests as a way of assessing intelligence in different groups of people.

ESTABLISHING THE SIZE OF GROUP
DIFFERENCES
In virtually all cases we shall consider, estimates of intelligence in one group will *not* be uniformly higher or lower than differences in another group. In fact, this is true of most human traits. What we need is some measure of the extent to which two populations

overlap. The difference between means in deviation units, d, does this.

Consider two arbitrary groups, with mean scores on some test M_1 and M_2, and with *within-group* standard deviations S_1 and S_2. The deviation score, d, is defined as[10]

$$d = \frac{M_1 - M_2}{\sqrt{\frac{S_1^2 + S_2^2}{2}\,10}}. \tag{11.1}$$

The d measure provides a picture of the extent to which two groups overlap. The larger the value of d, the less the overlap. This is illustrated in Figure 11.1, which shows the overlap between three groups that are ordered with respect to their means, and have identical standard deviations within each group.

The d measure is a measure of the size of an effect, just as the correlation coefficient, r, is a measure of the size of an effect. Before interpreting a finding that d is not large enough to be statistically reliable at the .05 or .01 level, it has to be shown that the study had adequate statistical power to detect the smallest difference of interest. All the concerns about power that applied to r, and were introduced in the previous chapter, also apply to d.

THE APPROPRIATENESS OF USING THE
SAME TEST IN DIFFERENT GROUPS
If we want to measure group differences on a physical variable, such as height or weight, the principle is simple. We use a physical device to make a physical measurement. If we want to compare, say, the heights and weights of Asians to the heights and weights of Africans, there is no concern that tape measures and scales would behave differently across groups. The problem is subtler when it comes to cognitive testing, because different types of people may systematically respond to a test in different ways, thus tapping different underlying psychological variables.

10 The equation shown applies to a contrast between two groups of equal size. The case of unequal group sizes requires a slight complication in equation 11.1, but poses no new conceptual issue.

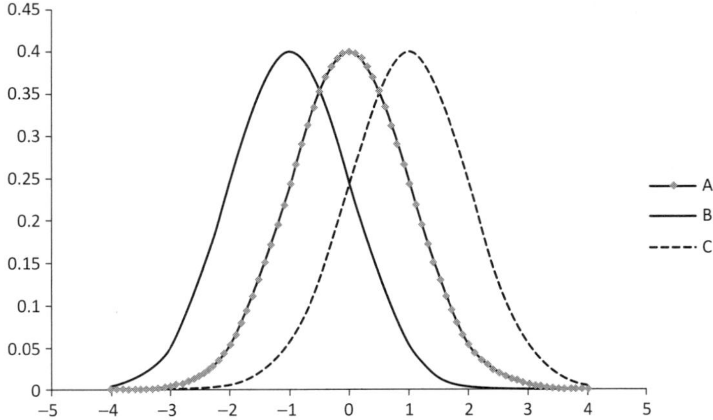

Figure 11.1. An illustration of the overlap between distributions. All distributions have an arbitrary standard deviation of 1. Distribution A has a mean at 0 on the abscissa, distribution B has a mean at −1, and distribution C has a mean at +1. The d (deviation) value for A – B is 1, for A – C is −1, and for B – C is −2. The amount of overlap decreases as the d value increases.

To illustrate this, imagine that we decide to develop a direction-taking test to measure people's ability to orient in space. The test might contain items like this:

Go to the flagpole to the north of your present position.
Then go east to the church.
Turn north at the church and proceed to the school.

We then see how long it takes people to get to the school, and how many deviations they make from the prescribed route.

Remember that we are not interested in direction-taking per se. We are interested in performance on the direction-taking test as a measure of a more general ability to orient in space.

If we use a contrast between the speeds with which men and women arrive at the school, we have implicitly assumed that men and women will approach the test in the same way. But there is evidence to the contrary. Men often approach problems in direction taking by constructing a mental map of the territory and the route through it. Women tend to memorize the directions and use them to follow a path.[11] The test evaluates a different underlying trait in men and in women, so comparing scores would be valid if we were interested in how well people did in direction finding, but not valid if we were interested in making an inference about men's and women's standing on an underlying latent trait of orienting ability.

In order to guard against such errors we have to have some way of showing that a test measures the same psychological trait in different groups. If we are dealing with a single test, and are concerned that different problems within the test tap different abilities in various groups, we look for evidence of *differential item functioning*.

The idea behind differential item functioning can be illustrated by another hypothetical test, a test of baseball knowledge. The more you know about baseball, the better able you will be to answer questions about baseball. The question "How many players are there on a team?" can be answered by anyone with the slightest knowledge of the game; the question "What is a squeeze play?" is a bit more challenging. Many Americans who have not thought about baseball since grammar school can answer the first question but not the second; a sports reporter would be able to answer

11 Hunt, 2002.

both. More generally, we should be able to order questions in terms of their difficulty.

Now suppose we give this test to two groups of people, Americans and Australians. Baseball is played in Australia, so some Australians know more about baseball than some Americans. The question is "Does the test measure the same thing, baseball knowledge, in both countries?" If it does, then the order of difficulty of items should be the same in each country, even though Australians, on the average, might answer fewer questions correctly. My intuition is that the order of item difficulty would be the same.

But let's go back to the direction-finding test, and this time the contrast is between men and women. Because the test measures orienting ability in men and verbal memory in women, there is no guarantee that the order of item difficulty would be the same. Suppose it is not. In that case we say that the test shows differential item functioning across groups. When differential item functioning is found, conclusions about group differences on a trait said to underlie a test cannot be drawn from observations of differences in test scores.

The simplest way to test for differential item functioning is to calculate the rank-order correlation between item difficulties within each group. Anything other than a fairly high value (.8 or above) is evidence for differential item functioning. If the items on a test have been selected using Item Response Theory (IRT; see Chapter 4), a more sophisticated test is possible. The item parameters must be the same in both groups.

COMPARING GROUPS USING TEST BATTERIES, SUCH AS THE WAIS

Differential item functioning refers to items within a test. Many studies attempt to draw conclusions about groups based on scores on a battery consisting of several tests. This would be the case, for instance, in a comparison of WAIS scores. In general, the purpose of the comparison will not be to compare raw scores, but to compare the groups on some underlying factor, such as general intelligence (g), that is derived from the scores on the individual tests. In technical terms, we want to determine group differences on a latent trait (g, R in the g-VPR model, Gf, Gc, etc.) from observations on the manifest test scores.

An important and deceptively simple-seeming case of such a comparison is *Spearman's hypothesis*, which Arthur Jensen attributes to the pioneering psychometrician Charles Spearman.[12] The conjecture is that differences between groups on virtually all cognitive tests are largely due to differences in g, general intelligence. For instance, suppose that we were to compare the grades of African American and White high school students in a variety of subjects – mathematics, language use, history, art, and so on. According to Spearman's hypothesis the differences between groups could largely be accounted for by differences in underlying general intelligence.

Spearman's hypothesis is a statement about group differences on a latent trait, g, rather than a difference on observable test scores. By definition, latent traits cannot be observed. So how do we evaluate the hypothesis? General intelligence, in the sense of g, is operationally defined as a factor underlying scores on several (observable) tests, such as the subtests of the WAIS. Jensen has developed a technique called the *method of correlated vectors* as a way to test Spearman's hypothesis.[13] As this method has been used widely, and erroneously, in the study of group differences, it is worthwhile understanding it. This serves as a good introduction to the more difficult task of understanding a better method.

If Spearman's hypothesis is valid, then those tests that are good measures of g should show large between-group differences, while tests that are measures of special abilities should show smaller differences. The extent to which a test is a measure of g is determined by its loading

12 Jensen, 1998, p. 372. Jensen credits the hypothesis to Spearman, but it appears to be Jensen's summary of Spearman's ideas on the topic.
13 Jensen, 1998.

on the first (general) factor in a factor analysis of a test battery (see Chapter 4). The extent to which groups differ on each of the tests within a battery is determined by the d statistic for comparing groups on that test. In order to apply the method of correlated vectors we compute the correlation between the test loadings and the d statistic, across tests. If the correlation is high, then the hypothesis is confirmed.

In spite of its popularity, the method of correlated vectors is seriously flawed. Depending upon the circumstances, it can either overstate the size of group differences on g when they are small[14] or, in other circumstances, understate them when they are present![15] This means that we will have to rethink many of the conclusions drawn by Jensen and others based upon its use. (It does not mean that these conclusions are wrong! It just means that they have to be held in abeyance until further analyses are done.) The reasons that the method is wrong are rather complicated, and so have been presented in Panel 11.2. Fortunately there is another method, MultiGroup Confirmatory Factor Analysis (MGCFA), that is much more satisfactory. Hopefully this method will receive wider use in the future.

This is not just a statistical nicety. There are many published conclusions that rest, somewhat shakily, on results obtained by using the method of correlated vectors. For instance, it has been used to make the very strong statement that African American and White differences in intelligence are due to differences along the g dimension.[16] The argument was that there is a fairly high correlation across subtests between (a) the g loading of the subtest and (b) the difference between White and African American scores on the subtest. At first glance, this is an argument for a difference between Whites and African Americans on g. But see Panel 11.2 for the problems of interpretation.

11.2. Aging

We all age. Binet assumed, and no one has disagreed, that cognitive competence increases with age up to early adulthood. At the other end of life, things are not so rosy. The incidence of dementia in people sixty-five and older is 10%, six times higher than the incidence in the population at large.[17] Dementia does not respect eminence. Ronald Reagan, the fortieth president of the United States, died with Alzheimer's disease at age ninety-three. He is believed by many to have suffered from early symptoms of the disease during his second term of office (1985–89), when he was in his late seventies. However, dementia is certainly not an inevitable feature of old age. Konrad Adenauer, the first chancellor of West Germany following World War II, is largely credited with guiding his country out of chaos and into a major place among industrial nations. He assumed office at seventy-three and left it at eighty-seven.

Theories of adult lives and aging stress how people find progressively more confined niches as they age. This is true in general, but there are exceptions. John Glenn (1921-) received a commission as a US Marine Corps aviator at age twenty-two, and served with distinction as a fighter pilot in both World War II and the Korean War. Following the Korean War he became a test pilot and had a brief interlude as a TV quiz show contestant. He was selected in the first cohort of American astronauts, and was the first American to orbit the Earth. Following his retirement from government service in 1964 (at age forty-three) he became a successful businessman in a field that had nothing to do with aviation. He developed a strong interest in politics, and served as a United States senator from 1974 until 1997. When he was seventy-seven he returned to space as a crew member on a space shuttle mission, thus becoming the oldest person to orbit the Earth.

14 Dolan & Hamaker, 2001; Dolan, Roorda, & Wicherts, 2004.
15 Ashton & Lee, 2005.
16 Nyborg & Jensen, 2000; Rushton & Jensen, 2005.
17 www.freemd.com/senile-dementia/incidence.htm, downloaded 18 November 2008.

Panel 11.2. The Method of Correlated Vectors and the Alternative, MGCFA

I first describe in somewhat more detail than in the main text just what the method of correlated vectors is. I then present the problems that it raises.

The first step in applying the method is to determine that the same relationships hold between tests within each group to be compared. This is evaluated by a statistical test called *congruence* that determines whether or not the two correlation (or covariance) matrices can be assumed to be identical in each group. If they appear to be identical, the congruence condition is said to be satisfied. In a nonstatistical sense, what this means is that the observable subtest scores are related to each other in the same way in each group. Consider the hypothetical direction-taking test described in the main text. If my intuitions are correct, this test would be highly correlated with a test of verbal memory in women, and with a test of rotational ability in men. The congruence condition would not be found.

Jensen assumed that failure of congruence would be evidence that the tests within a battery were measuring different things in each population, and therefore that Spearman's hypothesis could not be tested.

Assuming that congruence is satisfied, the next step is to factor analyze the combined data, extract a first factor, which is the operational definition of *g*, and correlate the factor loadings of each test with its associated *d* statistic, as described in the text.

A Dutch psychometrician, Conor Dolan, has pointed out that in order to test Spearman's hypothesis the data must satisfy a property called *measurement invariance*. The measurement invariance property is that the factor loadings for subtests should be identical within each group being compared. This ensures that two individuals, one from each group, who have identical scores on the latent traits (which is what we are interested in but cannot observe) also have identical scores on the test, which we can observe. In the examples given in the main text, measurement invariance would fail for the direction-finding test if it were to be incorporated into a test battery given to both men and women.

Dolan and his colleagues showed that the method of correlated vectors can produce positive findings in situations where measurement invariance does not hold.[*] Using a separate line of argument, Ashton and Lee have shown that the method can produce negative findings (the correlation between loadings and mean differences can approach zero) in situations in which there actually is a difference in *g*.[†]

Dolan advocated using *Multi-Group Confirmatory Factor Analysis* (MGCFA) to evaluate Spearman's hypothesis and similar conjectures. The technique is a variety of confirmatory factor analysis, the statistical method explained in Chapter 4, section 4.2. MGCFA is preferable to the method of correlated vectors in two ways. One is that it involves explicit tests for measurement invariance. The other, which is not negligible, is that it allows investigators to compare two hypotheses, rather than evaluating the weaker statement that a single hypothesis is a better than chance description of the data. The method of correlated vectors tests Spearman's hypothesis against chance, not against competing hypotheses.

The MGCFA technique has been known since the early 1980s. It requires relatively large samples from all groups, and calls for a good bit of expertise in the use of the required computer programs. Therefore, it is often not used when perhaps it should be. Hopefully this situation will change over time, as the flaws in the simpler method of correlated vectors become widely known.

[*] Dolan & Hamaker, 2001; Dolan, Roorda, & Wicherts, 2004.

[†] Ashton & Lee, 2005.

The message is straightforward. There are changes in cognitive competence over the adult years, both upward and downward. They are complex. They are also extremely important to understand, because age is a variable that affects every one of us.

11.2.1. *Issues*

Three different designs have been used in the study of aging. The simplest is the *cross-sectional* design, where the investigator takes measurements on people in different age groups, at roughly the same time. The good aspects of cross-sectional designs are that they are relatively easy to implement, compared to other alternatives, and that they provide a picture of differences in the cognitive competencies of different age groups in the population, as it exists at the time of testing. This information can be projected forward over short time spans. For instance, if we know the incidence of senile dementia in people seventy years and older as of 2010, and we know the number of people in the sixty-to-seventy age bracket, it is possible to estimate the incidence of senile dementia expected in 2020.

Cross-sectional designs pose problems of interpretation. It is difficult to obtain samples in which the participants differ only on age. For instance, elderly participants (seventy and over) will report having had less education, on the average, than younger adults. This reflects changes in society, rather than psychological changes in the individuals, but it produces an inevitable confound between age and education effects. The general principle is that in cross-sectional designs age effects are confounded with cohort (Flynn) effects discussed in Chapter 10. If we compare, in 2010, twenty-year-olds to seventy-year-olds, we are also comparing people in the 1990 birth cohort to people in the 1940 cohort. There is no way to tell whether the difference between the twenty- and seventy-year-olds is an age effect or a cohort effect.

Because cross-sectional studies measure each individual only once, there is also no way to distinguish between gradual and sudden changes in cognitive capability. To see this, consider two possible physiological events: gradual deterioration of the central nervous system (CNS) and sudden damage due, for instance, to stroke. Either could produce slowed decision-making. In a cross sectional design we would find that, on the average, decision-making processes slowed with age. However, because different people would be evaluated at each age, we would have no way of knowing how much of the difference was due to gradual deterioration, which affected everyone, and how much was because the older groups would contain more people who had suffered sudden CNS damage due to stroke.

In a *longitudinal design* the same people are studied across several time intervals. This makes it possible to observe age-related changes within an individual. The contrast between cross-sectional and longitudinal results is informative. Intelligence test scores show considerably less drop over the adult years in longitudinal studies than they do in cross-sectional studies. This is at least in part due to the confounding of age and cohort effects in a cross-sectional study.

Longitudinal studies are expensive and time-consuming. They are subject to strong recruitment effects, for people with low test scores are more likely to drop out than people with high test scores. This is particularly true if the study involves taking multiple measures, thus requiring a considerable investment in time on the part of the study participants. Nonrandom attrition effects occur. Unless allowance is made for this effect, aging may appear to be less debilitating than it actually is.[18]

The participants in a longitudinal study come from just one cohort. Therefore, the effects of general changes in society are mixed with the effects of aging. As an example, the percentage of women in Terman's study who followed professional careers was high for its time, but was much lower than the percentage of women following professional careers in the SMPY study, who were

---

18 See Madhyastha et al., 2009, for an example and discussion.

recruited fifty year later. Was this due to any psychological difference between women born around 1910 and those born around 1960, or was it due to the much greater career opportunities for young women in the 1980s than in the 1930s?

The gold standard is the cohort-sequential design, such as the Seattle Longitudinal Study described in Panel 9.2, in which investigators recruit people of different ages at the start, follow them as in a longitudinal study, and in addition periodically recruit new participants and follow them as well. This allows for a separate evaluation of cohort and aging effects, and provides for longitudinal studies of different cohorts. However, cohort-sequential designs are very difficult to arrange. Aside from the expense, the biggest problem is ensuring comparability of the samples developed at each phase of recruitment. In the Seattle Longitudinal Study participants were recruited from people enrolled in a health maintenance organization (HMO). If enrollments in the HMO have changed over the now fifty years of the study, recently recruited participants will not be comparable in all ways to earlier-recruited participants. There are also problems of selective attrition, as is the case in a longitudinal design.

These problems make the study of aging difficult. They do not make it impossible. The effects of aging will be discussed under three general headings: studies using psychometric techniques, studies concentrating on information-processing and physiological variables, and what turns out to be a very important, albeit amorphous, set of findings, "other cognitive changes."

11.2.2. *A Psychometric View of Aging*

Many psychometric studies of changes in intelligence with age have utilized Cattell and Horn's distinction between fluid and crystallized (Gf vs. Gc) intelligence. Horn summarized this work, as of the late twentieth century, by asserting that Gf peaks in the mid twenties and then falls fairly rapidly, with the fall accelerating in old age (sixty-five plus), while Gc peaks around thirty and

then is maintained at a surprisingly constant level until old age.[19] His conclusion has been widely accepted. The fact that age has different influences on fluid and crystallized intelligence is one of the strongest nonpsychometric arguments for the importance of making the Gf-Gc distinction, rather than collapsing Gc and Gf into a single construct, general intelligence (g).

In Carroll's expansion of the Gf-Gc model, crystallized and fluid intelligence are two of several broad second-stratum models, below g but less specialized than primary level abilities, such as vocabulary and image rotation. Other important second-stratum abilities are visual and auditory reasoning, short-term memory, and long-term memory retrieval. In a rather-less-cited part of his argument, Horn observed that all the second-stratum abilities except Gc show declines from roughly age thirty onward.

Horn relied heavily on cross-sectional studies to draw these conclusions. Such studies are confounded by cohort effects. This point is particularly troubling because the cohort effect is much stronger for measures of Gf than for measures of Gc.[20] If Gf has increased across cohorts, a cross-sectional study will show decrements in Gf with age. Therefore, the result of an abbreviated cross-sequential study of the Woodcock-Johnson testing program is of considerable interest.

The Woodcock-Johnson tests, mentioned briefly in Chapter 2, are battery-type tests generated from the Carroll-Cattell-Horn three-stratum model of intelligence. The testing program includes tests suitable for a wide range of ages, from early childhood to adulthood. The test batteries contain markers for Gf, Gc, and several other second-stratum abilities defined by the Cattell-Horn model. They also contain a measure of "broad cognitive ability," which is analogous to the general intelligence (third-stratum) factor in Carroll's extension of the model.[21]

---

19 Horn, 1985; see also Horn & Noll, 1994, and Cattell, 1987.
20 Flynn, 1987.
21 Carroll, 1993.

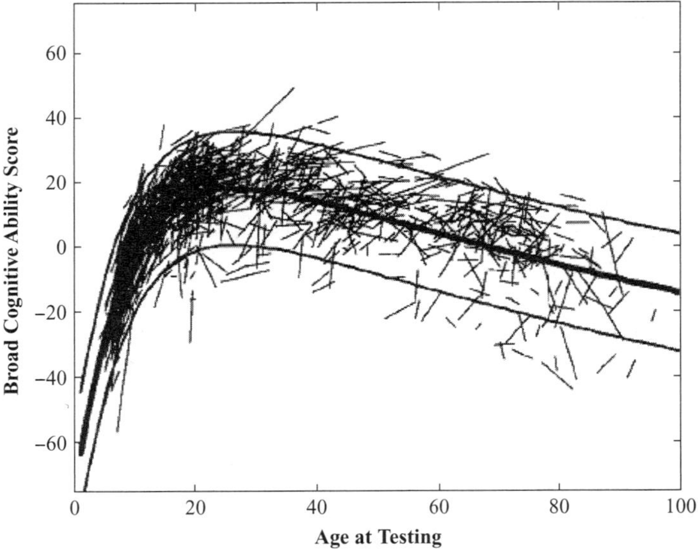

Figure 11.2. Broad cognitive ability (BCA) factor scores as a
function of age. The lines indicate scores at the two points of time
of testing. Heavy lines show quartiles. From McArdle et al., 2002,
Figure 8, reprinted with permission.

Because the different subtests have been calibrated using item response theory (Chapter 2), they provide a score that can be treated as a linear scale of the trait underlying each subtest. This makes it possible to talk about differences in the rate of decline of various measures of intelligence.[22]

The Woodcock-Johnson test was revised and renormed in 1990, to produce the WJ-R test.[23] The renorming was based on an (approximate) probability sample of the US population, containing about 6,500 cases. Subsequently J. J. McArdle, a professor at the University of Virginia, and his colleagues contacted and retested just under 1,200 of the original participants.[24] Chronological ages at the time of first testing ranged from two to ninety years. The interval between testing times ranged from one to five years. Figure 11.2 presents the raw scores for broad cognitive ability (*g*) as a function of age. There is a peak of intelligence in the early twenties, and a gradual decline thereafter. However, there are considerable individual differences. Some participants in their

seventies have scores that would be considered quite high for a twenty-five-year-old.

Different aspects of intelligence peak and decline at different rates. This is shown in Figure 11.3, which presents changes in Gf and Gc as a function of age. The two graphs clearly follow different trajectories of change over age. This point is reinforced by some numbers. Table 11.1 shows the peak age and the rate of decline (in a transformation of *z* scores, a point that need not concern us here). All the second-stratum broad abilities *except Gc* behave very much like Gf, cresting in the mid-twenties and then declining throughout the adult years. The exception, Gc, is important because Gc is a better predictor of workforce performance than Gf.

McCardle and colleagues' data clearly provides support for the three-stratum model as an appropriate way to understand the influence of age on intelligence. It is worth noting, though, that the effects in their data are not nearly as striking as the description of age-related declines presented in some discussions. This can be seen by contrasting Figures 11.2 and 11.3 with Horn's stylized presentation of the data, shown in Figure 11.4. Gc and Gf do follow different

22 Hunt, 2007, Chapter 10.
23 McGrew, Werder, & Woodcock, 1991.
24 McArdle et al., 2002.

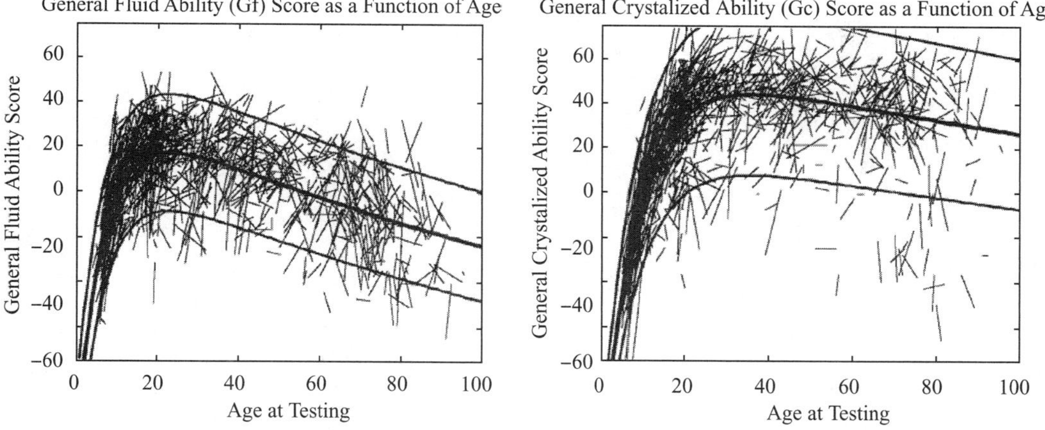

Figure 11.3. Age and change scores for Gf and Gc. Gf peaks sooner than Gc, but falls off more sharply. From McArdle et al., 2002, Figure 9, reprinted with permission.

courses over the life span, but the difference does not approach that shown in the stylized summary.

Schaie has reported data that complements the findings of McCardle and colleagues. Figure 11.5, based on data from the Seattle study, shows the cumulative age changes, from age twenty-five onward, for three different factors: verbal meaning, inductive reasoning, and general intellectual ability. These factors were chosen because an examination of the subtests on which they were based suggests that they should resemble the Gc, Gf, and "broad cognitive ability" (*g*) scales in the WJ-R battery. Comparing Figure 11.5 to Figures 11.2, 11.3, and 11.4, we see that the two studies are in agreement in showing that verbal/Gc measures are substantially less resistant to age than measures of inductive reasoning/Gf.

The studies disagree somewhat about precisely where the declines come. The McArdle study indicates declines starting in the mid-twenties for Gf and in the mid-thirties for Gc. The Seattle Longitudinal Study data shows declines starting

Table 11.1. Ages at peak value and rate of decline (in "W units," which are linearly related to the IRT logit scale) for various factors evaluated on the WJ-R test

WJ-R Composite	Age at Highest Value	Rate of Change per Year, Ages 20–75
Fluid reasoning (Gf)	22.8	−.5
Comprehension and knowledge (Gc)	35.6	−.01
Retrieval from long-term memory	18.1	−.4
Short-term memory	24.2	−.3
Processing speed	25.1	−.6
Auditory processing	22.7	−.4
Visual processing	24.5	−.4
Broad quantitative ability	29.0	−.3
Broad academic knowledge	29.8	−.3
Broad cognitive ability (*g*)	26.2	−.3

Source: Data from McArdle et al., 2002, Table 9, reprinted with permission.

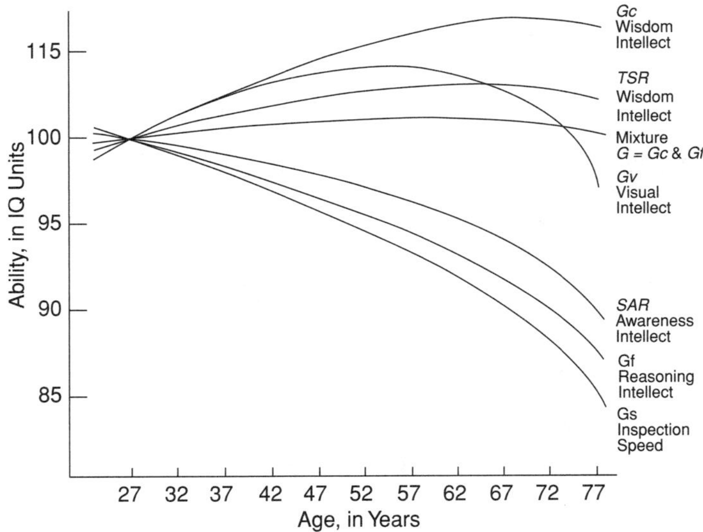

Figure 11.4. A stylized picture of the age trends for different broad second-level traits in the Gc-Gf model of intelligence. While the contrast between the Gf and Gc trends is maintained in Figure 11.3, the contrast is much less in the data than in the stylized depiction. From Horn, 1986, p. 52.

considerably later. The truth may lie somewhere in between. Age trends in the WJ-R renorming were confounded with cohort effects, which would lead to an overestimation of the deleterious effects of aging. In the Seattle Longitudinal Study participants have dropped out over time, so there is a bias toward continued participation by people with higher initial abilities. This would result in an understatement of the age effect.

There has been continuous debate about the extent to which the pervasiveness of the general intelligence factor increases with advanced age. This is called the *dedifferentiation hypothesis*. The hypothesis predicts that the correlations between measures of different types of intelligence, such as verbal and spatial-visual reasoning, will increase with age.

Powerful arguments can be advanced for the dedifferentiation hypothesis. Declines in intelligence are associated with declines in health. Injuries that influence the brain and nervous system should, on logical grounds alone, have widespread deleterious effects on cognitive performance. Non-pathological reductions in the prefrontal cortex and other areas associated with the working memory–attention–executive function complex, which are typical of aging, are associated with lower fluid intelligence scores.[25] Reduction in the capabilities of the working memory–attention complex should have a pervasive effect on almost all cognitive functions, which should lead to an increased influence of individual differences in g upon performance.

Despite this argument, the evidence for the dedifferentiation hypothesis is mixed. There is some support for an increase in correlations between cognitive variables with age in the Seattle Longitudinal Study.[26] However, inspection of the quartile lines in Figures 11.2 and 11.3 shows that there was little increase in the variance of g with age in the WJ-R sample. Other detailed multivariate studies of psychometric cognition and aging have produced evidence both for and against the dedifferentiation hypothesis.[27]

Psychometric studies of aging present a consistent pattern. Crystallized intelligence

25 See, for instance, Raz et al., 2008. A general review is provided by Kramer, Fabiani, & Colcomb, 2006.
26 Schaie, 2005, pp. 213–215.
27 de Frias et al., 2007; Juan-Espinosa et al., 2002; Tucker-Drob & Salthouse, 2008.

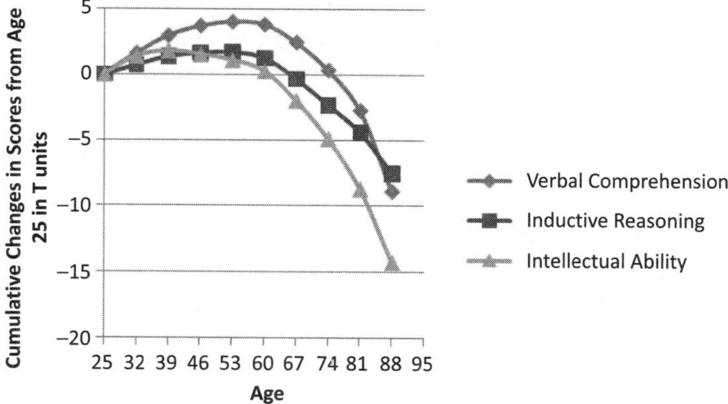

Figure 11.5. Cumulative age changes from age twenty-five for three different aspects of intelligence. Scores are shown in T units, where 10 is the variance at age twenty-five. Data from the Seattle Longitudinal Study (Schaie, 2005), Table 5.1. The "intellectual ability" scale is not an average of the other two. It includes measures of spatial reasoning and numerical skill, both of which show substantial decrements past middle age.

increases to a peak in early middle age, and remains constant throughout the adult working years. Fluid intelligence peaks somewhere in the young adult years and then, *on the average*, declines through the latter half of the working years and old age. However, some people have high fluid intelligence test scores well into late adulthood.

11.2.3. *Changes in Information-processing Capacity with Age*

The picture with respect to changes in information processing with age is quite clear. Cognition gets slower, and the working memory–attention–executive function complex does not function as well as it used to.

Cognitive slowing can be demonstrated using either psychometric or laboratory techniques. In psychometric studies of cognitive skills the examinee is asked to do something very simple, quickly, such as crossing out the "a's" in a text. Laboratory studies are a bit more complex. Choice reaction time and perceptual decision tasks (Chapter 6) are favorites. All methods demonstrate marked slowing with age. For example, in the three-stratum model perceptual speed is a second-level ability, on a

par with Gf and Gc. In the WJ-R study processing speed declined with age more rapidly than any other second-level ability, including Gf (Table 11.1). A large-scale survey of the UK population found marked slowing of both simple and choice reaction times with age, with choice reaction time being the more sensitive variable.[28]

There is a regular relationship between the time that young and old individuals take to accomplish a laboratory task such as a reaction time task. The time that young adults take to complete a task increases with task complexity, and the time that older people take to complete the same task is a multiplicative function of the time that the young adults take. The nature of the relationship is shown in Figure 11.6, for over 175 tasks and for multipliers ranging from 1 to 2. Algebraically, the relationship can be summarized by

$$L_{old} = aL_{young}, \tag{11.2}$$

where L is the latency of the task and a is a multiplier greater than 1.[29] The greater the age disparity, the greater the multiplier.

28 Der & Deary, 2006.
29 Cerella, 1990.

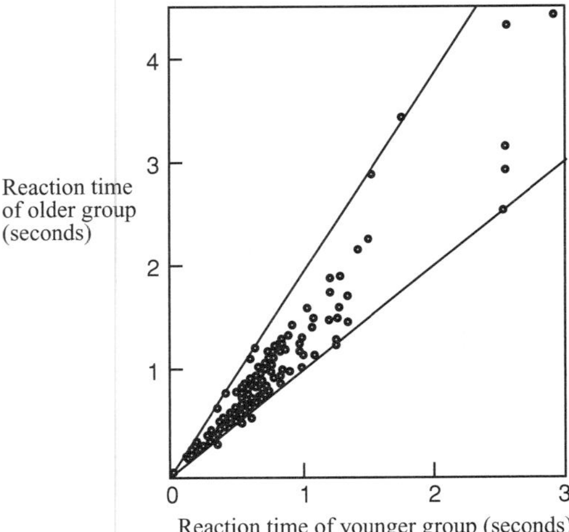

Figure 11.6. Reaction times lengthen with age. A summary of over 175 studies in which older and younger groups were compared on the same reaction time task. The time in seconds required by the older group is shown on the ordinate; the time required by the younger group is shown on the abscissa. From Cerella, 1985, Figure 1D, reprinted with permission.

While the fact of slowing is clear, both the reason for and the implications of slowing are less clear. It has been suggested that the reason for slowing is that as people age there is a decrease in the reliability of information transmission in the neural system.[30] Trying to pinpoint just why this should happen would lead us into a discussion of age effects on the brain, which is not our major concern. The implications of slowing are of concern.

Two models have been proposed.[31] Cognitive slowing might cause problems in other aspects of thought. For example, executive functioning, allocating attention to concurrent or nearly concurrent tasks (like driving a car while listening to the radio), is possible only if information can be evaluated as it comes in. A person whose cognitive processing is slowed is simply less able to keep up with the world. This can certainly be demonstrated in laboratory tasks. Whether it is a factor in familiar situations, in which people have developed strategies for dealing with relevant information processing, is another issue. Adults over fifty regularly play card games, and often play them quite well. On the other hand, they do get into accidents because they do not react quickly enough to an emerging situation.

In addition to whatever direct effects slowed cognitive processing has, slowing also serves as a marker for the general state of the nervous system. Therefore, slowed processing with age is important both in itself and as an indicator of general cognitive health.

Whichever of the two models is correct, it is clear that slowing is a major but not the entire cause of declines in intelligence with age. Figure 11.7 presents an idealization of results from a Swedish study in which changes in a general cognitive factor (*g*) were determined with and without statistical controls for changes in perceptual processing speed. Controlling for processing speed on perceptual tasks, such as figure identification, virtually eliminates the change in cognition from age fifty to sixty-five, and slows, but does not eliminate, the decline past sixty-five.[32]

As people age there is a breakdown in the working memory–control of attention–executive processing complex. This is shown by decreased performance on short-term memory tasks, greater susceptibility to interruption, and poorer control on dual tasks, such as simultaneously monitoring a stream of visual and auditory signals.[33] These behavioral measures are, in general (a) those that are most closely related to psychometric measures of *g* and Gf and (b) those that are supported by the frontal cortex–cingulate cortex–parietal cortex complex.

These results strongly suggest that the decline in the ability to deal with new problems (Gf) is caused by a reduced ability to construct and manipulate problem representations in working memory. The deficit is probably due to reduced functioning of

30 For example, see the model proposed by Myerson et al., 1990.
31 Hartley, 2006; Salthouse, 1996.
32 Finkel & Pedersen, 2004.
33 Hoyer and Verhaeghen, 2006; Kramer, Fabiani, & Colcombe, 2006; Salthouse et al., 2003.

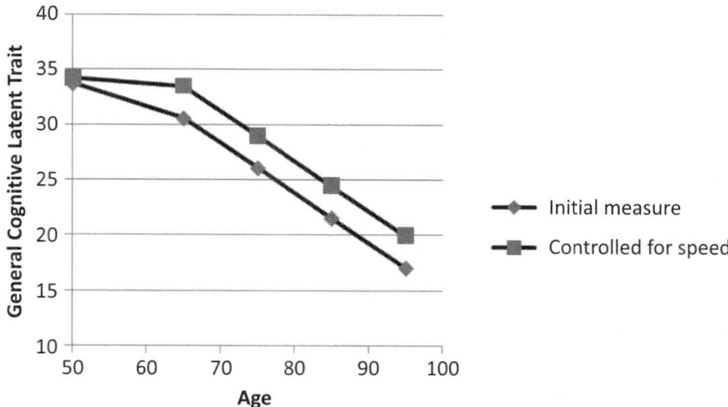

Figure 11.7. Changes in the level of a generalized cognitive trait (*g*) over the second half of the life span. The measurement of the latent trait has been set to a mean of 30 and a standard deviation of 10 to avoid negative numbers. The change is shown with and without statistical control for speed on perceptual tasks. Data from Finkel & Pedersen, 2004, Table 3.

the frontal-parietal system, which shows anatomical deterioration with age.[34] The failure in functioning appears to be general, rather than associated with a particular part of the working memory–control of attention complex.[35]

11.2.4. *Practical Knowledge, Experience, and Wisdom*

Given what has been presented so far, the reader may well have decided that somewhere around age forty-five people become slow, easily distracted, poorly focusing dunderheads. But how is it that men and women in their fifties and sixties occupy most of the important leadership positions in our society? Why are people advised to go to experienced physicians when physicians do not become experienced until their forties? Why do we routinely trust our lives to commercial airline captains, most of whom are in their fifties and sixties?

Experience counts . . . a lot. The typical test of crystallized intelligence (Gc) evaluates how well a person knows his or her society. The same Swedish longitudinal study that documented a drop in general cognitive functioning from age fifty onward found *increases* from age fifty to seventy-five in the extent to which people could answer general information questions.[36]

This finding is typical of many showing that Gc is either stable or increases until great age. The same thing is true of more pointed measures of functioning in life. In the Seattle Longitudinal Study participants were asked a number of questions about what the investigators refer to as "basic living skills." These varied from questions about personal finances to questions about how to cope with failures in household appliances. Figure 11.8 shows the results. There was very little decline in basic living skills until age sixty-five. This result is typical of several other studies that have investigated practical intelligence in the elderly.

Although they may have trouble dealing with the sorts of novel, out-of-context problems that populate IQ tests (and especially tests of Gf), people in midlife and beyond do quite well in dealing with realistic decision making.[37] On the other hand, the elderly do not do particularly well in made-up decision situations, especially when they are under time pressure. This could be due in part to general cognitive slowing, in part to the need to keep several factors in mind when making

---

34 Kramer, Fabiani, & Colcombe, 2006; Raz et al., 2008.
35 Salthouse, 1996, 2005.

36 Finkel & Pedersen, 2004.
37 Marsiske & Margrett, 2006; Sternberg, 2003a.

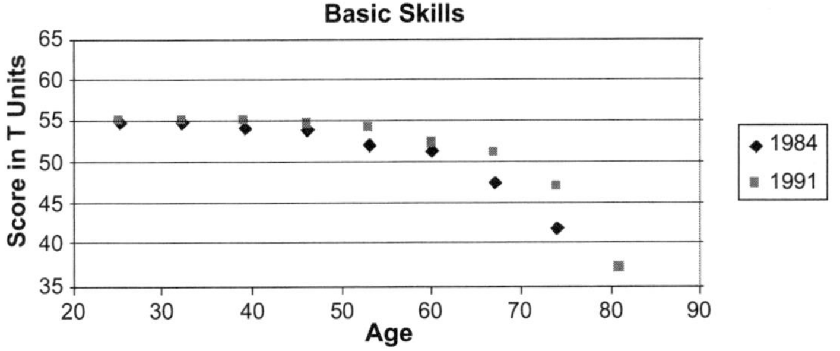

Figure 11.8. Scores on a test of basic living skills, measured on two different occasions. There is very little decline in basic living skills until past age sixty-five. Data from Schaie, 1996.

a complex decision, and in part to older individuals' tendency to stress accuracy rather than speed in decision-making situations.

Why is there a difference? Laboratory decision-making tasks are constructed to reveal the process of decision making, in situations where all participants have little prior experience with the problem at hand. Outside the laboratory, decision making is heavily influenced by the possession of relevant information.[38] People use the heuristics that are "condemned" in the laboratory, and they work.[39] The information-processing burden shifts from working memory to long-term memory and retrieval processes. The latter processes are relatively immune to age-related decline until quite late in life.

The heuristics used outside the laboratory rely upon the decision maker's having experience with similar decision-making situations – which is precisely what mature decision makers have. This sort of reasoning has been extended to what some have called "wisdom." The intuitive idea is that as you age you acquire wisdom – or at least, you should. But how do we distinguish wisdom from practical problem solving?

The theme that I have extracted from the literature is that practical problem solving and decision making involve problems that the individual faces in the here and now, while wisdom refers to thinking about broader, more ephemeral issues, often involving the course of society. For instance,

a group of German researchers have developed the Berlin Wisdom Theory, in which wisdom is defined as "knowing the rules and meaning of life."[40] Sternberg has defined wisdom as knowing how to apply creativity and intelligence for the common good, by balancing personal and societal interests.[41] Gerontologists claim that wisdom is more typical of the old than the young. That may be, but I would like to have clearer definitions and a better analysis of individual differences within the aged population before I would unequivocally associate age with wisdom.

11.2.5. *A Summary Comment on Aging, and a Remark on Healthy Aging*

The study of changes in intelligence with age has produced four well-established findings. They are:

1. Fluid intelligence decreases over the adult life span, while crystallized intelligence remains stable or even increases slightly until people are into the retirement years.
2. There is a generalized slowing of cognition with age. It is measurable as early as the forties, and can influence mental competencies outside of the laboratory as we approach the seventies and beyond. The slowing is pervasive.
3. There is a similar drop in the functioning of the working memory–attention

<hr>

38 Gigerenzer, 2000; Klein, 1998, 2009.
39 Klein, 2009.

40 Brugman, 2006.
41 Sternberg, 2003a.

control–executive functioning system over the life span. As is the case with general slowing of reactions, the degree of deficit accelerates past the mid-sixties.

4. Laboratory studies underestimate the effectiveness of older individuals when they are faced with familiar problems, especially in situations in which they have developed expertise. In such situations people in their forties and beyond, even into their sixties, may actually outperform younger individuals.

It is important not to romanticize the last finding. It refers to the performance of individuals who have experienced "healthy aging." While, as far as I can find out, this term has never been defined precisely, it clearly refers to two things.

First, the individual must not have experienced serious health problems that impact on cognition. These include, but are not limited to, cardiovascular problems and dementia-producing diseases, such as Alzheimer's disease and the later stages of Parkinson's disease. The dementias may unfold gradually, so any population of apparently healthy elderly people (arbitrarily, anyone over sixty) will include some pre-dementia cases. As the population ages the dementias will develop to the point that the individuals cannot live on their own. The high incidence of dementia in the elderly poses a major public health problem.

Second, in order to stay healthy the individual must remain engaged with society. Intelligence, like physical fitness, does not exist in a vacuum. It requires maintenance. Studies of healthy young adults[42] have shown that people vary in intellectual engagement, and that those who engage with the world are, in general, more intelligent than those who do not, where intelligence is measured by psychometric and laboratory studies. Whether engagement causes intelligence, or intelligence causes engagement, is hard to say. There are probably reciprocal influences.

Longitudinal studies of the elderly, such as the Seattle Longitudinal Study and the Swedish study of aging twins,[43] have shown that this trend is more pronounced as we grow older. Withdrawal and heightened anxiety are statistically associated with lower intelligence. This becomes a serious problem as people age, because the frequency of threatening life events will increase with advancing age. Loss of a job is far more threatening to a person of fifty or sixty than to one of twenty or thirty. Loss of a spouse becomes more likely with advancing age. How we handle such events may both tell a good deal about someone's present intelligence – in the conceptual rather than in the narrower psychometric sense – and have implications for maintenance of intelligence following the trauma.

11.3. Male-Female Differences in Intelligence

Are men smarter than women? Or is it the other way around? It depends on whom you ask, and how the question is framed.

Historically it has been assumed that men are generally more competent than women. This belief has been so widespread that some powerful women have felt that they should downplay either their ability or their femininity. Panel 11.3 presents some political examples that have stuck in my mind. Similar disparities are seen in other fields of accomplishment. When Charles Murray compiled a statistical analysis of major contributions in various fields he found the ratio of eminent men to eminent women ranged from 50:1 (mathematics) to 10:1 (literature).[44]

Historically, there have been entrenched rules limiting women's participation outside of home and hearth. In today's post-industrial society legal discrimination against women's participation in various social roles has been very much reduced. Informal social rules and attitudes dictating

42 Ackerman, 1996; Ackerman & Beier, 2001.

43 Schaie, 1996, 2005; Wetherell et al., 2002.
44 Murray, 2003.

Panel 11.3. Historic Examples and Historic Commentaries

Here are a few historic examples of accomplished women who have either hidden or downplayed their intellectual characteristics.

Hatshepsut (fifteenth century BCE), one of the very few women pharaohs, had herself depicted with a false beard, probably to preserve an image of a ruler. Some two millennia later Elizabeth I of England, one of the most powerful women who ever lived, famously described herself to her troops as "weak and feeble":

> *I know I have the body of a weak and feeble woman . . .*
> *Elizabeth I, speech to English army assembled to defend against a Spanish invasion, 1588**

Actually, Elizabeth was not all that uncertain about herself. It is not clear whether she actually spoke the words just quoted, or whether this quotation was made up by her advisors, in an early effort at public relations spin. In a better-documented speech to Parliament she had said

> *I thank God that I am endued with such qualities that if I were turned out of the Realm in my petticoat I were able to live in any place in Christendom.*
> *Elizabeth I, speech to Parliament, 1566[†]*

Given her career, I suspect that the second quote, rather than the first, better reflected Elizabeth I's self-image. The interesting thing is that either she felt it necessary to assert a "weakness of femininity" in the first quote, or, if she did not actually say this (and the historical record is weak here), it was necessary for her supporters, quoting her speech, to say that she said it.

The image of weak-willed femininity was still held in England two hundred years later, when Mary Wollstonecraft presented the first known argument for full female participation as movers and shakers in society. The second chapter of her book was titled "The Prevailing Opinion of a Sexual Character Discussed." It began

> *Many ingenious arguments have been brought forward to prove, that the two sexes, in the acquirement of virtue, ought to aim at attaining a very different character: or, to speak explicitly, women are not allowed to have sufficient strength of mind to acquire what really deserves the name of virtue.*
> *– Mary Wollstonecraft, opening lines of Chapter II of* A Vindication of the Rights of Women *. . . (1792)*

Wollstonecraft was certainly right about what people thought. Five years earlier the framers of the Constitution of the United States (1787), considered an extremely progressive political manifesto in its time, denied women the right to vote.

On the other hand, at the time Wollstonecraft was writing Catherine II ("the Great," 1729–96, ruled 1762–96) was Empress of all the Russias, and an autocrat's autocrat. She followed Elizabeth of Russia (1709–62, ruled 1741–62), who was a powerful figure herself.

Conflicts between women's actual accomplishments and widespread beliefs about the relative abilities of men and women are not just a modern phenomenon.

---

* Shapiro, 2006.
[†] Ibid.

differences in women's roles vary substantially across countries and across social groups within countries. Nevertheless, no modern society, and probably no past society, assigns exactly the same roles to men and women. The form of differentiation varies greatly, ranging from the substantial egalitarianism of modern Scandinavia to the much more rigid assignments of gender rules in conservative Islamic states.

Although societies vary in what they see as appropriate roles for men and women, there is one universal. Childbearing is dictated by biology. Child care is almost exclusively a female role, especially for younger children. This gender-differentiated role extends beyond caring for one's own children. Nursery, pre-school, and elementary school teachers are predominantly, although not exclusively, women.

Outside of the child-care role, assignments in modern industrial society are more equitable than they have been in past societies, but the extent of the gender differentiation varies over time and place. Men predominate in "traditionally masculine" fields, such as firefighting, police work, mechanical trades, military service, and aviation. There are more women than men in secretarial trades, nursing, and different varieties of interpersonal counseling. Some of these distributions of roles have seen rapid changes in the past fifty years. Medicine, for instance, was once almost exclusively a male occupation. Today women make up slightly over half the graduating classes from American medical schools.

The clergy provide an interesting case. Before 1950 women clergy were virtually unknown in the Catholic, Protestant, and Jewish faiths. Today women regularly serve as clergy in Protestant and Jewish communities. The Catholic Church forbids women to serve as priests. This distinction is interesting because the duties of the clergy are entirely intellectual and interpersonal. Strength, speed afoot, and the ability to orient in space, all characteristics that display strong sex differences, are irrelevant to the duties of a church leader.

Outside of child rearing, why should sex-role differentiation be so pervasive? Stories (with only indirect substantiation) about "man the hunter and woman the gleaner" present a plausible case for evolutionary differences in sex roles, based on men's superior size and strength. But why should these practices persist in modern society, where computer programming is far more important than hunting skill? Could it be that the differentiation is possibly due to male-female differences in cognition? Or are they due to social inertia, because we are still stuck with Neolithic thinking about what women can do?

These questions do not have easy answers. Diane Halpern, a professor at the Claremont Graduate Schools and a well-respected reviewer of the modern literature in the field, had this to say:

> *It seemed like a simple task when I started writing this book. . . . At the time it seemed to me that any between-sex differences in thinking abilities were due to socialization practices, artifacts and mistakes in the research, and bias and prejudice. After reviewing a pile of journal articles that stood several feet high, and numerous books and chapters that dwarfed the stack of the journal articles, I changed my mind. The task I had undertaken certainly wasn't simple and the conclusions that I had expected to make had to be revised.*
> *Halpern, 1986, Introduction*

The next few sections show why Halpern found the topic so complex.

11.3.1. General Intelligence I: The Evidence from Studies of Battery-type Tests

The case for differences between men and women in general intelligence, or *g*, rests on three pieces of evidence: the results from overall scores derived from battery-type tests, such as the IQ score derived from the Wechsler tests; the results from factorial studies in which individual scores are computed for the *g* factor derived from a variety of test batteries, including both avowed intelligence tests and batteries constructed for research purposes; and the results from studies of individual tests, such as the Raven Matrices tests, that purport to be measures of *g*. We will look first at the results from the battery-type tests, and then examine the results from the individual tests and some issues involving tests used for personnel screening.

Analyses of the adult standardization samples of the WAIS-III and WAIS-R generally show a small difference in IQ in favor of men. The results are consistent across countries, running from two to three IQ points in the United States and Canada[45] (in deviation units, $d = .19$) to four points ($d = .27$) in China and Japan.[46] These results are also close to the results obtained in earlier studies, showing consistency in time.[47] There is a somewhat similar picture when we look at children's data. IQ differences are on the order of one to two points in favor of boys in both the US and the Netherlands.[48]

These results are not exclusive to the Wechsler tests. Deary and his colleagues report an elegant example, involving data from the NLSY79, described in panel 9.9.[49] The data is of interest because the motivation for constructing the ASVAB, prediction of performance in the armed services, is rather different than the motivation for constructing the Wechsler tests, which were designed for use by clinical and educational psychologists.

Deary and colleagues contrasted the scores of brothers and sisters of the seventeen to twenty-three-year-olds who had taken the test, thus controlling for family background. The male-female difference in deviation scores on the AFQT, the general score derived from the ASVAB and a good measure of Gc, was $-.02$, a small, and not statistically reliable, finding in favor of females.

For the final piece of data, we look at a previously referenced, very large survey of over 70,000 schoolchildren in the United

Kingdom, who took the Cognitive Abilities Test battery at age eleven.[50] Two factors were derived from this test, a general intelligence factor and a residual verbal factor. No male-female differences were found on the general factor. There was a slight advantage for girls on the residual verbal factor.

What this review shows is either no difference or a very small difference in general intelligence in favor of males. Richard Lynn has argued that there is actually a greater male advantage in intelligence than the tests reveal.[51] His argument is based on two claims.

Lynn's first argument is that girls mature more rapidly than boys, and that cognitive competence increases with physiological age, rather than with calendar age. The male-female difference might be small, and even negative (reflecting a female advantage) prior to puberty, but a male advantage would appear after adolescence and continue throughout adulthood.

Lynn is correct that male-female differences are smaller in childhood than in adulthood, although not very much smaller. It is not clear whether this should be regarded as an artifact or simply an observation. By analogy, male-female discrepancies in height are smaller (and can show a female advantage) in childhood and not in adulthood, but this is not an artifact of the way we measure height; girls do get closer to their adult height than boys do in their pre-teen and early teen years. To the extent that cognitive growth mirrors physical growth, one could argue that girls are, in fact, smarter than boys during the elementary and middle school years, a point that should be taken into account in situations where entry into higher levels of education is determined by performance in the elementary years.

Lynn's second argument is that at all ages the tests are biased against men. He states,

The adult male advantage of around 4 IQ points obtained by averaging the verbal comprehension, reasoning and spatial

45 Longman, Sakofske, & Fung, 2007.
46 Dai et al., 1991; Hattori & Lynn, 1997.
47 Matarazzo et al., 1986, Snow & Weinstock, 1990.
48 Born & Lynn, 1994.
49 Deary, Irwing, et al., 2007.

50 Deary, Strand, Smith, & Fernandez, 2007.
51 Lynn, 1999.

Table 11.2. Selected scores and male-female comparison for brother-sister pairs in the NLSY79 data set

Test	Male Mean	Female Mean	*Effect Size in d Units (Male–Female)*
Word knowledge	22.3	22.9	−.07
Paragraph comprehension	9.2	10.0	−.21
Arithmetic reasoning	15.9	14.7	+.17
Mathematics knowledge	11.9	11.9	0.00
AFQT standardized score	−.034	+.034	−.02
AFQT g score	15.08	14.68	.06

Source: Data extracted from Deary et al., 2007, Table 1, with permission from Elsevier.

abilities is not generally found in the full scale IQ of the Wechsler tests or in the overall IQ of similar tests because the spatial abilities are typically under-represented in these tests.

Lynn, 1999, p. 2.

To what extent is this argument plausible? Summary scores, such as the widely used WAIS Full Scale, Verbal, and Performance (FSIQ, VIQ, PIQ) scores are determined by a weighted combination of scores on subtests. If men have higher scores on some subtests, and women on other subtests, then depending upon the weights assigned to each subtest you could produce a summary score that favored men over women or vice versa, simply by manipulating the weights assigned to the subtests. And it is certainly true that if a test battery omits an important ability on which there are male-female differences, then the balance of men and women's scores in an overall index will be different than it would have been had the omitted ability been evaluated.

Arthur Jensen has argued that the way out of this dilemma is to compare men's and women's measurements (factor scores) on g, defined as the primary factor extracted from a battery of tests of different aspects of intelligence. The argument is that the weighting of individual subtests will then be done by rational analysis of the data, rather than by using weights that were arbitrarily assigned to the subtests.[52]

The two approaches can lead to differences in the calculation of overall male-female differences. This is illustrated by Deary and colleagues' analysis of the NLSY79 data. Table 11.2 presents their data separately for male-female differences on the four subscales of the ASVAB used to compute the AFQT. As was mentioned earlier, the AFQT score showed essentially no difference between men and women.[53] However, when Deary and his colleagues applied Jensen's techniques, and computed male-female differences on a g index derived from factor analysis, there was a male advantage of .06 standard deviation units – not a lot, but still a reversal of the direction computed from the composite AFQT score.

Several researchers have conducted similar analyses of the WAIS and similar batteries. Some have found evidence for a small advantage in g for men. Most of these have relied on the method of correlated vectors, which, as was explained in section 11.1, is a questionable technique. Studies using the better-justified MGFCA procedure find no

52 See Chapter 4 for a detailed discussion of the logic of this approach.
53 The effect of composite scores upon an overall index, and upon the deviation scores of the index, is not determined solely by the weights of each component. The variance of the components and the correlation between the components are also important.

difference,[54] but these studies can be criticized for their low statistical power![55]

If there are any male-female differences in general intelligence indices derived from the commonly used battery-type tests, those differences are quite small.

No statistical analysis can address a stronger form of Lynn's argument, that appropriate subtests are not included at all. Women generally do better than men on verbal tests, and men may do markedly better than women on visual-spatial tests, especially those tests evaluating the R (rotational) aspect of visual-spatial reasoning in the g-VPR model. But does this mean that those batteries that are now widely used, such as the WAIS, "underrepresent" visual-spatial reasoning, as the quotation from Lynn implies?

To answer this question one would have to know what the proper representation of verbal, visual-spatial, and other traits is.

If the test battery as a whole is to be validated by its ability to predict performance in an applied setting, then the appropriateness of adding or subtracting a particular subtest can be determined by seeing if the addition improves accuracy of prediction. A powerful case can be made that adding spatial-visual tests might do this in some situations, but might not in others.[56] For that matter, there are some situations in which an argument can be made for ignoring spatial-visual

ability tests in favor of a more extended evaluation of verbal testing.

If the test is intended to measure intelligence, in the abstract, questions about what to include in a test battery are unanswerable without a theory of what intelligence is, *defined independently of the tests*. This illustrates (once again) the intellectual poverty of de facto acceptance of the argument that "intelligence is what the intelligence test tests."

11.3.2. *General Intelligence II: The Evidence from Tests Said to Be Markers for General Intelligence*

In theory, a way to study male-female differences while avoiding the problem of having to justify the composition of a test battery would be to look at men's and women's scores on a pure measure of g, and compare the scores obtained in an accurate sample of a large population, such as the population of a country, where the possibility of differential recruitment of men and women into the population would not be at issue. In practice, it is difficult, if not impossible, to find such a study. No pure measure of g exists; the best we have are progressive matrix tests. The most widely used of these, the Raven tests, do measure g, but in most populations they contain a significant visual-spatial reasoning component.[57]

Lynn has put the problem succinctly:

> *Few people will be persuaded that general intelligence can be so narrowly defined as to consist solely of fluid ability measured by the Progressive Matrices. General intelligence is generally regarded as consisting of a broader range of cognitive abilities which would include the verbal and spatial second order factors.*
>
> *– Lynn, 1999, p. 6*

This poses a problem when RPM scores are used to determine male-female differences in g. As will be documented later, there is substantial evidence that there are moderate to large male-female differences in

54 See Colom et al., 2000, and Dolan et al., 2006, for Spain; Jensen, 1998, Table 13.1, for American and United Kingdom data; and Van der Sluis, Derom, et al., 2008, for data from Belgium and the Netherlands. Nyborg (2005) reports a substantial male advantage, but he used a small sample of people who agreed to participate in extended testing, and hence may not have satisfied the requirement of having samples that were equally representative of men and women, due to recruitment effects.

55 Molenaar, Dolan, & Wicherts, 2009.

56 See Humphreys and Lubinski, 1996, for some of these arguments. The appropriate subtests to include in a composite battery depend upon what the battery is meant to do. The ASVAB legitimately has different subtests than the WAIS. If a test battery is to be used for personnel selection, substantial legal and ethical issues arise when changing a test battery results in differential changes in the frequency of prediction of success for men and women. It must be shown that these changes increase predictive validity.

57 Johnson & Bouchard, 2005a, Table 2; Palmer et al., 1985.

some types of visual-spatial reasoning. Any difference in RPM scores between men and women will reflect a difference both in *g* and in visual-spatial reasoning. Even if *g* is the predominant contributor to the RPM score, and there are no male-female differences in *g*, a moderate male-female difference in visual-spatial reasoning would produce a small difference in RPM scores.

The second problem is that the desired conclusion is a statement about differences in *g*, or lack of them, between men and women in general. Such a statement can be justified only if it is based on studies where the participants can be thought of as reasonably close to a probability sample of some defined large population.

A review of studies conducted prior to 1980 concluded that there were no male-female differences in RPM scores.[58] Lynn and Irwing properly criticized this review for having included a large number of convenience samples that made no claim of being representative of any national population. They then conducted two meta-analyses of their own, one based on the RPM and another, intended to represent college students, that contained studies using both the RPM and the more difficult Raven Advanced Progressive Matrices (RAPM).[59] They concluded that in adults men score higher than women by approximately .3 deviation units, which they regarded as equivalent to 4.5 to 5 points on the IQ scale. The male advantage was somewhat smaller in the early teen years, which would be in accord with Lynn's suggestion that prior to adolescence girls are both physically and cognitively more mature than boys of the same age.

Their conclusions must be taken with a grain of salt. Lynn and Irwing present their results as generalizations about male-female differences in RPM scores across countries. This means that the representation of male and female examinees in a study must be reasonably representative of males and females in the relevant country. At a minimum, the male:female ratio in the sample should be roughly equal to the likely male:female ratio in the population. Failure to meet this requirement is evidence that some unknown recruitment effect may be distorting the results. An unfortunate number of the studies upon which Lynn and Irwing base their case do not meet this criterion.

Here are a few examples. A study said to represent Israel was actually a study of children in a kibbutz, surely a nonrepresentative sample of modern Israel. A study involving 200 people was offered as representative of India, a nation of over one billion. A sample of Brazilians aged twenty to forty contained over 1,900 men and 740 women. This is a huge distortion of the male:female ratio for that age group. In another study a sample of "American college students" was actually taken from a single university, which stresses its preeminence in engineering and agriculture.[60] The male:female ratio in the study was approximately 9:2. According to records I obtained from the university's web site the enrollments of men and women were approximately equal during the time of the study. Such obvious deviations from representativeness make the application of meta-analytic techniques questionable. Additional criticisms have been made of the college student analysis, on other grounds.[61]

A somewhat different picture emerges from the rather scanty reports that have been made of standardization studies. In discussing the 1979 standardization of the RSPM, which analyzed data from a city that had a demographic profile resembling the national profile, rather than from a population sample, John Raven reported that there were no male-female differences in progressive matrix scores.[62] No mention is made of male-female differences in his discussion of British and American standardizations in the 1990s, but it is not clear whether a test for such differences was ever done. A collection of papers has been published that includes

58 Court, 1983.
59 Lynn & Irwing, 2004a, 2005.

60 Lynn & Irwing, 2004b.
61 Blinkhorn, 2005.
62 Raven, 2000.

reports of several national standardizations of the Raven tests, and a number of smaller studies, mostly of children and adolescents. No male-female differences are reported.[63]

A major point in Lynn's argument is that the difference in RPM scores shifts toward a male superiority from childhood to adolescence. Statistically, this would amount to an age x sex interaction. In seven of the eight studies of children and adolescents in which a comparison between the age nine to ten and age fifteen to sixteen scores could be made, there was a shift toward better male performance with increasing age.[64]

Two conclusions can be drawn from these frustratingly incomplete results. The first is that if there is any systematic difference between men's and women's scores on the Raven tests, it is a small one. Otherwise it would show up much more clearly in studies that do approximate national samples. The second is that the difference, if it does exist, could be due to either the g or the visual-spatial latent traits that underlie performance on progressive matrix items. Carlson and I were right when we stated our tenth principle for interpreting studies of group differences: investigators should be more willing than they are to say "We don't know."

11.3.3. *The Variance Issue*

If there is such a small difference in general intelligence (if any) between men and women, why do we care? What is all the fuss about?

Men's scores on measures of general intelligence are more variable than women's scores. This difference, combined with a small difference in mean scores, implies that there will be substantial differences between men and women at both extremes of the intelligence distribution, those of above-normal and below-normal intelligence. To explain this a brief excursion into the conceptual meaning of *variance* is needed.

Suppose we were to select a randomly chosen man or woman and try to guess his or her score on an intelligence test. Our best guess is the expected value, represented by $E(x_m)$ or $E(x_w)$, depending on whether we are talking about a man or a woman. Assuming a normal distribution for intelligence, this is the mean for the appropriate distribution; for men, $E(x_m) = \mu(x_m)$, where $\mu(x_m)$ represents the mean of the distribution of male scores. A similar expression applies for women, using the w subscript instead of m. However, we can also expect to miss by some amount, and the size of the misses will increase with the variability of the scores. Let $E(x_m - \mu(x_m))$ be the expected miss for men. (The same argument would follow for women, with w substituted for m.) The expected miss will be zero, because overestimates will balance out underestimates. However, the square of the misses, $(x_m - \mu(x_m))^2$, will always be non-negative (and will be positive unless all scores are equal to the mean score). The more widely the scores are distributed about the mean, the larger the value of the expected squared miss: $E((x_m - \mu(x_m))^2)$. This is the conceptual meaning of *variance*.

The relative variability in male and female distributions of scores is measured by the *variance ratio, VR,*

$$VR = \frac{E((x_m - \mu(x_m))^2)}{E((x_w - \mu(x_w))^2)}. \tag{11.2}$$

VR will be one if men's scores and women's scores are equally variable, greater than one if men's scores are more variable than women's, smaller if women's are more variable than men's.

In studies where the sample can be regarded as approximating a probability sample of the population, the male:female variance ratio has been found to be greater than one, both in overall scores (indicators of g) and in scores on subtests evaluating particular aspects of intelligence, such as verbal comprehension or spatial-visual reasoning. Here are some typical observations:

63 Raven & Raven, 2008.
64 Lynn & Irwing, 2004a, Table 1.

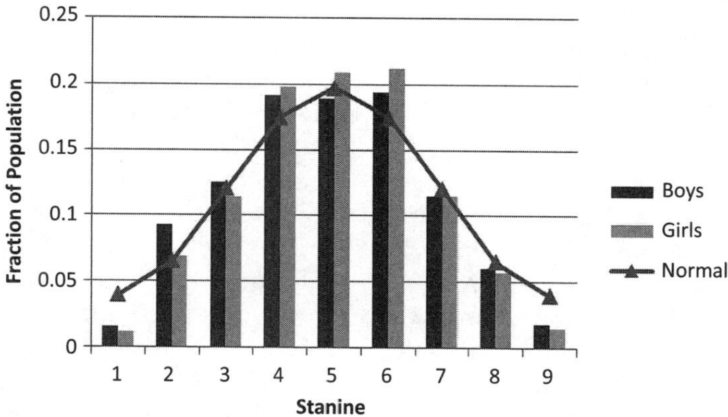

Figure 11.9. The distribution of CAT mean scores in a British sample of over 300,000 eleven-year-old schoolchildren. The normal distribution is shown as a reference point. Note the excess of boys at the extreme values (stanines 1–3 and 8–9) and the excess of girls in the middle stanines (4–6). Data from Strand et al., 2006, Appendix B.

1. The WAIS–III provides a general mental ability (GAI) index, defined by mean scores on the verbal and nonverbal reasoning subtests. The means for men and women, respectively, are 100.1 and 97.9, a difference of .147 standard deviation units. The standard deviations for men and women are 15.1 and 14.7, with a corresponding variance ratio of (15.1 / 14.76)² = 1.06.[65]

2. In the NAEP 2004 data for seventeen-year-olds, the mean scores for mathematics were men –308, women –305. The variance ratio was 1.23. For reading, the scores were men – 278, women – 293. The variance ratio was 1.33.[66]

3. In the 2001–03 period 320,000 eleven- to twelve-year-old children enrolled in United Kingdom schools took the Cognitive Assessment Test (CAT-III; see Chapter 2). The mean score across all subtests was 99.1 for boys and 99.9 for girls, an effect size of .05 in favor of girls. The variance ratio was 1.13.[67]

Figure 11.9 uses the British study to illustrate what this difference in variances implies for the overall distribution of scores. In this study there was a trivial difference in means between boys and girls, but a reasonably large variance ratio. The figure shows the distribution of boys' and girls' scores in *stanines*.[68] The standard normal curve (recalibrated to stanines) has been superimposed on this distribution. The girls' scores are *leptokurtic*, that is, somewhat more bunched-up than would be expected if they were normally distributed. The boys' scores are *platykurtic*, less bunched-up than would be expected. They are also slightly skewed to the left. As a result, there will be a higher percentage of boys than girls at both the high and low ends of the distribution, even when, as is the case in the UK data, there is virtually no difference in means.

---

65 Lange et al., 2006, Table 2.

66 Data downloaded from nces.ed.gov/nationsreportcard/lttnde/viewresults.asp, December 2008. The variance ratios were calculated from the standard errors, on the assumption that there was an equal number of men and women.

67 Strand, Deary, & Smith, 2006.

68 A stanine score is a linear transformation and quantization of a standard score. Stanines are defined for intervals 1–9, with 5 representing the mean, equivalent to a standard score of zero, and a standard deviation of 2. For stanines 2–8 the interval covered by a stanine has the width of one-half a standard deviation (stanine range of 1). For instance, stanine 5 covers the standard score interval $-2.5 \leq z < .25$. Stanine 6 covers the interval $.25 \leq z < .75$, and so forth. Stanine 9 covers the interval $1.75 \leq z < +\infty$, and stanine 1 covers the interval $-\infty < z < -1.75$.

Panel 11.4. An Illustration of the Effects of Small Differences in Means and Variances

The differences in intelligence test scores between men and women in both means and variances are small, in the absolute sense. In combination they imply substantial changes in the ratio of men to women at the extreme high and low ends of the distribution. This is important, because socioeconomic contributions (loosely, "eminence") may depend predominantly upon talent at the high end of the intelligence scale, while socioeconomic costs are created disproportionately by people at the low end of the distribution.*

The effects can be seen by comparing three distributions: the standard normal distribution (z, mean = 0, standard deviation = 1), which will be used to represent the female score distribution, F, and three possible male distributions. They are M1 (mean = .15 d units, standard deviation = 1), M2 (mean = 0, standard deviation = 1.05), and M3 (mean = .15 d units, standard deviation = 1.05). As a standard deviation of 1.05 corresponds to a variance ratio of 1.10, these values are in the range of empirically observed values for male-female mean differences and male:female variance ratios.

Figure 11.10 (a) shows the three M distributions, superimposed on the F distribution. There appears to be little difference between them. Figure 11.10 (b) presents the data from a different perspective. It shows the ratio of males to females at different points on the z scale, comparing the three M distributions to the F distribution, and assuming that there is an equal number of males and females in the population. This distribution is approximately correct for ages twenty to forty. The male:female ratios are close to one in the center of the z scale (i.e., the range of "normal" intelligence) and strikingly larger than one in both the upper and lower ranges.

* Gelade, 2009; Herrnstein & Murray, 1994; Murray, 1998, 2003.

This example illustrates a general principle. Slight differences in the means and variances of a distribution have little effect on the distribution of most of the scores, but can have substantial effects on the upper and lower tails of the distribution. Panel 11.4 and Figure 11.10 illustrate how large the effect can be. The combination of a slight difference in means and variances has very little effect on the distribution of intelligence test scores across men and women in the "generally normal" range, say from IQ equivalents of 80 to 120, which is where 80% of all scores lie, but can produce substantial differences in the frequencies of men and women among the top and bottom 10%.

The different frequencies of males and females at the extreme ends of the distributions have consequences for educational programs. Boys markedly outnumber girls in special education programs, and in other indices of low but not abnormal intelligence, by a ratio of about 2:1.[69] At the other end of the academic spectrum, unless there is an administrative decision to require equal numbers of boys and girls, boys usually outnumber girls in programs for gifted students. This was true in the Study of Mathematically Precocious Youth (SMPY), which was discussed in Chapter 10. Recall that part of this study involved three different cohorts, which can be described as being in the top 1 in 100, 1 in 200, and 1 in 10,000 in the

---

69 The ratio depends upon the criterion used for admission to the program. In the United States those states that offer fewer services, and hence have a stricter criterion for admission to the program, have higher M:F ratios (Coutinho & Oswald, 2005). Similar ratios have been reported for Europe (Skarbrevik, 2002).

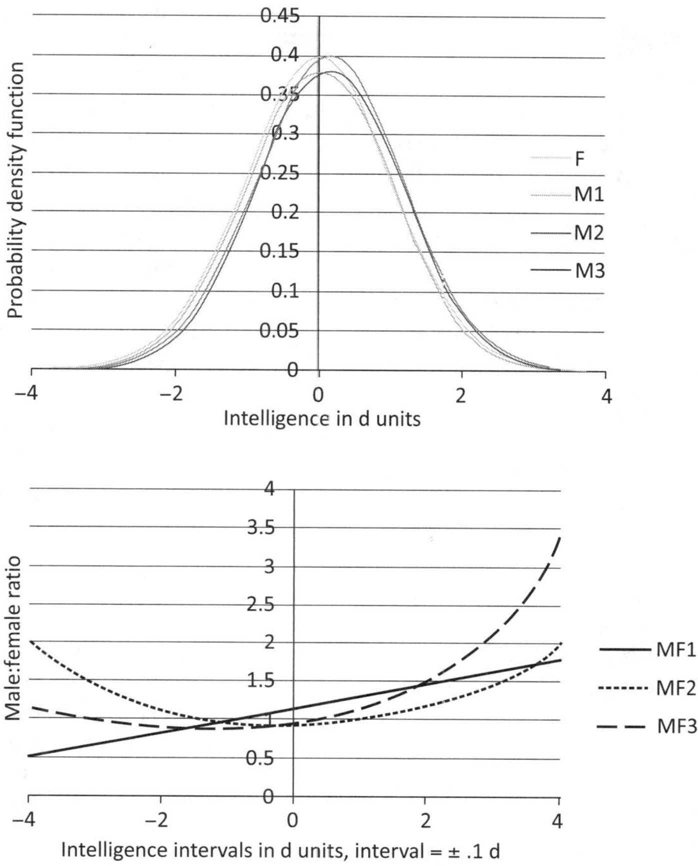

Figure 11.10. The effect of small differences in means and variances upon the distribution of scores at various points on the d scale.

distribution of SAT scores. The corresponding male:female ratios were 1.5:1, 2.1:1, and 11.2:1.

While differences in variance may be part of the explanation for the excess of men over women in the extremes of the intelligence distribution, this cannot be the whole story. On the positive end of the scale, a d scale value of 4 (IQ = 160) corresponds to the "1 in 10,000" cohort in the SMPY. According to Figure 11.10, the expected male:female ratio at this point should be 3.5, which is not even close to the 11:1 observed ratio. The observed male:female ratio in special education classes (roughly equivalent to $d = -2.5$, IQ = 78 and below) is also higher than would be expected on the basis of differences in variance alone.

Wendy Johnson and her colleagues at the University of Edinburgh have suggested a reason for the overrepresentation of males at the low end of the distribution.[70] They assumed that the distribution of intelligence actually consists of two distributions: a distribution of the intelligence of normally developing individuals, which is centered slightly above the IQ = 100 point, and a distribution of individuals who have been subjected to either biological or environmental disturbances that disrupt normal development. This distribution, which is considerably smaller than the first, is centered on the IQ = 80 point. Assuming that both distributions have a standard deviation of 15 IQ points, about 75% of the individuals in the disrupted group would have IQs above 70, the usual criterion for the mentally disabled. Therefore, the disrupted-development

70 Johnson, Carothers, & Deary, 2008, 2009.

population would consist largely of people whose intelligence was in the low normal, rather than the pathological, range. Johnson and colleagues further assumed that more males than females fall into the disrupted-development population. This is consistent with a great deal of data showing that males are generally more at risk for biological disruption than females.

Johnson and her colleagues also pointed out that greater male variability would be expected if the (yet unidentified) genes for general intelligence are located on the X chromosome, because the male genetic potential would then depend upon a smaller, and hence more variable, sample of the alleles for intelligence than would be the case for women, with two X chromosomes. The assumption is not unreasonable, for we know that genes leading to severe cognitive pathologies are overrepresented on the X chromosome. A direct test of the hypothesis will have to wait until the genes for normal variations in the genetic potential are located. Johnson and colleagues' assumptions are sufficient to account for deviations from the normal distribution in low scores from two Scottish surveys of intelligence in eleven-year-olds, taken in 1932 and 1947. Similar excesses of low scores have been observed in other data sets.

This leaves us without a proposal to explain the excess of males at the upper ends of the intelligence distribution. We take up this issue subsequently, in discussions of educational issues, in section 11.3.6. First we look at male-female differences on dimensions of intelligence other than *g*. Here we find much clearer differences.

11.3.4. *The Cognitive Differences between Men and Women*

Although there is at most a small difference between men and women in general intelligence, there are substantial differences along some of the dimensions of intelligence. In discussing these we will take a top down approach. We first look at the results from national surveys. These provide a broad-brush view of the nature of sex differences in

cognition, but do not provide details because the economics and logistics of very large testing programs rule out close examination of any one cognitive trait. We then look at psychometric research studies, which provide a more detailed look at individual traits, at the expense of not using nationally representative samples, but keeping the constraints of the conventional testing paradigm. Finally we look at laboratory studies using the techniques of cognitive psychology. These studies provide a much finer look at individual behavior, because they relax the constraints of the testing paradigm, at the cost of not studying correlations between traits, and using quite unrepresentative samples. These approaches complement each other, in much the same way that the progression from public health surveys to laboratory research provides complementary sources of information in the biomedical sciences.

We begin with a study of the way in which scores are distributed in the WAIS-III standardization sample. Most psychometric models assume that the scores are distributed in accordance with a multivariate normal distribution, but that is not necessarily the case. The profiles defined by the WAIS subtests could fall into patterns of similar scores, rather than being distributed smoothly across the mathematical space defined by possible test scores. For a geographic analogy, people's residences in the US are not characterized by a smooth distribution across the country; homes are clustered into cities and towns.

A technique known as *cluster analysis* has been used to identify five patterns in the WAIS standardization.[71] The clusters differ on two variables: overall performance level and whether people within the cluster obtain better scores on perceptual speed measures than would be expected given their overall level of performance. Women do not differ from men in overall performance, but they are overrepresented in clusters associated with high perceptual speed, which in effect means rapid recognition of simple visual figures.

71 Donders, Zhu, & Tulsky, 2001.

Table 11.3. *Male–female standard deviation unit (d) scores for effect size for different aspects of intelligence. The NLSY79 survey reported two scores for mathematics – arithmetical reasoning (use of numerical reasoning in problem solving) and mathematical knowledge. The same survey also reported two scores for the speed of conducting simple cognitive operations. One was a simple decoding operation; the other evaluated the examinee's speed of executing elementary numerical operations.*

Survey Code	Test Date	N	Reading Comp.	Mathematics	Nonverbal Reasoning	Spatial Ability	Perceptual Speed	Assoc. Memory
Project Talent	1960	73,425	−.15	.12	.04	.13	n.a.	−.32
NLS-72	1972	16,860	−.05	.24	−.22	n.a.	−.23	−.26
HS&B	1980	25,069	.002	.22	n.a.	.25	−.21	−.18
NLSY79	1980	11,914	−.18	.26, .08	n.a	n.a.	−.43, −.23	n.a.
NELS:88	1992	24,599	−.09	.03	n.a.	n.a.	n.a.	n.a.

Source: Data is from Hedges and Nowell, 1995, Tables 1 and 2.

A similar pattern has been found in studies of nationally representative adolescent populations. Table 11.3 shows the results from four national surveys of people who were tested when they were in high school, and who have since been followed through their early adult careers.[72] While there is some discrepancy between the results, which is probably due to differences in content between different tests, two trends stand out. Women do better than men in tests of reading comprehension, speed of simple perceptual operations, and tests of associative memory, in which examinees have to recall arbitrary associations, such as associating a picture and a number. Men do better than women on tests of visual-spatial reasoning and mathematics.

The results from the WAIS III indicate that in the adult years the female advantage in verbal operations disappears, but the advantage in tasks involving rapid, simple perceptual recognition and execution of simple cognitive operations (processing speed) remains.

These conclusions refer to very broadly defined abilities. Two psychometric research studies provide further detail, and, in the case of the second study, establish a theoretical framework for thinking about these results.

The Differential Aptitude Battery (DAT) is a battery of tests developed by the Educational Testing Service for research purposes. Figure 11.11 presents male-female differences on some of the subtests, calculated for four standardizations in the United States, spanning just over forty-three years. Results quite similar to those shown in Figure 11.11 have been obtained in Spain and in the United Kingdom.[73]

The consistency of the results is impressive. Women do somewhat better on tests of language skills (as opposed to reasoning about verbally presented material) and on tests of speed and accuracy of simple operations. Men do markedly better on tests involving the manipulation of visual images. Men also do slightly better on tests of verbal and abstract reasoning.

Johnson and Bouchard have placed results similar to these in the context of the g-VPR model.[74] In previous work (reviewed in Chapter 4, section 5) Johnson and Bouchard had shown that the g-VPR model provides a good fit to the MISTRA data (Chapter 8). They then removed the variance in scores associated with the g dimension, and analyzed the residual scores on the various tests. The residuals can be thought of as being the variation in test

72 Hedges & Nowell, 1995.

73 Colom & Lynn, 2004; Strand, Deary, & Smith, 2006.
74 Johnson & Bouchard, 2007a,b.

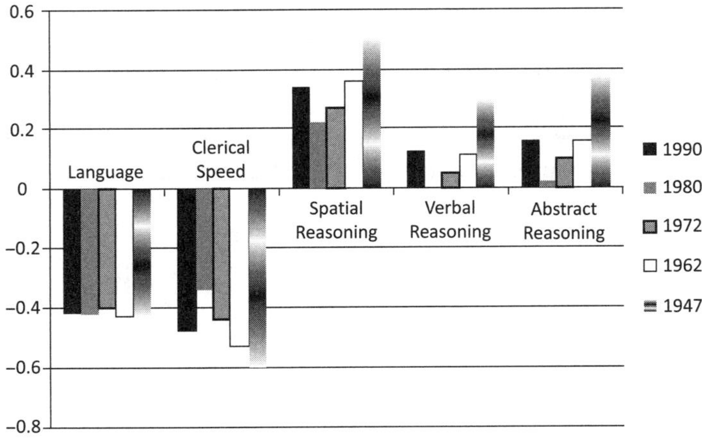

Figure 11.11. Male–female differences in *d* unit for selected subtests of the Differential Aptitude Battery, shown over standardizations from 1947 to 1990.

scores that *cannot* be ascribed to variations in general intelligence. The residual variation could be characterized by three orthogonal dimensions. The smallest of these, in terms of variance accounted for, was a "memory for content of passages" factor. This will not be discussed further. The other two factors are more interesting.

Figure 11.12 is a graphic model of Johnson and Bouchard's results, showing the two factors and their relation to the general intelligence (*g*) factor. The two residual factors are *bipolar* factors, in the sense that tests tend to have either high or low loadings on each of them. Johnson and Bouchard refer to these two dimensions as *verbal-rotational* and *focused-diffuse.*

The bipolar factors need special interpretation, for they are not quite the same as the ability factors identified in the original *g*-VPR model. Vocabulary tests and rotational tests were good markers for the respective ends of the verbal-rotational factor. What the result says is that in the MISTRA sample (adults!) *after general intelligence had been accounted for* people who knew lots of words tended to be poor at manipulating mental images, and vice versa. The focused-diffuse dimension contrasted people who did well on tasks that require concentration on visual diagrams with people who did well on tasks that involve comprehension of verbal argu-

ments and possession of information about the world.

Johnson and Bouchard measured male-female differences along each of the dimensions. They found only small, nonreliable differences on the *g* dimension. There were large differences (*d* values larger than .5) on the subsidiary dimensions. Women tended strongly toward the verbal ends of both bipolar dimensions, and tended to have superior memory for information presented during the testing session. Men tended to have higher scores on the "focused" (on visual objects) and "rotational" ends of the bipolar dimensions. Once again, though, it is important to remember that these differences refer to performance after removing variation due to general intelligence.

Johnson and Bouchard have offered an interesting summary and interpretation of their results.[75] They argue that whenever a person solves a problem he or she does so by combining general reasoning ability (i.e., *g*) with the particular mental tools they have on hand. For instance, many ostensibly visual-spatial problems can also be solved by verbal reasoning. The results just cited indicate that men and women differ somewhat in the quality of their mental tools; the verbal tools tend to be better

75 Johnson and Bouchard, 2007b.

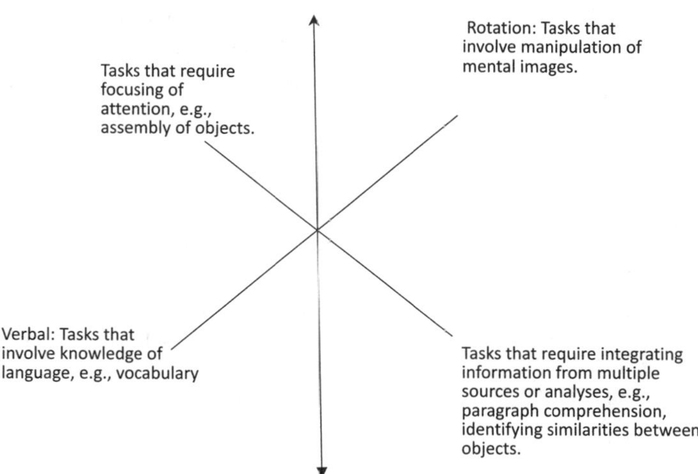

Figure 11.12. Johnson and Bouchard's model of general intelligence plus two bipolar factors (verbal-rotational and focus-diffuse). The bipolar factors represent a trade-off between opposing strengths.

for women, and the mental imaging and attention-focusing tools tend to be better for men. Rational application of general intelligence would thus lead men and women to adopt somewhat different strategies for problem solving. Therefore, even though men and women are essentially equal in general intelligence, they may differ in their performance on particular tests, because performance depends upon both general intelligence (for which there is no sex difference) and the residual abilities, where sex differences may be substantial.

Both the national surveys and the psychometric research studies indicate that the big differences between men and women are on perceptual and spatial-visual reasoning tasks – the P and R dimensions of the g-VPR model. (One could say much the same thing about the PS and Vz dimensions of the three-stratum model.) Laboratory studies amplify upon these results. Men tend to be better than women at tasks involving the manipulation of mental images. The prototypical example is a mental rotation task, in which two figures must be compared by moving them about "in the mind's eye." Women take longer to do this, on the average, and make more errors. The second type of task on which men's performance is generally better than women's performance is a field-independence task, where an observer is required to orient an object to the true vertical or horizontal, overcoming the effects of framing figures. Examples of these two types of task are shown in Figure 11.13. Men also do better than women on tasks involving judgment of real or imagined motion.[76]

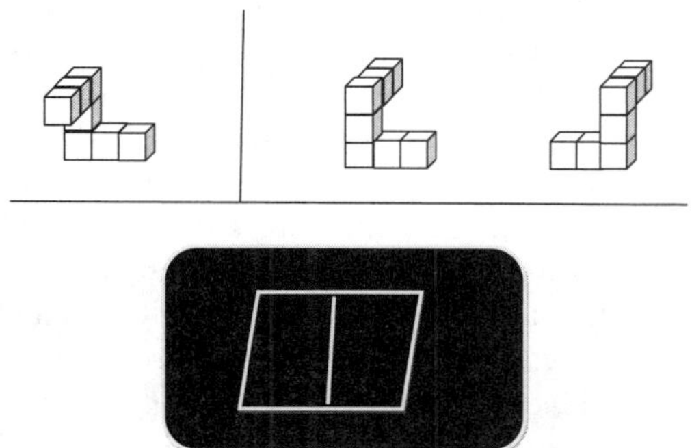

Figure 11.13. Illustrations of two visual-spatial reasoning tasks on which men tend to outperform women. See text for details.

76 Hunt et al., 1988; Kimura, 1999, Chapter 5; Law, Pellegrino, & Hunt, 1993.

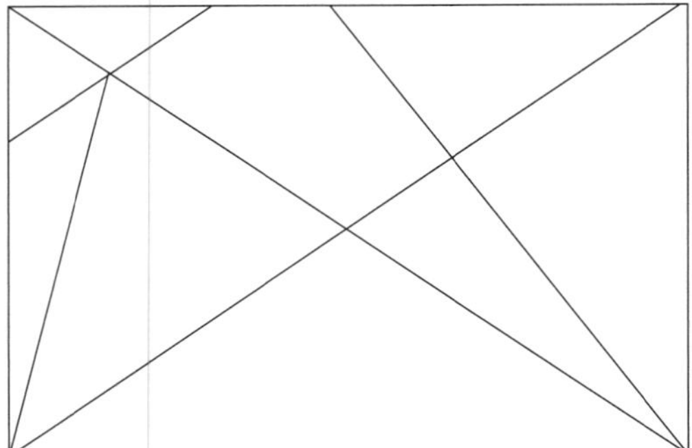

Figure 11.14. Detecting details in a complex picture. Count the triangles in the figure above. This task requires analysis of a static visual figure. Women tend to outperform men on this sort of task.

By contrast, there are many spatial-visual tasks that do not involve any of these skills. For instance, women tend to outperform men on tasks that require analysis of static visual figures. An example, where the task is to find a component within a picture, is shown in Figure 11.14.

A possibly related finding is that males do better than females in way finding, the ability to find locations and to maintain awareness of positions in the environment. This is true of both children and young adults, and appears to be related to performance on spatial orientation tasks, although the relationship is not a strong one. This result holds for imagined routes through environments, actual orienteering, and acquisition of knowledge of the environment through interaction with computer-generated virtual environments.[77]

The skills evaluated by these tasks have applications in everyday life. There are very large individual differences in our ability to find our way about the world. And, as would be expected from Johnson and Bouchard's analysis, way finding can be accomplished by visualizing the surrounding environment or by using strategies that rely on verbal memory. Men are more likely to use the first strategy, women the second.[78] There are also a number of practical situations in which

a person must visualize motion or changes in perspective while viewing a static display. These vary from analyzing gear trains to assembling objects from diagrammatic instructions – a task that will be familiar and perhaps frustrating to anyone who has purchased to-be-assembled furniture kits.

Such observations do not mean that "women can't (find their way in the woods, read maps, be architects, fly helicopters . . .) as well as men." The following qualifications should be kept in mind.

Virtually all tasks we encounter in daily life admit to multiple solutions. General intelligence is a far better predictor of performance than rotational ability, even though both are important. People can apply general intelligence to develop a problem-solving strategy that suits their particular strengths.

The claims for male superiority in rotation and related visual-spatial abilities refer to statistical trends. Assuming a deviation difference on a rotation task of .5, we would still expect 30% of the women to outperform 50% of the men. The differences in the frequencies of men and women, in favor of men, would be more extreme at higher levels of performance.

Visual-spatial abilities, like virtually all abilities, can be acquired through training. This is particularly true if the training can be focused on a narrow set of skills required for a particular task. On the average, women do not read maps as well as men.[79] Map reading is taught all the time, to both men and women, in contexts varying from sports orienteering to military training. The visual rotation task (Figure 11.13) was described as the prototypical task for illustrating male-female differences in rotation. Similarly, it can be used to illustrate age differences in rotation, which can be substantial over the adult years. People can be trained to perform this task. In one study in my own laboratory women in their fifties were trained to the level of performance typical of male undergraduates.[80] These are only two of

---

77 Choi & Silverman, 2003; Malinowski, 2001; Waller, Knapp, & Hunt, 2001.
78 See Hunt, 2002, for a review of the evidence.

79 Boardman, 1990.
80 Berg, Hertzog, & Hunt, 1982.

several examples that could be given of the acquisition of visual-spatial skills through training.[81]

Individual differences are generally not eliminated by training, although they may be reduced. This is what happened in the study in my laboratory; both men and women got better after five days of training, but there were still differences between them in their ability to do the spatial rotation task. Cognitive traits are not invariant, in the sense that height is. They are more like weight: they can be modified, but it can take a lot of work to do so. The amount of training required to reach a fixed level of performance will probably depend upon a person's initial performance level.

11.3.5. Male-Female Differences in Cognitive Traits Relevant to Education

This section discusses cognitive differences between men and women that have a direct impact upon education. The issue is important, because different educational avenues lead to markedly different careers in adulthood.

Psychologists and educators think about individual differences in different ways. Psychologists are interested in tasks that maximize individual differences in human behavior, try to characterize these differences, and, especially in recent years, try to relate behaviorally defined traits to biological systems. To illustrate, one of Johnson and Bouchard's arguments for preferring the g-VPR model of intelligence to the Gc-Gf model is that the behavioral distinctions in the g-VPR model map onto distinctions between brain systems, while those in the Gc-Gf model do not.

By contrast, educators think in terms of subject matter. They want to talk about cognitive traits associated with educational content. The biggest division of the curriculum is into topics that are broadly associated with language arts and topics associated with mathematics. Accordingly, to an educator

the most interesting individual differences are differences in the ability to deal with language and mathematics. "General reasoning" is too amorphous a concept, and, to an educator, perceptual and visual-spatial skills seem too microscopic.

We need to coordinate these two views, paying special attention to the ways in which male-female differences in cognitive experiences impact on education. A large study from Germany provides a good place to begin.[82]

Martin Brunner and two colleagues at the Max Planck Institute conducted a psychometric analysis of the data from a German testing program involving over 29,000 students, randomly selected from the seventeen-year-olds in the German school system. The study was exceptional both for the representativeness of the sample and for the care that the investigators paid to the technical issues concerning group differences that were described in the introduction to this chapter. They concluded that the data was best fit by a hierarchical model, consisting of a general factor (g) and a nested factor model, in which mathematics or verbal (reading) abilities contribute to overall mathematics or reading test scores. The traits of interest to educators, language and mathematical abilities, appear as specializations of a general reasoning factor, which is not a targeted educational variable.

Brunner and his colleagues then examined male-female differences along each dimension. The seventeen-year-old girls slightly outperformed the boys on the general reasoning and reading factors ($d = -.09$ for both comparisons), but the boys markedly outperformed the girls on the mathematical factor ($d = .94$). This conforms to the popular belief that boys are better than girls at mathematics, although, as we will show, this finding ought to be qualified.

Brunner and his colleagues then considered what their findings might imply for mathematics. They argued that mathematical problems are attacked with a

---

81 See Newcombe, 2007, for a further discussion of this issue.

82 Brunner, Krauss, & Kunter, 2008.

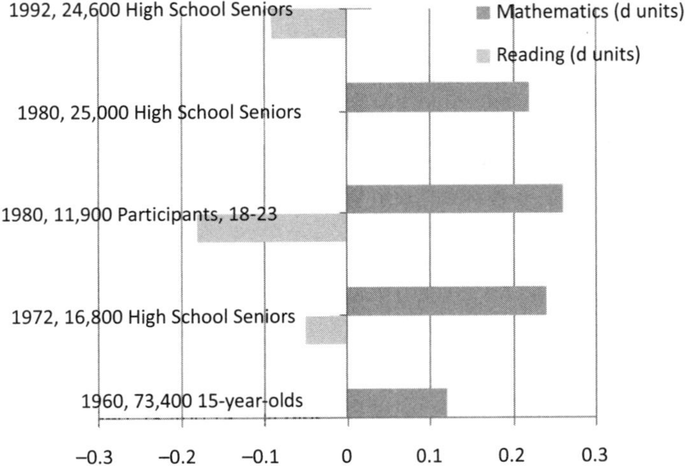

Figure 11.15. Male-female differences on various educational tests of reading and mathematics. All studies utilized large probability samples of the relevant US population. Positive numbers indicate a male advantage; negative numbers indicate a female advantage. Data from Hedges and Nowell, 1995, Table 2.

combination of general reasoning skills, in which men and women are essentially equivalent, and mathematics-specific skills, in which men, on the average, exceed women. As a result, men should do better than women in those areas of the curriculum that emphasize mathematics, providing that the mathematics involved is sufficiently specialized to emphasize mathematical rather than general reasoning skills.

Applying Brunner and colleagues' reasoning to the typical educational progression, what we should see is a progressive sharpening of differences between men and women in educational accomplishment as we move from the general education curriculum through the undergraduate university years, and then on to specialized education and career achievements in the Science, Technology, Engineering, and Mathematics (STEM) fields. That is what happens, but there are some important qualifications.

WHAT MEN AND WOMEN GET OUT
OF THE K-12 SYSTEM
In the United States public education is available to everyone from kindergarten through the twelfth grade. While there is some variation from state to state, attendance is usually compulsory through age six-

teen, and students are very strongly encouraged to complete the entire course, graduating at seventeen or eighteen. Similar public education programs exist in other developed countries.

Figure 11.15 presents a comparison of the scores achieved by high school age boys and girls on the cognitive tests used in several Department of Labor surveys during the last half of the twentieth century.[83] Throughout this period girls consistently outscored boys on tests involving language use, while boys outscored girls by a somewhat larger margin on tests of mathematical skills. Similar results have been obtained by the National Assessment of Educational Progress (NAEP). This test has been called "the nation's report card" for the evaluation of language, mathematics, and science skills. Somewhere between 70,000 and 100,000 students are evaluated each year. In the twelfth grade girls outscore boys in reading, while boys outscore girls in mathematics.[84]

International results are similar. The Program for International Student Assessment (PISA) is a program in which representative

83 Hedges & Nowell, 1995.
84 "Nation's Report Card," National Center for Education Statistics.

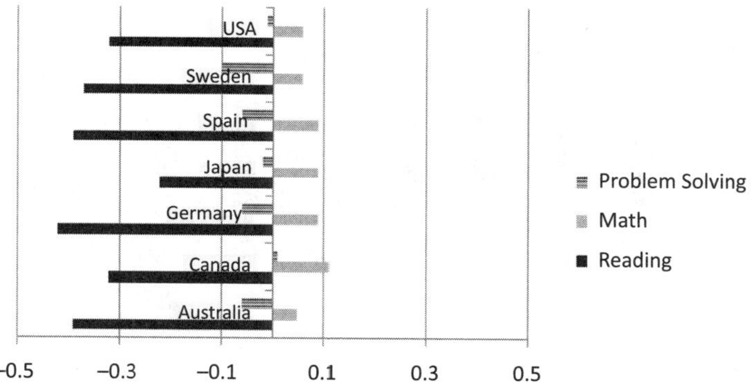

Figure 11.16. The difference between male and female scores on three of the 2003 PISA examinations. Differences are expressed in deviation units using a nominal standard deviation of 100, which is the intended standard deviation for the PISA examinations.

schools are selected, and fifteen-year-old children are evaluated on tests involving reading, mathematics, science, and problem solving. The problem-solving section presents realistic problems that do not depend upon specific academic knowledge, such as finding an efficient route on a bus line. Figure 11.16 shows the male-female deviation scores on the PISA reading, mathematics, and problem-solving tests, calculated for the United States and six other economically developed countries. The consistency in the pattern is striking. Across all countries males exceed females by a small amount (d's consistent, but less than .1) in mathematics, while females exceed males by a larger amount (d's around .3) in reading. On the problem-solving test, where an attempt was made to set problems that did not depend upon reading or mathematics skills, there was virtually no gender difference.

Figure 11.16 emphasizes the consistency of differences between boys and girls, but does not indicate the fact that the absolute level of achievement varies a great deal across countries. This variation is shown in Figure 11.17. The same pattern is evident in the science scores – small but consistent male-female differences and much larger differences between countries. Fifteen-year-old girls in Australia, Canada, Germany, Japan, and Sweden have higher mathemat-

ics and science scores than fifteen-year-old boys in Spain and the US.

One more point in the international data is worth noting. Because males typically display greater variance in scores than females, we would expect the differences between fifteen-year-old boys and girls to be greater at high levels of performance than it is on the average. This is the case. Averaged over countries, the d for male-female median mathematics scores is .10. At the ninety-fifth percentile it is .20.[85]

The data for K-12 educational achievement presents a remarkably consistent picture. At the end of the standard (and often compulsory) school period mid-teenage girls have greater language related skills than boys of their age, while the opposite is true of skills and knowledge in science and mathematics. In terms of deviation units the female advantage in language is greater than the male advantage in science and mathematics. It is important to remember that this is a statement about the extent to which the male and female score distributions differ with respect to each other. It is not a statement of differences in absolute skill, because there is no metric by which we can compare a difference in mathematical knowledge to a difference in language skill.

85 Machin & Pekkarinen, 2008.

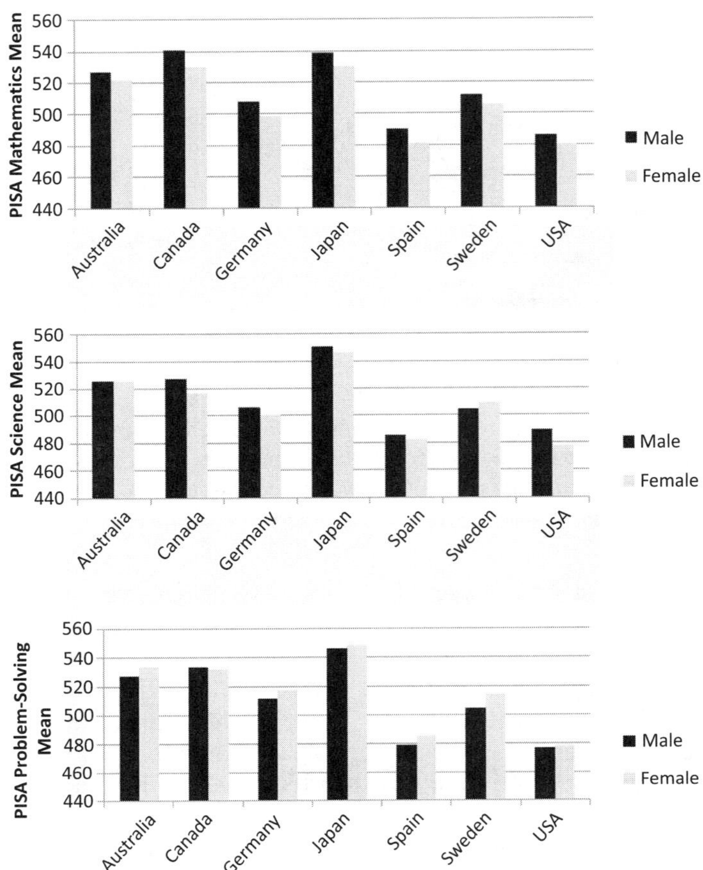

Figure 11.17. Mean scores of fifteen-year-old students in selected countries on the PISA 2003 tests of mathematics, science, and general problem solving. Data from the National Center for Educational Statistics, *Digest of Educational Statistics*, 2007, Table 389.

COLLEGE AND UNIVERSITY UNDERGRADUATE EDUCATION

College and university students represent an important population, because this population of young adults contains most of the people who will be leaders of society, both in the dramatic sense of providing a few highly visible leaders, and in the perhaps more important sense of providing the many business managers, entrepreneurs, technicians, and professionals who will constitute the economically and socially most productive segments of society.[86] As is well known, in the last fifty years there has been a tremendous expansion of social and economic opportunity for women within the college-educated segments of society. There is considerable reason to be interested in differences between the cognitive skills of men and women within this group.

It is important to remember, though, that results obtained by studies of people who are either in or about to enter undergraduate education do not necessarily generalize to the population at large. Since the early 1980s more women have enrolled in college than men. As of 2008, there were approximately three undergraduate men for every four women. This situation arises because at a given level of high school academic achievement a woman is more likely to take the first steps toward undergraduate education

86 Gelade, 2009.

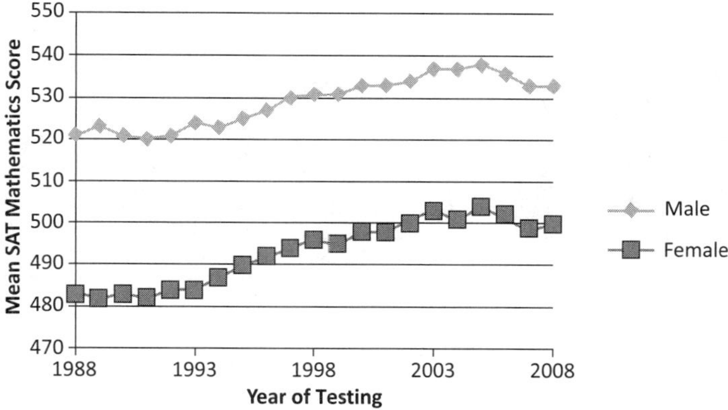

Figure 11.18. Mean SAT mathematics scores for men and women, from 1988 to 2008. The *d* values for these comparisons range from .33 to .41. *Source:* College Board Report, *College Bound Seniors, 2008.*

than a man is.[87] Accordingly, female undergraduates are a somewhat academically less select subpopulation of all women than male undergraduates are of all men. While this is not quite accurate, you can think of the two populations as being roughly the top 45% of men and the top 55% of women.

One implication of this is that male-female differences will be algebraically larger in the undergraduate population than in the high school population. The effect will be further exacerbated by the variance effects described earlier. Men's scores will be increased, overall, because of a high male:female ratio in the population of people who have high test scores. The excess of men with low test scores will not affect the undergraduate means, because people with low test scores are unlikely to enroll in undergraduate programs.

These trends are seen in the test scores of entering students. In the high school population, as a whole, the women's mean reading score is above the men's mean by about .2 standard deviation units, and men exceed women in mathematics test scores by about .1 standard deviation units. The 2008 SAT reading scores were 504 for men and 500 for women, while the mathematics scores were 533 for men and 504 for women. Using the nominal 100-point standard deviation for SAT sections, this translates into a trivial .04

d male advantage in reading, and a nontrivial .33 *d* advantage in the mathematics (now renamed "reasoning") portion of the test. This is the sort of magnification of male-female differences that would be expected because of the differential recruitment of men and women from the high school to the undergraduate population.

The male-female discrepancy in SAT mathematics scores is not a recent phenomenon. Figure 11.18 shows the SAT mathematics (SAT-M) scores of college-bound seniors from 1988 until 2008. Although the levels of scores for both men and women vary from year to year, the difference between means is remarkably consistent.

In 2005 an approximately equal number of men and women earned bachelor's degrees in Science, Technology, Engineering, and Mathematics (in the jargon of the US National Science Foundation, the STEM fields). This was a change from thirty years earlier, when the ratio of men to women earning bachelor's degrees in these fields was approximately 2:1.[88] However, because the undergraduate male:female ratio is 3:4, the 1:1 ratio in the STEM fields implies that a man is about 4/3 more likely to major in a STEM field than a women is. The extent to which this disparity is due to cognitive competence, personal interests, or social pressures is impossible to say.

---

87 Hunt & Madhyastha, 2008.

88 Source: National Science Foundation.

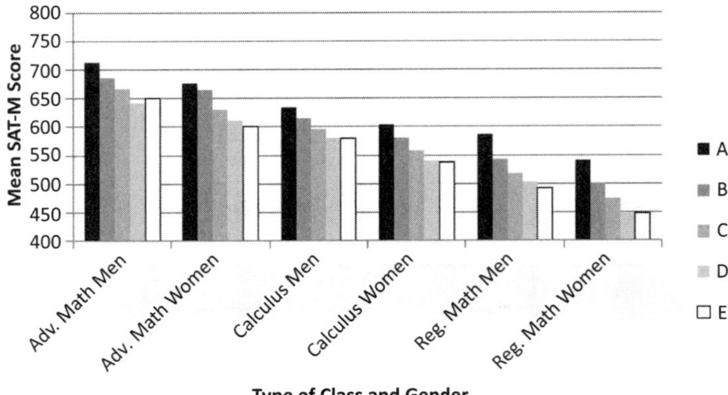

Figure 11.19. The relation between SAT-M scores, grades (A, B, C, D, E), and gender in three levels of college courses. Within course, men have higher SAT-M scores than women who have comparable grades. *Source:* Wainer & Steinberg, 1992.

Women are not entering the STEM fields and then dropping out because they find the work too difficult. Given constant SAT-M scores, women consistently outperform men in mathematics courses.[89] The difference can be striking. Figure 11.19 shows the results from a very large (N ∼ 49,000) study of college students in a variety of American universities.[90] SAT-M scores increase as a function of the level of mathematics involved. This reflects the unsurprising fact: people with high SAT-M scores are more willing to enroll in mathematics courses than people with low scores. Within each type of course, SAT-M scores increase as the course grade increases. This shows that the SAT-M is a valid predictor of accomplishments in mathematics classes. Both of these trends hold for men and for women.

But then we come to a paradox. Within each course and grade level, women receive *higher* grades than men, even though they have lower SAT-M scores. In terms of educational outcomes the difference can be substantial. Women who receive Bs have SAT-M scores lower than the men who receive Cs and Ds in the same class. This is a striking example of a general tendency for SAT scores to underpredict women's educational achievements in the early undergraduate years.

I have heard three explanations offered to explain the paradox. One is that the test is an objective measure of mathematics ability, while grades are a subjective measure based on the instructors' decisions. Therefore, men "really" possess more mathematics ability, but women are able to present a more favorable impression to instructors.

This explanation strikes me as a plausible argument for low correlations between test scores and grades in courses where there is a substantial subjective component to grading, such as a course in English literature, but I do not see how the argument applies to lower-division college mathematics courses, where right answers are clearly defined.

A second argument is that women simply work harder to get grades.

The most probable explanation is that women's stronger work motivation compensates for their lower test scores.
– Lynn & Irwing, 2004a, p. 495

Presumably what Lynn and Irwing meant was "lower ability as indexed by test scores" (which in this case referred to progressive matrix tests rather than the SAT), rather than to the test scores themselves, as the test scores per se are not involved in grade assignment. The motivational argument is

89　Clark & Grandy, 1984; Lynn & Mau, 2001; Ramist, Lewis, & McCamley-Jenkins, 1994; Wainer & Steinberg, 1992.
90　Wainer & Steinberg, 1992.

not unreasonable, for women do report doing more homework than men.[91] However, this implies a false dichotomy between intelligence and motivation as evidenced by behavior as a student. Talents such as good time management and establishing priorities among goals are part of intelligence, in the conceptual sense, as much as the talents required for taking tests.

A third possibility is that tests of mathematical aptitude, such as the SAT-M, are influenced by a psychological trait on which there are sex differences, but this trait either does not contribute to mathematical performance outside the test, or does so, but has more influence on test performance than it does on in-class performance. Visual-spatial ability, the R dimension of the g-VPR model, has been suggested as a possibility, both for the SAT and for progressive matrix tests.[92] Alternatively, there might be some ability that is not evaluated by the test, but that is important in the study of mathematics and is possessed by women more than by men. My comment about time management is an example of such an explanation.

When all is said and done, though, we just do not know what the link is between male-female differences in test performance and in performance in mathematics. The problem becomes more acute as we look at discrepancies between men and women at a higher level of analysis, the pursuit of careers in the STEM fields.

POSTGRADUATE EDUCATION
AND CAREER DEVELOPMENT

It is difficult to say anything succinct about male-female differences in postgraduate education and career development in general, because any statement has to be qualified by considering the field involved. Postgraduate education is itself so varied that general statements about how men and women progress through curricula as different as mathematics, education, medicine, and the law are equally suspect. What we can do, however, is to look at some of the

highly publicized differences in outcomes between men and women. Socially, what has been of particular concern is the scarcity of women in the Science, Technology, Engineering, and Mathematics (STEM) fields.

The disparity is longstanding. Charles Murray's statistical survey of five thousand years of human accomplishment uncovered very few eminent woman scientists or mathematicians.[93] This is hardly surprising, owing to restrictions on women's activities that were enforced by various human societies until modern times, and even now outside the industrially developed countries. Within these countries lifting of the restrictions is quite recent. In 1925 Cecelia Payne-Gaposchkin (1900–1979) became the first woman to receive a doctorate (in Astronomy, a STEM field) from Harvard University. A few years later, in 1934, Grace Hopper (1906–1992) became the first woman STEM graduate (in Mathematics) at Yale University. (Hopper later developed COBOL, one of the early computer programming languages, and was the first person to use the term "bug" to describe an error in program execution.) In 2007 Drew Gilpin Faust became the first woman president of Harvard. Hanna Holburn Gray served as acting president of Yale for one year in 1977. Things have changed, but perhaps not at breakneck speed. Harvard was founded in 1636, Yale in 1701.

The national picture is similar to that at Harvard and Yale. Figure 11.20 shows the percentages of women receiving doctorates in several relevant fields, contrasting 1977 and 2007. There has clearly been a great increase in the number of women receiving advanced degrees. However, the pattern for type of degree has changed very little over a thirty-year period marked by major advances in opportunities for women. Today women greatly outnumber the men who receive doctorates in Education, and are greatly outnumbered by them in Mathematics, the mathematically oriented physical sciences, and Engineering.

91 Mau & Lynn, 2000, 2001.
92 Casey et al., 1995; Lynn & Irwing, 2004a.

93 Murray, 2003.

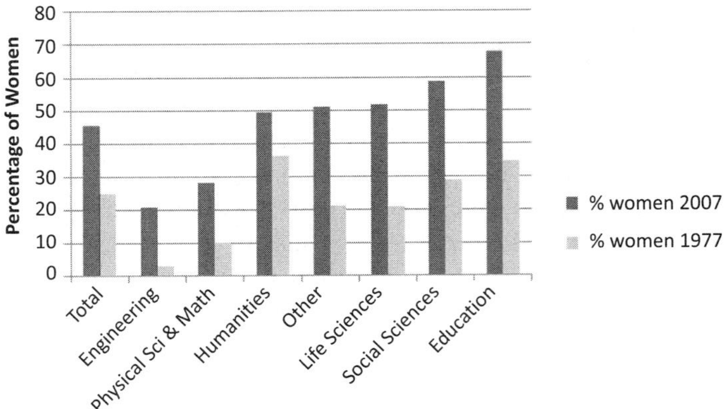

Figure 11.20. The percentages of women among the recipients of doctoral degrees, 1977 and 2007. *Source:* National Science Foundation Survey of Earned Doctorates, 2007.

Why have the higher reaches of the STEM fields remained so weighted toward men? In a widely publicized speech Faust's immediate predecessor at Harvard, the economist Larry Summers, proposed three reasons for the discrepancy. Two were social: the existence of conscious or unconscious prejudice on the part of hiring and promotion committees, and a preference for a personal lifestyle that is not compatible with the workaholic standards Summers associated with very high productivity in the STEM fields. The third was biological. Summers correctly observed that there is a striking disparity between the numbers of men and women who have very high scores on tests of mathematical ability and achievement. He then speculated that women's brains are organized in a way that makes acquiring the high level of analytic skills needed in STEM research more difficult for women than for men.[94]

Summers's remarks created such a firestorm that he subsequently resigned from the Harvard presidency. The incident is described in Panel 11.5. Going into all the possible social and biological reasons why women might be underrepresented in high-profile STEM positions is well beyond the scope of this book. The controversy does provide a good entry point for a more general discussion of why there might be differences in intelligence between men and women.

11.3.6. *The Causes of Cognitive Differences between Men and Women*

Professionals in the field were far more nuanced in their reaction to Summers's remarks than political figures and academic leaders. The American Psychological Association (APA) and the Association for Psychological Science (APS), the two professional organizations most involved, commissioned reports by people well known for their research in the field. The APA reports resulted in a book of contributed chapters, several of which I have cited.[95] The other report took up an entire issue in one of the APS's journals. Here are two sentences from its concluding paragraph.

There cannot be any single or simple answer to the many complex questions about sex differences in math and science.

Early experience, biological constraints, educational policy and cultural context each have effects, and these effects add and interact in complex and sometimes unpredictable ways.

– Halpern et al., 2007

94 See the earlier discussion of disparities between men and women in the SMPY program. For years men have outscored women on both the mathematical and verbal sections of the Graduate Record Examination (Grandy, 1999).

95 Ceci & Williams, 2007.

Panel 11.5. The Lawrence Summers Affair

On January 14, 2005, Lawrence Summers, at that time president of Harvard University, gave a speech addressing the fact that women are underrepresented in the STEM fields, and even more underrepresented at the top of those professions. Summers subsequently commented that he had been asked to be provocative. He was.

Summers proposed three causes for the discrepancy: conscious or unconscious prejudice against women, women's distaste for the intense professional commitments required to rise to the top of the STEM fields, and women's difficulty in acquiring mathematical and scientific reasoning skills. Summers noted that a relatively small percentage of women achieve high scores on tests of mathematical reasoning, and suggested that biological differences between men and women might contribute to the disparity in high-level mathematics skills.

Several prominent women scientists left the meeting in protest. The high-visibility magazine *Science* published a letter signed by seventy-three prominent academics protesting his statements.* The Harvard faculty voted no-confidence in Summers, and in 2006 he resigned his post, returning to his position as a Professor of Economics. He hardly retired to pasture. In January of 2009 he was appointed Chair of the Presidential Council of Economic Advisors, making him the chief White House advisor on economic matters.

Summers's remarks on women undoubtedly contributed to his more or less forced resignation, but it is unlikely that they were the only factors. By all accounts, Summers was a forceful executive in an institution that was accustomed to a great deal of collegiality and decentralized decision making. During his tenure at Harvard he clearly "rubbed a number of people the wrong way" as he sought what he perceived as urgently needed changes in an historic institution.† As is often the case, the incentive to take drastic action stemmed from several causes.

The politics behind Summers's resignation are not relevant to our discussion of intelligence. The letter to *Science* is, because it indicates both the passions that are involved in discussions of group differences in intelligence and the beliefs held by highly influential people who have not studied the topic in depth.

Here are two quotes from the letter to *Science*:

There is little evidence that those scoring in the very top of the range in standardized tests are likely to have more successful careers in science education. . . .

And

We are concerned by the suggestion that the status quo for women in science may be natural, inevitable, and unrelated to social factors.
Muller et al., 2005, p. 1043

Although the list of seventy-three signers of the letter included prominent academic scientists and science administrators, it did not include any of the major figures who do research on individual differences in cognition. I doubt that many of them would have signed the letter, for the first statement is demonstrably false. By 2005 the results of the Study of Mathematically Precocious Youth (i.e., people whose SAT-M scores were in the top 1%) were well known to professionals in the field. These results document the stunning success of people whose scores were "in the very top of the range in standardized tests." ‡

What about the second statement? Summers never said anything about the status quo being natural, inevitable, or

(continued)

Panel 11.5 *(continued)*

unrelated to social factors. On the contrary, he specifically listed two social factors that he thought contributed to the disparity: discrimination and conflicts between professional and family goals. The fact that Summers mentioned a possible biological explanation for differences in men's and women's intelligence was equated with a denial of social causes.

Evidently the academic leaders who signed the Muller letter felt that they knew what the truth is, for they either felt no need to consult with experts in the field, who would have been easily available to them, or they decided to disregard far more nuanced expert opinions.

* Muller et al., 2005.
† Bowley, 2006.
‡ Park, Lubinski, & Benbow, 2006.

Let us look at some arguments for social and biological causes.

SOCIAL CAUSES

Summers' thought that one of the reasons that there are more men than women in the STEM fields is that work in these fields is simply more interesting to men than to women. If Summers were correct, men should have a higher participation rate than women in the STEM fields even within a population of talented men and women, where ability to enter the field is not an issue, but interest is. And there is such a group, the SMPY participants, people who, in their teens, were in the top 1% of their cohort in terms of academic ability tests. The SMPY participants were contacted twenty years later, when they were in their thirties, to see where their careers had gone.

There were career differences between men and women. However, career choices were determined more by interest than by gender. It is a rough generalization, but not too far off the mark, to say that participants who had primary interests in things and abstract ideas tended to follow careers in mathematics and the sciences. Participants who had interests in people and social issues followed careers in the humanitarian/social issues–oriented professions. Participants also differed in the extent to which they valued careers or families. Those participants who had strong family orientations were underrepresented in the STEM professions, which are notoriously demanding of time.

Men tended to fall more into the "things-ideas-career" pattern, while women tended toward the "people-family orientation" pattern.[96] However, examples of each pattern occurred in both highly talented men and women. The codirectors of the SMPY, David Lubinski and Camilla Benbow, point out that difference between mens' and womens' interests alone would create disparities in the extent to which men and women choose to work in the STEM fields.[97]

The SMPY participants had acquired the cognitive talents they needed, but differed in interests. What about the more general issue of how men and women come to display disparities in mathematical aptitudes, and in language skills and visual-spatial reasoning?

Cognitive skills improve with practice, a psychological law that Diane Halpern[98] said is as certain as the law of gravity. (She was right.) Sex role differentiation is a fact in every society, although the restrictions placed on permissible gender roles have varied greatly both throughout history and across societies contemporaneously. There is considerable evidence that boys and girls do have different learning experiences that might impact on their acquisition of visual-spatial skills, and concomitantly of

96 Benbow et al., 2000; Ferriman, Lubinski, & Benbow, 2009; Lubinski et al., 2006; Wai, Lubinski & Benbow, 2005.
97 See Halpern et al., 2007, pp. 31–39, for a good discussion of these social issues.
98 Halpern et al., 2007, p. 4.

mathematics. A recent review[99] documented the following statements:

In American society parents are more likely to provide analytical, causal oriented explanations to boys than to girls.

Middle school children generally accept the stereotyped view that females do not do well in mathematics and spatially oriented tasks.

Male children begin to play and explore away from home at younger ages than girls do.

Mathematics and science teachers tend to direct their discussions more toward boys than girls.

Why do these differences arise? Is it because boys and girls draw forth different behaviors from the adults, or because the adults initiate these behaviors for either social or biological reasons? These are distal explanations; the proximal facts are that when people are provided differential learning experiences they will learn different things. Psychologists cannot conduct an experiment to prove that this is a cause of differences in men's and women's performance on mathematical tasks – for people cannot be randomly assigned to lifestyles! There is an interesting natural observation that is consistent with the differential learning explanation.

In forty of the forty-one countries that participated in the PISA mathematics assessment program fifteen-year-old males outperformed fifteen-year-old females.[100] The sizes of the differences varied considerably. Nations also vary in the extent to which they differentiate between male and female social roles, including education. These differences are reflected in the World Economic Forum's Gender Gap Index (GGI), which reflects the relative economic and social opportunities offered to men compared to those offered to women. The GGI correlates negatively ($r = -.55$) with the difference between men and women's scores on the 2003 PISA tests of mathematical competencies in fifteen-year-olds. The closer the economic and social opportunities for men and women are to being equal, the smaller the male advantage in mathematics.[101]

The differential learning explanation for male-female discrepancies in visual-spatial reasoning and (perhaps as a derivative) in mathematics is a compelling one. However, it fails to explain a sometimes overlooked fact. Why is it that the discrepancy in mathematics appears on tests but not in class work?

Two explanations have been offered – one that blames the tests and the other that, in a sense, blames society.

The explanation that blames the test itself has two aspects. One is that the test questions tend to be interpreted in different ways by men and women, and that the difference in interpretation hurts women's scores. To take an extreme example, suppose that all the word problems on a mathematics test used sports examples. If women were less familiar with sports than men are, they would be at a disadvantage not because they had lower mathematical skills but because they had difficulty mapping from the verbal statement of the problem to the appropriate mathematical model.

This argument may have had some validity at one time, but is unlikely to be valid today. All the major tests currently in use are subjected to elaborate statistical analyses to ensure that the tests measure the same underlying latent trait, whatever it is, in both men and women. This sort of error is far more likely to occur in a locally generated class examination than it is in a national testing program.

The second reason the tests could be blamed is that they might fail to measure (or fail to adequately weight) some trait that is required for performance in classroom mathematics, and that is possessed to a greater extent by women than by men. We have already encountered this

99 See Hyde, 2007, for detailed references.

100 National Center for Educational Statistics, *Digest of Educational Statistics*, 2008, Table 389. The exception was Thailand.

101 Guiso et al., 2008. See supporting online material for details of the computation. Interestingly, there is no correlation between the GCI and the male:female variance ratios in different populations (Machin & Pekkarinen, 2008).

sort of objection, in discussing Lynn and Irwing's hypothesis that there is a difference between test performance and classroom performance because women are more motivated to do well in class (or study more intelligently!). This seems to be likely.

The explanation that blames society is that stereotype threat, as described in the introductory section of this chapter, may depress women's test scores. The argument is that women think they will do poorly, and therefore give up more rapidly when faced with difficult mathematical problems. There is an elegant demonstration that this can happen. It involved a study of Asian women college students in a North American university.[102] The women first answered questions designed to emphasize either their Asian identities or their identities as women. They then attempted to solve mathematics problems. The idea was to produce two contrasting stereotypes – the belief that Asians do well in mathematics and the belief that women do poorly. The study worked; students who were induced to think of themselves as Asians did better than students who were induced to think of themselves as women, even though the assignment to different groups had been random.

Experiments like this show that the stereotype threat effect exists. There are substantial questions about the size of the effect in situations in which the test has real consequences, such as a college entrance examination. In such situations examinees' motivation to do well might override any anxiety introduced by stereotype threat. The evidence is that it can, for reminding women of their gender has little effect on their performance on either high-level or low-level real examinations in advanced placement and community college classes.[103] If stereotype threat can be overridden by motivation in these situations, it seems logical that it would be overridden in even higher-stakes situations, such as college entrance examinations. Direct evidence

on this topic is extremely hard to obtain because it would not be ethical to set up a testing condition (the stereotype threat situation) that was intended to lower the performance of one group of people relative to another. Statistical methods for detecting stereotype threat in high-stakes examinations without doing this have been suggested, but to my knowledge they have not been applied.[104]

All in all, it seems to me that the chief social reason for discrepancies between men's and women's performance in mathematics, and the concomitant and perhaps related discrepancy in visual-spatial reasoning, is simply a difference in interests. This difference causes girls to take fewer mathematics courses than boys, on beyond the primary grades. Because we learn what we practice, adult women are less likely than men to have acquired high levels of mathematical skill. Due to differences in interest, women are less likely than men to pursue careers in the STEM fields, even when they have developed the necessary cognitive skills.

This conclusion leaves two questions open: why do women develop different interests than men, and are there biological reasons for the discrepancy?

BIOLOGICAL REASONS FOR MALE-FEMALE DIFFERENCES IN COGNITION

Evolutionary psychologists have offered a widely held distal biological explanation for differences in cognition between men and women – the "man the hunter, woman the gatherer" explanation. In every society there are sex role differences that go beyond the childbearing difference forced by biology. The evolutionary psychologists conclude that these differences can be traced to an evolutionary advantage held by groups that, in prehistoric times, assigned the hunting role to males and the gatherer–child care role to females.

The story is that men in prehistoric societies ranged widely as they hunted, and that those men who were better hunters had a

102 Shih, Pittinsky, & Ambady, 1999.
103 Strickler & Ward, 2004.

104 Wicherts, Dolan, & Hessen, 2005.

reproductive advantage, either because their success gave them more access to females, or because their offspring were more likely to survive to reproductive age because good hunters could feed their children more reliably. This explanation also assumes that skills related to the R dimension of the *g*-VPR model, like the ability to judge the velocity of moving objects or to maintain orientation in space, aided in hunting. On the other hand, women are supposed to have primarily been gatherers of edible plants and small animals near the camp. A woman would have a reproductive advantage if she were a good gatherer, and so better able to feed her children. The final step is to assume that the ability to notice fine details, like an edible lizard in a bush or an edible berry amid shrubbery, would make for a better gatherer. Women's superior verbal abilities are explained by the assumption that women, being more dependent on others for protection of themselves and their offspring, had to be superior in social interchanges.[105]

The story is plausible. Slight reproductive advantages associated with various skills, acting over thousands of generations, could produce a substantial sexual imbalance in skills. However, the story is a story, not a fact. There is no direct evidence for it, because we know little, and probably never will know very much, about the behavioral characteristics of prehistoric *Homo sapiens*, let alone other hominid predecessors of our species. What we do know is inferred from indirect evidence, such as inferences about the rate of maturation of extinct hominids based on skeletal data, which then are used to infer the years required for protection of children, and then extrapolated to discussions of male-female roles in maintenance of children, foraging, and group protection. Analogies to the behaviors of existing human hunter-gatherer societies are frequently used.

Evolution certainly happened, and it could have happened this way. But the evidence is certainly, and of necessity, indirect.

There is another evolutionary story, based on social rather than biological mechanisms. The human brain is designed for general learning, a trait that is very useful in a species that occupies multiple ecological niches. Certain behavioral practices that produce better social and economic organization can lead to a competitive advantage at the level of the group, rather than the individual. Groups that adopt such practices are more likely to survive.[106] These practices include differentiation of male and female roles. Since humans are learners, males and females will acquire different, role-appropriate cognitive skills. The tendency will be accentuated over time, but the accentuation will be due to social rather than biological evolution. The difference in cognitive skills that appears in late adolescence is due to different learning experiences that have evolved historically, not physiological differences in brain structure that have evolved genetically.

This hypothesis emphasizes social history. It can be given a biological twist. It may be that boys learn more spatial skills because they explore more, and girls learn better verbal skills because they socialize more. This could be due to genetic influences on the tendency to explore each environment. Thus sex differences in cognition (and other differences between people) could be due to differential learning experiences, but the differential learning experiences themselves could be under genetic influence.[107]

I see no way to differentiate among these hypotheses. In fact, they are not mutually exclusive; all of them could have some truth. It is tautologically true that all human variations in behavior will be within the range of variation permitted by the genome; the most dedicated geneticist does not deny that humans are superb learners. We have learned to live with this ambiguity with respect to physical behaviors. No one denies that males are genetically predisposed to be able to swing sticks more rapidly than females, and no one denies that today's

105 Geary, 2005, 2007a,b.

106 Campbell, 1975; Wilson & Wilson, 2007, 2008.
107 Bouchard, 1999.

training methods routinely produce women tennis players who hit the ball harder than the men's champions of yesteryear.

The strict version of the genetic hypothesis, that men and women have evolved to have different cognitive abilities due to different physiological structures, rather than to different learning experiences, implies that there may be some physical difference between modern men and women that can be related to cognitive differences. Has such a physical difference been found?

Richard Lynn has pointed to one candidate difference.[108] Men have bigger brains than women. After allowing for body size, men's brain volumes average about 100 cm³ larger than women's brain volumes.[109] Within the sexes, brain volumes are positively correlated with intelligence test scores ($r \approx .35$; see Chapter 7). Lynn argues that the difference in brain size accounts for the difference in general intelligence. He has amplified this argument by observing that girls mature faster than boys, so that the difference in brain size does not appear until after adolescence. This parallels the development of the claimed difference in general intelligence.

The explanation is appealingly simple and probably incorrect.

The evidence for any substantial difference between men and women in general intelligence is extremely weak. Therefore, Lynn's argument leads to a paradox that, although not completely damning to Lynn's line of reasoning, certainly makes it seem implausible. There are brain size differences of about 20 cm³ between African- and European-derived populations in the United States, with the Europeans having larger brains after correction for body size. This is much smaller than the difference in brain volume between men and women. However, the difference in test scores between African-derived and European-derived Americans, roughly 15 points on the IQ scale, is four to five times larger than any reported difference

in test scores between men and women. This poses a contradiction, for it is not clear how a small brain size difference could produce a large IQ difference between races, while a large brain size difference produced a small IQ difference between men and women.[110]

The fact that the male-female brain size discrepancy and the discrepancy in general intelligence (if it exists) develop in parallel is not a strong argument for causation. There are many changes in the difference between girls and boys from childhood to adolescence. These include both hormonal changes that alter brain action and changes in social roles and experiences. Picking out one of many bivariate correlations and offering it as *the* explanation for a phenomenon, without a serious consideration of alternative hypotheses, is not a compelling scientific argument.

MALE-FEMALE DIFFERENCES IN BRAIN ORGANIZATION

A fairly strong case can be made for the existence of male-female differences in brain organization that are related to differences in cognition.

Neural pathways can be divided into the myelinated white matter pathways and the unmyelinated gray matter pathways. The white matter pathways connect relatively distant centers of the brain, while the gray matter pathways deal with local connections. There is a loose analogy to the distinction between highways and city streets.

Men have a higher proportion of white matter to gray matter than women do. In addition, women have somewhat larger connections between the hemispheres. This suggests that the male brain relies more on specialized processing centers in one or the other hemisphere than does the female brain, while the female brain spreads processing out across several possibly less powerful centers that perform the same or related functions. This is consistent with the observation that women have better

108 Lynn, 1994, 1999; Colom & Lynn, 2004.
109 Ankney, 1992

110 Macintosh, 1998, p. 184.

prospects of recovering from localized brain damage than men.[111]

These ideas have been supported by imaging studies, which have shown that when men and women are faced with the same problems, such as solving progressive matrix items, they show somewhat different patterns of activation, and that performance correlates with anatomical measurements, such as white/gray matter ratios, in different places in the brain.[112]

The finding that men's brains and women's brains are, on the average, active in different places during problem solving excited a good deal of comment in the press, because the idea that "brain studies show that men and women think in different ways" understandably arouses a good deal of popular interest. The finding should not be overinterpreted. Brain activities during problem solving will depend upon the strategy that the problem solver takes. It has been shown experimentally, and is not logically too surprising, that an individual can alter his or her brain activity by altering his or her problem-solving strategy.[113] It does not follow that men and women must adopt different problem-solving strategies because their brains are different, although it may be the case that differences in their brains predispose men and women to adopt different strategies. This conclusion does not lead to sweeping generalities, but that is the way it is!

Spatial orientation and navigation deserve special attention. These aspects of thought, part of the R in the g-VPR model, produce some of the largest, most consistent male-female differences in behavior. They also produce an interesting qualitative distinction. Men are more likely to orient themselves in space using geometric cues about the overall environment, while women are more likely to use landmark and route information.[114] The same difference in behavior is found when comparing differences in the way in which male and female rats explore unfamiliar environments.[115] The rat behavior has been associated with neural activation in the hippocampus and related structures deep in the medial temporal region of the brain. There are suggestions of differences in hippocampal structures between men and women, but the data is not yet definitive. As in the case of problem solving, orientation and navigation can be achieved by different strategies, and the strategy used will determine the brain region involved.

To summarize, there are differences both in the structures of male and female brains and in the ways in which the brain is used in different aspects of problem solving. The differences seem to be especially large when the problem to be solved has a spatial-visual component. But what causes these structural differences and differences in activity in the first place? The answer to this turns out to be genetic potential (of course!) interacting with hormonal balance during key periods of brain development.

The evidence for this comes from two sources: studies on nonhuman animals and studies of abnormal human development.

Manipulation of adrenal levels prenatally and postnatally can influence the display of typical male or typical female behavior in rats, including the extent of engagement in rough-and-tumble play and the patterns of behavior in maze exploration. Obviously, conducting an analogous experimental study on humans would not be ethical. What we can do is to study certain medical conditions in which unusual hormonal concentrations occur.

Congenital adrenal hyperplasia (CAH) is a genetic condition in which the adrenal gland fails to generate a key enzyme, causing unusual sensitivity to male hormones. The condition can occur in both boys and girls. It is treated by restoring the normal hormone balance. Female CAH patients tend to have higher scores on spatial orientation tests than normal females. Males with CAH (a

111 See Gur & Gur, 2007, and Kimura, 1999, Chapters 10 and 11, for further references and discussion.
112 Haier, Jung, et al., 2004, 2005.
113 Reichle, Carpenter & Just, 2000.
114 Hunt, 2002, Chapter 6; Maguire, Burgess, & O'Keefe, 1999.

115 Ohnishi et al., 2006.

less-studied group) tend to have lower scores than normal males. There are indications that this result generalizes to other behavior patterns in women, for female CAH patients display more masculine behaviors and interests than do normal girls and women, including such things as preferences for "male-appropriate" or "female-appropriate" toys.[116]

These results refer to effects of hormones on the developing brain. There is also evidence that circulating hormonal levels in adults will influence human cognition. The results are somewhat inconsistent, as the studies are difficult to do and generally involve small numbers of participants, a condition that invites null findings. Nevertheless, certain results seem to be reasonably well established.

In women, high levels of circulating estrogens facilitate tasks involving verbal fluency and/or short-term memory. The evidence is mixed for performance on visual-spatial reasoning, except for a consistent reduction in performance on mental rotation tasks. This has been established by two sources of data: studies of women tested at various times during their menstrual cycle, and studies of post-menopausal women who either are or are not receiving estrogen replacement therapy.[117]

Complementary results have been found in studies of testosterone. Testosterone appears to have a non-monotonic effect on spatial reasoning, enhancing spatial reasoning in women and men with low testosterone (a common condition in the elderly), but decreasing spatial reasoning abilities in men with normal or high testosterone levels. The cognitive effects are complicated by the fact that circulating testosterone levels are associated with a myriad of other effects, including increases in impulsivity and aggressive behavior. To get some idea of the complexity of the effect, contrasting effects of testosterone on spatial rotation have been reported in England, the United States,

and China.[118] The authors speculate that this is because of different emphases on speed versus accuracy of response in different cultures. The more general point is that in spatial-visual problem solving (which can be quite difficult) a hormonal effect could be on either the brain mechanisms required for the task itself or the brain mechanisms involved in selecting a problem-solving strategy.[119]

11.3.7. *A Summary but No Answers*

There is no simple answer to the question "What causes male-female differences in cognition?" There are biological differences between men's and women's brains, and these differences influence both verbal fluency and, to a somewhat greater degree, spatial orientation, way finding, and the manipulation of visual images – the V and R dimensions of the *g*-VPR model. However, biology is not destiny. Just as there is no doubt that there are biological predispositions that operate to produce a feminine or masculine trend in thought, there are social influences that can either accentuate or override these trends. Given motivation, humans are powerful learners, and learning itself influences brain organization.

Confused? You should be. Just as Diane Halpern said, the more you learn about sex differences in cognition, the less certain you are that you know the answers. Within very broad limits, biological and social influences produce tendencies toward certain cognitive and social behaviors. Once this is done, the behaviors themselves alter biological makeup and social status. Women, *on the average*, are somewhat more verbal and somewhat less spatially oriented than men, but there are male chatterboxes and female helicopter pilots.

There is one question that we can deal with. Are men more intelligent than women? The answer is clear.

It is the wrong question. Men and women have somewhat different brains. This leads

---

116 Berenbaum & Resnick, 2007; Kimura, 1999, Chapter 9; Puts et al., 2008.

117 Haussmann et al., 2000, and references therein; Halpern & Tan, 2001.

118 Yang et al., 2007.

119 Kimura, 1999, Chapter 9.

to somewhat different strengths and weaknesses in cognition. Any battery-type intelligence test will, by definition, consist of a mix of tasks, some that favor the feminine style of thinking and some that favor the masculine style. The particular mixtures found in battery-type tests, such as the WAIS, have been determined more by history than by any analysis of why one mix is better than another. There have also been powerful commercial forces that work against trying out any test battery that is too different from its predecessors. We should not disregard present batteries, and any male-female differences built into them, but we should not regard them as set in stone.

One could construct test batteries that favor males, favor women, or are neutral. There would be no way to say which of these mixes was best without specifying the purpose of the test. A test battery for the selection of pilots will not and should not look like a test battery for the selection of law school students.

Any individual test, including the much-used matrix tests, will evaluate *g* and test-specific features, a point that Spearman made a century ago. You can find a measure of general intelligence that is *g* and verbally loaded, and produce an advantage for females, or produce a measure of general intelligence that is *g* and loaded on spatial-visual reasoning, and find an advantage for males. Depending on the purpose for which the test is to be used, one or the other solution could be the correct one.

It is sensible to try to understand male-female differences in cognition. It is not sensible to ask whether men are smarter than women.

11.4. Race and Ethnicity

This section will deal with racial and ethnic differences in intelligence. The topic is probably the most controversial one in psychology. Jerry Carlson and I identified the following positions that have been taken:[120]

120 Hunt & Carlson, 2007a.

1. There are no differences in intelligence between racial and ethnic groups.
2. There are large differences in intelligence between racial and ethnic groups.
3. Differences in intelligence between groups exist and are social in origin.
4. Differences in intelligence between groups are genetic in origin.
5. There is no such thing as race.

The facts concerning racial and ethnic differences in IQ and similar test scores are clear. The causes and implications of these facts are not at all clear. Therefore, the scientific discussion can easily slip over into a heated dispute. The discussion and the dispute cannot be kept entirely apart. However, I believe (hope) the discussion here will shed more light than heat. To this end I will first spend some time setting up the problem and identifying the key variables, prior to presenting a picture of what I think is known. Being hyper-careful about the definition and scope of a subject may be somewhat boring, but in this case precision of thought is essential.

In previous discussions of the conceptual nature of intelligence, beyond the operational definition of a test score, the following points were made:

1. Although the requirements for intelligence vary somewhat across societies, there is a common core – for example, the ability to comprehend verbal arguments or to maintain orientation in space.
2. Intelligence tests and their analogs, such as personnel classification tests, are assessments of the cognitive skills required for success in industrial and post-industrial society. The test scores, although not perfect indicators of intelligence, are relevant in that society. They will be relevant to success in other societies to the extent that the tests tap the cognitive skills relevant for success in the target society. The extent of relevance has to be determined on a case-by-case basis.

3. Evaluating the sorts of skills required by the post-industrial societies is important, in itself. These societies dominate the globe now and will do so for the foreseeable future. Learning about intelligence as it is expressed in London, Madrid, or New York will have more impact on the human condition than learning about the expression of intelligence in small groups in the forests of South America. This is not to say that anthropological studies are uninteresting; they can be very informative. The point is just that even if it were shown that intelligence, as tested, is wholly confined to the post-industrial societies, the topic would still be important.

4. All cognitive skills are ultimately determined by biology. However, it is important to distinguish between genetic contributions, which establish potentials, and life experiences, which determine the extent to which a potential is realized. This can be very difficult to do. Measuring the size of the genetic contribution to variance in a particular society or subsociety is not the same as understanding it.

Do races and ethnic groups exist? It has been claimed that these are solely social distinctions. Because the definition of a group varies from time to time and place to place, it is argued, they cannot be biological natural kinds. Therefore, racial differences are not amenable to scientific study because the basic concept of race is ill-defined.[121] This argument has been buttressed by the fact that genetic diversity within groups is larger than genetic diversity between groups.[122]

The counterargument is that in fact, people identify and are identified with racial and ethnic groups. These distinctions are highly correlated with a clustering of social and biological variables. Socially, for instance, 68% of the residents of the United States who identify themselves as Hispanic are Catholics. Only 20% of the non-Hispanic residents are Catholic.[123] Therefore, Catholicism is statistically associated with ethnic identity, even though there are Hispanics who are not Catholic and Catholics who are not Hispanic. The same reasoning applies to genetic variation. While it is true that within-group genetic variation is greater than between-group variation, the amount of genetic variation between groups is quite sufficient, statistically, to make accurate assignments associating an individual with one of the three largest groups of origin in the United States – African, European, and East Asian.[124] There is also a high level of agreement between self-identification as White, Black, East Asian, or Latino and assignment of a person to clusters based upon similarities of their genomes.[125] While there is no one defining characteristic, other than self-identification, that assigns someone to a particular racial/ethnic group, identification of a person as a member of a racial/ethnic group will *probabilistically* tell us something about that person's standing on a variety of social and biological variables.

The key word is "probabilistic." Artificial Intelligence researchers have developed the idea of a "fuzzy" concept, a class in which membership is determined to varying degrees rather than being a binary property. The political concept *conservative* is a good example. An individual may espouse conservative beliefs with an intensity that varies with the topic. Race and ethnic membership are fuzzy concepts. There are no defining characteristics of a racial or ethnic group, but there are statistical tendencies.

The de facto definition of races and ethnic groups – that is, the extent to which a person has to possess the (fuzzy) properties in order to be designated a group member – varies over time and place. In modern American categorization the term "Asian-American" includes genetic Japanese who are fourth-generation Americans, who do not speak Japanese and have never been to Japan, along with green card holders

---

121 Fish, 2002; Smedley & Smedley, 2005.
122 Lewontin, 1974.
123 *New York Times*, 26 April 2007.
124 Bamshad et al, 2004.
125 Tang et al., 2005.

who just landed from Cambodia and speak marginal English. Similar examples could be offered for every other large racial and ethnic group in North America and Europe. Such variety means that for some purposes the classification of individuals into broad racial/ethnic groups is nearly useless. For other purposes it makes sense.

Knowledge about covariation between racial/ethnic identification and important social outcomes, such as health status, can serve as clues to tell us what variables to look at as we attempt to understand causal relationships. For instance, it is empirically the case that high blood pressure is more common in the African American than in the White community.[126] What is it in the African American genetic constitution or social practice that leads to high blood pressure? Questions like this ought to be investigated by the biomedical sciences.[127] Similarly, if there is a discrepancy in intelligence test scores between the African American and other American communities (and there is), seeking to understand the reasons for and implications of the discrepancy are legitimate issues for the psychological sciences.

Research on racial/ethnic distinctions can inform policy making. Most of the developed societies do make policy decisions about racial/ethnic groups. The United States, for instance, has developed an elaborate legal doctrine aimed at the prohibition of discrimination. Two American psychologists, A. & B. D. Smedley, writing in the *American Psychologist*, a high-impact journal, vehemently rejected the idea of race as a biological concept, and at the same time urged the government to continue to compile statistics on social inequality between races (and, by extension, ethnic groups) for the purpose of eliminating such inequalities.[128]

Such a position contains a contradiction. Policy makers should be informed of relevant scientific information, which should be considered along with other things when policy decisions are made. In the case of racial/ethnic differences, the scientific information needed can be obtained only by documenting the existence of ethnic differences in intelligence, understanding the implications of these differences, and inquiring into all possible causes, both social and biological. The Smedleys worried, with some reason, that such information could be used to justify discriminatory practices. This could happen; but if it does, it will be the result of political decisions combined with scientific findings, not the scientific findings themselves. I strongly believe that it is better to proceed with information rather than to proceed in ignorance.

In practice, investigators who study racial and ethnic differences face major obstacles. These obstacles have had an impact on the quality of research in the field. Let us see why.

11.4.1. *Issues of Quality in Research on Race and Ethnicity*

Racial and ethnic distinctions are both fuzzy, in the sense just defined, and inconsistent over time and place. Brazilians introduce distinctions that Americans do not, referring to people as white and black, but also as *Moreno*, *mestizo*, and *pardo*. The terms *Indian* and *Native American* are used today much more broadly than they were in the past. Given that the answer to the question "who is what?" changes over place and time, it is no wonder that it is hard to find how a behavioral capacity, such as intelligence, correlates with race and ethnicity.

Race and ethnicity are seldom causal variables in themselves. The only exceptions are in studies of the reactions of others to a person of a given race, and studies of the effects of self-identity on people's conceptions of themselves. In these situations the application of a label may itself be a stimulus that leads to action. Outside of such situations, a researcher who studies a correlation between racial/ethnic status and a test score is studying the correlation between the score and the many possibly causal variables

126 Information downloaded from www.americanheart
 .org/presenter.jhtml?identifier=4621, January 2009.
127 See Bamshad et al., 2004, for further examples.
128 Smedley & Smedley, 2005.

correlated with race and ethnicity. These include educational status, biological distinctions, health and wealth, and a variety of beliefs and behavioral practices. This complicates the assignment of causes for individual differences. The bivariate argument that "because racial/ethnic groups differ on possible cause X and outcome Y, cause X must produce group differences on Y" is an example of seizing on a bivariate correlation in the presence of collinearity. Such arguments should be regarded with great suspicion.

Differential recruitment is also a problem. In particular, college students, the default sample of convenience, are easy to study. However, college students are not a random sample of any racial or ethnic group, which makes generalizations tricky.

Finally, there are social (and sometimes legal) pressures restricting research on racial and ethnic groups. While *I* may think that the need to overcome ignorance overrides the possibility that a finding on race or ethnicity may be used to justify discrimination, there are other opinions. There are audiences who believe that anyone who reports racial/ethnic differences must be a racist, and concomitantly that anyone who reports a finding questioning the existence of racial and ethnic differences in intelligence must be on the side of the angels. There are also audiences who are longing to hear about racial differences in intelligence, because they want to use such findings to justify discriminating against, or not providing affirmative action for, an ethnic group. This has led both to a difficulty in getting funds to do good research in the field and to a temptation to oversimplify a finding, in order to tell different audiences what they want to hear.

I am not alone in my concerns. In the 1970s Lindzey, Loehlin, and Spuhler closed a widely respected review of racial difference in intelligence by saying

The design, execution, and reporting of studies of racial-ethnic differences in intelligence often leave much to be desired. The conclusions that we have attempted to draw from these data are often limited by this fact. We have been concerned privately by the number of instances in which the political and social preferences of the investigators apparently have grossly biased their interpretations of the data. Such distortions appear to be at least as prevalent at environmentalist as at hereditarian extremes.

Lindzey, Loehlin, & Spuhler, 1975, pp. 232–233

Writing over thirty years later, I am sorry that I have to say that Loehlin, Lindzey, and Spuhler are still correct. Bad research is itself a fuzzy concept. Very few studies are uniformly good or bad. In this field, more than in others, it is important to consider the strengths and weaknesses of a study before generalizing its findings. Panel 11.1 presented some cautions about research on group differences. I urge readers to consider their impact when evaluating a study on racial and ethnic groups, reported here or anywhere else.

11.4.2. *Coverage and Terminology*

For the most part, I will be concerned with the four major racial/ethnic groups in the United States, African Americans, Asian-Americans, Hispanics, and Whites. On occasion studies from other countries will be considered. These are the groups for which the most data has been gathered. In addition, these groups live in a large, post-industrial society; the vast majority of their members speak a common language, English, either as a first language or a strongly held second language; and they have generally comparable, although certainly not identical, living standards, compared to the contrast between, say, Whites in the United Kingdom and Africans in Somalia.

The four American groups have all the characteristics of a fuzzy class, defined on either social or biological variables. There is no one variable, or even one group of variables, that defines group membership. However, statistical clusterings based on either social or genetic variables do correspond closely to self-identification with a group.

In addition, these groups have a political identity. Laws, regulations, and government programs exist that distinguish among them in a variety of ways. As a consequence, the government keeps extensive statistics on characteristics of their health, education, and economic status. It is often important to consult these statistics in order to untangle issues due to collinearity.

Finally, a word about terminology.

Anyone who attempts to name racial/ethnic groups in the United States is shooting at a moving target. W. E. B. Du Bois (1868–1963), a leading social activist of the 1900–50 period and one of the founders of the National Association for the Advancement of Colored People (NAACP), referred to himself as a Negro. The term is proscribed today. The term "colored people" is part of the NAACP's name, but is now also proscribed. However, the term "people of color" is appropriate, at least as of 2010.

I will use the terms *African American* and *Black* interchangeably unless, of course, I am referring to a group outside the United States. In present US government documents *Hispanic* or *Latino* is used to refer to US residents who are immigrants from, or descendants of immigrants from, a Spanish- or Portuguese-speaking country in the Western Hemisphere. The term is also used for descendants of the Spanish/Mexican people who settled in California and the Southwest prior to the 1840s. Surprisingly, the government does not include in this term people whose family origin was Spain or Portugal, although this policy seems to be applied inconsistently. I will follow government usage, as it exists in 2010.

While I shall have to use the term *Asian-American* at times, especially when referring to government records, I will attempt to refer to more specific groups, such as the *Japanese*, as I believe that the current official designation *Asian-American* is far too broad.

White will be my catch-all term for all other groups. These are primarily American residents of European descent. There are substantial communities who have cultural and genetic ties to Armenia, Georgia, Iran, Israel, and other Middle Eastern nations, but they are all European-Americans to the US census! When appropriate I will refer to specific communities within the broad Asian and White designations.

11.4.3. *Test Score Gaps between Whites, African Americans, and Hispanics*

There is a long history of studies of racial/ethnic differences in test scores. In their 1975 review Lindzey, Loehlin, and Spuhler, citing earlier data by Yerkes, reported that in 1917–18, during World War I, the mean score on the Army tests for White recruits was 1.16 standard deviation units above the mean for African American recruits. Studies of enlistees in World War II and the Vietnam War[129] showed a 1.52 mean difference in favor of Whites. Lindzey and colleagues were careful to point out that this is not evidence that the Black-White differences in intelligence had increased from 1918 to the 1960s, because military enlistees are not a representative sample of the country, and because different recruitment/conscription standards were in effect in the two wars. However this is certainly not evidence for a presumed reduction in the difference!

In order to make a comparison between the scores of different groups we need to have data from a representative sample of the national population. Table 11.4 presents the results from several such surveys involving battery-type tests. There is some variety in the results, but not a great deal. The African American means are about 1 standard deviation unit (15 points on the IQ scale) below the White means, and the Hispanic means fall in between.

A similar picture is obtained from comparisons involving the Raven Progressive Matrices (RPM) tests. Figure 11.21 shows the median RPM test score obtained in a school district in the western United States, as a function of age and racial/ethnic group.[130] We see the same picture reflected in the scores on battery-type tests. Whites outscore African

129 Lindzey, Loehlin, & Spuhler, 1975, p. 143.
130 Raven, 2008a. J. Raven has recommended reporting RPM scores as percentiles, rather than in terms of summary statistics, such as means and variances. See Raven, 2008b, p. 60 (note 1.55), for a justification.

Table 11.4. *Values of (White mean – African American mean) and (White mean – Latino mean) in standard deviation units for a variety of cognitive tests, using cases where a reasonably large standardization sample has been obtained*

Population	Test Used	African American	Latino	Reference
WAIS III adult standardization	WAIS General Ability Index	.95	.65	Lange et al., 2006
NLSY79, men	AFQT	1.07		Scullin et al., 2000
NLSY79, women	AFQT	1.00		Scullin et al., 2000
NLSY79, all groups	AFQT	1.2	.93	Herrnstein & Murray, 1994, pp. 275, 278
Standardization sample	Wide Range Intelligence Test	.85	.51	Shields, Konold, & Glutting, 2004
Standardization sample	Woodcock-Johnson 3: General Intellectual Ability	1.05		Murray, 2007

Americans, and Hispanic scores fall somewhere in between.

In order to avoid recruitment effects, Table 11.4 cites studies using relatively large samples, where an attempt was made to obtain a sample representative of a defined population. The samples involved cover a wide range of people, from the five to sixty-five years age range in the Woodcock-Johnson standardization sample to the schoolchildren studied in the RPM standardization. Similar results can be found by averaging over the more than 150 studies that have used convenience samples.[131]

Similar differences are found internationally. Historically there have been a number of studies comparing Whites to other racial/ethnic groups in a variety of countries. Because there have been major changes in the economic and health status of many developing countries, the best course is probably to look at the recent literature rather than at that of over thirty years ago.

J. P. Rushton, Lynn, and a number of their colleagues have conducted a wide-ranging series of studies in which they use the Raven Progressive Matrices tests to evaluate group differences within various countries. All obtain the general results observed on the Raven standardization. Whites do better than Blacks, with other ethnic groups somewhere in between. The studies involved include a Roma–Serbian contrast in the Balkans,[132] White–Indian–mixed race–Black contrasts in South Africa,[133] and a contrast between Whites, Mestizos (mixed White–Native American), and Native Americans in Mexico.[134] In all these studies Whites and Asians obtain the highest scores, and Blacks the lowest, with other racial/ethnic groups falling in between.

The Mexican study provides a good example of this work, because it is somewhat more extensive than several of the other studies. Lynn and colleagues tested elementary school children, aged seven to ten, near Ensenada, in the state of Baja California. The ordering of means was what the experimenters had anticipated: Whites (IQ equivalent ~ 100), Mestizos (mixed Native

131 Herrnstein & Murray, 1994, p. 277; Jensen, 1998, p. 354. The Herrnstein and Murray citation gives references to specific studies. Jensen's citation does not, but it apparently refers to an analysis that he conducted.

132 Rushton, Cvorovic, & Bons, 2007.
133 Rushton & Skuy, 2000; Rushton, Skuy, & Fridjohn, 2003.
134 Lynn, Backhoff, & Contreras, 2005.

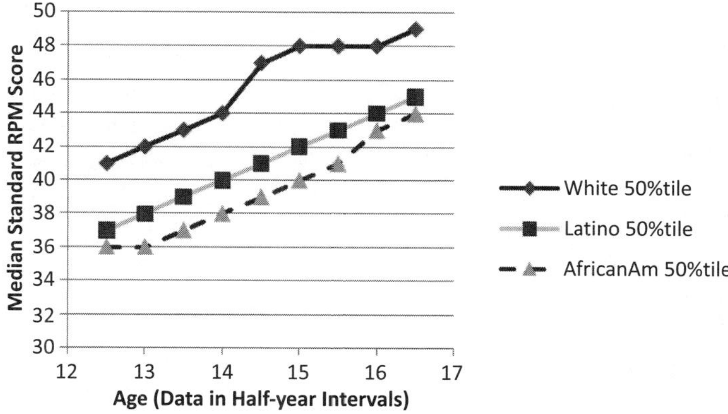

Figure 11.21. Raven Progressive Matrices scores in a school district in the western United States, as a function of age and racial/ethnic group. Data taken in the 1980s. *Source:* J. Raven, 2008b, Table 8.3.

American–White groups) (IQ equivalent $\sim$ 95), and Native Americans (IQ equivalent $\sim$ 83). (See Figure 11.22.) The authors point out that these results resemble those obtained in the United States, where Mexican immigrants have scores below Whites, and Native Americans tend to have still lower scores. The differences were substantial. Seven-year-old White and Mestizo children solved progressive matrix problems at a level not obtained by Native American children until they are nine or ten.

Lynn and colleagues' results for Mexicans in Mexico can be compared to Raven's results for Latinos in the southwestern United States. This is done in Figure 11.23, which shows a striking continuity in changes of test scores across ages, within each ethnic group.

Because the Raven tests are often referred to as measures of *g*, there is a temptation to interpret these results as showing that White populations possess general intelligence to a greater degree than nonwhite populations living in close proximity to the White groups. As Lynn himself has indicated, it is not appropriate to draw such a conclusion based on results from a single test. However, similar results implicating differences in *g* have also been found in European studies that used batteries of subtests designed to evaluate narrow cognitive functions. The populations compared included children from different immigrant

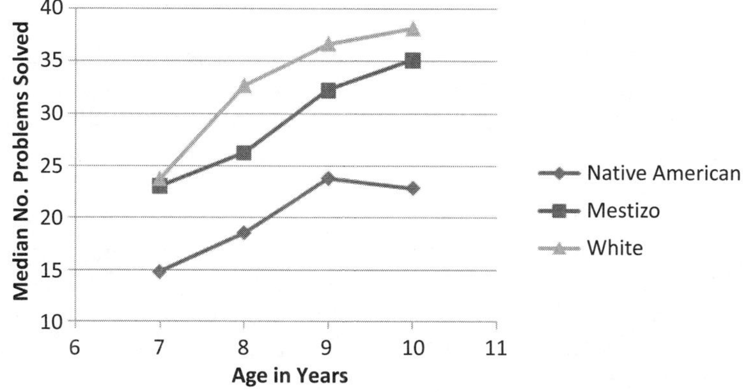

Figure 11.22. The median number of Raven's Standard Progressive Matrices problems solved by Native American, Mestizo, and White children in Mexico. Data from Lynn, Backhoff, & Contreras, 2005, Table 2.

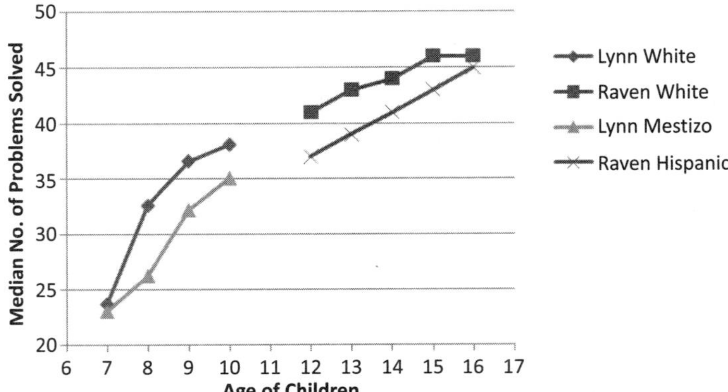

Figure 11.23. Median number of problems solved as a function of age and ethnicity. Data from Raven, 2008a, Table 8.2 (half-year intervals) and from Lynn, Backhoff, & Contreras, 2005, Table 2.

groups in Europe and adult immigrants from the Netherlands Antilles compared to native Dutch employees in the railway system in the Netherlands.[135]

11.4.4. *A Closer Look at the Nature of Racial/Ethnic Differences*

In the middle of the twentieth century a study was done on variations in first-grade children's intelligence that were associated with ethnic status and social class (SES).[136] The authors concluded that the level of intelligence was associated with SES, and that there were patterns of differential ability associated with ethnic groups. Asians were said to have high spatial ability, and Jewish children to have high verbal abilities. Since that time there have been several efforts to determine the nature of the differences in the intelligence of various racial/ethnic groups, beyond the omnibus statement that test scores vary from group to group.

Most of these studies have been presented as investigations of "Spearman's hypothesis." The strong version of this hypothesis is that all intergroup differences in intelligence are due to differences in general intelligence. The weak form is that the majority of these differences are due to general intelligence,

but that differences in lower-order factors (e.g., verbal and spatial-visual reasoning) may also contribute to group differences.[137]

Jensen summarized a number of studies testing Spearman's hypothesis that had been carried out through about 1995 using the method of correlated vectors. He concluded that the correlation between test loadings on a *g* factor and the Black-White differences in test scores is about .60, and considerably higher in some tests.[138] Jensen interpreted this as substantial support for the weak form of Spearman's hypothesis. He further concluded that spatial-visual reasoning, which tends to show fairly large Black-White differences, was responsible for the remaining differences.

Subsequently the Danish psychologist Helmut Nyborg collaborated with Jensen on a large study of African American–White differences among Vietnam veterans.[139] Because conscription was used during the Vietnam War the study participants were somewhat representative of men from the cohorts born in the United States during the 1940s and early 1950s. Nyborg and his colleagues updated Jensen's review and published further data testing a White-Hispanic contrast in the Vietnam veteran population.[140] These studies also reported

135 Helms-Lorenz, van de Vijver, & Poortinga, 2003; te Nijenhuis et al., 2004.
136 Lesser, Fifer, and Clark, 1965.

137 Jensen, 1998, p. 372.
138 Ibid., pp. 376 ff.
139 Nyborg & Jensen, 2001.
140 Hartmann, Kruuse, & Nyborg, 2007.

support for the weak form of the hypothesis, that racial/ethnic differences in cognitive skills are generally due to differences in g, but that other traits may be involved.

Nyborg and Jensen's conclusions, and many similar conclusions about differences between racial/ethnic groups, rest on the validity of the method of correlated vectors. Several questions have been raised about the technique. These are described in Panel 11.6. One of the most serious criticisms is that the method of correlated vectors tests a single hypothesis against "chance," the possibility that the correlation between g loadings and group differences would be produced by random assignment of numbers. A better question is whether Spearman's hypothesis fares well against competing hypotheses. Where a comparison has been made, the results have been equivocal. In the study of immigrant children cited earlier, the investigators also applied the method of correlated vectors, but instead of using g loadings they used "cultural loadings" assigned by having a panel of graduate students rate whether or not particular subtests were culturally loaded. Aggregated cultural ratings had a markedly higher correlation with group differences than the g loadings did.[141]

The conclusion that racial/ethnic group differences are primarily due to differences in g has been repeated several times in the secondary literature, in spite of the questions raised by Dolan's analyses. The Danish investigators who summarized the evidence after Jensen's 1998 summary did not even mention Dolan's work. Sometimes the summarizers have actually misstated Dolan's conclusions! When Rushton and Jensen published what they regarded as a summary of fifty years of studies of White-Black differences, they had this to say about Dolan's work:

The results statistically confirmed the conclusion derived from the method of correlated vectors regarding a "weak form"

[141] Helms-Lorenz, Van de Vijver, & Poortinga, 2003, Table 7. See particularly the lower right-hand entries, which summarize the complicated analyses.

of Spearman's hypothesis: Black–White group differences were predominantly on the g factor, although the groups also showed differences on some lower order factors (e.g., short-term memory and spatial ability) independent of g.
Rushton & Jensen, 2005, p. 248

Here is what the original authors said to summarize their work:

It is concluded that the Spearman correlation, as a test of the importance of g in B-W differences, lacks specificity. The results of the MGCFAs suggest that it is very difficult to distinguish between competing hypotheses concerning the latent sources of B-W differences.
Dolan & Hamaker, 2001, abstract

Where does this somewhat technical argument leave the substantive conclusion? Rushton and Jensen say that Spearman's hypothesis should be regarded as an empirical fact. The technical arguments and the various demonstrations by Dolan and his colleagues show that this is not the case. However, a demonstration of the weakness of the method should not be used to take another (indefensible) position – that group differences are independent of g. The results of the Dutch study that contrasted cultural and g differences as explanations for differences in test scores, although interesting, are in disagreement with several smaller studies from the United States. However, it is difficult to compare the degree of cultural difference between Native Dutch and immigrants, on the one hand, and between Whites and Blacks in the United States on the other.

It is probably the case that most group differences in cognitive skills are due in part to differences in general reasoning, but the extent is not clear. It would be nice to have a reanalysis of some of the key studies using appropriate statistical methods.

11.4.5. Group Differences on Educational Assessments

In the United States African American students have markedly lower educational achievement than Whites; Asian-Americans

Panel 11.6. The James Watson Affair

James Watson (1928–) is arguably America's most famous living scientist. In 1962 he, along with his colleague Francis Crick, received the Nobel Prize for their discovery of the structure of the DNA molecule. Their work sparked the explosion of discoveries in molecular biology that have continued to this day. Subsequently Watson left his appointment at Harvard to head the Cold Spring Harbor (New York) Laboratory, which he built into a major scientific institution. Late in his career Watson was a leading figure in the successful effort to catalog the human genome.

In 2007 Watson, who has always been an outspoken person, wrote an autobiography, *Avoid Boring People*. He was scheduled to give several public talks in England. Just prior to the talks he gave an interview to the (London) *Sunday Times*.* The following quotes are taken verbatim from the article:

1. *He is inherently gloomy about the prospect of Africa.*
2. *All our social policies are based on the fact that their intelligence is the same as ours, whereas all the testing says not really.*
3. *His hope is that everyone is equal, but "people who have had to deal with black employees find that this is not true."*
4. *There is no firm reason to anticipate that the intellectual capacities of peoples geographically separated in their evolution should prove to have evolved identically.*
5. *Our wanting to reserve equal powers of reason as some universal heritage of humanity will not be enough to make it so.*

A huge public furor ensued. The *New York Times* published a lengthy discussion of subsequent debates between Watson's supporters and critics. For some reason this appeared on the Arts page![†] Many of Watson's speaking engagements were cancelled abruptly. He was almost immediately removed as director of the Cold Spring Harbor Laboratory.

Let us look more closely at what Watson said. Statement (1) is a personal opinion that is shared by many, many knowledgeable observers. Statement (2) is probably a statement of fact. I know of no announced policy for various "Aid to Africa" programs that assumes that the intelligence of Africans is inherently and permanently limited. At the same time, many aid organizations have a realistic view of the state of the resources and teacher training in African schools. Intelligence test scores are generally lower in Africa, as is documented in the text of this chapter. Statement (3) is also a statement of fact. As references in this chapter have shown, in the United States the work performance evaluations of African Americans are, on the average, lower than the evaluations received by white workers. This is true for both objective and subjective evaluations. The difference is much less than the difference in test score averages. However, Watson's statement was certainly worded in a provocative manner. Statement (4) follows from well-established models of evolution and genetics. Populations separated in space, for many generations, and subject to somewhat different selection pressures will develop genetic distinctions, within the limits of genetic variability that permit viable phenotypes. This is as true for intelligence as for any other genetically influenced trait. Statement (5) is also a fact. Several Walt Disney movies notwithstanding, wishing for something does not make it so.

In 2008 I was privileged to attend a three-day seminar on "improving the brain" that had been arranged by the Cold

Spring Harbor Laboratory in honor of Watson's retirement. Watson discussed the incidents recounted here, with obvious bitterness. He felt that his remarks had been taken out of context.

The incident illustrates the extreme sensitivity of any discussion of racial, ethnic, or national differences in intelligence, especially if it is linked to a discussion of genetics. Watson's remarks, as printed (and the *London Times* has stood strongly behind their accuracy), seem to have been rather like the famous Rorsach ink blot test in clinical psychology. The people who dropped him from their speaking engagements read a racist interpretation into the remarks. I would want to have heard the entire interview before I made such an interpretation.

Given such strong sentiments, it is hardly surprising that policy makers, including many funders of scientific research, have backed away from inquiring about racial/ethnic differences in intelligence. This has inhibited inquiry and rational discussion, especially by those who hold an intermediate position on heredity – environment issues.

*   October 14, 2007.
†   *New York Times*, December 1, 2007, p. A17 and following.

have equivalent or slightly higher achievement; and, depending somewhat on the particular Hispanic group involved, Hispanic students' achievement falls between those of Whites and African Americans. The best data relevant to this question comes from the NAEP testing program, for an attempt is made to make the NAEP samples representative of the population of the US K-12 system, excluding those students who have significant mental or physical problems, and those students who are not proficient in English.[142] The effect is often referred to as the "gap" in white-minority educational achievement. Figure 11.24 shows the size of the gap for seventeen-year-olds during the 1990–2010 period, and, for comparison, the gap in the 1970s. The gap has been constant since roughly the 1990s, but is substantially smaller than it was in the 1970s. The narrowing of the gap is due to an increase in the performance of African American and Hispanic students. This probably reflects the benefits of the considerable national effort that has been invested in improving minority education since the 1960s.

The drop in the educational gap over time has been mirrored by a similar drop in the gap between African Americans and Whites on cognitive tests less tied to the educational curriculum. Charles Murray analyzed scores from the various standardizations of the Woodcock-Johnson (W-J) test battery that took place in 1976–77, 1986–88, and 1996–1999. Recall, from Chapter 2, that this test is designed to provide separate estimates of Gc and Gf. Unlike the educational data, the standardization sample for the W-J tests included people over a wide range of ages, and therefore birth cohorts. Murray concluded that the gap in W-J scores dropped substantially in the cohorts born from 1960 to 1970, and then stabilized at about .85 deviation units in subsequent years. This trend mirrors the change in educational achievement scores, for the cohorts born from the late 1950s through the early 1970s would be the seventeen-year-olds tested during the period that the NAEP gap was being reduced, and the cohorts born from 1970 onward reached the age of seventeen during the period that the NAEP gap was stable.

The gap in educational achievement has considerable social importance, because of

142 Grissmer, Flanagan, & Williamson, 1998. The exclusion is appropriate because the purpose of the NAEP is to track educational progress in typical American schools. NAEP results will understate the gap in the US population to the extent that African American and Hispanic students are overrepresented in the excluded groups.

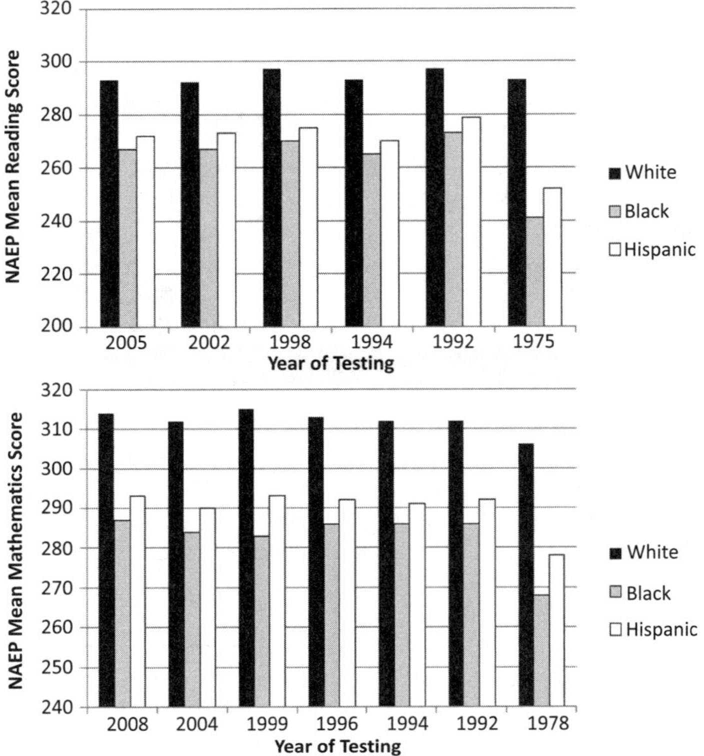

Figure 11.24. Mean NAEP scale scores for White, African American and Hispanic seventeen-year-olds. Material downloaded from nces.ed.gov/nationsreportcard/lttdata, October 2009.

the emphasis on education in the post-industrial workplace. Therefore, it is worth examining the gap itself and its changes in some detail.

After conducting extensive analyses of a variety of national educational assessments, Hedges and Nowell concluded that the reduction in the gap was largely due to a reduction in the proportion of African American students in the lowest ranks of the test scores. They did not find an increase in the proportion of African Americans in the highest ranks.[143] Consistent with this position, the achievement gap in the NAEP is mirrored by a similar gap in SAT scores, which indicates group differences in cognitive skill in the self-selected, but socially important, subset of students who intend to obtain education beyond high school (Figure 11.25). This is worrisome for those concerned

about group equality of rewards, for social and economic rewards are associated with higher levels of cognitive skills (see Chapter 10).

Although the White-Black test score gap is present in test scores of very young children, it widens markedly over the school years. This can be used to argue that either (a) African American children are not well prepared for school or (b) the schools are selectively failing to educate African American children. A good deal of light was shed on this issue in a tightly argued paper by Meredith Phillips, of the University of Chicago, and two of his colleagues, James Crouch and John Ralph.[144]

On the average, Black students enter elementary school with fewer of the skills required to benefit from formal instruction than do White students. Phillips and colleagues pointed out that it is important to

143 Hedges & Nowell, 1998, pp. 159–161, and their Tables 5–3 and 5B-2.

144 Phillips, Crouse, & Ralph, 1998.

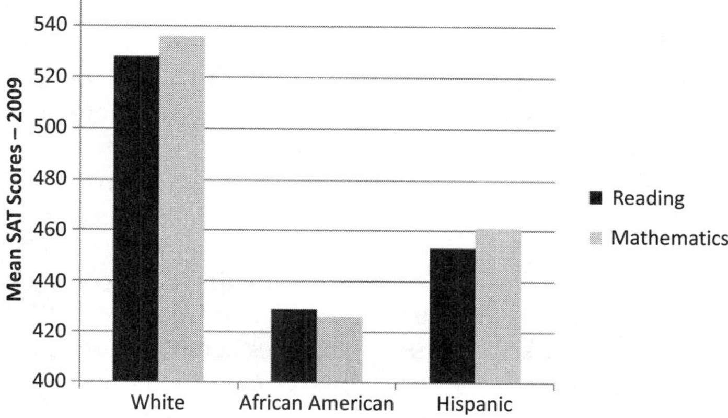

Figure 11.25. White, African American, and Hispanic mean scores on the SAT. The within-group standard deviation for this test is slightly over 100, making the White–African American gap approximately one *d* unit.

distinguish between the possibility that Black students fall further and further behind as they progress through the schools from the possibility that all students, of whatever race or ethnicity, who are initially poorly prepared fall further and further behind.

Figure 11.26 presents the results of some of Phillps and colleagues' analyses of the difference between Black and White achievement in reading and mathematics. The figure shows the size of the gap as computed directly from test scores at the beginning of second grade and at the end of high school, either with or without corrections for prior measures of achievement; on entering school (second graders, corrected for first grade scores); and measures taken in the ninth grade and earlier (twelfth graders, corrected for scores through the ninth grade). The size of the achievement gap was substantially reduced, although not quite eliminated, by considering the effects of the prior scores. Evidently differential reactions to schooling associated with race per se are only a small part of the causal factors that lead to a Black-White gap in student achievement.

Of course, this does not reduce the seriousness of the situation, but it does cast it in a different light. The effect of schooling

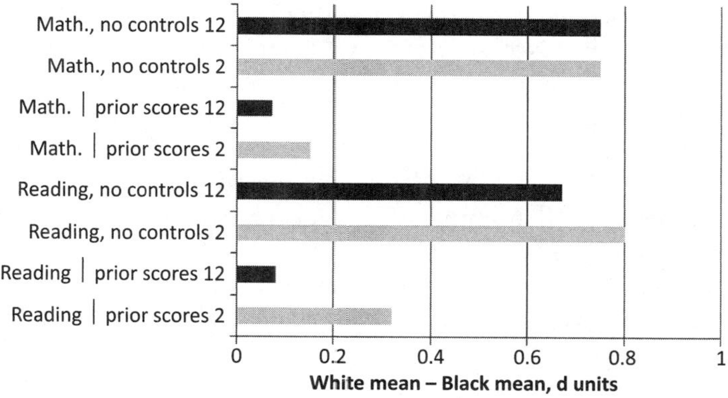

Figure 11.26. Difference in deviation score units between Black and White students' scores on achievement tests taken in the second and twelfth grades. The effect is shown with and without controls for differences between students in reading and mathematical skills assessed earlier. Data from Phillips, Crouse, & Ralph, 1998, Tables 7–4 and 7–5.

is certainly to increase cognitive skills. In the process of increasing those skills schooling increases the range of variation between those who were or were not initially well prepared for schooling.

11.4.6. *Group Differences in Cognitive Skills in the Workplace*

Three sources of data are available to study group differences in workplace performance: the test scores obtained by people applying for jobs, supervisors' ratings of on-the-job performance, and objective indices of performance. One can argue that the best measures of workplace performance would be the objective indices, that the supervisor's ratings would be next best, and that the test scores would be only indirect evidence of performance. Unfortunately the availability of the data produces the opposite ranking; it is fairly easy to study test scores and relatively expensive to obtain objective performance measures.

A great many of the studies of applicant test performance use data from the Wonderlic Personnel Test (WPT) and its current version, the WPT-R. As a brief reminder, people who take the WPT have to switch very rapidly from doing one simple task (simple mathematics word problems) to another (analyzing logical statements). The result is a sort of mental gymnastics for the working memory complex, as tasks and algorithms have to be switched rapidly. Not surprisingly, the WPT is a reasonable indicator of general intelligence. As it takes only twelve minutes, it is a cost-effective screening instrument.

Philip Roth, a professor at Clemson University, and his colleagues have conducted a meta-analysis of the WPT and some other data on applicant test scores.[145] When they combined the results from all jobs they found a White-Black d value of .99, and a White-Hispanic d of .83. Within jobs their estimate of the White-Black difference was .83 for jobs of low complexity, .72 for jobs of medium complexity, and .63 for jobs of high

complexity. The reduced d values could be expected on the basis of self-selection. It was not possible to analyze the White-Hispanic difference by job complexity, due to lack of data.

Meta-analyses have also been conducted on performance ratings.[146] The advantage in job performance, $d \approx .3$ in favor of Whites, is substantially less than the White advantage on test performance, $d \approx 1$. Black-White differences in job performance are larger when performance is evaluated by objective criteria, such as work samples and tests of job knowledge, than when supervisor ratings are used. The d values for such measures are in the .4–.5 range. This compares to d values for ratings of interpersonal skills, where the differences fall closer to .2.[147]

There is no contradiction between the findings on test performance and job performance. Within the population of applicants for a particular job differences in test scores are in the $d = .7$–.8 range. Predictive validity correlations range from .3 for jobs of low cognitive complexity, to .6 for jobs of high complexity. Multiplying .75 by either .6 or .3 provides a predicted d of either .45 or .22, depending upon the cognitive loading of the job and the performance rating.

Another way to estimate workplace success is to look at income. Income is important in itself, but it is only loosely tied to performance within an occupation, for many other variables, such as the type of position, noneconomic rewards, seniority, and area of the country also influence income.

White incomes are generally higher than the incomes of African Americans and Latinos. Based on their study of the NLSY79 data, Herrnstein and Murray claimed that the disparity between Black and White incomes virtually disappears after statistically controlling for intelligence, as indexed by AFQT scores.[148] However, they did not report separate analyses for men and women. A more detailed analysis of the

---

145 Roth et al., 2001.

146 McKay & McDaniel, 2006; Roth, Huffcut, & Bobko, 2003.
147 McKay & McDaniel, 2006.
148 Herrnstein & Murray, 1994, pp. 324–325.

NLSY79 data found that the relation between income and AFQT scores was essentially identical across the three racial groups – Whites, Blacks, and Hispanics – after making separate analyses for men and women. The same analyses indicate that the variation in income associated with AFQT scores was much smaller than Herrnstein and Murray had claimed that it was.[149]

In summary, it appears that there are gaps in job performance between Whites, African Americans, and Latinos (to the extent data is available), and that these gaps are about what would be predicted from the gaps in cognitive test scores and the correlation between test scores and performance.

11.4.7. *The Case of Asian-Americans*

Asians, a minority in America, but a plurality in the world, present a very different picture. Asian-Americans, as a group, have slightly higher cognitive test scores than do Whites. This is true both today and at a much earlier time, when Asian-Americans tended to have lower SES than they do today. They also have a pronounced pattern to their differences, on both intelligence tests and markers of educational achievement.

The fact that Asian-Americans tend to have high scores on intelligence tests is not a new observation. In the 1920–30 period Stanley Porteus (1883–1972), a professor of Psychology at the University of Hawaii, collected data showing that Japanese-Americans had higher intelligence test scores than did other groups.[150] At that time Japanese-Americans in Hawaii were considerably lower on the SES scale than they are today, so the relatively high test scores represented a reversal of the usually observed positive relation between IQ scores and SES.

The statement that Asian-Americans have higher average scores masks an important difference in the pattern of scores.

Asian-Americans tend to do better than Whites in Mathematics and visual-spatial reasoning, and tend to be somewhat below Whites in verbal scores. Figure 11.27 illustrates a typical finding, scores on the SAT for the period 1997–2007. Black scores are shown for comparison. The White-Asian difference is clear, and is also clearly much smaller than the Black-White difference.[151]

The US results are mirrored on the international scene. Of the forty-eight countries participating in the International Mathematics and Science Studies (TIMSS) in 2007, the top five countries were, in order of eighth-grade mathematics scores; China (Taipei), South Korea, Singapore, China (Hong Kong), and Japan. All five countries, and only those five countries, had test scores that were reliably higher than the scores for the United States. The PISA assessments show a similar picture. In the 2007 PISA mathematics assessments three out of the top five countries – Japan, South Korea, and Hong-Kong (People's Republic of China) – were from northeast Asia. While northeast Asian countries generally did well in the reading assessments, they were not nearly as dominant as they were in mathematics. Only Korea retained a position in the top five.[152]

These remarks refer strictly to northeast Asians – people who emigrated from, or whose forefathers emigrated from, China (including Taiwan), Japan, or Korea. The recent emigrations from Southeast Asian

149 Cawley et al, 1997, especially Table 8.5, and Cavallo, el-Abadi, & Heeb, 1998, Table 8.6. See also Figure 10.7 in this volume and the accompanying text.

150 Porteus, Dewey, & Bernreuter, 1930.

151 People who take the SAT are a self-selected population, so this comparison might be contaminated by recruitment effects, as discussed in section 11.1 of this chapter. In this case, however, recruitment probably works to underestimate the differences in the population, because the probability that an Asian-American or Black student will attempt to take the SAT is higher than the probability that a White student with equivalent high school examination scores will take the SAT. (Calculations by Tara Madhyastha and the author, based upon comparisons of the frequencies of various ethnic groups at different NAEP scoring levels and in the self-selected group taking the SAT.)

152 Hong Kong was tenth and Japan was tied with the tiny Duchy of Lichtenstein for the thirteenth position. Source: National Center for Educational Statistics, *Digest of Educational Statistics 2007*, Table 389.

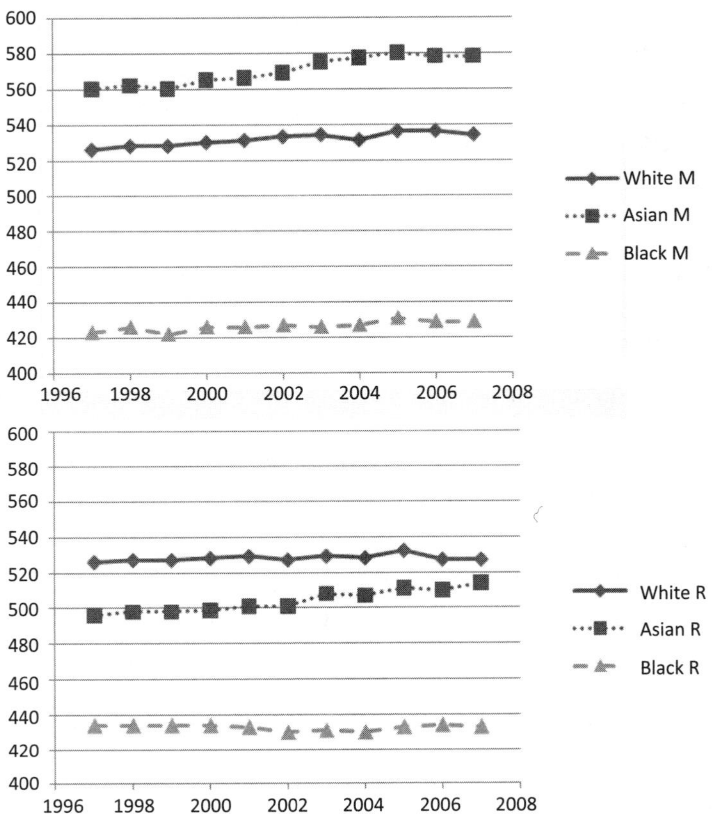

Figure 11.27. SAT scores for three racial/ethnic groups for the period 1997–2007. The top panel shows scores on the SAT-M (M code), the bottom shows the SAT-R (R code) scores. *Source:* College Board.

nations, such as Thailand, India, Indonesia, and the Philippines, are not reflected in most of the statistical comparisons. In fact, the current US census and educational practice of lumping all the Asian countries together, and further adding in emigrants from the Pacific Islands, is bound to confuse the statistical summaries. This is going to be a serious problem in the future, for there are studies indicating that educational performance and relevant social conditions vary considerably across different Asian groups.

In summary, there is little doubt that IQ scores and educational data present a consistent ordering of the major racial/ethnic groups in the United States, with (northeast) Asians slightly ahead of Whites, Hispanics about .5 to .7 deviation units below Whites, and African Americans from .8 to 1.1 deviation units below Whites. The picture has changed over time, but slowly. Two questions remain to be addressed; does this ordering matter, and if it does, what are its causes?

11.4.8. *Are the Tests Valid for Various Racial and Ethnic Groups within the Developed Societies?*

There have been numerous claims that cognitive tests do not fairly assess minorities. In one of the most famous of these disputes, *Larry P. vs. Ryles*,[153] a federal court forbade the use of intelligence tests to classify students as "educable mental retardates" and then channel them into special classes. (Ironically, eighty years earlier the French

153 *Larry P. v. Riles*, U.S. Court of Appeals, 1984, 793F.2d969 (9th Circuit).

Ministry of Education had commissioned Binet to develop tests for this purpose.) The courts' argument was that the tests were illegally discriminatory because when they were used a disproportionate percentage of African American children received IQ scores below 70, one of the criteria for retardation.

The reasoning used to win the *Larry P.* case is typical of the arguments made against relying on the various cognitive tests as valid indicators of the mental abilities of minority group members. Under what conditions might the argument be valid?

Return to the distinctions among three sets of cognitive skills; *assessed relevant skills,* those used both to take the test and to perform in school or the workforce; *assessed irrelevant skills* that can be used to take the test but are irrelevant to school and workplace performance; and *unassessed relevant skills,* cognitive (or other) skills that are relevant in the school and workplace, but are not evaluated by the tests. If only assessed relevant skills existed, the correlation between test scores and criterion performance in the school or workplace would approach 1.0. This, of course, is an unrealistic criterion, for no one thinks either that the tests are perfect or that success is determined solely by cognitive characteristics. An argument against testing different racial/ethnic groups cannot be made on the basis of imperfect testing.

The argument that the tests are not fair (to African Americans, Hispanics, or any other group) cannot rest on differential distributions of assessed relevant skills in the White and minority communities, because any prediction based only on these skills is a fair prediction. The argument has to be made on the basis of assessed irrelevant skills or unassessed relevant skills. Two conditions are possible:

a. the members of the affected minority group are less likely to possess assessed irrelevant skills than Whites are, or
b. the affected minority group members are more likely to possess unassessed relevant skills than Whites are.

If either of these conditions hold the tests are unfair, either because whites receive a boost due to their narrow test-taking skills, condition (a), or because minority group members do not receive appropriate credit for their unassessed relevant skills, condition (b).

Suppose condition (a) exists. Minority group members will have spuriously lower test scores than Whites because the White scores are elevated by their assessed irrelevant skills. The correlation between test scores and criterion performance, calculated only for white examinees, should be *lower* than the same correlation calculated within the minority group, because the White scores are affected by factors irrelevant to school and workplace (criterion) performance, while the minority scores are not. If a common prediction equation is developed for all examinees, regardless of race or ethnic status, the equation should overpredict White performance because the White scores are systematically and erroneously inflated. Minority performance will be underpredicted.

Suppose condition (b) exists: minorities exceed Whites in the possession of unassessed relevant skills. The correlation between test scores and criterion performance will be lower in the minority group than in Whites because the minority criterion performance scores have a source of variance that the White scores do not. If a common prediction equation is used, minority group performance will again be underpredicted, due to the minority group members' having unassessed but relevant cognitive skills.

In either case of unfairness, minority group scores should be underpredicted by an equation based on scores from all groups – the common prediction equation. Depending upon which case of unfairness occurs, the correlation between test and criterion performance may be either higher or lower when calculated for minority group members alone than for Whites alone.

This definition of fairness is restricted in two ways. The prediction equation must act only on test scores. If the prediction equation includes an adjustment for racial/ethnic status, by adding or subtracting a constant, predictions, but not correlations, will be adjusted appropriately. Whether or not such an adjustment should be made is a legal/ethical question rather than a scientific one, and will not be further discussed.

Psyohometric fairness has been defined entirely on the basis of statistical accuracy and skill possession. It is irrelevant to larger issues of social justice. It could be that when test scores are used to predict performance the appropriate equation systematically predicts lower criterion scores for minority group members than for Whites, and that in fact they have lower criterion scores, because they have not had the same opportunities Whites have had to acquire the necessary assessed, criterion-relevant skills. Such a situation is indeed unfair, in a global sense, and some form of affirmative action may be appropriate. Blaming an IQ or other cognitive test for this situation amounts to shooting the messenger. A test can only assess skill possessed at the time of testing; it cannot tell us how those skills came to be possessed.

How do the facts stand up to the criteria of fairness?

There is scant evidence that educational assessment tests are unfair, in the sense just defined. The validation data for the SAT provide a clear case. The correlation between SAT scores and first-year grade point average, the usual criterion for such studies, is .53 for Whites, .50 for Hispanics, and .47 for Blacks. While these small differences are statistically significant (with sample sizes of 10,000 or more per group), it is hard to imagine a situation where they would be of practical importance. What is even more telling is that African American and Hispanic grades in college are systematically overpredicted. This is not consistent with either condition of unfairness.[154]

Differences between White and minority group academic performance (White–minority group) are on the order of $d = .40$

for African Americans and .30 for Hispanics. These figures are substantially smaller than the corresponding differences in test performance, $d = 1.0$ and $d = .6 -.7$.[155] This is what one would expect, because the tests are imperfect predictors. Assuming a .5 predictive validity for educational tests such as the SAT, the expected d values for academic performance are .50 and .30–.35, not far from the observed differences.

I have found relatively few industrial studies that have reported a contrast between the predictive accuracy of tests for Whites and minority group members. A 2008 discussion of this issue by a knowledgeable researcher in the field[156] cited a study almost twenty years earlier as evidence that there is no difference in the predictive accuracy of industrial tests across racial and ethnic groups. The study in question[157] was a National Academy of Science review of yet earlier studies, involving a single test, the Department of Labor's General Aptitude Test Battery (GATB). Its authors concluded that test scores were equally predictive for both groups.[158] In my own searches I found one (!) recent study, of white-collar/managerial performance in a government agency. It concluded that various predictors of job success, including but not limited to cognitive tests, behaved in the same way for Black and White employees.[159]

In sum, the tests are accurate predictors of achievement for the three major racial/ethnic groups in the United States – Whites, African Americans, and Hispanics. The data for Asian-Americans is too scanty to make a firm statement, although there is some evidence that academic scores are underpredicted. Since test scores are higher

---

154 Mattern et al., 2008, Table 2. Correlations have been corrected for restriction in range.

155 Sackett, Borneman, & Connely, 2008.

156 Ibid.

157 Hartigan & Wigdor, 1989.

158 Many investigators must have had access to data relevant to this issue. For example, military studies have been reported in which it would have been impossible not to have obtained data that could be used to compare predictions across groups. Considering the amount of controversy over the question of test bias, it is surprising that the comparisons were not made.

159 Pulakos, Schmitt, & Chan, 1996.

for Asian-Americans than for Whites, this suggests that unfairness condition (b) holds: Asian-Americans may have more unassessed relevant cognitive skills than do Whites.

The differences in test scores across racial/ethnic groups almost certainly reflect a real difference in the distribution of cognitive skills across racial/ethnic lines. What might cause the difference?

11.4.9. *Social Causes for Disparities in the Distribution of Intelligence across Racial/Ethnic Lines*

Neither I nor anyone else knows the cause of the differences in indices of intelligence among various racial and ethnic groups. Furthermore, there almost certainly is not any single cause, and the causes may vary for different comparisons. We do have some leads.

Not surprisingly, the explanations fall into two broad categories – social and biological. The social ones will be discussed here, the biological ones in the next section.

EFFECTS THAT MAY ALTER THE
INTERPRETATION OF TEST SCORES
IN AFFECTED GROUPS
There have been a number of claims that the tests used for personnel screening are unfair because they contain questions that draw on cultural information not available, or less available, to Blacks, Hispanics, and Asians. While it is not generally acknowledged, this claim has to be made with the admittance that the relevant cultural information has predictive value for performance, for otherwise it would amount to unfairness condition (a), as defined in the previous section, and we have seen that condition (a) cannot be maintained. The argument has to be the "social justice" argument that the minority group members are less able to prepare for the tests than Whites are.

Arthur Jensen is one of the strongest critics of this claim.[160] He has applied the method of correlated vectors, with g loadings replaced by expert judgment of the extent to which questions or tests are culturally loaded, and concluded that the cultural loadings do not predict the extent of group differences on tests, subtests, and individual questions, while the g loadings do. Most of the studies Jensen considered compared Whites to African Americans in the United States. A substantial European study by Michelle Helms-Lorenz and her colleagues at the University of Tilburg, in the Netherlands,[161] which also used the method of correlated vectors, found that cultural loadings rather than g loadings were the best predictors of differences between racial/ethnic groups of Dutch children. The Dutch and the American studies do not necessarily conflict, for different ethnic groups were involved. In particular, many of the African immigrants to the Netherlands are relatively recent arrivals, while African Americans in the United States, with a few exceptions, have a history that goes back centuries.

In addition to conducting analyses of racial/ethnic differences on battery type tests, Jensen has pointed out that White–Black differences are found on tests that do not have obviously large cultural biases. For example, progressive matrix tests do not have obvious culture loadings, yet they produce fairly large racial/ethnic differences.

The matter is somewhat up in the air. However, the indeterminancy tells us something. If cultural unfairness were a major cause of racial/ethnic differences in test performance, we would not have as much trouble detecting it as seems to be the case. This does not mean that culture plays no part in determining test scores, particularly if the cultural differences are marked. For example, I would be suspicious of the use of the tests to evaluate intelligence in recent immigrants to a developed nation, although test scores might be useful as an index of assimilation. Whether it was desirable to use a valid, but in one sense "culturally unfair," test to screen applicants for jobs or academic programs would be a policy issue, not a scientific question.

---

160 This is discussed extensively in Jensen's 1980 book on the topic. Further discussions of more recent data can be found in Jensen, 1998, 359–367.

161 Helms-Lorenz, van de Vijver, & Poortinga, 2003.

This point was illustrated in an analysis of several studies of the workplace performance of various immigrant groups in the Netherlands.[162] Immigrants did indeed have lower test scores than ethnic Dutch. They also had lower scores in academic achievement and on a variety of workplace performance ratings. (Note the similarity to the American studies discussed earlier.) The authors then contrasted test scores and academic and workplace performance of successive generations of immigrants. The difference between the Dutch and non-Dutch groups was reduced in the second generation. As the immigrant-derived groups had more experience with the Dutch society they acquired the cognitive skills it valued. The test scores responded to the presence of these skills, and so did academic and workplace performance. There was a socially induced change in intelligence.

This brings us to a slightly different view of cultural bias on a measure of intelligence. If one is trying to understand or predict success in a certain society – usually a post-industrial society – then one's concern should be with the measurement of intelligence as defined by that society. Therefore, a certain amount of cultural bias in a test is appropriate. How much depends upon the situation. Troubles occur only if an investigator tries to define intelligence as something that is invariant across cultures.

A second argument for the idea that test scores are biased against minorities is that the testing situation itself is biased. Some years ago it was claimed that minorities, and especially minority children, would not communicate adequately with White examiners. Very little evidence has surfaced to support this idea, and in any case it would not apply strongly to a group testing situation. A more serious concern has to do with motivation. The idea is illustrated by the stereotype threat argument – that if minorities (or women) perceive a test as the sort of test on which they should do poorly, they will not put as much effort into

solving test questions.[163] The argument here is exactly the same as the argument presented to explain the fact that women tend to have lower scores than men on mathematics and visual-spatial tests. And the evidence is the same. Stereotype threat can be demonstrated in laboratory settings,[164] but not in field situations where success or failure has real consequences for the examinees.[165] The use of the MGCFA technique to evaluate stereotype threat effects in high-stakes testing has been suggested, but at present no such studies are available.[166]

A third argument is that minority group members may lack culturally relevant cognitive skills that are evaluated by conventional tests, but that they possess other important cognitive skills that are not evaluated by the tests. This is condition (b) in my categorization of unfair testing. It implies that the tests should underpredict minority performance. Such underprediction has not been reported for African Americans or Hispanics, either in academia or the workplace. There is a suggestion that condition (b) may apply to some Asian-Americans.

The claim that test scores are irrelevant or inaccurate in predicting minority group performance is contradicted by the evidence.

SOCIAL EXPLANATIONS: DEVELOPMENT
Some explanations for racial and ethnic differences in intelligence accept the validity of test scores as indicators of actual differences, and then seek to explain these differences in terms of social causes acting on cognitive development. In order to understand these explanations it helps to step back and consider how we develop intelligence.

Intelligence refers to the possession of a set of cognitive skills and knowledge that are useful in post-industrial society. These skills are not inherited directly, in the sense that eye color is inherited. They are produced by an interaction between a person's learning

---

162 Te Nijenhuis et al., 2004.

163 Steele & Aaronson, 1995, 1998; Suzuki & Aaronson, 2005.
164 Nguyen & Ryan, 2008.
165 Cullen, Hardison, & Sackett, 2004; Sackett, Hardison, & Cullen, 2004; Strickler & Ward, 2004.
166 Wicherts, Dolan, & Hessen, 2005.

capacity, which is initially genetically determined but soon influenced by what the person already knows, and social supports that facilitate the learning process. Initially these social supports are largely within-family, but as a person grows older the support network ranges from kindergarten to the university, church, and workplace, and from exploration of the playground to exploration of the World Wide Web. Cognitive skills are required to utilize these resources, so there is an important positive feedback loop. What you know already is a powerful predictor of what you are about to learn.

Human learning is an active process. It depends upon both the potential offered by the environment and the student's motivation and skill in interacting with the environment in a way that furthers the acquisition of learning. These statements apply equally to learning calculus, learning how to cook a soufflé, and learning how to hit a backhand overhead shot in tennis.

The next step is to apply these statements to racial/ethnic differences in intelligence and academic achievement.

Parental socioeconomic status (SES) is commonly pointed to as an indicator of social support (or lack thereof). Parental SES is confounded with racial/ethnic status. This is particularly true for recently arrived immigrants, who also may not be familiar with the dominant language. Chapter 9 reviewed the substantial evidence, from cultures as diverse as the rural Philippines and the American Midwest, showing that children from families that are disrupted and/or socioeconomically stressed are read to less, are less encouraged to do problem solving on their own, and generally tend to have lower intelligence test scores, even in the pre-school years. Home environments count.

Because home environment is strongly correlated with SES, one could argue that to a great extent the observed racial/ethnic disparities in cognitive skills are actually SES effects. This proposal has to be taken seriously, for the correlation between race/ethnicity and SES is substantial. In 2006 the percentages of families with children under eighteen who were below the poverty line was as follows:

White ...	9.5%
Black ...	33.0%
Hispanic ...	26.6%
Asian ...	12.0%

A lack of financial resources substantially constrains the amount of time and effort that adults can give to parenting. This undoubtedly takes its toll on the children. Recall that the gaps in cognitive achievement toward the end of high school can be predicted, on an individual basis, by the cognitive gap at the start of elementary school. The original gap is closely related to SES.

Nevertheless, there are three reasons for not accepting SES as the *sole* explanation for racial/ethnic disparities in intelligence. The first is statistical: SES measurements do not fully account for the differences in intelligence measures between groups. An SES argument also fails to account for the fact that the differences between groups on cognitive measures tend to be large for "culturally reduced" tests, such as the RPM tests.

Second, SES is itself confounded with intelligence. We then get a chicken- and-egg phenomenon. For children, parental SES is confounded with parental intelligence, and since intelligence is heritable to a significant degree, it is not clear whether an effect of parental SES on children's intelligence is due to social or biological inheritance.

Finally, and to me most compelling, socioeconomic status is a statistical abstraction. As such, it cannot cause anything. Intellectual development depends upon physical and social variables within the environment that are correlated with SES.

What might some of these variables be? One class of variables has already been implicated: parental practices. It has been estimated that in order to participate fully in school a child has to have learned to read approximately 9,000 words by the third grade. The child also has to have a good knowledge of the syntactical and semantic rules of the language that will be used in the school. A substantial portion of this knowledge is acquired via parental interaction, such as reading to children.[167] While there is less data for other skills, such as encouraging problem solving (at least that I am aware of), the same thing is likely to be true of elementary mathematics (e.g., counting) and general problem-solving skills.

Parenting practices are required to draw out biological potentials in young children.[168] The extent to which these are developed at the start of school is highly predictive of later development in school. As a general statement, for there obviously are exceptions, Black, White and Latino parents with low SES seem to be low on the time-consuming parental skills required to guide children toward independent problem solving. Asian parents with similar low SES give the practice of these skills high priority. This seems to be particularly true of Asian-Americans from the northeast Asian nations – China, Korea, and Japan.[169]

If this argument is correct, it ought to be possible to account for the gap in Black-White performance by considering the effect of these variables. This question was addressed in an analysis of data from the Panel Study on Income Dynamics (PSID), a longitudinal study being conducted by the Institute for Social Research of the University of Michigan. In 1997 extensive data was collected on the families involved who had dependent children age twelve and under. The children's cognitive skills were measured using age-appropriate tests, including several of the tests in the Woodcock-Johnson battery. Parental income and occupation and household wealth were measured. Mother's verbal skills were measured, using the paragraph comprehension subtest of the Woodcock-Johnson battery. This is a good marker for Gc. In addition, a number of measurements were made on the home environment itself, including parenting style and the quality of adult interactions with children.

The typical Black-White gap appeared when the children's cognitive scores were considered alone. However, it was greatly reduced, and no longer statistically reliable, after the family and home characteristics were considered. The three best predictors were occupational status of the head of the household (the higher prestige of the occupation, the better the child's scores), mother's score on the verbal comprehension test (the higher the mother's score, the higher the child's score), and the measures of the nature of the interactions with the child.[170]

The variables that best predict a child's scores are variables correlated with racial status. This is shown in Figure 11.28, which presents the *d* values associated with the four measures that were found most predictive of children's cognitive test scores. Black and White families differ on the key variables. This is an illustration of the general point that socioeconomic characteristics, rather than racial identity per se, are determiners of the Black-White gap in fairly young children.

What about group differences in older children and adults? The influence of family environments is diminished as children age. Therefore, we want to look at the interactions between students in different racial/ethnic groups and their schools, for the development of intelligence during this period depends on three things: biological potential (which can never be gainsaid), the quality of instruction, and the way in which the student interacts with the instruction.

Laurence Steinberg, a professor at Temple University, and his colleagues have conducted extensive studies of the attitudes of adolescents toward school.[171] Steinberg's group reached the following conclusions:

1. The dominant attitudes of the White peer group discourage high levels of school achievement. Conspicuous efforts toward studying are frowned upon. However, poor academic performance is also looked down upon. In general, it is OK to do well in school,

167 Wolf, 2007, Chapter 4.
168 Collins et al., 2000.
169 Corwyn & Bradley, 2008; Steinberg, 1996.

170 Yeung & Conley, 2008.
171 Steinberg, 1996.

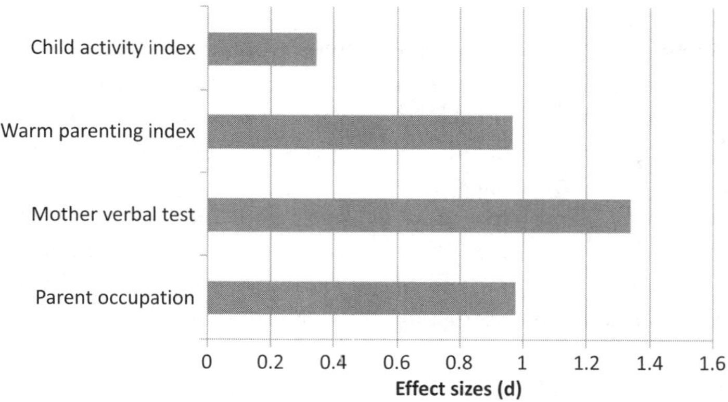

Figure 11.28. The effect sizes for White–Black contrasts on selected variables shown to predict the Black–White contrast on tests of cognitive skills. All effect sizes are reliable at the .05 level or lower. Calculations based on Yeung & Conley, 2008, Table 3. The selection of variables was based on regression analyses presented in that paper.

provided that you do not appear to be working hard at it.

2. Black and Hispanic students claim that high achievement would be valuable, but do not seem to be threatened by poor achievement. Considerable emphasis is placed upon behaviors that display group solidarity; "hanging out" is seen as important, studying is not.

3. Asian-American students believe in the importance of high achievement, and expect that it will be achieved only by sustained effort. This group was the only group that reported substantial discussion of class work between peers. The effect is highest in children who are immigrants or whose parents are immigrants from the three northeast Asian countries.

John Ogbu, an anthropologist at the University of California, Berkeley, reached much the same conclusion on the basis of ethnographic analyses of the attitudes of Black adolescents from well-to-do homes in a similar city. Support for Ogbu's conclusion was obtained in a survey of student feelings about high academic achievement. In general, Black tenth-graders saw social costs to academic achievement, especially if they

were in a predominantly Black school. Both Black and White teenagers believed that being in an honor society would threaten their chances of being part of the "in" crowd or being popular with the opposite sex, but these beliefs were much more common among Black students.[172]

This line of research has generated a great deal of debate. Several social commentators and activists, including African American activists, have accepted the findings and made efforts to change adolescent attitudes in the African American communities. Others have argued that the phenomenon is a result of socioeconomic status, rather than racial/ethnic attitudes. As a statistical phenomenon, though, this debate does not matter! If Blacks and Latinos are concentrated in lower SES groups, then any gap in performance that is based on the performance of students in general could appear either as an SES or a racial/ethnic disparity.

Finally, there is the question of the schools themselves. In extremely segregated societies, such as the American South prior to (forced) school integration in the 1950s or South Africa prior to the end of apartheid, schooling was separate and grossly unequal

---

172 Cook & Ludwig, 1998. Perhaps a way to improve American education is to keep the names of students on high school honor rolls a secret.

for Whites compared to non-Whites. That is no longer the situation today, in either country, but there is a correlation between racial/ethnic status, residential location, and the quality of schooling. For instance, in the United States schools in heavily Black, low SES areas tend not to be desirable positions for many teachers. Also, to the extent that school financing is dependent upon the local tax base, schools located in economically distressed areas are at a disadvantage. This is especially serious for attempts to control student/teacher ratios. At the gross level of measuring school quality by the amount of financing available per student, school funding seems to have little influence on outcomes. A finer-grained analysis provides a different picture.

As was shown earlier, the Black-White gap in cognitive skills upon finishing schooling is predictable, on an individual basis, from the gap upon entry to kindergarten. The size of the gap between groups, measured in deviation units, is substantially larger at the end of high school than at the beginning of the first grade. This suggests that the mathematical relationship is

$$d_f = cd_g + e, \qquad (11.3)$$

where d_g is the original black-white gap, d_f is the final gap, c is a constant greater than 1, and e is a residual term. Furthermore, the equation should hold for any educational transition.

Equation 11.3 implies that the Black-White gap grows steadily throughout the school years, which it does. This could be taken as evidence for social practices within the schools that place Black children at a disadvantage. However, a careful analysis of the patterns of accomplishment in both Black and White schoolchildren suggests a different conclusion.[173] Equation 11.3 applies not only to Black-White contrasts, but also to contrasts between White children who enter school in an advantaged or disadvantaged position. Less abstractly, the

gap in performance between students who were initially well or poorly prepared, prior to entering kindergarten or the first grade, increases steadily throughout the school years. Because Black children are more likely than White children to enter at a disadvantage, the progressively increasing gap between well-prepared and poorly prepared students, regardless of race, can appear as an increasing gap between Black and White students.

In sum, there are many social practices that have an impact on racial and ethnic differences in cognitive skills. They include parenting practices and cultural beliefs about the educational process. These in turn interact with issues of school financing and teacher behavior. It is extremely hard to quantify these various social variables. Furthermore, they are highly interactive and collinear, making an assignment of weights or evaluation of causal models difficult. I do not doubt, though, that the social environment of racial and ethnic groups has a major influence on the development of intelligence within those groups.

We might then ask why these differences in social environments arise in the first place. Here we enter the realm of speculation.

William Julius Wilson, a sociologist at the University of Chicago, has argued that since the end of segregation and legal discrimination the Black community has become increasingly bifurcated.[174] Middle-class Black families have seized expanded opportunities for economic, residential, and social improvement. To some extent this has led them to disengagement from the "ghettos," heavily Black areas in the inner cities. At the same time changes in the nature of work have led to a reduction in the employment opportunities available to less educated, less well-off people, regardless of their race or ethnicity. This trend has fallen heaviest on the Black community, because families there often did not have the financial and educational backing required to give their children the opportunity to acquire

173 Phillips et al, 1998.

174 Wilson, 1997.

the credentials that are becoming increasingly necessary for social advancement. In Wilson's terms there is now a permanent underclass that is not necessarily Black but tends to be heavily Black.

If we accept Wilson's sociological analysis, a psychological corollary follows from the Challenge Hypothesis stated in Chapter 1. An underclass that is divorced from the mainstream of the post-industrial society will fail to develop some of the cognitive skills that are required in that society. Since the divorce is not complete, there will be an overlap between the skills required in both the underclass society and the more general society. For instance, in modern America an inner-city Black may not speak the standard American English dialect, but he or she can develop the ability to comprehend it by watching television. The same thing cannot be said for the skills involved in mathematical or counterfactual reasoning. It is worth noting that in support of this explanation there are studies showing that there are no differences between Blacks and Whites in knowledge retrieval, providing that the opportunity for knowledge acquisition (of word definitions) is equal.[175]

Stanley Sue, a professor of Psychology at the University of California, Los Angeles, has offered a social-belief explanation for the predominance of Asian-Americans in both high test scores and academic and professional achievement.[176] Sue rejects the statement sometimes made that Asians in America are a modern example of successful migration. He agrees that they have indeed succeeded in some fields, but argues that a careful analysis of mental health indictors indicates that the success has been accompanied by a good deal of stress. He notes that Asian-American success has come primarily in fields such as engineering and medicine, where education and certification play a dominant role. Asian-Americans are less prominent in fields such as law and politics, where personal acceptance becomes a central issue.[177] Sue argues that a concentration on scientific and technical careers, combined with a traditional belief that hard work will lead to success, can account for much of the data on Asian-American cognitive accomplishments.

Ogbu presented an analysis somewhat similar to Sue's, but for African Americans.[178] Like Sue, Ogbu emphasized the importance of historically developed beliefs within the affected group as determinants of current behaviors. Ogbu then went on to distinguish between groups such as Asian-Americans, who were voluntary emigrants to the United States, and who arrived there with a historic belief in the efficacy of hard work, and African Americans, who were the descendants of an involuntary migration, and who came from a social group that, after several generations of slavery and discrimination, had not been given very much reason to believe that hard work would be followed by rewards.

I do not know of any similar analysis of the relations between cognitive achievement, current practices, and historical causes in the Hispanic community. In fact, I doubt that there can be such an analysis for the community as a whole, for it is composed of very different subcommunities. Puerto Ricans recently from Puerto Rico, Puerto Ricans who moved to the continental US from two to four generations ago, Cuban immigrants who left Cuba following the ascension of a communist dictatorship there in the 1950s, the descendants of Mexicans who moved to present-day California and the Southwest over two hundred years ago, and recently arrived immigrants and

175 Fagan & Holland, 2002, 2007.
176 See Sue and Okazaki, 1990, for a good discussion of Sue's ideas.

177 An exception has to be made for the State of Hawaii, where Asian-Americans are the majority ethnic group and, predictably, have dominated state politics. In the other forty-nine states only two Asian-Americans have been elected governor as of January 1, 2010. Both have served recently: Gary Locke (Chinese descent) in Washington State (1997–2005) and Bobby Jindal (Indian descent), elected Governor of Louisiana beginning in January 2008.
178 Ogbu, 2003.

children of recent immigrants from Latin America are very different people. Racial and ethnic designations are fuzzy concepts. In the case of American Hispanics the concept is very fuzzy indeed.

To sum up, there are powerful arguments and a good deal of evidence for the proposition that racial/ethnic differences in intelligence are influenced by a variety of social variables. There is no evidence pointing to a single explanatory variable, nor is there likely to be. Statistically, the variables are highly collinear, so that different causal models can be said to describe the data to very nearly the same degree of accuracy. In many cases what appears to be an important variable turns out to be a proxy for other variables. For instance, income and family wealth are statistically predictive of the Black-White gap, but when noneconomic family characteristics, such as parenting style, are statistically controlled for, the wealth-IQ relation disappears.[179] Logically, there are all sorts of reasons to expect interactions between variables. Trying to sort out the relationship between cognitive performance and contemporary indices of noncognitive behaviors is a data analyst's nightmare.

Social commentators disagree about how the present situation came to pass. Ogbu and Wilson disagree over whether the situation for African Americans has developed over two or three centuries or is due to developments in the last half-century. Sue falls somewhere in between, referring to beliefs held by an immigrant community that has been developing from successive waves of entrants for the last 150 years, but referring (somewhat generally) to social traditions that have a history of over a thousand years.

I do not think we are likely to resolve these issues. As is the case for evolutionary psychology's "man the hunter" hypothesis, the stories about the historic origins of present-day behavioral practices are reasonable, but to distinguish among them we would have to have access to historical data that has probably disappeared forever. More generally, rigorous methods of scientific analysis are difficult to apply to historic events. A social commentator may be able to convince us that his or her way of looking at the origins of racial/ethnic differences in intelligence is useful, but is unlikely to ever have either a sufficiently precise theory or sufficiently rich data to discriminate among different viewpoints.

11.4.10. *Biological Causes for Racial and Ethnic Differences*

Potential biological causes of racial/ethnic differences in intelligence may be either environmental or genetic.

Chapter 9 presented evidence on three of the most toxic environmental pathogens: exposure to lead, excessive use of alcohol and other psychoactive agents (alcohol is by far the biggest problem), and severe malnutrition. What data there is indicates that atmospheric and environmental lead exposure may be greater in the African American and Hispanic communities than in the White community. I know of no data for Asian communities, and in this case a distinction would have to be made between recent immigrant groups and others.

Alcohol abuse is more prevalent in the Black and Hispanic groups than in the White and Asian groups. Alcohol abuse is highly correlated with SES, thus confusing the issue. Failure to follow good dietary regimes is also a problem within the African American and Hispanic communities and, like alcohol abuse, is correlated with SES. Whether nutritional deficiencies in the two minority communities are severe enough to be a significant threat to cognitive development is debatable, although there certainly are international examples of severe malnutrition in Africa and Latin America.

What we lack are quantitative studies determining whether differential exposures to biologically hazardous environments (including self-induced ones) could account for the substantial gap in IQ scores between Whites and the two minority communities. The situation is not analogous

179 Yeung & Conley, 2008.

to the problem of discriminating between alternative accounts of history. Questions about the role that environmental hazards play in determining racial/ethnic differences in intelligence can be answered. As far as I know, though, the needed research has not been done.

There is a great deal of contention over the role that genetic differences play in establishing racial/ethnic differences in intelligence. The following two quotes summarize the conclusions of two recent reviewers:

> *For the race differences in IQ, we can be confident that genes play no role at all.*
> Nisbett, 2009, p. 197

> *. . . genetic and cultural factors carry the exact same weight in causing the mean Black-White difference in IQ as they do in causing individual differences in IQ, about 80% genetic-20% environmental by adulthood.*
> Rushston & Jensen, 2005, p. 279

There seems to be a difference of opinion.

The argument for genetic causes for group differences has been maintained by several serious researchers over the years. The three most prominent advocates of this position today are Arthur Jensen of the University of California, Berkeley; Richard Lynn of the University of Ulster; and J. Phillipe Rushton of the University of Western Ontario. The arguments they propose, which are essentially identical, were well presented in a 2005 paper by Rushton and Jensen.[180] Before discussing these claims, a comment about how genetic effects might influence racial/ethnic differences is in order.

No one inherits a test score. In order to make a direct argument for a genetic cause for group differences in intelligence one has to show that there is some biological characteristic that can account for differences in intelligence between the groups being discussed and that the characteristic is known or reasonably believed to be under genetic control. Two such characteristics have been proposed.

One is information-processing capacity, and especially speed of information processing, as measured by elementary cognitive tasks such as reaction time paradigms. Rushton and Jensen argue that there is a substantial difference in speed of processing between Whites and Blacks, in favor of Whites, and smaller differences between Whites and Asians, in favor of Asians. The evidence they offer is based largely on Jensen's studies of differences in reaction times between Whites and African Americans on fairly simple tasks.[181] However, a review of a wider range of studies of racial/ethnic differences in reaction time and other information-processing tasks found considerable inconsistency in results. The reviewers concluded that the difference between Blacks and Whites, which would be expected to be the largest difference, was on the order of $d \leq .20$.[182] Given that the correlation between speed-of-processing measures and IQ scores is around .5, after correction for various artifacts, the expected contribution of speed-of-processing measures to the Black-White test score gap would be .10, while the gap itself is on the order of 1.0. A lot remains to be explained.

Rushton and Jensen, and (in separate papers) Lynn have also proposed that the difference between groups in test scores is due to differences in brain size. Brain size does have a correlation of about .35 with intelligence within the White population. Brain size is almost entirely genetically determined.[183] Therefore, evidence for substantial differences between racial/ethnic groups in brain size would be an important link in an argument for a genetic basis for group differences in intelligence. However, such studies would be difficult

---

180 Rushton & Jensen, 2005.

181 Jensen, 1993. This study can be criticized for having given far fewer practice trials, fifteen, than is usual in reaction time studies. Studies within cognitive psychology have shown that speed measures become limiting factors in reaction time studies only after dozens, if not hundreds, of trials. See Ackerman, 1986, 1987, for a discussion.

182 Shepard & Vernon, 2008.

183 Baaré et al., 2001.

to arrange, due to the expense of obtaining brain images. Therefore, researchers interested in this topic have made estimates of brain size differences from external measures on the skull. This indirect method has its problems.

The correlation between intelligence and cranial capacity, estimated from measurements on the skull, drops to about .2, which is not surprising as brain size is substantially but imperfectly related to skull size. In studies by Rushton the difference between White adults and Black adults in cranial capacity is 43 cm^3, which corresponds to a d for cranial capacity of .46.[184] Combined with a .2 correlation, this leads to the conclusion that on the basis of skull size there should be a difference of $d = .09$ between Black and White test scores. If we accept the idea that brain size and processing speed are statistically independent, the expected gap due to these factors is then .19, still far below the observed value of 1.0.

Richard Lynn has argued that changes in intelligence over the past fifty years, the cohort (Flynn) effect described in Chapter 9, are probably due in part to changes in nutrition.[185] And he has used the correlation between cranial capacity and intelligence test scores to buttress his argument, for cranial capacity, unlike brain size, does have a substantial environmental component. To the extent that Lynn is right about nutrition, this would reduce the genetic effect upon intelligence associated with group differences in measurements on the skull.

As further evidence of a genetic basis for Black-White differences Rushton and Jensen point to various studies in which the method of correlated vectors was used to show that g loadings on tests correlate with Black-White differences and with heritability estimates. The ambiguities in the method of correlated vectors have already been commented upon.

Rushton and Jensen also make a good deal of what they refer to as "admixture studies," in which mixed-race groups are shown to have intelligence test scores intermediate between those of Whites and Blacks. In general, such studies are done outside of the United States, (e.g., in South Africa), where "Black" and "White" are more clearly defined groups than they are in the US. The mixed groups are generally intermediate on a variety of social and educational measurements. The studies are ambiguous unless these variables are controlled.

Rushton and Jensen, and in other writings (to be discussed in the next section) Lynn make a few more points, but these are their major ones. In general, I find their arguments not so much wrong as vastly overstated. But overstatement does not mean that there is no point to them. Rushton and Jensen present two conclusions.

1. They argue that the hypothesis that Black-White (and, by extension, Asian and Hispanic) differences in intelligence are entirely due to environment, the hypothesis they refer to as the 100% environment hypothesis, cannot be maintained.

2. They propose as an alternative "default hypothesis" that the Black-White difference is 80% due to genetic differences. They base this conclusion on the observation that within Whites intelligence test scores have a heritability coefficient of .8.

Rushton and Jensen (and Lynn) are correct in saying that the 100% environmental hypothesis cannot be maintained. Nisbett's extreme statement has virtually no chance of being true. However, the 100% environmental hypothesis is something of a stalking horse. Many researchers who are primarily interested in environmental differences associated with racial and ethnic differences in

---

184 This is based on the figures provided in Rushton, 1992, p. 405, text and Table 2. Rushton does not present a d value. I have calculated it by estimating standard deviations within groups provided in his Table 1, and then computing the average within-group variances. The mean difference was taken from the numbers given in the text, adjusted for military rank and sex.

185 Lynn, 1998.

intelligence would not be at all perturbed by an ironclad demonstration that, say, 3% of the gap is due to genetic differences. The real issue is over the identity and size of genetic and environmental influences on group differences in intelligence, not the existence of either one.

The 80% default hypothesis is an extreme and excessively precise statement. It is based on the assumption that the factors that contribute to the between-group differences are the same as the factors that contribute to within-group differences. This is doubtful. The genetic variability associated with the "continent of origin" distinction (races, for short) is much less than the variability between people with the same continent of origin. Estimates have placed the between-group correlation at from to 5% to 15% of the total variation within the human genome. On a statistical basis this is quite enough to identify genetic clusters associated with racial groupings.[186] There are certainly environmental differences between racial/ethnic groups. Do they amount to 5% of the total environmental variation in the United States population? Are the genetic and environmental variations associated with intelligence distributed between groups in exactly the same proportion as they are distributed within groups? We have no idea.

This is a topic about which there is a great deal of emotion and an unfortunate paucity of data. The direct evidence that we have for genetic effects does not come close to accounting for the size of the gap between White and African American test scores. Neither do environmental effects. And, unfortunately, the environmental evidence has often been presented as evidence that environmental effects do occur – which no advocate of genetic models has ever denied – but has not been presented in a way that permits a quantitative estimate of how important environmental effects are in determining group differences in intelligence in the population.

The questions raised by the existence of racial/ethnic group differences in intelligence are complex. The genome exerts both distal and proximal effects, so sometimes it is not clear whether a particular influence should be regarded as a genetic or an environmental one. Consider the case of parenting practices, shown to be an influence on a child's development of intelligence. If these practices are partly under control of the parents' genomes, and partly under the control of parental education, then the effect on the child could be called either environmental or genetic! Or an interaction between the two. Or we could say that the effect is genetic, but that it can be modified by education, just as any number of genetic disorders can be modified by medical treatment.

In spite of their complexity, questions like these are answerable. We can conduct quantitative searches for proximal and distal influences, on both the genetic and environmental sides. While we do not know, today, what genes are associated with intelligence, we will find them. When the genes are identified it will be possible to determine allele frequencies across different populations (with the caution that if the groups are in contact these frequencies will change over time!). Studies of environmental influences could go beyond the demonstration stage to the stage of making estimates of the size of these effects outside of the laboratory – once again remembering that we will be shooting at a moving target, for environments drift faster than gene frequencies.

This summary will probably not satisfy those who have taken strong stands on either side of the debate over racial and ethnic differences in intelligence. Bold hypotheses "rally the troops" and make great entrées for television talk shows. People who take intermediate positions are said to be "wishy-washy" or "afraid to say what they really think." Nevertheless, the issue is complex, and oversimplifications do not help. There are group differences in intelligence, they are important, and there are both scientific

186 Bamshad et al., 2004; Edwards, 2003; Tang et al., 2005.

and social reasons for trying to understand them. Plausible cases can be made for both genetic and environmental contributions to differences in intelligence. The evidence required to quantify the relative sizes of these contributions to group differences is lacking. The relative sizes of environmental and genetic influences will vary over time and place. Some of these influences may be amenable to change, while others will be resistant to change. The relevant questions can be studied. Denials or overly precise statements on either the pro-genetic or pro-environmental side do not move the debate forward. They generate heat rather than light.

And this is what I really believe!

11.5. The International Picture

Wealth and health are not distributed uniformly across nations; the countries of Europe and North America and their derivative oceanic cultures are best-off; Japan, Korea, and more recently China are closing the gap; sub-Saharan Africa is worst-off. The Middle East and South Asian nations and Latin America fall in between. Neither the genetic composition nor the socioeconomic histories of these regions are the same. To what extent is the present unequal distribution of health and wealth due to differences in the cognitive capacities of different peoples, and to what extent must these differences be taken into account as economies are developed over the globe?

This is an old question. Herodotus speculated about different temperaments of peoples in the fifth century BCE. From the seventeenth century until modern times economists have discussed the topic under the general title *human capital*. This term is used collectively to refer to the developed capabilities of a workforce, which can vary from being literate to having a high percentage of people with engineering degrees. It is generally agreed that human capital is very important in determining the economic potential of a state or nation. Political leaders are more likely to justify taxes to support schools by claiming that an educated population has a greater economic potential than by claiming that an uneducated population than by claiming that the educated have a moral and philosophical advantage.[187]

Economists seldom use the word "intelligence." They are interested in the distribution of developed skills in a society, and the implications of the distribution. How those skills came to be are of less concern to them. Economists are also well aware that for some people the word "intelligence" has connotations of fixed, genetically determined constraints on mental capacity. Anyone interested in influencing policies concerning "human capital" (the economists' euphemism for intelligence) is well advised to avoid using the word, for if someone does suggest that *intelligence* limits the socio-economic development of nations there is unnecessary Hell to pay. A spectacular case of this is presented in panel 11.6.

However, some people do look at the international distribution of intelligence, and do argue that the present-day (and presumably past and future) distribution of wealth, health, and happiness is due in part to differences in national intelligence. Richard Lynn, whose work on sex and race/ethnic differences was discussed earlier in this chapter, and Tutu Vanhanen, a Finnish economist, invigorated the field with the publication of two challenging books and some related papers. I shall be highly critical of their empirical work, and even more so of their interpretations. They do deserve credit for raising important questions in a way that has resulted in interesting and important findings. Before presenting the Lynn and Vanhanen research and studies that amplified and redirected it, let us consider the problems faced by any study of national intelligence.

---

187 Interestingly, this is a change in view. Thomas Jefferson argued for education on the grounds that it would make people better able to participate in political, not economic, life. There is some evidence that intelligence test scores are correlated with the relatively liberal values that have evolved (substantially!) from Jefferson's views of government and society. See Deary, Batty, & Gale, 2008.

11.5.1. *Methodological Issues*

Estimating the distribution of intelligence in a nation requires a probability sample of the residents in each nation and the use of tests that are valid in all the nations under review. These are stringent requirements. Representative national samples are hard to obtain in the most advanced post-industrial countries. The problem is virtually unsolvable in less developed countries, especially if these countries are subject to major unrest. As of 2010 there is no way that the governments of the war-torn countries of the Congo, Somalia, or Afghanistan could obtain a census or probability sample of all their residents, for any purpose.

It is often much easier to approximate a probability sample in a selected segment of the population, such as schoolchildren (the most likely accessible population) or, in some countries, registrants for military service. You then face three problems. The accessible populations may differ across countries; the estimates will apply only to the segment of the population involved; and the recruitment procedures that construct the accessible samples from the general population may differ across nations. The problem is particularly acute in the case of schoolchildren.

Consider the following contrast. In the United Kingdom essentially all children go to school, and the government has, from time to time, given well-standardized cognitive tests to students. In the Congo large parts of the country are cut off from government control, and schooling outside the major cities is haphazard at best. Inferences about national intelligence based upon studies of schoolchildren in the United Kingdom and the Congo would hardly be comparable.

These examples are extreme. Differential recruitment can occur in well-developed nations. South Korea reported that 42% of the participants in the Program for International Students Assessment (PISA) were girls; France reported 53 percent.[188] Any comparison between the PISA results from Korea and France would be confounded by male-female differences in sample recruitment.

Obtaining comparable and appropriate intelligence tests is equally challenging. The point has already been made that the tests are weighted toward evaluating skills that are relevant to the developed world, and that any test necessarily is partly an evaluation of the possession of test-taking skills. One has to be open to the possibility that outside the developed world people may not have had a chance to acquire the skills relevant to industrial and post-industrial society, and even that the people being examined may not have acquired the skills required to deal with the test-taking paradigm itself.

11.5.2. *Lynn and Vanhanen's Findings*

Lynn's position is set forward in numerous papers and in two books, both coauthored with the finnish economist Tutu Vanhanen.[189] The second book is basically an expansion of the first, with added data and analyses, none of which changes any of the conclusions of the first. I shall concentrate on the presentation in the second book, *IQ and Global Inequality*. Specific papers will be cited only if needed to make a point.

Lynn and Vanhanen regard intelligence as being largely a genetically determined trait. Although they do not say so precisely, their argument makes no sense unless they also regard the genetically defined reaction range as being narrow, as they are not optimistic about the effects of such things as improved education.

They believe that intelligence makes a contribution to indicators of national health and wealth both through its interaction with education and directly. Their argument is that intelligent people are more educable (which is certainly true) and that, in addition to the benefits of education, intelligent people are generally better reasoners, and hence more able to deal with the problems of a complex society. Lynn, in his numerous publications, has also made it clear

---

188 Rindermann, 2007.

189 Lynn & Vanhanen, 2002, 2006.

Table 11.5. Correlations between IQ estimates and selected indices of national well-being

Index of Quality of Life	*Correlation with IQ Estimate*
Gross national income/person (adjusted for local purchasing power)	.684
Adult literacy rate	.642
Tertiary education	.746
Life expectancy	.773
Democratization Index	.568

Note: Data selected from Lynn and Vanhanen, 2006, Table 6.1. Figures shown indicate the data based on 113 observed points.

that he regards intelligence test scores as equally valid across nations, including those nations usually referred to as "developing" or "Third World." For instance, he and Vanhanen include in their database test scores from the United States (mean IQ = 98), the United Kingdom (100), the Marshall Islands (84), China (105), Ghana (71), and Equatorial Guinea (59, to be discussed later).[190] Their statistical treatment gives all points equal validity.

Lynn and Vanhanen obtained estimates of IQs for each nation by searching various publication sources. This produced data for 113 countries. They estimated the IQs for another seventy-nine countries by using "comparison IQs" of "neighboring or other comparable countries." This provided them with three sets of data, 113 direct observations, 79 imputed data points, and a total of 192 data points, obtained by combining the first two sets.

In their main analyses Lynn and Vanhanen considered the relation between the IQ measures and five measures of, as they put it, "[t]he quality of human conditions." The measures of quality they used were gross national income per capita (corrected for local purchasing power), the adult literacy rate, the fraction of the population enrolling in tertiary education (college/university and beyond), life expectancy, and an index of democratization developed by Vanhanen from previous

work. This index can be thought of as a measure of the extent to which citizens of a country are free to participate in political life. The highest marks on the index (forty and above) were assigned to Belgium, Denmark, the Netherlands, and Switzerland. Most large European and North American countries scored in the mid-thirties. Dictatorships that (as of 2010) enforced a one-party state, such as China, Cuba, Kazakhstan, and North Korea, scored zero.

The variables were merged into a single quality of human conditions (QHC) index. Lynn and Vanhanen then calculated regression equations predicting the QHC index or one of its components from the IQ scores, in each of their three data sets. Additional analyses were also carried out, relating IQ scores to other social indices, such as measures of undernourishment and economic freedom. None of these analyses made any difference to Lynn and Vanhanen's conclusions, so I will concentrate on their central points.

Table 11.5 shows the correlations between the IQ estimates and the five indices of quality of human conditions. The correlations range from a high of .773 for life expectancy to a low of .568 for democratization. Given this level of correlation with the individual variables, it is inevitable that there will be a high correlation with the composite QHC index, and there is, .805 in the 113 observed data points.[191] The data presented is typical of a number of other analyses, all of

190 Lynn & Vanhanen, 2006, Table 4.3.

191 Lynn & Vanhanen, 2006, Table 7.1.

which make the same point. On a national basis the IQ estimate is a good predictor of socioeconomic indicators of quality of life. Lynn and Vanhanen reach a stronger conclusion, about causation, which I will discuss later.

Lynn and Vanhanen present one other set of analyses that are relevant to our concerns. They group countries by geographic area, note the predominant racial groups in those areas, and then calculate a representative value for IQ by race, based on this data. For instance, sub-Saharan Africans (i.e., Black, "Negroid" in some of Lynn's writings) are assigned a typical IQ of 67, East Asians receive 105, 99 for Europeans, and 90 for Southeast Asians. They further show that by assigning intermediate values to "mixed-race" groups, such as the Mestizos in some Latin American countries and "coloreds" in South Africa, they can produce an estimated IQ for the Latin American nations that predicts observed values.

Lynn and Vanhanen, and Lynn in other writings, draw three conclusions from their research.

1. The substantial correlations between IQ scores and various socioeconomic indicators shows that differences between countries in wealth, health, and to some extent happiness are very largely caused by differences in intelligence.
2. The differences in intelligence between nations are largely due to differences in the racial composition of the national and regional population.
3. While the differences have some environmental roots, the major differences are due to genetic inheritance. Nutritional differences are the most important environmental factors. They do allow some influence for education, but believe that it is not likely to be large.

Conclusions like this are bound to be controversial. Therefore, it is worth taking a closer look at the Lynn-Vanhanen data, and then looking at another analysis aimed at the same questions.

The Lynn and Vanhanen database for intelligence is highly suspect in one way, and accurate enough in another.

In both their publications Lynn and Vanhanen disregarded any question about the validity of various intelligence tests across different countries and cultures, and ignored considerations of differential sampling. In some cases their criteria for inclusion can only be described as a blunder. For instance, their data point for Equatorial Guinea, said to have a national IQ of 59 (which would be well into the mentally retarded range in a developed country), was taken from a report[192] that, while it did discuss Africa, stated clearly that the IQ 59 figure referred to children in a school for the developmentally disabled in Madrid! Many of the samples were grossly unrepresentative, and the criteria for selection of studies to include in their work were not made clear.

These concerns have led critics to claim that the data for developing countries is both unrepresentative and extremely suspect. In order to test this hypothesis Werner Wittmann and I conducted separate analyses of the data points for developed and developing countries, as presented in Lynn and Vanhanen's 2002 book.[193] We found that the residuals (i.e., the extent to which their predictions missed their targets) were much greater for developing than for developed countries. In much more detailed reviews which found many more problems of selectivity and scholarship in the Lynn and Vanhanen data set, Wicherts, Dolan, and van der Maas raised their estimate of the median sub-Saharan African's IQ of Lynn's estimate of 67 (an "educable mental retardate" in the jargon of clinicians in the developed countries) to 82.[194] Wicherts and his colleagues

192 Fernandez-Ballesteros et al., 1997.
193 Hunt & Wittmann, 2008.
194 Wicherts, Dolan, & van der Maas, 2010a. Wicherts, Dolan, and van der Maas based their calculations on a large number of studies using the Raven tests, in order to avoid problems involved in comparing different tests. Lynn and Meisenberg (2010) claimed that the studies Wicherts and his colleagues had used were not representative, and offered their own survey, which reinforced their original point. In a second paper Wicherts, Dolan, and van der Maas

pointed out that if you go backward in time by correcting for the increases in IQ scores over the past fifty years, this is the modern equivalent of the IQ of the Dutch just after World War II. The Wicherts and colleagues work showed that Lynn and Vanhanen's research was highly biased toward underestimation of countries in sub-Saharan Africa. Given that this was true of Africa, one has to be more than a little suspicious of the accuracy of their data for other developing countries.

In spite of these concerns, Lynn and Vanhanen's conclusions about the correlations between IQ estimates and measures of social well-being are probably correct. The spreads between nations in terms of various measures of social well-being are so wide that it is fairly easy to find a correlation between them. Also, as measures of social well-being are markedly collinear, a predictor that tracks one outcome measure will probably track them all. These points were illustrated by two researchers from George Mason University, Deborah Whetzel and Michael McDaniel. They assigned a value of 90 to all reported national IQs below 90 in the 2002 database. This arbitrary assumption was higher than the Wicherts and colleagues estimate, which was not available at the time that Whetzel and McDaniel did their analysis. All major trends in the 2002 data still held. I am virtually certain that the same thing would happen in the 2006 database, although I do not know of any such analysis.

There is a simple reason for the fact that correlations were obtained in spite of inaccurate data. Lynn and Vanhanen's results were driven by the sharp differences in both intelligence test scores and measures of social well-being between the European–North American–Northeast Asian (ENAMA) regions of the world and "the rest," largely sub-Saharan Africa and South Asia (SASA). The South America and the Middle East regions (SAME) generally fall somewhere between the other two regions, in terms of both intelligence test scores and indicators of well-being. However, substantial correlations, although lower than Lynn and Vanhanen reported, do hold within the developed countries, where the intelligence estimates are probably far more accurate.[195]

11.5.3. *A Much Closer Look: Rindermann's Analyses*

Lynn and Vanhanen rested their case largely on bivariate correlations between variables, which is a suspect procedure. They concluded that gross measures of educational accomplishment, such as the literacy rate or the number of people involved in tertiary education, were less important than intelligence as predictors of national well-being. A more detailed analysis of their own data, presented in Table 11.6, raises questions about this conclusion. The entries in Table 11.6 indicate the fraction of variance in the target variable (GNI per capita, life expectancy, or Democracy Index) that can be associated with various possible causal factors. For example, the first entry in the first row, .47, indicates that 47% of the variance in GNI per capita, across nations, can be statistically predicted from variations in the IQ estimate. That is impressive. The second entry in the first row, .07, modifies the impression considerably. It shows that after allowing for associations between IQ and GNI that can be predicted from rate of participation in tertiary education, only 7% of the variance in GNI is associated with IQ. The third entry in the row, .29, shows that 29% of the variance in GNI is associated with national differences in participation in tertiary education, after having allowed for differences in IQ.

Analyses such as those in Table 11.6 show the difficulty of interpreting bivariate correlations in situations where the variables involved are highly collinear. Suppose we regard participation in tertiary education as

(2010b) showed that Lynn and Meisenberg's techniques for selecting papers to cite were not related to measures of representativeness in the original research, and that they appeared to introduce a substantial bias toward underestimating the cognitive capacities of sub-Saharan populations.

195 Hunt & Wittmann, 2005.

Table 11.6. Squared correlations and partial correlations between target variables and IQ scores and education variables

Variable	IQ	IQ|Tertiary	Tertiary|IQ	IQ|Literacy	Literacy|IQ
GNI/capita	0.47	0.07	0.28	0.25	0.07
Life expect.	0.60	0.29	0.07	0.35	0.19
Democracy	0.32	0.01	0.25	0.11	0.09

Note: The calculations are based on the data presented in Lynn & Vanhanen, 2006, Table 6.1. GNI – gross national income; Life expect. – life expectancy at birth; Democracy – index of democratic institutions in a nation, developed by Vanhanen; Tertiary – fraction of population with some post-secondary education; Literacy – literacy rate.

an indicator of the general state of education in a country. One could argue that if the population as a whole has generally high intelligence the country will have a good school system, and as a result a high level of income per person. Or one could argue that because a country has a good school system the people will acquire high intelligence, and thus have high incomes. Or, as is more likely, there may be reciprocal influences between wealth, intelligence, and education.

We now turn to a study that dealt with such collinearities and ambiguities.

Heiner Rindermann, of the Otto-von-Guericke University in Germany, has carried out multivariate investigations of national cognitive skills, wealth, and well-being much further, and in a much more sophisticated way, than did Lynn and Vanhanen (or than I have done in my reanalysis of their data here.).[196] Lynn and Vanhanen paid relatively little attention to international assessments of educational data, such as the PISA studies, except to use them to validate their national intelligence estimates. (In general the correlations between the educational assessment data and the Lynn and Vanhanen intelligence estimates are in the .8–.9 range.) As Rindermann notes, researchers in intelligence and education use different words, but they all wind up generating tests that evaluate reasoning

and knowledge, albeit with somewhat different balances between the two.

The educational assessment data suffers from the disadvantage that it is restricted to children and adolescents, but it has several counterbalancing advantages. Compared to the intelligence data the educational samples are much larger and more representative of the countries involved. Where the samples appear to be unrepresentative, as in the case of differential participation rates by students across countries, statistics on the manner of unrepresentativeness are often available. These statistics can be used to make a revised estimate of a hypothetical national average. For example, if a country has low participation rates because it provides schools for only some of its children, the national estimate, based on the performance of schoolchildren, can be adjusted downward. Within a study, the same tests or tests that are "controllably different," as in the case of translations, are used in each country.

There is another important advantage to using educational rather than intelligence test data. In several countries comparable educational surveys have been carried out at different points in time. Longitudinal analysis can then be applied to determine what variables at time 1 best predict the state of a country at time 2. If the time period between evaluations is close to a generation (thirty years for humans), the best data for this prediction are the cognitive skills of school

196 Rindermann, 2007.

children at time 1, for they are the ones who will be running the society at time 2.

Rindermann first showed that there is a huge general factor for "national cognitive skill," calculated across countries. The Lynn and Vanhanen estimates load heavily on this factor, although they are not the best marker.[197] The centrality of this factor is amazing; the range of loadings is from .97 to 1.0! The reason that this is a bit surprising is that some of these tests were intended to cover special topics, such as reading or mathematics. On a cross-national basis, if the children read well they do math well (and vice versa).[198]

Rindermann then created a measure of national cognitive skill, based on the above analyses. He dropped the Lynn and Vanhanen data set from this analysis but, as the high factor loadings show, it could not have made much difference if it had been included.[199] On a regional basis Rindermann reconstructed, with much better data, the ENAMA-SASA-SAME groupings that Lynn and Vanhanen found. The lowest scores are found in sub-Saharan Africa. The only exception is Haiti in the Caribbean, where scores are also quite low. The two intermediate groups of scores are found in South Asia, the Middle East and North Africa, and in South America. The highest scores are found in northeast Asia, Europe, and North America.

Rindermann has reported a number of correlations between his cognitive skills index and indices of economic and political well-being. Some mirror the Lynn and Vanhanen data. For instance, the correlation with gross domestic product per capita (GDP/c) was .60, close to the Lynn-Vanhanen estimate. Other indicators show similar trends. The correlation with an index of economic freedom was .52, and with economic growth .44.

The correlation between the cognitive skills index and fertility (children per woman) was strongly negative, −.73. This is an important finding, because it may point the way to future changes in cognitive skills. As was pointed out in Chapter 9, there is a negative correlation between indices of intelligence and family size. Although family sizes are much larger in the developing than in the industrially developed countries, they are dropping as the developing nations become urbanized, probably because of many other social changes related to increasing socioeconomic opportunities for women. This may presage an increase in intelligence in the developing countries in coming generations. Only time will tell.

For those who like food for thought, the correlation between national cognitive skill and homicide rate was −.23, and the correlation between cognitive skill and the rate of solved homicide cases was .32. Smart populations produce moderately smart detectives.[200]

Because educational data was available over time, Rindermann was able to conduct causal analyses, in which he determined the extent to which a social or psychological variable measured at time 1 predicts social and psychological variables at time 2. His analysis relied on a technique called cross-lagged analysis, which made it possible to determine *standardized path coefficients*. These statistics can be interpreted as measuring the extent to which a raise of one standard deviation unit in a predicting variable will cause a raise, in standard deviation units, of a predicted variable. The analysis produced two interesting results.

The path coefficient between cognitive ability, measured in the 1960–70 period, and GDP/c, measured in 1998, was .29, which indicates that raising academic achievement by one deviation unit will "pay off" by

---

197 Rindermann, 2007, Table 1.

198 This does not mean that there are no variations in relative skill. Some countries are "tilted" toward high math scores or high language scores. See Wittmann, 2005. The same countries differ in level of performance, as defined by a mixture of mathematics, reading, and other scores. In a statistical analysis variations in level are much greater than variations in tilt.

199 The factor loading for the Lynn and Vanhanen estimates was .96. Rindermann's reason for dropping this data set was that it was a potpourri of measures taken at different times, and he wished to do longitudinal analyses.

200 Rindermann, 2008a, Figure 2.

increasing GDP/c by almost 30%, no small thing. Going the other way, the path coefficient from GDP/c in 1980 to cognitive ability in the 1990s was .21, indicating a feedback process. Investing in education does pay off in the future.[201] This conclusion has been strengthened by subsequent analyses, which showed that by far the best predictors of schoolchildren's cognitive competences are countries' general adult educational level, and the extent to which a country provides for early educational experiences, in preschool and kindergarten.[202]

A second set of path analyses focused on the relation between the national level of cognitive skill and political development.[203] Cognitive abilities measured in the 1960–70 period predicted levels of democratization, the rule of law, and political freedom in the 1990s. An interesting point was that in these analyses sheer level of education, as indexed by data on attendance at different levels, was generally as good a predictor as cognitive abilities, which could be considered a measure of educational accomplishment. Path coefficients were higher for the political than for the economic indicators. An increase of one standard deviation unit in cognitive abilities in the 1960s and 1970s was associated with a .71 deviation unit increase in the political freedom index in the 1990s. In this case there were no indications of reciprocal influence. Political freedom in the early period did not predict cognitive ability in the later period.

Dictators have a problem. In order to increase their nation's GDP/c they should invest in education. But if they do, it can come back to haunt them.

11.5.4. *Contrasting Lynn's Work and Rindermann's*

Because Lynn's work has been quoted widely by some authors, it is worth looking at the differences between the Lynn and Rindermann approaches.

Rindermann's work makes a compelling case that investment in education increases national cognitive skills, which in turn increase wealth, which allows for more investment in education. This leaves open the question of why some nations have gotten on the track toward success, and others have not.

Lynn and Vanhanen have no hesitation. The ENAMA-SASA-SAME grouping suggests to them an obvious correlation with race, especially since the lowest part of the SASA group is in sub-Saharan Africa.[204] They observe parallels with the within-country ordering of intelligence by racial/ethnic group: Asians, Whites, various mixed racial/ethnic groups, and then sub-Saharan Africans. They assign a major role to genetics, and also allow a role for nutrition, especially if children's malnutrition is extreme.

Rindermann's causal analysis is straightforward and believable. It accounts for a great deal of the variance in such variables as GDP/c, for the residual unexplained variance amounts to less than 20% of the total variance. Therefore, while you can always explain a finding by unmeasured variables, there is not much left to explain. I hope that future studies explore the effect of some physical environmental variables, such as nutrition, but this, presumably, will come.

Lynn's explanations cannot be ruled out, but he goes far beyond the data. To see this, let us consider some alternatives.

11.5.5. *How the International Differences Arose: Two "Just So" Stories*

Lynn and Vanhanen and Rindermann agree that cognitive skills vary across nations. Why? Lynn and Vanhanen, and Lynn in other writings,[205] have offered a distal explanation, which purports to explain how national differences arose in the genotype for intelligence. Their argument is that as people migrated northward away from early centers of civilization they encountered

201 Ibid., Figure 5.
202 Rindermann & Ceci, 2009.
203 Rindermann, 2008b.

204 Lynn & Vanhanen, 2006, Chapter 12.
205 Especially Lynn, 2006.

progressively harsher conditions due to cold and wide seasonal variations in the availability of food. Therefore, the selective pressure for high intelligence was stronger in the high northern latitudes. As a result the people in northern Europe and northeast Asia, and populations derived from them, such as the present North American and Australia–New Zealand populations, became smarter than those who had remained behind, in the more forgiving climate of the subtropics.

This sort of explanation can be interpreted as the regeneration of the justifications for European colonization. But an idea is not wrong just because the Victorians (and Herodotus!) thought it to be true. There have been attempts to fill out and modify Lynn's hypothesis. One pair of investigators has reported correlations between Lynn's IQ estimates and two graduate students' estimates of the skin colors of people in various countries. (The students had not been to the country in question.) Positive findings were interpreted as support for the hypothesis.[206] Another investigator, Sastsoi Kanazawa of the London School of Economics, has argued that Lynn is right in general, but that evolution was not due to the cold or seasonal change per se. It was due to the need to meet challenges that were not present in the evolutionary homeland from which mankind evolved, in the area occupied by present-day Ethiopia.[207]

Lynn supports his hypothesis by reference to group differences in brain size, estimated from studies of cranial capacity. Even if this data is accepted, the group differences in brain size and the correlations between brain size and intelligence are far too small to account for the large racial/ethnic differences in IQ scores. Besides, the fossil record indicates that human brain sizes have decreased over the past 20,000 years.[208] This coincides with the expansion of *Homo sapiens* into the high latitudes following the retreat of the glaciers. This is not in accord with Lynn's proposal that northern exposure, if you will, produced bigger brains.

Using the record of historical events, rather than modern test scores, Jared Diamond has proposed a quite different scenario.[209] He maintains that the problem-solving skills and general cultural knowledge of a people will be determined by the extent to which they are forced to confront other groups of people and exchange ideas with them. Prior to relatively modern times, geography posed substantial barriers to such exchanges, for pre-industrial groups found it difficult to move through unfamiliar ecologies.

To take one of Diamond's favorite examples, people who lived in the highlands of the island of New Guinea developed agriculture at about the same time it was developed in Mesopotamia. The New Guinea highlanders were isolated from the coast by harsh mountain and jungle conditions; Mesopotamia was at the hub of potential travel routes into China and India, Europe, and northern Africa. Except for agriculture, the New Guinea highlanders were stuck in the Stone Age until they were contacted in the 1930s. The development of agriculture in Mesopotamia was a major step in the history of civilization.

According to Diamond the European–northeast Asian peoples prospered intellectually because the major axis of the Eurasian land mass, East-West, facilitated communication, while the major axes of Africa and the Americas, North-South, presented major barriers to communication. The relevant communication took place over historic, not evolutionary, time. Diamond can be read as stressing social evolution of societies, not genetic evolution of individuals, as a major force in the development of intelligence.

We have two truly orthogonal explanations: the East-West one and the North-South one. Is there any evidence that can help us decide?

Personally, I am more impressed by Diamond's emphasis on the spread of ideas over

206 Templer & Arikawa, 2006.
207 Kanazawa, 2004, 2008.
208 Geary, 2005, p. 53.

209 Diamond, 1997.

historical time than by Lynn's ideas about presumed selective pressures on the genotype over evolutionary time. However, both Lynn's and Diamond's analyses are "just so" stories. Our present-day distribution of cognitive skills is the result of the unique history of humans on Earth. We can develop stories about how this distribution came to be. We can show that some are not in accord with the facts, but given only one history, over evolutionary or historic time, it is extremely unlikely that we will settle on one of several alternatives. What is the right one? We could answer this only by a careful analysis of the cognitive behavior of populations long since extinct. And this data we cannot have.

11.5.6. *Summing Up the Evidence for the Worldwide Distribution of Intelligence*

I have spent some time discussing Lynn and Vanhanen's work for two reasons. One is that their results have been widely publicized but, to my concern, too often accepted and too rarely carefully critiqued. The second one is that these findings are important.

Lynn and Vanhanen's critics have tended to reject their ideas out of hand, either because they see IQ scores as irrelevant outside of the industrial/post-industrial countries or because they are concerned about the weakness of many of the data points. Such criticisms miss the mark. IQ scores are not irrelevant as indicators of intelligence, in the conceptual sense, in the developing world; they are partially relevant. As Rindermann showed, IQ scores are so highly correlated with indices of educational achievement that, statistically, one can serve as a proxy for the other. Both are indicators of the extent to which a national population possesses the cognitive skills required in the post-industrial world. These indicators are important because the world is increasingly dominated by the developed countries, so the future of developing countries is tied to the extent that they can acquire the skills needed in post-industrial society.

Lynn and Vanhanen are investigating a question that deserves serious study.

Therefore, it is not surprising that they close both of their books with policy recommendations. They believe that genetic constrictions are so great that, although modest improvements may be made by improved nutrition, not very much can be done to improve human capital in the poorer nations. They are especially pessimistic about the sub-Saharan African nations. They say

> *The persistence of differences in intelligence between nations is inevitable, and so, too, will be the consequences: the persistence of national differences in wealth. Or, as St. John put it 2000 years ago, "poor you have always with you."*
> *Lynn and Vanhanen, 2006, p. 293*

Lynn and Vanhanen's conclusion is a good example of a mindset for defeat. We have a problem; it's hard to solve; let's regard it as unsolvable. Rindermann's analysis shows that they have badly undervalued the effects of investment in education. I, personally, agree with Diamond that the important thing is to have an exchange of ideas in a population – something that is related to but more than formal education. So I have a very different view.

Can we do something to improve the intelligence of the poorer, often desperately poorer, peoples of the world? I wrote this chapter the week that Barack Obama was inaugurated President of the United States. My question was answered by the signature slogan of his campaign:

> *Yes we can!*
> *Barack Obama, in many speeches during the 2008 US presidential campaign.*

Whether we actually will do anything to improve cognitive skills on an international scale is a policy decision, and as such beyond the scope of this book

11.6. Closing Comments on Group Differences in Intelligence

Intelligence does vary with demography.

As we age, our information-processing mechanisms deteriorate. The speed of mental processing slows, and our ability to control attention lessens. Until great age, though, these effects do not begin to match the beneficial effects of practice. Your fifty-five-year-old surgeon may not be as quick as a physician just out of medical school, but the experienced surgeon is likely to recognize a situation more rapidly than a neophyte, and to be much more efficient at dealing with it. Your fifty-five-year-old airplane pilot may not have the same capacity to control attention that he or she had thirty years ago, but the experienced pilot knows better what to attend to, and has a library of experiences that can be drawn on. Fluid intelligence, Gf, may be a dramatic thing to study in the laboratory, but in everyday life there is a great deal to be said for Gc. The quickest way to solve a problem is to recognize that you have seen it before and already know the answer.

These trends are important. The population is aging. Sheer economics dictates that we will have to utilize an older workforce. When life expectancies approach ninety, neither the individual nor the society can afford retirement at sixty. Designers of future workplaces must take account of the changing nature of cognition during the second half of life.

Men and women do not think alike; a statement that may be a revelation to psychologists but certainly will not surprise novelists. There is little, if any, average difference in general reasoning between men and women. In defiance to the novelists' intuitions, when it comes to general reasoning men are more variable than women.

Just as aging is a matter of degree, so is thinking like a man or a woman. Over and over again in this chapter I have used the word "tend." That is important. Women tend to rely more on verbal thinking, men tend to be better at spatial-visual reasoning. There is plenty of overlap. Nevertheless, I think that we will continue to see that most helicopter pilots are men.

Why these differences occur is still a topic of research. The brain size hypothesis put forward so strongly by Lynn and Rushton appears to me to be a nonstarter. Differences in brain structure and hormonal influence are far more likely causal factors. Given the influence of prenatal and neonatal hormone circulation upon brain development, these causes are probably intertwined. And then there are the social causes – differential experience and different values for social roles. These differences have their influence; and they have their reasons for being, both in the past and in today's society. My own belief is that individuals should be as free as possible to choose their social roles, within the limits of their own capacity, and that other people should respect those choices. At this point we are getting into the realm of social belief, rather than a discussion of the science of human intelligence, so I will say no more.

Suppose it were possible to take those cognitive skills that are required to "make it" in modern, post-industrial society and to assign every person in the world a number, reflecting how many of those skills he or she had. (If we had the ultimate IQ test, we could do this!) We would find that within countries some racial/ethnic groups had a lower distribution of numbers than other groups had. As in the case of male-female differences, there would be substantial overlap, although probably not as much as the overlap in the distribution of numbers between men and women. What would we find across countries, and more particularly, within the developed countries?

The northeast Asian and White ethnic groups would have almost equal numbers. Which group had the highest average would probably depend upon whether we weighed verbal skills more heavily than spatial-mathematical skills or vice versa. What is the best weighting? It depends upon whether you are looking for the next Einstein or the next Shakespeare.

African-derived groups, "Blacks" in a jargon that ignores the fact that there are Melanesian and Australian-Papuan groups that are every bit as dark as Africans but are genetically distant from them, would almost certainly tend (that word again) to have lower numbers on a test of skills required to make it in post-industrial society. Some of these skills are undoubtedly relevant to all societies, but we have little idea what the mix is. Genetically, the African-derived groups cluster differently from other groups, but the classification is fuzzy, especially when different racial/ethnic groups have been living close to each other for generations. Socially, the groups that have low scores are generally those groups that have the least contact with post-industrial society. This remark applies both to national groups and to segments of a national society that are segregated from each other, or from schooling and social opportunities, to any degree.

Are these racial/ethnic distinctions important? Yes, because to the extent that members of a group wish to participate in the industrial and post-industrial society, they have to have the skills that society utilizes. Are the distinctions inevitable? Some professors and some politicians have proclaimed, loudly, that they know the answer to this question. However, those people who are so certain seem to disagree rather vehemently about whether the answer is "yes" or "no." I do not expect them to agree with each other, any more than I expect that the Pope and Shiite Islam's Grand Ayatollahs will agree on the nature of God.

It could be that there are genetic constraints that make inequality of cognition across groups inevitable. This hypothesis can never be ruled out, for doing so would require proving the null hypothesis and, as any good statistics instructor will tell you, that is a logical impossibility. It is worth remembering that *no genes related to the difference in cognitive skills across the various racial and ethnic groups have ever been discovered*. The argument for genetic differences has been carried forward largely by circumstantial evidence. Of course, tomorrow afternoon genetic mechanisms produc-

ing racial and ethnic differences in intelligence might be discovered, but there have been a lot of investigations, and tomorrow has not come for quite some time now.

A number of social and environmental causes for racial/ethnic differences in intelligence have been proposed. Some refer to the physical environment: health, nutrition, and exposure to atmospheric toxins. Some refer to the social environment. These include constraints imposed by the general society, such as lack of adequate schools (particularly a problem in developing countries, but certainly a problem in the industrially developed ones) or discriminatory practices. In other cases the constraints are imposed by the group's own mores. Examples would be having more children than a family can raise effectively, differential discrimination within a group (think of fundamentalist Islam's view of women's education), and attitudes within a peer group toward short-term achievement as opposed to long-term achievement in education.

The causes of differences in cognition between old and young, men and women, and various racial/ethnic groups should be investigated. We have made legal and practical distinctions between these categories in the past, we do so now, and we probably will do so in the future. Retirement regulations, antidiscrimination policies, social support for mothers and their children, and different forms of affirmative action are all part of a rational society. Demographic differences in intelligence are relevant to these policies, regulations, and programs. It is best if science informs policy makers, so inquiry is appropriate. On the policy makers' side, scientists should not be restricted in their inquiries because the results might be inconvenient. On the scientist's side, the results must be fully and honestly reported, regardless of the scientists' personal beliefs about social policy.

CHAPTER 12

Summary and Prospectus

It's tough to make predictions, especially about the future.

– attributed to Yogi Berra,
American sports figure[1]

A colleague of mine once observed that the ending sections of all scientific discussions could be collapsed to a single word – *much*. Much has been learned and much remains to be learned. That is certainly true of intelligence. But let us be more specific.

12.1. A Summary

Scientific research on intelligence is just over a century old. There has been progress; it just has not been as rapid as we might have hoped. A great deal of this research has come in spurts. As in many other sciences, these spurts have occurred when technological or historic developments open up new sources of relevant data. In research on human intelligence that has happened three times. The development of group testing initiated by the Army Alpha examination in World War I showed that valid intelligence measures could be obtained without expensive one-on-one interviews. The result was an explosion of applications, and data, in both academic and industrial settings. In the 1930s the development of mathematical techniques for handling multivariate data made possible the evaluation of sophisticated psychometric models of human intelligence. The impetus of this development was magnified with the development of computers, which made computation-heavy methods of analysis possible. Since about 1985 we have been busy digesting data from a new source – the extensive neuroscientific measurements that are now possible, These include noninvasive techniques for looking directly at indicators of functioning in the normal brain. So what have we learned from all this?

Chapter 1 presented a view of intelligence as a concept, and as it is assessed by IQ and related tests. I argued, in agreement with several other authors (especially Robert Sternberg, but with echoes of

---

1 The quotation has also been attributed to the physicist and Nobel Prize winner Niels Bohr.

Raymond Cattell), that intelligence should be thought of as the collection of cognitive skills and knowledge required to achieve success in one's society. Some of these skills are common to all human societies, and some of them have varying degrees of relevance depending on the society. Our present cognitive tests evaluate some of the cognitive skills and knowledge needed in modern industrial and post-industrial societies. Without making any statement about the moral values involved, the practical fact is that these skills are important worldwide, for there are far more societies interested in becoming industrial or post-industrial cultures than there are developed societies that want to revert to farming and herding, let alone to being gleaners and hunter-gatherers.

Chapter 2 introduced the tests. My examples were certainly not exhaustive, but I think that they will give readers an idea of what the tests are like. In that discussion I argued strongly, and not for the only time, that the biggest restriction on intelligence testing has been an acceptance of intelligence as something that has to be demonstrated within the "Drop in from the Sky" test paradigm.

In Chapter 3 I presented an overview of the distinction between behavioral theories of intelligence and theories based on findings in the neurosciences. I concluded that there is room for both of them. Chapter 4 expanded on this by discussing the concepts of psychometric analysis and the models of intelligence that have been developed using psychometric tools. I made the (somewhat controversial) assumption that the theory you want depends upon what you want to do with it. If the goal is to understand how intelligence is derived from biological variables, then the g-VPR model is useful. If the goal is to understand how intelligence is used in society, then the g and three-stratum Gc-Gf models have much to recommend them. The two goals are equally legitimate and can be explored with equal scientific rigor.

Chapter 5 presented theories that are outside the psychometric mode. I concluded that, in spite of the publicity that it has generated, there is little empirical support for Howard Gardner's Multiple Intelligence theory. I take no stand on how useful it is as an inspiration for educators. Robert Sternberg's Theory of Successful Intelligence is rooted in empirical data, and has clear connections to the use of information about intelligence in society. Psychometric theories are silent on this point. While many of the individual studies in support of Sternberg's theory are, in my opinion, not as strong as they have been made out to be, the overall support cannot be disregarded. A special strength of this theory is that it can be expanded to evaluating behavior outside of the testing situation.

In that chapter I also shed a small tear for J. P. Das's PASS model of intelligence, which may not have received the attention, evaluation, and expansion that it should have. The reasons seem to me more historic and social than intellectual.

Chapter 6 discussed the relationship between behavioral measures of human information processing and intelligence, as defined by test scores. It was concluded that there are two major components of the information-processing underpinnings of intelligence: cognitive processing speed and individual differences in the functioning of the working memory–control of attention complex. I questioned whether it is useful to try to break down these relationships more finely. I think it is not; others may disagree.

Chapter 7 discussed the brain structures shown to be involved in intelligent action. It is clear that there is no "center of intelligence" in the brain. Intelligent behavior depends upon the functioning of a coordinated system involving many parts of the brain. Certain regions are more involved in cognitive behavior than others. The frontal lobe and parts of the parietal lobe are especially prominent in cognition. But the whole brain is needed. And yes, bigger-brained people are smarter, and smarter people have brains that function more efficiently than less-smart people. This is true in the literal sense of efficiency; more intelligent people show less brain metabolism, not more, than less intelligent people when both are presented with the same problem.

Chapter 8 discussed the very strong evidence for a genetic contribution to intelligence, from Quantitative Behavior Genetics, and the lack of evidence from Molecular Genetics that could identify the gene-intelligence link. This is a point where time will tell. We need more studies of the molecular genetic link. We do not need any more studies trying to tie down the value of heritability coefficients in the general population. It was important to determine that the heritability coefficient is not zero and that it is not one. Where does it fall in between? That number will vary over time and place.

Chapter 9 turned the argument around, by presenting evidence for a myriad of physical and social environmental variables that affect intelligence. These include atmospheric lead, how much alcohol your mother consumed when you were *in utero*, and how good and how extensive your schooling was. The point was made that intelligence develops with cognitive engagement; some people acquire wisdom as they go through life, others just have experiences.

Chapter 10 presented the benefits of intelligence, including its influence on educational achievement, social achievement, and such mundane things as income and occupation. Contrary to widespread beliefs, intelligence does not just predict academic success. It predicts workplace and academic success about equally well. The prediction is not perfect, but it is better than any other predictor we have today, most definitely including personality tests. It was also pointed out in this chapter that there is no support whatsoever for the idea that the very intelligent are social nerds, or that once you have an adequate supply of intelligence other personality traits become more important. Intelligent people, as indicated by test scores, tend to be successful people, and the more intelligence you have, the brighter your prospects.

Chapter 11 discussed group differences in intelligence. As we grow older we grow slower, in a literal sense, and have less control over the attention–working memory complex. That is the bad news. The good news is that older people know more. Elders may solve by memory a problem that the young have to work out for themselves. Recollection and analogy to previously solved problems are powerful aids in thinking.

There are differences in the ways that men and women think, but they lie much more along a verbal-spatial reasoning axis than in general intelligence. For some unknown reason, though, men are more variable in their general reasoning powers than women are.

With respect to racial/ethnic and national distinctions: yes, there are considerable differences between some groups in the possession of general cognitive skills, the *g* dimension of intelligence. These differences are related to the socioeconomic and educational achievements of group members, on both the national and international levels. While some environmental causes for group differences have been uncovered, their effects are insufficient to account for the observed differences between groups and nations. Arguments have been made assigning the causes to genetic differences, but no example of an actual genetic mechanism causing group differences has ever been found.

I closed Chapter 11 with a brief discussion of the problems involved in studying this topic in the context of understandably heated social concerns about the existence of, or implications of, racial and ethnic differences in intelligence.

That is where we have been. Now where are we going?

12.2. The Future

Yogi was right, predicting about the future is difficult. I will try anyway.

Science advances when one of three things happens. A scientific discovery may open up new sources of relevant data. Developments in solid-state, low-temperature physics led to today's imaging technology, which opened a huge new source of data for the neuroscientists. Or a new idea, perhaps imported from another field, may bring about a new way of looking at known facts. Darwin's Theory of Evolution, developed after studying finches, turtles, and beetles, has profoundly altered the way we think about differences in behavior between men and women. Then there is the third way to change. Sometimes a genius comes along, someone who arrives at a time when the old ideas are not quite working and who has the creativity and breadth of thought to put everything together. Newton, Darwin, and Einstein qualify, but there aren't that many other examples at their level of accomplishment.

There are two reasons for studying intelligence: to understand how individual differences in cognitive capability come about, and to understand what those differences mean in our society. The two purposes are similar in two ways. They are both legitimate scientific goals, and they both require some way of describing variations in intelligence.

I think that our present descriptions of intelligence are pretty good. After all, they are the culmination of over a century of careful thought. It turns out that if you want to look down from intelligence to the brain, the g-VPR theory may be best; if you want to think about how intelligence is used in society, the g model, some version of the three-stratum theory, or of Sternberg's Theory of Successful Intelligence may be most useful. This will depend upon the context in which the study is conducted. Note the difference. Understanding how the brain produces individual differences in cognition is a single goal, and a single description may be appropriate. Understanding how intelligence is used "in society" involves disparate goals for disparate situations, and different descriptions may be needed. I do not find this particularly bothersome. I do find Procrustean attempts to make one model fit all situations a bit annoying.

What about new sources of data? With respect to the brain-mind connection we have every reason to be optimistic. Advances in imaging, biochemistry, and molecular biology have and will continue to open up huge new fields of data for psychological inquiry. The biggest constraint on advances here may be the expense involved. The equipment and techniques are very expensive now, but that may change. One thing will not change. Studies of individual differences require lots of people, committing a lot of their time. Time is money.

What about new data on the social development and uses of intelligence? I am a bit optimistic here, even though spectacular new machinery like that used by neuroscientists is not on the horizon. There are two things that have to be done. First, we must break down the artificial boundary between the study of personality and the study of intelligence. In the world, the two work together. There are examples where this is already being done, notably in the work of Ackerman and in the major longitudinal studies, such as the Seattle Longitudinal Study and the Study of Mathematically Precocious Youth. I am optimistic that this sort of research will develop. But then comes the next issue.

We have to break out of the rigid paradigm of thinking of intelligence as something to be measured only in a formal testing session, the "Drop in from the Sky" paradigm. That paradigm has its uses, and it has had its day. We may be on the edge of a technological breakthrough that will allow us to do just this. In the modern world people leave a great many electronic tracks as they move about. Banking and credit companies know a great deal about people's movements and spending habits. Centralized medical records are already widespread in Europe, and the United States is moving toward creating such databases. Studies have already been reported in which people's movement through space was tracked by analyzing records of calls on cell phones.[2] Special electronic badges have been used to record nonverbal communication during social mixers and business meetings.[3] The resulting data banks contain a tremendous amount of information that, potentially,

2 Song et al., 2010.
3 Pentland, 2010.

could be used to construct models of how intelligence is developed and used in the world outside of both the laboratory and the testing paradigm. The result might be breakthroughs in our understanding of the social aspects of intelligence that will rival the breakthroughs achieved by the use of imaging technologies and genetics to understand the biological aspects of intelligence.

The use of central databases and tracking technologies raise serious issues about privacy and accountability. If society sees sufficient value in expanding our knowledge of how cognition is used in everyday life, then these problems can be solved. Will they be solved? That depends on how well those interested in the study of intelligence make their case.

Then there is that last way of advancing – finding the genius who puts it all together. What we need is that person who will bring his or her one-in-ten-million intelligence to bear on the problem. According to the latest *Digest of Educational Statistics*, approximately 700,000 people graduate from US four-year institutions annually. Let us double this to allow for geniuses outside the United States. We can expect the necessary genius to obtain a bachelor's degree sometime in the next ten to fifteen years. Then the trick will be to interest them in the Psychology of Intelligence.

I hope this book will help.

References

Abad, F. J., Colom, R., Juan-Espinosa, M., & Garcia, L. F. (2003) Intelligence differentiation in adult samples. *Intelligence*, 31 (2), 157–166.

Ackerman, P. L. (1986) Individual differences in information processing: An investigation of intellectual abilities and task performance during practice. *Intelligence*, 10, 101–139.

Ackerman, P. L. (1987) Individual differences in skill learning: An integration of psychometric and information processing perspectives. *Psychological Bulletin*, 102 (1), 3–27.

Ackerman, P. L. (1996) A theory of adult intellectual development: Personality, interests, and knowledge. *Intelligence*, 22 (2), 227–257.

Ackerman, P. L. (2000) Domain-specific knowledge as the "dark matter" of adult intelligence: Gf/Gc, personality, and interest correlates. *Journal of Gerontology: Psychological Sciences*, 55B, 69–84.

Ackerman, P. L., & Beier, M. E. (2001) Trait complexes, cognitive investment, and domain knowledge. In R. J. Sternberg & Elena L. Grigorenko (Eds.), *The psychology of abilities, competences, and expertise.* Cambridge: Cambridge University Press, pp. 1–30.

Ackerman, P. L., & Beier, M. E. (2006) Determinants of domain knowledge and independent study learning in an adult sample. *Journal of Educational Psychology*, 98 (2), 366–381.

Ackerman, P. L., Beier, M. E., & Boyle, M. O. (2002) Individual differences in working memory within a nomological network of cognitive and perceptual speed abilities. *Journal of Experimental Psychology: General*, 131 (3), 567–589.

Ackerman, P. L., Beier, M. E., Boyle, M. O. (2005) Working memory and intelligence: The same or different constructs? *Psychological Bulletin*, 131 (1), 30–60.

Ackerman, P. L., & Heggestad, E. D. (1997) Intelligence, personality, and interests: Evidence for overlapping traits. *Psychological Bulletin*, 121 (2), 219–245.

Ackerman, P. L., & Rolfhus, E. L. (1999) The locus of adult intelligence: Knowledge, abilities, and nonability traits. *Psychology and Aging*, 14 (2), 314–330.

Alarcon, M., Plomin, R., Fulker, D. W., Corley, R., & DeFries, J. C. (1999) Molarity, not modularity: Multivariate genetic analysis of specific cognitive abilities in parents and their 16-year-old children in the Colorado Adoption Project. *Cognitive Development*, 14 (1), 175–193.

Alfonso, V. C., Flanagan, D. C., & Radwan, S. (2005) The impact of the Cattell-Horn-Carroll theory on test development and interpretation of cognitive and academic abilities. In D. P.

Flanagan & P. L. Harrison (Eds.), *Contemporary intellectual assessment: Theories, tests, and issues*. New York: Guilford, pp. 185–202.

Allahyar, M., & Hunt, E. (2003) The assessment of spatial orientation using virtual reality techniques. *International Journal of Testing*, 3 (3), 263–275.

Amsel, E., Langer, R., & Loutzenhiser, L. (1991) Do lawyers reason differently from psychologists? A comparative design for studying expertise. In R. J. Sternberg & P. A. Frensch (Eds.), *Complex problem solving: Principles and mechanisms*. Hillsdale, NJ: Erlbaum, pp. 223–250.

Anastasi, A. (1956) Intelligence and family size. *Psychological Bulletin*, 53 (3), 187–209.

Anderson, D. R. (1998) Educational television is not an oxymoron. *Annals of the American Academy of Political and Social Sciences*, 557, 24–38.

Anderson, J. R. (1996) ACT: A simple theory of complex cognition. *American Psychologist*, 51 (4), 355–365.

Ando, J., Ono, Y., & Wright, M. J. (2001) Genetic structure of spatial and verbal working memory. *Behavior Genetics*, 31, 615–624.

Ankney, C. D. (1992) Sex differences in brain size: The mismeasure of women too? *Intelligence*, 16 (3–4), 329–336.

Arija, V., Esparo, G., Fernandez-Ballart, J., Murphy, M. M., Wachs, T. D., & McCabe, G. (2001) Relation of maternal intelligence and schooling to offspring nutritional intake. *International Journal of Behavioral Development*, 25 (5), 444–449.

Ashton, M. C., & Lee, K. (2005) Problems with the method of correlated vectors. *Intelligence*, 33 (4), 431–434.

Atkinson, R. C. (2005) College admissions and the SAT: A personal perspective. *Observer (Magazine of the Association for Psychological Science)*, 18 (5), 15–22.

Baaré, W. E. C., Hulshoff Pol, H. E., Boomsma, D. I., Posthuma, D., Geus, deE. J. C., Schnack, H. G., et al. (2001) Quantitative genetic modeling of human brain morphology variation. *Cerebral Cortex*, 11, 816–824.

Baddeley, A. D. (1968) A three-minute reasoning test based on grammatical transformation. *Psychonomic Science*, 10, 341–342.

Baddeley, A. D. (1986) *Working Memory*. Oxford: Oxford University Press.

Baddeley, A. D., & Hitch, G. (1974) Working memory. In G. Bower (Ed.), *Recent advances in learning and motivation (vol. 8)*. New York: Academic Press, pp. 47–90.

Baghurst, P. A., McMichael, A. J., Wigg, N. R., Vimpani, G. V., et al. (1992) Environmental exposure to lead and children's intelligence at the age of seven years. *New England Journal of Medicine*, 327 (18), 1279–1284.

Balter, M. (2006) Bruce Lahn profile: Links between brain genes, evolution, and cognition challenged. *Science*, 314 (22 December), 1872.

Baltes, P. B., & Smith, J. (1990) Towards a psychology of wisdom and its ontogenesis. In R. J. Sternberg (Ed.), *Wisdom: Its origins, nature, and development*. Cambridge: Cambridge University Press, pp. 87–120.

Baltes, P. B., & Staudinger, U. M. (2000) Wisdom. *American Psychologist*, 55 (1), 122–136.

Bamshad, M., Wooding, S., Salisbury, B. A., & Stephens, J. C. (2004) Deconstructing the relationship between genetics and race. *Nature Reviews: Genetics*, 5 (August), 598–604.

Barnett, W. S. (1998) Long-term cognitive and academic effects of early childhood education of children in poverty. *Preventive Medicine: An International Journal Devoted to Practice and Theory*, 27 (2), 204–207.

Bar-On, R., Tranel, D., Denburg, N. L., & Bechara, A. (2003) Exploring the neurological substrate of emotional and social intelligence. *Brain: A Journal of Neurology*, 126 (8), 1790–1800.

Bartlett, J. (1980) *Familiar Quotations* (15th edition, edited by E. Beck). Boston: Little Brown.

Batty, G. D., Der, G., Macintyre, S., & Deary, I. J. (2006) Does IQ explain socioeconomic inequalities in health? Evidence from a population based cohort study in the west of Scotland. *British Medical Journal*, 332 (7541), 1–5.

Bayless, S., & Stevenson, J. (2007) Executive functions in school-age children born very prematurely. *Early Human Development*, 84 (4), 247–254.

Bayley, N. (1968) Behavioral correlates of mental growth: Birth to 36 years. *American Psychologist*, 23 (1), 1–17.

Bayley, N. (2005) *Bayley Scales of Infant and Toddler Development* (3rd edition). San Antonio, TX: Harcourt Assessment.

Beaujean, A. (2005) Heritability of cognitive abilities as measured by mental chronometric tasks: A meta-analysis. *Intelligence*, 33 (2), 187–201.

Becker, J. B., Berkley, K. J., Geary, N., Hampson, E., Herman, J. P., & Young, E. (Eds.) (2008)

Sex differences in the brain: From genes to behavior. Oxford: Oxford University Press.

Beer, J. S., Shimamura, A. P., & Knight, R. T. (2004) Frontal lobe contributions to executive control of cognitive and social behavior. In M. S. Gazzaniga (Ed), *The cognitive neurosciences* (3rd ed.). Cambridge, MA: MIT Press, pp. 1091–1104.

Benbow, C. P., Lubinski, D., Shea, D. L., & Eftekhari-Sanjani, H. (2000) Sex differences in mathematical reasoning: Ability at age 13. *Psychological Science*, 11 (6), 474–480.

Benbow, C. P., & Stanley, J. C. (1996) Inequity in equity: How "equity" can lead to inequity for high-potential students. *Psychology, Public Policy, and Law*, 2 (2), 249–292.

Berenbaum, S. A., & Resnick, S. (2007) The seed of career choice: Prenatal sex hormone effects. In S. I. Ceci & W. M. Williams (Eds.), *Why aren't there more women in science: Top researchers debate the evidence*. Washington, DC: American Psychological Association, 147–157.

Berg C., Hertzog, C., & Hunt, E. (1982) Age differences in the speed of mental rotation. *Developmental Psychology*, 18 (1), 95–107.

Berg, L. M. (2007) Socioeconomic factors and substandard parenting. *Social Service Review*, 81 (3), 485–522.

Bethge, H.-J., Carlson, J. S., & Wiedl, K. H. (1982) The effect of dynamic assessment procedures on Raven Matrices performance, visual search behavior, test anxiety, and test orientation. *Intelligence*, 6 (1), 89–97.

Binet, A., & Simon, T. (1905) The development of intelligence in children. *L'Annee Psychologique*, 11, 163–191.

Birnbaum, A. (1968) Some latent trait models and their use in inferring an examinee's ability. In F. M. Lord & M. R. Novick, *Statistical theories of mental test scores*. Reading, MA: Addison-Wesley, pp. 397–479.

Bittner, A. C., Carter, R. C., Kennedy, R. S., & Harveson, M. M. (1986) Performance evaluation tests for environmental research (PETER): Evaluation of 114 measures. *Perceptual and Motor Skills*, 63 (2, pt. 2), 683–708.

Bjerkedal, T., Kristensen, P., Skjeret, G. A., & Brevik, J. L. (2007) Intelligence test scores and birth order among young Norwegian men (conscripts) analyzed within and between families. *Intelligence*, 35 (5), 503–514.

Black, P., Harrison, G., Ley, C., Marshall, B., & Wiliam, D. (2003) *Assessment for learning*. New York: Open University Press (McGraw-Hill).

Black, P., & Wiliam, D. (1998) Assessment and classroom learning. *Assessment in Education*, 5 (1), 7–17.

Blackwell, D. L., & Lichter, D. T. (2000) Mate selection among married and cohabiting couples. *Journal of Family Issues*, 21 (3), 275–302.

Blair, C. (2006) How similar are fluid cognition and general intelligence? A developmental neuroscience perspective on fluid cognition as an aspect of human cognitive ability. *Behavioral and Brain Sciences*, 29 (2), 109–125.

Blair, C., Gramson, D., Thorne, S., & Baker, D. (2005) Rising mean IQ: Cognitive demand of mathematics education for young children, population exposure to formal schooling, and the neurobiology of the prefrontal cortex. *Intelligence*, 33 (1), 93–106.

Bledsoe, C., Houle, R., & Sow, P. (2007) High fertility Gambians in low fertility Spain: The dynamics of child accumulation across transnational space. *Demographic Research*, 16, Article 12.

Blinkhorn, S. (2005) A gender bender. *Nature*, 438 (3 November), 31–32.

Boardman, D. (1990) Graphicacy revisited: Mapping abilities and gender differences. *Educational Review*, 42 (1), 57–64.

Bollen, K. A. (1994) *Testing structural equation models*. Newbury Park, CA: Sage.

Boomsma, D., Busjahn, A., & Peltonen, L. (2002) Classical twin studies and beyond. *Nature Reviews Genetics*, 3, 872–882.

Boring, E. G. (1923) Intelligence as the tests test it. *New Republic*, 35 (June 6), 35–37.

Born, M. Ph., & Lynn, R. (1994) Sex differences on the Dutch WISC–R: A comparison with the USA and Scotland. *Educational Psychology*, 14 (2), 249–254.

Bornkessel, I. D., Fiebach, C. J., & Friederici, A. D. (2004) On the cost of syntactic ambiguity in human language comprehension: An individual differences approach. *Cognitive Brain Research*, 21 (1), 11–21.

Bouchard, T. J., Jr. (1997) IQ similarities in twins reared apart: Findings and responses to critics. In R. J. Sternberg & E. Grigorenko (Eds.), *Intelligence, heredity, and environment*. Cambridge: Cambridge University Press, pp. 126–160.

Bouchard, T. J., Jr. (1999) Genes, environment, and personality. In S. J. Ceci & W. M. Williams (Eds.), *The nature-nurture debate:*

The essential readings. Malden, MA: Blackwell, pp. 97–103.

Bouchard, T. J., Jr. (2009). Strong inference: A strategy for advancing psychological science. In K. McCartney & R. Weinberg (Eds.), *Experience and development: A festschrift in honor of Sandra Wood Scarr*. London: Taylor and Francis, pp. 39–59.

Bowen, W. G., & Bok, D. (1998) *The shape of the river: Long-term consequences of considering race in college and university admissions*. Princeton, NJ: Princeton University Press.

Bowley, G. (2006) Out of his league. When Larry Summers got to Harvard he saw lazy, leftish professors inflating grades in what looked like an outdated Yugoslav workers' co-operative. The faculty saw a bumptious, ill-educated boor hijacking their university. Graham Bowley looks at why Harvard's president had to go. *Financial Times*, (13 May 2006), p. 19.

Bradley, R. H. (1993) Children's home environments, health, behavior, and intervention efforts: A review using the HOME Inventory as a marker measure. *Genetic, Social, and General Psychology Monographs*, 119 (4), 437–490.

Bransford, J. D., Brown, A. L., & Cocking, R. R. (Eds.) (1999) *How people learn: Brain, mind, experience and school*. Washington, DC: National Academy Press.

Brim, O. G., Jr. (1965) American attitudes toward intelligence tests. *American Psychologist*, 20 (2) (February 1965), 125–130.

Broadhurst, C. L., Cunnane, S. C., & Crawford, M. A. (1998) Rift valley lake fish and shellfish provided brain-specific nutrition for early Homo. *British Journal of Nutrition*, 79 (1), 3–21.

Brody, L. C., & Blackburn, C. C. (1996) Nurturing exceptional talent: SET as a legacy of SMPY. In C. P. Benbow & D. Lubinski (Eds.), *Intellectual talent: Psychometric and social issues*. Baltimore: Johns Hopkins University Press, pp. 246–267.

Brody, N. (1992) *Intelligence* (2nd ed.) New York: Academic Press.

Brody, N. (2003) Construct validation of the Sternberg Triarchic Abilities Test: Comment and reanalysis. *Intelligence*, 31 (4), 319–329.

Brody, N. (2004) What cognitive intelligence is and what emotional intelligence is not. *Psychological Inquiry*, 15 (3), 234–238.

Brody, N. (2006) Geocentric theory: A valid alternative to Gardner's theory of multiple intelligences. In J. A. Schaler (Ed.), *Howard Gardner under fire: The rebel psychologist faces his critics*. Chicago: Open Court, pp. 73–94.

Brokaw, T. (1998) *The greatest generation*. New York: Random House.

Bronfenbrenner, U., & Ceci, S. J. (1994) Nature-nurture reconceptualized in developmental perspective: A bioecological model. *Psychological Review*, 101 (4), 566–586.

Bronfenbrenner, U., McClelland, P., Wethington, E., Moen, P., & Ceci, S. J. (1996) *The state of Americans*. New York: Free Press.

Brothers, J. (1981) Large versus small families. *Good Housekeeping* (February).

Brugman, G. M. (2006) Wisdom and aging. In J. E. Birren & K. W. Schaie (Eds.), *Handbook of the psychology of aging* (6th edition). Burlington, MA: Elsevier, pp. 445–476.

Brunner, M., Krauss, S., & Kunter, M. (2008) Gender difference in mathematics: Does the story need to be rewritten? *Intelligence*, 36 (5), 401–421.

Burden, M. J., Jacobson, S. W., Sokol, R. J., & Jacobson, J. L. (2005) Effects of prenatal alcohol exposure on attention and working memory at 7.5 years of age. *Alcoholism: Clinical and Experimental Research*, 29 (3), 443–452.

Burns, N. R., & Nettlebeck, T. J. (2003) Inspection time in the structure of cognitive abilities: Where does it fit? *Intelligence*, 31 (3), 237–255.

Burton, L., & Fogarty, G. J. (2003) The factor structure of visual imagery and spatial ability. *Intelligence*, 31 (3), 289–318.

Butterworth, B. (2006) Mathematical expertise. In K. A. Ericsson, N. Charness, P. J. Feltovich, & R. R. Hoffman (Eds.), *The Cambridge handbook of expertise and expert performance*. Cambridge: Cambridge University Press, 553–568.

Cabeza, R., & Nyberg, L. (2000) Imaging cognition II: An empirical review of 275 PET and fMRI studies. *Journal of Cognitive Neuroscience*, 12 (1), 1–47.

Campbell, D. T. (1975) On the conflicts between biological and social evolution and between psychology and moral tradition. *American Psychologist*, 30 (12), 1103–1126.

Campbell, F. A., Pungello, E. P., Miller-Johnson, S., Burchinal, M., & Ramey, C. T. (2001) The development of cognitive and academic abilities: Growth curves from an early childhood educational experiment. *Developmental Psychology*, 37 (2), 231–242.

Campbell, J. P., & Knapp, D. (Eds.), (2001) *Exploring the limits in personnel selection and classification*. Mahwah, NJ: Erlbaum.

Caplan, D., Waters, G., & Alpert, N. (2003) Effects of age and speed of processing on rCBF correlates of syntactic processing in sentence comprehension. *Human Brain Mapping*, 19 (2), 112–231.

Caporael, L. R. (1976) Ergotism: The satan loosed in Salem? *Science*, 192 (4234; 2 April), 21–26.

Capron, C., & Duyme, M. (1989) Assessment of effects of socio-economic status on IQ in a full cross-fostering study. *Nature*, 340 (623), 552–554.

Capron, C., & Duyme, M. (1996) Effect of socio-economic status of biological and adoptive parents on WISC-R subtest scores of their French adopted children. *Intelligence*, 22 (3), 259–276.

Carlson, J. S., & Wiedl, K. H. (1992) Principles of dynamic testing: The application of a specific model. *Learning and Individual Differences*, 4, 153–166.

Carpenter, P. A., Just, M. A., & Shell, P. (1990) What one intelligence test measures: A theoretical account of processing in the Raven Progressive Matrix Test. *Psychological Review*, 97 (3), 404–431.

Carroll, J. B. (1993) *Human cognitive abilities*. Cambridge: Cambridge University Press.

Carroll, J. B. (1995) Reflections on Stephen Jay Gould's *The Mismeasure of Man* (1981): A retrospective review. *Intelligence*, 21, 121–134.

Casey, M. B., Nuttall, R. I., Pezaris, E., & Benbow, C. P. (1995) The influence of spatial ability on gender differences in mathematics college entrance test scores across diverse samples. *Developmental Psychology*, 31, 697–705.

Cattell, R. B. (1940) Effects of human fertility trends upon the distribution of intelligence and culture. In *Intelligence in nature and nurture: Thirty ninth yearbook of the national society for the study of education, Part I*. Bloomington, IL: Society for the Study of Education, pp. 221–233.

Cattell, R. B. (1957) *Personality and motivation: Structure and measurement*. Yonkers-on-Hudson, NY: World Book Co.

Cattell, R. B. (1971) *Abilities: Their structure, growth, and action*. Boston: Houghton Mifflin.

Cattell, R. B. (1987) *Intelligence: Its structure, growth, and action*. New York: North-Holland.

Cavallo, A., el-Abbadi, H., & Heeb, R. (1998) The hidden gender restriction: The need for proper controls when testing for racial discrimination. In B. Devlin, S. E. Fienberg, D. P. Resnick, & K. Roeder (Eds.), *Intelligence, genes, and success: Scientists respond to The Bell Curve*. New York: Springer-Verlag, pp. 193–214.

Cawley, J., Conneeley, K., Heckman, J., & Vytlactil, E. (1997) Cognitive ability, wages, and meritocracy. In B. Devlin, S. Fienberg, D. Resnick, & K. Roeder (Eds.), *Intelligence, genes, and success: Scientists respond to The Bell Curve*. New York: Springer-Verlag, pp. 179–192.

Ceci, S. J. (1990) *On intelligence . . . more or less: A bio-ecological treatment on intellectual development*. Englewood Cliffs, NJ: Prentice-Hall.

Ceci, S. J., & Liker, J. (1986) A day at the races: A study of IQ, expertise, and cognitive complexity. *Journal of Experimental Psychology: General*, 115, 255–266.

Ceci, S. J., & Liker, J. (1987) A day at the races: A study of IQ, expertise, and cognitive complexity. *Journal of Experimental Psychology: General*, 116, 90.

Ceci, S. J., & Papierno, P. B. (2005) The rhetoric and reality of gap closing: When the "have nots" gain but the "haves" gain even more. *American Psychologist*, 60, 149–160.

Ceci, S. J., & Williams, W. M. (1997) Schooling, intelligence, and income. *American Psychologist*, 52 (10), 1051–1058.

Ceci, S. J., & Williams, W. M. (Eds.) (2007) *Why aren't there more women in science: Top researchers debate the evidence*. Washington, DC: American Psychological Association.

Cerella, J. (1985) Information processing rates in the elderly. *Psychological Bulletin*, 98, 67–93.

Cerella, J. (1990) Ageing and information-processing rate. In J. Birren & K. Schaie (Eds.), *Handbook of the psychology of aging* (third edition). New York: Academic Press, pp. 201–222.

Chabris, C. F. (1999) Prelude or requiem for the 'Mozart Effect'. *Nature*, 400 (26 August), 826–827.

Chamorro-Premuzic, T., Furnham, A., & Ackerman, P. L. (2006) Incremental validity of the typical intellectual engagement scale as a predictor of different academic performance measures. *Journal of Personality Assessment*, 87 (3), 261–268.

Chen, J.-Q., & Gardner, H. (2005) Assessment based on multiple-intelligences theory. In D. P. Flanagan & P. L. Harrison (Eds.), *Contemporary intellectual assessment: Theories, tests, and issues*. New York: Guilford, pp. 77–102.

Chiodo, L. M., Covington, C., Sokol, R. J., Hannigan, J. H., Jannise, J., Ager, J., Greenwald, M., & Delaney-Black, V. (2007) Blood lead levels and specific attention effects in young children. *Neurotoxicology and Teratology*, 29 (5), 538–546.

Choi, J., & Silverman, I. (2003) Processes underlying sex differences in route-learning strategies in children and adolescents. *Personality and Individual Differences*, 34 (7), 1153–1166.

Chorney, M. J., Chorney, K., Seese, N., Owen, M. J., Daniels, J., McGuffin, P., Thompson, L. A., Detterman, D. K., Benbow, C., Lubinski, D., Eley, T., & Plomin, R. (1998) A quantitative trait locus associated with cognitive ability in children. *Psychological Science*, 19 (3), 159–166.

Church, A. T., & Katigbak, M. S. (1991) Home environment, nutritional status, and maternal intelligence as determinants of intellectual development in rural Philippine preschool children. *Intelligence*, 15 (1), 49–78.

Clark, M. J., & Grandy, J. (1984) Sex differences in the academic performance of scholastic aptitude test takers. College Board Report 84–8. New York: College Entrance Examination Board.

Clarke, J., & Haughton, H. (1975) A study of intellectual impairment and recovery rates in heavy drinkers in Ireland. *British Journal of Psychiatry*, 126, 178–184.

Cohen, J. (1988) *Statistical power analysis for the behavioral sciences* (2nd edition). Hillsdale, NJ: Erlbaum.

Cole, M. (2005) Cross-cultural and historical perspectives on the developmental consequences of education. *Human Development*, 48, 195–216.

Cole, M., Gay, J., Glick, J., & Sharp, D. W. (1971) *The cultural context of learning and thinking: An exploration of experimental anthropology*. New York: Basic Books.

Collins, W. A., Maccoby, E. E., Steinberg, L., Hetherington, E. M., & Bornstein, M. H. (2000) Contemporary research on parenting: The case for nature and nurture. *American Psychologist*, 55 (2), 218–232.

Colom, R., Abad, F. J., Garcia, L. F., & Juan-Espinosa, M. (2002) Education, Wechsler's Full Scale IQ, and g. *Intelligence*, 30 (5), 449–462.

Colom R., Abad F.J., Quiroga, M-A., Shih, P. C., & Flores-Mendoza, C. (2008) Working memory and intelligence are highly related constructs, but why? *Intelligence*, 36 (6), 584–606.

Colom, R., Abad, F. J., Rebollo, I., & Shih, P. C. (2005) Memory span and general intelligence: A latent variable approach. *Intelligence*, 33 (6), 623–642.

Colom, R., Aluja-Fabregat, A., & Garcia-Lopez, O. (2002) Tendencias de emparejamiento selectivo en inteligencia, dureza de character, extraversion e inestabilidad emocional. *Psychothemia*, 14 (1), 154–158.

Colom, R., Escorial, S., & Rebollo, I. (2004) Sex differences on the progressive matrices are influenced by sex differences on spatial ability. *Personality and Individual Differences*, 37 (6), 1289–1293.

Colom, R., Haier, R. J., Head, K., Álvarez-Linera, J., Quiroga, M-A., Shih, P. C., & Jung, R. E. (2009) Gray matter correlates of fluid, crystallized, and spatial intelligence: Testing the P-Fit model. *Intelligence*, 37 (2), 124–135.

Colom, R., Juan-Espinosa, M., Abad, F., & Garcia, L. F. (2000) Negligible sex differences in general intelligence. *Intelligence*, 28 (1), 57–68.

Colom, R., Jung, R. E., & Haier, R. J. (2006) Finding the g-factor in brain structure using the method of correlated vectors. *Intelligence*, 34 (6), 561–570.

Colom, R., & Lynn, R. (2004) Testing the developmental theory of sex differences in intelligence on 12–18 year olds. *Personality and Individual Differences*, 36 (1), 75–82.

Colom, R., Rebollo, I., Palacios, A., Juan-Espinosa, M., & Kyllonen, P. C. (2004) Working memory is (almost) perfectly predicted by g. *Intelligence*, 32 (3), 277–296.

Committee on Prospering in the Global Economy: An Agenda for American Science and Technology. (2007) *Rising above the gathering storm: Energizing and employing America for a brighter economic future*. Washington, DC: National Academies Press.

Connor, P. D., Sampson, P. D., Bookstein, F. I., Barr, H. M., & Streissguth, A. P. (2001) Direct and indirect effects of prenatal alcohol damage on executive function. *Developmental Neuropsychology*, 18 (3), 331–354.

Conway, A. R. A. (2005) Cognitive mechanisms underlying intelligence: A defense of a reductionist approach. In O. Wilhelm & R. W. Engle (Eds.), *Handbook of understanding and measuring intelligence*. Thousand Oaks, CA: Sage, pp. 47–60.

Cook, P. J. & Ludwig, J. (1998) The burden of acting black: Do black adolescents disparage academic achievement? In C. Jencks & P. Meredith (Eds.), *The black-white test score gap*. Washington, DC: Brookings, pp. 375–400.

Cooke, A., Grossman, M., DeVita, C., Gonzalez-Atavales, J., Moore, P., Chen, W., Gee, J., & Detre, J. (2006) Large scale network for sentence processing. *Brain and Language*, 96 (1), 14–36.

Coon, H., Fulker, D. W., DeFries, J. C., & Plomin, R. (1990) Home environment and cognitive ability of 7-year-old children in the Colorado Adoption Project: Genetic and environmental etiologies. *Developmental Psychology*, 26 (3), 459–468.

Corwyn, R. F., & Bradley, R. H. (2008) The panethnic Asian label and predictors of eighth-grade student achievement. *School Psychology Quarterly*, 23 (1), 90–106.

Counter, S. A., Buchanan, L. H., & Ortega, F. (2005) Neurocognitive impairment in lead-exposed children of Andean lead-glazing workers. *Journal of Occupational Environmental Medicine*, 47 (3), 306–312.

Court, H. (1983) "Sex differences in performance on Raven's Progressive Matrices": A review. *Alberta Journal of Educational Research*, 29 (1), 54–74.

Coutinho, M. J. & Oswald, D. P. (2005) State variation in gender disproportionality in special education: Findings and recommendations. *Remedial and Special Education*, 26 (1), 7–15.

Cowley, J., Connelley, K., Heckman, J., & Vytlacil, E. (1998) Cognitive ability, wages, and meritocracy. In B. Devlin, S. E. Fienberg, D. P. Resnick, & K. Roeder (Eds.), *Intelligence, genes, and success: Scientists respond to The Bell Curve*. New York: Springer-Verlag, 179–192.

Coyle, T. R., & Pillow, D. R. (2008) SAT and ACT predict college GPA after removing *g*. *Intelligence*, 36 (6), 719–729.

Credé, M., & Kuncel, N. R. (2008) Study habits, skills, and attitudes: The third pillar supporting collegiate academic performance. *Perspectives on Psychological Science*, 3 (6), 425–453.

Cree, E. H. (Michael Levien, editor) (1982) *Naval Surgeon*. New York: Dutton.

Cronbach, L. J. (1957) The two disciplines of scientific psychology. *American Psychologist*, 12, 671–684.

Cronbach, L. J. (1996) Acceleration among the Terman males: Correlates in midlife and after. In C. P. Benbow & D. J. Lubinski (Eds.), *Intellectual talent: Psychometric and social issues*. Baltimore, MD: Johns Hopkins University Press, 179–191.

Cronbach, L. J., & Snow, R. E. (1977) *Aptitudes and instructional methods: A handbook for research on interactions*. New York: Irvington.

Cullen, M. J., Hardison, C. M., & Sackett, P. R. (2004) Using SAT-grade and ability-job performance relationships to test predictions derived from stereotype threat theory. *Journal of Applied Psychology*, 89 (2), 220–230.

Dai, X., Ryan, J. J., Paolo, A. M., & Harrington, R. G. (1991) Sex differences on the Wechsler Adult Intelligence Scale-Revised for China. *Psychological Assessment*, 32 (2), 282–284.

Damasio, A. R. (1994) *Descartes' error: Emotion, reason, and the human brain*. New York: Grosset/Putman.

Damasio, A. R. (1998) Emotion in the perspective of an integrated nervous systems. *Brain Research Reviews*, 26, 83–86.

Damasio, H., Grabowski, T., Randall, F., Galaburda, A. M., & Damasio, A. R. (1994) The return of Phineas Gage: Clues about the brain from the skull of a famous patient. *Science*, 264 (20 May), 1102–1104.

Daneman, M., & Carpenter, P. A. (1980) Individual differences in working memory and reading. *Journal of Verbal Learning and Verbal Behavior*, 19 (4), 450–466.

Daneman, M., & Carpenter, P. A. (1983) Individual differences in integrating information between and within sentences. *Journal of Experimental Psychology: Learning, Memory, and Cognition*, 9, 561–584.

Daneman, M., & Merikle, P. M. (1996) Working memory and language comprehension: A meta-analysis. *Psychonomic Bulletin, and Review*, 3 (4), 422–483.

Das, J. P., Naglieri, J. A., & Kirby, J. R. (1994) *Assessment of cognitive processes: The PASS theory of intelligence*. Boston: Allyn and Bacon.

Deary, I. J. (1994) Sensory discrimination and intelligence: Postmortem or resurrection? *American Journal of Psychology*, 107 (1), 95–115.

Deary, I. J. (2000) *Looking down on human intelligence: From psychometrics to the brain*. Oxford: Oxford University Press.

Deary, I. J., Batty, G., & Gale, R. (2008) Bright children become enlightened adults. *Intelligence*, 19 (1), 1–6.

Deary, I. J., & Der, G. (2005) Reaction time, age, and cognitive ability: Longitudinal findings from age 16 to 63 years in representative population samples. *Aging, Neuropsychology, and Cognition*, 12, 187–215.

Deary, I. J., Der, G., & Shenkin, S. D. (2005) Does mother's IQ explain the association between birth weight and cognitive ability in childhood? *Intelligence*, 33 (5), 445–454.

Deary, I. J., & Egan, V., Gibson, G. J., Austin, E. J., Brand, C. R., & Kellaghan, T. (1996) Intelligence and the differentiation hypothesis. *Intelligence*, 23 (2), 105–132.

Deary, I. J., Ferguson, K. J., Bastin, M. E., Barrow, G. W. S., Reid, L. M., Seckl, J. R., Wardlaw,

J. M., & MacLullich, A. M. J. (2007) Skull size and intelligence, and King Robert Bruce's IQ. *Intelligence*, 35 (6), 519–528.

Deary, I. J., Irwing, P., Der, G., & Bates, T. (2007) Brother-sister differences in the g factor in intelligence: Analysis of full, opposite-sex siblings from the NLSY 1979. *Intelligence*, 35 (5), 451–456.

Deary, I. J., Stough, C. (1996) Intelligence and inspection time: Achievements, prospects, and problems. *American Psychologist*, 51 (6), 599–608.

Deary, I. J., Strand, S., Smith, P., & Fernandes, C. (2007) Intelligence and educational achievement. *Intelligence*, 35 (1), 13–21.

Deary, I. J., Whalley, L. J., Lemmon, H., Crawford, J. R., & Starr, J. M. (2000) The stability of individual differences in mental ability from childhood to old age: Follow-up of the 1932 Scottish Mental Survey. *Intelligence*, 28 (1), 49–55.

deFrias, C. M., Lovden, M., Lindenberger, U., & Nisson, L.-G. (2007) Revisiting the dedifferentiation hypothesis with longitudinal multicohort data. *Intelligence*, 35, 381–392.

Demetriou, A. (2002) The development of mental processing: Efficiency, working memory and thinking. *Monographs of the Society for Research in Child Development*, 67 (1), vii–154.

Demetriou, A., Kui, Z. X., Spanoudis, G., Christou, C., Kyriakides, L., & Platsidou, M. (2005) The architecture, dynamics, and development of mental processing: Greek, Chinese, or Universal? *Intelligence*, 33 (2), 109–141.

Der, G., & Deary, I. J. (2006) Age and sex differences in reaction time in adulthood: Results from the United Kingdom Health and Lifestyle Survey. *Psychology and Aging*, 21 (1), 62–73.

Derksen, J., Kramer, I., & Katzko, M. (2002) Does a self-report measure for emotional intelligence assess something different than general intelligence? *Personality and Individual Differences*, 32 (1), 37–48.

Detterman, D. K. (1991) Reply to Deary and Pagliari: Is g intelligence or stupidity? *Intelligence*, 15 (2), 251–255.

Detterman, D. K., & Daniel, M. H. (1989) Correlations of mental tests with each other and with cognitive variables are highest in low IQ groups. *Intelligence*, 13, 349–360.

Detterman, D. K., & Spry, K. M. (1988) Is it smart to play the horses? Comment on "A day at the races: A study of IQ, expertise, and cognitive complexity." *Journal of Experimental Psychology: General*, 117 (1), 91–95.

Detterman, D. K., & Thompson, L. A. (1997) What is so special about special education? *American Psychologist*, 52 (10), 1082–1090.

Deutsch, G. K., Dougherty, R. F., Bammer, R., Siok, W. T., Gabrieli, J. D., & Wandell, B. (2005) Children's reading performance is correlated with white matter structure measured by diffusion tensor imaging. *Cortex*, 41, 354–363.

Devlin, B., Fienberg, S. E., Resnick, D. P., & Roeder, K. (Eds.) (1998) *Intelligence, genes, and success: Scientists respond to The Bell Curve.* New York: Springer-Verlag.

Diamond, J. (1997) *Guns, germs and steel: The fates of human societies.* San Francisco: Norton.

Dick, D. M., Aliev, F., Kramer, J., Wang, J. C., Hinrichs, A., Bertelsen, S., Kuperman, S., Schukit, M., Nurnberger, J., Jr., Edenberg, H. J., Porjesz, B., Begleiter, H., Hesselbrock, V., Goate, A., & Bierut, L. (2007) Association of CHRM2 with IQ: Converging evidence for a gene influencing intelligence. *Behavior Genetics*, 37 (2), 265–272.

Dickens, W. T., & Flynn, J. R. (2001) Heritability estimates vs. large environmental effects: The IQ paradox resolved. *Psychological Review*, 108 (3), 346–369.

Dobzhanzky, T. (1937) *Genetics and the origin of species.* New York: Columbia University Press.

Dodrill, C. B. (1981) An economical method for the evaluation of general intelligence in adults. *Journal of Consulting and Clinical Psychology*, 49 (5), 668–673.

Dodrill, C. B., & Warner, M. H. (1988) Further studies of the Wonderlic Personnel Test as a brief measure of intelligence. *Journal of Consulting and Clinical Psychology*, 56 (1), 145–147.

Dolan, C. V., Colom, R., Abad, F. J., Wicherts, J. M., Hessen, D. J., & Van Der Sluis, S. (2006) Multi-group covariance and mean structure modeling of the relationship between the WAIS-III common factors and sex and educational attainment in Spain. *Intelligence*, 34, 193–210.

Dolan, C. V., & Hamaker, E. L. (2001) Investigating Black-White differences in psychometric IQ: Multi-group confirmatory factor analyses of the WISC-R and the K-ABC and a critique of the method of correlated vectors. In F. Columbus (Ed.), *Advances in psychology research, Volume 6.* Hauppauge, NY: Nova Science Publishers, 31–59.

Dolan, C. V., Roorda, W., & Wicherts, J. M. (2004) Two failures of Spearman's hypothesis: The GATB in Holland and the JAT in South Africa. *Intelligence*, 32 (2), 155–173.

Dombrowski, S. C., Noonan, K., & Martin, R. P. (2007) Low birth weight and cognitive outcomes: Evidence for a gradient relationship in an urban, poor, African American birth cohort. *School Psychology Quarterly*, 22 (1), 26–43.

Donders, J., Zhu, J., & Tulsky, D. (2001) Factor Index score patterns in the WAIS-III standardization sample. *Assessment*, 8 (2), 193–203.

Duckworth, A. L., & Seligman, M. E. P. (2005) Self-discipline outdoes IQ in predicting academic performance of adolescents. *Psychological Science*, 16 (12), 939–944.

Duncan, J., Burgess, P., & Emslie, H. (1995) Fluid intelligence after frontal lobe lesions. *Neuropsychologia*, 33 (3), 261–268.

Duncan, J., Emslie, H., Williams, P., & Johnson, R. (1996) Intelligence and the frontal lobe: The organization of goal directed behavior. *Cognitive Psychology*, 30 (3), 257–303.

Duncan, J., Seitz, R. J., Kolodny, J., Bor, D., Herzog, H., Ahmed, A., Newell, F. N., & Emslie, H. (2000) A neural basis for general intelligence. *Science*, 289 (5478), 457–460.

Dweck, C. S. (2006) *Mindset: The new psychology of success*. New York: Random House.

Dye, M. W. G., Green, C. S., & Bavelier, D. (2009) Increasing speed of processing with action video games. *Current Directions in Psychological Science*, 18 (6), 321–326.

Earles, J. A., & Ree, M. J., (1992) The predictive validity of the ASVAB for training. *Educational and Psychological Measurement*, 52, 721–725.

Edwards, A. L. (1959) *Objective approaches to personality assessment*. Princeton, NJ: Princeton University Press.

Edwards, A. W. F. (2003) Human genetic diversity: Lewontin's fallacy. *BioEssays*, 25, 798–801.

Eichenbaum, H. (2004) An information processing framework for memory representation by the hippocampus. In M. S. Gazzaniga (Ed.), *The cognitive neurosciences* (3rd edition). Cambridge, MA: MIT Press, pp. 679–690.

Elliott, C. D. (1986) The factorial structure and specificity of the British Ability Scales. *British Journal of Psychology*, 77 (2), 175–185.

Embretson, S., & Reise, S. P. (2000) *Item response theory for psychologists*. Mahaw, NJ: Erlbaum.

Engle, R. W., Tuholski, S. W., Laughlin, J. E., & Conway, A. R. A. (1999) Working memory, short-term memory, and general fluid intelligence: A latent variable approach. *Journal of Experimental Psychology: General*, 128 (3), 309–331.

Ericsson, K. A. (Ed.) (1996) *The road to excellence: The acquisition of expert performance in the arts and sciences, sports, and games*. Mahwah, NJ: Erlbaum.

Ericsson, K. A. (2003) The search for general abilities and basic capacities: Theoretical implications from the modifiability and complexity of mechanisms mediating expert performance. In R. J. Sternberg & E. L. Grigorenko (Eds.), *Abilities, competence, and expertise*. Cambridge: Cambridge University Press, pp. 93–125.

Ericsson, K. A., Charness, N., Feltovich, P. J., & Hoffman, R. R. (2006) *The Cambridge handbook of expertise and expert performance*. Cambridge: Cambridge University Press.

Ericsson, K. A., Krampe, R. Th., & Tesch-Romer, C. (1993) The role of deliberate practice in the acquisition of expert performance. *Psychological Review*, 100 (3), 363–406.

Esbjorn, B. H., Hansen, B. M., Greisen, G., & Mortensen, E. L. (2006) Intellectual development in a Danish cohort of prematurely born preschool children: Specific or general difficulties? *Journal of Developmental, Behavioral Pediatrics*, 27 (6), 477–484.

Evans, P. D., Gilbert, S. L., Mekel-Bobrov, N., Vallender, E. J., Anderson, J. R., Vaez-Azizi, L., Tishkoff, S. A., Hudson, R. R., & Lahn, B. T. (2005) *Microcephalin*, a gene regulating brain size, continues to evolve adaptively in humans. *Science*, 309 (9 September), 1717–1720.

Fagan, J. F., & Holland, C. R. (2002) Equal opportunity and racial differences in IQ. *Intelligence*, 30 (4), 361–387.

Fagan, J. F., Holland, C. R., & Wheeler, K. (2007) The prediction, from infancy, of adult IQ and achievement. *Intelligence*, 35 (3), 225–231.

Feldman, R. D. (1982) *Whatever happened to the quiz kids? Perils and profits of growing up gifted*. Chicago: Chicago Review Press.

Fenner, J. N. (2005) Cross-cultural estimation of the human generation interval for use in genetics-based population divergence studies. *American Journal of Physical Anthropology*, 128 (2), 415–423.

Fernandez-Ballesteros, R., Juan-Espinosa, M., Colom, R., & Calero, M. D. (1997) Contextual and personal sources of individual differences in intelligence. In J. S. Carlson, J. Kingma, & W. Tomic (Eds.), *Advances in cognition and educational practice: Reflections on the concept of intelligence*. London: JAI Press, 221–274.

Ferriman, K., Lubinski, D., & Benbow, C. P. (2009) Work preferences, life values, and personal views of top math/science graduates and the profoundly gifted: Developmental changes and gender differences during emerging adulthood and parenthood. *Journal of Personality and Social Psychology*, 97 (3), 517–532.

Finkel, D., & Pedersen, N. L. (2000) Contribution of age, genes, and environment to the relationship between perceptual speed and cognitive ability. *Psychology and Aging*, 15 (1), 56–64.

Finkel, D., & Pedersen, N. L. (2004) Processing speed and longitudinal trajectories of change for cognitive abilities: The Swedish adoption/twin study of aging. *Aging, Neuropsychology, and Cognition*, 11 (2, 3), 325–345.

Fish, J. M. (2002a) *Race and intelligence: Separating science from myth*. Mahwah, NJ: Erlbaum.

Fish, J. M. (2002b) The myth of race. In J. M. Fish (Ed.), *Race and intelligence: Separating science and myth*. Mahwah, NJ: Erlbaum, pp. 113–141.

Fisk, A. D., & Schneider, W. (1983) Category and word search: Generalizing search principles to complex processing. *Journal of Experimental Psychology: Learning, Memory, Cognition*, 9, 177–195.

Flynn, J. R. (1984) The mean IQ of Americans: Massive gains 1932 to 1978. *Psychological Bulletin*, 95 (1), 29–51.

Flynn, J. R. (1987) Massive IQ gains in 14 nations: What IQ tests really measure. *Psychological Bulletin*, 10 (2), 171–192.

Flynn, J. R. (1991) *Asian Americans: Achievement beyond IQ*. Mahwah, NJ: Erlbaum.

Flynn, J. R. (2007) *What is intelligence?* Cambridge: Cambridge University Press.

Ford, R. T. (2008) *The race card: How bluffing about bias makes race relations worse*. New York: Farrar, Strauss, Giroux.

Fox, S., & Spector, P. E. (2000) Relation of emotional intelligence, practical intelligence, general intelligence, and trait affectivity with interview outcomes: It's not all just 'G.' *Journal of Organizational Behavior*, 21 (Special Issue), 203–220.

Freebody, P., & Tirre, W. C. (1985) Achievement outcomes of two reading programmes: An instance of aptitude-treatment interaction. *British Journal of Educational Psychology*, 55 (1), 53–60.

Frey, M. C., & Detterman, D. K. (2004) Scholastic assessment or g? The relationship between the scholastic assessment test and general cognitive ability. *Psychological Science*, 15 (6), 373–378.

Friederici, A. D., Opitz, B., & von Cramon, D. Y. (2000) Segregating semantic and syntactic aspects of processing in the human brain: An fMRI investigation of different word types. *Cerebral Cortex*, 10 (7), 698–705.

Furnham, A. (2001) Self-estimates of intelligence: Culture and gender difference in self and other estimates of both general (g) and multiple intelligences. *Personality and Individual Differences*, 31 (8), 1381–1405.

Gajdusek, D. C., & Zigas, V. (1957) Degenerative disease of the nervous system in New Guinea: The endemic occurrence of kuru in the native population. *New England Journal of Medicine*, 257 (20), 974–978.

Galton, F. (1869) *Hereditary genius: An inquiry into its laws and consequences*. London: MacMillan.

Ganis, G., Thompson, W. L., Mast, F., & Kosslyn, S. M. (2004) The brain's mind's images: The cognitive neuroscience of mental imagery. In M. S. Gazzaniga (Ed.), *The cognitive neurosciences (3rd edition)*. Cambridge, MA: MIT Press, pp. 931–941.

Gardner, H. (1983) *Frames of mind: The theory of multiple intelligences*. New York: Basic Books.

Gardner, H. (1993a) *Multiple intelligences: The theory in practice*. New York: Basic Books.

Gardner, H. (1993b) *Creating minds: An anatomy of creativity seen through the lives of Freud, Einstein, Picasso, Stravinsky, Eliot, Graham, and Gandhi*. New York: Basic Books.

Gardner, H. (1999) Who owns intelligence? *Atlantic Monthly*, 383 (February 1999), 67–76.

Gardner, H. (2006a) Replies to my critics: Reply to Nathan Brody. In J. A. Schaler (Ed.), *Howard Gardner under fire: The rebel psychologist faces his critics*. Chicago: Open Court, pp. 297–300.

Gardner, H. (2006b) On failing to grasp the core of MI theory: A reply to Visser et al. *Intelligence*, 34 (5), 503–505.

Gardner, H., Kornhaber, M. L., & Wake, W. K. (1996) *Intelligence: Multiple perspectives*. New York: Harcourt Brace.

Garlick, D. (2002) Understanding the nature of the general factor of intelligence: The role of individual differences in neural plasticity as an explanatory mechanism. *Psychological Review*, 109, 116–136.

Geary, D. C. (2005) *The origin of mind: Evolution of brain, cognition, and general intelligence.* Washington, DC: American Psychological Association.

Geary, D. C. (2007a) Educating the evolving mind: Conceptual foundations for an evolutionary educational psychology. In J. C. Carlson & J. L. Levine (Eds.), *Educating the evolving mind.* Charlotte, SC: Information Age Press, pp. 177–203.

Geary, D. C. (2007b) An evolutionary perspective on sex differences in science and mathematics. In S. J. Ceci & W. M. Williams (Eds.), *Why aren't there more women in science: Top researchers debate the evidence.* Washington, DC: American Psychological Association, 173–188.

Geiser, S., & Studley, R. (2002) UC and the SAT: Predictive validity and differential impact of the SAT I and SAT II at the University of California. *Educational Assesment*, 8 (1), 1–26.

Gelade, G. A. (2009) IQ, cultural values, and the technological achievements of nations. *Intelligence*, 36 (6), 711–718.

Gentner, D., & Gentner, D. R. (1983) Flowing waters or teeming crowds: Mental models of electricity. In D. Gentner & A. L. Stevens (Eds.), *Mental models.* Hillsdale, NJ: Erlbaum, pp. 99–129.

Gigerenzer, G. (2000) *Adaptive thinking: Rationality for the real world.* Oxford: Oxford University Press, 2000.

Gignac, G. E. (2006) The WAIS-III as a nested factors model: A useful alternative to the more conventional oblique and higher-order models. *Journal of Individual Differences*, 27 (2), 73–86.

Goff, M., & Ackerman, P. L. (1992) Personality-intelligence relations: Assessment of typical intellectual engagement. *Journal of Educational Psychology*, 84, 537–552.

Goldberg, R. A., Schwartz, S., & Stewart, M. (1977) Individual differences in cognitive processes. *Journal of Educational Psychology*, 69 (1), 9–14.

Goldman, S. M., Tanner, C. M., Oakes, D., Bhudhikanok, G. S., Gupta, A., & Langston, J. W. (2006) Head injury and Parkinson's disease risk in twins. *Annals of Neurology*, 60 (1), 65–72.

Goleman, D. (1995) *Emotional intelligence.* New York: Bantam Books.

Goodwin, D. K. (2005) *Team of rivals: The political genius of Abraham Lincoln.* New York: Simon and Schuster.

Gopnik, A., Meltzoff, A. N., & Kuhl, P. K. (1999) *The scientist in the crib: Mind, brains, and how children learn.* New York: Morrow.

Gorey, K. M. (2001) Early childhood education: A meta-analytic affirmation of the short- and long-term benefits of educational opportunity. *School Psychology Quarterly*, 16 (1), 9–30.

Gosso, M. F., van Belzen, M., de Geus, E. J. C., Polderman, J. C., Heutink, P., Boomsma, D. I., & Posthuma, D. (2006) Association between the CHRM2 gene and intelligence in a sample of 304 Dutch families. *Genes, Brain, Behavior*, 5 (8), 577–584.

Gosso, M. F., de Geuss, E. J. C., van Belzen, M. J., Polderman, T. C., Heutink, P., Boomsma, D. I., & Poshuma, D. (2006) The SNAP-25 gene is associated with cognitive ability: Evidence from a family-based study in two independent Dutch cohorts. *Molecular Psychiatry*, 11 (9), 878–886.

Gottfredson, L. S. (1986) Occupational aptitude patterns match: Development and implications for a theory of job aptitude requirements. *Journal of Vocational Behavior*, 29 (monograph), 254–291.

Gottfredson, L. S. (1997) Why g matters: The complexity of everyday life. *Intelligence*, 24 (1), 79–132.

Gottfredson, L. S. (1998) Jensen, Jensenism, and the sociology of intelligence. *Intelligence*, 26 (3), 291–299.

Gottfredson, L. S. (2002) g: Highly general and highly practical. In R. J. Sternberg & E. L. Grigorenko (Eds.), *The general factor of intelligence: How general is it?* Mahwah, NJ: Erlbaum, pp. 331–381.

Gottfredson, L. S. (2003a) Dissecting practical intelligence: Its claims and evidence. *Intelligence*, 31 (4), 343–398.

Gottfredson, L. S. (2003b) On Sternberg's "Reply to Gottfredson." *Intelligence*, 31 (4), 415–424.

Gottfredson, L. S. (2005) Suppressing intelligence research: Hurting those we intend to help. In R. H. Wright & N. Cummings (Eds.), *Destructive trends in mental health: The well-intentioned path to harm.* New York: Routledge, 155–186.

Gottfredson, L. S. (2007a) Applying double standards to "divisive" ideas: Commentary on Hunt and Carlson (2007). *Perspectives on Psychological Science*, 2 (2), 216–220.

Gottfredson, L. S. (2007b) Innovation, fatal accidents, and the evolution of general intelligence. In M. J. Roberts (Ed.), *Integrating the mind: Domain general vs domain specific processes in higher cognition.* New York: Psychology Press, 387–425.

Gotz M. J., Johnstone, E. C., & Ratcliffe, S. G. (1999) Criminality and antisocial behaviour in unselected men with sex chromosome abnormalities. *Psychological Medicine*, 29 (4), 953–962.

Gould, S. J. (1981) *The mismeasure of man.* New York: Basic Books.

Gould, S. J. (1996) *The mismeasure of man* (Rev. Ed.). Boston: Norton.

Grandy, J. (1999) *GRE trends and profiles: Statistics about GRE © test examinees by gender, age, and ethnicity* (second edition). GRE No. 96-07. Princeton, NJ: Educational Testing Service.

Gray, J. R., Chabris, C. F., & Braver, T. S. (2003) Neural mechanisms of general fluid intelligence. *Nature Neuroscience*, 6, 316–322.

Greenfield, P. M. (1998) The cultural evolution of IQ. In U. Neisser (Ed.), *The rising curve: Long-term gains in IQ and related measures.* Washington, DC: American Psychological Association, 81–123.

Grigorenko, E. L., Meier, E., Lipka, J., Muhatt, G., Yanez, E., & Sternberg, R. J. (2004) Academic and practical intelligence: A case study of the Yup'ik in Alaska. *Learning and Individual Differences*, 14 (4), 183–207.

Grissmer, D., Flanagan, A., & Williamson, S. (1998) Why did the Black-White score gap narrow in the 1970s and 1980s? In C. Jenks & M. Philips (Eds.), *The Black-White test score gap.* Washington, DC: Brookings Institute, 182–226.

Grudnik, J. L., & Kranzler, J. (2001) Meta-analysis of the relationship between intelligence and inspection time. *Intelligence*, 29 (6), 523–535.

Guerrero, L. M. K. (2009) *The impact of lead contamination in children of Callao – Peru.* Lima: Fundacion Cayetano Heredia.

Guiso, L., Monte, F., Sapienza, P., & Zingales, L. (2008) Culture, gender, and math. *Science*, 320 (30 May), 1164–1165.

Gur, R. C., & Gur, R. E. (2007) Neural substrates for sex differences in cognition. In S. J. Ceci & W. M. Williams (Eds.), *Why aren't there more women in science: Top researchers debate the evidence.* Washington, DC: American Psychological Association, pp. 189–198.

Gustafsson, J.-E. (1984) A unifying model for the structure of intellectual abilities. *Intelligence*, 8 (3), 179–203.

Habib, R. J., McIntosh, A. R., & Tulving, E. (2000) Individual differences in the functional neuroanatomy of verbal discrimination learning revealed by positron emission tomography. *Acta Psychologia*, 105 (2), 141–157.

Haier, R. J. (2009) Neuro-intelligence, neurometrics, and the next phase of brain imaging studies. *Intelligence*, 27 (2), 121–123.

Haier, R. J., & Benbow, C. P. (1995) Sex differences and lateralization in temporal lobe glucose metabolism during mathematical reasoning. *Developmental Neuropsychology*, 11, 405–414.

Haier, R. J., Colom, R., Schroeder, D. H., Condon, C. A., Tang, C., Eaves, E., & Head, K. (2009) Gray matter and intelligence factors: Is there a neuro-g? *Intelligence*, 37 (2), 136–144.

Haier, R. J., Jung, R. E., Yeo, R. A., Head, K., & Alkire, M. T. (2004) Structural brain variation and general intelligence. *Neuroimage*, 23, 425–433.

Haier, R. J., Jung, R. E., Yeo, R. A., Head, K., & Alkire, M. T. (2005) The new neuroanatomy of general intelligence: Sex matters. *Neuroimage*, 25, 320–327.

Haier, R. J., Siegel, B. V., Neuchterlein, K. H., Hazlett, E., Wu, J. C., Paek, J., Browning, H. L., & Buchsbaum, M. S. (1988) Cortical glucose metabolic rate correlates of abstract reasoning and attention studied with positron emission tomography. *Intelligence*, 12 (2), 199–217.

Haier, R. J., Siegel, B. V., Tang, C., Abel, L., et al. (1992) Intelligence and changes in regional cerebral glucose metabolic rate following learning. *Intelligence*, 16 (3–4), 415–426.

Haier, R. J., White, N. S., Alkire, M. T. (2003) Individual differences in general intelligence correlate with brain function during nonreasoning tasks. *Intelligence*, 31 (5), 429–441.

Hakstian, A. R., & Cattell, R. B. (1978) Higher-stratum ability structures on a basis of twenty primary abilities. *Journal of Educational Psychology*, 70 (5), 667–689.

Halpern, D. F. (1986) *Sex differences in cognitive abilities* (1st edition). Hillsdale, NJ: Erlbaum.

Halpern, D. F. (2000) *Sex differences in cognitive abilities* (2nd edition). Hillsdale, NJ: Erlbaum.

Halpern, D. F., Benbow, C. P., Geary, D. C., Gur, R. C., Hyde, J. S., & Gernsbacher, M. A. (2007) The science of sex differences in science and mathematics. *Psychological Science in the Public Interest*, 6 (1), 1–51.

Halpern, D. F., & Tan, U. (2001) Stereotypes and steroids: Using a psychobiosocial model to understand sex differences in cognitive abilities. *Brain and Cognition*, 45 (3), 392–414.

Harden, K. P., Turkheimer, E., & Loehlin, J. C. (2007) Genotype by environment interaction in adolescents' cognitive aptitude. *Behavior Genetics*, 37, 273–283.

Harrs, M., & Hatano, G. (Eds.) (1999) *Learning to read and write: A cross-linguistic perspective*. New York: Cambridge University Press.

Hartigan, J. A., & Wigdor, A. K. (Eds.) (1989) *Fairness in employment testing: Validity generalization, minority issues, and the General Aptitude Test Battery*. Washington, DC: National Academies Press.

Hartley, A. (2006) Changing role of the speed of processing construct in the psychology of aging. In J. E. Birren & K. W. Schaie (Eds.), *Handbook of the psychology of aging* (6th edition). Burlington, MA: Elsevier, pp. 183–207.

Hartmann, P., Kruuse, N. H. S., & Nyborg, H. (2007) Testing the cross-racial generality of Spearman's hypothesis in two samples. *Intelligence*, 35 (1), 47–57.

Hattori, K., & Lynn, R. (1997) Male-female differences on the Japanese WAIS-R. *Personality and Individual Differences*, 23 (3), 531–533.

Haussmann, M., Slabbekoorn, D., Van Goozen, S. H. M., Cohen-Kettenis, P. T., & Güntürkün, O. (2000) Sex hormones affect spatial abilities during the menstrual cycle. *Behavioral Neuroscience*, 114 (6), 1245–1250.

Hayes, B. (2007) Trains of thought. *American Scientist*, 95 (2), 108–113.

Hazlett, H. C. (2005) Klinefelter Syndrome. In S. Goldstein & C. R. Reynolds (Eds.), *Handbook of neurodevelopmental and genetic orders in adults*. New York: Guilford Press, pp. 367–382.

Hearnshaw, L. S. (1979) *Cyril Burt, psychologist*. London: Hodder & Stoughton.

Hedges, L. V., & Nowell, A. (1995) Sex differences in mental test scores, variability, and numbers of high-scoring individuals. *Science*, 270, 365–367.

Hedges, L. V., & Nowell, A. (1998) Black-White test score convergence since 1965. In C. Jenks & M. Phillips (Eds.), *The black-white test score gap*. Washington: Brookings Institute, 129–181.

Hedlund, J., Forsythe, G. B., Horvath, J. A., Williams, W. M., Snook, S., & Sternberg, R. J. (2003) Identifying and assessing tacit knowledge: Understanding the practical intelligence of military leaders. *The Leadership Quarterly*, 14, 117–140.

Hedlund, J., Wilt, J. M., Nebel, K. L., Ashford, S. J., & Sternberg, R. J. (2006) Assessing practical intelligence in business school admissions: A supplement to the graduate admissions test. *Learning and Individual Differences*, 16, 101–127.

Hegarty, M., Just, M. A., & Morrison, I. R. (1988) Mental models of mechanical systems: Individual differences in qualitative and quantitative reasoning. *Cognitive Psychology*, 20, 191–236.

Hegarty, M., & Waller, D. A. (2005) Individual differences in spatial abilities. In P. Shah & A. Miyake (Eds.), *The Cambridge handbook of visuospatial thinking*. New York: Cambridge University Press, pp. 121–169.

Heitz, R. P., Unsworth, N., & Engle, R. W. (2005) Working memory capacity, attention control, and fluid intelligence. In O. Wilhelm & R. W. Engle (Eds.), *Handbook of understanding and measuring intelligence*. Thousand Oaks, CA: Sage, pp. 61–78.

Helms-Lorenz, M., Van de Vijver, F. J. R., & Poortinga, Y. H. (2003) Cross-cultural differences in cognitive performance and Spearman's hypothesis: g or c? *Intelligence*, 31 (1), 9–29.

Herrnstein, R. J., & Murray, C. (1994) *The Bell Curve: Intelligence and class structure in American life*. New York: The Free Press.

Hick, W. E. (1952) On the rate of gain of information. *Quarterly Journal of Experimental Psychology*, 4, 11–26.

Hill, L., Chorney, M. J., Lubinski, D., Thompson, L. A., & Plomin, R. (2002) A quantitative trait locus not associated with cognitive ability in children: A failure to replicate. *Psychological Science*, 13 (6), 561–562.

Hill, N., & Schneider, W. (2006) Brain changes and the development of expertise: Neuroanatomical and neurophysiological evidence about skill-based adaptations. In K. A. Ericsson, N. Charness, P. J. Feltovich, & R. R. Hoffman, *The Cambridge handbook of expertise and expert performance*. Cambridge: Cambridge University Press, pp. 653–682.

Hines, M. (2007) Do sex differences in cognition cause the shortage of women in science? In S. J. Ceci & W. M. Williams (Eds.), *Why aren't there more women in science: Top researchers debate the evidence*. Washington, DC: American Psychological Association, 101–112.

Hoeft, F., Ueno, T., Reiss, A. L., Meyler, A., Whitfield-Gabrieli, S., Glover, G. H., Keller, T. A., Kobayashi, N., Mazaika, P., Jo, B., Just, M. A., & Gabrieli, J. D.E. (2007) Prediction of children's reading skills using behavioral, functional, and structural neuroimaging measures. *Behavioral Neuroscience*, 121 (3), 602–613.

Holohan, C. K., & Sears, R. R. (1995) *The gifted group in later maturity*. Stanford, CA: Stanford University Press.

Horn, J. L. (1985) Remodeling old models of intelligence. In B. B. Wolman (Ed.), *Handbook of intelligence: Theories, measurements, and applications*. New York: Wiley, pp. 267–300.

Horn, J. L. (1986) Intellectual ability concepts. In R. L. Sternberg (Ed.), *Advances in the psychology of human intelligence, Vol. 3*. Hillsdale, NJ: Erlbaum, pp. 35–78.

Horn, J. L. (1998) A basis for research on age differences in cognitive capabilities. In J. J. McArdle & R. W. Woodcock (Eds.), *Human cognitive abilities in theory and practice*. Mahwah, NJ: Erlbaum, pp. 57–91.

Horn J. L. & Noll, J. (1994) A system for understanding cognitive capabilities: A theory and the evidence on which it is based. In D. Detterman (Ed.), *Current topics in human intelligence: Vol. 4. Theories of intelligence*. Norwood, NJ: Ablex, pp. 151–204.

Horn, J. L., & Stankov, L. (1982) Auditory and visual factors in intelligence. *Intelligence*, 6 (2), 165–185.

Howard, A., & Bray, D. W. (1988) *Managerial lives in transition: Advancing age and changing times*. New York: Guilford Press.

Hoyer, W. J., & Verhaeghen, P. (2006) Memory aging. In J. W. Birren & K. W. Schaie (Eds.), *Handbook of the psychology of aging* (6th edition). Amsterdam: Elsevier, 209–232.

Huarte de San Juan, J. (1575/1991) *Examen de ingenios para las ciencias* (edición Felisa Fresco Otero). Madrid: Espasa-Calpa S. A.

Hubbs-Tait, L., Nation, J. R., Krebs, N. F., & Bellinger, D. C. (2005) Neurotoxicants, micronutrients, and social environments: Individual and combined effects on children's development. *Psychological Science in the Public Interest*, 6 (3), 57–121.

Humphreys, L. G., & Lubinski, D. J. (1996) Assessing spatial visualization: An underappreciated ability for many school and work settings. In C. P. Benbow & D. J. Lubinski (Eds.), *Intellectual talent: Psychometric and social issues*. Baltimore, MD: Johns Hopkins University Press, pp. 116–140.

Hunt, E. (1980) Intelligence as an information processing concept. *British Journal of Psychology*, 71 (4), 449–474.

Hunt, E. (1987) The next word on verbal ability. In P. A. Vernon (Ed.), *Speed of information processing and intelligence*. New York: Ablex, pp. 347–392.

Hunt, E. (1995a) The role of intelligence in modern society. *American Scientist*, 83 (July-August), 356–368.

Hunt, E. (1995b) *Will we be smart enough? A cognitive analysis of the coming workforce*. New York: Russell Sage.

Hunt, E. (1997) Nature vs. nurture: The feeling of *vujà dé*. In R. J. Sternberg & E. Grigorenko (Eds.), *Intelligence, heredity, and environment*. Cambridge: Cambridge University Press, pp. 531–551.

Hunt, E. (2002) *Thoughts on thought*. Mahwah, NJ: Erlbaum.

Hunt, E. (2004) Multiple views of multiple intelligence. *Contemporary Psychology*, 46 (1), 5–7.

Hunt, E. (2007) *The mathematics of behavior*. Cambridge: Cambridge University Press.

Hunt, E. (2008) Applying the theory of successful intelligence to education – The good, the bad, and the ogre: Commentary on Sternberg et al. (2008). *Perspectives on Psychological Science*, 3 (6), 509–515.

Hunt, E., & Agnoli, F. (1991) The Whorfian hypothesis: A cognitive psychology perspective. *Psychological Review*, 98 (3), 377–389.

Hunt, E., & Carlson, J. (2007a) Considerations relating to the study of group differences in intelligence. *Perspectives in Psychological Science*, 2 (2), 194–213.

Hunt, E., & Carlson, J. (2007b) Reply to commentators. *Perspectives in Psychological Science*, 2 (2), 224–226.

Hunt, E., & Carlson, J. (2007c) The standards for conducting research on topics of immediate social relevance. *Intelligence*, 35 (5), 393–399.

Hunt, E., Frost, N., & Lunneborg, C. E. (1973) Individual differences in cognition: A new approach to intelligence. In G. S. Bower (Ed.), *Advances in learning and motivation (vol. 7)*. New York: Academic Press, pp. 87–123.

Hunt, E., & Lansman, M. (1986) A unified model of attention and problem solving. *Psychological Review*, 93, 446–461.

Hunt, E., & Lunneborg, C. E., & Lewis, J. (1975) What does it mean to be high verbal? *Cognitive Psychology*, 7, 194–227.

Hunt, E., & Madhyastha, T. M. (2008) Recruitment modeling: An analysis and application to the study of male-female differences in intelligence. *Intelligence*, 36 (6), 653–663.

Hunt, E., & Minstrell, J. (1994) A cognitive approach to the teaching of physics. In K.

McGilly (Ed.), *Classroom lessons: Integrating cognitive theory in the classroom*. Cambridge, MA: MIT Press, pp. 51–74.

Hunt E., & Minstrell, J. (1996) Effective instruction in science and mathematics: Psychological principles, social constraints. *Issues in Education: Contributions from Educational Psychology*, 2 (2), 123–162.

Hunt, E., Pellegrino, J. W., Frick, R. W., Farr, S., & Alderton, D. (1988) The ability to reason about movement in the visual field. *Intelligence*, 12, 77–100.

Hunt, E., & Wittmann, W. (2008) National intelligence and national prosperity. *Intelligence*, 36 (1), 1–9.

Hunt, S. (2007) *Hiring for success: The art and science of staffing assessment and employee selection*. San Francisco: Pfieffer.

Hunter, J. E., & Schmidt, F. L. (1990) *Methods of meta-analysis: Correcting error and bias in scientific findings*. Newbury Park, CA: Sage.

Hutchins, E. (1983) Understanding micronesian navigation. In D. Gentner & A. L. Stevens (Eds.), *Mental models*. Hillsdale, NJ: Erlbaum, pp. 191–226.

Hyde, J. S. (2007) Women in science: Gender similarities in abilities and sociocultural forces. In S. J. Ceci & W. M. Williams (Eds.), *Why aren't there more women in science: Top researchers debate the evidence*. Washington, DC: American Psychological Association, pp. 131–145.

Hyde, J. S., Lindberg, S. M., Linn, M. C., Ellis, A. B., & Williams, C. C. (2008) Gender similarities characterize math performance. *Science*, 321 (25 July), 494–495.

Hyman, R. (1953) Stimulus information as a determinant of reaction-time. *Journal of Experimental Psychology*, 45, 188–196.

Inlow, J. K., & Restifo, L. L. (2004) Molecular and comparative genetics of mental retardation. *Genetics*, 166 (2), 835–881.

Irwing, P., Hamza, A., Khaleefa, O., & Lynn, R. (2008) Effects of abacus training on the intelligence of Sudanese children. *Personality and Individual Differences*, 45 (7), 694–696.

Irwing, P., & Lynn, R. (2005) Sex differences in means and variabilities on the progressive matrices in university students: A meta-analysis. *British Journal of Psychology*, 96, 505–524.

Isaacson, W. (2003) *Benjamin Franklin: An American life*. New York: Simon and Schuster.

Jackson, D. N., & Rushton, J. P. (2006) Males have greater *g*: Sex differences in general mental ability from 100,000 17- to 18-year-olds on the Scholastic Assessment Test. *Intelligence*, 34 (5), 479–486.

Jacoby, L. L., Toth, J. P., & Yonelinas, A. P. (1993) Separating conscious and unconscious influences on memory: Measuring recollections. *Journal of Experimental Psychology: General*, 122 (2), 139–154.

Jaeggi, S. M., Buschkeuhl, M., Jonides, J., & Perrig, W. J. (2008) Improving fluid intelligence with training on working memory. *Proceedings of the National Academy of Science*, 105 (19), 6829–6833.

Jarvik, L. F., Klodin, V., & Matsuyama, S. S. (1973) Human aggression and the extra Y chromosome: Fact or fantasy? *American Psychologist*, 28 (8), 574–682.

Jensen, A. R. (1969) How much can we boost IQ and scholastic achievement? *Harvard Educational Review*, 39 (1), 1–123.

Jensen, A. R. (1974) Kinship correlations reported by Sir Cyril Burt. *Behavior Genetics*, 4 (1), 1–28.

Jensen, A. R. (1980) *Bias in mental testing*. New York: Free Press.

Jensen, A. R. (1993) Spearman's hypothesis tested with chronometric information-processing tasks. *Intelligence*, 17 (1), 47–77.

Jensen, A. R. (1997) The puzzle of non-genetic variance. In R. J. Sternberg & E. Grigorenko (Eds.), *Intelligence, heredity, and environment*. Cambridge: Cambridge University Press, pp. 42–88.

Jensen, A. R. (1998) *The g factor: The science of mental ability*. Westport, CT: Praeger Publishers/Greenwood Publishing Group.

Jensen, A. R. (2002) Psychometric g: Definition and substantiation. In R. J. Sternberg & E. L. Grigorenko (Eds.), *The general factor of intelligence: How general is it?* Mahwah, NJ: Erlbaum, pp. 39–53.

Jensen, A. R. (2006) *Clocking the mind: Mental chronometry and individual differences*: Amsterdam: Elsevier.

Johnson, W. (2007) Genetic and environmental influences on behavior: Capturing all the interplay. *Psychological Review*, 114 (2), 423–440.

Johnson, W., & Bouchard, T. J., Jr. (2005a) The structure of human intelligence: It is verbal, perceptual, and image rotation (VPR), not fluid and crystallized. *Intelligence*, 33 (4), 393–416.

Johnson, W., & Bouchard, T. J. Jr. (2005b) Constructive replication of the visual perceptual image-rotation model in Thurstone's (1941) battery of 60 tests of mental ability. *Intelligence*, 33 (4), 417–430.

Johnson, W., & Bouchard, T. J., Jr. (2007a) Sex differences in mental abilities: *g* masks the dimensions on which they lie. *Intelligence*, 35 (1), 23–39.

Johnson, W., & Bouchard, T. J., Jr. (2007b) Sex differences in mental ability: A proposed means to link them to brain structure and functioning. *Intelligence*, 35 (3), 197–209.

Johnson, W., Bouchard, T. J., Jr., Krueger, R. F., McGue, M., & Gottesman, I. I. (2004) Just one *g*: Consistent results from three test batteries. *Intelligence*, 32, 95–107.

Johnson, W., Bouchard, T. J., Jr., McGue, M., Segal, N. L., Tellegen, A., Keyes, M., & Gottesman, I. I. (2007) Genetic and environmental influences on the Verbal-Perceptual-Image Rotation (VPR) model of the structure of mental abilities in the Minnesota study of twins reared apart. *Intelligence*, 35 (6), 542–562.

Johnson, W., Carothers, A., & Deary, I. J. (2008) Sex differences in variability in general intelligence: A new look at an old question. *Perspectives on Psychological Science*, 3 (6), 518–531.

Johnson, W., Carothers, A., & Deary, I. J. (2009) A role for the X chromosome in sex differences in variability in general intelligence. *Perspectives on Psychological Science*, 4 (6), 598–611.

Johnson, W., te Nijenhuis, J., & Bouchard, T. J., Jr. (2007) Replication of the hierarchical visual-perception-rotation model in De Wolff and Buiten's (1963) battery of 46 tests of mental ability. *Intelligence*, 35 (3), 69–81.

Johnson-Laird, P. N., & Byrne, M. J. B. (1991) *Deduction*. Hillsdale, NJ: Erlbaum.

Jones, B. M. (1971) Verbal and spatial intelligence in short and long term alcoholics. *Journal of Nervous and Mental Disease*, 154 (4), 292–297.

Jones, S. M., & Zigler, E. (2002) The Mozart effect: Not learning from history. *Journal of Applied Developmental Psychology*, 23 (3), 355–372.

Jöreskog, K. G., & Sörboom, D. (1979) *Advances in factor analysis and structural equation modeling*. Cambridge, MA: Abt Books.

Juan-Espinosa, M., Garcia, L. F., Escorias, S., Rebollo, I., Colom, R., & Abad, F. J. (2002) Age dedifferentiation hypothesis: Evidence from the WAIS III. *Intelligence*, 30 (5), 395–408.

Jung, R. E., & Haier, R. J. (2007) The parieto-frontal integration theory (P-FIT) of intelligence: Converging neuroimaging evidence. *Behavioral and Brain Sciences*, 30, 135–187.

Just, M. A., & Carpenter, P. A. (1985) Cognitive coordinate systems: Accounts of mental rotation and individual differences in spatial ability. *Psychological Review*, 92 (2), 137–172.

Just, M. A., & Carpenter, P. A. (1992) A capacity theory of comprehension: Individual differences in working memory. *Psychological Review*, 99, 122–149.

Just, M. A., Carpenter, P. A., & Keller, T. A. (1996) The capacity theory of comprehension: New frontiers of evidence and arguments. *Psychological Review*, 104 (4), 773–780.

Just, M. A., Carpenter, P. A., Keller, T. A., Eddy, W. A., Martijn, F., van Dijl, J. M., Suda, K., Schatz, G. et al. (1996) Brain activation modulated by sentence comprehension. *Science*, 274 (5284), 114–116.

Kanaya, T., Scullin, M. H., & Ceci, S. J. (2003) The Flynn Effect and U. S. policy: The impact of rising IQ scores on American society via mental retardation diagnoses. *American Psychologist*, 58 (10), 778–790.

Kanazawa, S. (2004) General intelligence as a domain-specific adaptation. *Psychological Review*, 111 (2), 512–523.

Kanazawa, S. (2008) Temperature and evolutionary novelty as forces behind the evolution of general intelligence. *Intelligence*, 36 (2), 99–108.

Kane, M. J., Brown, L. H., McVay, J. C., Silvia, P. J., Myin-Germeys, I., & Kwapil, T. R. (2007) For whom the mind wanders, and when: An experience-sampling study of working memory and executive control in daily life. *Psychological Science*, 18 (7), 614–621.

Kane, M. J., & Engle, R. W. (2002) The role of prefrontal cortex in working memory capacity, executive attention, and general fluid intelligence: An individual differences perspective. *Psychonomic Bulletin and Review*, 9 (4), 637–671.

Kane, M. J., Hambrick, D. Z., Conway, A. R. A., & Engle, R. W. (2001) The generality of working memory capacity: A latent variable approach. *Journal of Experimental Psychology: General*, 130, 169–183.

Kane, M. J., Hambrick, D. Z., Tuholski, S. W., Wilhelm, O., Payne, T. W., & Engle, R. W. (2004) The generality of working memory capacity: A latent variable approach to verbal and visual-spatial working memory span and reasoning. *Journal of Experimental Psychology: General*, 133, 189–217.

Kaplan, C. (1996) Predictive validity of the WPPSI-R: A four year follow-up study. *Psychology in the Schools*, 33 (3), 211–220.

Karama, S., Ad-Dab'bagh, Y., Haier, R. J., Deary, I. J., Lyttelton, O. C., Lepage, C., & Evans, A. C. (2009) The Brain Development Cooperative Group: Positive association between cognitive ability and cortical thickness in a representative US sample of 6 to 18 year olds. *Intelligence*, 37 (2), 145–155.

Kaufman, A. S. (2001) Do low levels of lead produce IQ loss in children? A careful examination of the literature. *Archives of Clinical Neuropsychology*, 16, 303–341.

Kimura, D. (1999) *Sex and cognition.* Cambridge, MA: MIT Press.

Kintsch, W. (1998) *Comprehension: A paradigm for cognition.* New York: Cambridge University Press.

Kirschner, P. A., Sweller, J., & Clark, R. E. (2006) Why minimal guidance during instruction does not work: An analysis of the failure of constructivist, discovery, problem-based, experiential, and inquiry-based teaching. *Educational Psychologist*, 41, 75–86.

Klein, G. (1998) *Sources of power: How people make decisions.* Cambridge, MA: MIT Press.

Klein, G. (2009) *Streetlights and shadows.* Cambridge, MA: MIT Press.

Kobrin, J. L., Patterson, B. F., Shaw, E. J., Mattern, K. D., & Barbuti, S. M. Validity of the SAT for predicting first year college grade point average. College Board Research Report 2008-5. New York: The College Board.

Koenig, K. A., Frey, M. C., & Detterman, D. K. (2008) ACT and general cognitive ability. *Intelligence*, 36 (2), 153–160.

Kornhauser, A. W. (1918) The economic standing of parents and the intelligence of their children. *Journal of Educational Psychology*, 9 (3), 159–164.

Kosslyn, S. M. (1980) *Image and mind.* Cambridge, MA: Harvard University Press.

Kosslyn, S. M. (1994) *Image and brain.* Cambridge, MA: MIT Press.

Kotchick, B. A., & Forehand, R. (2002) Putting parenting in perspective: A discussion of the contextual factors that shape parenting practices. *Journal of Child and Family Studies*, 11 (3), 255–269.

Kovarik, W. (2005) Ethyl leaded gasoline: How a classic occupational disease became an international public health disaster. *International Journal of Occupational Health*, 11 (4), 384–397.

Kovas, Y., Haworth, C. M. A., Dale, P. S., & Plomin, R. (2007) The genetic and environmental origins of learning abilities and disabilities in the early school years. *Monographs of the Society for Research in Child Development*, 72 (3), vii–160.

Kramer, A. F., Fabiani, M., & Colcombe, S. J. (2006) Contributions of cognitive neuroscience to the understanding of behavior and aging. In J. E. Birren & K. W. Schaie (Eds.), *Handbook of the psychology of aging*, 6th edition. Burlington, MA: Elsevier, 57–83.

Kremen, W. S., Jacobsen, K. C., Xian, H., Eisen, S. A., Eaves, L. J., Tsuang, M. T., & Lyons, M. J. (2007) Genetics of verbal working memory processes: A twin study of middle-aged men. *Neuropsychology*, 21 (5), 569–580.

Kristensen, P., & Bjerkedal, T. (2007) Explaining the relation between birth order and intelligence. *Science*, 316 (5832), 1717.

Kroc, R., Howard, R., Hull, P., & Woodard, D. (1997) Graduation rates: Do students' academic program choices make a difference? Paper presented at the 37th Annual Forum of the Association for Institutional Research (Orlando, FL, May 1997). Dowloaded from aer.arizona.edu/enrollment%20management/ whitepapers/graduation_rates.htm, December 2008.

Kronman, A. T. (2007) Against political correctness: A liberal's cri de coeur. *Yale Alumni Masgazine*, 71 (1), September-October.

Kuncel, N. R., & Hezlett, S. A. (2007) Standardized tests predict graduate students' success. *Science*, 315 (23 February), 1080–1081.

Kuncel, N. R., Hezlett, S. A., & Ones, D. S. (2004) Academic performance, career potential, creativity, and job performance: Can one construct predict them all? *Journal of Personality and Social Psychology*, 86 (1), 148–161.

Kyllonen, P. C. (1993) Aptitude testing inspired by information processing: A test of the four sources model. *Journal of General Psychology*, 120 (3), 375–405.

Kyllonen, P. C., & Christal, R. E. (1990) Reasoning ability is (little more than) working memory capacity?! *Intelligence*, 14, 389–433.

Kyllonen, P. C., & Stephens, D. L. (1990) Cognitive abilities as determinants of success in acquiring logic skills. *Learning and Individual Differences*, 2 (2), 129–160.

Lai, C. S. L., Fisher, S. E., Hurst, J. A., Vargha-Khadem, F., & Monaco, A. P. (2001) A forkhead-domain gene is mutated in a severe speech and language disorder. *Nature*, 413 (6855), 519–523.

Lam, L. T., & Kirby, S. (2002) Is emotional intelligence an advantage? An exploration of emotional intelligence. *The Journal of Social Psychology*, 142 (1), 133–143.

Lange, R. T., Chelune, G. J., Taylor, M. J., Woodward, T. S., & Heaton, R. K. (2006) Development of demographic norms for four new WAIS-III/WMS-III indexes. *Psychological Assessment*, 19 (2), 174–181.

Lanphear, B. P., Khoury, J., Yolton, K., Baghurst, P., and eleven further authors. (2005) Low-level environmental lead exposure and children's intellectual function: An international pooled analysis. *Environmental Health Perspectives*, 113 (7), 894–899.

Larson, G. E., Haier, R. J., LaCasse, L., & Hazen, K. (1995) Evaluation of a "mental effort" hypothesis for correlations between cortical metabolism and intelligence. *Intelligence*, 21 (3), 267–278.

Larson, G. E., & Saccuzzo, D. P. (1989) Cognitive correlates of intelligence: Toward a process theory of g. *Intelligence*, 13 (1), 5–31.

Lave, J. (1988) *Cognition in practice*. Cambridge: Cambridge University Press.

Law, D. J., Pellegrino, J. W., & Hunt, E. B. (1993) Comparing the tortoise and the hare: Gender differences and experience in dynamic spatial reasoning tasks. *Psychological Science*, 4 (1), 35–40.

Leckliter, I. N., & Matarazzo, J. D. (1989) The influence of age, education, IQ, gender, and alcohol abuse on the Halstead-Reitan Neuropsychological Test Battery performance. *Journal of Clinical Psychology*, 145 (4), 484–512.

Lee, H. L., Devlin, J. T., Shakeshaft, C., Stewart, L. H., Brennan, A., Glensman, J., Pitcher, K., Crinion, J., Mechelli, A., Frackowiak, R. S. J., Green, D. W., & Price, C. J. (2007) Anatomical traces of vocabulary acquisition in the adolescent brain. *Journal of Neuroscience*, 27 (5), 1184–1189.

Legree, P. J., Pifer, M. E., & Grafton, F. C. (1996) Correlations among cognitive abilities are lower for higher ability groups. *Intelligence*, 23 (1), 45–57.

Lemann, N. (1999) *The big test: The secret history of American meritocracy*. New York: Farrar, Strous, and Giroux.

Lesser, G. S., Fifer, G., & Clark, D. H. (1965) Mental abilities of children from different social-class and cultural groups. *Monographs of the Society for Research in Child Development*, 30 (4), 1–115.

Levidow, B. (1993) The effect of high school physics instruction on measures of general knowledge and reasoning ability. Unpublished Ph.D. dissertation, University of Washington.

Lewontin R. C. (1974) *The genetic basis of evolutionary change*. New York: Columbia University Press.

Lidz, C., & Elliot, J. (Eds.) (2000) *Dynamic assessment*. New York: JAI Press.

Lindzey, G., Loehlin, J. C., & Spuhler, J. (1975) *Racial differences in intelligence*. San Francisco: Freeman.

Lippmann, W. (1922a) The mental age of Americans. *New Republic*, 32 (412) (25 October), 213–215.

Lippmann, W. (1922b) The mental age of Americans. *New Republic*, 32 (413) (1 November), 246–248.

Loehlin, J. C. (1998) Wither dysgenics? Comment on Lynn and Preston. In U. Neisser (Ed.), *The rising curve: Long-term gains in IQ and related measures*. Washington, DC: American Psychological Association, 389–398.

Loehlin, J. C. (2004) *Latent variable models: An introduction to factor, path, and structural equation analysis*. Mahwah, NJ: Erlbaum.

Loehlin, J. C., Horn, J. M., & Ernst, J. L. (2007) Genetic and environmental influences on adult life outcomes: Evidence from the Texas Adoption Project. *Behavior Genetics*, 37 (3), 463–476.

Loehlin, J. C., Horn, J. M., & Willerman, L. (1997) The Texas Adoption Project. In R. J. Sternberg E. Grigorenko (Eds.), *Intelligence, heredity, and environment*. Cambridge: Cambridge University Press, pp. 105–125.

Logie, R. H. (1995) *Visuo-spatial working memory*. Hove, UK: Erlbaum.

Lohman, D., & Hagen, E. P. (2001) *Cognitive abilities test: Form 6*. Chicago: Riverside Press.

Longman, R. S., Sakofske, D. H., & Fung, T. S. (2007) WAIS-III percentile scores by education and sex for U. S. and Canadian populations. *Assessment*, 14 (4), 426–432.

Lopez, A., Atran, S., Coley, J. D., Medin, D. L., & Smith, E. E. (1997) The tree of life: Universal and cultural features of folkbiological taxonomies and inductions. *Cognitive Psychology*, 32 (3), 251–295.

Lord, F. M. (1956) A study of speed factors in tests and academic grades. *Psychometrika*, 52 (6), 505–510.

Lord, F. M., & Novick, M. R. (1968) *Statistical theories of mental test scores*. Reading, MA: Addison-Wesley.

Lubinski, D., & Benbow, C. P. (2006) Study of mathematically precocious youth after

35 years: Uncovering antecedents for the development of math-science expertise. *Perspectives on Psychological Science*, 1 (4), 316–345.

Lubinski, D., Benbow, C. P., Webb, R. M., & Bleske-Rechek, A. (2006) Tracking exceptional human capital over two decades. *Psychological Science*, 17 (3), 194–199.

Luciano, M., Smith, G. A., Wright, M. J., Geffen, G. M., Geffen, L. B., & Martin, N. (2001) On the heritability of inspection time and its covariance with IQ: A twin study. *Intelligence*, 29 (6), 443–457.

Luciano, M., Wright, M. J., Duffy, D. L., Wainwright, M. A., Zhu, G., Evans, D. M., Geffen, G. M., Montgomery, G. W., & Martin, N. G. (2006) Genome-wide scan of IQ finds significant linkage to a quantitative trait locus on 2q. *Behavior Genetics*, 36 (1), 45–55.

Luciano, M., Wright, M. J., Smith, G. A., Geffen, G. M., Geffen, L. B., & Martini, N. G. (2001) Genetic covariance among measures of information processing speed, working memory, and IQ. *Behavior Genetics*, 31 (6), 581–592.

Luders, E., Narr, K. L., Thompson, P. M., & Toga, A. W. (2009) Neuroanatomical correlates of intelligence. *Intelligence*, 37 (2), 156–163.

Luria, A. R. (1962/1980) *Higher cortical functions in man* (second edition, revised and expanded). New York: Basic Books. (English version, original in Russian.)

Lynn, R. (1990) The role of nutrition in secular increase in intelligence. *Personality and Individual Differences*, 11 (3), 273–285.

Lynn, R. (1994) Sex differences in intelligence and brain size: A paradox resolved. *Personality and Individual Differences*, 17, 257–271.

Lynn, R. (1998) The decline of genotypic intelligence. In U. Neisser (Ed.), *The rising curve: Long-term gains in IQ and related measures*. Washington, DC: American Psychological Association, pp. 333–354.

Lynn, R. (1999) Sex differences in intelligence and brain size: A developmental theory. *Intelligence*, 27 (1), 1–12.

Lynn, R. (2006) *Race differences in intelligence: An evolutionary analysis*. Augusta, GA: Washington Summit Publishers.

Lynn, R., Allik, J., & Irwing, P. (2004) Sex differences on three factors identified in Raven's Standard Progressive Matrices. *Intelligence*, 32 (4), 411–424.

Lynn, R., Backhoff, E., & Contreras, L. A. (2005) Ethnic and racial differences on the standard progressive matrices in Mexico. *Journal of Biosocial Sciences*, 37, 107–113.

Lynn, R., & Harvey, J. (2008) The decline of the world's IQ. *Intelligence*, 36 (2), 112–120.

Lynn, R., & Hattori, K. (1990) The heritability of intelligence in Japan. *Behavior Genetics*, 20 (4), 545–546.

Lynn, R., & Irwing, P. (2004a) Sex differences on the progressive matrices: A meta-analysis. *Intelligence*, 32 (5), 481–498.

Lynn, R., & Irwing, P. (2004b) Sex differences on the advanced progressive matrices in college students. *Personality and Individual Differences*, 37 (1), 219–223.

Lynn, R., & Irwing, P. (2005) Sex differences in means and variability on the progressive matrices in university students: A meta-analysis. *British Journal of Psychology*, 96, 505–524.

Lynn, R., & Mau, W.-C. (2001) Ethnic and sex differences in the predictive validity of the Scholastic Achievement Test for college grades. *Psychological Reports*, 88 (3, pt. 2), 1099–1104.

Lynn, R., & Meisenberg, G. (2010) The average IQ of sub-Saharan Africans: Comments on Wicherts, Dolan, and van der Maas. *Intelligence*, 38 (1), 21–29.

Lynn, R., & Owen, K. (1994) Spearman's hypothesis and test score differences between White, Indian, and Blacks in South Africa. *The Journal of General Psychology*, 121 (1), 27–36.

Lynn, R., & Van Court, M. (2004) New evidence of dysgenic fertility for intelligence in the United States. *Intelligence*, 32 (2), 193–201.

Lynn, R., & Vanhanen, T. (2002) *IQ and the wealth of nations*. Westport, CT: Praeger.

Lynn, R., & Vanhanen, T. (2006) *IQ and global inequality*. Augusta, GA: Washington Summit Publishers.

MacDonald, M. C., Just, M. A., & Carpenter, P. A. (1992) Working memory constraints on the processing of syntactic ambiguity. *Cognitive Psychology*, 24, 56–98.

Mace, R. (2008) Reproducing in cities. *Science*, 319 (8 February), 764–766.

Machin, S., & Pekkarinen, T. (2008) Global sex differences in test score variability. *Science*, 322 (28 November), 1331–1332.

Macintosh, N. J. (1995) *Cyril Burt: Fraud or framed?* Oxford: Oxford University Press.

Macintosh, N. J. (1998) *IQ and human intelligence*. Oxford: Oxford University Press.

MacLeod, C. M., Hunt, E., & Mathews, N. N. (1978) Individual differences in the verification of sentence-picture relationships. *Journal of Verbal Learning and Verbal Behavior*, 17, 493–507.

Madhyastha, T. M., Hunt, E., Deary, I. J., Gale, C. R., & Dykiert, D. (2009) Recruitment modeling applied to longitudinal studies of group differences in intelligence. *Intelligence*, 37 (4), 422–427.

Maguire, E. A., Burgess, N., & O'Keefe, J. (1999) Human spatial navigation: Cognitive maps, sexual dimorphism, and neural substrates. *Current Opinion in Neurobiology*, 9 (2), 171–177.

Maguire, E. A., Spiers, H. J., Good, C. D., Hartley, T., Frackowiak, R. S., & Burgess, N. (2003) Navigation expertise and the human hippocampus: A structural brain imaging analysis. *Hippocampus*, 13, 250–259.

Malinowski, J. C. (2001) Mental rotation and real-world wayfinding. *Perceptual and Motor Skills*, 92 (1), 19–30.

Marsiske, M., & Margrett, J. A. (2006) Everyday problem solving and decision making. In J. E. Birren & K. W. Schaie (Eds.), *Handbook of the Psychology of Aging* (6th edition). Burlington, MA: Elsevier, 315–342.

Marvis, C. B. (2007) Language and communicative development in Williams' syndrome. *Mental Retardation and Developmental Disabilities Research Reviews*, 13 (1), 3–15.

Matarazzo, J. D. (1972) *Wechsler's measurement and appraisal of adult intelligence*. Baltimore: Williams and Wilkins.

Matarazzo, J. D., Bornstein, R. A., McDermott, P. A., & Noonan, J. V. (1986) Verbal IQ vs. performance IQ difference scores in males and females from the WAIS–R standardization sample. *Journal of Clinical Psychology*, 42 (6), 965–974.

Mathews, N. N., Hunt, E., & MacLeod, C. M. (1980) Strategy choice and strategy training in sentence-picture verification. *Journal of Verbal Learning and Verbal Behavior*, 19, 531–538.

Matte, T. D., Bresnahan, M., Begg, M. D., & Susser, E. (2001) Influence of variation in birth weight within normal range and within sibships on IQ at age 7 years: Cohort study. *British Medical Journal*, 323 (7308), 310–314.

Mattern, K. D., Pattern, B. F., Shaw, E. J., Kobrin, J. F., & Barbuti, S. M. (2008) Differential validity and prediction of the SAT. College Board Research Report 2008-4. New York: College Entrance Examination Board.

Matthews, G., Zeidner, M., & Roberts, R. D. (2005) Emotional intelligence: An elusive ability? In O. Wilhelm & R. W. Engle (Eds.), *Handbook of understanding and measuring intelligence*. Thousand Oaks, CA: Sage, pp. 79–99.

Mau, W.-C., & Lynn, R. (2000) Gender differences in homework and test scores in mathematics, reading and science at tenth and twelfth grade. *Psychology, Evolution, Gender*, 2 (2), 119–125.

Mau, W.-C., Lynn, R. (2001) Gender differences on the Scholastic Aptitude Test, the American College Test, and college grades. *Educational Psychology*, 21 (2), 133–136.

Mauger, P. A., Kolmodin, C. A. (1975) Long-term predictive validity of the scholastic aptitude test. *Journal of Educational Psychology*, 67 (6), 847–851.

Max, J. E., Manes, F. F., Robertson, B. A. M., Mathews, K., Fox, P. T., & Lancaster, J. (2005) Prefrontal and executive attention network lesions and the development of attention-deficit/hyperactivity symptomatology. *Journal of the American Academy of Child and Adolescent Psychiatry*, 44 (5), 443–450.

Mayer, J. D., Salovey, P., & Caruso, D. R. (2004) Emotional intelligence: Theory, findings, and implications. *Psychological Inquiry*, 15 (3), 197–215.

Mayer, R. E. (2002) Should there be a three-strikes rules against pure discovery learning? The case for guided methods of instruction. *American Psychologist*, 59 (1), 14–19.

McArdle, J. J. (1998) Contemporary statistical models for examining test-bias. In J. J. McCardle & R. W. Woodcock (Eds.), *Human cognitive abilities: Theory and practice*. Mahwah, NJ: Erlbaum, pp. 157–196.

McArdle, J. J., Ferrer-Caja, E., Hamagami, F., & Woodcock, R. W. (2002) Comparative longitudinal structural analyses of the growth and decline of multiple intellectual abilities over the life span. *Developmental Psychology*, 38 (1), 115–142.

McDaniel, M. A. (2005) Big-brained people are smarter: A meta-analysis of the relationship between in vivo brain volume and intelligence. *Intelligence*, 33 (4), 337–346.

McDaniel, M. A., Moregson, F. P, Finnegan, E. B., Campion, M. A., & Braverman, E. P. (2001) Use of situational judgment tests to predict job performance: A clarification of the literature. *Journal of Applied Psychology*, 86 (4), 730–740.

McGrew, K. S. (2005) The Cattell-Horn-Carroll theory of cognitive abilities. In D. P. Flanagan & P. L. Harrison, *Contemporary intellectual assessment: Theories, tests, and issues.* New York: Guilford, pp. 136–181.

McGrew, K. S., Werder, J. K., & Woodcock, R. W. (1991) *Woodcock-Johnson technical manual.* Allen, TX: DLM Teaching Resources.

McGrew, K. S., & Woodcock, R. W. (2001) *Technical manual: Woodcock Johnson III.* Itasca, IL: Riverside Press.

McGue, M. (1999) Behavior genetic models of alcoholism and drinking. In K. E. Leonard & H. T. Blaine (Eds.), *Psychological theories of drinking and alcoholism* (2nd ed.). New York. Guilford Press, pp. 372–421.

McGue, M., Bouchard, T. J., Jr., Iacono, W. G., & Lykken, D. T. (1993) Behavioral genetics of cognitive ability: A life-span perspective. In R. Plomin & G. E. McClearn (Eds.), *Nature, nurture, and psychology.* Washington, DC: American Psychological Association, pp. 59–76.

McHenry, J. J., Hough, L. M., Toquam, J. L., Hanson, M. A., & Ashworth, S. (1990) Project A validity results: The relationship between predictor and criterion domains. *Personnel Psychology*, 43 (2), 335–354.

McKay, P. F., & McDaniel, M. A. (2006) A reexamination of black-white mean differences in work performance: More data, more moderators. *Journal of Applied Psychology*, 91 (3), 538–544.

Mekel-Bobrov, N., Gilbert, S. L., Evans, P. D., Vallender, E. J., Anderson, J. R., Hudson, R. R., Tishkoff, S. A., & Lahn, B. T. (2005) Ongoing adaptive evolution of *ASPM*, a brain size determinant in *Homo sapiens. Science*, 309 (9 September), 1720–1722.

Mekel-Bobrov, N., Posthuma, D., Gilbert, S. L., Lind, P., Gosso, M. F., Luciano, M., Harris, S. E., Bates, T. C., Polderman, T. J. C., Whalley, L. J., Fox, H., Starr, J. M., Evans, P. D., Montgomery, G. W., Fernandes, C., Heutnik, P., Martin, N. G., Boomsma, D. I., Deary, I. J., Wright, M. J., de Geuss, E. J. C., & Lahn, B. T. (2007) The ongoing adaptive evolution of *ASPM* and *Microcephalin* is not explained by increased intelligence. *Human Molecular Genetics*, 16 (6), 600–608.

Mervis, C. B. (203) Williams syndrome: 15 years of psychological research. *Developmental Neuropsychology*, 23 (1–2), 1–12.

Messick, S., & Jungeblut, A. (1981) Time and method in coaching for the SAT. *Psychological Bulletin*, 89 (2), 191–216.

Meyer, D. E., & Kieras, D. E. (1997) A computational theory of executive cognition processes and multi-task performance. Part 1: Basic mechanisms. *Psychological Review*, 104 (1), 3–65.

Milne, A. A. (1926) *Winnie-the-Pooh.* London: Methuen.

Milner, B. (2005) The medial temporal-lobe amnesic syndrome. *Psychiatric Clinics of North America*, 28 (3), 599–611.

Milner, B., Corkin, S., & Teuber, H. L. (1968) Further analysis of the hippocampal amnesic syndrome: 14-year follow-up study of H. M. *Neuropsychologia*, 6, 215–234.

Minstrell, J. (2001) The role of the teacher in making sense of classroom experience and effecting better learning. In S. M. Carver & D. Klahr (Eds.), *Cognition and instruction: 25 years of progress.* Mahwah, NJ: Erlbaum, pp. 121–150.

Moeser, S. D. (1988) Cognitive mapping in a complex building. *Environment and Behavior*, 20 (1), 21–49.

Moffat, S. D., Kennedy, K. M., Rodrigue, K. M., & Raz, N. (2007) Extrahippocampal contributions to age differences in human spatial navigation. *Cerebral Cortex*, 17 (6), 1274–1282.

Molenaar, D., Dolan, C. V., & Wicherts, J. M. (2009) The power to detect sex differences in IQ test scores using Multi-Group Covariance and Means Structural Analysis. *Intelligence*, 37 (4), 396–404.

Molfese, V., DeLalla, L. F., & Bunce, D. (1997) Prediction of the intelligence test scores of 3- to-8-year old children by home environment, socioeconomic status, and biomedical risks. *Merrill-Palmer Quarterly*, 41 (2), 219–234.

Mortensen, L. H., Sorensen, T. I. A., & Gronbaek, M. (2005) Intelligence in relation to later beverage preference and alcohol intake. *Addiction*, 100 (10), 1445–1452.

Moselhy, H., Georgiou, G., & Kahn, A. (2001) Frontal lobe changes in alcoholism: A review of the literature. *Alcohol and Alcoholism*, 36 (5), 357–368.

Muller, C. B., et al. (72 additional signatures) (2005) Gender difference and performance in science. *Science*, 307 (18 February), 1043.

Murray, C. A. (1998) *Income inequality and IQ.* Washington, DC: American Enterprise Institute.

Murray, C. A. (2003) *Human accomplishment.* New York: Harper.

Murray, C. A. (2005) The inequality taboo. *Commentary*, 120 (2), 13–22.

Murray, C. (2007) The magnitude and components of change in the black-white IQ difference from 1920 to 1991: A birth cohort analysis of the Woodcock-Johnson standardizations. *Intelligence*, 35, 305–318.

Murray, C. A (2008) *Real education: Four simple truths for bringing America's schools back to reality*. New York: Random House.

Myerson, J., Hale, S., Wagstaff, D., Poon, L. W., & Smith, G. A. (1990) The information-loss model: A mathematical theory of age-related cognitive slowing. *Psychological Review*, 97, 475–487.

Naglieri, J. A. (2005) The Cognitive Assessment System. In D. P. Flanagan & L. Harrison (Eds.), *Contemporary intellectual assessment: Theories, tests, and issues*. New York: Guilford Press, pp. 441–460.

Nathawat, S. S., & Puri, P. (1995) A comparative study of MZ and DZ twins on Level I and Level II mental abilities and personality. *Journal of the Indian Academy of Applied Psychology*, 21, 87–92.

Needleman, Herbert L., Gunnoe, C., Leviton, A., Reed, R., Peresie, H., Maher, C., & Barret, P. (1979) Deficits in psychologic and classroom performance of children with elevated dentine lead levels. *New England Journal of Medicine*, 300 (13), 689–695.

Neisser, U., Boodoo, G., Bouchard, T. J., Jr., Boykin, A. W., Brody, N., Ceci, S. J., Halpern, D. F., Loehlin, J. C., Perloff, R., Sternberg, R. J., & Urbina, S. (1996) Intelligence: Knowns and unknowns. *American Psychologist*, 51 (2), 77–101.

Neisser, U. (Ed.) (1998) *The rising curve: Long term gains in IQ and related measures*. Washington, DC: American Psychological Association.

Nettlebeck, T. (1987) Inspection time and intelligence. In P. A. Vernon (Ed.), *Speed of information processing and intelligence*. Norwood, NJ: Ablex, pp. 295–346.

Nettlebeck, T. (2001) Correlations between inspection time and psychometric ability: A personal interpretation. *Intelligence*, 29, 459–474.

Neubauer, A. (2000) Physiological approaches to human intelligence. *Psychologische Beitrage*, 42 (2), 161–173.

Neubauer, A. C., Fink, A., & Schrausser, D. G. (2001) Intelligence and neural efficiency: The influence of task content and sex on brain–IQ relationship. *Intelligence*, 30 (6), 515–536.

Neubauer, A. C., Grabner, R. H., Fink, A., & Neuper, C. (2005) Intelligence and neural efficiency: Further evidence of the influence of task content and sex on the brain-IQ relationship. *Cognitive Brain Research*, 25 (1), 217–225.

Newcombe, N. S. (2007) Taking science seriously: Straight thinking about spatial sex differences. In S. J. Ceci & W. M. Williams (Eds.), *Why aren't there more women in science: Top researchers debate the evidence*. Washington, DC: American Psychological Association, pp. 69–77.

Newcombe, R., Milne, B. J., Caspi, A., Poulton, R., & Moffitt, T. E. (2007) Birthweight predicts IQ: Fact or artifact? *Twin Research and Human Genetics*, 10 (4), 581–586.

Newell, A. (1990) *Unified theories of cognition*. Cambridge, MA: Harvard University Press.

Nguyen, H.-H. D., & Ryan, A. M. (2008) Does stereotype threat affect test performance of minorities and women? A meta-analysis of experimental evidence. *Journal of Applied Psychology*, 93 (6), 1314–1334.

Nickerson, R. S. (2010) *Mathematical reasoning: Patterns, problems, conjectures, and proof*. New York: Psychology Press.

Nisbett, R. E. (2009) *Intelligence and how to get it*. New York: Norton.

Nyborg, H. (2005) Sex-related differences in general intelligence, g, brain size and social status. *Personality and Individual Differences*, 39 (3), 497–509.

Nyborg, H., & Jensen, A. R. (2000) Black-white differences on various psychometric tests: Spearman's hypothesis tested on American Armed Services veterans. *Personality and Individual Differences*, 28 (3), 593–599.

Nyborg, H., & Jensen, A. R. (2001) Occupation and income related to psychometric g. *Intelligence*, 29 (1), 45–55.

Oberauer, K. (2003) The multiple faces of working memory: Storage, processing, and coordination. *Intelligence*, 31 (2), 167–193.

Ogbu, J. (2003) *Black American students in an affluent suburb: A study of academic disengagement*. Mahwah, NJ: Erlbaum.

O'Grady, K. E. (1983) A confirmatory maximum likelihood factor analysis of the WAIS-R. *Journal of Consulting and Clinical Psychology*, 51 (6), 826–831.

Ohnishi, T., Matsuda, H., Hirakata, M., & Ugawa, Y. (2006) Navigation ability dependent neural activation in the human brain: An fMRI study. *Neuroscience Research*, 55 (4), 361–369.

O'Toole, B. I. (1990) Intelligence and behaviour and motor vehicle accident mortality. *Accident Analysis and Prevention*, 22 (3), 211–221.

Pal, S., Shyam, R., & Singh, R. (1997) Genetic analysis of general intelligence 'g': A twin study. *Personality and Individual Differences*, 22 (5), 779–780.

Palmer, J., MacLeod, C. M., Hunt, E., & Davidson, J. (1985) Information processing correlates of reading. *Journal of Memory and Language*, 24, 59–88.

Park, G., Lubinski, D., & Benbow, C. P. (2006) Ability differences among people who have commensurate degrees matter for scientific productivity. *Psychological Science*, 19 (10), 957–961.

Park, G., Lubinski, D., & Benbow, C. P. (2007) Contrasting intellectual patterns predict creativity in the arts and sciences: Tracking intellectually precocious youth over 25 years. *Psychological Science*, 10 (11), 948–952.

Parker, E. S., Parker, D. A., & Harford, T. C. (1991) Specifying the relationship between alcohol use and cognitive loss: The effects of frequency of consumption and psychological distress. *Journal of Studies on Alcohol*, 52 (4), 366–373.

Pennock-Roman, M. (1994) College major and gender differences in the prediction of college grades. College Board Report 94–2. New York: College Entrance Examination Board.

Pentland, A. (2010) To signal is human. *American Scientist*, 98 (May–June), 204–211.

Peter, L. J. (1969) *The Peter Principle*. New York: Morrow.

Petrill, S. A. (2002) The case for general intelligence: A behavior genetics perspective. In R. J. Sternberg & E. L. Grigorenko (Eds.), *The general factor of intelligence: How general is it?* Mahwah, NJ: Erlbaum, pp. 281–298.

Petrill, S. A., Lipton, P. A., Hewitt, J. K., Plomin, R., Cherny, S. S., Corley, R., & DeFries, J. C. (2004) Genetic and environmental contributions to general cognitive ability through the first 16 years of life. *Developmental Psychology*, 40 (5), 805–812.

Phillips, M., Brooks-Gunn, J., Duncan, G. J., Klebanov, P., & Crane, J. (1998) Family background, parenting practices, and the Black-White test score gap. In C. Jenks & M. Phillips (Eds.), *The black-white test score gap*. Washington, DC: Brookings Institute, pp. 103–145.

Phillips, M., Crouse, J., & Ralph, J. (1998) Does the black-white test score gap widen after children enter school? In C. Jenks & M. Phillips (Eds.), *The black-white test score gap*. Washington, DC: Brookings Institute, pp. 229–272.

Piazza, M., & Dehaene, S. (2004) From number neurons to mental arithmetic: The cognitive neuroscience of number sense. In M. S. Gazzaniga (Ed.), *The cognitive neurosciences* (3rd edition). Cambridge, MA: MIT Press, pp. 865–875.

Pind, J., Gunnarsdóttir, E. K., & Jóhannesson, H. S. (2003) Raven's standard progressive matrices: New school age norms and a study of the test's validity. *Personality and Individual Differences*, 34, 375–386.

Plomin, R., DeFries, J. C., McClearn, G. E., & McGuffin, P. (2008) *Behavioral Genetics* (5th edition). New York: Worth Publishers.

Plomin, R., Fulker, D. W., Corley, R., & DeFries, J. C. (1997) Nature, nurture, and cognitive development from 1 to 16 years: A parent-offspring adoption study. *Psychological Science*, 8 (6), 442–447.

Plomin, R., Kennedy, J. K. J., & Craig, I. W. (2006) The quest for quantitative trait loci associated with intelligence. *Intelligence*, 34 (6), 513–526.

Plucker, J. A. (1999) Is the proof in the pudding? Reanalysis of Torrance's (1958 to present) longitudinal data. *Creativity Research Journal*, 12 (2), 103–114.

Polderman, T. J. C., Posthuma, D., De Sonneville, L. M. J., Stins, J. F., Verhulst, F. C., & Boomsma, D. I. (2007) Genetic analysis of the stability of executive functioning during childhood. *Biological Psychology*, 76 (1–2), 11–20.

Polderman, T. J. C., Stins, J. F., Posthuma, D., Gasso, M. F., Verhulst, F. C., & Boomsma, D. I. (2006) The phenotypic and genotypic relation between working memory speed and capacity. *Intelligence*, 34 (6), 549–560.

Pollitt, E., Gorman, K. S., Patrice, L., Martorell, R., et al. (1993) Early supplementary feeding and cognition: Effects over two decades. *Monographs of the Society for Research in Child Development*, 58 (7), v-99.

Poltrock, S. E. (1977) Models of temporal order discrimination. Unpublished Ph.D. dissertation, University of Washington.

Poltrock, S. E., & Brown, P. (1984) Individual differences in visual imagery and spatial ability. *Intelligence*, 8 (2), 93–138.

Poretus, S. D., Dewey, D. M., & Bernreuter, R. G. (1930) Race and social differences in performance tests. *Genetic Psychology Monographs*, 8, 95–208.

Posner, M. I., Boies, S. E., Eichelman, W. H., & Taylor, R. L. (1969) Retention of visual and name codes of single letters. *Journal of Experimental Psychological Monographs*, 79, 1–16.

Posner, M. I., & Rothbart, M. K. (2007) *Educating the human brain*. Washington, DC: American Psychological Association.

Posner, M. I., Sheese, B. E., Odludas, Y., & Tang, Y. Y. (2006) Analyzing and shaping human attentional networks. *Neural Networks*, 19 (9), 1422–1429.

Posthuma, D., de Geus, E. J. C., & Boomsma, D. I. (2001) Perceptual speed and IQ are associated through common genetic factors. *Behavior Genetics*, 31 (6), 593–602.

Posthuma, D., de Geus, E. J. C., & Boomsma, D. I. (2004) Genetic contributions to anatomical, behavioral, and neurophysiological indices of cognition. In R. Plomin, J. C. DeFries, I. W. Craig, & P. McGuffin (Eds.), *Behavioral genetics in the postgenomic era*. Washington, DC: American Psychological Association, pp. 141–161.

Posthuma, D., Luciano, M., de Geus, E. J. C., Wright, M. J., Slagboom, P. E., Montgomery, G. W., Boomsma, D. I., & Martin, N. G. (2005) A genomewide scan for intelligence identifies quantitative trait loci on 2q and 6p. *American Journal of Human Genetics*, 77, 318–326.

Prat, C. S., Keller, T. A., & Just, M. A. (2007) Individual differences in sentence comprehension: A functional magnetic resonance imaging investigation of syntactic and lexical processing demands. *Journal of Cognitive Neuroscience*, 19 (12), 1950–1963.

Preston, S. H. (1998) Differential fertility by IQ and the IQ distribution of a population. In U. Neisser (Ed.), *The rising curve: Long-term gains in IQ and related measures*. Washington, DC: American Psychological Association, pp. 317–338.

Pulakos, E. D., Schmitt, N. A., & Chan, D. (1996) Models of job performance: An examination of ratee race, ratee gender, and rater level effects. *Human Performance*, 9 (2), 103–119.

Puts, D. A., McDaniel, M. A., Jordan, C. L., & Breedlove, S. M. (2008) Spatial ability and prenatal androgens: Meta-analyses of congenital adrenal hyperplasia and digit ratio (2D:4D). *Archives of sexual behavior*, 37 (1), 100–111.

Raftery, A. E. (1995) Bayesian model selection in sociological research. *Sociological Methodology*, 25, 111–163.

Ramist, L., Lewis, C., & McCamley-Jenkins, L. (1994) Student group differences in predicting college grades: Sex, language, and ethnic groups. College Board Research Report 93–1. New York: College Entrance Examination Board.

Rauscher, F. H., Shaw, G. L., & Ky, K. N. (1993) Music and spatial task performance. *Nature*, 365 (14 October), 365.

Raven, J. (1989) The Raven Progressive Matrices: A review of national norming studies and ethnic and socioeconomic variation within the United States. *Journal of Educational Measurement*, 26 (1), 1–16.

Raven, J. (2000) The Raven's Progressive Matrices: Change and stability over culture and time. *Cognitive Psychology*, 41 (1), 1–48.

Raven, J. (2008a) Change and stability in RPM scores over culture and time: The story at the turn of the century. In J. Raven & J. Raven (Eds.), *Uses and abuses of intelligence: Spearman and Raven's Quest for Non-Arbitrary Metrics*. New York: Royal Fireworks Press, pp. 213–258.

Raven, J. (2008b) The Raven Progressive Matrices Tests: Their theoretical basis and measurement model. In J. Raven & J. Raven (Eds.), *Uses and abuses of intelligence: Spearman and Raven's Quest for Non-Arbitrary Metrics*. New York: Royal Fireworks Press, pp. 14–68.

Raven, J. (2008c) Intelligence, engineered ability, and the destruction of life on Earth. In J. Raven & J. Raven (Eds.), *Uses and abuses of intelligence: Spearman and Raven's Quest for Non-Arbitrary Metrics*. New York: Royal Fireworks Press, pp. 431–471.

Raven, J. (2008d) Psychometrics, cognitive ability, and occupational performance. In J. Raven & J. Raven (Eds.), *Uses and abuses of intelligence: Spearman and Raven's Quest for Non-Arbitrary Metrics*. New York: Royal Fireworks Press, pp. 472–518.

Raven, J., & Raven, J. (Eds.), (2008) *Uses and abuses of intelligence: Studies advancing Spearman and Raven's quest for non-arbitrary metrics*. New York: Royal Fireworks Press.

Raven, J. C. (1938) Progressive Matrices: A perceptual test of intelligence. London: H. K. Lewis.

Raz, N., Lindenberger, U., Ghisletta, P., Rodrigue, K. M., Kennedy, K. M., & Acker, J. D. (2008) Neuroanatomical correlates of fluid intelligence in healthy adults and persons with vascular risk factors. *Cerebral Cortex*, 18 (3), 718–726.

Reader, S. M., & Laland, K. N. (2002) Social intelligence, innovation, and enhanced brain size in primates. *Proceedings of the National Academy of Sciences*, 99, 4436–4441.

Ree, M. J., & Earles, J. A. (1991) The stability of *g* across different methods of estimation. *Intelligence*, 15 (3), 271–278.

Reich, R. (1991) *The work of nations: Preparing ourselves for 21st century capitalism*. New York: Knopf.

Reichle, E. D., Carpenter, P. A., & Just, M. A. (2000) The neural basis of strategy and skill in sentence-picture verification. *Cognitive Psychology*, 40 (3), 261–295.

Reynolds, C., Baker, L. A., & Pedersen, N. L. (2000) Multivariate models of mixed assortment: Phenotypic assortment and social homogamy for education and fluid ability. *Behavior Genetics*, 30 (6), 455–476.

Reynolds, C. A., Finkel, D., McArdle, J. J., Gatz, M., Berg, S., & Pedersen, N. L. (2005) Quantitative genetic analysis of latent growth curve models of cognitive abilities in adulthood. *Developmental Psychology*, 41 (1), 1–16.

Rhode, T. E., & Thompson, L. A. (2007) Predicting academic achievement with cognitive ability. *Intelligence*, 35 (1), 83–92.

Rindermann, H. (2007) The g factor of international cognitive ability comparisons: The homogeneity of results in PISA, TIMSS, PIRLS, and IQ tests across nations. *European Journal of Personality*, 21 (5), 667–706.

Rindermann, H. (2008a) Relevance of education and intelligence at the national level for the economic welfare of people. *Intelligence*, 36 (2), 127–142.

Rindermann, H. (2008b) Relevance of education and intelligence for the political development of nations: Democracy, the rule of law, and political liberty. *Intelligence*, 36 (4), 306–322.

Rindermann, H., & Ceci, S. J. (2009) Educational policy and country outcomes in international cognitive competence studies. *Perspectives on Psychological Science*, 4 (6), 551–577.

Rips, L. J. (1994) *The psychology of proof: Deductive reasoning in human thinking*. Cambridge, MA: MIT Press.

Robb, G. P., Bernardoni, L. C., & Johnson, R. W. (1972) *Assessment of individual mental ability*. Scranton, PA: Intext Educational Publishers.

Roberts, R. D., Goff, G. N., Anjoul, F., Kyllonen, P. C., Pallier, G., & Stankov, L. (2000) The Armed Services Vocational Aptitude Battery (ASVAB): Little more than acculturated learning (Gc)!? *Learning and Individual Differences*, 12 (1), 81–103.

Robinson, N. M. (1996) Acceleration as an option for the highly gifted adolescent. In C. P. Benbow & D. J. Lubinski (Eds.), *Intellectual talent: Psychometric and social issues*. Baltimore, MD: Johns Hopkins University Press, pp. 169–178.

Rodgers, J. L., Cleveland, H. H., van den Ourd, E., & Rowe, D. C. (2000) Resolving the debate over birth order, family size, and intelligence. *American Psychologist*, 55 (6), 599–612.

Rosen, A. C., Prull, M. W., Gabrieli, J. D. E., Stoub, T., O'Hara, R., Friedman, L., Yesavage, J. A., & deToledo-Morrell, L. (2003) Differential associations between entorhinal and hippocampal volumes in older adults. *Behavioral Neuroscience*, 117 (6), 1150–1160.

Rosenberg, N. A., Pritchard, J. K., Weber, J. L., Cann, H. M., Field, K. K., Zhivotovsky, L. A., & Feldman, M. A. (2002) Genetic structure of human populations. *Science*, 298 (20 December), 2381–2385.

Ross, J., Zinn, A., & McCauley, E. (2000) Neurodevelopmental and psychosocial aspects of Turner Syndrome. *Mental Retardation and Developmental Disabilities Research Reviews*, 6, 135–141.

Roth, P. L., Bevier, C. A., Bobko, P., Switzer, F. S. III, & Tyler, P. (2001) Ethnic group differences in cognitive ability in employment and educational settings: A meta-analysis. *Personnel Psychology*, 54 (2), 297–330.

Roth, P. L., Huffcutt, A. I., & Bobko, P. (2003) Ethnic group differences in measures of job performance: A new meta-analysis. *Journal of Applied Psychology*, 88 (4), 694–706.

Rowe, D. C. (2004) Assessing genotype-environment interactions and correlations in the postgenomic era. In R. Plomin, J. C. DeFries, I. W. Craig, & P. McGuffin (Eds.), *Behavioral genetics in the postgenomic era*. Washington, DC: American Psychological Association, pp. 71–86.

Rushton, J. P. (1992) Cranial capacity related to sex, rank, and race in a stratified sample of 6325 U. S. Military personnel. *Intelligence*, 16, 401–413.

Rushton, J. P. (1994) Sex and race differences in cranial capacity from international labour office data. *Intelligence*, 19 (3), 281–294.

Rushton, J. P. (2008) Testing the genetic hypothesis of group mean IQ differences in South Africa: Racial admixture and cross-situational consistency. *Personality and Individual Differences*, 44 (3), 768–776.

Rushton, J. P., & Ankney, C. D. (1996) Brain size and cognitive ability: Correlations with age, sex, social class, and race. *Psychonomic Bulletin and Review*, 3 (1), 21–36.

Rushton, J. P., Cvorovic, J., & Bons, T. A. (2007) General mental ability in South Asians: Data from three Roma (Gypsy) communities in Serbia. *Intelligence*, 35 (1), 1–12.

Rushton, J. P., & Jensen, A. R. (2005) Thirty years of research on race differences in cognitive ability. *Psychology, Public Policy, and Law*, 11 (2), 235–294.

Rushton, J. P., & Osborne, R. T. (1995) Genetic and environmental contributions to cranial capacity in Black and White adolescents. *Intelligence*, 20 (1), 1–13.

Rushton, J. P., & Skuy, M. (2000) Performance on Raven's Matrices by African and White university students in South Africa. *Intelligence*, 28 (4), 251–265.

Rushton, J. P., Skuy, M., & Fridjhon, P. (2003) Performance on Raven's Advanced Progressive Matrices by African, East Indian, and White engineering students in South Africa. *Intelligence*, 31 (2), 123–137.

Rushton, J. P., Vernon, P. A., & Bons, T. A. (2007) No evidence that polymorphisms of brain regulator genes *Microcephalin* and *ASPM* are associated with general mental ability, head circumference, or altruism. *Evolutionary Biology*, 3 (2), 157–160.

Sackett, P. R., Borneman, M. J., & Connelley, B. S. (2008) High-stakes testing in higher education and employment. *American Psychologist*, 6 (4), 215–227.

Sackett, P. R., Hardison, C. M., & Cullen, M. J. (2004) On interpreting stereotype threat as accounting for African American–White differences on cognitive tests. *American Psychologist*, 59 (1), 7–13.

Sackett, P. R., Kuncel, N. R., Arenson, J. J., Cooper, S. R., & Waters, S. D. (2009) Does socioeconomic status explain the relationship between admissions tests and post-secondary academic performance? *Psychological Bulletin*, 135 (1), 1–22.

Saklofske, D. H., Yang, Z., Zhu, J., & Austin, E. J. (2008) Spearman's law of diminishing returns in normative samples for the WISC-IV and WAIS-III. *Journal of Individual Differences*, 29 (1), 57–69.

Salovey, P., & Grewal, D. (2005) The science of emotional intelligence. *Current Directions in Psychological Science*, 14 (6), 281–285.

Salovey, P., & Mayer, J. D. (1990) Emotional intelligence. *Imagination, Cognition and Personality*, 9 (3), 185–211.

Salthouse, T. A. (1996) The processing-speed theory of adult age differences in cognition. *Psychological Review*, 103 (3), 403–428.

Salthouse, T. A. (2005) Relations between cognitive abilities and measures of executive functioning. *Neuropsychology*, 19 (4), 532–545.

Salthouse, T. A., Atkinson, T. M., & Berish, D. E. (2003) Executive functioning as a potential mediator of age-related cognitive decline in normal adults. *Journal of Experimental Psychology: General*, 132 (4), 566–594.

Sampson, P. D., Kerr, B., Olson, H. C., Streissguth, A. P., Hunt, E. B., & Barr, H. M. (1997) The effects of prenatal alcohol exposure on adolescent cognitive processing: A speed-accuracy tradeoff. *Intelligence*, 24 (2), 329–353.

Santy, P. A. (1994) *Choosing the right stuff: The psychological selection of astronauts and cosmonauts*. Westport, CT: Praeger.

Sarason, I. G. (1980) *Test anxiety: Theory, research, and applications*. Mahwah, NJ: Erlbaum.

Scarr, S., & Weinberg, R. A. (1976) IQ performance of black children adopted by white families. *American Psychologist*, 31, 726–739.

Scarr, S., & Weinberg, R. A. (1977) Intellectual similarities within families of both adopted and biological children. *Intelligence*, 1 (2), 170–191.

Scarr, S., & Weinberg, R. A. (1983) The Minnesota Adoption Studies: Genetic differences and malleability. *Child Development*, 54 (2), 260–267.

Schaie, K. W. (1996) *Intellectual development in adulthood: The Seattle longitudinal study*. Cambridge: Cambridge University Press.

Schaie, K. W. (2005) *Developmental influences on adult intelligence*. Oxford: Oxford University Press.

Schaie, K. W., & Strother, C. R. (1968) A cross-sequential study of age changes in cognitive behavior. *Psychological Bulletin*, 70 (6), 671–680.

Schaler, J. A. (Ed.) (2006) *Howard Gardner under fire: The rebel psychologist faces his critics*. Chicago: Open Court.

Schiff, M., & Lewontin, R. (1986) *Education and class*. Oxford: Clarendon Press.

Schmidt, F. L., & Hunter, J. E. (1998) The validity and utility of selection methods in personnel psychology: Practical and theoretical implications of 85 years of research findings. *Psychological Bulletin*, 124 (2), 262–274.

Schnakenberg, R. (2004) *Distory: A treasury of historical insults*. New York: St. Martin's Press.

Schneider, W., & Shiffrin, R. M. (1977) Controlled and automatic processing: I. Detection, search, and attention. *Psychological Review*, 84 (1), 1–66.

Schooler, C. (1998) Environmental complexity and the Flynn effect. In U. Neisser (Ed.), *The *rising curve: Long-term gains in IQ and related measures.* Washington, DC: American Psychological Association, pp. 67–79.

Schottenbauer, M. A., Momenan, R. M., Kerick, M. H., & Hommer, D. W. (2007) Relationships among aging, IQ, and intracranial volume in alcoholics and control subjects. *Neuropsychology*, 3, 337–345.

Schrank, F. A. (2005) The Woodcock-Johnson III tests of cognitive abilities. In D. P. Flanagan & P. L. Harrison (Eds.), *Contemporary intellectual assessment: Theories, tests, and issues.* New York: Guilford, pp. 371–401.

Scullin, M. H., Peters, E., Williams, W. M., & Ceci, S. J. (2000) The role of IQ and education in predicting later labor market outcomes. *Psychology, Public Policy, and the Law,* 6 (1), 63–89.

Segal, N. L. (2000) Virtual twins: New findings on within-family environmental influences on intelligence. *Journal of Educational Psychology,* 92 (3), 442–448.

Segal, N. L., & Hershberger, S. L. (2005) Virtual twins and intelligence: Updated and new analyses of within-family environmental influences. *Personality and Individual Differences,* 39 (6), 1061–1073.

Semendeferi, K., Lu, A., Schenker, N., & Damasio, H. (2002) Humans and great apes share a large frontal cortex. *Nature Neuroscience,* 5 (3), 272–276.

Shallice, T. (2004) The fractionation of supervisory control. In M. S. Gazzaniga (Ed.), *The cognitive neurosciences* (3rd ed.). Cambridge, MA: MIT Press, pp. 943–956.

Shapiro, F. R. (2006) *The Yale book of quotations:* New Haven, CT: Yale University Press.

Shaw, P., Greenstein, D., Lerch, J. Clasen, L., Lenroot, R., Gogtay, N., Evans, A., Rapoport, J., & Giedd, J. (2006) Intellectual ability and cortical development in children and adults. *Nature,* 440 (30 March), 676–679.

Shepard, L. D., & Vernon, P. A., (2008) Intelligence and speed of information-processing: A review of 50 years of research. *Personality and Individual Differences,* 44 (3), 535–551.

Shields, J., Konold, T. R., & Glutting, J. J. (2004) Validity of the Wide Range Intelligence Test: Differential effects across race/ethnicity, gender, and education level. *Journal of Psychoeducational Assessment,* 22, 287–303.

Shih, M., Pittinsky, T. L., & Ambady, N. (1999) Stereotype susceptibility: Identity salience and shifts in quantitative performance. *Psychological Science,* 10 (1), 80–83.

Shoda, Y., Mischel, W., & Peake, P. K. (1990) Predicting adolescent cognitive and self-regulatory competencies from pre-school delay of gratification: Identifying diagnostic conditions. *Developmental Psychology,* 26 (6), 978–986.

Shute, V. J., Gawlick-Grendell, L. A., Young, R. K., & Burnham, C. (1996) An experiential system for learning probability: Stat Lady description and evaluation. *Instructional Science,* 24 (1), 25–46.

Sigman, M., & Whaley, S. E. (1998) The role of nutrition in the development of intelligence. In U. Neisser (Ed.), *The rising curve: Long term gains in IQ and related measures.* Washington, DC: American Psychological Association, pp. 155–182.

Simonton, D. K. (1984) *Genius, creativity, and leadership: Historiometric inquiries.* Cambridge, MA: Harvard University Press.

Simonton, D. K. (2001) Predicting presidential performance in the United States: Equation replication and recent survey results. *Journal of Social Psychology,* 141 (3), 293–308.

Simonton, D. K. (2006) Presidential IQ, openness, intellectual brilliance, and leadership: Estimates and correlations for 42 U. S. chief executives. *Political Psychology,* 27 (4), 511–526.

Skarbrevik, K. J. (2002) Gender differences among students found eligible for special education. *European Journal of Special Needs Education,* 17 (2), 97–107.

Skodak, M., & Skeels, H. M. (1949) A final follow-up study of one hundred adopted children. *Journal of General Psychology,* 75, 85–125.

Smedley, A., & Smedley, B. D. (2005) Race as biology is fiction, racism as a social problem is real: Anthroplogical and historical perspectives on the social construction of race. *American Psychologist,* 60 (1), 16–26.

Smith, D. I., & Kirkham, R. W. (1982) Relationship between intelligence and driving record. *Accident Analysis and Prevention,* 14 (6), 439–442.

Smith, E. E., & Jonides, J. (1999) Storage and executive processes in the frontal lobes. *Science,* 283 (5408), 1657–1661.

Snow, R. E. (1982) Education and intelligence. In R. J. Sternberg (Ed.), *Handbook of human intelligence.* New York: Cambridge University Press, pp. 493–585.

Snow, R. E. (1996) Aptitude development and education. *Psychology, Public Policy, and Law,* 2 (3/4), 536–560.

Snow, W. G., & Weinstock, J. (1990) Sex differences among non-brain-damaged adults on the Wechsler Adult Intelligence Scales: A review of the literature. *Journal of Clinical and Experimental Neuropsychology*, 126 (6), 873–886.

Song, C., Qu, Z., Blumm, N., & Barabási, A.-L. (2010) Limits of predictability in human mobility. *Science*, 327 (5698), 1018–1021.

Spearman, C. (1904) General intelligence, objectively determined and measured. *American Journal of Psychology*, 15, 201–293.

Spearman, C. (1923) *The nature of "intelligence" and the principles of cognition*. London: Methuen.

Spearman, C. (1927) *The abilities of man*. London: MacMillan.

Spelke, E. S. (2005) Sex differences in intrinsic aptitude for mathematics and science? A critical review. *American Psychologist*, 60 (9), 950–958.

Stankov, L., & Horn, J. L. (1980) Human abilities revealed through auditory tests. *Journal of Educational Psychology*, 72 (1), 21–44.

Stanley, J. (1996) In the beginning: The study of mathematically precocious youth (SMPY). In C. P. Benbow & D. Lubinski (Eds.), *Intellectual talent: Psychometric and social issues*. Baltimore, MD: Johns Hopkins University Press, pp. 225–235.

Steele, C. M., & Aaronson, J. (1995) Stereotype threat and the intellectual test performance of African Americans. *Journal of Personality and Social Psychology*, 69, 791–811.

Steele, C. M., & Aaronson, J. (1998) Stereotype threat and the test performance of academically successful African Americans. In C. Jencks & P. Meredith (Eds.), *The black-white test score gap*. Washington, DC: Brookings, pp. 401–427.

Stein, Z., Susser, M., Saenger, G., & Marolla, F. (1972) Nutrition and mental performance. *Science*, 178 (4062), 708–713.

Steinberg, R., with Brown, B. B., & Dornbusch, S. M. (1996) *Beyond the classroom: Why school reform has failed and what parents need to do*. New York: Simon & Schuster.

Sternberg, R. J. (1977a) *Intelligence, information processing, and analogical reasoning: The componential analysis of human abilities*. Hillsdale, NJ: Erlbaum.

Sternberg, R. J. (1977b) Component processes in analogical reasoning. *Psychological Review*, 84, 353–378.

Sternberg, R. J. (1981) Intelligence and entrenchment. *Journal of Educational Psychology*, 73 (1), 1–16.

Sternberg, R. J. (1990) *Metaphors of mind*. Cambridge: Cambridge University Press.

Sternberg, R. J. (1996) *Successful intelligence: How practical and creative intelligence determines success in life*. New York: Simon & Schuster.

Sternberg, R. J. (2003a) *Wisdom, intelligence, and creativity synthesized*. Cambridge: Cambridge University Press.

Sternberg, R. J. (2003b) Issues in the theory and measurement of successful intelligence: A reply to Brody. *Intelligence*, 31 (4), 331–338.

Sternberg, R. J. (2004) Culture and intelligence. *American Psychologist*, 59 (5), 325–338.

Sternberg, R. J. (2006) The Rainbow Project: Enhancing the SAT through assessments of analytical, practical, and creative skills. *Intelligence*, 34 (4), 312–350.

Sternberg, R. J. (2007) Finding students who are wise, practical, and creative. *The Chronicle of Higher Education*, July 6, 2007, 1311.

Sternberg, R. J., Ferrari, M., Clinkenbeard, P. R., & Grigorenko, E. L. (1996) Identification, assessment, and instruction of gifted children: A construct validation of a triarchic model. *Gifted Child Quarterly*, 40, 129–137.

Sternberg, R. J., Forsythe, G. B., Hedlund, J., Horvath, J. A., Wagner, R. K., Williams, W. M., Snook, S. A., & Grigorenko, E. L. (2000) *Practical intelligence in everyday life*. New York: Cambridge University Press.

Sternberg, R. J., & Grigorenko, E. L. (2007) The difficulty of escaping preconceptions in writing an article about the difficulty of escaping preconceptions: Commentary on Hunt and Carlson (2007). *Perspectives in Psychological Science*, 2 (2), 221–223.

Sternberg, R. J., Grigorenko, E. L., Ferrari, M., & Clinkenbeard, P. (1999) A triarchic analysis of an aptitude treatment interaction. *European Journal of Psychological Assessment*, 15 (1), 1–11.

Sternberg, R. J., Grigorenko, E. L., & Kidd, K. K. (2005) Intelligence, race, and genetics. *American Psychologist*, 60 (1), 46–59.

Sternberg, R. J., Grigorenko, E. L., & Zhang, L.-F. (2008) Styles of learning and thinking matter in instruction and assessment. *Perspectives on Psychological Science*, 3 (6), 486–506.

Sternberg, R. J., Nokes, K., Geissler, P. W., Prince, R., Katcha, F., Bundy, D. A., & Grigorenko, E. L. (2001) The relationship between academic and practical intelligence: A case study in Kenya. *Intelligence*, 29, 401–418.

Sternberg, S. (1966) High speed scanning in human memory. *Science*, 153, 652–654.

Sticht, T. G. (Ed.) (1975) *Reading for working: A functional literacy anthology:* Alexandria, VA: Human Resources Research Organization.

Sticht, T. G., Armstrong, W. B., Hickey, D. T., & Caylor, J. S. (1987) *Cast-off youth: Policy and training methods from the military experience.* New York: Praeger.

Stoolmiller, M. (1999) Implications of the restricted range of family environments for estimates of heritability and nonshared environment in behavior-genetic adoption studies. *Psychological Bulletin*, 125 (4), 392–409.

Strand, S., Deary, I. J., & Smith, P. (2006) Sex differences in cognitive ability tests: A UK national picture. *British Journal of Educational Psychology*, 76, 463–480.

Strickler, L. J., & Ward, W. C. (2004) Stereotype threat, inquiring about test takers' ethnicity and gender, and standardized test performance. *Journal of Applied Social Psychology*, 34 (4), 665–693.

Sue, S., & Okazaki, S. (1990) Asian-American educational achievements: A phenomenon in search of an explanation. *American Psychologist*, 45 (8) (August), 913–920.

Sullivan, E. V., & Marsh, L. (2003) Hippocampal volume deficits in alcoholic Korsakoff's syndrome. *Neurology*, 61 (12), 1716–1719.

Sunderland, A., Harris, J. E., & Baddeley, A. D. (1983) Do laboratory tests predict everyday memory? A neuropsychological study. *Journal of Verbal Learning and Verbal Behavior*, 22 (3), 341–357.

Suzuki, L., & Aaronson, J. (2005) The cultural malleability of intelligence and its impact on the racial/ethnic hierarchy. *Psychology, Public Policy, and the Law*, 11 (2), 320–327.

Tang, H., Quertermous, T., Rodriguez, B., Kardia, S. L. R., Zhu, X., Brown, A., Pankow, J. S., Province, M. A., Hunt, S. C., Boerwinkle, E., Schork, N. J., & Risch, N. J. (2005) Genetic structure, self-identified race/ethnicity, and confounding in case-control association studies. *American Journal of Human Genetics*, 76, 268–275.

Tannenbaum, A. J. (1996) The IQ controversy and the gifted. In C. P. Benbow & D. Lubinski (Eds.), *Intellectual talent.* Baltimore: Johns Hopkins University Press, pp. 44–82.

te Nijenhuis, J., De Jong, M.-J., Evers, A., & Van Der Flier, H. (2004) Are cognitive differences between immigrants and majority groups diminishing? *European Journal of Personality*, 18, 405–434.

te Nijenhuis, J., van Vianen, A. E. M, & van der Flier, H. (2007) Score gains on g-loaded tests: No g. *Intelligence*, 35, 283–300.

Teasdale, T. W., & Owen, D. R. (1986) The influence of paternal social class on intelligence and educational level in male adoptees and non-adoptees. *British Journal of Educational Psychology*, 56 (1), 3–12.

Teasdale, T. W., & Owen, D. R. (2000) Forty-year secular trends in cognitive abilities. *Intelligence*, 28 (2), 115–120.

Teasdale, T. W., & Owen, D. R. (2008) Secular declines in cognitive test scores: A reversal of the Flynn Effect. *Intelligence*, 36 (2), 121–126.

Templer, D., & Arikawa, H. (2006) Temperature, skin color, per capita income, and IQ: An international perspective. *Intelligence*, 34 (2), 121–127.

Terman, L. M., & Oden, M. H. (1959) *The gifted group at mid-life: Thirty-five years' follow-up of the superior child.* Palo Alto, CA: Stanford University Press.

Thorndike, R. L., & Hagen, E. (1959) *Ten thousand careers.* New York: Wiley.

Thurstone, L. L. (1938) *Primary mental abilities.* Chicago: University of Chicago Press.

Thurstone, L. L., & Thurstone, T. G. (1941) Factorial studies of intelligence. *Psychometric Monographs*, 94 No. 2.

Toomey, R., Lyons, M. J., Eisen, S. A., Xian, H., Chantarujikapong, S., Seidman, L. J., Faraone, S. V., & Tsuang, M. T. (2003) A twin study of the neuropsychological consequences of stimulant abuse. *Archives of General Psychiatry*, 60 (3), 303–310.

Tucker-Drob, E., & Salthouse, T. A. (2008) Adult age trends in the relations among cognitive traits. *Psychology and Aging*, 23 (2), 453–480.

Tuddenham, R. D. (1948) Soldier intelligence in World Wars I and II. *American Psychologist*, 3 (2), 54–56.

Tulving, E., Habib, R., Nyberg, L., Lepage, M., & McIntosh, A. R. (1999) Positron emission tomography correlations in and beyond medial temporal lobes. *Hippocampus*, 9 (1), 71–82.

Turkheimer, E. (1991) Individual and group differences in adoption studies of IQ. *Psychological Bulletin*, 110 (3), 392–405.

Turkheimer, E., Haley, A., Waldron, M., D'Onofrio, B., & Gottesman, I. (2003) Socioeconomic status modifies heritability of IQ in young children. *Psychological Science*, 14 (6), 623–628.

Van Der Maas, H. L. J., Dolan, C. V., Grasman, R. P. P. P, Wicherts, J. M., Huizenga, H. M., & Raijmakers, M. E. J. (2006) A dynamical model of general intelligence: The positive manifold of intelligence by mutualism. *Psychological Review*, 113 (4), 842–861.

Van der Sluis, S., Derom, C., Thiery, E., Bartels, M., Polderman, T. J. C., Verhulst, F. C., Jacobs, N., van Gestel, S., deGeus, J. C., Dolan, C., Boomsma, D. I., & Posthuma, D. (2008) Sex differences on the WISC-R in Belgium and the Netherlands. *Intelligence*, 36 (1), 48–67.

Van der Sluis, S., Willemsen, G., De Geus, E. J. C., Boomsma, D. I., & Posthuma, D. (2008) Gene-environment interaction in adult IQ scores: Measures of past and present environment. *Behavior Genetics*, 38 (4), 348–360.

Van Ijzendoorn, M. H., Juffer, F., & Klein Poelhuis, C. W. (2005) Adoption and cognitive development: A meta-analytic comparison of adopted and nonadopted children's IQ and school performance. *Psychological Bulletin*, 131 (2), 301–316.

van Leeuwen, M., van den Berg, S. M., & Boomsma, D. I. (2008) A twin-family study of general IQ. *Learning and Individual Differences*, 18 (1), 76–88.

van Rijn, S., Aleman, A., Swaab, H., Vink, M., Sommer, I., & Kahn, R. S. (2008) Effects of an extra X chromosome on language lateralization: An fMRI study with Klinefelter men (47, XXY). *Schizophrenia Research*, 101 (1–3), 17–25.

Vasquez, M. J. T., & Jones, J. M. (2006) Increasing the number of psychologists of color: Public policy issues for affirmative diversity. *American Psychologist*, 61, 132–142.

Venter, J. C., et al. (over 200 coauthors) (2001) The sequence of the human genome. *Science*, 291, 1304–1351.

Vernon, P. A., Wickett, J. C., Bazana, P. G., & Stelmack, R. M. (2000) The neuropsychology and neurophysiology of human intelligence. In R. J. Sternberg (Ed.), *Handbook of intelligence*. New York: Cambridge University Press, pp. 245–265.

Vernon, P. E. (1964) *The structure of human abilities*. London: Methuen.

Vernon, P. E. (1965) Ability factors and environmental influences. *American Psychologist*, 20, 723–733.

Vernon, P. E. (1979) *Intelligence: Heredity and environment*. San Francisco: Freeman.

Visser, B. A., Ashton, M. C., & Vernon, P. A. (2006) Beyond *g*: Putting multiple intelligences theory to the test. *Intelligence*, 34 (5), 487–502.

Wachs, T. D., McCabe, G. (2001) Relation of maternal intelligence and schooling to offspring nutritional intake. *International Journal of Behavioral Development*, 25 (5), 444–449.

Wai, J., Lubinski, D., & Benbow, C. (2005) Creativity and occupational accomplishments among intellectually precocious youths: An age 13 to 33 longitudinal study. *Journal of Educational Psychology*, (97) 3, 484–492.

.Wainer, H., & Steinberg, L. S. (1992) Sex differences in performance on the mathematics section of the Scholastic Aptitude Test: A bidirectional validity study. *Harvard Educational Review*, 62 (3), 323–336.

Waller, D., Beall, A. C., & Loomis, J. M. (2004) Using virtual environments to assess directional knowledge. *Journal of Environmental Psychology*, 24 (1), 105–116.

Waller, D., Knapp, D., & Hunt, E. (2001) Spatial representations of virtual mazes: The role of visual fidelity and individual differences. *Human Factors*, 43 (1), 147–158.

Wasserman, G. A., Liu, X., Popovac, D., Factor-Litvak, P., Line, J., Waternaux, C., LoIacono, N., & Graziano, J. H. (2000) The Yugoslavia prospective lead study: Contributions of prenatal and postnatal lead exposure to early intelligence. *Neurotoxicology and Teratology*, 22, 811–828.

Watson, J. D. (2003) *DNA: The secret of life*. New York: Knopf.

Watson, J. D., & Crick, F. H. C. (1953) Molecular structure of nucleic acids: A structure for deoxyribose nucleic acid. *Nature*, 4356 (25 April), 737.

Webb, R. M., Lubinsky, D., & Benbow, C. P. (2002) Mathematically facile adolescents with math/science aspirations. *Journal of Educational Psychology*, 97, 484–492.

Wechsler, D. (1975) Intelligence defined and undefined: A relativistic appraisal. *American Psychologist*, 30 (2), 135–139.

Weinberg, R. A., Scarr, S., & Waldman, I. D. (1992) The Minnesota Transracial Adoption Study: A follow-up of IQ test performance at adolescence. *Intelligence*, 16 (1), 117–135.

Wetherell, J. L., Reynolds, C. A., Gatz, M., & Pedersen, N. L. (2002) Aging, cognitive performance and cognitive decline in normal aging. *Journal of Gerontology: Psychological Sciences*, 57B, 246–255.

Whalley, L. J., & Deary, I. J. (2001) Longitudinal cohort study of childhood IQ and survival up to age 76. *British Medical Journal*, 322 (7 April), 1–5.

Whetzel, D. L., & McDaniel, M. A. (2006) Prediction of national wealth. *Intelligence*, 34 (5), 449–458.

Wicherts, J. M., Dolan, C. V., & Hessen, D. J. (2005) Stereotype threat and group differences in test performance: A question of measurement invariance. *Journal of Personality and Social Psychology*, 89 (5), 696–716.

Wicherts, J. M., Dolan, C. V., & van der Maas, H. L. J. (2010a) A systematic literature review of the average IQ of Africans. *Intelligence*, 39 (1), 1–20.

Wicherts, J. M., Dolan, C. V., & van der Maas, H. L. J. (2010b) The dangers of unsystematic selection methods and the representativeness of 46 samples of African test-takers. *Intelligence*, 38 (1), 30–37.

Wigdor, A. K., & Green, B. F., Jr. (1991) *Performance assessment in the workplace*. Washington, DC: National Academy Press.

Willcut, E. G., DeFries, J. C., Pennington, B. F., Smith, S. D., Caron, L. R., & Olson, R. K. (2004) Genetic eitiology of comorbid reading difficulties and ADHD. In R. Plomin, J. C. DeFries, I. W. Craig, & P. McGuffin (Eds.), *Behavioral genetics in the postgenomic era*. Washington, DC: American Psychological Association, pp. 227–246.

Willerman, L., Schultz, R., Rutledge, J. N., & Bigler, E. D. (1991) In vivo brain size and intelligence. *Intelligence*, 15 (2), 223–228.

Wilson, D. S., & Wilson, E. O. (2007) Rethinking the theoretical foundations of sociobiology. *Quarterly Review of Biology*, 82, 327–348.

Wilson, D. S., & Wilson, E. O. (2008) Evolution "for the good of the group." *American Scientist*, 96, 378–389.

Wilson, W. J. (1997) *When work disappears: The world of the new urban poor*. New York: Knopf.

Winship, C., & Korenman, S. (1997) Does staying in school make you smarter? The effect of education on IQ in *The Bell Curve*. In B. Devlin, S. E. Fienberg, D. P. Resnick, & K. Roeder (Eds.), *Intelligence, genes, and success: Scientists respond to The Bell Curve*. New York: Springer-Verlag, pp. 215–234.

Witelson, S. F., Beresh, H., & Kigar, D. L. (2006) Intelligence and brain size in 100 postmortem brains: Sex, lateralization and age factors. *Brain: A Journal of Neurology*, 129 (2), 386–398.

Witelson, S. F., Kigar, D. L., & Harvey, T. (1999) The exceptional brain of Albert Einstein. *The Lancet*, 353 (19 June), 2150–2153.

Witkin, H. A., Mednick, S. A., Schulsinger, F., Bakkestrøm, E., Christiansen, K. O., Goodenough, D. R., Hirschorn, K., Lundstren, C., Owen, D. R., Philip, J., Rubin, D. B., & Stocking, M. (1976) Criminality in XYY and XXY men. *Science*, 193 (4253) (13 August), 547–555.

Wittmann, W. W. (2005) Group differences in intelligence and related measures. In O. Wilhelm & R. Engle (Eds.), *Handbook of understanding and measuring intelligence*. London: Sage, pp. 223–240.

Wolf, M. (2007) *Proust and the squid: The story and science of the reading brain*. New York: Harper.

Wonderlic Corporation (2007) *Wonderlic Personnel Test normative report*. Libertyville, IL: Wonderlic, Inc.

Wonderlic, E. F., & Wonderlic, C. F. (1992) *Wonderlic Personnel Test user's manual*. Libertyville, IL: Wonderlic Personnel Test, Inc.

Woods, R. P., Freimer, N. B., de Young, J. A., Fears, S. C., Sicotte, N. L., Service, S. K., Valentino, D. J., Toga, A. W., & Mazziotta, J. C. (2006) Normal variants of *microcephalin* and *ASPM* do not account for brain size variability. *Human Molecular Genetics*, 15 (12), 2025–2029.

Yang, C.-F.J., Hooven, C. K., Boynes, M., Gray, P. B., & Pope, H. G., Jr. (2007) Testosterone levels and mental rotation in Chinese men. *Hormones and Behavior*, 51 (3), 373–378.

Yeung, W. J., & Conley, D. (2008) Black-White achievement gap and family wealth. *Child Development*, 79 (2), 303–324.

Zadeh, L. A. (1965) Fuzzy sets. *Information and Control*, 8, 338–353.

Zajonc, R. B. (1983) Validating the confluence model. *Psychological Bulletin*, 93 (3), 457–480.

Zajonc, R. B., Marcus, H. L., & Marcus, G. B. (1979) The birth order puzzle. *Journal of Personality and Social Psychology*, 37 (8), 1325–1341.

Zerjal, T., Tyler-Smith, C., et al. (21 additional authors) (2003) The genetic legacy of the Mongols. *American Journal of Human Genetics*, 72 (3), 719–722.

Zigler, E., & Styfco, S. J. (1997) A "Head Start" in what pursuit? IQ versus social competence as the objective of early intervention. In B. Devlin, S. E. Fienberg, D. P. Resnick, & K.

Roeder (Eds.), *Intelligence, genes, and success: Scientists respond to The Bell Curve.* New York: Springer-Verlag, pp. 281–314.

Zimmerman, F. J., Chirstakis, D. A., & Meltzoff, A. N. (2007) Associations between media viewing and language development in children under age 2 years. *The Journal of Pediatrics*, 151 (4), 364–368.

Zuboff, S. (1988) *In the age of the smart machine: The future of work and power.* New York: Basic Books.

Zwick, R., & Green, J. G. (2007) New perspectives on the correlation of SAT scores, high school grades, and socioeconomic factors. *Journal of Educational Measurement*, 44 (1), 23–45.

Author Index

Subject Index